Hoover's Online is your source for business information that works.

Millions of businesspeople use Hoover's Online every day for research, analysis, and prospecting. Hoover's updates information daily on thousands of companies and hundreds of industries worldwide.

USE HOOVER'S ONLINE FOR:

• **COMPANY RESEARCH**
Overview
History
Competitors
News
Products
Location(s)
Financials
Stock data

• **INDUSTRY RESEARCH**
Quick synopsis
Leading companies
Analysis of trends
Associations
Glossary of terms
Research reports

• **PROSPECTING**
Search by industry,
location, sales, keyword
Full officer lists
Company history
Financials

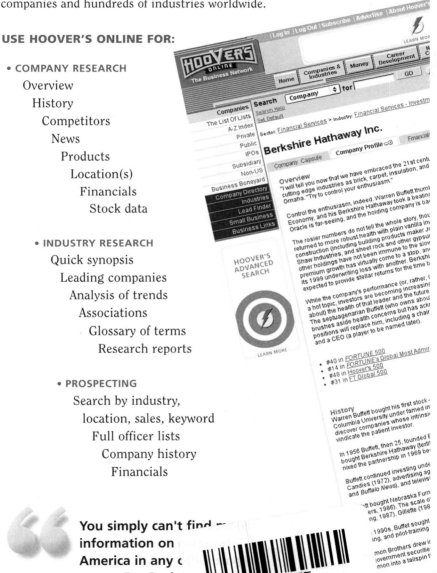

You simply can't find ~
information on
America in any ~
source." —Busine

D1089255

For accurate online business in~...ation, visit us at www.hoovers.com

Hoover's Texas 500

A GUIDE TO THE
TOP TEXAS COMPANIES

BUSINESS PRESS

Hoover's Texas 500: A Guide to the Top Texas Companies is intended to provide readers with accurate and authoritative information about the enterprises covered in it. Hoover's asked all companies and organizations profiled to provide information. Many did so; some did not. The information contained herein is as accurate as we could reasonably make it. In many cases we have relied on third-party material that we believe to be trustworthy, but were unable to independently verify. We do not warrant that the book is absolutely accurate or without error. Readers should not rely on any information contained herein in instances where such reliance might cause loss or damage. The publisher, the editors, and their data suppliers specifically disclaim all warranties, including the implied warranties of merchantability and fitness for a specific purpose. This book is sold with the understanding that neither the publisher, the editors, nor any content contributors are engaged in providing investment, financial, accounting, legal, or other professional advice.

The financial data (Historical Financials & Employees section) in this book are from a variety of sources. Media General Financial Services, Inc., provided selected data for the Historical Financials sections for most publicly traded companies. For the remainder of the public companies, for private companies, and for historical information on public companies prior to their becoming public, we obtained information directly from the companies or from trade sources deemed to be reliable. Hoover's, Inc., is solely responsible for the presentation of all data.

Many of the names of products and services mentioned in this book are the trademarks or service marks of the companies manufacturing or selling them and are subject to protection under US law. Space has not permitted us to indicate which names are subject to such protection, and readers are advised to consult with the owners of such marks regarding their use. Hoover's is a trademark of Hoover's, Inc.

BUSINESS PRESS

10 9 8 7 6 5 4 3 2 1

Publishers Cataloging-in-Publication Data

Hoover's Texas 500: A Guide to the Top Texas Companies

Includes indexes.

1. Business enterprises — Directories. 2. Corporations — Directories.

HF3010 338.7

Hoover's Company Information is also available on America Online, Bloomberg Financial Network, CNBC on MSN Money, EBSCO, Factiva, FORTUNE, Hoover's Online, LexisNexis, NewsEdge, ProQuest, The Washington Post, and other Web sites.

A catalog of Hoover's products is available on the World Wide Web at www.hoovers.com.

ISBN 1-57311-078-7

Hoover's Texas 500 is produced for Hoover's Business Press by Sycamore Productions, Inc., Austin, Texas, using Quark, Inc.'s QuarkXPress 4.04; EM Software, Inc.'s Xtags 4.1; and fonts from Adobe's Clearface, Futura, and Myriad families. Cover design is by Jim Neeley. Electronic prepress and printing were done by Edwards Brothers Incorporated, Ann Arbor, Michigan. Text paper is 60# Arbor.

US AND WORLD DIRECT SALES

Hoover's, Inc.
5800 Airport Blvd.
Austin, TX 78752
Phone: 512-374-4500
Fax: 512-374-4501
e-mail: orders@hoovers.com

EUROPE

William Snyder Publishing Associates
5 Five Mile Drive
Oxford OX2 8HT
England
Phone & fax: +44-186-551-3186
e-mail: snyderpub@cs.com

HOOVER'S, INC.

Founder: Gary Hoover
Chairman: Patrick J. Spain
President and CEO: Jeffrey Tarr
EVP, Corporate Strategy and Development: Carl G. Shepherd

EDITORIAL

Managing Editor: Nancy Regent
Assistant Managing Editor: Valerie Pearcy
Editorial Operations Manager: Ashley Schrump
Director, Financial Information: Dennis Sutton
Senior Editors: Rachel Brush, Margaret Claughton, Paul Geary, Joe Grey, Kathleen Kelly, Mary Mickle Morales
Assistant Senior Editors: Larry Bills, Angela Boeckman, Joe Bramhall, Michaela Drapes, Chris Huston, Joe Simonetta
Associate Editors: Joy Aiken, Sally Alt, Graham Baker, Jason Cother, Bobby Duncan, Carrie Geis, Todd Gernert, Allan Gill, Gregg Gordon, Melanie Hall, Matt Saucedo, Vanita Trippe, Jennifer Westrom, Randy Williams, David Woodruff
Contributing Editor: Travis Brown
Senior Writers: David Hamerly, Stuart Hampton
Writers: Linnea Anderson, James Bryant, Ryan Caione, Jason Cella, Danny Cummings, Tom Elia, Michael Gaworecki, Guy Holland, Laura Ivy, Andreas Knutsen, Anne Law, Diane Lee, Josh Lower, John MacAyeal, Nell Newton, Sheri Olander, Amanda Palm, Elizabeth Paukstis, Rob Reynolds, Seth Shafer, Tim Walker, Chris Zappone
Financial Editors: Adi Anand, Gabe Hascoll, Joel Sensat
QC Editor, MasterList: John Willis
Chief Copyeditor: Emily Weida Domaschk
Assistant Editors: Tommy Ates, Lesley Epperson Dings, Jeanette Herman, Julie Krippel, Michael McLellan, David Ramirez, Christopher Sovine, Bronwen Taylor, Daysha Taylor
Editorial Assistants: Anita Carrillo, Jana Cummings, Travis Irby, Jay Koenig, Michelle Medina, Peter Moore, Anna Porlas, Kcevin Rob, Amy Schein, Leslie Westmoreland
QA Editor: Anthony Staats
Research Coordinator: Jim Harris
Library Coordinator: Kris Stephenson
Interns: Daniel Croll, Tom Moore

PRINT PRODUCTS DIVISION

Director, Print Products: Dana Smith
Distribution Manager: Rhonda Mitchell
Fulfillment and Shipping Manager: Michael Febonio
Shipping Clerk: James H. Taylor IV

ABOUT HOOVER'S, INC.

Hoover's, Inc. (Nasdaq: HOOV) provides online business information and tools to help business-people get their jobs done. Hoover's information is available through its destination site Hoover's Online (http://www.hoovers.com); through co-branding agreements with other online services; and through customized applications developed for enterprise information portals. Hoover's investors include AOL Time Warner (NYSE: AOL), Media General (AMEX: MEGA), and Knowledge Universe, through its Knowledge Net Holdings and Nextera Enterprises (Nasdaq: NXRA) units. Hoover's is headquartered in Austin, Texas, and has offices in New York City and San Francisco.

Abbreviations

AFL-CIO – American Federation of Labor and Congress of Industrial Organizations
AMA – American Medical Association
AMEX – American Stock Exchange
ARM – adjustable-rate mortgage
ATM – asynchronous transfer mode
ATM – automated teller machine
CAD/CAM – computer-aided design/computer-aided manufacturing
CASE – computer-aided software engineering
CD-ROM – compact disc – read-only memory
CEO – chief executive officer
CFO – chief financial officer
CISC – complex instruction set computer
CMOS – complementary metal-oxide semiconductor
COO – chief operating officer
DAT – digital audiotape
DOD – Department of Defense
DOE – Department of Energy
DOS – disc operating system
DOT – Department of Transportation
DRAM – dynamic random access memory
DVD – digital versatile disk/digital videodisk
EPA – Environmental Protection Agency
EPROM – erasable programmable read-only memory
EPS – earnings per share
ESOP – employee stock ownership plan
EU – European Union
EVP – executive vice president
FCC – Federal Communications Commission
FDA – Food and Drug Administration
FDIC – Federal Deposit Insurance Corporation
FTC – Federal Trade Commission
FTP – file transfer protocol
GATT – General Agreement on Tariffs and Trade
GDP – gross domestic product
GUI – graphical user interface
HMO – health maintenance organization
HR – human resources
HTML – hypertext markup language
ICC – Interstate Commerce Commission
IPO – initial public offering
IRS – Internal Revenue Service
ISDN – integrated services digital network
kWh – kilowatt-hour
LAN – local-area network

LBO – leveraged buyout
LCD – liquid crystal display
LNG – liquefied natural gas
LP – limited partnership
Ltd. – limited
mips – millions of instructions per second
MW – megawatt
NAFTA – North American Free Trade Agreement
NASA – National Aeronautics and Space Administration
Nasdaq – National Association of Securities Dealers Automated Quotations
NATO – North Atlantic Treaty Organization
NYSE – New York Stock Exchange
OCR – optical character recognition
OECD – Organization for Economic Cooperation and Development
OEM – original equipment manufacturer
OPEC – Organization of Petroleum Exporting Countries
OS – operating system
OSHA – Occupational Safety and Health Administration
OTC – over-the-counter
PBX – private branch exchange
PCMCIA – Personal Computer Memory Card International Association
P/E – price-to-earnings ratio
RAM – random access memory
R&D – research and development
RBOC – regional Bell operating company
RISC – reduced instruction set computer
REIT – real estate investment trust
ROA – return on assets
ROE – return on equity
ROI – return on investment
ROM – read-only memory
S&L – savings and loan
SEC – Securities and Exchange Commission
SEVP – senior executive vice president
SIC – Standard Industrial Classification
SPARC – scalable processor architecture
SVP – senior vice president
VAR – value-added reseller
VAT – value-added tax
VC – venture capitalist
VP – vice president
WAN – wide-area network
WWW – World Wide Web

Contents

List of Lists

HOOVER'S RANKINGS

Companies Profiled

ABOUT *HOOVER'S TEXAS 500:* A GUIDE TO THE TOP TEXAS COMPANIES

Welcome to the third edition of *Hoover's Texas 500.* Since we published the most recent edition (entitled *Hoover's Guide to the Top Texas Companies*) we've had requests for an updated version. As part of our mission to make business information readily accessible, we have responded. We hope you find this edition useful.

The Texas economy is based on businesses as diverse as the state's landscape. Companies range from some of the largest business enterprises in the world (Exxon Mobil), to those that have a secure perch as the largest in their industry (Halliburton, ClubCorp), to the upstarts of the high-tech world (National Instruments, Vignette), to the quintessentially Texan (King Ranch).

This book is the result of a search of our extensive database of business information for companies headquartered in Texas. We looked for the biggest, the best, the fastest growing, and the most interesting.

We present coverage in this edition of 500 companies — 100 of them in our two-page profile format with a company overview and history and 10 years of financial and employment information. The remaining 400, found in the section titled Key Texas Companies, are presented with shorter summaries and one-year sales information. The Texas 500 are a measure of the health of the state's economy. For the most part, they are the largest businesses, although we have included companies that do not report sales (such as investment firm Hicks, Muse, Tate & Furst) but are recognized as key players on the business front.

In addition to *Hoover's Texas 500,* Hoover's offers its premier four-title series of Handbooks featuring coverage of 2,375 companies: *Hoover's Handbook of American Business* (in two volumes), *Hoover's Handbook of Emerging Companies, Hoover's Handbook of Private Companies,* and *Hoover's Handbook of World Business.*

We also encourage you to visit Hoover's Online (www.hoovers.com), which provides coverage of some 12 million business enterprises. The goal of our Web site is to provide one location that addresses all the needs of business professionals. Hoover's has partnered with other prestigious business information and service providers to bring you the best business information, services, and links in one place. Additionally, Hoover's Company Information is available on other Web sites, including The Washington Post, LexisNexis, and online services Bloomberg Financial Network, Factiva, and America Online.

We believe that anyone who buys from, sells to, invests in, lends to, competes with, interviews with, or works for a company should know as much as possible about that enterprise. Together, *Hoover's Texas 500* and the other Hoover's products represent the most complete source of basic corporate information readily available to the general public.

This book is divided into five sections:

1. "Using the Profiles" describes the contents of our profiles and explains the ways in which we gather and compile our data.

2. "A List-Lover's Compendium" contains lists of the largest, smallest, best, most, and other superlatives related to the companies in this book.

3. The Profiles section comprises 100 profiles of the largest and most interesting Texas enterprises, arranged alphabetically.

4. In the Key Texas Companies section are summary overviews of 500 companies (including the companies with in-depth profiles in the book). The page number of the full profile is listed on the summary page for quick reference.

5. Three indexes complete the book: In addition to the main index, which contains the names of brands, companies, and people mentioned in the profiles, the companies are also indexed by industry group and headquarters location.

As always, we hope you find our books useful. We invite your comments via telephone (512-374-4500), fax (512-374-4501), mail (5800 Airport Blvd., Austin, Texas 78752), or e-mail us at (comments@hoovers.com).

The Editors
Austin, Texas
December 2001

USING THE PROFILES

ORGANIZATION

The profiles and the summary overviews that follow are presented in alphabetical order. This alphabetization is generally word by word, which means that Oak Technology precedes Oakley, Inc. We have shown the full legal name of the enterprise at the top of the page, unless the name is too long, in which case you will find it above the address in the Locations section of the profile. If a company name is also a person's name, such as Jack Henry & Associates, Inc., it will be alphabetized under the first name. All company names (past and present) used in the profiles are indexed in the main index in the book. Basic financial data are listed under the heading Historical Financials & Employees: this includes the exchange where a company's stock is traded if it is public, the ticker symbol used by the stock exchange, and the company's fiscal year-end.

The annual financial information contained in the profiles is current through fiscal year-ends occurring as late as July 2001. We have included certain nonfinancial developments, such as officer changes, through November 2001.

OVERVIEW

In this section we have tried to give a thumbnail description of the company and what it does. The overview will usually include information on the company's strategy, reputation, and ownership. We have also provided a brief history, including the founding date and the names of the founders whenever possible.

OFFICERS

Here we list the names of the people who run the company, insofar as space allows. In the case of public companies, we have shown the ages and pay of key officers. In some cases the published data are for the previous year, although the company has announced promotions or retirements since year-end. The pay represents cash compensation, including bonuses, but excludes stock option programs.

While companies are free to structure their management titles any way they please, most modern corporations follow standard practices. The ultimate power in any corporation lies with the shareholders, who elect a board of directors, usually including officers or company insiders as well as individuals from outside the firm. The chief officer, the person on whose desk the buck stops, is usually called the chief executive officer (CEO). Often, he or she is also the chairman of the board.

Because corporate management has become more complex, it is now common for the CEO to have a right-hand person who oversees the day-to-day operations of the company, allowing the CEO plenty of time to focus on strategy and long-term issues. This right-hand person is usually designated the chief operating officer (COO) and is often the president of the company. In other cases one person is both chairman and president.

A multitude of other titles exists, including chief financial officer (CFO), chief administrative officer, and vice chairman (VC). We include the CFO, the chief legal officer, and the chief human resources or personnel officer, if possible. Our best advice is that officers' pay levels are clear indicators of who the board of directors thinks are the most important members of the management team. The Officers section also includes the name of the company's auditing (accounting) firm, where available.

The people named in the profiles and Officers section are also included in the main index.

LOCATIONS

Here we include the company's headquarters, street address, telephone and fax numbers, and Web site, as available. The back of the book includes an index of companies by headquarters locations.

In some cases we have also included information on the geographical distribution of the company's business, including sales and profit data. Note that these profit numbers, like those in the Products/Operations section below, are usually operating or pretax profits rather than net profits. Operating profits are generally those before financing costs (interest income and payments) and before taxes, which are considered costs attributable to the whole company rather than to one division or part of the world. For this reason the net income figures (in the Historical Financials & Employees section) are usually much lower, since they are after interest and taxes. Pretax profits are after interest but before taxes.

PRODUCTS/OPERATIONS

This section lists as many of the company's products, services, brand names, divisions, subsidiaries, and joint ventures as we could fit.

We have tried to include all its major lines and all familiar brand names. The nature of this section varies by company and amount of information available. If the company publishes sales and profit information by type of business, we have included it. The brand, division, and subsidiary names are listed in the main index.

COMPETITORS

In this section we have listed companies that compete with the profiled company. This feature is included as a quick way to locate similar companies and compare them.

HISTORICAL FINANCIALS & EMPLOYEES

Here we have tried to present as much data about each enterprise's financial performance as we could compile in the allocated space. While the information varies somewhat from industry to industry, the following information is generally present.

A ten-year table, with relevant annualized compound growth rates, covers:

- **Sales** — fiscal year sales (year-end assets for most financial companies)
- **Net Income** — fiscal year net income (before accounting changes)
- **Income as a percent of sales** — fiscal year net income as a percent of sales (as a percent of assets for most financial firms)
- **Earnings Per Share** — fiscal year earnings per share (EPS)
- **Stock price** — the high, low, and close for the fiscal year
- **P/E** — high and low price/earnings ratio
- **Dividends Per Share** — fiscal year dividends per share
- **Book Value Per Share** — fiscal year-end book value (common shareholders' equity per share)
- **Employees** — fiscal year-end or average number of employees

The information on the number of employees is intended as an aid to the reader interested in knowing whether a company has a long-term trend of increasing or decreasing employment. As far as we know, we are the only company that publishes this information in print format.

The numbers at the top of each column in the Historical Financials & Employees section give the month and the year in which the company's fiscal year actually ends. Thus, a company with a March 31, 2001, year-end is shown as 3/01.

Key year-end statistics in this section generally show the financial strength of the enterprise, including:

- Debt ratio (total debt as a percent of combined total debt and shareholders' equity)
- Return on equity (net income divided by the average of beginning and ending common shareholders' equity)
- Cash and cash equivalents
- Current ratio (ratio of current assets to current liabilities)
- Total long-term debt (including capital lease obligations)
- Number of shares of common stock outstanding
- Dividend yield (fiscal year dividends per share divided by the fiscal year-end closing stock price)
- Dividend payout (fiscal year dividends divided by fiscal year EPS)
- Market value at fiscal year-end (fiscal year-end closing stock price multiplied by fiscal year-end number of shares outstanding)
- Research and development as a percentage of sales
- Advertising as a percentage of sales

Per share data have been adjusted for stock splits. The data for most public companies have been provided to us by Media General Financial Services, Inc. Other public and private company information was compiled by Hoover's, which takes full responsibility for the content of this section.

KEY TEXAS COMPANIES

Each of the 400 shorter summary overviews contains the company's name, headquarters address, phone and fax numbers, and Web address (where available); the names of the chief executive officer (CEO), chief financial officer (CFO), and chief human resources officer (HR); the company's fiscal year-end; the most recent annual sales figure available; the sales change over the prior year; the number of employees; and the stock symbol and exchange (if public). Also included are an overview of company operations and ownership and a list of key competitors.

Hoover's
Texas 500

TEXAS ECONOMIC OUTLOOK

OVERVIEW OF THE TEXAS ECONOMY AND BUSINESS ENVIRONMENT

By the office of Carole Keeton Rylander, Comptroller of Public Accounts*

The Texas economy is slowing, as it has been for most of the past three years. This slow-down, paralleling the deceleration in the US economy, shows the state economy performing as expected. Fortunately, Texas' employment and income numbers, at least for now, show the state continuing to prosper. The percentage of Texas' economy tied to the oil and gas industry has shrunk to only 8.5%, less than one-third of the oil/gas peak proportion in the early 1980s. Overall, with the contributions of strengthening energy and communications sectors, Texas' non-farm employment is now growing at a year-over-year rate of 2.7%. Construction and the sector made up of transportation, communications, and utilities, with annual growth rates of 5.0% and 4.3%, respectively, have been leading the pack. According to the US Bureau of Economic Analysis, Texas ranked fourth among the states in the rate of personal income growth and second to California in the dollar increase in personal income for the most recently available period.

Areas with economies more tightly linked to high-tech industries have had a head start in the comparison game. The US Department of Commerce reported that technology industries have accounted for a full one-third of economic growth in the US over the past five years, while representing just 8% of total economic production, as measured by gross product. The same report notes a hundred-fold increase in the number of Internet users since 1994. In Texas today, high-tech industries slightly exceed oil and gas as a percentage of the economy, reaching 8.9% of total gross state product, versus 8.5% for oil and gas.

Although the Texas economy remains vigorous, certain trends suggest that a mild slowdown is underway, as expected. The comptroller forecasts that Texas' real gross state product, the most complete measure of state economic activity, will rise by 4.3% in 2001 and about an average of 4.2% annually in 2002 and 2003, compared to actual growth rates of 7.1%, 5.0%, and 6.1% annually for the last three years.

PRODUCTIVITY GROWTH IS THE KEY

A question often posed about today's Texas economy is how has it been able to continue rolling along with low inflation, in light of very low unemployment and rapid income growth. The answer lies partly in strong productivity growth, enhanced in part by easier communication and information sharing rooted in technological improvements. The "New Economy," roughly meaning an economy tied more to information and electronic usage than in the past, is making radical changes in the service sector, where an increasing number of services is being offered online. For many, mobile telephones allow continuous links to offices and customers. Paying bills and sending messages take less time. Ordering products, researching information, and receiving reports can be done quickly and more easily than in the recent past. People spend less time standing in line or waiting for supplies or services, leaving more time for productive work. Through its e-Texas project, the Comptroller's Office itself is focusing on making state government services more readily available online. Texas has seen annual per-worker productivity increases of 3.1% over the past four years, increases that are partially spurred on by rapid technological advancements in computers and communications.

KEY TEXAS INDICATORS

The state is:

#2 In total resident population for 2000 (20,851,820)
#2 in 1999 (20,044,141)

#2 In employed civilian labor force for 2000 (9,887,000)
#2 in 1999 (9,734,000)

#3 In Gross State Production for 1999 ($687.3 billion)
#3 in 1998 ($645.2 billion)

#16 In unemployment rate for 2000 (4.2%)
#15 in 1999 (4.6%)

#23 in per capita personal income for 2000 ($27,871)
#26 in 1999 ($26,858)

Source: Carole Keeton Rylander, Texas Comptroller of Public Accounts

*Published Fall 2001

Have these productivity improvements nearly run their course, or are they just getting up to speed? According to this research, the Internet economy is growing at 15 times the growth rate of the national economy and in 2000 became larger in dollar terms than the life insurance or automobile sales industries. Productivity requires an ongoing flow of new discoveries and applications, and the Federal Reserve Bank and a leading provider of business data, the WEFA Group, anticipate that the rate of productivity growth will continue or even increase over the next three years.

The rationale for at least three more years of productivity growth, at a time when businesses and consumers are scaling back their economic optimism, is that investment will continue to be spawned by falling technology prices. Also, the lag time between cost reductions and corporate restructuring has shortened, allowing technological advancements already available to keep contributing to productivity growth.

Texas already has a greater rate of productivity than the national average. Texas' gross product per worker ratio has exceeded that of the nation for at least 30 years (save 1987, a Texas recession year). This is largely because Texas has a higher concentration of oil and gas, refining, and petrochemical industries, and the heavy investment in these capital-intensive industries results in a relatively small number of workers. The concentration of oil and gas in Texas is four times that of the national average, benefitting Texas' productivity relative to that for the nation as a whole.

Part of Texas' economic strength may be traced to the almost indefinable entrepreneurial spirit of its workforce, whereby gross state product growth consistently exceeds what would be expected by employment growth alone. That is, Texas elicits proportionately more economic production from an additional job than the national average. While Texas' employment growth rate has outpaced the US by 0.9 percentage points over the past four years, the state's gross product has grown even faster, leading the national gross domestic product growth rate on average by 1.9 percentage points.

OIL AND GAS INDUSTRY: HIGHER FUEL PRICES ARE SLOW TO HELP

Price volatility of oil and gas over the past 20 years has caused potential investors to be wary about investments in exploration. Capital for oil investment remains tight. On top of this, the time delay between investment and production, increasing production quotas for OPEC nations,

and the risk of drilling an unsuccessful well have kept investors skittish. This lack of investment capital, combined with a labor shortage caused by the strong national economy, has held mining employment statewide at 145,000, up less than 1% over the past year. Slow erosion, down to a total of 140,000 jobs by 2005, is forecast.

As technological improvements mean fewer workers are required, the oil and gas industry doesn't offer high hopes for new jobs: Texas oil production is less than half of its 1982 level and has declined by 4.5% annually over the past five years. Natural gas production, likewise, is now only 53% of its 1982 level, declining about 2% per year over the past five years. Consequently, the overall oil and gas industry — including refining, petrochemicals and oil field machinery — fell below ten percent of the Texas economy in 1998.

CONSTRUCTION EMPLOYMENT: UP MORE THAN 50% SINCE 1993

The Texas construction industry has been the fastest-growing sector of the Texas economy over the past three years. Comparatively low building costs, combined with steady net migration spawned by the state's out-performance of the national economy, have kept up the demand for new construction. With 560,400 employees, the Texas construction industry now accounts for 5.9% of the state's non-farm workers, its highest proportion since the mid-1980s.

Although local markets vary, aggregate housing supply statewide has been catching up with demand, causing residential and nonresidential construction activity to slip back a bit. However, Texas per-capita housing starts still exceed the national rate, reflecting the continuing effects of strong positive migration. The total value of single-family residential permits more than tripled in the Houston and Dallas metropolitan areas in the 1990s, while rising more than six times in the Austin-San Marcos metropolitan area. Construction permit values are affected largely by vacancy rates, rates of overbuilding, the demand for housing in the area, and the particular stage of a building cycle in which a local area finds itself.

The state's construction industry will cool in 2001 and 2002. The demand for single-family housing construction could be crimped a bit more than the market for multifamily housing, such as apartments. An expected dip in wage growth could shift more potential buyers away from houses and to apartments, making the outlook for multifamily construction more robust than the outlook for single-family construction.

In sum, total statewide housing starts are expected to drop back a bit (by 1.5%) in 2001, but the demand for housing construction should increase again in 2002 and 2003.

The slowdown in Texas construction has been inching downward just enough to alleviate a labor shortage that suppressed the industry over the past couple of years. The Federal Reserve Bank of Dallas reports the strong building activity in recent years is softening the market for new properties in many areas. The comptroller forecasts continuing construction employment growth, albeit at much slower rates, over the next five years.

The growth rate for construction industry employment is expected to diminish to 1.7% in 2001, 1.3% in 2002, and 1.6% in 2003. After seven years of growth rates averaging 6.6% annually, these rates may appear anemic to some. Even so, the number of construction jobs will grow over the next three years by about 26,000.

FOR MANUFACTURING, IT'S HIGH TECH AGAIN

With a national economic slowdown braking demand, year-to-year manufacturing employment growth is slowing. Propping up manufacturing over this period has been solid growth in building materials, driven by the construction industry.

Layoffs among high-tech manufacturers, resulting from a flood of semiconductors in the market, was the primary reason behind the state's loss of manufacturing jobs. Largely because of high-tech jobs, overall Texas manufacturing employment rose during the 1990s, eclipsing the nation's increase over the same period. More dramatically, real gross state product in the manufacturing sector exploded.

This explosive pace was unsustainable with the glut of computer and electronic components on the market. Rapid technological advances caused computer prices to plummet 26% a year over the past five years. Computer manufacturing employment in Texas has declined, accompanied by a decline in electronics manufacturing employment.

The outlook for Texas manufacturing over the next three years is for job growth to resume, based on the assumption that international markets will continue to strengthen, given that exports are now a crucial variable in Texas' manufacturing growth. Based on national export market forecasts, the Comptroller's Office expects 10% average annual increases in Texas exports from 2000 through 2003. Exports will take up much of the slack in the demand for manufactured goods, even if the domestic market for manufactured goods weakens.

Computers and electronics will be the focus of

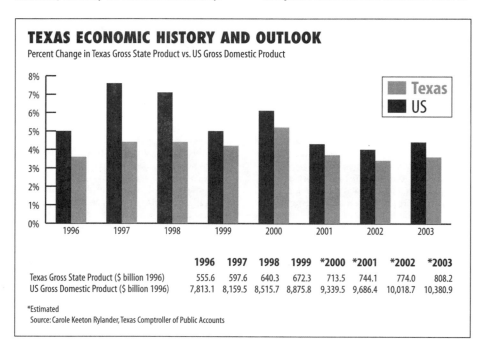

TEXAS ECONOMIC HISTORY AND OUTLOOK

Percent Change in Texas Gross State Product vs. US Gross Domestic Product

	1996	1997	1998	1999	*2000	*2001	*2002	*2003
Texas Gross State Product ($ billion 1996)	555.6	597.6	640.3	672.3	713.5	744.1	774.0	808.2
US Gross Domestic Product ($ billion 1996)	7,813.1	8,159.5	8,515.7	8,875.8	9,339.5	9,686.4	10,018.7	10,380.9

*Estimated

Source: Carole Keeton Rylander, Texas Comptroller of Public Accounts

Texas' manufacturing growth over the next three years. Overall, durable goods manufacturing accounts for more than 60% of Texas' manufacturing employment. In large part because of demand for electronics and computers, overall durable goods manufacturing jobs will grow by about 2.2% annually over the next three years.

Nondurable goods manufacturing has seen five years of declining employment. The decline was due to job losses in the apparel and textile industries, which lost about one-third of their total jobs. Most of these losses, chalked up to international competition, have run their course, so nondurable goods manufacturers are forecast to see net job growth in 2001 and an average annual growth of 0.9% in 2002 and 2003. Most of this growth will be in the expanding range of plastics products fabricated in Texas.

RETAIL GROWTH DECLINING

Even though the vibrant growth rates of Internet sales receive press coverage, the online retailing industry still represents only 2% of national retail trade. This leaves an abundant opportunity for continued growth. Because of continued job and income growth, the outlook for retail sales also remains healthy. However, a more volatile stock market will suppress consumer optimism, which eventually will affect consumers' willingness to spend. This is one of the reasons that the comptroller's forecast anticipates retail sales growth declining through 2003.

Wholesalers and retailers will add jobs over the next three years, particularly those supplying export markets. The rate will slow somewhat, with indications of flagging consumer optimism. Retail trade is laboring harder for gains, corporate debt is at high levels, and the stock market turned more bearish. Employment growth in trade will slide from 3.2% in 2000 to slightly over two percent per year through 2003. Nearly a quarter of Texas' nonfarm jobs are in trade, and this proportion is expected to remain relatively stable over the next few years.

FOR TRANSPORTATION AND COMMUNICATIONS, IT'S ALSO HIGH TECH

Transportation, communications, and public utilities (TCPU) will continue to be one of the fastest-growing Texas industries. The fastest growth will be in the communications sector, where job growth will roll along at 6.1% annually through 2003. This will be driven in part by the unrelenting growth of cellular and Internet communications, with particularly active growth in

high-speed Internet access connections such as digital subscriber lines (DSL). New telecommunications devices and services are far from saturating the Texas market, but intense competition has brought down prices and reduced profit margins for the industry. As a result, gross state product growth in the industry has stepped back a bit from its 10% annual growth during the last three years of the 1990s.

Transportation jobs, now up by 4.2% from a year ago, will advance another 4% annually because of expanding air travel and growing domestic and export markets requiring more shipments of manufactured goods. Utilities employment, on the other hand, is expected to be flat in 2001 and shrink in the next two years. Even though there will be expansions in electrical capacity fueled largely by the recent deregulation of the industry, job opportunities in utilities will be held back because of the capital-intensive, rather than jobs-oriented, nature of this sector. In sum, transportation/communications/public utilities, now employing 6% of all Texas nonfarm workers, will account for more than 11% of net new Texas jobs through 2003.

FINANCE, INSURANCE, AND REAL ESTATE: BACKED BY INVESTMENTS AND HOUSING

Banks took advantage of consumer optimism and sustained low inflation to substantially increase their loan portfolios during the late 1990s. Over the last three years, Texas banks and savings institutions have been expanding their employment at rates not seen since the boom of the early 1980s. The solid growth is beginning to soften, as increased numbers of loan defaults have occurred. Lenders are searching for diversity across industries in their loan portfolios, making loans often harder to get in areas dominated by a single industry. Fee and loan income should keep banking employment opportunities robust in 2001, at a growth rate of 3.7%, before stepping back in 2002 and 2003 in response to a generally quieter economy.

The insurance industry, too, has experienced three very strong years in Texas, with annual employment growth rates averaging 3.4%. However, with personal income growth slowing, inflation rising, and debt levels up, the Texas insurance industry will see employment growth slip, dropping to about 1.6% annually from 2000 to 2003.

Texas real estate values rose much faster than the rate of inflation in the 1990s. According to the Texas A&M Real Estate Center, the median sale price of homes in Texas was $144,900 in

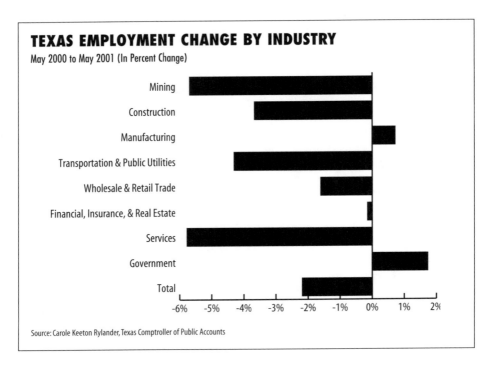

TEXAS EMPLOYMENT CHANGE BY INDUSTRY
May 2000 to May 2001 (In Percent Change)

Mining
Construction
Manufacturing
Transportation & Public Utilities
Wholesale & Retail Trade
Financial, Insurance, & Real Estate
Services
Government
Total

-6%   -5%   -4%   -3%   -2%   -1%   0%   1%   2%

Source: Carole Keeton Rylander, Texas Comptroller of Public Accounts

2000, based on Multiple Listing Service (MLS) data for the first three-quarters of the year, compared to $104,400 in 1995. This represents a robust 6.8% increase in the average MLS house's value per year, considerably outstripping the rate of inflation. If housing prices had increased at the rate of the consumer price index, which rose only 2.4% a year over the period, the value of the average Texas residential house would have increased by only $12,800 in five years, rather than the $40,500 shown in the MLS data. The importance of location and cycles to real estate value is certainly true of Texas real estate; while some geographic pockets experienced colossal increases in total value, others barely budged.

The real estate and finance sector, which includes stockbrokers, will experience the economic cooling that is suppressing insurance employment growth over the next two years, only more so. Leveraged (or margin) debt is at a near-record high, forcing the sale of stock shares when margin calls occur, and adding to stock and commodity market volatility. Stock price volatility and fickle consumer confidence have already cooled employment growth in investment finance. Although the real estate and finance sector will add jobs through 2003, the toll of a more

shaky economy is to limit job growth to 0.3% in 2001 and just over 1% annually in 2002 and 2003. Real estate and finance was one of the fastest-growing Texas sectors in 1998, with 8.4% job growth, before slowing to 5.3% in 1999 and 4.4% in 2000.

Overall employment growth in Texas' finance, insurance, and real estate industry should step back from 3.4% in 2000 to about 1 to 1.5% annually over the 2000-2003 period.

SERVICES TO CONTINUE 3.2% ANNUAL GROWTH

Whether we have entered a "new economy" operating under a new set of electronic commerce rules, or one grounded in old conventional economic forces, service jobs will continue to provide the bulk of job growth to the Texas economy. Most of these jobs will be in traditional occupations. About 14% of the total job growth in the Texas economy over the next three years will be in business services, with 8% in health services and 8% more in engineering, accounting, and research. Another 9% will be in miscellaneous services such as repair, amusements, membership organizations, and personal services. All combined, services will account for 39% of the new

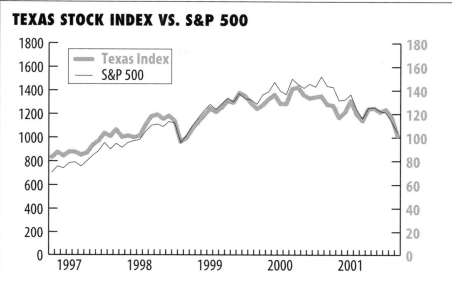

TEXAS STOCK INDEX VS. S&P 500

Legend:
- Texas Index
- S&P 500

MAKEUP OF THE TEXAS STOCK INDEX

The Texas Stock Index is based on the 100 largest publicly traded employers in Texas measured by their average number of workers annually. For a complete list of companies that make up the index, see pages 25-26 in A List-Lover's Compendium.

Source: Carole Keeton Rylander, Texas Comptroller of Public Accounts; Standard and Po's

jobs over the next three years. An additional 48% of the new jobs are in other service-producing industries, such as trade, transportation, utilities, finance, real estate, and government, leaving only about one out of eight nonfarm jobs to be generated in goods-producing industries.

The most rapid growth in the service industry will be in sectors most closely tied to new technological improvements, with engineering, accounting, and research services showing the fastest growth of any sector of the Texas economy, rising 6% per year through 2003.

The business services sector, including temporary and consulting services, is expected to add 4% more jobs annually. Repair services will grow faster than the overall economy, at about 3.2% per year, but health services, which boomed in the early and mid-1990s, will just slightly eclipse the economy's overall rate of job growth. While the aging of the population favors rapid growth in health care services, efforts to control costs in the face of rising pharmaceutical prices will hold health services employment growth to about 2.5% annually. Overall, services employment will account for about 84,000 new jobs per year through

2003, with average annual job growth rates of about 3%.

GOVERNMENT

Government will once again have the slowest job growth rate among the five major service-producing industries. Federal government employment has shrunk in response to defense cutbacks, but most of this has run its course. Because of the "hiccup" created in 2000 as workers were hired to conduct the decennial population census, federal jobs in Texas increased for the first year since the 1990 census. Federal employment will decline again in 2001, and in 2002 it will be about where it was in 1999, just shy of 185,000 jobs.

Most government jobs in Texas are not at the federal level. State government employment should rise at about half the rate of population growth, as it has over the past five years, adding about 0.8% job growth annually. Local government, with job growth rates of just under 2% annually, will account for 90% of new government jobs in Texas and continue to reflect the ongoing shift of government services to local areas.

EXPORTS TAKE MORE OF TEXAS AROUND THE GLOBE

Texas exports will account for 14% of the state's 2000 gross product, up from 11% 10 years ago, despite the economic pummeling and later recovery of the important Mexican and Asian markets over the past decade. The increasing role of international trade in Texas' economy means it will be shaped by international events more than ever, and the comptroller's economic forecast is not expecting exports to retreat anytime soon. As the recovering economies of developing nations, specifically Mexico, take off, exports are expected to account for an even greater share of the state economy, rising nearly a half percentage point per year. In twenty years, the proportion of Texas' economy owing to exports will be 22%.

Exports are relatively more important to the Texas economy than is the case nationwide. Although Texas has only a bit over 7% of the nation's population, for every dollar of US exports, 13 cents are generated from exports originating in Texas. Texas ranks third among the states in both per capita exports and the proportion of total gross state product from exports (exceeded in each case by Vermont and Washington).

Underlying this export intensity is the state's proximity to Mexico, which receives the lion's share of Texas' exports. According to the most recent data available, 45% of Texas exports are destined for Mexico, and 48% of US exports to Mexico originate in Texas. Four industries account for two-thirds of total Texas exports: electronics, industrial machinery (including computers), chemicals, and transportation equipment.

Vicente Fox's election to the presidency of Mexico shows signs of stimulating increased economic activity across the border. Recent US moves to resume normal trading relations with China, as evidenced by granting China "most favored nation" status, should be particularly beneficial for the state's technology-based exports.

INTERNATIONAL MIGRATION EXCEEDS DOMESTIC MIGRATION

During the 1990s, Texas added an average of 139,000 people per year from net migration. About 77,000 of these (or 56%) were international migrants, a large share of them from Mexico. The great majority of international migrants, including both legal and, to the extent the Census Bureau can measure, illegal immigrants, take up residence in one of the state's large cities, according to the Bureau of the Census. The Houston metropolitan area has received the most net

---

NONFARM EMPLOYMENT JUNE 2000-JUNE 2001 RANKED BY STATE

Total Employment in June 2001

California	14,817,000
TEXAS	**9,669,100**
New York	8,725,500
Florida	7,299,800
Illinois	6,058,500
Pennsylvania	5,743,800
Ohio	5,650,400
Michigan	4,670,400
Georgia	4,051,200
New Jersey	4,023,100
Total US	**132,383,000**

Change in Nonfarm Employment by Number

California	+310,300
Florida	228,800
TEXAS	**221,400**
New York	92,400
Georgia	75,600
Colorado	60,000
Virginia	56,100
Pennsylvania	52,900
Nevada	51,700
Massachusetts	50,100
Total US	**414,000**

Percentage Change in Nonfarm Employment

Nevada	+5.0
Florida	3.2
Wyoming	2.8
Colorado	2.7
TEXAS	**2.3**
Alaska	2.3
California	2.1
Idaho	2.1
New Mexico	2.1
Georgia	1.9
Total US	**0.3**

Source: Carole Keeton Rylander, Texas Comptroller of Public Accounts

---

international migration (about 23,000 annually), while Dallas is second at about 14,000. El Paso, McAllen-Edinburg-Mission, and Ft. Worth-Arlington round out the top five Texas metros for international migrants.

With continued net domestic migration, as well as a birth rate exceeding the national average, Texas is expected to increase its representation in the US House of Representatives from 30 to 32 following the 2000 census. Overall, the state's population is expected to increase from 20.8 million in 2000 to 21.9 million in 2003.

WHERE ARE THE NEW TEXANS FROM?

During the 1990s, Texas' population increased by a record 3.7 million, reaching a total of 20.8 million by the end of the decade. Over this period the majority of the state's population growth was due to natural increase, i.e. births minus deaths. But nearly 45% of the increase reflected the net in-migration of persons from other states and other parts of the world. Since Texas' birth rate is only somewhat above the national average, net migration is the major factor that allows Texas' population to grow faster than the national average.

Net migration, however, is the difference between two huge flows into or out of a given geographic area. For two reasons, we usually concentrate on net migration in analyzing and projecting Texas' population growth. First, because of the availability of the Census Bureau's annual population estimates, we can easily calculate updated net migration figures by taking the annual population change and then subtracting natural increase (births minus deaths) during the period. Second, as noted above, although net migration reflects only the difference between two large flows into and out of a state, it is the net difference between these two flows that is the primary determinant of state population growth relative to the US.

The majority of the persons who moved into the state during this period are from nine states — California, Florida, Louisiana, Oklahoma, Illinois, New Mexico, Colorado, Georgia, and Arkansas — and from other countries. As many Texans would expect, California, with 11% of the in-migrants, leads the list of states. But 21.5% of the new Texas residents come from the four surrounding states of Louisiana, Oklahoma, New Mexico, and Arkansas, plus our near-neighbor Colorado. Another 9.3% of the new Texans during this period originated from the two large Sun Belt states of Florida and Georgia. Finally, reflecting national trends, in-migration from foreign countries is playing an increasing role in migration into Texas. A total of 7.1% of the total were from other parts of the world, a large share coming from Mexico.

This pattern of migration is generally consistent with the measurement of migration trends across the world using the "gravity model" of population attraction. The gravity model predicts that migration between any two areas is positively related to the product of the areas' populations and inversely related to the distance between the two areas. Thus, given the relatively close proximity, the large migration flows between Texas and surrounding states as well as Colorado and Mexico are expected. In addition, even though they are relatively far away, both California and Florida contain large populations that facilitate migrant flows between Texas and the other two most populated Sun Belt states.

As predicted by the gravity model, the destination of out-migrants from the state looks almost identical to the origin of in-migrants. More than 11.2% of the Texas out-migrants moved to California. Another 23% moved to the four surrounding states plus Colorado, and 10.6% went to Florida and Georgia.

Finally, 5.8% of the out-migrants moved to foreign countries, again a large share going to Mexico, during this period. Even with this large outflow, however, Texas remained a net importer of new residents during this period because of its relatively healthy economy.

Hoover's
Texas 500

A List-Lover's Compendium

The 500 Companies in *Hoover's Texas 500*
Ranked by Sales

Rank	Company	Sales ($ mil.)	Rank	Company	Sales ($ mil.)
1	Exxon Mobil Corporation	228,439	51	Clear Channel Communications, Inc.	5,345
2	Enron Corp.	100,789	52	Baker Hughes Incorporated	5,234
3	SBC Communications Inc.	51,476	53	Tesoro Petroleum Corporation	5,104
4	Equilon Enterprises LLC	50,010	54	Blockbuster Inc.	4,960
5	Compaq Computer Corporation	42,383	55	RadioShack Corporation	4,795
6	Conoco Inc.	38,737	56	Suiza Dairy Group	4,660
7	USX-Marathon Group	33,859	57	Cooper Industries, Inc.	4,460
8	Dell Computer Corporation	31,888	58	Genesis Energy, L.P.	4,325
9	J. C. Penney Company, Inc.	31,846	59	Temple-Inland Inc.	4,286
10	Shell Oil Company	29,671	60	Encompass Services Corporation	4,099
11	Dynegy Inc.	29,445	61	Lyondell Chemical Company	4,036
12	Reliant Energy, Incorporated	29,339	62	Texas Lottery Commission	3,940
13	TXU Corp.	22,009	63	Administaff, Inc.	3,709
14	El Paso Corporation	21,950	64	D.R. Horton, Inc.	3,654
15	SYSCO Corporation	21,785	65	Group 1 Automotive, Inc.	3,586
16	ExxonMobil Chemical Company	21,503	66	Lennox International Inc.	3,247
17	Reliant Resources, Inc.	19,792	67	Gulf States Toyota, Inc.	3,158
18	AMR Corporation	19,703	68	Burlington Resources Inc.	3,147
19	Motiva Enterprises LLC	19,446	69	TEPPCO Partners, L.P.	3,088
20	Electronic Data Systems Corporation	19,227	70	Enterprise Products Partners L.P.	3,049
21	Ultramar Diamond Shamrock	17,061	71	The Neiman Marcus Group, Inc.	3,016
22	Valero Energy Corporation	14,671	72	Smith International, Inc.	2,761
23	Fleming Companies, Inc.	14,444	73	Kinder Morgan, Inc.	2,714
24	Kimberly-Clark Corporation	13,982	74	CompuCom Systems, Inc.	2,711
25	Frito-Lay, Inc.	12,881	75	Commercial Metals Company	2,661
26	Waste Management, Inc.	12,492	76	Sabre Inc.	2,617
27	Texas Instruments Incorporated	11,875	77	Randall's Food Markets, Inc.	2,585
28	Halliburton Company	11,856	78	Service Corporation International	2,565
29	EOTT Energy Partners, L.P.	11,614	79	CellStar Corporation	2,476
30	American General Corporation	11,063	80	Brinker International, Inc.	2,474
31	McLane Company, Inc.	10,542	81	Pizza Hut, Inc.	2,469
32	Continental Airlines, Inc.	9,899	82	MAXXAM Inc.	2,448
33	7-Eleven, Inc.	9,346	83	Wyndham International, Inc.	2,422
34	Burlington Northern Santa Fe	9,205	84	Apache Corporation	2,284
35	USAA	8,550	85	Pennzoil-Quaker State Company	2,271
36	H. E. Butt Grocery Company	8,200	86	Michaels Stores, Inc.	2,249
37	Equistar Chemicals, LP	7,495	87	CHRISTUS Health	2,200
38	AdvancePCS, Inc.	7,024	88	The Minute Maid Company	2,200
39	Adams Resources & Energy, Inc.	7,022	89	Kaiser Aluminum Corporation	2,170
40	Compaq Global Services	6,993	90	Goodman Manufacturing Company	2,160
41	Army and Air Force Exchange Service	6,992	91	Zale Corporation	2,068
42	Centex Corporation	6,711	92	Affiliated Computer Services, Inc.	2,064
43	Plains All American Pipeline, L.P.	6,641	93	Frontier Oil Corporation	2,045
44	Plains Resources Inc.	6,575	94	Metals USA, Inc.	2,022
45	CompUSA Inc.	6,321	95	Sammons Enterprises, Inc.	2,000
46	The University of Texas System	5,943	96	Quexco Incorporated	2,000
47	The Turner Corporation	5,800	97	Southern Union Company	1,933
48	Suiza Foods Corporation	5,756	98	Trinity Industries, Inc.	1,904
49	Anadarko Petroleum Corporation	5,686	99	Dr Pepper/Seven Up Bottling Group	1,900
50	Southwest Airlines Co.	5,650	100	EGL, Inc.	1,861

Source: Hoover's, Inc., Database, November 2001

Rank	Company	Sales ($ mil.)	Rank	Company	Sales ($ mil.)
101	Whole Foods Market, Inc.	1,839	151	Sterling Chemicals Holdings, Inc.	1,078
102	American National Insurance	1,838	152	Ocean Energy, Inc.	1,074
103	Imperial Sugar Company	1,821	153	ClubCorp, Inc.	1,069
104	Weatherford International, Inc.	1,814	154	UICI	1,051
105	Quanta Services, Inc.	1,793	155	Global Marine Inc.	1,040
106	The Texas A&M University System	1,792	156	VarTec Telecom, Inc.	1,020
107	Benchmark Electronics, Inc.	1,705	157	NCI Building Systems, Inc.	1,018
108	Integrated Electrical Services, Inc.	1,672	158	Memorial Hermann Healthcare	1,003
109	Mitchell Energy & Development	1,672	159	Tauber Oil Company	1,000
110	Rent-A-Center, Inc.	1,602	160	Minyard Food Stores, Inc.	1,000
111	Brookshire Grocery Company	1,600	161	Vought Aircraft Industries, Inc.	1,000
112	Comfort Systems USA, Inc.	1,591	162	JPI	1,000
113	Belo Corp.	1,589	163	Petro Stopping Centers, L.P.	983
114	BJ Services Company	1,555	164	TIG Specialty Insurance Solutions	979
115	Flowserve Corporation	1,538	165	Harte-Hanks, Inc.	961
116	BMC Software, Inc.	1,504	166	Ben E. Keith Company	959
117	Pilgrim's Pride Corporation	1,499	167	Stage Stores, Inc.	952
118	Greyhound Lines, Inc.	1,498	168	Dal-Tile International Inc.	952
119	EOG Resources, Inc.	1,490	169	The Beck Group	950
120	Glazer's Wholesale Drug Company	1,480	170	Stewart Information Services	936
121	Pier 1 Imports, Inc.	1,412	171	Quanex Corporation	934
122	Grocers Supply Co. Inc.	1,400	172	Crescent Real Estate Equities Company	923
123	Builders FirstSource, Inc.	1,400	173	NL Industries, Inc.	922
124	Cooper Cameron Corporation	1,387	174	Pride International, Inc.	909
125	Noble Affiliates, Inc.	1,381	175	Rush Enterprises, Inc.	897
126	Pillowtex Corporation	1,350	176	Noble Drilling Corporation	883
127	Texas Health Resources	1,340	177	Baylor Health Care System	875
128	The Men's Wearhouse, Inc.	1,334	178	Key Energy Services, Inc.	866
129	Nabors Industries, Inc.	1,327	179	Texas Petrochemicals LP	859
130	US Oncology, Inc.	1,324	180	Pioneer Natural Resources Company	853
131	Texas Industries, Inc.	1,252	181	Atmos Energy Corporation	850
132	Lincoln Property Company	1,251	182	IMCO Recycling Inc.	847
133	Triad Hospitals, Inc.	1,236	183	Kevco, Inc.	840
134	Transocean Sedco Forex Inc.	1,230	184	David Weekley Homes	828
135	Austin Industries Inc.	1,217	185	The La Quinta Companies	823
136	Software Spectrum, Inc.	1,213	186	Triangle Pacific Corp.	823
137	Shell Services International	1,200	187	Williamson-Dickie Manufacturing	820
138	Hunt Consolidated Inc.	1,200	188	AmeriCredit Corp.	818
139	Contran Corporation	1,200	189	Kinder Morgan Energy Partners, L.P.	816
140	Mary Kay Inc.	1,200	190	The Freeman Companies	801
141	H. B. Zachry Company	1,195	191	Methodist Health Care System	795
142	Valhi, Inc.	1,192	192	Cinemark USA, Inc.	786
143	Daisytek International Corporation	1,190	193	Austin Energy	783
144	Stewart & Stevenson Services, Inc.	1,153	194	Cirrus Logic, Inc.	779
145	National-Oilwell, Inc.	1,150	195	Trammell Crow Company	761
146	Holly Corporation	1,142	196	GameStop, Inc.	757
147	Cameron Ashley Building Products	1,138	197	Consolidated Container Company LLC	755
148	i2 Technologies, Inc.	1,126	198	Concentra, Inc.	752
149	GSC Enterprises, Inc.	1,111	199	Brookshire Brothers, LTD.	750
150	Perot Systems Corporation	1,106	200	Carlson Restaurants Worldwide Inc.	750

The 500 Companies in *Hoover's Texas 500*
Ranked by Sales (continued)

Rank	Company	Sales ($ mil.)	Rank	Company	Sales ($ mil.)
201	Hines Interests L.P.	750	251	CEC Entertainment, Inc.	506
202	FreshPoint, Inc.	732	252	Fossil, Inc.	504
203	Fiesta Mart, Inc.	730	253	Alliance Data Systems Corporation	503
204	Academy Sports & Outdoors, Ltd.	720	254	N.F. Smith & Associates, LP	500
205	Crescent Operating, Inc.	717	255	Associated Materials Incorporated	499
206	El Paso Electric Company	702	256	Grant Prideco, Inc.	499
207	Affiliated Foods Incorporated	700	257	Pogo Producing Company	498
208	FFP Marketing Company, Inc.	688	258	Atrium Companies, Inc.	496
209	Consolidated Graphics, Inc.	683	259	Luby's, Inc.	493
210	Cullen/Frost Bankers, Inc.	683	260	BancTec, Inc.	488
211	NCH Corporation	680	261	Aviall, Inc.	486
212	Diamond Offshore Drilling, Inc.	659	262	Snelling and Snelling, Inc.	481
213	Palm Harbor Homes, Inc.	651	263	International Bancshares Corporation	479
214	Fairchild Dornier Corporation	650	264	Veritas DGC Inc.	477
215	Crown Castle International Corp.	649	265	EmCare Holdings Inc.	471
216	Rowan Companies, Inc.	646	266	SWS Group, Inc.	471
217	Lone Star Technologies, Inc.	645	267	McCoy Corporation	467
218	TNP Enterprises, Inc.	644	268	HCC Insurance Holdings, Inc.	466
219	E-Z Mart Stores, Inc.	641	269	Home Interiors & Gifts, Inc.	460
220	Newmark Homes Corp.	641	270	Hastings Entertainment, Inc.	458
221	Plains Cotton Cooperative Association	633	271	F.Y.I. Incorporated	458
222	Hanover Compressor Company	604	272	VHA Inc.	442
223	XTO Energy Inc.	601	273	Centex Construction Products, Inc.	441
224	Cactus Feeders, Inc.	600	274	Haggar Corp.	433
225	Darr Equipment Company	600	275	Norwood Promotional Products, Inc.	431
226	Whataburger, Inc.	600	276	The Gambrinus Company	425
227	David McDavid Auto Group	596	277	The Bombay Company, Inc.	422
228	La Quinta Corporation	595	278	National Instruments Corporation	410
229	Ancira Enterprises	589	279	DuPont Photomasks, Inc.	408
230	Tuesday Morning Corporation	587	280	Camden Property Trust	404
231	Santa Fe International Corporation	584	281	U.S. Concrete, Inc.	395
232	United Supermarkets, Inc.	575	282	Frozen Food Express Industries, Inc.	392
233	American Homestar Corporation	574	283	Vinson & Elkins L.L.P.	387
234	American Plumbing and Mechanical	569	284	Riviana Foods Inc.	382
235	FelCor Lodging Trust Incorporated	557	285	Marketing Specialists Corporation	381
236	TTI, Inc.	555	286	Elcor Corporation	379
237	Fresh America Corp.	555	287	L.D. Brinkman and Co.	378
238	TRT Holdings	550	288	Prodigy Communications Corporation	376
239	Foxworth-Galbraith Lumber Company	540	289	Parker Drilling Company	376
240	Interlogix, Inc.	540	290	Clarent Hospital Corporation	369
241	Lower Colorado River Authority	538	291	Cabot Oil & Gas Corporation	369
242	ENSCO International Incorporated	534	292	Vignette Corporation	367
243	MMI Products, Inc.	530	293	American Realty Investors, Inc.	366
244	Newfield Exploration Company	527	294	Garden Ridge Corporation	365
245	Landry's Restaurants, Inc.	521	295	Southwestern Energy Company	364
246	Capstead Mortgage Corporation	520	296	Cash America International, Inc.	364
247	Dallas Semiconductor Corporation	517	297	Helen of Troy Limited	361
248	University of Houston System	515	298	Kinetic Concepts, Inc.	354
249	Kirby Corporation	513	299	Dynacare Inc.	353
250	Justin Industries, Inc.	510	300	Central Freight Lines, Inc.	350

The 500 Companies in *Hoover's Texas 500*
Ranked by Sales (continued)

Rank	Company	Sales ($ mil.)	Rank	Company	Sales ($ mil.)
301	Hollywood Casino Corporation	348	351	Dynamex Inc.	252
302	Prentiss Properties Trust	348	352	Southwestern Life Holdings Inc.	251
303	Fulbright & Jaworski L.L.P.	343	353	Trilogy	250
304	Pioneer Companies, Inc.	341	354	The Dunlap Company	250
305	SEACOR SMIT Inc.	340	355	Coastal Bancorp, Inc.	249
306	Northern Border Partners, L.P.	340	356	Weiner's Stores, Inc.	249
307	Eye Care Centers of America, Inc.	338	357	Jenkens & Gilchrist, P.C.	249
308	Keystone Consolidated Industries, Inc.	338	358	U S Liquids Inc.	248
309	Dave & Buster's, Inc.	332	359	Radiologix, Inc.	247
310	Nuevo Energy Company	332	360	Packaged Ice, Inc.	244
311	Triton Energy Limited	329	361	Darling International Inc.	243
312	Hotel Reservations Network, Inc.	328	362	Boy Scouts of America	242
313	ICO, Inc.	325	363	Hispanic Broadcasting Corporation	238
314	ProMedCo Management Company	325	364	Evercom, Inc.	235
315	Pitt-Des Moines, Inc.	318	365	Universal Compression Holdings, Inc.	233
316	Southwest Bancorporation of Texas	315	366	Southwest Texas State University	232
317	Southwest Research Institute	315	367	Stevens Transport Inc.	231
318	Baker Botts L.L.P.	312	368	Silverleaf Resorts, Inc.	231
319	Transportation Components, Inc.	311	369	W-H Energy Services, Inc.	230
320	Warren Electric Group, Ltd.	310	370	Ennis Business Forms, Inc.	229
321	Patterson-UTI Energy, Inc.	308	371	Cornell Companies, Inc.	226
322	Oceaneering International, Inc.	308	372	Electrolux L.L.C.	226
323	Vallen Corporation	306	373	NATCO Group Inc.	225
324	Enbridge Energy Partners, L.P.	306	374	TETRA Technologies, Inc.	225
325	Oil States International, Inc.	305	375	Cooperative Computing	224
326	King Ranch, Inc.	300	376	The Meridian Resource Corporation	223
327	Blue Bell Creameries L.P.	300	377	Powell Industries, Inc.	223
328	Sun Coast Resources Inc.	300	378	Southern Methodist University	218
329	Friona Industries, L.P.	300	379	Travis Boats & Motors, Inc.	218
330	Aegis Communications Group, Inc.	295	380	Alamo Group Inc.	216
331	National Western Life Insurance	293	381	Monarch Dental Corporation	211
332	Brazos Electric Power Cooperative	290	382	Argonaut Group, Inc.	210
333	WebLink Wireless, Inc.	290	383	TDIndustries, Ltd.	204
334	Gadzooks, Inc.	288	384	Texas Regional Bancshares, Inc.	203
335	Pure Resources, Inc.	287	385	Efficient Networks, Inc.	202
336	Allegiance Telecom, Inc.	285	386	Hunt Building Corporation	200
337	Encore Wire Corporation	284	387	Commemorative Brands, Inc.	200
338	Pentacon, Inc.	284	388	Ultrak, Inc.	200
339	Crown Group, Inc.	283	389	Tandy Brands Accessories, Inc.	199
340	Baylor University	275	390	EZCORP, Inc.	197
341	Golfsmith International, L.P.	275	391	Ace Cash Express, Inc.	197
342	InterVoice-Brite, Inc.	275	392	Furr's Restaurant Group, Inc.	196
343	Weingarten Realty Investors	274	393	Sterling Bancshares, Inc.	196
344	The Houston Exploration Company	271	394	H.D. Vest, Inc.	194
345	Grey Wolf, Inc.	269	395	XeTel Corporation	193
346	EEX Corporation	262	396	Travelocity.com Inc.	193
347	The Container Store	260	397	The York Group, Inc.	193
348	University of North Texas	257	398	KCS Energy, Inc.	192
349	Lufkin Industries, Inc.	255	399	Transcontinental Realty Investors, Inc.	192
350	CompX International Inc.	253	400	E. W. Blanch Holdings, Inc.	191

The 500 Companies in *Hoover's Texas 500*
Ranked by Sales (continued)

Rank	Company	Sales ($ mil.)	Rank	Company	Sales ($ mil.)
401	Gundle/SLT Environmental, Inc.	191	451	Prime Medical Services, Inc.	131
402	Denali Incorporated	190	452	Xanser Corporation	128
403	Swift Energy Company	190	453	Kaneb Services LLC	128
404	Overhill Corporation	189	454	Magnum Hunter Resources, Inc.	128
405	Range Resources Corporation	187	455	INSpire Insurance Solutions, Inc.	127
406	Industrial Holdings, Inc.	186	456	Texas Rangers Baseball Club	127
407	TransTexas Gas Corporation	183	457	Houston Astros Baseball Club	122
408	DXP Enterprises, Inc.	183	458	La Madeleine French Bakery & Cafe	121
409	Classic Communications, Inc.	182	459	Spinnaker Exploration Company	121
410	Cal Dive International, Inc.	181	460	LDB Corp.	120
411	Dallas Cowboys Football Club, Ltd.	181	461	EXE Technologies, Inc.	116
412	The Staubach Company	180	462	Express One International, Inc.	115
413	Hydril Company	180	463	Lancer Corporation	114
414	Denbury Resources Inc.	179	464	El Paso Energy Partners, L.P.	112
415	Mattress Giant Corporation	178	465	Carreker Corporation	110
416	Arena Brands Inc.	175	466	Clayton Williams Energy, Inc.	110
417	American Rice, Inc.	171	467	Castle Dental Centers, Inc.	106
418	AMRESCO, INC.	171	468	First Cash Financial Services, Inc.	106
419	Taco Cabana, Inc.	171	469	3TEC Energy Corporation	103
420	Comstock Resources, Inc.	169	470	Silicon Laboratories Inc.	103
421	Excel Communications, Inc.	166	471	Souper Salad, Inc.	97
422	GAINSCO, INC.	165	472	Multimedia Games, Inc.	97
423	Dril-Quip, Inc.	164	473	Angelo State University	95
424	Seitel, Inc.	164	474	AMX Corporation	94
425	Synagro Technologies, Inc.	163	475	Vari-Lite International, Inc.	94
426	Carriage Services, Inc.	163	476	CARBO Ceramics Inc.	93
427	Pegasus Solutions, Inc.	162	477	Alamosa Holdings, Inc.	83
428	Horizon Offshore, Inc.	161	478	Half Price Books	80
429	Inet Technologies, Inc.	159	479	Houston Rockets	79
430	Samuels Jewelers, Inc.	158	480	Input/Output, Inc.	78
431	Kaneb Pipe Line Partners, L.P.	156	481	Dallas Stars L.P.	73
432	Play-By-Play Toys & Novelties, Inc.	153	482	San Antonio Spurs, Ltd.	67
433	Mannatech, Incorporated	150	483	Pizza Inn, Inc.	64
434	AXIA Incorporated	150	484	San Juan Basin Royalty Trust	60
435	Ascent Assurance, Inc.	150	485	Dallas Mavericks	60
436	Prize Energy Corp.	150	486	Schlotzsky's, Inc.	59
437	Entrust Inc.	148	487	Hugoton Royalty Trust	57
438	El Chico Restaurants, Inc.	148	488	Calloway's Nursery, Inc.	54
439	ACS Dataline, LP	145	489	VTEL Corporation	38
440	New Century Equity Holdings Corp.	145	490	ILEX Oncology, Inc.	28
441	Panda Energy International, Inc.	144	491	Tanox, Inc.	13
442	First Financial Bankshares, Inc.	144	492	Active Power, Inc.	5
443	ACR Group, Inc.	136	493	Texas Southern University	*
444	HORIZON Pharmacies, Inc.	136	494	St. Luke's Episcopal Hospital	*
445	United Surgical Partners International	136	495	Wingate Partners	**
446	Luminant Worldwide Corporation	135	496	Hicks, Muse, Tate & Furst Incorporated	**
447	Atwood Oceanics, Inc.	135	497	Blue Cross and Blue Shield of Texas Inc.	*
448	Horizon Health Corporation	134	498	Sevin Rosen Funds	**
449	MetaSolv, Inc.	132	499	Texas Pacific Group	**
450	CMS Oil and Gas Company	131	500	Austin Ventures, L.P.	**

*Sales not available
**Investment and venture capital firms generally do not report revenues.

The 500 Companies in *Hoover's Texas 500*
Ranked by Employees

Rank	Company	Employees	Rank	Company	Employees
1	J. C. Penney Company, Inc.	267,000	51	Randall's Food Markets, Inc.	17,650
2	SBC Communications Inc.	215,088	52	Conoco Inc.	17,600
3	Exxon Mobil Corporation	123,000	53	Suiza Dairy Group	17,500
4	Electronic Data Systems	122,000	54	TXU Corp.	16,540
5	AMR Corporation	116,054	55	McLane Company, Inc.	16,120
6	Frito-Lay, Inc.	100,000	56	Texas Health Resources	16,000
7	Blockbuster Inc.	95,800	57	Landry's Restaurants, Inc.	16,000
8	Compaq Computer Corporation	94,600	58	Reliant Energy, Incorporated	15,633
9	Halliburton Company	93,000	59	Transocean Sedco Forex Inc.	15,600
10	The University of Texas System	79,430	60	Triad Hospitals, Inc.	15,500
11	Brinker International, Inc.	78,500	61	Integrated Electrical Services, Inc.	15,500
12	Kimberly-Clark Corporation	66,300	62	The Neiman Marcus Group, Inc.	15,400
13	Administaff, Inc.	62,140	63	Pilgrim's Pride Corporation	15,400
14	Waste Management, Inc.	57,000	64	Trinity Industries, Inc.	15,300
15	Continental Airlines, Inc.	54,300	65	El Paso Corporation	15,000
16	Army and Air Force Exchange Service	54,000	66	Whataburger, Inc.	15,000
17	H. E. Butt Grocery Company	50,000	67	Temple-Inland Inc.	14,800
18	RadioShack Corporation	43,600	68	ExxonMobil Chemical Company	14,600
19	SYSCO Corporation	43,000	69	Pier 1 Imports, Inc.	14,600
20	Texas Instruments Incorporated	42,400	70	Stage Stores, Inc.	14,021
21	Dell Computer Corporation	40,000	71	Luby's, Inc.	14,000
22	Burlington Northern Santa Fe	39,600	72	Quanta Services, Inc.	13,260
23	Clear Channel Communications, Inc.	36,350	73	Equilon Enterprises LLC	13,000
24	Cooper Industries, Inc.	34,250	74	Centex Corporation	13,000
25	Encompass Services Corporation	34,000	75	Rent-A-Center, Inc.	12,554
26	The Freeman Companies	34,000	76	Pillowtex Corporation	12,500
27	7-Eleven, Inc.	33,400	77	The Men's Wearhouse, Inc.	12,000
28	Michaels Stores, Inc.	33,000	78	Memorial Hermann Healthcare	12,000
29	USX-Marathon Group	30,892	79	Baylor Health Care System	12,000
30	Compaq Global Services	30,000	80	Weatherford International, Inc.	11,900
31	Fleming Companies, Inc.	29,567	81	MAXXAM Inc.	11,560
32	Service Corporation International	29,326	82	Shell Oil Company	11,140
33	Southwest Airlines Co.	29,274	83	F.Y.I. Incorporated	11,000
34	Wyndham International, Inc.	28,000	84	H. B. Zachry Company	11,000
35	Greyhound Lines, Inc.	24,700	85	GameStop, Inc.	11,000
36	Baker Hughes Incorporated	24,500	86	Comfort Systems USA, Inc.	10,959
37	Lennox International Inc.	24,000	87	Brookshire Grocery Company	10,500
38	ClubCorp, Inc.	24,000	88	Flowserve Corporation	10,000
39	The Texas A&M University System	23,000	89	Sabre Inc.	10,000
40	USAA	22,000	90	TRT Holdings	10,000
41	Affiliated Computer Services, Inc.	21,000	91	Smith International, Inc.	9,892
42	Enron Corp.	20,600	92	Aegis Communications Group, Inc.	9,500
43	Zale Corporation	20,000	93	Key Energy Services, Inc.	9,300
44	Ultramar Diamond Shamrock	20,000	94	BJ Services Company	9,265
45	Carlson Restaurants Worldwide Inc.	20,000	95	Contran Corporation	9,000
46	CompUSA Inc.	19,700	96	EGL, Inc.	9,000
47	Whole Foods Market, Inc.	18,500	97	Lyondell Chemical Company	8,900
48	Suiza Foods Corporation	18,000	98	Harte-Hanks, Inc.	8,849
49	Nabors Industries, Inc.	17,980	99	Concentra, Inc.	8,800
50	CEC Entertainment, Inc.	17,802	100	Pride International, Inc.	8,700

Source: Hoover's, Inc., Database, November 2001

The 500 Companies in *Hoover's Texas 500*
Ranked by Employees (continued)

Rank	Company	Employees	Rank	Company	Employees
101	Pennzoil-Quaker State Company	8,428	151	United Supermarkets, Inc.	5,000
102	NCH Corporation	8,404	152	Rowan Companies, Inc.	4,917
103	Commercial Metals Company	8,378	153	Lincoln Property Company	4,900
104	University of Houston System	8,300	154	Academy Sports & Outdoors, Ltd.	4,748
105	Methodist Health Care System	8,100	155	Hollywood Casino Corporation	4,720
106	Cinemark USA, Inc.	8,000	156	St. Luke's Episcopal Hospital	4,700
107	Dr Pepper/Seven Up Bottling Group	8,000	157	Consolidated Graphics, Inc.	4,700
108	CHRISTUS Health	8,000	158	Metals USA, Inc.	4,700
109	Motiva Enterprises LLC	8,000	159	Clarent Hospital Corporation	4,670
110	Kaiser Aluminum Corporation	7,800	160	AdvancePCS, Inc.	4,534
111	Perot Systems Corporation	7,800	161	Souper Salad, Inc.	4,500
112	Goodman Manufacturing Company	7,750	162	Gadzooks, Inc.	4,458
113	US Oncology, Inc.	7,716	163	Consolidated Container Company LLC	4,400
114	Dal-Tile International Inc.	7,524	164	Blue Cross and Blue Shield of Texas	4,400
115	Fiesta Mart, Inc.	7,500	165	Texas Industries, Inc.	4,400
116	La Quinta Corporation	7,500	166	AmeriCredit Corp.	4,392
117	The La Quinta Companies	7,500	167	Veritas DGC Inc.	4,300
118	American General Corporation	7,500	168	American National Insurance	4,300
119	BMC Software, Inc.	7,330	169	NCI Building Systems, Inc.	4,250
120	Trammell Crow Company	7,300	170	The Turner Corporation	4,200
121	Cooper Cameron Corporation	7,300	171	ProMedCo Management Company	4,200
122	Belo Corp.	7,245	172	Petro Stopping Centers, L.P.	4,186
123	Minyard Food Stores, Inc.	7,155	173	Palm Harbor Homes, Inc.	4,180
124	Valhi, Inc.	7,110	174	Atrium Companies, Inc.	4,100
125	Quexco Incorporated	7,000	175	CompuCom Systems, Inc.	4,100
126	Dave & Buster's, Inc.	6,600	176	Stewart & Stevenson Services, Inc.	4,100
127	Alliance Data Systems Corporation	6,500	177	Reliant Resources, Inc.	4,100
128	University of North Texas	6,447	178	Diamond Offshore Drilling, Inc.	4,000
129	Tuesday Morning Corporation	6,340	179	American Homestar Corporation	3,934
130	Williamson-Dickie Manufacturing	6,300	180	Eye Care Centers of America, Inc.	3,900
131	Hastings Entertainment, Inc.	6,245	181	Haggar Corp.	3,856
132	Benchmark Electronics, Inc.	6,158	182	E-Z Mart Stores, Inc.	3,845
133	Brookshire Brothers, LTD.	6,000	183	Justin Industries, Inc.	3,826
134	i2 Technologies, Inc.	6,000	184	Grant Prideco, Inc.	3,825
135	Austin Industries Inc.	6,000	185	Kinder Morgan, Inc.	3,801
136	Group 1 Automotive, Inc.	5,830	186	Imperial Sugar Company	3,800
137	Marketing Specialists Corporation	5,800	187	BancTec, Inc.	3,700
138	Dynegy Inc.	5,778	188	Equistar Chemicals, LP	3,700
139	EmCare Holdings Inc.	5,700	189	Cornell Companies, Inc.	3,673
140	Stewart Information Services	5,627	190	Fairchild Dornier Corporation	3,650
141	Dynacare Inc.	5,500	191	D.R. Horton, Inc.	3,631
142	Santa Fe International Corporation	5,500	192	Mary Kay Inc.	3,600
143	Furr's Restaurant Group, Inc.	5,400	193	El Chico Restaurants, Inc.	3,600
144	American Plumbing and Mechanical	5,200	194	Silverleaf Resorts, Inc.	3,561
145	Builders FirstSource, Inc.	5,160	195	Parker Drilling Company	3,542
146	Vought Aircraft Industries, Inc.	5,000	196	Norwood Promotional Products, Inc.	3,500
147	The Bombay Company, Inc.	5,000	197	Anadarko Petroleum Corporation	3,500
148	Central Freight Lines, Inc.	5,000	198	ENSCO International Incorporated	3,400
149	Taco Cabana, Inc.	5,000	199	Cullen/Frost Bankers, Inc.	3,394
150	National-Oilwell, Inc.	5,000	200	Interlogix, Inc.	3,344

Rank	Company	Employees	Rank	Company	Employees
201	Quanex Corporation	3,302	251	Monarch Dental Corporation	2,100
202	Allegiance Telecom, Inc.	3,249	252	EZCORP, Inc.	2,100
203	Glazer's Wholesale Drug Company Inc.	3,200	253	Tesoro Petroleum Corporation	2,100
204	Valero Energy Corporation	3,180	254	Crown Castle International Corp.	2,100
205	Southern Union Company	3,105	255	Fossil, Inc.	2,044
206	SEACOR SMIT Inc.	3,100	256	Pegasus Solutions, Inc.	2,003
207	Patterson-UTI Energy, Inc.	3,062	257	Lufkin Industries, Inc.	2,000
208	Cash America International, Inc.	3,035	258	GSC Enterprises, Inc.	2,000
209	Oceaneering International, Inc.	3,000	259	Software Spectrum, Inc.	2,000
210	The Dunlap Company	3,000	260	Associated Materials Incorporated	2,000
211	Commemorative Brands, Inc.	3,000	261	Vinson & Elkins L.L.P.	2,000
212	Excel Communications, Inc.	3,000	262	Radiologix, Inc.	2,000
213	Noble Drilling Corporation	2,943	263	Dallas Semiconductor Corporation	1,991
214	Oil States International, Inc.	2,805	264	Packaged Ice, Inc.	1,954
215	Dynamex Inc.	2,800	265	DuPont Photomasks, Inc.	1,950
216	Hines Interests L.P.	2,800	266	Industrial Holdings, Inc.	1,925
217	La Madeleine French Bakery & Cafe	2,781	267	Rush Enterprises, Inc.	1,900
218	Riviana Foods Inc.	2,745	268	WebLink Wireless, Inc.	1,899
219	Hanover Compressor Company	2,700	269	Atmos Energy Corporation	1,885
220	Global Marine Inc.	2,700	270	Crescent Operating, Inc.	1,851
221	Southwest Research Institute	2,673	271	Kirby Corporation	1,850
222	Cameron Ashley Building Products	2,669	272	Keystone Consolidated Industries, Inc.	1,830
223	Frozen Food Express Industries, Inc.	2,647	273	Golfsmith International, L.P.	1,800
224	Hunt Consolidated Inc.	2,600	274	Garden Ridge Corporation	1,800
225	MMI Products, Inc.	2,590	275	Fulbright & Jaworski L.L.P.	1,800
226	National Instruments Corporation	2,511	276	Transportation Components, Inc.	1,790
227	The Minute Maid Company	2,500	277	Burlington Resources Inc.	1,783
228	Electrolux L.L.C.	2,500	278	IMCO Recycling Inc.	1,755
229	FreshPoint, Inc.	2,500	279	Camden Property Trust	1,735
230	Blue Bell Creameries L.P.	2,500	280	Lower Colorado River Authority	1,724
231	Foxworth-Galbraith Lumber Company	2,500	281	Denali Incorporated	1,710
232	McCoy Corporation	2,500	282	Cooperative Computing	1,700
233	NL Industries, Inc.	2,500	283	The York Group, Inc.	1,667
234	Kinetic Concepts, Inc.	2,400	284	Centex Construction Products, Inc.	1,665
235	United Surgical Partners International	2,400	285	Gulf States Toyota, Inc.	1,650
236	Ace Cash Express, Inc.	2,397	286	Universal Compression Holdings, Inc.	1,650
237	Lone Star Technologies, Inc.	2,358	287	International Bancshares Corporation	1,634
238	Vignette Corporation	2,330	288	FFP Marketing Company, Inc.	1,622
239	Baylor University	2,318	289	Kinder Morgan Energy Partners, L.P.	1,600
240	Sammons Enterprises, Inc.	2,300	290	Weiner's Stores, Inc.	1,557
241	Grey Wolf, Inc.	2,300	291	L.D. Brinkman and Co.	1,550
242	UICI	2,300	292	Apache Corporation	1,546
243	CompX International Inc.	2,270	293	Samuels Jewelers, Inc.	1,535
244	Kevco, Inc.	2,238	294	Alamo Group Inc.	1,535
245	VarTec Telecom, Inc.	2,238	295	TDIndustries, Ltd.	1,500
246	Arena Brands Inc.	2,200	296	JPI	1,500
247	ICO, Inc.	2,199	297	ACS Dataline, LP	1,500
248	Carriage Services, Inc.	2,186	298	The Container Store	1,500
249	Ennis Business Forms, Inc.	2,181	299	Baker Botts L.L.P.	1,500
250	Ben E. Keith Company	2,160	300	Lancer Corporation	1,452

Rank	Company	Employees	Rank	Company	Employees
301	Darr Equipment Company	1,450	351	El Paso Electric Company	1,000
302	Southern Methodist University	1,432	352	Plains Cotton Cooperative Association	1,000
303	Stevens Transport Inc.	1,425	353	Castle Dental Centers, Inc.	985
304	NATCO Group Inc.	1,411	354	Classic Communications, Inc.	970
305	Hydril Company	1,400	355	HCC Insurance Holdings, Inc.	958
306	TETRA Technologies, Inc.	1,362	356	Texas Regional Bancshares, Inc.	953
307	Austin Energy	1,361	357	Schlotzsky's, Inc.	941
308	Cirrus Logic, Inc.	1,356	358	Synagro Technologies, Inc.	918
309	Powell Industries, Inc.	1,314	359	Plains All American Pipeline, L.P.	915
310	Southwest Bancorporation of Texas	1,313	360	HORIZON Pharmacies, Inc.	903
311	Travelocity.com Inc.	1,300	361	Hispanic Broadcasting Corporation	903
312	CellStar Corporation	1,300	362	Gundle/SLT Environmental, Inc.	901
313	Dril-Quip, Inc.	1,262	363	Mattress Giant Corporation	900
314	Darling International Inc.	1,242	364	Pioneer Companies, Inc.	895
315	Tandy Brands Accessories, Inc.	1,224	365	Daisytek International Corporation	880
316	Overhill Corporation	1,200	366	Mitchell Energy & Development Corp.	875
317	Texas Southern University	1,200	367	American Realty Investors, Inc.	867
318	Home Interiors & Gifts, Inc.	1,200	368	Pioneer Natural Resources Company	853
319	Grocers Supply Co. Inc.	1,200	369	EOG Resources, Inc.	850
320	EOTT Energy Partners, L.P.	1,200	370	Atwood Oceanics, Inc.	850
321	U S Liquids Inc.	1,200	371	TNP Enterprises, Inc.	836
322	VHA Inc.	1,200	372	Aviall, Inc.	817
323	Half Price Books	1,200	373	TEPPCO Partners, L.P.	798
324	LDB Corp.	1,200	374	Enterprise Products Partners L.P.	782
325	InterVoice-Brite, Inc.	1,196	375	Cal Dive International, Inc.	758
326	Sterling Chemicals Holdings, Inc.	1,180	376	TIG Specialty Insurance Solutions	748
327	New Century Equity Holdings Corp.	1,175	377	Pentacon, Inc.	740
328	Elcor Corporation	1,163	378	Input/Output, Inc.	736
329	E. W. Blanch Holdings, Inc.	1,154	379	Crescent Real Estate Equities Company	707
330	Xanser Corporation	1,131	380	First Financial Bankshares, Inc.	706
331	Kaneb Services LLC	1,131	381	Travis Boats & Motors, Inc.	701
332	SWS Group, Inc.	1,121	382	Frontier Oil Corporation	700
333	Entrust Inc.	1,108	383	King Ranch, Inc.	700
334	David McDavid Auto Group	1,100	384	The Beck Group	687
335	Plains Resources Inc.	1,100	385	Adams Resources & Energy, Inc.	685
336	Vallen Corporation	1,100	386	Coastal Bancorp, Inc.	661
337	Affiliated Foods Incorporated	1,100	387	XTO Energy Inc.	651
338	Sterling Bancshares, Inc.	1,094	388	Ascent Assurance, Inc.	650
339	First Cash Financial Services, Inc.	1,090	389	Trilogy	650
340	INSpire Insurance Solutions, Inc.	1,087	390	Luminant Worldwide Corporation	648
341	Horizon Health Corporation	1,085	391	Inet Technologies, Inc.	640
342	Crown Group, Inc.	1,060	392	XeTel Corporation	632
343	TTI, Inc.	1,055	393	EXE Technologies, Inc.	630
344	AXIA Incorporated	1,054	394	Ancira Enterprises	625
345	Ocean Energy, Inc.	1,051	395	Warren Electric Group, Ltd.	613
346	Jenkens & Gilchrist, P.C.	1,050	396	Kaneb Pipe Line Partners, L.P.	600
347	Pitt-Des Moines, Inc.	1,024	397	Fresh America Corp.	590
348	W-H Energy Services, Inc.	1,015	398	Alamosa Holdings, Inc.	582
349	David Weekley Homes	1,010	399	Noble Affiliates, Inc.	576
350	The Staubach Company	1,000	400	MetaSolv, Inc.	574

The 500 Companies in *Hoover's Texas 500*
Ranked by Employees (continued)

Rank	Company	Employees	Rank	Company	Employees
401	Play-By-Play Toys & Novelties, Inc.	574	451	Dallas Stars L.P.	200
402	Ultrak, Inc.	568	452	Triton Energy Limited	195
403	Helen of Troy Limited	558	453	Southwestern Life Holdings Inc.	187
404	Newmark Homes Corp.	543	454	TransTexas Gas Corporation	186
405	Southwestern Energy Company	536	455	Swift Energy Company	181
406	DXP Enterprises, Inc.	532	456	Hunt Building Corporation	170
407	Holly Corporation	521	457	CMS Oil and Gas Company	170
408	Express One International, Inc.	500	458	CARBO Ceramics Inc.	168
409	Cactus Feeders, Inc.	500	459	Active Power, Inc.	167
410	Snelling and Snelling, Inc.	500	460	Panda Energy International, Inc.	164
411	Boy Scouts of America	487	461	KCS Energy, Inc.	164
412	Carreker Corporation	477	462	The Meridian Resource Corporation	163
413	Encore Wire Corporation	474	463	EEX Corporation	162
414	Horizon Offshore, Inc.	467	464	Pogo Producing Company	161
415	Prodigy Communications Corporation	455	465	Multimedia Games, Inc.	152
416	Friona Industries, L.P.	450	466	Sun Coast Resources Inc.	150
417	Argonaut Group, Inc.	435	467	Prize Energy Corp.	139
418	Efficient Networks, Inc.	430	468	Range Resources Corporation	139
419	AMX Corporation	418	469	Seitel, Inc.	128
420	Prime Medical Services, Inc.	400	470	The Houston Exploration Company	110
421	ACR Group, Inc.	400	471	San Antonio Spurs, Ltd.	100
422	Vari-Lite International, Inc.	397	472	Houston Astros Baseball Club	100
423	U.S. Concrete, Inc.	375	473	Clayton Williams Energy, Inc.	96
424	H.D. Vest, Inc.	375	474	Tanox, Inc.	95
425	ILEX Oncology, Inc.	361	475	Magnum Hunter Resources, Inc.	95
426	Hotel Reservations Network, Inc.	360	476	Hicks, Muse, Tate & Furst Incorporated	85
427	Newfield Exploration Company	348	477	Dallas Mavericks	85
428	GAINSCO, INC.	339	478	Houston Rockets	75
429	Texas Lottery Commission	335	479	Texas Pacific Group	75
430	Cabot Oil & Gas Corporation	323	480	Nuevo Energy Company	67
431	Texas Petrochemicals LP	316	481	FelCor Lodging Trust Incorporated	51
432	VTEL Corporation	312	482	3TEC Energy Corporation	50
433	Mannatech, Incorporated	304	483	Comstock Resources, Inc.	48
434	Dallas Cowboys Football Club, Ltd.	300	484	Spinnaker Exploration Company	46
435	The Gambrinus Company	300	485	Tauber Oil Company	45
436	Brazos Electric Power Cooperative, Inc.	295	486	Wingate Partners	20
437	Evercom, Inc.	289	487	Capstead Mortgage Corporation	17
438	N.F. Smith & Associates, LP	287	488	Sevin Rosen Funds	14
439	Northern Border Partners, L.P.	280	489	Austin Ventures, L.P.	8
440	Genesis Energy, L.P.	260	490	El Paso Energy Partners, L.P.	*
441	Silicon Laboratories Inc.	256	491	Enbridge Energy Partners, L.P.	*
442	Calloway's Nursery, Inc.	250	492	Hugoton Royalty Trust	*
443	American Rice, Inc.	250	493	Angelo State University	*
444	Texas Rangers Baseball Club	250	494	Pizza Hut, Inc.	*
445	Denbury Resources Inc.	242	495	Prentiss Properties Trust	*
446	National Western Life Insurance	228	496	San Juan Basin Royalty Trust	*
447	Pure Resources, Inc.	228	497	Shell Services International	*
448	Weingarten Realty Investors	222	498	Southwest Texas State University	*
449	AMRESCO, INC.	218	499	Transcontinental Realty Investors, Inc.	*
450	Pizza Inn, Inc.	211	500	Triangle Pacific Corp.	*

*No employees reported

The Top 100 Companies in One-Year Sales Growth in *Hoover's Texas 500*

Rank	Company	One-Year Sales Growth (%)	Rank	Company	One-Year Sales Growth (%)
1	Efficient Networks, Inc.	1,266.2	51	Transocean Sedco Forex Inc.	89.7
2	Alamosa Holdings, Inc.	818.9	52	San Juan Basin Royalty Trust	89.3
3	Tanox, Inc.	807.1	53	Comstock Resources, Inc.	88.0
4	Anadarko Petroleum Corporation	711.0	54	Crown Castle International Corp.	87.7
5	Prize Energy Corp.	695.2	55	Newfield Exploration Company	86.7
6	3TEC Energy Corporation	391.4	56	EOG Resources, Inc.	85.9
7	Active Power, Inc.	390.0	57	Valero Energy Corporation	84.3
8	Interlogix, Inc.	343.7	58	Magnum Hunter Resources, Inc.	83.2
9	Pegasus Solutions, Inc.	325.0	59	Grey Wolf, Inc.	82.9
10	Vignette Corporation	311.1	60	Lone Star Technologies, Inc.	82.6
11	Frontier Oil Corporation	306.1	61	Pogo Producing Company	81.0
12	AdvancePCS, Inc.	256.9	62	MetaSolv, Inc.	80.7
13	Spinnaker Exploration Company	253.9	63	Horizon Offshore, Inc.	80.3
14	EGL, Inc.	212.7	64	W-H Energy Services, Inc.	80.3
15	Synagro Technologies, Inc.	188.7	65	The Houston Exploration Company	79.7
16	Allegiance Telecom, Inc.	187.8	66	Houston Rockets	79.2
17	Encompass Services Corporation	164.9	67	Mitchell Energy & Development	79.0
18	Luminant Worldwide Corporation	158.3	68	N.F. Smith & Associates, LP	77.3
19	Evercom, Inc.	155.5	69	Calloway's Nursery, Inc.	77.0
20	Enron Corp.	151.3	70	XTO Energy Inc.	76.1
21	Reliant Resources, Inc.	148.2	71	Adams Resources & Energy, Inc.	75.8
22	Triangle Pacific Corp.	137.7	72	Apache Corporation	75.6
23	U.S. Concrete, Inc.	135.0	73	Entrust Inc.	74.2
24	Southern Union Company	132.4	74	Grant Prideco, Inc.	74.1
25	Transportation Components, Inc.	132.2	75	Swift Energy Company	74.0
26	Clayton Williams Energy, Inc.	128.3	76	TransTexas Gas Corporation	73.5
27	Enterprise Products Partners L.P.	126.4	77	Hugoton Royalty Trust	71.4
28	Cabot Oil & Gas Corporation	122.5	78	H. B. Zachry Company	70.7
29	Denbury Resources Inc.	119.9	79	Universal Compression Holdings, Inc.	70.7
30	Silicon Laboratories Inc.	119.8	80	American Plumbing and Mechanical	70.4
31	Travelocity.com Inc.	112.0	81	Tesoro Petroleum Corporation	70.1
32	El Paso Corporation	107.4	82	Equilon Enterprises LLC	70.1
33	Nabors Industries, Inc.	106.6	83	The Meridian Resource Corporation	68.5
34	Patterson-UTI Energy, Inc.	103.2	84	Silverleaf Resorts, Inc.	66.8
35	Hotel Reservations Network, Inc.	102.7	85	JPI	66.7
36	Genesis Energy, L.P.	100.1	86	Administaff, Inc.	64.0
37	Quexco Incorporated	100.0	87	XeTel Corporation	63.9
38	Clear Channel Communications	99.6	88	Classic Communications, Inc.	63.6
39	Prodigy Communications	99.2	89	The Beck Group	62.7
40	Oil States International, Inc.	97.3	90	Greyhound Lines, Inc.	62.2
41	i2 Technologies, Inc.	97.2	91	Integrated Electrical Services, Inc.	61.4
42	Samuels Jewelers, Inc.	94.4	92	AmeriCredit Corp.	60.5
43	Benchmark Electronics, Inc.	94.2	93	Hunt Consolidated Inc.	60.0
44	Quanta Services, Inc.	93.7	94	TEPPCO Partners, L.P.	59.6
45	United Surgical Partners	92.6	95	Motiva Enterprises LLC	59.4
46	Reliant Energy, Incorporated	91.7	96	San Antonio Spurs, Ltd.	59.3
47	Dynegy Inc.	90.8	97	Consolidated Container Company	59.2
48	Hanover Compressor Company	90.5	98	Noble Affiliates, Inc.	55.8
49	Kinder Morgan Energy Partners, L.P.	90.4	99	Transcontinental Realty Investors	55.7
50	Dr Pepper/Seven Up Bottling Group	90.0	100	Kinder Morgan, Inc.	55.5

Note: These rates are for sales growth for the most current fiscal year and may have resulted from acquisitions or one-time gains.
Source: Hoover's, Inc., Database, November 2001

The Top 100 Companies in One-Year Income Growth in *Hoover's Texas 500*

Rank	Company	One-Year Net Income Growth (%)	Rank	Company	One-Year Net Income Growth (%)
1	Burlington Resources Inc.	67,400.0	51	Temple-Inland Inc.	97.0
2	Denbury Resources Inc.	2,991.3	52	Quanta Services, Inc.	96.1
3	Valero Energy Corporation	2,271.3	53	Noble Drilling Corporation	96.0
4	Crescent Real Estate Equities	2,156.4	54	AmeriCredit Corp.	94.7
5	Anadarko Petroleum Corporation	1,794.4	55	Transocean Sedco Forex Inc.	86.7
6	NATCO Group Inc.	1,183.3	56	San Juan Basin Royalty Trust	86.2
7	ENSCO International	1,174.6	57	Enterprise Products Partners L.P.	83.3
8	Consolidated Container Company	1,002.8	58	Administaff, Inc.	79.8
9	KCS Energy, Inc.	865.1	59	Alamo Group Inc.	77.0
10	National-Oilwell, Inc.	773.3	60	Rent-A-Center, Inc.	73.4
11	Reliant Resources, Inc.	581.0	61	Carreker Corporation	72.2
12	Holly Corporation	544.7	62	Hugoton Royalty Trust	71.3
13	MetaSolv, Inc.	515.4	63	Benchmark Electronics, Inc.	65.8
14	El Paso Energy Partners, L.P.	502.9	64	Coastal Bancorp, Inc.	65.4
15	Synagro Technologies, Inc.	500.0	65	NCH Corporation	61.8
16	Southern Union Company	416.2	66	Southwest Bancorporation of Texas	61.7
17	Nabors Industries, Inc.	396.0	67	The Men's Wearhouse, Inc.	59.5
18	Equistar Chemicals, LP	378.1	68	Kirby Corporation	59.3
19	Calloway's Nursery, Inc.	325.0	69	Shell Oil Company	58.0
20	The Meridian Resource Corporation	317.2	70	Valhi, Inc.	55.1
21	Newfield Exploration Company	298.5	71	Kinder Morgan Energy Partners, L.P.	52.7
22	Pogo Producing Company	295.0	72	Cornell Companies, Inc.	50.9
23	Noble Affiliates, Inc.	287.1	73	Newmark Homes Corp.	47.7
24	Horizon Offshore, Inc.	276.5	74	Hanover Compressor Company	45.3
25	XeTel Corporation	266.7	75	Stewart & Stevenson Services, Inc.	45.1
26	Apache Corporation	255.0	76	El Paso Electric Company	44.2
27	The Houston Exploration Company	246.7	77	Triton Energy Limited	41.6
28	Veritas DGC Inc.	246.2	78	CARBO Ceramics Inc.	41.0
29	Clear Channel Communications	243.2	79	Dallas Semiconductor Corporation	39.7
30	Dynegy Inc.	230.0	80	Cal Dive International, Inc.	37.9
31	Swift Energy Company	213.0	81	Adams Resources & Energy, Inc.	37.5
32	Baker Hughes Incorporated	207.2	82	Dal-Tile International Inc.	36.6
33	Cabot Oil & Gas Corporation	200.0	83	Kaneb Services LLC	36.0
34	Electronic Data Systems	171.6	84	SYSCO Corporation	34.0
35	Mitchell Energy & Development	164.5	85	F.Y.I. Incorporated	33.8
36	Clayton Williams Energy, Inc.	157.4	86	Inet Technologies, Inc.	33.0
37	Ultramar Diamond Shamrock	156.5	87	Encompass Services Corporation	32.9
38	Conoco Inc.	155.6	88	Helen of Troy Limited	32.1
39	Daisytek International Corporation	153.3	89	ProMedCo Management Company	31.1
40	XTO Energy Inc.	150.5	90	Dell Computer Corporation	30.7
41	H.D. Vest, Inc.	150.0	91	7-Eleven, Inc.	30.3
42	Dave & Buster's, Inc.	134.6	92	Smith International, Inc.	28.4
43	Exxon Mobil Corporation	124.0	93	Silicon Laboratories Inc.	27.3
44	Texas Instruments Incorporated	117.5	94	Global Marine Inc.	27.3
45	Seitel, Inc.	117.0	95	Southwest Airlines Co.	27.1
46	HCC Insurance Holdings, Inc.	112.7	96	Pier 1 Imports, Inc.	26.8
47	Gadzooks, Inc.	109.8	97	Michaels Stores, Inc.	26.0
48	U.S. Concrete, Inc.	106.1	98	CEC Entertainment, Inc.	24.8
49	Randall's Food Markets, Inc.	104.1	99	Sterling Bancshares, Inc.	24.3
50	Atmos Energy Corporation	102.8	100	RadioShack Corporation	23.5

Note: These rates are for net income for the most current fiscal year and may have resulted from acquisitions or one-time gains.
Source: Hoover's, Inc., Database, November 2001

The Top 100 Companies in One-Year Employment Growth in *Hoover's Texas 500*

Rank	Company	One-Year Employment Growth (%)	Rank	Company	One-Year Employment Growth (%)
1	Pegasus Solutions, Inc.	1,064.5	51	Southwest Bancorporation of Texas	40.6
2	Travelocity.com Inc.	550.0	52	Inet Technologies, Inc.	40.0
3	Interlogix, Inc.	386.8	53	Centex Construction Products, Inc.	39.9
4	Efficient Networks, Inc.	246.8	54	Classic Communications, Inc.	38.6
5	AdvancePCS, Inc.	230.9	55	Alamo Group Inc.	37.4
6	Alamosa Holdings, Inc.	219.8	56	Ascent Assurance, Inc.	36.8
7	El Paso Corporation	219.1	57	Horizon Offshore, Inc.	35.8
8	Vignette Corporation	207.8	58	Southern Union Company	35.2
9	Dr Pepper/Seven Up Bottling Group	166.7	59	Hotel Reservations Network, Inc.	34.3
10	Anadarko Petroleum Corporation	144.6	60	The Meridian Resource Corporation	33.6
11	Dynegy Inc.	124.7	61	Dallas Cowboys Football Club, Ltd.	33.3
12	i2 Technologies, Inc.	114.3	62	Kinder Morgan Energy Partners, L.P.	33.3
13	Transocean Sedco Forex Inc.	113.7	63	Group 1 Automotive, Inc.	32.5
14	Clear Channel Communications, Inc.	105.9	64	Tanox, Inc.	31.9
15	Entrust Inc.	103.3	65	TRT Holdings	31.9
16	Patterson-UTI Energy, Inc.	98.1	66	Grey Wolf, Inc.	31.8
17	VarTec Telecom, Inc.	90.1	67	Overhill Corporation	31.6
18	Hanover Compressor Company	88.4	68	Smith International, Inc.	31.5
19	Greyhound Lines, Inc.	84.3	69	Spinnaker Exploration Company	31.4
20	Allegiance Telecom, Inc.	82.1	70	Crown Group, Inc.	30.9
21	N.F. Smith & Associates, LP	76.1	71	American Plumbing and Mechanical	30.0
22	Silicon Laboratories Inc.	73.0	72	National Instruments Corporation	28.4
23	Quanta Services, Inc.	71.0	73	Samuels Jewelers, Inc.	27.9
24	Active Power, Inc.	70.4	74	Administaff, Inc.	27.3
25	Crown Castle International Corp.	68.0	75	Fairchild Dornier Corporation	26.6
26	National-Oilwell, Inc.	68.0	76	Valero Energy Corporation	26.3
27	Fossil, Inc.	68.0	77	Key Energy Services, Inc.	25.1
28	Synagro Technologies, Inc.	63.6	78	United Supermarkets, Inc.	25.0
29	Hollywood Casino Corporation	62.8	79	ACS Dataline, LP	25.0
30	ILEX Oncology, Inc.	61.2	80	The Staubach Company	25.0
31	Memorial Hermann Healthcare System	60.0	81	Alliance Data Systems Corporation	25.0
32	U.S. Concrete, Inc.	56.9	82	Dallas Semiconductor Corporation	24.9
33	Triton Energy Limited	54.8	83	Michaels Stores, Inc.	24.5
34	Zale Corporation	53.8	84	Tandy Brands Accessories, Inc.	24.0
35	Newfield Exploration Company	53.3	85	Carreker Corporation	23.9
36	Landry's Restaurants, Inc.	51.9	86	ProMedCo Management Company	23.5
37	Oil States International, Inc.	51.9	87	Central Freight Lines, Inc.	23.5
38	Lone Star Technologies, Inc.	51.7	88	The Beck Group	22.7
39	Silverleaf Resorts, Inc.	51.7	89	H. B. Zachry Company	22.2
40	Grant Prideco, Inc.	47.7	90	Ennis Business Forms, Inc.	21.8
41	Pride International, Inc.	47.5	91	BJ Services Company	21.7
42	MetaSolv, Inc.	46.8	92	Aegis Communications Group, Inc.	21.5
43	Nabors Industries, Inc.	46.8	93	Atwood Oceanics, Inc.	21.4
44	Texas Southern University	44.9	94	Kimberly-Clark Corporation	21.0
45	Baylor University	44.9	95	Prize Energy Corp.	20.9
46	AmeriCredit Corp.	44.1	96	GAINSCO, INC.	20.2
47	Veritas DGC Inc.	43.3	97	The Turner Corporation	20.0
48	Taco Cabana, Inc.	42.9	98	Half Price Books	20.0
49	Flowserve Corporation	42.9	99	NCI Building Systems, Inc.	19.7
50	New Century Equity Holdings Corp.	41.9	100	Integrated Electrical Services, Inc.	19.2

Note: These rates are for employees for the most current fiscal year and may have resulted from acquisitions or one-time gains.
Source: Hoover's, Inc., Database, November 2001

The Texas 100: Texas Stock Index Companies

Company	Headquarters	Business Description
Energy Sector		
Baker Hughes, Inc.	Houston	Oil field services
BP Amoco Corp.	Chicago	Oil and gas exploration, production
Chevron USA Inc.	San Francisco	Oil and gas operations
The Dow Chemical Co., Inc.	Midland, MI	Chemicals
E.I. Du Pont De Nemours & Co.	Wilmington, DE	Chemicals
Exxon Mobil Corp.	Irving, TX	Oil exploration, production
Fluor Corp.	Irvine, CA	Construction, diversified services
Halliburton Co.	Dallas	Oil field services
Lyondell Chemical Co.	Houston	Petrochemicals
Phillips Petroleum Co.	Bartlesville, OK	Oil and gas operations
Reliant Energy, Inc.	Houston	Electric utility
Schlumberger	New York	Oil field services and utilities metering
Shell Transport & Trading Co.	London	Oil and gas operations
Texas Utilities Co.	Dallas	Electric utility
Ultramar Diamond Shamrock	San Antonio	Natural gas utility, refining, convenience stores
Entertainment/Travel Sector		
American Airlines Inc.	Fort Worth, TX	Airline, travel agency, telemarketing
Brinker International, Inc.	Dallas	Restaurant
Continental Airlines, Inc.	Houston	Airline
Darden Restaurants Inc.	Orlando, FL	Restaurant
Delta Air Lines, Inc.	Atlanta	Airline
Luby's Cafeterias, Inc.	San Antonio	Restaurant
The Sabre Group	Fort Worth, TX	Travel, reservations
Southwest Airlines Co.	Dallas	Airline
Tricon Restaurants International	Louisville, KY	Restaurant
High-Tech Sector		
Advanced Micro Devices Inc.	Sunnyvale, CA	Chipmaker
Alcatel USA Inc.	Plano, TX	Telecom equipment
ATT Communications Inc.	New York	Telecommunications
Bell Canada Enterprises	Montreal	Telecommunications
The Boeing Co.	Seattle	Aerospace, defense
Compaq Computer Corp.	Houston	Computer maker/seller
Dell Computer Corp.	Round Rock, TX	Computer maker/seller
IBM	Armonk, NY	Computer maker/software developer
Lockheed Martin Corp.	Bethesda, MD	Aerospace, defense
Lucent Technologies Inc.	Murray Hill, NJ	Telecom equipment
Motorola Inc.	Schaumburg, IL	Telecom equipment, chips
Nortel Networks	Brampton, Ontario	Telecom equipment
Northrup Grumman	Los Angeles	Aerospace, defense
Raytheon	Lexington, MA	Aerospace, defense
Southwestern Bell Communications	San Antonio	Telecommunications
Sprint Corp.	Kansas City, MO	Telecommunications
Texas Instruments Inc.	Dallas	Chipmaker
Textron	Providence, RI	Aircraft
Verizon Communications	New York	Telecommunications
WorldCom	Clinton, MS	Telecommunications
Other Manufacturing Sector		
Coca Cola Enterprises	Atlanta	Bottler
Goodyear Tire & Rubber Co.	Akron, OH	Tires
Iowa Beef Packers Inc.	Dakota Dunes, SD	Food processor
International Paper	Purchase, NY	Pulp and paper
PepsiCo Inc.	Purchase, NY	Food processor
Pilgrim's Pride	Pittsburg, TX	Chicken producer
Temple-Inland Forest Products, Inc.	Diboll, TX	Wood products, banking
Trinity Industries Inc.	Dallas	Metal products
VF Corp.	Greensboro, NC	Clothing

Note: The 100 largest publicly traded employers in Texas measured by their average number of workers during 1999 make up the Texas Stock Index. See page 7 for a historical look at the index.

Source: Carole Keeton Rylander, Texas Comptroller of Public Accounts, January 2001

The Texas 100: Texas Stock Index Companies (continued)

Company	Headquarters	Business Description
Retail Sector		
7-Eleven, Inc.	Dallas	Convenience store
Albertson's Inc.	Boise, ID	Food
AutoZone Inc.	Memphis	Auto parts
Best Buy Co. Inc.	Eden Prairie, MN	Consumer electronics
Dillard's Inc.	Little Rock, AR	Department store
Gap Inc.	San Francisco	Clothing
The Home Depot	Atlanta	Home improvement
J.C. Penney Co., Inc.	Plano, TX	Department store, drugstore
Kmart Corp.	Troy, MI	General merchandise
The Kroger Co.	Cincinnati	Food
Lowe's Home Centers, Inc.	North Wilkesboro, NC	Home improvement
May Department Stores	St. Louis	Department store
The Neiman Marcus Group Inc.	Dallas	Department store
Office Depot	Delray Beach, FL	Office supplies
O'Reilly Automotive	Springfield, MO	Auto parts
Radio Shack	Fort Worth, TX	Consumer electronics
Safeway, Inc.	Pleasanton, CA	Food
Sears, Roebuck and Co.	Hoffman Estates, IL	General merchandise
Target Stores	Minneapolis	General merchandise
Walgreen Co.	Deerfield, IL	Drugstore chain
Wal-Mart Stores Inc.	Bentonville, AR	General merchandise
Winn-Dixie	Jacksonville	Food
Services And Finance Sector		
Adecco Employment Services, Inc.	Lausanne, Switzerland	Employment
Administaff Inc.	Kingwood, TX	Employee benefits
Aetna Inc.	Hartford, CT	Insurance
Allstate Insurance Co.	Northbrook, IL	Insurance
ABM Industries Incorporated	San Franciso	Janitorial services
Bank of America, NA	Charlotte, NC	Banking
Bank One NA	Columbus, OH	Banking
Borg-Warner, Inc.	Chicago	Security services
Citigroup	New York	Banking
Columbia HCA	Nashville	Hospital management
Electronic Data Systems Corp.	Plano, TX	Business services
Federal Express Corp.	Memphis	Shipping
J.P. Morgan Chase	New York	Banking
Kelly Services Inc.	Troy, MI	Employment
Labor Ready Inc.	Tacoma, WA	Employment
Manpower Inc.	Milwaukee	Employment
Personnel Group of America	Charlotte, NC	Employment
Service Master Inc.	Downers Grove, IL	Employment
Sitel Corp.	Baltimore	Teleservices
Spherion Corp.	Fort Lauderdale, FL	Employment
United Parcel Service	Atlanta, GA	Shipping
Viacom International	New York	Broadcasting, video rental
Wells Fargo & Co.	San Francisco	Banking
West TeleServices Corp.	Omaha, NE	Teleservices
Xerox Corp.	Stamford, CT	Document processing

Companies in *Hoover's Texas 500* by Metropolitan Area

Abilene	Sales ($ mil.)
Patterson-UTI Energy, Inc.	308
First Financial Bankshares, Inc.	144

Amarillo	Sales ($ mil.)
Affiliated Foods Incorporated	700
Cactus Feeders, Inc.	600
Hastings Entertainment, Inc.	458
Friona Industries, L.P.	300

Austin	Sales ($ mil.)
Dell Computer Corporation	31,888
The University of Texas System	5,943
Temple-Inland Inc.	4,286
Texas Lottery Commission	3,940
Southern Union Company	1,933
Whole Foods Market, Inc.	1,839
Austin Energy	783
Cirrus Logic, Inc.	779
American Plumbing and Mechanical, Inc.	569
Interlogix, Inc.	540
Lower Colorado River Authority	538
McCoy Corporation	467
Norwood Promotional Products, Inc.	431
National Instruments Corporation	410
DuPont Photomasks, Inc.	408
Prodigy Communications Corporation	376
Vignette Corporation	367
National Western Life Insurance Company	293
Golfsmith International, L.P.	275
Trilogy	250
Southwest Texas State University	232
Cooperative Computing Holding Company	224
Travis Boats & Motors, Inc.	218
Commemorative Brands, Inc.	200
EZCORP, Inc.	197
XeTel Corporation	193
Samuels Jewelers, Inc.	158
ACS Dataline, LP	145
Prime Medical Services, Inc.	131
Silicon Laboratories Inc.	103
Multimedia Games, Inc.	97
Schlotzsky's, Inc.	59
VTEL Corporation	38
Active Power, Inc.	5

College Station	Sales ($ mil.)
The Texas A&M University System	2,620
Blue Bell Creameries L.P.	300

Corpus Christi	Sales ($ mil.)
Whataburger, Inc.	600

Dallas-Fort Worth	Sales ($ mil.)
Exxon Mobil Corporation	228,439
J. C. Penney Company, Inc.	31,846
TXU Corp.	22,009
AMR Corporation	19,703
Electronic Data Systems Corporation	19,227
Fleming Companies, Inc.	14,444
Kimberly-Clark Corporation	13,982
Frito-Lay, Inc.	12,881
Texas Instruments Incorporated	11,875
Halliburton Company	11,856
7-Eleven, Inc.	9,346
Burlington Northern Santa Fe Corporation	9,205
AdvancePCS, Inc.	7,024
Army and Air Force Exchange Service	6,992
Centex Corporation	6,711
CompUSA Inc.	6,321
The Turner Corporation	5,800
Suiza Foods Corporation	5,756
Southwest Airlines Co.	5,650
Blockbuster Inc.	4,960
RadioShack Corporation	4,795
Suiza Dairy Group	4,660
D.R. Horton, Inc.	3,654
Lennox International Inc.	3,247
The Neiman Marcus Group, Inc.	3,016
CompuCom Systems, Inc.	2,711
Sabre Inc.	2,617
CellStar Corporation	2,476
Brinker International, Inc.	2,474
Pizza Hut, Inc.	2,469
Commercial Metals Company	2,441
Wyndham International, Inc.	2,422
Michaels Stores, Inc.	2,249
CHRISTUS Health	2,200
Zale Corporation	2,068
Affiliated Computer Services, Inc.	2,064
Sammons Enterprises, Inc.	2,000
Blue Cross and Blue Shield of Texas Inc.	2,000
Quexco Incorporated	2,000
Trinity Industries, Inc.	1,904
Dr Pepper/Seven Up Bottling Group, Inc.	1,900
Rent-A-Center, Inc.	1,602
Belo Corp.	1,589
Builders FirstSource, Inc.	1,580
Flowserve Corporation	1,538
Greyhound Lines, Inc.	1,498
Glazer's Wholesale Drug Company Inc.	1,480
Atmos Energy Corporation	1,442
Pier 1 Imports, Inc.	1,412
Pillowtex Corporation	1,350

Source: Hoover's, Inc., Database, November 2001

Companies in *Hoover's Texas 500* by Metropolitan Area (continued)

Dallas-Fort Worth (continued)	Sales ($ mil.)
Texas Health Resources	1,340
Texas Industries, Inc.	1,252
Lincoln Property Company	1,251
Triad Hospitals, Inc.	1,236
Austin Industries Inc.	1,217
Software Spectrum, Inc.	1,213
Contran Corporation	1,200
Hunt Consolidated Inc.	1,200
Mary Kay Inc.	1,200
Valhi, Inc.	1,192
Daisytek International Corporation	1,190
Holly Corporation	1,142
Cameron Ashley Building Products, Inc.	1,138
i2 Technologies, Inc.	1,126
GSC Enterprises, Inc.	1,111
Perot Systems Corporation	1,106
ClubCorp, Inc.	1,069
UICI	1,051
VarTec Telecom, Inc.	1,020
Minyard Food Stores, Inc.	1,000
JPI	1,000
Vought Aircraft Industries, Inc.	1,000
TIG Specialty Insurance Solutions	979
Ben E. Keith Company	959
Dal-Tile International Inc.	952
The Beck Group	950
Crescent Real Estate Equities Company	923
Baylor Health Care System	875
Pioneer Natural Resources Company	853
IMCO Recycling Inc.	847
Kevco, Inc.	840
The La Quinta Companies	823
Triangle Pacific Corp.	823
Williamson-Dickie Manufacturing Company	820
AmeriCredit Corp.	818
The Freeman Companies	801
Cinemark USA, Inc.	786
Trammell Crow Company	761
GameStop, Inc.	757
Consolidated Container Company LLC	755
Concentra, Inc.	752
Carlson Restaurants Worldwide Inc.	750
FreshPoint, Inc.	732
Crescent Operating, Inc.	717
FFP Marketing Company, Inc.	688
NCH Corporation	680
Palm Harbor Homes, Inc.	651
Lone Star Technologies, Inc.	645
TNP Enterprises, Inc.	644
XTO Energy Inc.	601
Darr Equipment Company	600
David McDavid Auto Group	596
La Quinta Corporation	595
Tuesday Morning Corporation	587
Santa Fe International Corporation	584
FelCor Lodging Trust Incorporated	557
TTI, Inc.	555
Fresh America Corp.	555
TRT Holdings	550
Foxworth-Galbraith Lumber Company	540
Kaneb Services LLC	537
ENSCO International Incorporated	534
Capstead Mortgage Corporation	520
Dallas Semiconductor Corporation	517
Justin Industries, Inc.	510
CEC Entertainment, Inc.	506
Fossil, Inc.	504
Alliance Data Systems Corporation	503
Associated Materials Incorporated	499
Atrium Companies, Inc.	496
BancTec, Inc.	488
Aviall, Inc.	486
Snelling and Snelling, Inc.	481
EmCare Holdings Inc.	471
SWS Group, Inc.	471
Home Interiors & Gifts, Inc.	460
F.Y.I. Incorporated	458
Haggar Corp.	445
VHA Inc.	442
Centex Construction Products, Inc.	441
The Bombay Company, Inc.	422
Frozen Food Express Industries, Inc.	392
Marketing Specialists Corporation	381
Elcor Corporation	379
L.D. Brinkman and Co.	378
American Realty Investors, Inc.	366
Cash America International, Inc.	364
Dynacare Inc.	353
Hollywood Casino Corporation	348
Prentiss Properties Trust	348
Keystone Consolidated Industries, Inc.	338
Dave & Buster's, Inc.	332
Triton Energy Limited	329
Hotel Reservations Network, Inc.	328
ProMedCo Management Company	325
Aegis Communications Group, Inc.	295
WebLink Wireless, Inc.	290
Gadzooks, Inc.	288
Allegiance Telecom, Inc.	285
Encore Wire Corporation	284
Crown Group, Inc.	283
InterVoice-Brite, Inc.	275
The Container Store	260
University of North Texas	257
CompX International Inc.	253
Dynamex Inc.	252
Southwestern Life Holdings Inc.	251
The Dunlap Company	250
Jenkens & Gilchrist, P.C.	249
Radiologix, Inc.	247

Companies in *Hoover's Texas 500* by Metropolitan Area (continued)

Dallas-Fort Worth (continued)	Sales ($ mil.)
Packaged Ice, Inc.	244
Darling International Inc.	243
Boy Scouts of America	242
Hispanic Broadcasting Corporation	238
Evercom, Inc.	235
Stevens Transport Inc.	231
Silverleaf Resorts, Inc.	231
Ennis Business Forms, Inc.	229
Electrolux L.L.C.	226
Southern Methodist University	218
Monarch Dental Corporation	211
TDIndustries, Ltd.	204
Efficient Networks, Inc.	202
Ultrak, Inc.	200
Tandy Brands Accessories, Inc.	199
Ace Cash Express, Inc.	197
Furr's Restaurant Group, Inc.	196
H.D. Vest, Inc.	194
Travelocity.com Inc.	193
Transcontinental Realty Investors, Inc.	192
E. W. Blanch Holdings, Inc.	191
Overhill Corporation	189
Range Resources Corporation	187
Dallas Cowboys Football Club, Ltd.	181
The Staubach Company	180
Denbury Resources Inc.	179
Mattress Giant Corporation	178
Arena Brands Inc.	175
AMRESCO, INC.	171
Comstock Resources, Inc.	169
Excel Communications, Inc.	166
GAINSCO, INC.	165
Pegasus Solutions, Inc.	162
Inet Technologies, Inc.	159
Kaneb Pipe Line Partners, L.P.	156
Mannatech, Incorporated	150
Ascent Assurance, Inc.	150
Prize Energy Corp.	150
Entrust Inc.	148
El Chico Restaurants, Inc.	148
Panda Energy International, Inc.	144
HORIZON Pharmacies, Inc.	136
United Surgical Partners International, Inc.	136
Luminant Worldwide Corporation	135
MetaSolv, Inc.	132
Horizon Health Corporation	128
Xanser Corporation	128
Magnum Hunter Resources, Inc.	128
INSpire Insurance Solutions, Inc.	127
Texas Rangers Baseball Club	127
La Madeleine French Bakery & Cafe	121
EXE Technologies, Inc.	116
Express One International, Inc.	115
Carreker Corporation	110
First Cash Financial Services, Inc.	106

	Sales ($ mil.)
AMX Corporation	94
Vari-Lite International, Inc.	94
CARBO Ceramics Inc.	93
Half Price Books	80
Dallas Stars L.P.	73
Pizza Inn, Inc.	64
San Juan Basin Royalty Trust	60
Dallas Mavericks	60
Hugoton Royalty Trust	57
Calloway's Nursery, Inc.	54

El Paso	Sales ($ mil.)
Petro Stopping Centers, L.P.	983
El Paso Electric Company	702
Helen of Troy Limited	361
Hunt Building Corporation	200

Houston	Sales ($ mil.)
Enron Corp.	100,789
Equilon Enterprises LLC	50,010
Compaq Computer Corporation	42,383
Conoco Inc.	38,737
USX-Marathon Group	33,859
Shell Oil Company	29,671
Dynegy Inc.	29,445
Reliant Energy, Incorporated	29,339
El Paso Corporation	21,950
SYSCO Corporation	21,785
ExxonMobil Chemical Company	21,503
Reliant Resources, Inc.	19,792
Motiva Enterprises LLC	19,446
Waste Management, Inc.	12,492
EOTT Energy Partners, L.P.	11,614
American General Corporation	11,063
Continental Airlines, Inc.	9,899
Equistar Chemicals, LP	7,495
Adams Resources & Energy, Inc.	7,022
Compaq Global Services	6,993
Plains All American Pipeline, L.P.	6,641
Plains Resources Inc.	6,575
Anadarko Petroleum Corporation	5,686
Baker Hughes Incorporated	5,234
Cooper Industries, Inc.	4,460
Genesis Energy, L.P.	4,325
Encompass Services Corporation	4,099
Lyondell Chemical Company	4,036
Administaff, Inc.	3,709
Group 1 Automotive, Inc.	3,586
Gulf States Toyota, Inc.	3,158
Burlington Resources Inc.	3,147
TEPPCO Partners, L.P.	3,088
Enterprise Products Partners L.P.	3,049
Smith International, Inc.	2,761
Kinder Morgan, Inc.	2,714
Randall's Food Markets, Inc.	2,585
Service Corporation International	2,565

Companies in *Hoover's Texas 500* by Metropolitan Area (continued)

Houston (continued)	Sales ($ mil.)
MAXXAM Inc.	2,448
Apache Corporation	2,284
Pennzoil-Quaker State Company	2,271
BJ Services Company	2,234
The Minute Maid Company	2,200
Kaiser Aluminum Corporation	2,170
Goodman Manufacturing Company, L.P.	2,160
Frontier Oil Corporation	2,045
Metals USA, Inc.	2,022
American National Insurance Company	1,838
Imperial Sugar Company	1,821
Weatherford International, Inc.	1,814
Quanta Services, Inc.	1,793
Benchmark Electronics, Inc.	1,705
Integrated Electrical Services, Inc.	1,672
Comfort Systems USA, Inc.	1,591
BMC Software, Inc.	1,504
EOG Resources, Inc.	1,490
Grocers Supply Co. Inc.	1,400
Cooper Cameron Corporation	1,387
Noble Affiliates, Inc.	1,381
The Men's Wearhouse, Inc.	1,334
Nabors Industries, Inc.	1,327
US Oncology, Inc.	1,324
Transocean Sedco Forex Inc.	1,230
Shell Services International	1,200
Stewart & Stevenson Services, Inc.	1,153
National-Oilwell, Inc.	1,150
Sterling Chemicals Holdings, Inc.	1,078
Ocean Energy, Inc.	1,074
Global Marine Inc.	1,040
NCI Building Systems, Inc.	1,018
Memorial Hermann Healthcare System	1,003
Tauber Oil Company	1,000
Stage Stores, Inc.	952
Stewart Information Services Corporation	936
Quanex Corporation	934
Mitchell Energy & Development Corp.	934
NL Industries, Inc.	922
Pride International, Inc.	909
Noble Drilling Corporation	883
Texas Petrochemicals LP	859
David Weekley Homes	828
Kinder Morgan Energy Partners, L.P.	816
Methodist Health Care System	795
Hines Interests L.P.	750
Fiesta Mart, Inc.	730
Academy Sports & Outdoors, Ltd.	720
Consolidated Graphics, Inc.	683
Diamond Offshore Drilling, Inc.	659
Crown Castle International Corp.	649
Rowan Companies, Inc.	646

EGL, Inc.	644
Newmark Homes Corp.	641
St. Luke's Episcopal Hospital	640
Hanover Compressor Company	604
American Homestar Corporation	574
MMI Products, Inc.	530
Newfield Exploration Company	527
Landry's Restaurants, Inc.	521
University of Houston System	515
Kirby Corporation	513
N.F. Smith & Associates, LP	500
Grant Prideco, Inc.	499
Pogo Producing Company	498
Veritas DGC Inc.	477
HCC Insurance Holdings, Inc.	466
Oceaneering International, Inc.	417
Camden Property Trust	404
U.S. Concrete, Inc.	395
Vinson & Elkins L.L.P.	387
Riviana Foods Inc.	382
Parker Drilling Company	376
Clarent Hospital Corporation	369
Cabot Oil & Gas Corporation	369
Garden Ridge Corporation	365
Southwestern Energy Company	364
Fulbright & Jaworski L.L.P.	343
Pioneer Companies, Inc.	341
SEACOR SMIT Inc.	340
Northern Border Partners, L.P.	340
Nuevo Energy Company	332
ICO, Inc.	325
Pitt-Des Moines, Inc.	318
Southwest Bancorporation of Texas, Inc.	315
Baker Botts L.L.P.	312
Transportation Components, Inc.	311
Warren Electric Group, Ltd.	310
Vallen Corporation	306
Enbridge Energy Partners, L.P.	306
Oil States International, Inc.	305
King Ranch, Inc.	300
Sun Coast Resources Inc.	300
Pentacon, Inc.	284
Weingarten Realty Investors	274
The Houston Exploration Company	271
Grey Wolf, Inc.	269
EEX Corporation	262
Coastal Bancorp, Inc.	249
Weiner's Stores, Inc.	249
U S Liquids Inc.	248
Universal Compression Holdings, Inc.	233
W-H Energy Services, Inc.	230
Cornell Companies, Inc.	226
NATCO Group Inc.	225
TETRA Technologies, Inc.	225
The Meridian Resource Corporation	223

Companies in *Hoover's Texas 500*
by Metropolitan Area (continued)

Houston (continued)	Sales ($ mil.)
Powell Industries, Inc.	223
Sterling Bancshares, Inc.	196
The York Group, Inc.	193
KCS Energy, Inc.	192
Gundle/SLT Environmental, Inc.	191
Denali Incorporated	190
Swift Energy Company	190
Industrial Holdings, Inc.	186
TransTexas Gas Corporation	183
DXP Enterprises, Inc.	183
Cal Dive International, Inc.	181
Hydril Company	180
American Rice, Inc.	171
Dril-Quip, Inc.	164
Seitel, Inc.	164
Synagro Technologies, Inc.	163
Carriage Services, Inc.	163
Horizon Offshore, Inc.	161
AXIA Incorporated	150
ACR Group, Inc.	136
Atwood Oceanics, Inc.	135
CMS Oil and Gas Company	131
Houston Astros Baseball Club	122
Input/Output, Inc.	122
Spinnaker Exploration Company	121
El Paso Energy Partners, L.P.	112
Castle Dental Centers, Inc.	106
3TEC Energy Corporation	103
Houston Rockets	79
Texas Southern University	61
Tanox, Inc.	13

Killeen	Sales ($ mil.)
McLane Company, Inc.	10,542

Laredo	Sales ($ mil.)
International Bancshares Corporation	479
LDB Corp.	120

Longview	Sales ($ mil.)
Pilgrim's Pride Corporation	2,215

Lubbock	Sales ($ mil.)
Plains Cotton Cooperative Association	633
United Supermarkets, Inc.	575
Alamosa Holdings, Inc.	83

McAllen	Sales ($ mil.)
Texas Regional Bancshares, Inc.	203

Odessa	Sales ($ mil.)
Key Energy Services, Inc.	866
Pure Resources, Inc.	287
Clayton Williams Energy, Inc.	110

San Angelo	Sales ($ mil.)
Angelo State University	95

San Antonio	Sales ($ mil.)
SBC Communications Inc.	51,476
Ultramar Diamond Shamrock Corporation	17,061
Valero Energy Corporation	14,671
USAA	8,550
H. E. Butt Grocery Company	8,200
Clear Channel Communications, Inc.	5,345
Tesoro Petroleum Corporation	5,104
H. B. Zachry Company	1,195
Harte-Hanks, Inc.	961
Rush Enterprises, Inc.	897
Cullen/Frost Bankers, Inc.	683
Fairchild Dornier Corporation	650
Ancira Enterprises	589
Luby's, Inc.	467
The Gambrinus Company	425
Kinetic Concepts, Inc.	354
Eye Care Centers of America, Inc.	338
Southwest Research Institute	315
Alamo Group Inc.	216
Argonaut Group, Inc.	210
Taco Cabana, Inc.	171
Play-By-Play Toys & Novelties, Inc.	153
New Century Equity Holdings Corp.	145
Lancer Corporation	114
Souper Salad, Inc.	97
San Antonio Spurs, Ltd.	67
ILEX Oncology, Inc.	28

Texarkana	Sales ($ mil.)
E-Z Mart Stores, Inc.	641

Tyler	Sales ($ mil.)
Brookshire Grocery Company	1,600
Brookshire Brothers, LTD.	750
Lufkin Industries, Inc.	255
Classic Communications, Inc.	182

Waco	Sales ($ mil.)
Central Freight Lines, Inc.	350
Brazos Electric Power Cooperative, Inc.	290
Baylor University	275

Hoover's
Texas 500

THE COMPANY PROFILES

7-ELEVEN, INC.

OVERVIEW

"If convenience stores are open 24 hours, why the locks on their doors?" If anyone knows, it's 7-Eleven. The Dallas-based company (formerly The Southland Corporation) operates nearly 5,700 7-Eleven convenience stores in more than 30 states and Canada (more than half are franchised). Stores range from 2,400-3,000 sq. ft. and sell about 2,500 items. Less than half of its stores offer gasoline (mostly Citgo brand), and its merchandise (including Slurpees, beer, perishables, and tobacco items) accounts for about 70% of sales.

Worldwide, 7-Eleven operates or franchises more than 20,000 stores throughout North America and 16 other countries. Seven-Eleven Japan, 51%-owned by retailer Ito-Yokado (which also owns about 73% of 7-Eleven), runs about 8,500 7-Eleven stores in Japan and Hawaii under a license agreement. 7-Eleven has an interest in some 300 stores in Mexico.

To boost sales 7-Eleven has increased its offerings of fresh foods (deli items, salads, and baked goods) and rolled out new products, including breakfast foods and various cappuccino products. The company is testing Web-based cash machine/kiosks for purchasing event tickets, money transfers, and other e-commerce services. It believes its large store base can serve as convenient distribution points for other products as well.

HISTORY

Claude Dawley formed the Southland Ice Company in Dallas in 1927 when ice was a precious necessity during Texas summers for storing and transporting food. Dawley bought four other Texas ice plant operations with backing from Chicago utility magnate Martin Insull. The purchases included Consumers Ice, where Joe Thompson had increased profits by selling chilled watermelons off the truck docks.

After the Dawley enterprise was underway, a dock manager in Dallas began stocking a few food items for customers. (Ice docks were exempt from Texas' blue laws and could operate even on Sundays.) He relayed the idea to Thompson, then running the ice operations, who adopted it at all company locations.

Thompson promoted the grocery operations by calling them Tote'm Stores and erecting totem poles by the docks. In 1928 he added gas stations to some store locations.

Insull bought out Dawley in 1930, and Thompson became president. He expanded Southland's operations even as the company operated briefly under the direction of bankruptcy court (1932-34). Having become the largest dairy retailer in the Dallas/Fort Worth area, in 1936 the company began its own dairy, Oak Farms, to supply some of its milk (sold in 1988). Ten years later the company changed its name to The Southland Corporation and adopted the store name 7-Eleven, a reference to the stores' hours of operation at the time.

After Thompson died in 1961, his eldest son, John, became president. John opened stores in Colorado, New Jersey, and Arizona in 1962 and in Utah, California, and Missouri in 1963. The company introduced the Slurpee, a fizzy slush drink, in 1965. Southland franchised the 7-Eleven format in the UK (1971) and in Japan (1973).

To supply its gas pumps, in 1983 the company purchased Citgo, a gasoline refining and marketing business with about 300 gas stations. It soon sold a 50% interest of the business to the Venezuelan government-owned oil company, Petroleos de Venezuela (PDVSA), in 1986.

In 1988 John and his two brothers borrowed heavily to buy 70% of Southland's stock in an LBO. Stymied by debt, the company sold its remaining 50% stake in Citgo to PDVSA in 1990. However, Southland defaulted on $1.8 billion in publicly traded debt later that year and filed for bankruptcy protection. The company then persuaded bondholders to restructure its debt and take 25% of its stock, clearing the way for the purchase of 70% of Southland in 1991 by its Japanese partner, Ito-Yokado. Company veteran Clark Matthews was named CEO that year.

From 1991 to 1993 sales declined as Southland closed stores, renovated others, and upgraded its merchandise. In 1998 Southland began testing in-store electronic banking kiosks, which allow users to cash checks, pay bills, and transfer funds. New store openings and acquisitions (Christy's in New England, red D marts in Indiana) added 299 more units that year.

Southland changed its name to 7-Eleven in 1999 to better reflect the lone business of the company. In early 2000 Ito-Yokado raised its stake in 7-Eleven to nearly 73%. COO Jim Keyes (a 15-year veteran who began managing 7-Eleven's Citgo gasoline business) replaced Matthews as CEO in April 2000.

Chairman: Masatoshi Ito
Vice Chairman: Toshifumi Suzuki
Co-Vice Chairman: Clark J. Matthews II
President, CEO, and Director: James W. Keyes
SVP, International Liaison, and Director:
Masaaki Asakura
SVP, General Counsel, and Secretary: Bryan F. Smith Jr.
SVP, Merchandising and Development: Gary Rose
SVP, Store Operations: Rodney A. Brehm
VP, CFO, Controller, and Chief Accounting Officer:
Donald E. Thomas
VP, E-Commerce and Business Development:
Michael J. Gade
VP, Merchandising Integration: Dave Podeschi
VP, Gasoline Supply: Gary Lockhart
VP, Information Systems: Linda Svehlak
VP, National Sales and Marketing: Nancy A. Smith
VP, Planning: Rick Updyke
VP, Merchandising: Jeffrey S. Hamill
Director of Human Resources: Joe Eulberg
Auditors: PricewaterhouseCoopers LLP

LOCATIONS

HQ: 2711 N. Haskell Ave., Dallas, TX 75204
Phone: 214-828-7011   **Fax:** 214-828-7848
Web: www.7-eleven.com

PRODUCTS/OPERATIONS

2000 Sales

	% of total
Gasoline	29
Tobacco products	18
Non-alcoholic drinks	16
Beer & wine	8
Candy & snacks	6
Food service	4
Baked goods	3
Dairy products	3
Other	13
Total	**100**

COMPETITORS

Allsup's	Phillips Petroleum
Casey's General Stores	Pilot
Chevron	QuikTrip
Clark Retail Group	Racetrac Petroleum
Cumberland Farms	Royal Dutch/Shell
Dairy Mart	Sheetz
Eckerd	Shell
Exxon Mobil	Swifty Serve
Gate Petroleum	Texaco
H-E-B	Tosco
Holiday Companies	Ultramar Diamond
Kiel Brothers	Shamrock
Krause Gentle	Uni-Marts
Kroger	United Petroleum
Loblaw	USX-Marathon
Minyard Food Stores	Walgreen
Murphy Oil	Wawa
The Pantry	

HISTORICAL FINANCIALS & EMPLOYEES

NYSE: SE FYE: December 31	Annual Growth	12/91	12/92	12/93	12/94	12/95	12/96	12/97	12/98	12/99	12/00
Sales ($ mil.)	1.7%	8,010	7,426	5,851	5,767	5,754	5,907	6,000	6,214	8,252	9,346
Net income ($ mil.)	3.1%	83	(131)	71	92	271	90	70	74	83	108
Income as % of sales	—	1.0%	—	1.2%	1.6%	4.7%	1.5%	1.2%	1.2%	1.0%	1.2%
Earnings per share ($)	(2.2%)	1.20	(1.60)	0.85	1.10	3.25	1.00	0.80	0.85	0.90	0.98
Stock price - FY high ($)	—	15.16	21.25	38.44	33.75	23.59	24.69	18.44	15.16	13.75	21.25
Stock price - FY low ($)	—	4.69	5.94	14.84	19.06	14.38	12.19	8.59	7.81	7.97	8.00
Stock price - FY close ($)	(0.8%)	9.38	15.16	33.75	22.50	16.56	14.84	10.63	9.53	8.91	8.75
P/E - high	—	13	—	45	31	12	22	22	25	14	20
P/E - low	—	4	—	17	17	7	11	10	13	8	8
Dividends per share ($)	—	0.00	0.00	0.00	0.00	0.00	0.00	0.00	0.00	0.00	0.00
Book value per share ($)	—	(14.76)	(16.08)	(15.23)	(14.11)	(10.57)	(9.62)	(8.80)	(7.83)	(6.82)	0.78
Employees	(2.7%)	42,616	35,646	32,406	30,417	30,523	29,532	30,323	32,368	33,687	33,400

STOCK PRICE HISTORY

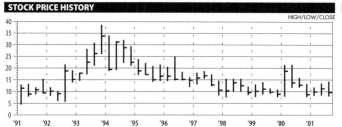

HIGH/LOW/CLOSE

2000 FISCAL YEAR-END

Debt ratio: 95.2%
Return on equity: —
Cash ($ mil.): 133
Current ratio: 0.72
Long-term debt ($ mil.): 1,641
No. of shares (mil.): 105
Dividends
 Yield: —
 Payout: —
Market value ($ mil.): 917

ADAMS RESOURCES & ENERGY, INC.

OVERVIEW

While the name Tennessee is now synonymous with NFL team-owner Bud Adams, his oil and gas business remains deeply rooted in Texas. Houston-based Adams Resources & Energy and its subsidiaries market crude oil and petroleum products, which account for about 99% of the company's sales. The company explores for and produces oil and gas, mainly in Texas, and has proved reserves of about 8.6 billion cu. ft. of natural gas and 626,000 barrels of oil.

Adams Resources Exploration (Exco) explores for and produces oil and gas primarily onshore on third party properties in Texas. GulfMark Energy purchases crude oil and transports it via company-owned trucks, third-party vehicles, common carrier pipelines, and barges. GulfMark primarily serves oil producers in Texas and off the coast of Louisiana.

Other subsidiaries include Service Transport, which operates tanker trucks that haul petrochemicals and other hazardous liquids throughout the continental US and Canada. Ada Resources purchases, stores, transports, and sells motor fuels and lubrication oils for service stations, including CITGO, Conoco, and Phillips. Bayou City Pipelines operates two crude oil pipelines off the coast of Louisiana. Adams Resources Marketing is a wholesale purchaser, distributor, and marketer of natural gas, serving 100 independent producers primarily offshore in the Gulf of Mexico.

The company has also expanded in the Northeast through the formation of the New England Energy Group. Adams, who owns the NFL's Tennessee Titans, controls about 50% of Adams Resources.

HISTORY

Born in Bartlesville, Oklahoma, in 1923 K. S. "Bud" Adams founded Ada Oil in 1947 to explore for and produce oil and gas. These operations, with some real estate holdings, formed the core of what became Adams Resources when the company went public in 1974. An investment in coal in Illinois and Kentucky led to $65 million in losses in 1981 and the closure of those operations. In 1992 Adams Resources bought GulfMark Energy, a crude oil trading company that specialized in oil transport and the marketing of specialty grades of crude.

When intrastate trucking was deregulated in 1995, Adams Resources faced new competition in Texas, where it made 40% of its trucking sales. The company had to cut prices that year, and transportation earnings fell 30%. Adams Resources enjoyed greater production from a series of successful gas wells in the Austin Chalk region in 1996, and the company and partner Nuevo Energy added three wells in Austin Chalk the next year.

Adams Resources completed a 7.5-mile offshore Louisiana crude oil pipeline in 1998 that boosted the company's Gulf of Mexico crude oil throughput by more than 15,000 barrels per day.

The company expanded its operations in 1999 by setting up Adams Resources Marketing as a wholesale purchaser, distributor, and marketer of natural gas. In connection with the formation of the new company, Adams Resources Marketing hired almost all of the personnel formerly employed by Houston-based gas marketer

H&N Gas Ltd. In addition Adams Resources Marketing signed a service agreement with H&N to administer H&N's existing contracts.

In 2000 Adams Resources ramped up operations in the US Northeast by forming New England Energy Group, a regional retail marketer of natural gas and other energy products. Also in 2000 the company expanded its crude oil operations into Michigan and California. Adams Resources also signed a joint venture deal with Oklahoma-based energy producer The Williams Companies. The deal teamed Adams subsidiary Gulfmark Energy Marketing and Williams Energy Marketing & Trading to form Williams-Gulfmark Energy Co. for purchase, distribution and marketing of crude oil from the Gulf of Mexico.

In 2000 Adams Resources signed an agreement with British Petroleum (BP) to transport fuels and lubricants to BP outlets in southeastern Texas and Southern Louisiana. Revenues skyrocketed during 1999 and 2000 thanks to rising crude oil prices, but the company was hurt in 2001 as the crude oil market became highly volatile.

OFFICERS

Chairman, President, and CEO: K. S. Adams Jr., age 78, $320,213 pay
VP Finance and Director; President, Gulfmark Energy and Adams Resources Marketing GP:
Richard B. Abshire, age 48, $399,961 pay
VP Land Transportation and Director; President, Service Transport Company: Claude H. Lewis, age 57
President, Ada Resources: Lee A. Beauchamp, age 49
President, Adams Resources Exploration:
James Brock Moore III, age 61, $171,261 pay
Director Human Resources: Jay Grimes
Auditors: Arthur Andersen LLP

LOCATIONS

HQ: 4400 Post Oak Pkwy., Ste. 2700, Houston, TX 77027
Phone: 713-881-3600 **Fax:** 713-881-3491

Adams Resources produces oil and gas in Texas and Louisiana; markets oil and gas products on the Gulf Coast and in New England; and provides energy transportation services throughout the US and Canada.

PRODUCTS/OPERATIONS

2000 Sales

	$ mil.	% of total
Marketing	6,980	99
Transportation	36	1
Oil & gas	6	—
Total	7,022	100

Selected Subsidiaries
Ada Crude Oil Company
Ada Mining Corporation
Adams Resources Exploration Corporation
Adams Resources Marketing, Ltd. (natural gas marketing)
Ada Resources, Inc. (petroleum products marketing)
Ada Resources Marketing, Inc. (wholesale natural gas marketing)
Bayou City Pipelines, Inc.
Buckley Mining Corporation
CJC Leasing, Inc.
Classic Coal Corporation
GulfMark Energy, Inc. (crude oil marketing)
New England Energy Group (retail natural gas marketing)
Service Transport Company (liquid chemicals and petroleum products transport)

COMPETITORS

Abraxas Petroleum
Anadarko Petroleum
Apache
Bass Enterprises
BP
Cabot Oil & Gas
Chevron
EOG
Exxon Mobil
Howell
Mitchell Energy & Development
Phillips Petroleum
Pioneer Natural Resources
Pogo Producing
Royal Dutch/Shell
Texaco

HISTORICAL FINANCIALS & EMPLOYEES

AMEX: AE FYE: December 31	Annual Growth	12/91	12/92	12/93	12/94	12/95	12/96	12/97	12/98	12/99	12/00
Sales ($ mil.)	57.2%	120	550	695	635	831	1,497	1,963	1,974	3,996	7,022
Net income ($ mil.)	19.3%	2	4	2	3	1	6	6	2	6	9
Income as % of sales	—	1.5%	0.8%	0.2%	0.5%	0.1%	0.4%	0.3%	0.1%	0.2%	0.1%
Earnings per share ($)	18.7%	0.45	1.00	0.35	0.72	0.29	1.34	1.36	0.55	1.51	2.10
Stock price - FY high ($)	—	4.00	6.50	6.13	10.75	10.00	13.88	18.38	14.75	11.38	21.06
Stock price - FY low ($)	—	2.25	3.00	4.00	4.44	4.88	5.63	11.63	5.25	5.81	8.13
Stock price - FY close ($)	16.7%	3.50	5.13	4.50	9.88	7.13	12.25	14.38	5.75	8.50	14.00
P/E - high	—	9	36	18	15	34	10	14	27	8	10
P/E - low	—	5	17	11	6	17	4	9	10	4	4
Dividends per share ($)	—	0.00	0.00	0.00	0.03	0.05	0.07	0.10	0.10	0.10	0.13
Book value per share ($)	21.8%	1.78	2.11	2.47	3.16	3.74	5.42	6.66	7.14	8.53	10.50
Employees	10.0%	291	309	322	377	378	403	512	565	643	685

STOCK PRICE HISTORY

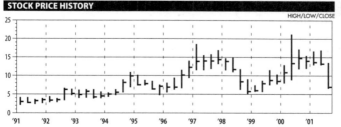

HIGH/LOW/CLOSE

2000 FISCAL YEAR-END

Debt ratio: 21.2%
Return on equity: 21.9%
Cash ($ mil.): 36
Current ratio: 1.08
Long-term debt ($ mil.): 12
No. of shares (mil.): 4
Dividends
 Yield: 0.9%
 Payout: 6.2%
Market value ($ mil.): 59

ADMINISTAFF, INC.

OVERVIEW

Administaff helps its client companies administer their businesses with fewer staff. One of the leading professional employer organizations (PEOs) in the country, the Kingwood, Texas-based company handles payroll and benefits administration, health and workers' compensation insurance programs, and employee recruiting for small and midsized companies. In a system known as employee leasing, clients' employees are put on Administaff's payroll, and then "leased" back to the client for a fee.

Most of its 4,000 client companies are engaged in the business services, financial services, and health care industries. Administaff has three service centers in Atlanta, Dallas, and Houston, as well as 35 sales offices in 19 major US markets. Its business in Texas accounts for about 50% of sales.

To offer immediate and more personalized services for its clients, the company runs Administaff Assistant, an online service and resource Web site where its client companies and their employees can access and update payroll information, create reports, and receive online training. It also runs the bizzport Internet portal, where clients can purchase goods and services from vendors like BANK ONE, Continental Airlines, Dell, and IBM or from other Administaff clients.

The company continues to expand by adding offices in new territories, with a long-term expansion goal of having 90 offices serving 40 markets. It is also building a fourth service center in Los Angeles. It hopes to handle human resource services for about 10% of the small businesses in the US.

Investor Lang Gerhard owns about 21% of the company, and American Express has a 15% stake. Administaff co-founder and CEO Paul Sarvadi owns 13%, and CFO Richard Rawson owns 5% of the company.

HISTORY

Gerald McIntosh and Paul Sarvadi founded Administaff in 1986. The two entrepreneurs saw growth potential in employee leasing, despite the industry's image problems. (Sarvadi had worked for James Borgelt, who founded several Dallas-area employee leasing firms and was sentenced to three years in prison in 1996 for stealing from clients.)

By 1991 Administaff had become one of the largest employee leasing companies in the US. That year it joined 17 other leasing companies in filing a suit against the Texas State Board of Insurance, which had tried to prohibit leasing companies from buying workers' compensation insurance. Regulators claimed leasing companies were touting their services as a way to avoid high workers' comp premiums. In 1993 a compromise law allowed employee leasing companies to buy workers' comp insurance based on the clients' on-the-job accident history.

With about 1,500 clients, Administaff went public in 1997. The following year the company formed a marketing agreement with American Express, under which the travel and financial services giant refers smaller business clients to Administaff for a fee.

Administaff entered the world of barter in 1999 when it signed a services agreement with Web developer Luminant Worldwide. Under the agreement, Admnstaff provided human resource services to Luminant in exchange for e-commerce consulting services.

Administaff began offering Web-based services in 1999 with Administaff Assistant.

The company launched Internet portal site bizzport in 2000. It also formed several co-marketing deals designed to provide extra perks to its clients' employees. Among the companies it signed agreements with were Web florist FTD.com (for special pricing on flowers and other gifts), Continental Airlines (for travel bonuses), and Spiegel Catalog (for special pricing and reward programs on Spiegel merchandise).

Also in 2000 Administaff opened new offices in New Jersey and Maryland, and added offices in Atlanta, Los Angeles, San Francisco, and Washington, DC.

The company continued to expand in 2001, adding new offices in Boston and San Diego. It also continued to sign co-marketing agreements, including deals with e-Realty.com and Wells Fargo Home Mortgage. By 2001 the company's client roster had grown to more than 4,000 companies.

OFFICERS

President and CEO: Paul J. Sarvadi, age 44,
$521,035 pay
EVP Administration, CFO, and Treasurer:
Richard G. Rawson, age 52, $585,335 pay
EVP Client Services: A. Steve Arizpe, age 43,
$455,777 pay
EVP Sales and Marketing: Jay E. Mincks, age 47,
$409,467 pay
VP Client Services Coordination: Gwen Fey
VP e-Commerce Development: Randall H. McCollum,
age 56
VP Enterprise Project Management: Samuel G. Larson,
age 39
VP eService Operations: Jeff W. Hutcheon
VP Finance and Controller: Douglas S. Sharp, age 39
VP Benefits and Corporate Human Resources: Howard
G. Buff
VP Human Resource Services: Constance Hall Barnaba
VP Legal, General Counsel, and Secretary:
John H. Spurgin II, age 54, $358,212 pay
VP Sales Administration: Roger L. Gaskamp
VP Technology Solutions and Chief Technology Officer:
David C. Dickson
VP Sales: John F. Orth
Auditors: Ernst & Young LLP

LOCATIONS

HQ: 19001 Crescent Springs Dr., Kingwood, TX 77339
Phone: 281-358-8986   **Fax:** 281-358-3354
Web: www.administaff.com

Administaff has 35 offices in 19 markets around the US.

PRODUCTS/OPERATIONS

2000 Clients

	% of total
Business services	25
Finance, insurance & real estate	16
Medical services	9
Engineering, accounting & legal	8
Manufacturing	8
Construction	7
Retail trade	6
Wholesale trade	6
Transportation	4
Other	11
Total	**100**

Selected Services
Benefits and payroll administration
eBusiness services
Employee recruiting and selection
Employer liability management
Health insurance programs
Performance management
Personnel records management
Training and development
Workers' compensation programs

COMPETITORS

ADP
EPIX
Express Personnel
Gevity HR

Paychex
TEAM Mucho
TeamStaff
TTC

HISTORICAL FINANCIALS & EMPLOYEES

NYSE: ASF FYE: December 31	Annual Growth	12/91	12/92	12/93	12/94	12/95	12/96	12/97	12/98	12/99	12/00
Sales ($ mil.)	32.2%	300	409	496	564	716	900	1,214	1,683	2,261	3,709
Net income ($ mil.)	84.0%	0	0	2	4	1	3	7	9	9	17
Income as % of sales	—	0.0%	0.0%	0.4%	0.7%	0.2%	0.3%	0.6%	0.5%	0.4%	0.5%
Earnings per share ($)	29.0%	—	—	—	—	—	—	0.27	0.31	0.34	0.58
Stock price - FY high ($)	—	—	—	—	—	—	—	13.25	26.47	17.25	44.56
Stock price - FY low ($)	—	—	—	—	—	—	—	6.88	10.81	5.56	10.38
Stock price - FY close ($)	28.1%	—	—	—	—	—	—	12.94	12.50	15.13	27.20
P/E - high	—	—	—	—	—	—	—	47	83	51	72
P/E - low	—	—	—	—	—	—	—	25	34	16	17
Dividends per share ($)	—	—	—	—	—	—	—	0.00	0.00	0.00	0.00
Book value per share ($)	18.7%	—	—	—	—	—	—	2.30	2.99	2.99	3.85
Employees	26.5%	—	—	12,000	16,000	16,220	25,000	30,205	34,819	48,800	62,140

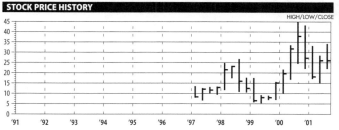

STOCK PRICE HISTORY
HIGH/LOW/CLOSE

2000 FISCAL YEAR-END
Debt ratio: 0.0%
Return on equity: 18.2%
Cash ($ mil.): 70
Current ratio: 1.39
Long-term debt ($ mil.): 0
No. of shares (mil.): 27
Dividends
  Yield: —
  Payout: —
Market value ($ mil.): 746

ADVANCEPCS, INC.

OVERVIEW

Health plans farming out their pharmacy operations turn to AdvancePCS, the largest independent pharmacy benefits provider in the US (Medco, a subsidiary of pharmaceutical company Merck, is larger.). The company, based in Irving, Texas, was formed when Advance Paradigm bought PCS Health Systems from Rite Aid.

The firm provides pharmacy and health management services to health plan sponsors covering more than 75 million enrollees. The company's services include mail-order and online pharmacies, disease management programs (for asthma, diabetes, and congestive heart failure), and a broad system of information management capabilities. Subsidiaries Innovative Medical Research and Baumel-Eisner Neuromedical Institute provide a range of clinical trials, outcomes research, and health survey services.

The company has grown quickly both through acquisitions and the aggressive courting of such groups as the United Mine Workers and the Oklahoma State Education Employees Group Insurance Board. AdvancePCS includes among its clients many Blue Cross and Blue Shield organizations, insurance companies and HMOs, corporate employers, labor unions, and state and local governments.

AdvancePCS is looking for more growth over the next few years as more patients switch to mail-order drug delivery, cutting out local pharmacies and saving on distribution costs. Also, as more high-tech drugs hit the market, the company sees a chance to enhance sales and profits by handling the delivery and administration of these expensive and complex treatments.

HISTORY

David Halbert, a former energy company executive, founded Advance Health Care in 1986 as a mail-order pharmacy. His brother Jon, formerly of Bear Stearns, became COO in 1988. In 1992 the company began building a retail pharmacy network. The next year Advance Health Care bought Paradigm Pharmacy Management, a benefits management subsidiary of Blue Cross and Blue Shield of Maryland. This acquisition enabled the company to strike bargains with drug companies and to attract cost-conscious managed care clients. After the acquisition, the company was renamed Advance Paradigm and moved into integrated health benefits management. The company went public in 1996.

Advance Paradigm had been expanding its customer base through marketing and acquisitions. In keeping with the industry's focus on disease management, it also began acquiring clinical trial and research companies (Innovative Medical Research and Baumel-Eisner Neuromedical Institute, 1998). In 1998 Advance Paradigm launched its online pharmacy operations. In 1999 it bought Foundation Health System's (now Health Net) pharmacy benefit management operations, adding about 27 million members to its system.

In 2000 Advance Paradigm purchased PCS Health Systems from Rite Aid. Rite Aid had acquired PCS from Eli Lilly, but was forced to sell it for a loss to reduce debt. Founded in 1969 as Pharmaceutical Card System, PCS was the first pharmacy benefit management company in the

US. PCS entered the mail-order pharmacy business in 1996 when it opened a distribution center in Fort Worth, Texas. After the merger, the two companies became AdvancePCS. In 2000 the company acquired pharmacy benefits manager FFI Health Services, and it invested in Consumer Health Interactive, a Web-based health services marketing company.

In 2001 AdvancePCS launched a specialty pharmacy business unit, AdvancePCS SpecialtyRx, by acquiring specialty pharmacy provider TheraCom and forming a joint venture with specialty pharmacy and distribution company Priority Healthcare. The new division is devoted to offering services to patients who need expensive and technologically advanced drugs to treat complex diseases.

Also in 2001 AdvancePCS teamed with pharmacy benefits companies Express Scripts and Merck-Medco to form RxHub, an electronic exchange that will link patients' doctors with pharmacies, pharmacy benefit managers, and health plans. Later in 2001 the company renewed its contract with the Blue Cross and Blue Shield Association Federal Employee Program, which serves more than 4 million customers.

OFFICERS

Chairman and CEO: David D. Halbert, $984,615 pay (prior to merger)
Vice Chairman, e-Business and Technology: Jon S. Halbert, $527,692 pay (prior to merger)
President and Director: David A. George, $437,199 pay (prior to merger)
EVP, Client Management: Joseph J. Filipek Jr., age 45, $338,338 pay (prior to merger)
EVP, Financial Operations: Thomas J. Garrity
EVP, Business Development and CFO: T. Danny Phillips, age 41, $407,153 pay
SVP, Operations: Ernest Buys, age 58
SVP, Legal, Government Affairs, and Marketing and General Counsel: Susan de Mars
SVP, Clinical Operations: Andrew Garling
SVP and Chief Information Officer: Mitch Henry
SVP, Corporate Affairs and Secretary: Laura I. Johansen
SVP, Pharma Relations: Rudy Mladenovic
SVP, Mail Services: Phil Pearce
SVP, Strategic Initiatives: Jeffrey G. Sanders
SVP, Sales: John H. Sattler, age 48
SVP, Corporate Accounts and Product Management: Dan Segedin
SVP, Pharmacy Network Administration: Doug Stephens
SVP and Chief Human Resources Officer: Steven C. Mizell
Director, Public Relations: Blair Jackson
Auditors: Arthur Andersen LLP

LOCATIONS

HQ: 5215 N. O'Connor St., Ste. 1600, Irving, TX 75039
Phone: 972-830-6199   **Fax:** 972-830-6196
Web: www.advparadigm.com

AdvancePCS operates throughout the US.

PRODUCTS/OPERATIONS

2001 Sales

	$ mil.	% of total
Data services	6,011	86
Mail services	714	10
Clinical & other	299	4
Total	**7,024**	**100**

COMPETITORS

Caremark
Chronimed
Express Scripts
Merck
MIM
National Medical Health Card Systems
Owen Healthcare
Rite Aid
Walgreen

HISTORICAL FINANCIALS & EMPLOYEES

Nasdaq: ADVP FYE: March 31	Annual Growth	3/92	3/93	3/94	3/95	3/96	3/97	3/98	3/99	3/00	3/01
Sales ($ mil.)	115.5%	7	12	23	66	125	252	477	775	1,968	7,024
Net income ($ mil.)	—	(0)	(0)	(0)	0	1	3	8	13	21	23
Income as % of sales	—	—	—	—	0.0%	0.8%	1.2%	1.7%	1.6%	1.0%	0.3%
Earnings per share ($)	36.8%	—	—	—	—	—	0.18	0.35	0.55	0.85	0.63
Stock price - FY high ($)	—	—	—	—	—	—	12.63	20.38	33.88	34.75	59.25
Stock price - FY low ($)	—	—	—	—	—	—	3.88	5.44	8.50	11.13	9.50
Stock price - FY close ($)	69.1%	—	—	—	—	—	6.63	19.81	31.59	11.88	54.27
P/E - high	—	—	—	—	—	—	57	46	55	36	76
P/E - low	—	—	—	—	—	—	18	12	14	11	12
Dividends per share ($)	—	—	—	—	—	—	0.00	0.00	0.00	0.00	0.00
Book value per share ($)	42.1%	—	—	—	—	—	2.72	2.84	3.28	4.62	11.12
Employees	74.3%	—	—	—	—	282	336	697	891	1,370	4,534

STOCK PRICE HISTORY

HIGH/LOW/CLOSE

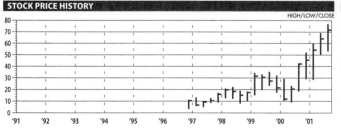

2001 FISCAL YEAR-END

Debt ratio: 67.2%
Return on equity: 9.0%
Cash ($ mil.): 110
Current ratio: 0.80
Long-term debt ($ mil.): 830
No. of shares (mil.): 36
Dividends
  Yield: —
  Payout: —
Market value ($ mil.): 1,980

AFFILIATED COMPUTER SERVICES

OVERVIEW

Affiliated Computer Services (ACS) makes money out of the mundane. The Dallas-based company generates nearly half of its sales from its business process outsourcing division, which processes, scans, and analyzes company documents such as health care invoices and financial transactions. ACS's services include data processing (loan and mortgage, accounts payable), systems integration, network management, Internet/intranet development, supply chain management, and custom programming. The company also offers program management, processing services, and consulting for state and local governments' health and human services agencies. ACS serves more than 10,000 clients worldwide through more than 250 offices throughout the US, Europe, Central and South America, and the Middle East.

Commercial clients, such as Motorola and Blue Cross and Blue Shield, bring in about two-thirds of sales. The rest comes from contracts with various agencies of the US government, including the Senate, the Labor Department, and the National Security Agency.

The company has acquired more than 50 businesses since its founding in 1988, including its $825 million purchase of Lockheed Martin's IMS subsidiary.

Founder and chairman Darwin Deason owns 12% of ACS, and controls about 45% of the voting power.

HISTORY

In 1967 Darwin Deason took over a company called Affiliated Computer Services (ACS). Eight years later he sold that company to Dallas-based MTech, but stayed on as its president. Under Deason, ACS helped MTech become the US's largest provider of financial data processing. When MTech was bought by General Motors subsidiary Electronic Data Systems in 1988, Deason left to start an entirely new ACS.

The new company was created as a financial computer services provider, focused on processing bank transactions. Its 1992 acquisition of Dataplex ushered the company into business process outsourcing, and ACS went public two years later. ACS's 1995 acquisition of The Systems Group extended the company's offerings to include professional services.

The company continued pursuing its rapid rate of growth throughout the late 1990s, building a string of acquisitions that included Intelligent Solutions (1997), Computer Data Systems (1997), Betac International (1998), and Canmax's retail systems subsidiary (1998). In 1998 ACS agreed to buy the Unclaimed Property Services Division of State Street Corporation. Early the following year it acquired information technology (IT) services company BRC Holdings. Deason also stepped down as CEO (he remains chairman), passing the reigns to president Jeffrey Rich, a former Citibank investment banker. Later in 1999 ACS bought Consultec, a provider of IT services for state health programs, from General American Life in a $105 million deal.

In 2000 the company sold its ATM business for about $180 million. It also boosted its government outsourcing capabilities with the acquisition of Intellisource Group. Additionally, it bought Birch & Davis, a provider of management and consulting services to federal and state government agencies that manage government health care programs, for approximately $75 million.

Also in 2000 ACS's Defense business unit signed a deal with J.S. Wurzler Underwriting Managers to provide a total risk management service, offering online security services and insurance against potential losses from business outages caused by online security breaches.

In 2001 ACS acquired Lockheed Martin's IMS subsidiary, which provides outsourcing services to municipal and state governments, for $825 million. Also that year ACS acquired the business process outsourcing services unit of National Processing Company, which was a subsidiary of National Processing, Inc. for $42 million. The unit provides health care claim, credit card application, and airline lift ticket processing.

Also in 2001 it bought Systems & Computer Technology's Global Government Solutions unit, a provider of outsourcing services to local and state governments, for $85 million. It also acquired Tyler Technologies' subsidiary Business Resources Corporation, a provider of records management, document workflow, and imaging services to state and local governments, for $71 million.

OFFICERS

Chairman: Darwin Deason, age 61, $2,010,045 pay
President, CEO, and Director: Jeffrey A. Rich, age 41, $1,500,000 pay
COO and Director: Mark A. King, age 44, $933,000 pay
EVP, General Counsel, Secretary, and Director: William L. Deckelman Jr., age 44
EVP, Global Business Development; Director: Henry G. Hortenstine, age 57, $750,000 pay
EVP; Group President, Government Services: Harvey Braswell, $582,596 pay
SVP, Human Resources: Lora Villarreal
Group President, Business Process Solutions: Lynn Blodgett, $486,000 pay
Group President, IT Solutions: Donald G. Liedtke
Auditors: PricewaterhouseCoopers LLP

LOCATIONS

HQ: Affiliated Computer Services, Inc.
2828 N. Haskell Ave., Dallas, TX 75204
Phone: 214-841-6111   **Fax:** 214-821-8315
Web: www.acs-inc.com

Affiliated Computer Services has more than 200 offices worldwide.

PRODUCTS/OPERATIONS

2001 Sales

	$ mil.	% of sales
Business process outsourcing	974	47
Systems integration services	649	31
Technology outsourcing	441	22
Total	**2,064**	**100**

Selected Services

Business process outsourcing
  Accounts payable and accounts receivable administration
  Benefits and claims administration
  Check processing
  Customer care and support
  Invoice processing
  Loan processing and administration
  Merchandise fulfillment
  Records storage and retrieval
  Shareholder support
  Supply chain management
  Trade marketing
Professional support
  Contract programming
  Network design and installation
  Systems conversion
  Systems development
  Telecommunications integration
Technology outsourcing
  Call center support
  Client/server support
  Desktop support
  Hardware and software procurement
  Help desk support
  Network management, support, and maintenance
  Online and batch data processing
  Telemarketing support

COMPETITORS

Accenture	First Data
ADP	Fiserv
BISYS	IBM
Cambridge Technology	Perot Systems
Cap Gemini	SAIC
Computer Sciences	Unisys
EDS	

HISTORICAL FINANCIALS & EMPLOYEES

NYSE: ACS FYE: June 30	Annual Growth	6/92	6/93	6/94	6/95	6/96	6/97	6/98	6/99	6/00	6/01
Sales ($ mil.)	33.8%	150	189	271	313	397	625	1,189	1,642	1,963	2,064
Net income ($ mil.)	44.4%	5	10	12	18	24	39	54	86	109	134
Income as % of sales	—	3.3%	5.0%	4.5%	5.6%	6.0%	6.2%	4.6%	5.2%	5.6%	6.5%
Earnings per share ($)	23.0%	—	—	—	0.71	0.85	1.05	1.11	1.66	2.07	2.46
Stock price - FY high ($)	—	—	—	—	15.75	26.88	32.00	39.75	51.75	53.00	77.68
Stock price - FY low ($)	—	—	—	—	8.50	13.88	19.50	21.50	22.38	31.00	32.63
Stock price - FY close ($)	29.5%	—	—	—	15.25	23.50	28.00	38.50	50.63	33.13	71.91
P/E - high	—	—	—	—	21	31	30	35	29	24	29
P/E - low	—	—	—	—	11	16	18	19	13	14	12
Dividends per share ($)	—	—	—	—	0.00	0.00	0.00	0.00	0.00	0.00	0.00
Book value per share ($)	27.6%	—	—	—	4.05	8.60	9.71	10.44	12.33	14.35	17.51
Employees	32.6%	—	2,200	2,200	2,800	5,580	7,030	12,300	15,700	18,500	21,000

STOCK PRICE HISTORY

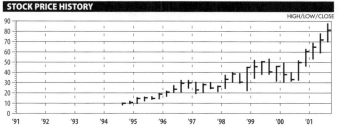

HIGH/LOW/CLOSE

2001 FISCAL YEAR-END

Debt ratio: 42.3%
Return on equity: 16.8%
Cash ($ mil.): 243
Current ratio: 2.88
Long-term debt ($ mil.): 649
No. of shares (mil.): 51
Dividends
  Yield: —
  Payout: —
Market value ($ mil.): 3,637

AMR CORPORATION

AMR's American Airlines is taking on the world. The #2 airline in the US based on revenue passenger miles (behind UAL's United Airlines), Fort Worth, Texas-based American flies to some 170 destinations (including those served by code-sharing partners) in the Caribbean, the Pacific Rim, Europe, and the Americas. The airline, which has a fleet of more than 700 jetliners (mostly Boeings), has hubs at Dallas/Fort Worth's DFW, Chicago's O'Hare, and in Miami and San Juan, Puerto Rico. AMR also owns commuter carrier American Eagle.

Internationally, American Airlines leads Oneworld, an extensive marketing alliance that includes British Airways, Cathay Pacific, Qantas, and others. It also has code-sharing agreements with carriers such as China Eastern Airlines and Japan Airlines.

Early in 2001 AMR responded to UAL's then-pending purchase of US Airways with some dealmaking of its own. It acquired the assets of bankrupt rival TWA and agreed to buy some East Coast assets of US Airways that were to be sold upon that carrier's acquisition by UAL. But antitrust regulators at the US Department of Justice moved to block the UAL-US Airways transaction, and the companies called the deal off. AMR's agreement to buy the US Airways assets also was terminated. But for AMR, all's well that ends well: Once it absorbs TWA's assets, American Airlines is expected to surpass UAL's United Airlines to become the largest US carrier.

Also in 2001 two hijacked American Airlines aircraft were crashed by terrorists in attacks in New York and Washington, DC. In anticipation of reduced demand for air travel, AMR announced it would cut back on its flights by 20% and lay off some 20,000 workers (about 17% of its workforce).

In 1929 Sherman Fairchild created a New York City holding company called the Aviation Corporation (AVCO), combining some 85 small airlines in 1930 to create American Airways. In 1934 the company had its first dose of financial trouble after the government suspended private airmail for months. Corporate raider E. L. Cord took over and named the company American Airlines.

Cord put former AVCO manager C. R. Smith in charge, and American became the leading US airline in the late 1930s. The Douglas DC-3, built to Smith's specifications, was introduced by American in 1936 and became the first commercial airliner to pay its way on passenger revenues alone.

After WWII American bought Amex Airlines, which flew to northern Europe, but another financial crisis prompted Amex's sale in 1950. The airline introduced Sabre, the first automated reservations system, in 1964. Smith left American four years later to serve as secretary of commerce in the Johnson administration.

In 1979, the year after airline industry deregulation, American moved to Dallas/Fort Worth. Former CFO Bob Crandall became president in 1980 (and later, CEO). Using Sabre to track mileage, he introduced the industry's first frequent-flier program (AAdvantage). In 1982 American created AMR as its holding company. After acquiring commuter airline Nashville Eagle in 1987, AMR established American Eagle.

After ducking a 1989 takeover bid by Donald Trump, AMR bought routes to Japan, Latin America, and London from other carriers. American's 1994 attempt to simplify pricing led to a fare war that hurt industry profits. Tragedy struck American Eagle that year — two crashes resulted in 83 deaths. The next year American's 16-year fatality-free flying record ended when an airliner crashed into a mountain near Cali, Colombia, killing 160.

In 1996 AMR spun off nearly 20% of Sabre. The airline announced plans for a code-sharing pact with British Airways (BA) that sparked a wave of alliances, including Oneworld.

Crandall retired in 1998 and was replaced by Donald Carty. To focus on its airlines, AMR sold its executive aviation services, ground services, and call center units in 1999. In 2000 AMR sold its Canadian Airlines stake to Air Canada and spun off the rest of Sabre.

In 2001 AMR moved to become a stronger competitor to UAL by agreeing to buy troubled rival TWA and some US Airways operations. The company paid $742 million for TWA's assets, and AMR formed TWA Airlines LLC to oversee TWA's operations while they were being integrated with American's.

Also in 2001 American lost two aircraft that were used in terrorist attacks on the World Trade Center in New York and the Pentagon in Washington, DC. In anticipation of reduced demand for air travel, AMR announced a 20% reduction in flights and layoffs of at least 20,000 employees. Later that same year, another American Airlines jet crashed in New York, killing all 260 passengers.

OFFICERS

Chairman, President, and CEO, AMR and American Airlines: Donald J. Carty, age 54, $2,124,375 pay
Vice Chairman, AMR and American Airlines: Robert W. Baker, age 56
EVP Customer Service, AMR and American Airlines: Daniel P. Garton, age 43, $1,037,132 pay
EVP Marketing and Planning, AMR and American Airlines: Michael W. Gunn, age 55, $1,037,310 pay
EVP Operations, AMR and American Airlines: Gerard J. Arpey, age 42, $1,037,209 pay
SVP and General Counsel, AMR and American Airlines: Anne H. McNamara, age 53
SVP Finance and CFO, AMR and American Airlines: Thomas W. Horton, age 39
SVP Government Affairs, American Airlines: William K. Ris Jr.
SVP Human Resources, American Airlines: Susan M. Oliver
SVP Information Technology and Chief Information Officer, American Airlines: Monte E. Ford
SVP Maintenance and Engineering, American Airlines: Dan P. Huffman
SVP Miami, Caribbean, and Latin America, American Airlines: Peter J. Dolara
SVP Planning, American Airlines: Henry C. Joyner
VP and Controller, American Airlines: Douglas G. Herring
Auditors: Ernst & Young LLP

LOCATIONS

HQ: 4333 Amon Carter Blvd., Fort Worth, TX 76155
Phone: 817-963-1234   **Fax:** 817-967-9641
Web: www.amrcorp.com

AMR Corporation's American Airlines serves about 170 cities in the Caribbean, Europe, North America, Latin America, the Pacific Rim. Subsidiary American Eagle serves an additional 70 destinations.

2000 Sales

	$ mil.	% of total
US	13,881	70
Latin America	2,907	15
Europe	2,338	12
Pacific	577	3
Total	**19,703**	**100**

PRODUCTS/OPERATIONS

2000 Sales

	$ mil.	% of total
Passenger		
American Airlines	16,377	83
AMR Eagle Holding	1,452	7
Cargo	721	4
Other	1,153	6
Total	**19,703**	**100**

COMPETITORS

AirTran Holdings	Legend Airlines	UAL
Alaska Air	Mesa Air	UPS
America West	Mesaba Holdings	US Airways
Continental	Northwest	Virgin Atlantic
Delta	SkyWest	
Greyhound	Southwest	

HISTORICAL FINANCIALS & EMPLOYEES

NYSE: AMR FYE: December 31	Annual Growth	12/91	12/92	12/93	12/94	12/95	12/96	12/97	12/98	12/99	12/00
Sales ($ mil.)	4.8%	12,887	14,396	15,816	16,137	16,910	17,753	18,570	19,205	17,730	19,703
Net income ($ mil.)	—	(240)	(935)	(110)	228	167	1,016	985	1,314	985	813
Income as % of sales	—	—	—	—	1.4%	1.0%	5.7%	5.3%	6.8%	5.6%	4.1%
Earnings per share ($)	—	(1.79)	(6.27)	(1.12)	1.13	1.05	5.60	5.39	7.52	6.26	5.03
Stock price - FY high ($)	—	15.89	17.93	16.29	16.26	17.93	21.79	29.62	40.20	33.72	39.44
Stock price - FY low ($)	—	9.89	12.15	12.40	10.75	11.93	15.20	17.49	20.39	23.49	21.93
Stock price - FY close ($)	10.7%	15.75	15.08	14.97	11.90	16.59	19.69	28.72	26.54	29.95	39.19
P/E - high	—	—	—	—	14	14	3	5	5	5	7
P/E - low	—	—	—	—	10	10	2	3	3	4	4
Dividends per share ($)	—	0.00	0.00	0.00	0.00	0.00	0.00	0.00	0.00	0.00	0.00
Book value per share ($)	6.1%	27.75	22.21	28.22	22.27	24.35	31.14	35.89	41.51	46.26	47.19
Employees	(0.0%)	116,300	119,300	118,900	109,800	110,000	88,900	90,600	92,000	124,421	116,054

STOCK PRICE HISTORY

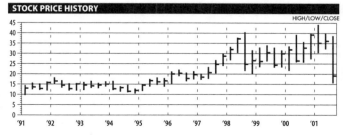

HIGH/LOW/CLOSE

2000 FISCAL YEAR-END

Debt ratio: 43.3%
Return on equity: 11.6%
Cash ($ mil.): 89
Current ratio: 0.74
Long-term debt ($ mil.): 5,474
No. of shares (mil.): 152
Dividends
  Yield: —
  Payout: —
Market value ($ mil.): 5,959

ANADARKO PETROLEUM

OVERVIEW

Leaving behind its Anadarko Basin roots, Houston-based Anadarko Petroleum has ventured far afield to become one of the world's largest independent oil and gas exploration and production companies. The company, which has expanded significantly with the acquisition of fellow independent Union Pacific Resources, has proved reserves of more than 2 billion barrels of oil equivalent and daily production of about 570,000 barrels equivalent.

More than half of Anadarko's reserves are located in the US, where it operates in Alaska, Texas, Louisiana, the midcontinent and Rocky Mountain regions, and the Gulf of Mexico. It also operates five gas-gathering systems (more than 2,500 miles of pipeline) in the midcontinent. Internationally, the company has substantial oil and gas interests in Algeria's Sahara Desert, Guatemala, Venezuela, and western Canada. It has gained a stake in the Middle East by purchasing Gulfstream Resources Canada, which has operations in Oman and Qatar.

Since Anadarko became independent in 1986, the company's reserves have shifted from being more than 90% natural gas to being evenly split between gas and crude oil, largely because of oil discoveries in the Gulf of Mexico and Algeria.

HISTORY

In 1959 the Panhandle Eastern Pipe Line Company set up Anadarko (named after the Anadarko Basin, which stretches from northwest Texas through western Oklahoma to southern Kansas) to carry out its gas exploration and production activities. The new company was also formed to take advantage of a ruling by the Federal Power Commission (now the Federal Energy Regulatory Commission) to set lower price ceilings for producing properties owned by pipeline companies.

The company grew rapidly during the early 1960s, largely because of its gas-rich namesake. It bought Ambassador Oil of Fort Worth, Texas, in 1965 — adding interests in 19 states in the US and Canada. The firm also relocated from Kansas to Fort Worth.

Anadarko began offshore exploration in the Gulf of Mexico in 1970 and focused there early in the decade. After moving to Houston in 1974, Anadarko increased its oil exploration activities when the energy crisis led to higher gas prices. A deal with Amoco (now part of BP) led to major finds on Matagorda Island, off the Texas coast, in the early 1980s.

To realize shareholder value, Panhandle spun off Anadarko in 1986 — separating transmission from production. At the time more than 90% of Anadarko's reserves were natural gas. The next year Anadarko made new discoveries in Canada.

Low domestic natural gas prices led Anadarko overseas. It signed a production-sharing agreement with Algeria's national oil and gas firm, SONATRACH, in 1989. The deal covered 5.1 million acres in the Sahara. Two years later Anadarko began operating in the South China Sea and in Alaska's North Slope.

Back home, the company spent $190 million in 1992 for properties in West Texas, and in 1993 it began divesting noncore assets. Along with some of its partners, the company also discovered oil in the Mahogany Field off the Louisiana coast. Production from Mahogany began in 1996.

In 1997 Anadarko added exploration acreage in the North Atlantic and Tunisia. The next year it made two major oil and gas discoveries in the Gulf of Mexico. Anadarko decided to sell some of its noncore Algerian assets in 1999 and teamed up with Texaco in a joint exploration program in the Gulf of Mexico, offshore Louisiana. The next year the company acquired Union Pacific Resources in a $5.7 billion stock swap. The deal more than doubled Anadarko's proved reserves. Also in 2000 the company signed a production-sharing agreement with the former Soviet Republic of Georgia for offshore exploration of the Georgian Black Sea.

Anadarko expanded its presence in western Canada in 2001 by buying Berkley Petroleum for more than $1 billion in cash and assumed debt; a smaller purchase that year, Gulfstream Resources Canada, landed Anadarko in the Persian Gulf and added 70 million barrels of oil equivalent to its reserves.

OFFICERS

Chairman and CEO: Robert J. Allison Jr., age 62,
$3,725,000 pay
Vice Chairman: George Lindahl III, age 55
President and COO: John N. Seitz, age 50,
$2,079,583 pay
EVP Administration: Charles G. Manley, age 57,
$1,047,417 pay
EVP Exploration and Production: William D. Sullivan,
age 45
EVP Finance and CFO: Michael E. Rose, age 54,
$1,091,667 pay
SVP Domestic Operations: Rex Alman III, age 50
SVP Marketing and Minerals: Richard J. Sharples,
age 54
SVP Strategy and Planning: Michael D. Cochran, age 59
SVP Worldwide Business Development:
Bruce H. Stover, age 52
VP and Controller: James R. Larson, age 51
VP and General Counsel: J. Stephen Martin, age 45
VP and Treasurer: Albert L. Richey, age 52
VP Algeria: Tony Meyer
VP Canada: Bob Daniels
VP Corporate Services: Donald R. Willis, age 51
VP Engineering and Technology: Mark L. Pease, age 45
VP Exploration: Jim Emme
VP Government Relations and Public Affairs:
Gregory M. Pensabene, age 51
VP Human Resources: Richard A. Lewis, age 57
Auditors: KPMG LLP

LOCATIONS

HQ: Anadarko Petroleum Corporation
17001 Northchase Dr., Houston, TX 77060
Phone: 281-875-1101   **Fax:** 281-874-3385
Web: www.anadarko.com

2000 Sales

	$ mil.	% of total
US	4,835	85
Canada	447	8
Algeria	271	5
Other countries	133	2
Total	**5,686**	**100**

PRODUCTS/OPERATIONS

2000 Sales

	$ mil.	% of total
Marketing	2,823	50
Gas	1,591	28
Oil & condensate	948	17
Natural gas liquids	264	5
Minerals & other	60	—
Total	**5,686**	**100**

COMPETITORS

Adams Resources	Hunt Consolidated
Apache	Key Energy
BP	Mitchell Energy &
Burlington Resources	Development
Cabot Oil & Gas	Phillips Petroleum
Chesapeake Energy	Pioneer Natural Resources
Chevron	Pogo Producing
Devon Energy	Royal Dutch/Shell
EOG	Texaco
Exxon Mobil	

HISTORICAL FINANCIALS & EMPLOYEES

NYSE: APC FYE: December 31	Annual Growth	12/91	12/92	12/93	12/94	12/95	12/96	12/97	12/98	12/99	12/00
Sales ($ mil.)	36.9%	337	375	476	483	434	569	673	560	701	5,686
Net income ($ mil.)	42.9%	32	27	117	41	21	101	107	(42)	43	807
Income as % of sales	—	9.6%	7.3%	24.6%	8.5%	4.8%	17.7%	15.9%	—	6.1%	14.2%
Earnings per share ($)	33.9%	0.30	0.25	1.03	0.35	0.18	0.85	0.89	(0.41)	0.25	4.16
Stock price - FY high ($)	—	16.56	16.44	25.88	29.25	27.06	34.44	38.38	44.88	42.75	75.95
Stock price - FY low ($)	—	10.75	9.25	12.81	18.50	17.81	23.38	25.38	24.75	26.25	27.56
Stock price - FY close ($)	21.9%	12.00	14.69	22.69	19.25	27.06	32.38	30.34	30.88	34.13	71.08
P/E - high	—	55	66	74	84	150	41	43	—	171	17
P/E - low	—	36	37	37	53	99	28	28	—	105	6
Dividends per share ($)	3.2%	0.15	0.15	0.15	0.15	0.15	0.15	0.15	0.19	0.20	0.20
Book value per share ($)	18.5%	5.81	5.94	7.37	7.64	7.58	8.38	9.17	10.29	11.84	26.79
Employees	16.1%	910	910	970	1,085	1,076	1,229	1,386	1,476	1,431	3,500

STOCK PRICE HISTORY

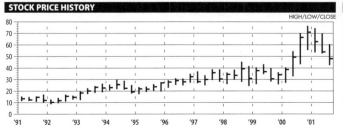

HIGH/LOW/CLOSE

2000 FISCAL YEAR-END

Debt ratio: 37.0%
Return on equity: 20.4%
Cash ($ mil.): 199
Current ratio: 1.13
Long-term debt ($ mil.): 3,984
No. of shares (mil.): 253
Dividends
  Yield: 0.3%
  Payout: 4.8%
Market value ($ mil.): 18,005

APACHE CORPORATION

Apache's oil patch is the planet Earth. Based in Houston, Apache is an independent oil and gas exploration and production company with operations in the US as well as Australia, Canada, China, Egypt, Poland. The company has proved reserves of more than 1 billion barrels of oil equivalent.

About 80% of Apache's reserves are in North America: the Gulf of Mexico, the Gulf Coast of Texas and Louisiana, the Permian Basin in West Texas, the Anadarko Basin in Oklahoma, and western Canada. The company owns or has interests in more than 5,000 gas wells and 8,500 oil wells.

Although Apache has been dumping non-strategic properties, including its Ivory Coast operations, it hasn't stopped buying. It has expanded its Gulf of Mexico operations with the acquisition of Occidental Petroleum's continental shelf properties, and its Canadian operations have been augmented with purchases from Fletcher Challenge Energy and Phillips Petroleum.

HISTORY

Originally, Raymond Plank wanted to start a magazine. Then it was an accounting and tax-assistance service. Plank and his co-founding partner, Truman Anderson, had no experience in any of these occupations, but their accounting business succeeded. In the early 1950s Plank and Anderson branched out again, founding APA, a partnership to invest in new ventures, including oil and gas exploration. The partnership founded Apache Oil in Minnesota in 1954. Investors put up the money, and Apache managed the drilling, spreading the risk over several projects.

As problems with government regulations in the oil industry mounted during the 1960s, Apache diversified into real estate. The real estate operations were pivotal in driving a wedge between Plank and Anderson. In 1963 Anderson called a board meeting to ask the directors to fire Plank. Instead, Anderson resigned, and Plank took over.

Apache's holdings soon encompassed 24 firms, including engineering, electronics, farming, and water-supply subsidiaries. Understanding that its fortunes were tied to varying oil and gas prices, the company reassessed its diversified structure in the 1970s. When the energy crisis rocketed oil prices skyward, Apache sold its non-energy operations, which would have been hurt by the price increases.

Apache formed Apache Petroleum in 1981 as an investment vehicle to take advantage of tax laws favoring limited partnerships. Initially the strategy was a success, but it fell victim in the mid-1980s to a one-two punch: Oil prices sank like a rock, and Congress put an end to the tax advantage. After suffering its first loss in 1986, Apache reorganized into a conventional exploration and production company.

Still under Plank's leadership, the company began steadily buying oil and gas properties and companies in 1991. That year it purchased oil and gas sites with more than 100 million barrels of reserves from Amoco and put the wells back into production. By buying Hadson Energy Resources, which operated fields in western Australia, Apache gained entry into the relatively unexplored region in 1993.

In 1995 Apache merged with Calgary, Canada-based DEKALB Energy (later renamed DEK Energy) and continued picking up properties. It bought $600 million worth of US reserves from Texaco that year. In 1996 it expanded its Chinese operations and bought Phoenix Resource Companies, which operated solely in Egypt. A 1998 agreement with Texaco expanded its Chinese acreage thirtyfold. Apache also bought oil and gas properties and production facilities in waters off western Australia from a Mobil unit.

Apache joined with FX Energy and Polish Oil & Gas in 1998 to begin exploratory drilling in Poland. It also worked with XCL and China National Oil & Gas Exploration & Development in Bohai Bay, though the project was slowed by a dispute between Apache and XCL over costs. In 1999 Apache bought Gulf of Mexico assets from a unit of Royal Dutch/Shell and acquired oil and gas properties in western Canada from Shell Canada. That year Apache sold its Ivory Coast oil and gas holdings for $46 million.

Still shopping, however, Apache agreed in 2000 to buy assets in western Canada and Argentina with proved reserves of more than 700 billion cu. ft. of natural gas equivalent from New Zealand's Fletcher Challenge Energy. To help pay for the $600 million acquisition, which closed in 2001, Apache sold $100 million in stock to Shell, which acquired other Fletcher Challenge Energy assets. Apache bought the Canadian assets of Phillips Petroleum for $490 million in 2000 and acquired the Egyptian assets of Repsol YPF for $410 million in 2001.

Chairman and CEO: Raymond Plank, $1,400,000 pay
President, COO, and Director: G. Steven Farris, age 52, $1,300,000 pay
EVP and CFO: Roger B. Plank, age 44, $523,750 pay
EVP Business Development and Exploration and Production Services: Lisa A. Stewart, age 43, $501,250 pay
EVP Eurasia and New Ventures: John A. Crum, age 48
SVP and General Counsel: Zurab S. Kobiashvili, age 58
VP and Treasurer: Matthew W. Dundrea, age 47
VP and Controller: Thomas L. Mitchell, age 40
VP Exploration and Production Technology: Michael Bahorich, age 44
VP Human Resources: Jeffrey M. Bender, age 49
VP Investor Relations: Robert J. Dye, age 45
VP Public and International Affairs: Anthony R. Lentini Jr., age 51
VP Tax: Jon W. Sauer
Regional VP and Managing Director, Australia: James K. Bass
Regional VP, Offshore Region: Jon A. Jeppesen
Regional VP, Midcontinent Region: Rodney S. Myers
Regional VP, Canada; President Apache Canada: Floyd R. Price
Regional VP, Southern Region: Danny E. Shultz
Regional VP, Egypt: Rodney J. Eichler
Staff VP, Oil and Gas Marketing: Kevin J. Ikel
Auditors: Arthur Andersen LLP

LOCATIONS

HQ: 2000 Post Oak Blvd., Ste. 100, Houston, TX 77056
Phone: 713-296-6000   **Fax:** 713-296-6496
Web: www.apachecorp.com

2000 Sales

	$ mil.	% of total
US	1,375	60
Egypt	361	16
Canada	332	14
Australia	223	10
Adjustments	(7)	—
Total	**2,284**	**100**

PRODUCTS/OPERATIONS

2000 Sales

	$ mil.	% of total
Oil	1,147	50
Natural gas	1,093	48
Natural gas liquids	51	2
Adjustments	(7)	—
Total	**2,284**	**100**

COMPETITORS

Adams Resources	EEX Corporation	Pioneer
Amerada Hess	El Paso	Royal
Anadarko	Enron	Dutch/Shell
BP	EOG	Shell
Burlington	Exxon Mobil	Texaco
Resources	Forest Oil	TransTexas Gas
Chesapeake	KCS Energy	Ultramar
Energy	Kerr-McGee	Diamond
Chevron	Nuevo Energy	Shamrock
Conoco	Ocean Energy	Unocal
Devon Energy	Phillips	XTO Energy

HISTORICAL FINANCIALS & EMPLOYEES

NYSE: APA FYE: December 31	Annual Growth	12/91	12/92	12/93	12/94	12/95	12/96	12/97	12/98	12/99	12/00
Sales ($ mil.)	22.9%	357	423	463	538	750	976	1,181	876	1,300	2,284
Net income ($ mil.)	40.0%	35	48	37	43	20	121	155	(129)	201	713
Income as % of sales	—	9.7%	11.3%	8.1%	8.0%	2.7%	12.4%	13.1%	—	15.4%	31.2%
Earnings per share ($)	25.0%	0.76	1.02	0.67	0.65	0.28	1.38	1.65	(1.34)	1.72	5.67
Stock price - FY high ($)	—	20.75	22.13	33.50	29.25	31.00	37.88	45.06	38.75	49.94	74.19
Stock price - FY low ($)	—	12.00	12.00	17.63	22.25	22.25	24.38	30.13	21.06	17.63	32.13
Stock price - FY close ($)	17.9%	15.88	18.75	23.38	25.00	29.50	35.13	35.06	25.31	36.94	70.06
P/E - high	—	27	22	50	45	111	27	26	—	29	13
P/E - low	—	16	12	26	34	79	17	18	—	10	5
Dividends per share ($)	0.0%	0.28	0.28	0.28	0.28	0.28	0.28	0.28	0.28	0.35	0.28
Book value per share ($)	13.6%	9.39	10.12	12.87	13.28	14.11	16.86	18.53	18.43	23.42	29.68
Employees	6.5%	875	875	844	1,182	1,285	1,256	1,287	1,281	1,429	1,546

STOCK PRICE HISTORY

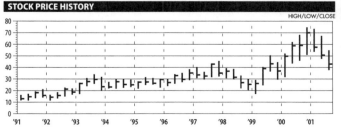

HIGH/LOW/CLOSE

2000 FISCAL YEAR-END

Debt ratio: 36.9%
Return on equity: 24.6%
Cash ($ mil.): 37
Current ratio: 1.14
Long-term debt ($ mil.): 2,193
No. of shares (mil.): 127
Dividends
  Yield: 0.4%
  Payout: 4.9%
Market value ($ mil.): 8,863

BAKER HUGHES INCORPORATED

OVERVIEW

Baker Hughes has the drill down pat. The Houston-based company provides products and services to the worldwide oil field and process equipment industries. The company helps energy companies locate oil and gas reserves and provides drill bits, drilling fluids, and other equipment used in the drilling process. Baker Hughes also makes submersible pumps that deliver oil to the well's surface and provides equipment and services to maintain oil and gas wells. Baker Petrolite makes oil field specialty chemicals, as well as chemicals for the refining and wastewater industries.

Baker Hughes is starting to make a comeback along with the increasing price of oil. With its rig counts at a 10-year high, the company is hoping for a renewed gusher of cash as the increase in per-barrel prices prompts oil companies to reinvest in exploration and production. The company has also been helped by the doubling of natural gas prices. Baker Hughes has tried unsuccessfully to sell its Baker Process division (waste-separation equipment), so it is planning to sell it off in parts.

HISTORY

Howard Hughes Sr. developed the first oil well drill bit for rock in 1909. Hughes and partner Walter Sharp opened a plant in Houston, and their company, Sharp & Hughes, soon had a near monopoly on rock bits. When Sharp died in 1912, Hughes bought his partner's half of the company, incorporating as Hughes Tool. Hughes held 73 patents when he died in 1924; the company passed to Howard Hughes Jr.

It is estimated that between 1924 and 1972 Hughes Tool provided Hughes Jr. with $745 million in pretax profits, which he used to diversify into movies (RKO), airlines (TWA), and Las Vegas casinos. In 1972 he sold the company to the public for $150 million. After 1972 the company expanded into tools for aboveground oil production. In 1974, under the new leadership of chairman James Leach, Hughes bought the oil field equipment business of Borg-Warner.

In 1913 drilling contractor Carl Baker organized the Baker Casing Shoe Company in California to collect royalties on his three oil tool inventions. The firm began to make its own products in 1918, and during the 1920s it expanded nationally, opened global trade, and formed Baker Oil Tools (1928). The company grew in the late 1940s and the 1950s as oil drilling boomed.

During the 1960s Baker prospered, despite fewer US well completions. Foreign sales increased. From 1963 to 1975 Baker bought oil-related companies Kobe, Galigher, Ramsey Engineering, and Reed Tool.

US expenditures for oil services fell between 1982 and 1986 from $40 billion to $9 billion. In 1987 both Baker and Hughes faced falling revenues. The two companies merged to form Baker Hughes. By closing plants and combining operations, the venture became profitable by the end of 1988. The company bought

Eastman Christensen (the world leader in directional and horizontal drilling equipment) and acquired the instrumentation unit of Tracor Holdings in 1990.

Baker Hughes spun off BJ Services (pumping services) to the public in 1991 and sold the Eastern Hemisphere operations of Baker Hughes Tubular Services (BHTS) to Tuboscope. It sold the Western Hemisphere operations of BHTS to ICO the following year.

Also in 1992 Baker Hughes bought Teleco Oilfield Services, a pioneer in directional drilling techniques, from Sonat. In 1995 Baker Hughes sold EnviroTech Pumpsystems to the Weir Group of Glasgow, Scotland. In 1996 company veteran Max Lukens became CEO. He replaced James Woods as chairman the next year.

Baker Hughes allied with Schlumberger's oil field service operations in 1996. In a move to boost its oil field chemicals business the company bought Petrolite in 1997 and rival Western Atlas for $3.3 billion in 1998, strengthening its land-based seismic data business (#1 in that market) and testing business. A downturn in the Asian economy, disruptions from tropical storms, and slumping oil prices caused oil companies to reduce demand for Baker Hughes' products. The company suffered a big loss in 1998 and in response trimmed its workforce by about 15% in 1999. It also put its separation-equipment business up for sale.

In 2000 Lukens stepped down after accounting blunders caused the company to restate earnings. Company director and Newfield Exploration CEO Joe Foster replaced him as acting CEO until Michael Wiley was named to that office. Baker Hughes combined its seismic oil and gas exploration business with that of Schlumberger Limited to create Western GECO in early 2001.

OFFICERS

Chairman, President, and CEO: Michael E. Wiley,
age 50, $338,070 pay
SVP, Finance and Administration and CFO:
George S. Finley, age 50, $410,481 pay
**SVP and COO; President, Baker Hughes Oilfield
Operations:** Andrew J. Szescila, age 53, $471,507 pay
VP and General Counsel: Alan R. Crain, age 49
VP and Controller: Alan J. Keifer, age 45, $191,386 pay
VP, Human Resources: Greg Nakanishi, age 49
Auditors: Deloitte & Touche LLP

LOCATIONS

HQ: 3900 Essex Ln., Ste. 1200, Houston, TX 77027
Phone: 713-439-8600   **Fax:** 713-439-8699
Web: www.bakerhughes.com

Baker Hughes has 77 manufacturing plants worldwide,
63% of which are in the US.

2000 Sales

	$ mil.	% of total
US	2,035	39
UK	349	7
Venezuela	290	6
Norway	279	5
Canada	277	5
Other countries	2,004	38
Total	**5,234**	**100**

PRODUCTS/OPERATIONS

2000 Sales

	$ mil.	% of total
Oil field	4,911	94
Processing	323	6
Total	**5,234**	**100**

Selected Operations

Baker Atlas (downhole data acquisition, processing and
analysis; pipe recovery)
Baker Hughes INTEQ (directional drilling,
measurement, and drilling fluids)
Baker Oil Tools (completion, workover, and fishing
technologies and services)
Baker Petrolite (specialty chemicals for petroleum,
transportation, and refining)
Centrilift (electric submersible pumps and downhole
oil/water separation)
Hughes Christensen (oil well drill bits)
Western GECO (30%, seismic exploration services, field
development and management)

COMPETITORS

Ahlstrom	ONDEO Nalco
BJ Services	Outokumpu
FMC	Petroleum Geo-Services
Compagnie Générale de	Sandvik
Géophysique	Schlumberger
Halliburton	Smith International
Hercules	Svedala Industri
Ingersoll-Rand	USFilter
Krauss-Maffei	Veritas DGC
Kværner	Weatherford International
Nabors Industries	

HISTORICAL FINANCIALS & EMPLOYEES

NYSE: BHI FYE: December 31	Annual Growth	9/91	9/92	9/93	9/94	9/95	9/96	9/97	*12/98	12/99	12/00
Sales ($ mil.)	7.1%	2,828	2,539	2,702	2,505	2,638	3,028	3,685	6,312	4,547	5,234
Net income ($ mil.)	(5.7%)	174	5	59	43	105	176	97	(297)	33	102
Income as % of sales	—	6.1%	0.2%	2.2%	1.7%	4.0%	5.8%	2.6%	—	0.7%	2.0%
Earnings per share ($)	(14.4%)	1.26	0.00	0.34	0.22	0.57	1.23	0.63	(0.92)	0.10	0.31
Stock price - FY high ($)	—	31.00	26.00	29.63	24.88	23.75	35.63	47.25	44.13	36.25	43.38
Stock price - FY low ($)	—	20.75	15.88	17.75	17.00	16.75	18.38	29.50	15.00	15.00	19.63
Stock price - FY close ($)	6.0%	24.50	23.38	23.50	18.63	20.38	30.38	43.81	17.63	21.06	41.56
P/E - high	—	25	—	87	29	35	29	67	—	363	140
P/E - low	—	16	—	52	20	25	15	42	—	150	63
Dividends per share ($)	0.0%	0.46	0.46	0.46	0.46	0.46	0.46	0.46	0.58	0.46	0.46
Book value per share ($)	(2.2%)	11.17	11.87	11.47	11.63	10.64	11.69	15.38	9.78	9.31	9.13
Employees	1.6%	21,300	19,600	18,400	14,700	15,200	16,800	21,500	32,300	27,326	24,500

* Fiscal year change

STOCK PRICE HISTORY

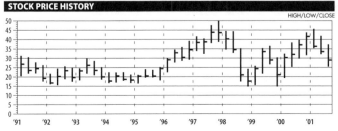

HIGH/LOW/CLOSE

2000 FISCAL YEAR-END

Debt ratio: 40.2%
Return on equity: 3.3%
Cash ($ mil.): 35
Current ratio: 2.52
Long-term debt ($ mil.): 2,050
No. of shares (mil.): 334
Dividends
    Yield: 1.1%
    Payout: 148.4%
Market value ($ mil.): 13,869

BELO CORP.

OVERVIEW

In this case, old news is good news. Dallas-based Belo Corp. (formerly A.H. Belo Corporation), the oldest continuously operated business in Texas, publishes four daily newspapers and owns a string of television stations in larger markets throughout the US. Its flagship, *The Dallas Morning News,* is among the 10 largest newspapers in the US, with a daily circulation of about 520,000. Other publications include *The Providence Journal* (Rhode Island) and *The Press-Enterprise* (Riverside, California).

Belo's television operations include 18 company-owned and two managed stations, as well as two regional cable news channels (Texas Cable News, Northwest Cable News). The company also operates about 35 Web sites.

Belo concentrates on building clusters in three major operating areas: Texas, the Southwest, and the Pacific Northwest. Chairman and CEO Robert Decherd and his family own about 12% of the company.

HISTORY

Alfred Horatio Belo joined the *Galveston Daily News* in Texas in 1865 and bought the paper in 1876. He later sent young George Dealey to North Texas to find a good locale for a sister paper. Dealey liked the prospects of a small prairie town named Dallas, and in 1885 *The Dallas Morning News* was born.

In the 1920s the firm started the state's first network radio station (1922), and new owner Dealey gave the company its present name (1926). The Dallas paper thrived, and in the early 1950s A. H. Belo bought a Dallas television station. The company went public in 1981 and began acquiring other TV stations. In 1987 Belo president Robert Decherd was named chairman and CEO.

Belo purchased its Dallas newspaper competitor, the *Times-Herald,* in 1991 and shut it down, making *The Dallas Morning News* the city's only daily. In 1996 Belo started its second major paper in the Dallas-Fort Worth metroplex, the *Arlington Morning News,* to compete with the *Fort Worth Star-Telegram,* owned by Walt Disney (since sold to Knight Ridder). That year it also bought a stake in *The Press-Enterprise,* a Southern California newspaper. (It acquired the remaining interest in 1997.)

In 1997 Belo bought The Providence Journal Company in a $1.5 billion deal that included *The Providence Journal* (leading newspaper in Rhode Island and southeastern Massachusetts), several television stations, and some cable network holdings. Also that year it bought a TV station and a radio station (KENS-TV and KENS-AM) in San Antonio from E. W. Scripps for $75 million plus Belo's 56% stake in the Television Food Network. In 1998 WFAA, Belo's Dallas TV station, became the first in the US to begin regular broadcasts of high-definition digital signals.

In 1999 the company launched Texas Cable News (TXCN), a 24-hour regional news network reaching about 600,000 subscribers in the Dallas area. It also established a new media unit (Belo Interactive) to focus on Internet initiatives and bought KVUE-TV (Austin, Texas) from Gannett in exchange for KXTV (Sacramento). Later that year Belo spent approximately $24 million for a 12% stake in the Dallas Mavericks professional basketball team.

The company relented in 2000 and sold the stake to the Mavericks majority owner Mark Cuban for $34 million. The company also changed its name from A.H. Belo Corporation to Belo Corp.

In 2001 the company acquired Spokane, Washington's KSKN-TV, a WB/UPN affiliate, for about $5 million in cash, and KTTU-TV, a UPN affiliate in Tucson, Arizona, for $18 million in cash. Also that year Belo announced plans to launch Charlotte News Channel, a 24-hour local cable news channel in Charlotte, North Carolina, in partnership with Time Warner Cable, a division of media giant AOL Time Warner. The new channel is expected to be on the air by early 2002.

Boosting its online presence that year, the company's Internet subsidiary, Belo Interactive, teamed with one-to-one messaging services provider Strategy.com to launch My News to offer personalized news to users via e-mail, the Internet, mobile phones, pagers or fax.

OFFICERS

Chairman, President, and CEO: Robert W. Decherd, age 49, $1,499,100 pay
SEVP: Michael J. McCarthy, age 56, $725,500 pay
EVP and CFO: Dunia A. Shive, age 40
EVP Media Operations: John L. Sander, age 59
SVP Business Development: Colleen B. Brown, age 42
SVP: Donald Cass Jr., age 35
SVP Finance: David S. Boone, age 41
SVP Human Resources: Marian Spitzberg, age 52
VP and Chief Technology Officer: Jon Roe
Publisher Emeritus, The Dallas Morning News, and Director: Burl Osborne, age 63, $987,300 pay
Publisher and CEO, The Dallas Morning News: James M. Moroney, age 44
General Counsel and Secretary: Guy H. Kerr, age 48
Director Human Resources: Joe Daume
Auditors: Ernst & Young LLP

LOCATIONS

HQ: 400 S. Record St., Dallas, TX 75202
Phone: 214-977-6606   **Fax:** 214-977-7655
Web: www.belo.com

PRODUCTS/OPERATIONS

2000 Sales

	$ mil.	% of total
Newspaper publishing	873	55
Broadcasting	700	44
Interactive Media	10	—
Other	14	1
Adjustments	(8)	—
Total	**1,589**	**100**

Local Marketing Agreements
KBEJ (UPN; San Antonio)
KTTU-TV (UPN; Tucson, AZ)

Owned Television Stations
KASW-TV (WB; Phoenix)
KENS-TV (CBS; San Antonio)
KGW-TV (NBC; Portland, OR)
KHOU-TV (CBS; Houston)
KING-TV (NBC; Seattle-Tacoma)
KMOV-TV (CBS; St. Louis)
KMSB-TV (FOX; Tucson, AZ)
KONG-TV (Independent; Seattle-Tacoma)
KREM-TV (CBS; Spokane, WA)
KSKN-TV (UPN/WB; Spokane, WA)
KTVB-TV (NBC; Boise, ID)
KTVK-TV (Independent; Phoenix)
KVUE-TV (ABC; Austin, TX)
WCNC-TV (NBC; Charlotte, NC)
WFAA-TV (ABC; Dallas-Fort Worth)
WHAS-TV (ABC; Louisville, KY)
WVEC-TV (ABC; Hampton-Norfolk, VA)
WWL-TV (CBS; New Orleans)

Selected Newspapers
The Dallas Morning News
Denton Record-Chronicle (Texas)
The Press-Enterprise (Riverside, CA)
The Providence Journal (Rhode Island)

COMPETITORS

Cox Enterprises
E. W. Scripps
Fisher Communications
Gannett
Hearst-Argyle Television
Knight Ridder
New York Times
Sinclair Broadcast Group
Tribune
Washington Post

HISTORICAL FINANCIALS & EMPLOYEES

NYSE: BLC FYE: December 31	Annual Growth	12/91	12/92	12/93	12/94	12/95	12/96	12/97	12/98	12/99	12/00
Sales ($ mil.)	15.6%	432	516	545	628	735	824	1,248	1,407	1,434	1,589
Net income ($ mil.)	32.0%	12	37	51	69	67	88	83	65	178	151
Income as % of sales	—	2.9%	7.2%	9.4%	11.0%	9.1%	10.6%	6.6%	4.6%	12.4%	9.5%
Earnings per share ($)	25.3%	0.17	0.48	0.63	0.85	0.84	1.06	0.71	0.52	1.50	1.29
Stock price - FY high ($)	—	8.44	11.72	13.25	14.31	18.38	20.88	28.06	28.47	24.50	20.00
Stock price - FY low ($)	—	6.06	7.66	9.69	10.78	13.91	15.50	16.63	13.94	16.38	12.31
Stock price - FY close ($)	8.2%	7.88	10.50	13.25	14.13	17.38	17.44	28.06	19.94	19.06	16.00
P/E - high	—	50	24	21	16	21	20	39	54	16	16
P/E - low	—	36	16	15	12	16	14	23	26	11	10
Dividends per share ($)	8.9%	0.13	0.14	0.14	0.15	0.16	0.21	0.22	0.24	0.26	0.28
Book value per share ($)	16.7%	3.05	3.59	4.28	4.81	5.08	5.11	10.65	10.49	11.71	12.28
Employees	11.9%	2,627	2,788	2,863	3,082	3,489	3,760	6,760	6,920	7,612	7,245

STOCK PRICE HISTORY

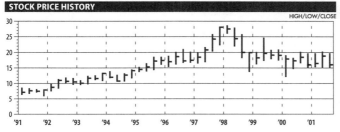

HIGH/LOW/CLOSE

2000 FISCAL YEAR-END

Debt ratio: 57.0%
Return on equity: 11.0%
Cash ($ mil.): 88
Current ratio: 1.39
Long-term debt ($ mil.): 1,790
No. of shares (mil.): 110
Dividends
  Yield: 1.8%
  Payout: 21.7%
Market value ($ mil.): 1,758

BLOCKBUSTER INC.

OVERVIEW

Anxious parent Viacom has decided to coddle Blockbuster a little longer. The media giant never achieved the synergy it had anticipated with the world's largest home video rental chain and sold 18% of the Dallas-based company to the public in 1999. Viacom planned to shed its remaining 82% stake (96% of voting power) to Viacom shareholders as soon as the shares hit $20 or more, but decided to keep the company thanks to a turnaround in the retailer's core video rental business. While Blockbuster owns or franchises about 7,800 Blockbuster Video outlets in the US and 27 other countries (renting more than 1 billion videos, DVDs, and video games each year) it has had a hard time sustaining growth as more people are building their own video libraries, accessing pay-per-view channels, and buying satellite dishes.

Chairman and CEO John Antioco has helped Blockbuster's bottom line by negotiating revenue-sharing agreements with film studios instead of buying copies from them for around $65 a piece. It allows Blockbuster to stock more copies for less and take in 60%-70% of all rental revenues. It also has prompted an antitrust lawsuit against the company, filed by two small video store operators in Texas. However Blockbuster has announced that it will likely start phasing out those revenue-sharing agreements when they expire, an announcement that has been bitterly received in Hollywood. The move is primarily brought on by the growing popularity of DVD rentals, which are not part of the revenue agreements.

A major marketing deal with traditional industry enemy DIRECTV creates another competitive concern for mom-and-pop video stores.

Blockbuster wants to cash in on the Internet as well, with its Blockbuster.com Web site. The site provides movie news and information and allows customers to reserve video rentals and pay for them online.

HISTORY

After selling his computing services company, David Cook turned to operating flashy, computerized video rental stores, opening his first in 1985 and adopting the moniker Blockbuster Entertainment in 1986. Entrepreneur Wayne Huizenga took over in 1987, injecting $18 million into Blockbuster and buying the company outright by the end of the year. Huizenga's acquisitions rapidly expanded the number of Blockbuster stores to 130. Other acquisitions (including Major Video, a 175-store chain, and Erol's, the US's third-largest video chain) increased the number of stores to 1,500 by 1990.

Blockbuster became the largest video renter in the UK in 1992 through the purchase of 875-unit Cityvision. It also branched into music retailing that year when it bought the Sound Warehouse and Music Plus chains and created Blockbuster Music. The following year it acquired a majority stake in Spelling Entertainment, then was itself acquired in 1994 by Viacom for $8.4 billion. Viacom took Spelling Entertainment under its wing and formed a division for its new chain of video stores called Blockbuster Entertainment Group. Following the deal, Huizenga left the company (he's now chairman of AutoNation).

Over the next few years, Blockbuster experienced a rash of poor business decisions and executive departures starting with Steven Berrard (CEO after Viacom's 1994 takeover), who resigned in 1996 to head Huizenga's used-car operations. Wal-Mart veteran Bill Fields replaced him and started promoting the retailer as a neighborhood entertainment center, selling videotapes (instead of renting them), books, CDs, gift items, and music. After closing 50 music outlets in 1996, the company moved its headquarters from Florida to Dallas in 1997, a move many employees refused to make.

Fields resigned later that year and John Antioco replaced him. Antioco's reign began with Viacom taking a $300 million charge related to the turmoil at Blockbuster. He immediately started unraveling many of Fields' efforts, especially his focus on non-rental operations. Antioco also set the video rental industry on its ear in 1997 by forcing the movie studios into a revenue-sharing agreement that replaced the standard practice of buying rental copies. It not only saved money, it allowed Blockbuster to stock more copies for less.

The company finished returning to its rental roots by selling Blockbuster Music in 1998. By 1999 Blockbuster's revenue-sharing deal with the studios was taking its toll on smaller video stores, two of which filed an antitrust lawsuit against the company. Viacom spun off a minority stake in Blockbuster later that year, and the company split into three new operating units that oversee its retail outlets, e-commerce operations, and database and brand marketing.

In 2001 Blockbuster struck a deal with RadioShack that gives the electronics retailer space in Blockbuster outlets to sell its wares.

OFFICERS

Chairman, President, and CEO: John F. Antioco, age 51, $3,605,000 pay
EVP and CFO: Larry J. Zine, age 46, $776,228 pay
EVP and Chief Marketing Officer: James Notarnicola, age 49
EVP, General Counsel, and Secretary: Edward B. Stead, age 54
EVP; Chief Merchandising Officer, Worldwide Store Operations: Dean M. Wilson, age 43
EVP and President, New Media Division: Mark T. Gilman, age 37
EVP; COO, North America Operations: Michael K. Roemer, age 52, $693,033 pay
EVP; President, Worldwide Stores Division: Nigel Travis, age 51, $899,301 pay
Auditors: PricewaterhouseCoopers LLP

LOCATIONS

HQ: 1201 Elm St., Dallas, TX 75270
Phone: 214-854-3000   **Fax:** 214-854-4848
Web: www.blockbuster.com

2000 Sales

	% of total
US	81
International	19
Total	**100**

PRODUCTS/OPERATIONS

2000 Sales

	$ mil.	% of total
Rentals	4,161	84
Merchandise	705	14
Other	94	2
Total	**4,960**	**100**

COMPETITORS

Best Buy	MTS
Borders	Musicland
Circuit City	Trans World Entertainment
DIRECTV	Video Update
Hastings Entertainment	Wherehouse
Hollywood Entertainment	Entertainment
Movie Gallery	

HISTORICAL FINANCIALS & EMPLOYEES

NYSE: BBI FYE: December 31	Annual Growth	12/91	12/92	12/93	12/94	12/95	12/96	12/97	12/98	12/99	12/00
Sales ($ mil.)	13.9%	—	—	—	—	—	2,942	3,314	3,893	4,464	4,960
Net income ($ mil.)	—	—	—	—	—	—	78	(318)	(337)	(69)	(76)
Income as % of sales	—	—	—	—	—	—	2.6%	—	—	—	—
Earnings per share ($)	—	—	—	—	—	—	—	—	—	(0.44)	(0.43)
Stock price - FY high ($)	—	—	—	—	—	—	—	—	—	17.13	14.88
Stock price - FY low ($)	—	—	—	—	—	—	—	—	—	11.38	6.88
Stock price - FY close ($)	(37.4%)	—	—	—	—	—	—	—	—	13.38	8.38
P/E - high	—	—	—	—	—	—	—	—	—	—	—
P/E - low	—	—	—	—	—	—	—	—	—	—	—
Dividends per share ($)	300.0%	—	—	—	—	—	—	—	—	0.02	0.08
Book value per share ($)	(1.9%)	—	—	—	—	—	—	—	—	35.00	34.33
Employees	7.8%	—	—	—	—	—	—	—	82,400	89,700	95,800

STOCK PRICE HISTORY

HIGH/LOW/CLOSE

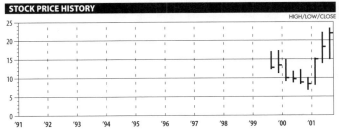

2000 FISCAL YEAR-END

Debt ratio: 15.9%
Return on equity: —
Cash ($ mil.): 194
Current ratio: 0.71
Long-term debt ($ mil.): 1,137
No. of shares (mil.): 175
Dividends
  Yield: 1.0%
  Payout: —
Market value ($ mil.): 1,467

BMC SOFTWARE, INC.

BMC Software plays tweak-a-boo with corporate mainframe and networked computers. The Houston-based company's more than 450 software tools are designed to speed up and monitor databases, eliminate unplanned outages, predict and remove computer bottlenecks, and recover system assets. Despite a hearty push into the networked computer world, mainframe-related tools and services still account for nearly 65% of software sales. BMC sells to credit card companies, banks, and airlines, as well as to government agencies; its customers include Dow Corning, Home Depot, and Wachovia.

The company is expanding through the acquisitions of rival software makers such as Boole & Babbage and New Dimension, which is based in Israel. BMC is also touting its current lines geared to handle e-business management.

Chairman Max Watson, who has overseen the company's transformation beyond its monolithic-sized hardware specialty roots, believes that treating employees well is the best motivation. Consistently rated as one of America's best places to work, BMC features whimsical offices with hammocks and cowskin-lined elevators, and a self-contained campus stocked with a dry cleaner, a hairdresser, and other stores catering to workers' needs.

HISTORY

BMC, one of the few profitable software companies not operated by its founders, was launched in 1980 by Scott Boulett, John Moores, and Dan Cloer. Their initials gave the company its name. Its first product — and most that followed — improved communications between IBM databases with connected terminals and PCs.

Through an aggressive telemarketing campaign boasted of internally as "telemuscle," the company's utility software was snapped up by a chunk of the *FORTUNE* 500, which used it to boost the performance of wall-sized IBM mainframes and database systems. The company started an international expansion in 1984, opening an office in Germany. BMC went public in 1988.

Two years later COO Max Watson replaced Richard Hosley as president and CEO. Hosley stayed on as VC until 1992 when Watson assumed that title as well. Moores, the only founder who held a position with the company, resigned as chairman that year (a 35% stake in BMC that Moores sold that year helped the entrepreneur found rival software company NEON Systems, where he remains chairman, and become majority owner of the San Diego Padres professional baseball team).

In the early 1990s Watson navigated BMC's transition toward networked PC systems as corporate customers began eschewing mainframes. The company continued to take its product development cues from IBM, where Watson had worked for 14 years. As Big Blue developed new technology, BMC would act quickly to release utilities that improved performance for that new technology.

In 1994 BMC bought PATROL Software, adding a network-based performance optimiza-

tion product that would later become one of the company's flagship lines. The next year the company doubled the size of its marketing. In 1995 BMC launched a lawsuit against Moores for luring away company executives to help run his growing software ventures (the two sides acrimoniously settled in 1999).

Using alliances and acquisitions to expand, the company in 1996 forged an alliance with Sun Microsystems to develop platform management software. The company bought software specialist DataTools in 1997 and system performance analysis software specialist BGS Systems in 1998.

The next year the company doubled its size when it bought rival management software maker Boole & Babbage for about $900 million, and Israeli software developer New Dimension Software for about $675 million. Along with these acquisitions came a corporate reinvention that included a new logo and revamped product divisions. That year the company began tailoring its management software for the e-commerce market.

In 2000 BMC increased its e-commerce offerings by acquiring Evity, a provider of Web transaction monitoring services. Early in 2001, Watson brought Robert Beauchamp on board, passing the president and CEO titles to him. Watson will remain chairman until April of 2001. Also that year the company announced it would cut 6% of its workforce (about 440 jobs).

Chairman: B. Garland Cupp, age 60
President, CEO, and Director: Robert E. Beauchamp,
age 41, $877,987 pay
SVP and Chief Technology Officer: Kirill Tatarinov,
age 36
SVP, General Counsel, and Secretary:
Robert H. Whilden Jr., age 66
SVP, BMC Ventures: Jeffrey S. Hawn, age 37,
$384,499 pay
SVP, Field Operations, Americas: Debra A. Tummins,
age 49, $753,714 pay
SVP, Field Operations, International:
Darroll Buytenhuys, age 53, $617,510 pay
SVP, Operations: Dan Barnea, age 56, $649,942 pay
VP, CFO, and Chief Accounting Officer: John W. Cox,
age 42
VP and Treasurer: Stephen B. Solcher, age 40
**VP and General Manager, Distributed Data
Management:** Gene Austin
**VP and General Manager, Business Information
Integration:** Renee Bacherman
VP and General Manager, PATROL Infrastructure:
Pete DiStefano
**VP and General Manager, PATROL Network
Management:** Andrew Burger
VP and General Manager, PATROL Platform Solutions:
Carl Coken
VP, Human Resources: Johnnie Horn
Auditors: Arthur Andersen LLP

LOCATIONS

HQ: 2101 City West Blvd., Houston, TX 77042
Phone: 713-918-8800   **Fax:** 713-918-8000
Web: www.bmc.com

BMC Software has operations in more than 30 countries.

2001 Sales

	$ mil.	% of total
US	821	55
Other countries	683	45
Total	**1,504**	**100**

PRODUCTS/OPERATIONS

2001 Sales

	$ mil.	% of total
License	892	59
Maintenance	524	35
Professional services	88	6
Total	**1,504**	**100**

COMPETITORS

Ascential Software	NetIQ
Candle Corporation	Network Associates
Computer Associates	Oracle
Compuware	Software AG
Hewlett-Packard	Software AG, Inc.
IBM	Sun Microsystems
IONA Technologies	Sybase
Landmark Systems	Symantec
NEON Systems	

HISTORICAL FINANCIALS & EMPLOYEES

NYSE: BMC FYE: March 31	Annual Growth	3/92	3/93	3/94	3/95	3/96	3/97	3/98	3/99	3/00	3/01
Sales ($ mil.)	25.9%	189	239	289	345	429	563	731	1,304	1,719	1,504
Net income ($ mil.)	(1.5%)	49	65	57	78	106	164	166	363	243	42
Income as % of sales	—	25.8%	27.4%	19.6%	22.5%	24.6%	29.1%	22.7%	27.8%	14.1%	2.8%
Earnings per share ($)	(3.8%)	0.24	0.32	0.27	0.38	0.50	0.76	0.77	1.45	0.77	0.17
Stock price - FY high ($)	—	9.88	10.52	8.88	8.72	15.34	25.50	42.13	60.25	86.63	51.38
Stock price - FY low ($)	—	4.13	4.66	4.84	5.03	6.91	12.69	19.81	30.13	30.00	13.00
Stock price - FY close ($)	12.4%	7.53	6.11	7.72	7.97	13.69	23.06	41.91	37.06	49.38	21.50
P/E - high	—	41	33	33	23	29	31	51	39	113	302
P/E - low	—	17	15	18	13	13	15	24	19	39	76
Dividends per share ($)	—	0.00	0.00	0.00	0.00	0.00	0.00	0.00	0.00	0.00	0.00
Book value per share ($)	29.2%	0.73	1.06	1.22	1.52	1.92	2.73	3.68	5.92	7.28	7.32
Employees	28.2%	782	909	987	1,185	1,444	1,813	2,777	4,914	6,677	7,330

STOCK PRICE HISTORY

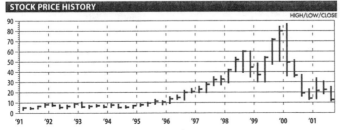

2001 FISCAL YEAR-END

Debt ratio: 0.0%
Return on equity: 2.4%
Cash ($ mil.): 146
Current ratio: 1.09
Long-term debt ($ mil.): 0
No. of shares (mil.): 248
Dividends
   Yield: —
   Payout: —
Market value ($ mil.): 5,334

BRINKER INTERNATIONAL, INC.

OVERVIEW

Brinker International can't do much for your broken heart, but it can help you get your baby back, baby back (ribs). The Dallas-based restaurateur operates several chains of concept eateries, including the southwestern-themed Chili's Grill & Bar (with its famous Baby Back Ribs), Italian family-style Romano's Macaroni Grill, and casual Mexican diner On The Border Mexican Grill & Cantina. Of its nearly 1,150 units, Brinker's flagship Chili's accounts for about 750 locations. In addition to its core operations, Brinker is working to build a number of smaller chains, such as its Corner Bakery Cafe (Old World breads and quick foods), Cozymel's Coastal Mexican Grill, and Maggiano's Little Italy.

In the often-fickle world of casual dining,

Brinker's Chili's chain has experienced continued popularity, buoyed by an aggressive national marketing campaign. CEO Ronald McDougall has shut down or sold restaurant concepts that weren't working, such as Grady's American Grill, Kona Ranch, and Wildfire. In their place he developed concepts that didn't face competition from big chains, including Big Bowl, which serves Asian cuisine and was created in partnership with Lettuce Entertain You Enterprises. (Brinker gained complete control of Big Bowl in 2001.) With Phil Romano, founder of Romano's, Brinker also has developed Eatzi's Market & Bakery, a high-end take-out and grocery business. The company is focusing its growth on company-owned restaurants.

HISTORY

Norman Brinker pioneered the so-called casual-dining segment in 1966 when he opened his first Steak & Ale in Dallas. In 1971 he took the company public and watched it grow to more than 100 locations by 1976 when Pillsbury bought the chain.

After serving as president of Pillsbury Restaurant Group (which included Burger King, Poppin' Fresh Restaurants, and Steak & Ale), Brinker left in 1983 to take over Chili's, a chain of southwestern-styled eateries founded by Larry Lavine in 1975. With plans to develop the company into a major chain, Brinker took Chili's public in 1984. The company began recruiting joint venture and franchise partners. It also expanded the Chili's menu to include items such as fajitas, staking the company's growth on aging baby boomers who were looking for something more than fast food.

Stymied in attempts to regain control of his former S&A Restaurant (later bought by Metromedia) and to acquire fast-food chains such as Taco Cabana and Flyer's Island Express, Brinker decided to focus on the casual, low-priced restaurant market. In 1989 Chili's acquired Knoxville, Tennessee-based Grady's Goodtimes, as well as Romano's Macaroni Grill, a small Italian chain founded by Texas restaurateur Phil Romano in 1988. Reflecting the expansion of its restaurant offerings, the company changed its name to Brinker International in 1990.

Brinker introduced Spageddies (a casual, lower-priced pasta restaurant) in 1992. With two Italian-cuisine chains in his network, the entrepreneur began to take on rival Olive Garden. Brinker suffered a major head injury in 1993 while playing polo, leaving him comatose

for two weeks. Despite the traumatic event and poor early prognosis, he made a rapid recovery and returned to running the company. In 1994 Brinker International expanded to cash in on the popularity of Mexican food. It acquired Cozymel's Coastal Mexican Grill that year and bought the 21-unit On The Border Mexican-food chain in 1995.

That year Brinker retired as CEO (though he remained chairman) and was replaced by Ronald McDougall. McDougall sold Grady's and Spageddies to Quality Dining, as they no longer fit the company's overall strategy, and acquired two restaurant concepts (Corner Bakery and Maggiano's Little Italy) from Rich Melman's Lettuce Entertain You Enterprises for $67 million. With Romano in 1996, the company opened a test location (in Dallas) of Eatzi's Market & Bakery, a gourmet grocery takeout concept to capitalize on the public's increasing desire not to cook.

In 1998 Brinker announced plans to open as many as 1,500 Corner Bakery shops over a 10-year period. In 1999 Brinker began expanding further overseas, venturing into Guatemala, Saudi Arabia, and Mexico.

In 2000 the company made plans to open as many as 140 new restaurants during the next two years, including locations in Puerto Rico and Qatar. With an emphasis on company-owned restaurants, Brinker purchased 47 Chili's and On The Border restaurants from New England Restaurant Co. and 39 Chili's restaurants from Sydran Group in 2001. It also acquired Sydran's rights to develop locations in all or part of 14 western states.

OFFICERS

Chairman: Norman E. Brinker, age 69
Vice Chairman and CEO: Ronald A. McDougall, age 58, $2,336,078 pay
President and COO: Douglas H. Brooks, age 48, $1,490,352 pay
EVP, Chief Administrative Officer, Secretary, and General Counsel: Roger F. Thomson, age 51, $720,395 pay
EVP and CFO: Charles M. Sonsteby
EVP and Chief Strategic Officer: Starlette B. Johnson
SVP Corporate Development: Roy E. Study
SVP and Chief Information Officer: Jodie N. Ray
President, Mexican Concepts and On The Border: Kenneth D. Dennis, age 47
President, Chili's Grill & Bar Concepts: Todd E. Diener, age 43, $649,316 pay
President, Romano's Macaroni Grill: John C. Miller, age 45
President, Maggiano's Little Italy Concept: Mark F. Tormey, age 46
President, Corner Bakery Cafe Concept: David Wolfgram, age 42
VP Property Development: Kevin B. Connell
VP Risk and Loss Control: Lisa F. Dickson
VP Accounting Services: David R. Doyle
VP Information Technology: Johnny R. Earl
VP Human Resources: Stan A. Fletcher
VP Human Resources: Larry H. Ford
VP Information Technology: Laurie A. Gaines
Auditors: KPMG LLP

LOCATIONS

HQ: 6820 LBJ Fwy., Dallas, TX 75240
Phone: 972-980-9917   **Fax:** 972-770-4139
Web: www.brinker.com

Brinker International operates about 1,150 restaurants in Australia, Austria, Bahrain, Canada, Egypt, Guatemala, Indonesia, Kuwait, Lebanon, Malaysia, Mexico, Peru, The Philippines, Saudi Arabia, South Korea, the UK, United Arab Emirates, the US, and Venezuela.

PRODUCTS/OPERATIONS

Selected Restaurant Concepts
Big Bowl (Asian food)
Chili's Grill & Bar (Southwestern-themed)
Corner Bakery Cafe (retail Old World bakery and quick foods)
Cozymel's Coastal Mexican Grill (upscale Mexican dining)
Eatzi's Market & Bakery (takeout and catering)
Maggiano's Little Italy (1940s-style Italian diner)
On the Border Mexican Grill & Cantina (casual-style Mexican food)
Romano's Macaroni Grill (family-style Italian dining)

COMPETITORS

Advantica Restaurant Group
American Hospitality Concepts
American Restaurant Group
Applebee's
Avado Brands
Bertucci's
Carlson Restaurants Worldwide
Darden Restaurants
El Chico Restaurants
Landry's
Lettuce Entertain You
Lone Star Steakhouse
Metromedia
Outback Steakhouse
Panera Bread
Prandium
Quality Dining
RARE Hospitality
Ruby Tuesday
Uno Restaurant

HISTORICAL FINANCIALS & EMPLOYEES

NYSE: EAT FYE: Last Wednesday in June	Annual Growth	6/92	6/93	6/94	6/95	6/96	6/97	6/98	6/99	6/00	6/01
Sales ($ mil.)	18.9%	519	653	879	1,042	1,163	1,335	1,574	1,871	2,160	2,473
Net income ($ mil.)	16.7%	36	49	62	73	34	61	69	79	118	145
Income as % of sales	—	6.9%	7.5%	7.0%	7.0%	3.0%	4.5%	4.4%	4.2%	5.5%	5.9%
Earnings per share ($)	17.2%	0.34	0.46	0.55	0.65	0.29	0.54	0.68	0.77	1.17	1.42
Stock price - FY high ($)	—	12.24	16.46	22.47	17.34	12.67	12.67	16.42	20.43	24.01	31.30
Stock price - FY low ($)	—	7.47	9.20	13.34	9.84	7.92	7.09	9.09	10.46	13.26	18.84
Stock price - FY close ($)	11.4%	9.79	15.24	14.01	11.51	10.01	9.50	12.84	18.34	19.76	25.85
P/E - high	—	36	36	38	26	42	23	23	23	20	22
P/E - low	—	22	20	23	15	26	13	13	12	11	13
Dividends per share ($)	—	0.00	0.00	0.00	0.00	0.00	0.00	0.00	0.00	0.00	0.00
Book value per share ($)	14.8%	2.61	3.25	3.92	4.60	5.25	5.35	6.01	6.69	7.72	9.05
Employees	12.1%	28,000	29,000	38,000	37,500	39,900	47,000	53,000	62,300	71,000	78,500

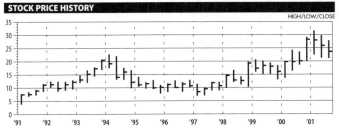

STOCK PRICE HISTORY HIGH/LOW/CLOSE

2001 FISCAL YEAR-END
Debt ratio: 20.4%
Return on equity: 17.5%
Cash ($ mil.): 13
Current ratio: 0.57
Long-term debt ($ mil.): 231
No. of shares (mil.): 100
Dividends
 Yield: —
 Payout: —
Market value ($ mil.): 2,572

BURLINGTON NORTHERN SANTA FE

OVERVIEW

It's true that Santa leaves trains as gifts for little boys, but Burlington Northern Santa Fe (BNSF) is a big boy now and has to buy its own rolling stock. Based in Fort Worth, Texas, BNSF is spending millions of dollars to buy locomotives and upgrade track and yard facilities.

The second-largest US railroad behind Union Pacific, BNSF makes tracks through 28 states in the West, Midwest, and Sun Belt regions of the US and in two Canadian provinces. Trackage rights (which allow BNSF to operate its trains on another railroad's tracks) account for 7,500 miles of BNSF's 33,500-mile system.

Knowing that there's more than one way to get a new train, BNSF agreed in 1999 to merge with Canadian National Railway to form the largest railroad in North America. But the companies called off the transaction because of a US moratorium on rail mergers — upheld by an appeals court — that would have delayed the deal's completion until at least 2002.

HISTORY

Burlington Northern was largely created by James Hill, who bought the St. Paul & Pacific Railroad in Minnesota in 1878. By 1893 Hill had completed the Great Northern Railway, extending from St. Paul to Seattle. The next year he gained control of Northern Pacific (chartered in 1864), which had been built between Minnesota and Washington. In 1901, with J.P. Morgan's help, Hill acquired the Chicago, Burlington & Quincy (Burlington), whose routes included Chicago-St. Paul and Billings, Montana-Denver-Fort Worth, Texas-Houston. The Spokane, Portland & Seattle Railway (SP&S), completed in 1908, gave Great Northern an entrance to Oregon.

Hill intended to merge Great Northern, Northern Pacific, SP&S, and Burlington under his Morgan-backed Northern Securities Company, but in 1904 the Supreme Court found that Northern Securities had violated the Sherman Antitrust Act. The holding company was dissolved, but Hill controlled the individual railroads until he died in 1916. Hill's railroads produced well-known passenger trains: Great Northern's Empire Builder (now operated by Amtrak) began service in 1929, and in 1934 Burlington Zephyr was the nation's first streamlined passenger diesel.

After years of deliberation, the Interstate Commerce Commission allowed Great Northern and Northern Pacific to merge in 1970, along with jointly owned subsidiaries Burlington and SP&S. The new company, Burlington Northern (BN), acquired the St. Louis-San Francisco Railway in 1980, adding more than 4,650 miles to its rail network.

BN formed Burlington Motor Carriers (BMC) in 1985 to manage five trucking companies it had acquired. It sold BMC in 1988 and spun off Burlington Resources, a holding company for its nonrailroad businesses.

In 1995 Burlington Northern Santa Fe (BNSF) was created in a $4 billion merger of BN and Santa Fe Pacific (SFP), founded in 1859. BN's strength lay in transporting manufacturing, agricultural, and natural resource commodities, and SFP specialized in intermodal shipping (combining train, truck, and ship). SFP (originally the Atchison, Topeka & Santa Fe) had taken the name Santa Fe Pacific in 1989 after its forced sale of Southern Pacific. In 1996 BNSF acquired Washington Central Railroad, adding a third connection between central Washington and the Pacific Coast.

In 1997 BNSF customers protested when it couldn't come up with enough cars and locomotives for grain shipping; a year later BNSF rival Union Pacific (UP) was in trouble with clogged rail lines. The problems led the two companies to open a joint dispatching center in Houston to help unsnarl traffic. The effort proved successful, and in 1999 BNSF and UP began to combine dispatching in Southern California; the Kansas City, Missouri area; and Wyoming's Powder River Basin.

In 1999 BNSF agreed to merge with Canadian National Railway, but the deal was terminated in 2000 after a US moratorium on rail mergers was upheld on appeal. BNSF began offering intermodal service in 2000 between the US and Monterrey, Queretaro, and Mexico City, Mexico, its first such US-Mexico service.

In 2001 BNSF became the first US railroad to use the Internet to purchase fuel (via the American Petroleum Exchange). Another first followed, albeit a more dubious one: To settle the first federal lawsuit against workplace genetic testing, BNSF agreed to drop its testing program. Without their knowledge, employees who had been diagnosed with carpal tunnel syndrome were tested for genetic defects.

Also in 2001 BNSF announced plans to join with a group of chemical and plastics companies to build a 13-mile rail line southeast of Houston in order to compete with UP for petrochemical shipping business.

Chairman: Robert D. Krebs, age 58, $601,496 pay
President, CEO, and Director: Matthew K. Rose, age 41, $615,761 pay
EVP and CFO: Thomas N. Hund, age 47, $261,210 pay
EVP and Chief Marketing Officer: Charles L. Schultz, age 53, $482,443 pay
EVP Law and Chief of Staff: Jeffrey R. Moreland, age 56, $185,148 pay
EVP Operations: Carl R. Ice, age 44, $409,422 pay
VP and Chief Information Officer: Bruce E. Freeman
VP and Controller: Dennis R. Johnson, age 49
VP and Senior Regulatory Counsel: Richard E. Weicher
VP and General Tax Counsel: Shelley J. Venick
VP Automotive: Ricci Gardner
VP Corporate Relations: Richard A. Russack
VP E-Business: Kathleen Regan
VP Government Affairs: A. R. Endres Jr.
VP Human Resources: Gloria Zamora
VP Investor Relations and Corporate Secretary: Marsha K. Morgan
VP Law and General Counsel: Gary L. Crosby
VP Network Development: Peter J. Rickershauser
Director Investor Relations: Kathie Farrell
Assistant Secretary: Sue Rombach
Auditors: PricewaterhouseCoopers LLP

LOCATIONS

HQ: Burlington Northern Santa Fe Corporation
2650 Lou Menk Dr., 2nd Fl., Fort Worth, TX 76131
Phone: 817-333-2000   **Fax:** 817-352-7171
Web: www.bnsf.com

Burlington Northern Santa Fe operates in 28 states and in two Canadian provinces.

PRODUCTS/OPERATIONS

2000 Sales

	$ mil.	% of total
Intermodal	2,654	29
Carload	2,577	28
Coal	2,131	23
Agricultural commodities	1,257	14
Automotive	493	5
Other	93	1
Total	**9,205**	**100**

Selected Railway Subsidiaries
BN Leasing Corporation
Burlington Northern International Services, Inc.
Burlington Northern Railroad Holdings, Inc.
Burlington Northern Santa Fe Manitoba, Inc.
Burlington Northern Worldwide, Inc.
The Dodge City and Cimarron Valley Railway Company
Electro Northern, Inc.
Los Angeles Junction Railway Company
Northern Radio Limited
Oklahoma City Junction Railway Company
Rio Grande, El Paso and Santa Fe Railroad Company
Santa Fe Pacific Insurance Company
Santa Fe Pacific Railroad Company (Act of Congress)
SFP Pipeline Holdings, Inc.
Star Lake Railroad Company
Western Fruit Express Company
Winona Bridge Railway Company

COMPETITORS

APL	Landstar System
Canadian National Railway	Norfolk Southern
Canadian Pacific	Schneider National
CNF	Union Pacific
CSX	U.S. Xpress
J. B. Hunt	Werner

HISTORICAL FINANCIALS & EMPLOYEES

NYSE: BNI FYE: December 31	Annual Growth	12/91	12/92	12/93	12/94	12/95	12/96	12/97	12/98	12/99	12/00
Sales ($ mil.)	8.1%	4,559	4,630	4,699	4,995	6,183	8,187	8,413	8,941	9,100	9,205
Net income ($ mil.)	—	(306)	299	296	426	92	889	885	1,155	1,137	980
Income as % of sales	—	—	6.5%	6.3%	8.5%	1.5%	10.9%	10.5%	12.9%	12.5%	10.6%
Earnings per share ($)	60.7%	—	—	—	—	0.22	1.90	1.88	2.43	2.44	2.36
Stock price - FY high ($)	—	—	—	—	—	28.22	30.01	33.61	35.67	37.94	29.56
Stock price - FY low ($)	—	—	—	—	—	23.48	24.48	23.39	26.88	22.88	19.06
Stock price - FY close ($)	1.7%	—	—	—	—	25.97	28.76	30.95	34.25	24.25	28.31
P/E - high	—	—	—	—	—	50	16	18	15	15	13
P/E - low	—	—	—	—	—	41	13	12	11	9	8
Dividends per share ($)	—	—	—	—	—	0.00	0.40	0.40	0.42	0.48	0.48
Book value per share ($)	11.2%	—	—	—	—	11.21	12.93	14.51	16.52	17.98	19.10
Employees	2.5%	31,760	31,204	30,502	30,711	45,500	43,000	44,500	42,900	41,600	39,600

STOCK PRICE HISTORY

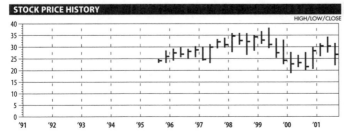

HIGH/LOW/CLOSE

2000 FISCAL YEAR-END

Debt ratio: 46.9%
Return on equity: 12.5%
Cash ($ mil.): 11
Current ratio: 0.45
Long-term debt ($ mil.): 6,614
No. of shares (mil.): 392
Dividends
  Yield: 1.7%
  Payout: 20.3%
Market value ($ mil.): 11,086

BURLINGTON RESOURCES INC.

OVERVIEW

The bulk of Burlington Resources' resources is in the form of natural gas (82% of its total reserves). Houston-based Burlington Resources is one of the largest independent oil and gas companies in the US, having proved reserves of more than 7.6 trillion cu. ft. of natural gas equivalent. It is also a major natural gas producer in North America. A holding company for a number of operating companies, Burlington Resources is engaged in oil and gas exploration, development, production, and marketing.

North American activities account for most of the company's sales, and its top gas-producing region is the San Juan Basin of New Mexico and Colorado. Burlington Resources also operates in the deepwater provinces of the Gulf of Mexico and the midcontinent region of the US, where it has wells in the Williston Basin in the Dakotas and Montana, Oklahoma's Anadarko Basin, Texas' Permian Basin, and Wyoming's Wind River Basin.

The company has also moved into western Canada with the purchase of Poco Petroleums (renamed Burlington Resources Canada Energy). Abroad, Burlington Resources has operations in the East Irish Sea and North Sea, Asia, Latin America, and North and West Africa.

HISTORY

Burlington Resources got its start in 1864 when President Abraham Lincoln granted Burlington Northern's predecessor, Northern Pacific Railway, the land and rights-of-way to construct a transcontinental railroad. After the railroad was completed, Northern Pacific retained major land holdings and mineral rights, including the largest private coal reserve in the US, 1.5 million acres of forest, and one of the country's largest reserves of natural gas and oil (discovered in 1951 on Burlington Northern's property in the Williston Basin of North Dakota).

In 1980 the company set up Milestone Petroleum to manage its oil and gas assets. Burlington Northern acquired the El Paso Company and Southland Royalty between 1983 and 1985; it merged these oil and gas firms with Milestone to form Meridian Oil.

During the 1980s, under the leadership of chairman Richard Bressler, Burlington Northern refocused its efforts on its railroad business. However, faced with the possibility of a long strike by railroad workers, Bressler moved to create two companies to protect the group's profits: Burlington Northern would manage the railroad activities, and Burlington Resources (spun off in 1988) would hold all the other interests of the enterprise.

The company spun off El Paso Natural Gas, a gas distribution company, in 1992 to focus exclusively on oil and gas operations. In 1994 Burlington Resources launched an exploration growth strategy that included ramping up its operations in the Gulf of Mexico. To avoid confusion, Meridian Oil's operations were subsumed under the Burlington Resources name in 1996, and the company subsequently divested nonstrategic oil and gas properties.

To position itself as a "super independent" with vast resources and a global reach, Burlington Resources acquired independent oil and gas exploration and production company Louisiana Land and Exploration (LL&E) in 1997. LL&E had been founded in 1926 by speculator Edward Simms to explore for oil on Louisiana coastal property owned by Henry Timken and a group of Midwesterners. During the 1950s and 1960s LL&E acquired other properties across the US, and in the 1980s it bought properties in Australia, Colombia, Indonesia, Mexico, and the UK. By 1997 it had production and exploration operations not only in Louisiana and the Gulf of Mexico, but also in Algeria, offshore Indonesia, Venezuela, the North Sea, and the Madden Gas Field in Wyoming. The company also owned 600,000 acres of land in southern Louisiana and about 200 shallow-water and deepwater leases.

In 1998 Burlington Resources, Canada's Talisman Energy, and Sonatrach of Algeria successfully tested a wildcat well in the Berkine Basin of Algeria. Burlington Resources also signed an agreement with Hydrocarbon Resources, a subsidiary of Centrica, to transport and process natural gas from undeveloped gas fields in the UK's East Irish Sea. In 1999 Burlington Resources moved into western Canada by buying Calgary-based Poco Petroleums Ltd. in a $2.5 billion deal.

In 2000 the company moved into West Africa by acquiring a 25% stake in fields operated by Agip SpA off the coast of Gabon. The next year Burlington Resources agreed to buy properties in western Canada that had net proved reserves of 297 billion cu. ft. of gas equivalent from Petrobank Energy and ATCO Gas.

OFFICERS

Chairman, President, and CEO: Bobby S. Shackouls, age 50, $1,729,038 pay
SVP and CFO: Steven J. Shapiro, age 48
SVP, Exploration, BROG GP: John A. Williams, age 56, $712,500 pay
SVP, Law and Administration: L. David Hanower, age 41, $617,538 pay
VP and Treasurer: Daniel D. Hawk
VP and Controller: Joseph P. McCoy
VP and General Counsel: Frederick J. Plaeger
VP, Acquisitions: Thomas B. Nusz
VP, Corporate Affairs: Gavin H. Smith
VP, Gulf Coast Division: Hunter L. Malson
VP, Human Resources and Administration: William Usher
VP, International, Houston: Gregory M. Larberg
VP, International, London: Richard E. Fraley
VP, Internal Audit: Dane E. Whitehead
VP, Investor Relations and Corporate Communications: Ellen R. DeSanctis
VP, Marketing: Clifford Scott Kirk
VP, Mid-Continent Division: Barry J. Winstead
President and CEO, BROG GP: Randy L. Limbacher, age 42, $712,500 pay
President, Burlington Resources Canada Energy: Mark E. Ellis
Auditors: PricewaterhouseCoopers LLP

LOCATIONS

HQ: 5051 Westheimer, Ste. 1400, Houston, TX 77056
Phone: 713-624-9500   **Fax:** 713-624-9645
Web: www.br-inc.com

Burlington Resources operates primarily in the US (Colorado, Louisiana, Montana, New Mexico, North Dakota, Oklahoma, Texas, Wyoming) and Canada.

2000 Sales

	$ mil.	% of total
North America	2,976	95
Other regions	171	5
Total	**3,147**	**100**

PRODUCTS/OPERATIONS

2000 Reserves

	Billion cu. ft.	% of total
Gas	6,233	82
Oil	1,409	18
Total	**7,642**	**100**

Major Subsidiaries
Burlington Resources Canada Energy Ltd.
Burlington Resources Oil & Gas Company LP
The Louisiana Land and Exploration Company

COMPETITORS

Adams Resources	Koch
Anadarko Petroleum	Mitchell Energy &
Apache	Development
BP	Ocean Energy
Calpine	Phillips Petroleum
Conoco	Pioneer Natural Resources
Devon Energy	Royal Dutch/Shell
EOG	Talisman Energy
Exxon Mobil	TOTAL FINA ELF
Helmerich & Payne	Unocal
Kerr-McGee	Vintage Petroleum

HISTORICAL FINANCIALS & EMPLOYEES

NYSE: BR FYE: December 31	Annual Growth	12/91	12/92	12/93	12/94	12/95	12/96	12/97	12/98	12/99	12/00
Sales ($ mil.)	6.7%	1,754	1,141	1,249	1,055	873	1,293	2,000	1,637	2,065	3,147
Net income ($ mil.)	14.1%	205	258	256	154	(280)	255	319	86	1	675
Income as % of sales	—	11.7%	22.6%	20.5%	14.6%	—	19.7%	16.0%	5.3%	0.0%	21.4%
Earnings per share ($)	8.2%	1.54	1.95	1.53	1.20	(1.47)	1.88	1.79	0.48	0.01	3.12
Stock price - FY high ($)	—	43.75	43.63	53.88	49.63	42.25	53.50	54.50	49.63	47.63	52.88
Stock price - FY low ($)	—	32.88	33.00	36.50	33.13	33.63	35.13	39.75	29.44	29.50	25.75
Stock price - FY close ($)	4.1%	35.25	40.00	42.38	35.00	39.25	50.38	44.81	35.81	33.06	50.50
P/E - high	—	28	22	35	41	—	28	30	103	4,763	17
P/E - low	—	21	17	24	28	—	19	22	61	2,950	8
Dividends per share ($)	(2.6%)	0.70	0.65	0.54	0.55	0.55	0.55	0.55	0.55	0.55	0.55
Book value per share ($)	(2.6%)	22.11	18.67	20.11	20.30	17.54	18.68	17.07	17.01	15.03	17.40
Employees	(9.4%)	4,347	1,705	1,729	1,846	1,796	2,004	1,819	1,678	1,997	1,783

STOCK PRICE HISTORY

HIGH/LOW/CLOSE

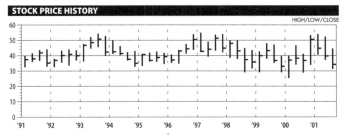

2000 FISCAL YEAR-END

Debt ratio: 38.0%
Return on equity: 19.3%
Cash ($ mil.): 132
Current ratio: 1.33
Long-term debt ($ mil.): 2,301
No. of shares (mil.): 216
Dividends
 Yield: 1.1%
 Payout: 17.6%
Market value ($ mil.): 10,886

CASH AMERICA INTERNATIONAL

OVERVIEW

King of the pawns, Fort Worth, Texas-based Cash America International is #1 worldwide (EZCORP comes in at #2) with about 470 pawnshops in the US, 42 in the UK, and 11 in Sweden. Cash America makes high-interest (up to 300%) loans to its customers, who pony up collateral (electronics, cameras, firearms, and other merchandise, except in the UK, where only jewelry and precious metals can be pawned). About 30% of the loans are not redeemed and the collateral is sold; Cash America also sells new merchandise.

The company's Mr. Payroll subsidiary offers check cashing, money orders, bill paying, money transfers, and other services through kiosks located within convenience stores and other locations. The unit has about 150 company-owned and franchised sites in 20 states, including locations in Texaco, Conoco, and BP service stations as well as in Allsups, Cracker Barrel, EZ Mart, and Jet 24 stores.

Subsidiary Rent-A-Tire, which is on the selling block, provides tire rent-to-own services in Arizona, Louisiana, Oklahoma, and Texas. InnoVentry, a joint venture with Wells Fargo that offered automated check cashing services to customers without bank accounts, has ceased operations.

Cash America has built its business by serving a market that typically avoids commercial banks and credit cards. It has focused on customer service, providing personal attention to people with lower incomes. The company continues to expand by opening new branches and by franchising to independent pawnshops.

HISTORY

When Jack Daugherty was a student, he hocked his guitar to finance dates. In 1970, after quitting school, he opened a pawnshop that was so successful he used the proceeds to invest in oil. When oil took a downturn, he returned to the pawn business, incorporating Cash America in 1984; it went public in 1987. The company began to expand rapidly in the late 1980s and early 1990s, both through acquisitions and through construction of new stores. After adding several stores in Texas it moved into the Southeast and then up the East Coast.

Cash America expanded overseas when it bought UK-based Harvey & Thompson Ltd. in 1992; two years later, the company acquired Sweden's Svensk Pantbelaning. Also in 1994, Cash America acquired Mr. Payroll Corporation, the largest convenience store-based check-cashing service in the US. It continued its expansion into non-pawn services when it acquired Rent-A-Tire in 1995.

Operational problems, including a failed retail venture, caused a brief downturn in 1995, but Cash America refocused on its core business and recovered in 1996. As part of a low-cost expansion program, the next year the firm introduced a Cash America franchise plan to independent pawnshop owners. Over the next two years, Cash America expanded further in Texas and Utah.

In 1998 Mr. Payroll rolled out automated check-cashing machines that identified customers by their facial features; it formed an alliance with Crestar to supplement the bank's Virginia supermarket branches with the machines. That year the company also launched its Rent-A-Tire subsidiary in Texas. Also in 1998 the company acquired the Doc Holliday's chain of pawn shops, which operated about 40 stores in Colorado, North Carolina, Oklahoma, South Carolina, Tennessee, and Texas, as well as smaller chains in Cincinnati and Chicago.

In 1999 Cash America expanded its automated check cashing business, participating in InnoVentry, a joint venture with Wells Fargo. Late that year following his second heart attack, Daugherty announced he would step down as CEO. He was succeeded by president Dan Feehan. Daugherty remained chairman.

In 2000 Cash America got plenty of publicity (presumably unwanted) when its nine-story headquarters in downtown Fort Worth was slammed by a tornado. The company is renovating the building, whose other tenants had included an FBI bureau.

InnoVentry ceased operations in 2001. Also that year Cash America announced plans to sell Rent-A-Tire.

Chairman: Jack R. Daugherty, age 53
President, CEO, and Director: Daniel R. Feehan, age 50, $442,496 pay
EVP and CFO: Thomas A. Bessant Jr., age 42, $200,494 pay
EVP, Administration: Robert D. Brockman, age 46, $209,384 pay
EVP, Business Development: Michael D. Gaston, age 56, $216,370 pay
EVP, Foreign Operations; CEO, Rent-A-Tire: James H. Kauffman, age 56, $317,643 pay
EVP, Information Technology: William R. Horne, age 58
EVP, U.S. Operations, Western Division: Jerry D. Finn, age 54
EVP, Secretary, and General Counsel: Hugh A. Simpson, age 41, $200,494 pay
Auditors: PricewaterhouseCoopers LLP

LOCATIONS

HQ: Cash America International, Inc.
1600 W. 7th St., Fort Worth, TX 76102
Phone: 817-335-1100 **Fax:** 817-335-1119
Web: www.cashamericaonline.com

PRODUCTS/OPERATIONS

2000 Sales

	$ mil.	% of total
Finance and service charges	115	32
Sale of merchandise	227	62
Rental	17	5
Check cashing	4	1
Other lending fees and royalties	1	—
Total	**364**	**100**

Selected Subsidiaries
CAII Pantbelaning AB (Sweden)
Cash America Financial Services, Inc.
Cash America Franchising, Inc.
Cash America Holding, Inc.
Cash America International, Inc.
Cash America Management L.P.
Cash America of Missouri, Inc.
  Vincent's Jewelers and Loan, Inc.
Cash America Pawn, Inc. of Ohio
Cash America, Inc.
Cash America, Inc. of Alabama
Cash America, Inc. of Colorado
Cash America, Inc. of Illinois
Cash America, Inc. of Indiana
Cash America, Inc. of Kentucky
Cash America, Inc. of North Carolina
Cash America, Inc. of Oklahoma
Cash America, Inc. of South Carolina
Cash America, Inc. of Tennessee
Cash America, Inc. of Utah
Cash America Pawn L.P.
Doc Holliday's Pawnbrokers & Jewelers, Inc.
  Longhorn Pawn & Gun, Inc.
Express Cash International Corporation
Florida Cash America, Inc.
Georgia Cash America, Inc.
Harvey & Thompson Limited (UK)
Mr. Payroll Corporation

COMPETITORS

Ace Cash Express	Greenland Corp.
Cattles	Grow Biz
DGSE Companies	PawnMart
EZCORP	Provident Financial
First Cash Financial Services	World Acceptance

HISTORICAL FINANCIALS & EMPLOYEES

NYSE: PWN FYE: December 31	Annual Growth	12/91	12/92	12/93	12/94	12/95	12/96	12/97	12/98	12/99	12/00
Sales ($ mil.)	11.4%	138	185	225	262	254	281	303	343	373	364
Net income ($ mil.)	—	11	13	14	16	(7)	16	17	13	4	(2)
Income as % of sales	—	7.9%	7.0%	6.1%	5.9%	—	5.6%	5.5%	3.7%	1.0%	—
Earnings per share ($)	—	0.45	0.45	0.48	0.54	(0.24)	0.54	0.66	0.48	0.15	(0.07)
Stock price - FY high ($)	—	9.81	12.88	11.00	10.13	9.75	8.50	13.75	20.88	15.94	13.00
Stock price - FY low ($)	—	6.00	7.25	6.38	7.50	4.63	4.75	8.00	9.00	6.75	3.63
Stock price - FY close ($)	(8.4%)	9.63	10.88	9.38	9.88	5.50	8.50	12.94	15.19	9.75	4.38
P/E - high	—	23	27	22	18	—	15	20	41	106	—
P/E - low	—	14	15	13	14	—	9	12	18	45	—
Dividends per share ($)	2.5%	0.04	0.05	0.05	0.05	0.05	0.05	0.05	0.05	0.05	0.05
Book value per share ($)	6.2%	4.21	5.46	5.87	6.46	6.12	6.35	6.89	7.46	7.42	7.24
Employees	9.9%	1,300	1,700	1,530	2,475	2,200	2,635	2,787	3,035	3,061	3,035

STOCK PRICE HISTORY

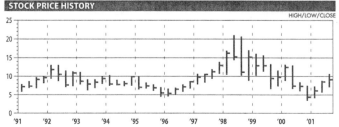

HIGH/LOW/CLOSE

2000 FISCAL YEAR-END
Debt ratio: 48.0%
Return on equity: —
Cash ($ mil.): 5
Current ratio: 6.93
Long-term debt ($ mil.): 165
No. of shares (mil.): 25
Dividends
  Yield: 1.1%
  Payout: —
Market value ($ mil.): 108

CELLSTAR CORPORATION

OVERVIEW

CellStar is good at helping everyday conversations reach new heights. Carrollton, Texas-based CellStar is a leading independent wholesale cellular phone distributor (it competes fiercely with Brightpoint). The company makes 80% of its sales to customers outside North America, primarily from countries that lack wireline telecom infrastructure. It distributes products from Nokia, Ericsson, Motorola, and other manufacturers to retailers, carriers, and exporters; the company also operates retail outlets in Asia, Europe, and Latin America. CellStar has sold all but two of its US stores to help combat declining income. It also provides inventory and logistics management, packaging, and wireless activation services.

CellStar continues to streamline its operations to boost profits and beef up electronic commerce capabilities through its online ordering system and NetXtreme inventory system.

Founder Alan Goldfield and his wife own 35% of the company.

HISTORY

Alan Goldfield started Dallas record store National Tape and Record Center in 1969, later selling car stereos and accessories. In 1981 he formed a relationship with Audiovox that led to a 1984 joint venture to distribute cell phones; in 1988 it began selling phones in Wal-Mart's Sam's Clubs. The company changed its name to CellStar and went public in 1993.

In the early 1990s CellStar opened operations in Mexico, soon branched into other Latin American markets, and became the first company authorized to distribute wireless phones in China (it must buy and sell locally made products and deal in local currency). By 1995 CellStar had 150 retail outlets, and within a year it added 200 more. But rapid expansion depressed earnings.

In 1996 CellStar sold 331 centers located in Sam's Club to MCI and shifted its focus to wholesale. The company started wholesale operations in the UK (1996) and Shanghai and Indonesia (1997), and made acquisitions in Sweden and Poland (1998).

Income fell in fiscal 1998 as CellStar recorded a $29 million investment charge, and shareholder litigation alleging that CellStar had padded sales numbers hit hard when the company settled for $14.5 million. The SEC launched an investigation into the company's finances that year. Also in 1998 CellStar signed an agreement with the Beijing Radio Telecommunications Bureau to be its sole supplier of Motorola cellular phones and accessories and to operate Motorola branded sales outlets for the Bureau. Also in 1998 CellStar introduced an e-commerce site, allowing commercial customers to order mobile phones and accessories via the Internet.

In 1999 CellStar sold all but two of its US retail stores to Baby Bell SBC Communications, cut 10% of its workforce, and consolidated Latin American and North American operations. It bought Dutch distributor Montana Telecommunications that year. Also in 1999 it entered a strategic alliance with Boston Communications Group to market prepaid cellular phones and phone services to international clients.

In 1999 CellStar signed a strategic alliance agreement with Arcoa Communications, Taiwan's largest telecommunications retail store chain, to serve as the primary supplier of Motorola-licensed handsets and accessories to Arcoa's retail stores. CellStar strengthened its ties with Arcoa in early 2000 when it bought a small stake in the Taiwanese retailer.

Despite belt-tightening, CellStar suffered losses for fiscal 2000. Also that year the company signed a joint venture agreement with Asian Internet content provider chinadotcom to provide fulfillment, sales, and distribution for chinadotcom's Wireless Access Protocol (WAP) Internet service. Also in 2000 CellStar signed a deal with Amazon.com to provide logistics, fulfillment support, and service activations for the online retailer's new wireless phones store.

In 2001 Goldfield announced his retirement as chairman and CEO. Board member James L. Johnson was named chairman and Terry S. Parker, former president and COO of CellStar, was named CEO. Goldfield became chairman emeritus. Also in 2001, the SEC dropped its investigation of CellStar.

Chairman: James L. Johnson, age 73
CEO and Director: Terry S. Parker, age 56
President and COO: Dale H. Allardyce, age 51, $400,000 pay
SVP, CFO, and Treasurer: Austin P. Young, age 60, $350,000 pay
SVP, General Counsel, and Secretary: Elaine Flud Rodriguez, age 44
Chairman and CEO, CellStar (Asia) Corporation Ltd.: A. S. Horng, age 43, $866,778 pay
VP and Controller: Raymond L. Durham, age 39
Director, Human Resources: Scott Campbell
Auditors: KPMG LLP

LOCATIONS

HQ: 1730 Briercroft Ct., Carrollton, TX 75006
Phone: 888-466-5000   **Fax:** 888-896-0576
Web: www.cellstar.com

CellStar operates in Argentina, Chile, China, Colombia, Hong Kong, Mexico, the Netherlands, Peru, Singapore, Sweden, Taiwan, the UK, and the US.

2000 Sales

	$ mil.	% of total
Asia/Pacific	1,025	41
Latin America	636	26
North America	499	20
Europe	316	13
Total	**2,476**	**100**

PRODUCTS/OPERATIONS

Suppliers

Audiovox	Motorola
Ericsson	Nokia
Kenwood	Samsung
Kyocera	

Services
Inventory management (order processing, purchasing, returns, and repairs)
Logistics management (tri-party purchasing and custom invoicing)
Multiparty marketing
Package design
Supply chain management
Testing and repair
Web-based procurement (NetXtreme)
Wireless service activation

Selected Subsidiaries
A&S Air Service, Inc.
Audiomex Export Corp.
Celular Express S.A. de C.V. (Mexico)
Florida Properties, Inc.
National Auto Center, Inc.
Sizemore International B.V. (Netherlands Antilles)
Shanghai CellStar International Trading Co. Ltd. (China)
Sunrise Mobil Sdn Bhd (Malaysia)
Systar Corporation Ltd. (Taiwan)

COMPETITORS

Andrew	Circuit City	SANYO
Corporation	Hello Direct	SED
Audiovox	Matsushita	International
Best Buy	Communication	Sony
Brightpoint	NTT DoCoMo	TESSCO
Casio Computer	Oki Electric	

HISTORICAL FINANCIALS & EMPLOYEES

Nasdaq: CLST FYE: November 30	Annual Growth	11/91	11/92	11/93	11/94	11/95	11/96	11/97	11/98	11/99	11/00
Sales ($ mil.)	41.0%	113	181	275	518	812	948	1,483	1,996	2,334	2,476
Net income ($ mil.)	—	(0)	0	8	16	23	(6)	54	14	69	(59)
Income as % of sales	—	—	—	2.9%	3.1%	2.8%	—	3.6%	0.7%	3.0%	—
Earnings per share ($)	—	—	—	—	0.30	0.41	(0.11)	0.89	0.24	1.12	(0.99)
Stock price - FY high ($)	—	—	—	—	6.92	12.38	9.75	24.94	18.81	13.50	13.13
Stock price - FY low ($)	—	—	—	—	3.04	5.38	1.92	3.71	3.00	5.00	1.63
Stock price - FY close ($)	(19.7%)	—	—	—	6.17	8.75	3.90	12.94	6.44	9.66	1.66
P/E - high	—	—	—	—	23	30	—	28	78	12	—
P/E - low	—	—	—	—	10	13	—	4	13	4	—
Dividends per share ($)	—	—	—	—	0.00	0.00	0.00	0.00	0.00	0.00	0.00
Book value per share ($)	14.8%	—	—	—	1.38	1.93	1.80	2.75	3.02	4.17	3.14
Employees	12.0%	—	524	700	1,250	2,008	1,010	1,100	1,100	1,425	1,300

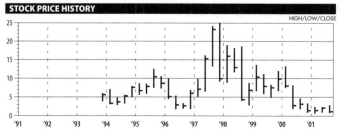

STOCK PRICE HISTORY

HIGH/LOW/CLOSE

2000 FISCAL YEAR-END

Debt ratio: 44.2%
Return on equity: —
Cash ($ mil.): 77
Current ratio: 1.52
Long-term debt ($ mil.): 150
No. of shares (mil.): 60
Dividends
  Yield: —
  Payout: —
Market value ($ mil.): 100

CENTEX CORPORATION

OVERVIEW

Centex has built its way to the top: The Dallas-based company's Centex Homes unit is one of the largest US home builders, along with Lennar, behind industry leader Pulte Homes. Centex also buys and develops land, provides mortgage loans and insurance to home buyers, and offers commercial contracting and construction services.

Centex Homes, which targets both first-time buyers and move-up buyers, builds houses that range in price from $49,000 to $1.5 million. The average price is $206,000. The company operates in 23 states and Washington, DC. Almost 90% of its homes are single-family detached houses; townhomes and condominiums make up the balance. Centex also has holdings in Latin America and the UK, including British builder Fairclough Homes, and it owns Cavco Industries, a leading builder of manufactured homes.

The company's commercial building arm, Centex Construction Group, has projects in both the private sector (such as office and apartment buildings) and public sector (such as schools and government buildings). Almost a quarter of the group's sales are derived from the construction of health care facilities.

Centex has cemented its position among the top domestic home builders by offering home-related products and services. Its 65%-owned subsidiary, Centex Construction Products, makes and sells gypsum wallboard, aggregates, and ready-mix concrete. CTX Mortgage makes loans to about 70% of its parent's homebuyers. The firm's Centex HomeTeam unit provides pest control, security, and lawn services.

HISTORY

Tom Lively and Ira Rupley, who built their first large subdivision near Dallas in 1949, founded home builder Centex the next year. Centex's first outside of Texas project was a development of 7,000 houses near Chicago. By 1960 it had built 25,000 houses.

Branching out from home building, Centex built its first cement plant in 1963 and established four more over the next 25 years. Centex expanded into commercial construction with the 1966 purchase of Dallas contractor J. W. Bateson (founded 1936). In the 1970s it picked up other general contractors, moving into Florida, California, and Washington, DC. To combine home building with home financing, Centex began mortgage banking in 1973, and when oil prices soared during the 1970s, the enterprising company formed subsidiary Cenergy to go digging for petroleum (spun off in 1984).

Centex increasingly built outside its Southwest territory — from 28% of all new homes in 1979 to 45% in 1984. Larry Hirsch, a New York-reared lawyer who had headed a Houston cement and energy company, became COO in 1984 (and CEO in 1988). The early 1980s were a boom time for Texas real estate as deregulation spurred S&Ls to make loans — any loans. The market became overbuilt, and when oil prices collapsed in 1986 and 1987, credit dried up. With the spectacular failure of several Texas S&Ls, the Texas real estate market crashed. Centex was pinched, but it survived on sales from less-depressed areas of the US.

Centex Development was established in 1987 as a custodian for land the company could not develop during the bust. Centex created Centex Rodgers Construction that year to focus on construction of medical facilities. In 1994 the company took its construction products division public and sold off its S&Ls.

In 1995 Centex entered ventures to build luxury houses in the UK and living centers for sufferers of Alzheimer's disease and memory disorders. The next year Centex purchased parts of security firm Advanced Protection Systems and pest-control company Environmental Safety Systems — both are now part of Centex HomeTeam.

The company was selected by *Builder* and *Home* magazines in 1997 to build the Home of the Future, showcasing cutting-edge products and design. On the other end of the housing spectrum, Centex acquired 80% of manufactured-home maker Cavco Industries (it bought the rest in 2000). The next year Cavco bought manufactured home retailer AAA Homes. In 1998 Centex entered Ohio and New Jersey by acquiring Wayne Homes and Calton Homes, respectively.

The next year Centex went further abroad: It bought UK builder Fairclough Homes (operating in the North West, Midlands, and South East) from AMEC for $175 million.

In 2000 Centex joined other leading home builders to form HomebuildersXchange, a supply chain services Web site, but the project soon collapsed. The next year Centex expanded in the Midwest by acquiring Detroit home builder Selective Group. It also acquired City Homes, a Dallas luxury townhome and condo builder.

OFFICERS

Chairman and CEO: Laurence E. Hirsch, age 55, $3,200,000 pay
Vice Chairman: David W. Quinn, age 59, $3,375,000 pay
EVP; Chairman and CEO, Centex Homes: Timothy R. Eller, age 52, $3,749,000 pay
EVP and CFO: Leldon E. Echols, age 45, $1,275,000 pay
EVP, Chief Legal Officer, General Counsel, and Secretary: Raymond G. Smerge, age 57, $1,042,000 pay
SVP Administration: Michael S. Albright
SVP Finance: Lawrence Angelilli
SVP Strategic Planning and Marketing: Robert S. Stewart
VP and Treasurer: Vicki A. Roberts
VP, Controller, and Financial Strategy: Mark A. Blinn
VP Corporate Communications: Sheila E. Gallagher
Chairman, President, and CEO, Centex Construction Group; Chairman, Centex Rooney Construction: Bob L. Moss, age 53
Auditors: Arthur Andersen LLP

LOCATIONS

HQ: 2728 N. Harwood, Dallas, TX 75201
Phone: 214-981-5000 **Fax:** 214-981-6859
Web: www.centex.com

Centex builds houses in 79 markets in 23 states and the District of Columbia. It also invests in home building activities in Latin America and the UK.

PRODUCTS/OPERATIONS

2001 Sales

	$ mil.	% of total
Home building		
Conventional homes	4,356	65
Manufactured homes	126	2
Contracting & construction services	1,291	19
Financial services	464	7
Construction products	441	7
Investment real estate	33	—
Total	**6,711**	**100**

COMPETITORS

Barratt Developments
Beazer Homes
Countrywide Credit
David Weekley Homes
Del Webb
D.R. Horton
FleetBoston
Fluor
Foster Wheeler
GE Capital
George Wimpey

Hovnanian Enterprises
KB Home
Lennar
M.D.C. Holdings
MGIC Investment
M I
Schottenstein Homes
NVR
Peter Kiewit Sons'
PMI Group

Pulte Homes
Rollins
Ryland
SBC Communications
Taylor Woodrow
Toll Brothers
Turner Corporation
Tyco International
Whiting-Turner

HISTORICAL FINANCIALS & EMPLOYEES

NYSE: CTX FYE: March 31	Annual Growth	3/92	3/93	3/94	3/95	3/96	3/97	3/98	3/99	3/00	3/01
Sales ($ mil.)	13.4%	2,166	2,503	3,215	3,278	3,103	3,785	3,976	5,155	5,956	6,711
Net income ($ mil.)	26.3%	35	61	85	92	53	107	145	232	257	282
Income as % of sales	—	1.6%	2.4%	2.7%	2.8%	1.7%	2.8%	3.6%	4.5%	4.3%	4.2%
Earnings per share ($)	26.5%	0.56	0.96	1.29	1.51	0.91	1.80	2.36	3.75	4.22	4.65
Stock price - FY high ($)	—	13.75	17.31	22.88	16.19	18.00	21.00	41.63	45.75	42.88	46.20
Stock price - FY low ($)	—	8.47	9.94	13.38	10.06	11.75	12.63	16.75	26.38	17.50	20.63
Stock price - FY close ($)	14.7%	12.09	15.81	15.44	12.13	15.50	17.63	38.13	33.38	23.81	41.65
P/E - high	—	25	18	18	11	19	11	17	12	10	10
P/E - low	—	15	10	10	7	13	7	7	7	4	4
Dividends per share ($)	5.4%	0.10	0.10	0.10	0.10	0.10	0.10	0.12	0.16	0.16	0.16
Book value per share ($)	14.4%	8.49	9.29	10.56	11.90	12.71	14.40	16.65	20.17	24.14	28.60
Employees	10.0%	5,500	6,500	8,430	6,395	6,186	8,926	10,259	13,161	13,368	13,000

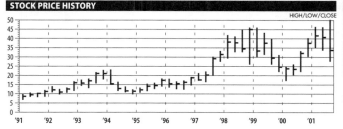

STOCK PRICE HISTORY

HIGH/LOW/CLOSE

2001 FISCAL YEAR-END

Debt ratio: 67.3%
Return on equity: 18.0%
Cash ($ mil.): 58
Current ratio: 4.09
Long-term debt ($ mil.): 3,520
No. of shares (mil.): 60
Dividends
  Yield: 0.4%
  Payout: 3.4%
Market value ($ mil.): 2,496

CINEMARK USA, INC.

OVERVIEW

Thanks to Cinemark, you can see the movie stars of Tinsel Town at a Tinseltown. Plano, Texas-based Cinemark USA operates more than 270 theaters with more than 2,900 screens (some larger theaters go by the Tinseltown moniker). About 15% of its theaters are discount cinemas and nearly 20% offer online ticketing. All of Cinemark's theaters are multiplexes (89% have eight or more screens), many of which sport neon color schemes not found in nature.

The company prefers to build new theaters in midsized markets or in suburbs of major cities where the Cinemark theater is the only game in town. The company now focuses almost exclusively on building stadium-seating-style theaters.

Cinemark's theaters can be found in 33 states and 12 other countries, primarily in Latin America. Despite signs of improvement, the company continues to struggle along with the rest of its industry.

Chairman and CEO Lee Roy Mitchell owns 24% of the company's stock and controls all of its voting shares. Invesment firm Cypress Merchant Banking Partners owns 42% and CGI Equities owns 18%.

HISTORY

Lee Roy Mitchell and partner Paul Broadhead founded Cinemark in 1985; by the end of 1989, Cinemark had about 660 screens in 18 states. Mitchell set a company goal of 1,000 screens by 1992 and, in addition to constructing its own theaters, Cinemark made acquisitions to achieve its goal.

In 1992 Cinemark built its first megaplex, Hollywood USA — featuring 15 movie screens, a pizzeria, and an arcade. As the multiplex became one of its most profitable theaters, the company added more to its portfolio. Cinemark also started developing a Latin American presence in 1992, building theaters in Mexico and Chile. It formed a joint venture in 1995 to build theaters in Argentina, and in 1996 created three more joint ventures for theaters in Brazil, Ecuador, and Peru.

Meanwhile, Cinemark continued to add megaplexes; it opened 12 theaters with 165 screens (an average of about 14 screens per theater) in 1997. That year Cinemark signed a deal with high-tech theater developer IMAX to build 12 IMAX 3-D movies theaters as part of Cinemark multiplexes in the US, Mexico, and South America.

Also in 1997 the company formed a joint venture with Japan's Shochiku Co. Ltd. to develop multiplex theaters in Japan. The company continued its Asian expansion in 1998 when it signed a joint venture deal with Core Pacific Development Co., Ltd., one of Taiwan's largest real estate development companies to develop multiplex cinemas in that country.

In the first half of 1998, the company added 223 more screens, including 64 in Latin America. Later that year a group of wheelchair users sued the company, claiming the front-row spaces reserved for them in Cinemark's stadium-seating theaters were uncomfortably close to screens. (A US Court of Appeals sided with the theater chain in 2000 and the US Supreme Court refused to hear the plaintiffs' appeal.) At the end of 1998 the company moved its headquarters from Dallas to suburban Plano, Texas.

Cinemark entered the world of online sales in early 2000 when it teamed with Dallas-based e-commerce software company Vectrix.com to sell movie tickets in real time over the Internet at Cinemark's Web site.

In 2001 the company announced it would build a 4-screen, stadium-seating theater in Park City, Utah. In conjunction with that announcement the company said it had signed an agreement with the Sundance Film Festival to make the Park City multiplex the official "Home of the Sundance Film Festival." The agreement runs through 2006.

Also in 2001 the company acquired 42 screens in San Antonio from Regal Cinemas. Later that year Cinemark announced plans to build a 15-screen multiplex at the South Center Mall in South Dallas. The announcement came after several years of delays due to financial setbacks at the mall. The theater is scheduled to open in 2003.

OFFICERS

Chairman and CEO: Lee Roy Mitchell, age 64, $431,378 pay
Vice Chairman, EVP, and Secretary: Tandy Mitchell, age 50
President and COO: Alan W. Stock, age 40, $422,179 pay
SVP, Director of Operations: Robert F. Carmony, age 43
SVP, Treasurer, CFO, and Assistant Secretary: Robert D. Copple, age 42, $308,272 pay
VP General Counsel: Michael Cavalier, age 34
VP Construction: Don Harton, age 43
VP Purchasing: Walter Hebert, age 55
VP Marketing: Randy Hester, age 48
VP Film Licensing: John Lundin, age 51
VP Real Estate and Assistant Secretary: Margaret E. Richards, age 42
VP Information Systems: Philip Wood, age 37
President, Cinemark International: Tim Warner, $342,355 pay
Director Human Resources: Brad Smith
Auditors: Deloitte & Touche LLP

LOCATIONS

HQ: 3900 Dallas Pkwy., Ste. 500, Plano, TX 75093
Phone: 972-665-1000   **Fax:** 972-665-1004
Web: www.cinemark.com

Cinemark USA has theaters in Argentina, Brazil, Canada, Chile, Colombia, Costa Rica, Ecuador, El Salvador, Honduras, Nicaragua, Mexico, Peru, and the US.

2000 Sales

	$ mil.	% of total
US	599	76
Mexico	62	8
Brazil	61	8
Other countries	67	8
Adjustments	(3)	—
Total	**786**	**100**

PRODUCTS/OPERATIONS

2000 Sales

	$ mil.	% of total
Admissions	511	65
Concessions	236	30
Other	39	5
Total	**786**	**100**

COMPETITORS

AMC Entertainment
Carmike Cinemas
GC Companies
Loews Cineplex
  Entertainment
National Amusements
Regal Cinemas
United Artists Theatre

HISTORICAL FINANCIALS & EMPLOYEES

Private FYE: December 31	Annual Growth	12/91	12/92	12/93	12/94	12/95	12/96	12/97	12/98	12/99	12/00
Sales ($ mil.)	19.1%	—	195	240	283	299	342	435	571	713	786
Net income ($ mil.)	—	—	6	10	7	13	15	15	11	1	(10)
Income as % of sales	—	—	2.9%	4.1%	2.5%	4.4%	4.3%	3.5%	1.9%	0.1%	—
Employees	6.6%	—	—	5,100	5,500	7,000	6,500	7,000	8,000	8,000	8,000

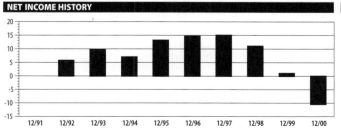

NET INCOME HISTORY

2000 FISCAL YEAR-END

Debt ratio: 94.1%
Return on equity: —
Cash ($ mil.): 20
Current ratio: 0.25
Long-term debt ($ mil.): 778

CLEAR CHANNEL

OVERVIEW

In a media landscape dominated by flashy Internet companies, it's tempting to dismiss radio and billboards as yesterday's news. But don't write off these media pioneers just yet — Clear Channel Communications is a reminder that the health of radio and billboards is still vigorous. The San Antonio-based company's 1999 acquisitions of Jacor Communications elevated it to the #2 spot in US radio station ownership. In 2000 the company ascended to the #1 position in radio station ownership with its $23.8 billion acquisition of AMFM. Clear Channel also is one of the world's largest outdoor advertising companies.

Nationwide, the company owns, programs, or sells airtime for nearly 1,200 stations (including pending transactions). Clear Channel also has equity stakes in more than 240 radio stations internationally and owns 26% of Hispanic Broadcasting (one of the largest Spanish-language radio broadcasters in the US). Its acquisition of Jacor brought more than 50 syndicated programs (*Rush Limbaugh, The Dr. Laura Program*) under its umbrella. Clear Channel also operates 19 US TV stations.

The company's outdoor advertising activities encompass some 700,000 outdoor advertising displays (billboards, transit displays) across the globe. Clear Channel also boasts investments in international outdoor advertising companies in 43 countries.

Not content to dominate just the airwaves, Clear Channel has expanded into live entertainment through its acquisition of events producer and promoter SFX Entertainment (now Clear Channel Entertainment). Thomas Hicks of Dallas-based leverage buyout firm Hicks, Muse, Tate & Furst owns about 9% of Clear Channel; CEO L. Lowry Mays, about 5%.

HISTORY

In 1972 investment banker L. Lowry Mays found himself in a predicament. Investors looking to buy a San Antonio radio station had reneged on the financing that he had arranged for them, leaving Mays in a tight spot. He turned to local car dealer B. J. "Red" McCombs, and the two decided to buy the station themselves. The pair bought three more radio stations in 1973 and another station two years later. In 1975, after leaving investment banking to devote his time to radio stations, Mays changed the company's name from San Antonio Broadcasting to Clear Channel Communications (a moniker borrowed from the term for a high-powered station that has exclusive use of its frequency).

The company went public in 1984, and Clear Channel soon earned a reputation for buying unsuccessful stations and turning them around. By the mid-1980s its collection of radio stations numbered 16. Reluctant to pay the high prices asked for radio stations in the late 1980s, Clear Channel temporarily bowed out of radio acquisitions and tried its luck in the TV market. The company created subsidiary Clear Channel Television in 1988; by 1992 it had purchased seven TV stations.

After the Federal Communications Commission loosened restrictions on radio station ownership in 1992, Clear Channel resumed the expansion of its radio empire. By 1994 its portfolio included 35 radio stations and nine TV stations. The company expanded internationally in 1995 through its purchase of a half interest in the Australian Radio Network. It also dipped a toe in the US Spanish-language radio market, buying 20% of Heftel Broadcasting (the company later was renamed Hispanic Broadcasting, and Clear Channel's stake now stands at 26%).

When regulations on nationwide radio station ownership were lifted in 1996, Clear Channel wasted no time in extending its reach into radio. By the end of 1997, it owned or programmed 175 radio stations and 18 TV stations. It also crossed the threshold of the outdoor advertising industry with acquisitions of Eller Media in 1997 and Universal Outdoor Holdings and UK-based More Group in 1998. Clear Channel's foray into outdoor advertising was largely responsible for the company's 93% increase in sales in 1998. Its $4 billion purchase of Jacor Communications in 1999 marked the company's largest acquisition to date and positioned Clear Channel as the second-largest radio station owner in the country. In 2000 it completed an even larger acquisition: a $23.8 billion buyout of rival AMFM.

Also in 2000 the company bought SFX Entertainment (renamed Clear Channel Entertainment in 2001), the largest events producer and promoter in the US. The following year Clear Channel (and other radio operators) stopped streaming Webcast signals from many of its stations after the American Federation of Television and Radio Artists signed a contract guaranteeing its members 300% of fees for Internet commercials.

Chairman and CEO: L. Lowry Mays, age 65, $4,000,000 pay
President, COO, and Director: Mark P. Mays, age 37, $2,157,500 pay
EVP, CFO, and Director: Randall T. Mays, age 35, $2,155,000 pay
SVP Finance: Juliana F. Hill, age 31
SVP and Chief Accounting Officer: Herbert W. Hill Jr., age 41
SVP Labor and Employment: Demetra Koelling
SVP, General Counsel, and Secretary: Kenneth E. Wyker, age 39
Chairman and CEO, Radio Group: Randy Michaels, age 48, $1,804,412 pay
CEO, Eller Media and Director: Karl Eller, age 72, $907,200 pay
President and COO, Eller Media: Paul Meyer, age 58
President and COO, Radio Group: John E. Hogan
SVP Mid-Atlantic Radio Operations: Jim Shea
SVP Midwest Radio Operations: Dave Crowl
SVP Plains/Northwest Radio Operations: Jay Meyers
SVP Northeast Radio Operations: Rob Williams
SVP Southeast Radio Operations: Peter Ferrara
SVP Southwest Radio Operations: J.D. Freeman
SVP Southwest/Central Radio Operations: John Cullen
SVP West Coast Radio Operations: Jim Donahoe
Auditors: Ernst & Young LLP

LOCATIONS

HQ: Clear Channel Communications, Inc.
200 E. Basse, San Antonio, TX 78209
Phone: 210-822-2828   **Fax:** 210-822-2299
Web: www.clearchannel.com

Clear Channel Communications has operations in Asia, Australia, Europe, North America, and South America.

PRODUCTS/OPERATIONS

2000 Sales

	% of total
Broadcasting	45
Outdoor advertising	32
Live entertainment	17
Other	6
Total	**100**

Selected Radio Investments
Australian Radio Network (50%, Australian radio stations)
Golden Rose (32%, UK radio stations)
Grupo Acir Communicaciones (40%, radio broadcasting in Mexico)
Hispanic Broadcasting Corporation (26%, US Spanish-language radio broadcaster)
New Zealand Radio Network (33%, New Zealand radio stations)
Radio 1 (50%, Norwegian radio stations)
Radio Bonton (50% ownership, FM radio station in the Czech Republic)

COMPETITORS

ABC	Gannett
Ackerley Group	Hearst-Argyle Television
Citadel Communications	Infinity Broadcasting
Cox Radio	Lamar Advertising
Cumulus Media	Sinclair Broadcast Group
Donrey	Spanish Broadcasting
Emmis Communications	Westwood One
Entercom	

HISTORICAL FINANCIALS & EMPLOYEES

NYSE: CCU FYE: December 31	Annual Growth	12/91	12/92	12/93	12/94	12/95	12/96	12/97	12/98	12/99	12/00
Sales ($ mil.)	63.4%	64	82	118	173	244	352	697	1,351	2,678	5,345
Net income ($ mil.)	82.6%	1	4	9	22	32	38	64	54	73	249
Income as % of sales	—	1.7%	5.2%	7.7%	12.7%	13.1%	10.7%	9.1%	4.0%	2.7%	4.7%
Earnings per share ($)	45.1%	0.02	0.04	0.08	0.16	0.23	0.26	0.34	0.22	0.22	0.57
Stock price - FY high ($)	—	0.99	1.81	4.61	6.50	11.06	22.63	39.94	62.31	91.50	95.50
Stock price - FY low ($)	—	0.67	0.86	1.62	3.93	6.27	10.19	16.81	31.00	52.00	43.88
Stock price - FY close ($)	55.7%	0.90	1.63	4.60	6.34	11.03	18.06	39.72	54.50	89.25	48.44
P/E - high	—	50	45	58	41	48	87	111	271	339	162
P/E - low	—	34	22	20	25	27	39	47	135	193	74
Dividends per share ($)	—	0.00	0.00	0.00	0.00	0.00	0.00	0.00	0.00	0.00	0.00
Book value per share ($)	83.8%	0.22	0.26	0.72	0.95	1.18	3.34	8.89	17.01	29.78	51.82
Employees	52.8%	800	1,150	1,354	1,549	1,779	3,219	5,400	7,000	17,650	36,350

STOCK PRICE HISTORY

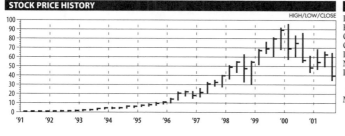

HIGH/LOW/CLOSE

2000 FISCAL YEAR-END

Debt ratio: 25.0%
Return on equity: 1.2%
Cash ($ mil.): 197
Current ratio: 1.10
Long-term debt ($ mil.): 10,100
No. of shares (mil.): 586
Dividends
   Yield: —
   Payout: —
Market value ($ mil.): 28,369

CLUBCORP, INC.

OVERVIEW

It's always tee time at ClubCorp. The Dallas-based holding company is the world's largest operator of golf courses, private clubs, and resorts. The company owns or manages a collection of about 220 resorts, country club and golf facilities, and city clubs spanning nearly a dozen countries. Under the leadership of billionaire founder and chairman Robert Dedman (named by *Forbes* magazine as one of the 400 wealthiest Americans), ClubCorp's properties have grown to include Mission Hills Country Club near Palm Springs, California, and North Carolina's Pinehurst Resort and Country Club

(site of the 1999 US Open). ClubCorp also owns 25% of ClubLink, a leading Canadian developer and operator of golf courses.

In addition, ClubCorp has a 30% stake in PGA European Tour Courses, an operator of tournament golf courses across Europe. Striving to stay on top of the game, the company has been acquiring new properties and is building new ones in a joint venture with golf legend Jack Nicklaus. Dedman and his family own about 75% of ClubCorp; investment firm The Cypress Group, nearly 15%.

HISTORY

Though his childhood in Depression-era Arkansas was dominated by intense poverty, ClubCorp founder Robert Dedman knew how to dream big. At a young age he vowed to become "very, very rich," and the scrappy Dedman embarked on achieving that goal by earning a college scholarship, obtaining a law degree, and eventually launching a flourishing Dallas law practice.

Dedman's law firm was successful, but he realized that it wouldn't bring him the $50 million he wanted to earn by age 50. In 1957 he formed Country Clubs, Inc., to venture into the country club business. At that time, doctors and lawyers working on a volunteer basis were managing most clubs, and Dedman believed his new company could bring professional management expertise to these facilities. The company opened its first country club, Dallas' Brookhaven Country Club, in 1957. Through the subsequent purchase of 20 more clubs, Country Clubs refined its management style, implementing unique practices such as reducing playing time on the golf course and developing specialized training for club staff.

In 1965 the company expanded into city and athletic clubs and assumed the Club Corporation of America name. The expansion drive that followed fueled a 30% growth rate that the company maintained from the 1960s through the 1980s. In 1985 the company was restructured and divided into a handful of separate companies owned by the newly formed Club Corporation International holding company.

In 1988 the company bought an 80% interest in Franklin Federal Bancorp. The bank's club properties had initially caught his eye, but Dedman also believed that the 400,000 members of his clubs might prove fertile ground for the marketing of financial services. In 1996, however, Club Corporation International sold

the financial institution to Norwest. Although Franklin Federal was turning a profit, losses from investment in derivatives, coupled with the bank's inability to compete with larger competitors, prompted the company to sell the bank and refocus on its core club and resort business.

In 1996 Japanese cookie-maker Tohato sued the company, claiming that it intentionally mismanaged the Pinewild Country Club. Pinewild was owned by Tohato, managed by Club Corporation International, and located next door to Club Corporation International's Pinehurst Resort and Country Club. Tohato alleged that the company's mismanagement was part of a scheme to eventually buy Pinewild at a reduced price. The case was eventually settled, but the nasty legal wrangling that ensued cast a pall over the impending 1999 US Open at Pinehurst.

In 1998 the company was reincorporated as ClubCorp International, Inc. It expanded its international base that year by purchasing nearly 30% of PGA European Tour Courses. The company also entered into a joint venture with Jack Nicklaus to develop three dozen new golf courses.

The company shortened its moniker to ClubCorp in 1999. Among the additions ClubCorp made to its holdings that year were 22 properties acquired from The Meditrust Companies. The company also increased its ownership of Canadian club developer ClubLink to 25%. An influx of funds for further expansion came in 1999 after investment firm The Cypress Group took a 15% stake. In 2000 the company took a 9% stake in Lifecast.com, which will develop members-only Web sites for ClubCorp's properties.

OFFICERS

Chairman: Robert H. Dedman Sr., age 75, $342,689 pay
President and CEO: Robert H. Dedman Jr., age 43, $535,600 pay
COO: James M. Hinckley, age 45, $370,200 pay
CFO: Jeffrey P. Mayer, age 44
SVP People Strategy Department: Kim Besse
EVP Strategic Operations: Albert E. Chew III
EVP: Mark W. Dietz, age 47
EVP: James E. Maser, age 63
EVP, Secretary and General Counsel: Terry A. Taylor, age 45
EVP ClubCorp Resorts, Inc: Patrick A. Corso, age 50, $363,548 pay
EVP Sales ClubCorp USA, Inc: Frank C. Gore, age 51, $343,755 pay
EVP Domestic Club Operations; ClubCorp USA Inc.: Douglas T. Howe
EVP Development: Murray S. Siegel
Chief Information Officer: Colby H. Springer
Auditors: KPMG LLP

LOCATIONS

HQ: 3030 LBJ Fwy., Ste. 700, Dallas, TX 75234
Phone: 972-243-6191   **Fax:** 972-888-7338
Web: www.clubcorp.com

ClubCorp has operations worldwide.

PRODUCTS/OPERATIONS

2000 Sales

	% of total
Country club & golf facilities	47
Business & sports clubs	24
Resorts	21
Real estate & international operations	8
Total	**100**

Selected Clubs
The Athletic and Swim Club at Equitable Center (New York)
Barton Creek Resort and Country Club (Texas)
Columbia Tower Club (Washington)
Drift Golf Club (UK)
Firestone Country Club (Ohio)
Golden Bear Golf Club (South Carolina)
Inverrary Country Club (Florida)
Kingwood Cove Golf Club (Texas)
Lakelands Gold Club (Australia)
Metropolitan Club (Illinois)
Mission Hills Country Club (California)
Pinehurst Resort and Country Club (North Carolina)
Teal Bend Golf Club (California)

COMPETITORS

American Golf
Club Med
Golf Trust of America
Hillman
Hilton
Hyatt
National Golf Properties
ResortQuest International
Sandals Resorts
Silverleaf Resorts
Starwood Hotels & Resorts

HISTORICAL FINANCIALS & EMPLOYEES

Private FYE: Last Wed. in Dec.	Annual Growth	12/91	12/92	12/93	12/94	12/95	12/96	12/97	12/98	12/99	12/00
Sales ($ mil.)	4.0%	751	884	1,200	773	761	784	840	851	1,028	1,069
Net income ($ mil.)	—	—	19	41	15	(11)	29	122	38	12	(16)
Income as % of sales	—	—	2.1%	3.4%	1.9%	—	3.7%	14.5%	4.5%	1.1%	—
Employees	9.1%	—	12,000	13,000	19,200	19,800	19,000	20,000	21,000	23,000	24,000

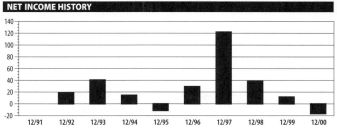

NET INCOME HISTORY

2000 FISCAL YEAR-END
Debt ratio: 54.2%
Return on equity: —
Cash ($ mil.): 25
Current ratio: 0.78
Long-term debt ($ mil.): 643

COMMERCIAL METALS COMPANY

OVERVIEW

Vertical integration keeps Commercial Metals Company's (CMC) sales from falling flat. The Dallas-based company's manufacturing division operates four steel minimills, 26 steel fabrication plants, and 22 concrete products warehouses. The unit also operates a heat-treating facility and plants that manufacture steel joists, castellated beams, and fence posts. CMC's recycling segment operates 33 secondary metals-processing plants that sort, shred, shear, and pulverize ferrous and nonferrous metals into bales that are sold to steel mills, lead smelters, copper refineries, ingot manufacturers, and others. Subsidiary Howell Metal Company manufactures copper tubing.

CMC's marketing and trading segment operates through 17 international trading offices. It brokers industrial products that include primary and secondary metals, fabricated metals, chemicals, and industrial minerals to customers in the steel, nonferrous metals, metal fabrication, chemical, refractory, and transportation industries.

Despite the gloomy outlook for the steel industry, CMC has managed to make a profit in nearly every quarter for the past 23 years. The company's vertical integration allows for a flagging segment to be compensated for by another's success in tough times. For example, when scrap prices are low, CMC's recycling centers feel the pain, but the company's minimills rake it in. When steel prices are hurt by the dumping of cheap imports, CMC's marketing and trading arm continues to make money.

HISTORY

Russian immigrant Moses Feldman moved to Dallas in 1914 and founded scrap metal company American Iron & Metal the next year. In the 1920s Feldman suffered a heart attack, and his son Jake helped out with the business. Low metal prices hurt the company during the Depression. In 1932 Jake formed a two-man brokerage firm, Commercial Metals Company (CMC), which was combined as a partnership with his father's scrap metal operations. Moses Feldman died in 1937. CMC was incorporated in 1946 and began buying related businesses during the 1950s.

CMC was listed on the American Stock Exchange in 1960. It soon expanded geographically, buying a stake in Texas steelmaker Structural Metals (1963). In 1965 it formed Commercial Metals Europa (the Netherlands), its first overseas subsidiary, and Commonwealth Metal (New York). By 1966 CMC was one of the world's top three scrap metal companies. It bought copper tube manufacturer Howell Metals (Virginia) in 1968, the remainder of Structural Metals, and major stakes in seven affiliated businesses. Over 10 years, CMC opened trading offices around the world. Business continued to grow throughout the 1970s. The company added a small minimill in Arkansas (1971) and certain assets of General Export Iron and Metal in Texas (1976).

CMC began trading on the New York Stock Exchange in 1982. The next year the company bought Connors Steel (Alabama), its third minimill. By the end of 1984 CMC was operating 20 metal recycling plants from Texas to Florida.

The company modernized its minimills in the 1990s. CMC acquired small scrap-metal operations and Shepler's, a concrete-related products business, in 1994. Also that year CEO Stanley Rabin completed the $50 million purchase of Owen Steel (a South Carolina minimill), which expanded CMC's reach into the Mid-Atlantic and Southeast. The company wrapped up a $30 million capital improvement program at its Alabama minimill in 1995 — just in time to ride a strong steel market to record profits.

Although a correction in the steel and metals industry depressed prices in 1996, CMC achieved record sales and profits that fiscal year. However, both dipped the next year, with lower steel and scrap prices widely attributed to an influx of foreign imports. CMC strengthened its vertical integration in 1997 by acquiring Allegheny Heat Treating (heat-treatment services to steel mills) and two auto salvage plants in Florida.

During 1998 CMC moved into the Midwest, buying a metals recycling company in Missouri. It boosted global operations by purchasing a metals trading firm in Australia and entering a joint venture with Trinec, a Czech Republic steel mill, to sell steel products in Germany. The next year CMC completed construction of a rolling mill in South Carolina and renovations at an Alabama plant; both were expected to reduce production-related costs and increase efficiency to help counter slumping steel prices.

In 2000 CMC picked up three rebar fabricators — two in California (Fontana Steel and C&M Steel), and one in Florida (Suncoast Steel).

OFFICERS

Chairman, President, and CEO: Stanley A. Rabin, age 62, $1,080,000 pay
VP and CFO: William B. Larson, age 47
VP; President and COO, CMC Steel Group: Clyde P. Selig, age 68, $659,000 pay
VP; President, Fabrication Plants, CMC Steel Group: Hugh M. Ghormley, age 71, $622,100 pay
VP; President, Howell Metal Company: A. Leo Howell, age 79, $940,000 pay
VP; President, Marketing and Trading Segment: Murray R. McClean, age 52
VP; President, Secondary Metals Processing Division: Harry J. Heinkele, age 68
VP, General Counsel, and Secretary: David M. Sudbury, age 55
Chairman and CEO, CMC Steel Group: Marvin Selig, age 77, $880,000 pay
President, Cometals: Eliezer Skornicki
President, Commonwealth Metal: Eugene L. Vastola
President, Dallas Trading Division: J. Matthew Kramer
President, International Division: Kevin S. Aitken
Treasurer: Louis A. Federle, age 51
Controller: Malinda G. Passmore, age 41
Asst. Controller: Milton L. Davis
Director, Human Resources: Jesse Barnes
Auditors: Deloitte & Touche LLP

LOCATIONS

HQ: 7800 Stemmons Fwy., Dallas, TX 75247
Phone: 214-689-4300   **Fax:** 214-689-5886
Web: www.commercialmetals.com

CMC operates manufacturing and recycling facilities throughout the US; it has 17 trading offices in Australia, Germany, Hong Kong, Singapore, Switzerland, the UK, and the US.

2000 Sales

	$ mil.	% of total
US	1,782	67
Other countries	879	33
Total	**2,661**	**100**

PRODUCTS/OPERATIONS

2000 Sales

	$ mil.	% of total
Manufacturing	1,356	50
Marketing & trading	903	33
Recycling	462	17
Adjustments	(60)	—
Total	**2,661**	**100**

COMPETITORS

AK Steel Holding Corporation
Bethlehem Steel
BHP Billiton
Birmingham Steel
Blue Tee
Chaparral Steel
Connell Limited Partnership
Keywell
LTV
Metal Management
Nucor
OmniSource
Oregon Steel Mills
Quanex
Roanoke Electric Steel
Rouge Industries
Schnitzer Steel
Tube City
USX-U.S. Steel
Worthington Industries

HISTORICAL FINANCIALS & EMPLOYEES

NYSE: CMC FYE: August 31	Annual Growth	8/91	8/92	8/93	8/94	8/95	8/96	8/97	8/98	8/99	8/00
Sales ($ mil.)	9.7%	1,161	1,166	1,569	1,666	2,117	2,322	2,258	2,368	2,251	2,661
Net income ($ mil.)	16.2%	12	13	22	26	38	46	39	43	47	46
Income as % of sales	—	1.0%	1.1%	1.4%	1.6%	1.8%	2.0%	1.7%	1.8%	2.1%	1.7%
Earnings per share ($)	16.2%	0.84	0.87	1.46	1.75	2.51	3.01	2.54	2.82	3.22	3.25
Stock price - FY high ($)	—	16.69	18.94	28.50	30.00	29.13	33.25	33.50	36.00	34.19	33.94
Stock price - FY low ($)	—	12.09	13.03	16.78	21.00	23.38	23.00	27.13	24.13	19.69	22.13
Stock price - FY close ($)	7.4%	14.72	17.25	28.31	26.75	28.25	30.13	30.75	24.38	30.63	27.94
P/E - high	—	20	22	20	17	12	11	13	13	11	10
P/E - low	—	14	15	11	12	9	8	10	8	6	7
Dividends per share ($)	3.2%	0.39	0.39	0.39	0.46	0.48	0.48	0.52	0.52	0.52	0.52
Book value per share ($)	9.2%	14.44	14.91	15.96	17.01	19.73	22.20	24.04	26.18	29.05	31.93
Employees	9.5%	3,709	3,834	3,904	4,353	6,272	6,700	7,150	7,350	7,581	8,378

STOCK PRICE HISTORY

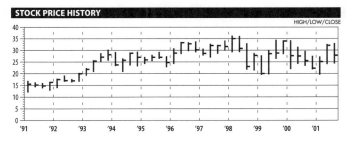

HIGH/LOW/CLOSE

2000 FISCAL YEAR-END

Debt ratio: 38.4%
Return on equity: 11.0%
Cash ($ mil.): 20
Current ratio: 1.63
Long-term debt ($ mil.): 262
No. of shares (mil.): 13
Dividends
  Yield: 1.9%
  Payout: 16.0%
Market value ($ mil.): 368

COMPAQ COMPUTER CORPORATION

OVERVIEW

Strangely enough, at Compaq Computer (the world's leading personal computer maker) it's no longer PC to talk PCs. The Houston-based company has blossomed into the third-largest global computer company, behind IBM and Hewlett-Packard. Corporate purchases of computers, including servers, storage products, and related services, account for half of sales. Compaq's other products range from business and consumer PCs to handheld computers. The company sells to businesses, consumers, government agencies, and schools.

CEO Michael Capellas is leading a charge against competition that's bigger (IBM) and faster (Dell) with a blue-collar attitude and an eye on the Internet. The affable executive has walked a fine line of reform, attempting to widen the company's product offerings while streamlining its operations. The result: Increasing emphasis on products at the high end (servers, storage systems) and low end (handhelds, MP3 players), and cost-cutting measures that include the revamping of manufacturing processes and personnel cuts. Capellas is also shifting the company's focus toward software and consulting services, moving Compaq out of ancillary hardware operation such as microprocessors.

Despite some success in growing its services business, the company has felt the pinch of a flagging PC market and now plans to pool its resources with a long-time competitor. Hewlett-Packard has agreed to buy Compaq in a stock deal initially valued at $25 billion. Capellas will be president of the combined company.

HISTORY

Joseph "Rod" Canion and two other ex-Texas Instruments engineers started Compaq Computer in Houston in 1982 to manufacture and sell portable IBM-compatible computers. Compaq's first portable was developed from a prototype the three sketched on a paper place mat when they first discussed the idea.

Compaq shipped its first computer in 1982, and in 1983 (the year it went public) it recorded sales of $111 million — unprecedented growth for a computer startup. The success was due in part to emphasis on leading-edge technology. That year Benjamin Rosen was named chairman. Also in 1983 the company introduced a 28-pound portable computer — 18 months before IBM did — and in 1986 it was first to release a computer based on Intel's 386 chip. However, Compaq delayed the debut of its laptop until 1988 to improve the display and battery technology. It was quickly successful.

To sell its products, Compaq capitalized on the extensive base of dealers and suppliers built up around the IBM PC. Rather than create a large sales force, it gave exclusive rights to dealers for sales and service of its products and by 1990 had networks in 152 countries.

Economic recession and stiff price competition slashed Compaq's revenues in 1991. Canion was forced to resign as CEO. He was replaced with German-born Eckhard Pfeiffer, the company's COO and a former marketing head at Texas Instruments.

Pfeiffer took a no-nonsense approach to battle the glut of IBM cloners, cutting gross profit margins nearly in half. The move caused an intense price war. When the dust settled in 1994, Compaq had passed Big Blue to lead the world in PC sales.

In 1996 Compaq reorganized divisions to reflect a more global emphasis. In 1998 Compaq bought high-end hardware and Web search engine (AltaVista) specialist Digital Equipment in efforts to boost its service prowess. The assimilation of Digital eventually resulted in the trimming of 15,000 jobs and restructuring costs that contributed to a loss for the year. To intensify a head-to-head battle with Dell's booming direct sales, Compaq began using the Internet to sell PCs to businesses.

In 1999 Compaq intensified its Internet focus by forming AltaVista Company and purchasing online retailer Shopping.com. But bottom-line results came too slowly for Compaq's board, which pressured Pfeiffer to resign in the wake of disappointing earnings and shareholder suits. Rosen assumed the interim CEO post. Compaq chose COO Michael Capellas, who had joined the company in 1998, as its new president and CEO. Capellas issued more layoffs and made the Internet the company's primary objective.

In 2000 Compaq bought distribution operations from PC reseller Inacom to form the Custom Edge direct sales unit. The next year the company announced that it would cut its workforce by 12% or about 8,500 jobs. Trying to shift its emphasis from hardware to services, Compaq later in 2001 announced plans to sell its Alpha microprocessor operations to Intel. Later that year Hewlett-Packard agreed to acquire Compaq in a stock deal initially valued at about $25 billion.

Chairman Emeritus: Benjamin M. Rosen
Chairman, President, and CEO: Michael D. Capellas,
  age 46, $5,040,971 pay
EVP, Global Business Units: Michael J. Winkler, age 55,
  $1,296,147 pay
EVP, Worldwide Sales and Service: Peter Blackmore,
  age 53, $1,370,024 pay
SVP and CFO: Jeff Clarke
SVP and Chief Technology Officer: Shane V. Robison,
  age 47
SVP and General Counsel: Thomas C. Siekman, age 59
SVP; General Manager, Business Critical Server Group:
  Howard D. Elias, age 43
**SVP; General Manager, Industry Standard Server
  Group:** Mary T. McDowell, age 36, $1,190,988 pay
SVP, Access Business Group: Michael J. Larson, age 47,
  $2,029,745 pay
**SVP, Global Business Solutions and Chief Information
  Officer:** Robert V. Napier, age 54
**SVP, Human Resources, Organization, and
  Environment:** Yvonne R. Jackson, age 51
SVP, Marketing and Strategy: Douglas B. Fox, age 53
SVP, Strategic Planning: Jesse J. Greene Jr., age 56
SVP, Supply Chain Management: George Devlin, age 46
VP and COO, EMEA: Rob Walker
VP and Treasurer: Ben K. Wells
Auditors: Ernst & Young LLP

LOCATIONS

HQ: 20555 State Hwy. 249, Houston, TX 77070
Phone: 281-370-0670   **Fax:** 281-514-1740
Web: www.compaq.com

Compaq Computer has operations in nearly 60
countries. Its principal manufacturing facilities are in
Brazil, the UK, and the US.

2000 Sales

	$ mil.	% of total
US	18,966	45
Other countries	23,417	55
Total	**42,383**	**100**

PRODUCTS/OPERATIONS

2000 Sales

	$ mil.	% of total
Enterprise Computing	14,316	34
Commercial PC	13,136	31
Consumer PC	7,586	18
Compaq Global Services	6,993	16
Other	352	1
Total	**42,383**	**100**

COMPETITORS

Acer	Gateway	Samsung
Apple Computer	Hewlett-Packard	Siemens
Bull	Hitachi	SGI
Computer	Intel	Sony
Sciences	IBM	Sun
Dell Computer	Matsushita	Microsystems
eMachines	NCR	Toshiba
EMC	NEC	Unisys
Fujitsu	Oki Electric	

HISTORICAL FINANCIALS & EMPLOYEES

NYSE: CPQ FYE: December 31	Annual Growth	12/91	12/92	12/93	12/94	12/95	12/96	12/97	12/98	12/99	12/00
Sales ($ mil.)	32.9%	3,271	4,100	7,191	10,866	14,755	18,109	24,584	31,169	38,525	42,383
Net income ($ mil.)	17.7%	131	213	462	867	789	1,313	1,855	(2,743)	569	569
Income as % of sales	—	4.0%	5.2%	6.4%	8.0%	5.3%	7.3%	7.5%	—	1.5%	1.3%
Earnings per share ($)	14.2%	0.10	0.17	0.01	0.68	0.60	0.87	1.19	(1.71)	0.34	0.33
Stock price - FY high ($)	—	4.95	3.32	5.05	8.43	11.35	17.43	39.78	44.75	51.25	34.88
Stock price - FY low ($)	—	1.47	1.48	2.78	4.83	6.23	7.18	14.20	22.94	18.25	14.30
Stock price - FY close ($)	26.9%	1.76	3.25	4.92	7.90	9.60	14.88	28.25	42.00	27.06	15.05
P/E - high	—	50	20	505	12	18	19	32	—	146	100
P/E - low	—	15	9	278	7	10	8	12	—	52	41
Dividends per share ($)	—	0.00	0.00	0.00	0.00	0.00	0.00	0.00	0.05	0.08	0.10
Book value per share ($)	18.7%	1.53	1.67	2.10	2.82	3.45	4.49	6.21	6.73	8.76	7.15
Employees	26.3%	11,600	11,300	10,541	14,372	17,055	18,900	32,656	71,000	85,100	94,600

STOCK PRICE HISTORY

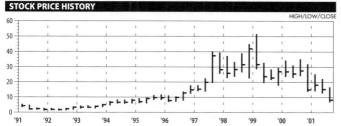

HIGH/LOW/CLOSE

2000 FISCAL YEAR-END

Debt ratio: 4.5%
Return on equity: 4.2%
Cash ($ mil.): 2,569
Current ratio: 1.31
Long-term debt ($ mil.): 575
No. of shares (mil.): 1,689
Dividends
  Yield: 0.7%
  Payout: 30.3%
Market value ($ mil.): 25,419

COMPUCOM SYSTEMS, INC.

OVERVIEW

CompuCom Systems pieces together the computing puzzle. The Dallas-based company provides desktop, mobile, and wireless computers, networking equipment, peripherals, and software to nearly 6,000 corporations. CompuCom also offers consulting, distribution, help desk support, and other information technology services (10% of sales). Its product vendors include Compaq (30% of product sales), IBM (26%), Hewlett-Packard (20%), Microsoft, and Palm.

CompuCom's services business, which offers a variety of consulting, integration, help desk, asset management, and network management assistance, has hovered around 10% of sales each of the past three years, despite a strategic push into that market. (The company has nearly quadrupled its service personnel since 1995).

To counter sagging profits, CompuCom implemented a major restructuring to reduce costs. It created distribution centers close to supplier manufacturing sites and closed down all of its sales offices — more than 60 — in favor of virtual offices.

Investment and management firm Safeguard Scientifics owns 53% of the company.

HISTORY

Stanley Sternberg founded CompuCom Systems in Michigan in 1981 to make factory automation products. Originally called CytoSystems, the company changed its name in 1983 to Machine Vision International (MVI) to reflect its focus on designing artificial vision systems for computers. Its main customers were Detroit automakers, which used MVI's automated inspection guidance systems to control industrial robots.

By the mid-1980s MVI was one of the largest machine vision companies in the US. In 1984 Safeguard Scientifics bought 31.5% of the company; Safeguard had been founded in 1953 by Warren Musser and Frank Diamond to raise funds for small, promising businesses. To raise more capital for MVI, Safeguard and MVI's management took the company public in 1985. However, MVI soon ran into trouble as the machine vision industry slowed down. General Motors, the company's biggest customer, cut its orders, and MVI lost more than $13 million in 1986.

The following year MVI acquired New Jersey-based computer retailer TriStar Data Systems and Office Automation. The company moved its headquarters to New Jersey, changed its name to CompuCom Systems, and refocused on selling and supporting microcomputers.

CompuCom exited the machine vision business in 1988. It acquired CompuShop, a Dallas-based computer retailer, from Bell Atlantic the same year. CompuCom then relocated to Dallas.

In 1989 the company named Avery More (EVP of an Apple Computer reseller) president and co-CEO along with CompuShop CEO James Dixon. Safeguard extended its interest in the company that year to 66% (now 53%).

In 1991 CompuCom flirted with retailing but decided to abandon the market and focus on direct sales to corporate customers.

CompuCom expanded its networking business when it bought network integrator MicroSolutions in 1992 and International Micronet Systems two years later. When More left the company in 1993 to start his own venture capital firm, COO and reseller channel veteran Ed Anderson became CEO.

In 1995 the company bought network integrators in New Jersey and Texas. CompuCom and Unisys joined forces the next year to provide support services for multiple manufacturer desktop and network systems. The company also won a contract in 1996 to establish and operate two computer stores for the State of California (one in Los Angeles, the other in San Francisco). The next year the company added software management to its list of services.

In 1998, when sales expenses grew faster than revenues, the company laid off close to 10% of its workforce. The reorganization was partly to blame for a drop in profits that year.

Boosting its sales in 1999, CompuCom bought the resale products business of rival ENTEX Information Services (now part of Siemens) for $137 million. That year the company merged its ClientLink applications development subsidiary with Internet security services specialist E-Certify. Anderson left CompuCom to become president and CEO of E-Certify; later in 1999 a veteran of Computer Sciences Corporation, Edward Coleman, took over the CEO position.

Coleman assumed additional duties in 2000 when CompuCom's president and chief operating officer Thomas Lynch resigned his position. The following year the company acquired MicroAge Technology Services for $81 million.

OFFICERS

Chairman: Harry Wallaesa
President, CEO, and Director: J. Edward Coleman, age 49, $1,177,090 pay
SVP and Chief Information Officer: Don Flores
SVP and Chief Technology Officer: David W. Hall
SVP, Finance, CFO, Secretary, and Director: M. Lazane Smith, age 46, $589,320 pay
SVP, Consulting and Strategic Planning: Terry Schechinger
SVP, Human Resources: David A. Loeser, age 46, $400,000 pay
SVP, Marketing and Engagement Services: Patricia Hope Griffith
SVP, Sales: Anthony F. Pellegrini, age 58, $357,734 pay
SVP, Services: John F. McKenna, age 37, $400,090 pay
VP, Business Development and Supply Chain Management: Thomas Ducatelli
VP, Business Systems: Gary M. Samuelson
VP, Consulting Western Region: Mark Sandson
VP, Enterprise Help Desk: Meg Frantz
VP, Finance, Treasurer, and Controller: Daniel L. Celoni
VP, Financial Operations: Mark J. Loder
VP, Infrastructure: Jim H. Carey
VP, Integration and Distribution Services: John DiMuzio
VP, Outsourcing Business Development: Charles Jarrow
VP, Outsourcing Southern Region: Terence L. Jonker
Auditors: KPMG LLP

LOCATIONS

HQ: 7171 Forest Ln., Dallas, TX 75230
Phone: 972-856-3600 **Fax:** 972-856-5395
Web: www.compucom.com

CompuCom Systems has operations in New Jersey, North Carolina, Ohio, and Texas.

PRODUCTS/OPERATIONS

2000 Sales

	$ mil.	% of total
Products	2,439	90
Services	272	10
Total	**2,711**	**100**

Products
Computers
Mobile and wireless computing products
Networking equipment
Peripherals
Software

Services
Asset tracking
Configuration
Consulting
Distribution
Field engineering
Help desk support
Network management
Networking support
Product procurement
Software management

COMPETITORS

Accenture
Comark
Compaq
Computer Sciences
EDS
Hewlett-Packard
Ingram Micro

IBM
Merisel
Siemens
Software Spectrum
Tech Data
Unisys

HISTORICAL FINANCIALS & EMPLOYEES

Nasdaq: CMPC FYE: December 31	Annual Growth	12/91	12/92	12/93	12/94	12/95	12/96	12/97	12/98	12/99	12/00
Sales ($ mil.)	19.9%	529	713	1,016	1,256	1,442	1,995	1,950	2,255	2,908	2,711
Net income ($ mil.)	0.2%	5	7	11	15	21	31	35	0	12	5
Income as % of sales	—	0.9%	1.0%	1.1%	1.2%	1.4%	1.5%	1.8%	0.0%	0.4%	0.2%
Earnings per share ($)	(6.2%)	0.16	0.22	0.29	0.34	0.45	0.61	0.71	(0.01)	0.22	0.09
Stock price - FY high ($)	—	3.56	2.88	4.63	7.25	10.63	13.88	11.13	9.75	5.63	7.69
Stock price - FY low ($)	—	1.31	1.44	2.19	2.75	3.13	6.25	4.00	2.25	2.75	0.91
Stock price - FY close ($)	(6.1%)	2.25	2.19	4.06	3.13	9.50	10.75	8.25	3.50	4.13	1.28
P/E - high	—	22	13	13	17	20	21	15	—	26	85
P/E - low	—	8	6	6	6	6	9	5	—	13	10
Dividends per share ($)	—	0.00	0.00	0.00	0.00	0.00	0.00	0.00	0.00	0.00	0.00
Book value per share ($)	16.3%	1.22	1.39	1.78	2.80	3.14	3.61	4.56	4.43	4.64	4.73
Employees	16.2%	1,061	1,156	1,542	1,975	2,615	3,700	4,300	4,800	5,000	4,100

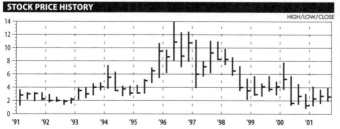

STOCK PRICE HISTORY
HIGH/LOW/CLOSE

2000 FISCAL YEAR-END

Debt ratio: 0.0%
Return on equity: 2.4%
Cash ($ mil.): 15
Current ratio: 1.57
Long-term debt ($ mil.): 0
No. of shares (mil.): 49
Dividends
  Yield: —
  Payout: —
Market value ($ mil.): 62

CONOCO INC.

OVERVIEW

Conoco is spinning a cocoon of oil and gas assets to secure its long-term growth. The Houston-based integrated energy company is engaged in oil and gas exploration, production, refining, marketing, and transportation. It has exploration activities in 20 countries. With proved reserves of about 3.7 billion barrels of oil equivalent, Conoco has major holdings in the Gulf of Mexico, South Texas, the North Sea, Venezuela, and Indonesia. The company gained 1 billion barrels of oil equivalent in proved reserves in 2001 by buying Gulf Canada Resources.

Conoco processes crude oil at four refineries in the US and one in the UK. It also has stakes in a refinery in Germany, two in the Czech Republic, and one in Malaysia, and it operates some 6,000 miles of pipeline. Conoco sells gasoline, diesel fuel, and other petroleum products through 5,000 outlets in the US, almost 2000 in Europe, and more than 100 in Thailand, under the Conoco, Jet, Seca, and Turkpetrol brands.

The company also is winging its way into power generation and wholesale marketing. Its Conoco Global Power unit markets and trades electricity and natural gas, and it develops and builds power plants, including a cogeneration plant in Texas for former parent DuPont.

Conoco is using its long-term oil-producing assets in the North Sea and Venezuela to fuel the expansion of its international exploration and production activities.

HISTORY

Isaac Elder Blake, an Easterner who had lost everything on a bad investment, came to Ogden, Utah, and founded Continental Oil & Transportation (CO&T) in 1875.

In 1885 CO&T merged with Standard Oil's operations in the Rockies and was reincorporated in Colorado as Continental Oil. The company tightened its grip on the Rocky Mountain area and by 1906 had taken over 98% of the western market. Its monopoly ended in 1911 when the US Supreme Court ordered Standard to divest several holdings: Continental was one of 34 independent oil companies created in 1913.

Seeing opportunity in autos, Continental built a gas station in 1914. Two years later it got into oil production when it bought United Oil, and by 1924 it had become fully integrated by merging with Mutual Oil, which owned production, refining, and distribution assets. Continental's biggest merger came in 1929 when it merged with Marland Oil of Oklahoma.

Continental expanded in the 1950s and 1960s, acquiring oil fields in Africa, the Middle East, and South America. It also bought gas station chains (SOPI, Jet, Seca, and others) across Europe.

Continental then diversified, acquiring American Agricultural Chemicals in 1963 and Consolidation Coal (Consol) in 1966. Restructuring in the 1970s into Conoco Chemical, Consol, and two petroleum divisions, the firm ramped up oil exploration and entered ventures to develop uranium. In 1979 it changed its name to Conoco.

In the late 1970s, Conoco undertook joint ventures with chemical titan DuPont and was acquired by DuPont in 1981 to forestall hostile takeover attempts by Mobil and Seagram. In the midst of a worldwide oil crisis, DuPont saw Conoco as a reliable source of crude oil. DuPont sold off $1.5 billion of Conoco's assets and absorbed Conoco Chemicals.

During the 1980s Conoco made big oil finds in the Gulf of Mexico, the North Sea, Indonesia, and Ecuador, but by 1990 it was spread thin among 30 countries. It refocused on 15 countries, including high-risk areas: It formed a venture with LUKOIL in 1991 to look for oil in the Russian Arctic and a 1996 deal to drill in disputed waters off Vietnam. Its largest overseas investment, a Malaysian refinery, was finished in 1998. Conoco began to pursue opportunities in electric power in 1995.

In 1998 DuPont spun off Conoco in what was the US's largest-ever IPO at the time (DuPont had completely divested its 70% stake by the next year). Meanwhile, oil prices dropped, and the newly independent Conoco laid off workers and slashed capital spending by about 20%.

The company announced major oil finds in offshore Venezuela and in the Gulf of Mexico in 1999, and in the North Sea in 2000. That year Conoco also acquired North Sea assets from Norsk Hydro and began expanding its oil exploration in Vietnamese waters.

In 2001 joint venture partners Conoco and Petronas agreed to acquire Statoil's 15% stake in the Melaka refinery in Malaysia, in which Conoco already held a 40% share. Later that year Conoco expanded its natural gas reserves by buying Gulf Canada Resources for $4.3 billion in cash and $2 billion in assumed debt.

Chairman, President, CEO, and Director:
  Archie W. Dunham, age 62, $4,200,000 pay
SEVP, Corporate Strategy and Development:
  Gary W. Edwards, age 59, $1,886,200 pay
EVP, Exploration and Production: Robert E. McKee III,
  age 54, $1,596,000 pay
EVP, Refining, Marketing, Supply, and Transportation:
  Jimmy W. Nokes, age 54, $1,219,200 pay
SVP, Finance and CFO: Robert W. Goldman, age 58,
  $747,400 pay
**SVP, Government Affairs, Corporate Strategy, and
  Communications:** J. Michael Stinson, age 57
SVP, Legal and General Counsel: Rick A. Harrington,
  age 56
**President, Exploration and Production, Africa, Asia
  Pacific, and Middle East:** Jim D. McColgin
President, Exploration and Production, Americas:
  Gary A. Merriman
President, Exploration and Production, Europe:
  Steven M. Theede
President, Refining and Marketing, Asia Pacific:
  George W. Paczkowski
President, Refining and Marketing, Europe:
  W. Rick Hamm
President, Refining and Marketing, North America:
  Richard W. Severance
VP, Business Development: Philip L. Frederickson
VP, Exploration and Production, Technology:
  John R. Hopkins
VP, Human Resources: Thomas C. Knudson, age 54
VP, Investor Relations: Thomas R. Henkel
**VP, Refining, Marketing, Supply and Transportation,
  Technology:** L. Duane Wilson
**VP and General Manager, Exploration and Production;
  Chairman and Managing Director, Conoco (U.K.)
  Ltd.:** George E. Watkins
Auditors: PricewaterhouseCoopers LLP

LOCATIONS

HQ: 600 N. Dairy Ashford, Houston, TX 77079
Phone: 281-293-1000   **Fax:** 281-293-1440
Web: www.conoco.com

2000 Sales

	$ mil.	% of total
Downstream		
US	17,556	43
Other countries	12,801	31
Upstream		
US	6,271	15
Other countries	4,497	11
Adjustments	(2,388)	—
Total	**38,737**	**100**

PRODUCTS/OPERATIONS

2000 Sales

	$ mil.	% of total
Refined products	23,627	61
Crude oil	6,894	18
Natural gas	5,785	15
Other	2,431	6
Total	**38,737**	**100**

COMPETITORS

Ashland	Occidental	Southern
BP	PETROBRAS	Company
Chevron	PDVSA	Sunoco
Eni	PEMEX	Texaco
Enron	Phillips	TOTAL FINA
Exxon Mobil	Petroleum	ELF
Kerr-McGee	Royal	Unocal
Norsk Hydro	Dutch/Shell	USX-Marathon

HISTORICAL FINANCIALS & EMPLOYEES

NYSE: COC FYE: December 31	Annual Growth	12/91	12/92	12/93	12/94	12/95	12/96	12/97	12/98	12/99	12/00
Sales ($ mil.)	10.4%	15,851	16,065	15,035	13,956	14,695	18,779	20,447	16,995	27,039	38,737
Net income ($ mil.)	10.2%	795	316	755	422	575	863	1,097	450	744	1,902
Income as % of sales	—	5.0%	2.0%	5.0%	3.0%	3.9%	4.6%	5.4%	2.6%	2.8%	4.9%
Earnings per share ($)	156.4%	—	—	—	—	—	—	—	—	1.17	3.00
Stock price - FY high ($)	—	—	—	—	—	—	—	—	—	29.38	29.94
Stock price - FY low ($)	—	—	—	—	—	—	—	—	—	20.75	19.00
Stock price - FY close ($)	16.3%	—	—	—	—	—	—	—	—	24.88	28.94
P/E - high	—	—	—	—	—	—	—	—	—	25	10
P/E - low	—	—	—	—	—	—	—	—	—	17	6
Dividends per share ($)	300.0%	—	—	—	—	—	—	—	—	0.19	0.76
Book value per share ($)	23.8%	—	—	—	—	—	—	—	—	7.28	9.01
Employees	3.2%	—	—	—	—	—	—	16,000	16,650	16,700	17,600

STOCK PRICE HISTORY

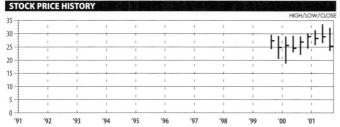

HIGH/LOW/CLOSE

2000 FISCAL YEAR-END

Debt ratio: 42.4%
Return on equity: 37.4%
Cash ($ mil.): 342
Current ratio: 0.81
Long-term debt ($ mil.): 4,138
No. of shares (mil.): 624
Dividends
  Yield: 2.6%
  Payout: 25.3%
Market value ($ mil.): 18,069

CONTINENTAL AIRLINES, INC.

OVERVIEW

Not content to drift, Continental Airlines plans to keep building on its six continuous years of profits. Based in Houston, the fifth-largest US carrier (behind United, American, Delta, and Northwest) offers 2,200 daily flights to more than 135 domestic and more than 90 international destinations, primarily from hubs in Cleveland, Houston, and Newark, New Jersey. Regional feeder Continental Express also operates out of those hubs with more than 1,000 daily departures to more than 115 US cities. Subsidiary Continental Micronesia serves the western Pacific from its hub in Guam.

The carrier is courting business travelers, upgrading and expanding its fleet, adding re-gional jets to its Continental Express fleet, and expanding international service.

Continental has an extensive marketing alliance with Northwest that includes code-sharing and shared frequent-flyer programs. Northwest, which in 2001 sold back shares that gave it a 55% voting stake in Continental, retains a 5% equity interest and the right to block the sale of Continental to a third party.

In anticipation of a reduced demand in air travel resulting from terrorist attacks on New York and Washington, DC, in September 2001, Continental is reducing its long-term flight schedule. The reduction has also forced the airline to lay off more than 21% of its workforce.

HISTORY

Varney Speed Lines, the fourth airline begun by Walter Varney, was founded in 1934. It became Continental Airlines three years later when Robert Six, whose own airline had folded during the Depression, bought 40% of the carrier. Six convinced his father-in-law, chairman of drugmaker Charles Pfizer Co., to lend him $90,000 for the stake in Varney.

In 1951 Continental spent $7.6 million to update its fleet, a sum equal to its profit that year. It was a bold move for a small airline in an industry moving toward ever-larger aircraft. Two years later Continental merged with Pioneer Airlines, adding routes to 16 cities in Texas and New Mexico. It also added jets in the late 1950s to compete on cross-country routes. To maintain its small Boeing 707 fleet, Continental developed a maintenance system that enabled it to fly the planes 15 hours a day, seven days a week.

In 1962 the carrier suffered its first crash. The next year it moved its headquarters from Denver to Los Angeles. A transport service contract with the US military during the Vietnam War led to the formation of Air Micronesia in 1968.

Economic downturn, industry deregulation, and rising fuel costs left Continental with a string of losses in the late 1970s (it would lose more than $500 million between 1978 and 1983). Over the objections of Continental's unions, Frank Lorenzo's Texas Air bought the company in 1982.

Texas Air had been founded in 1947 to provide service within Texas, and by 1970 it also flew to the West Coast and Mexico. Bankrupt two years later, the company was acquired by Lorenzo, who returned it to profitability by 1976 — just in time for airline deregulation in 1978.

When Continental's union employees went on strike in 1983, Lorenzo maneuvered the airline into Chapter 11. It emerged from bankruptcy in 1986 as a low-fare carrier with the industry's lowest labor costs. That year Texas Air bought Eastern Air Lines, People Express, and Frontier Airlines.

In 1990 Lorenzo resigned as head of the company, and Texas Air changed its name to Continental Airlines Holdings. With fuel prices soaring because of the Mideast conflict, Continental again filed for bankruptcy. Gordon Bethune became CEO in 1994 and piloted Continental to a comeback with an investment by Air Partners/Air Canada and with a reduction in routes and staff. In 1996 regional subsidiary Continental Express began replacing turboprops with jets from Embraer.

In 1997 Bethune's honeymoon with employees ended as the pilots union negotiated for an accelerated pay-raise schedule; a five-year contract was ratified in 1998. That year Northwest Airlines paid $370 million for 13.5% of Continental, beating a takeover bid from Delta. Meanwhile, Continental bought 20 Boeing aircraft and acquired stakes in airlines in Colombia and Panama.

The next year Continental launched its first Mideast route (to Tel Aviv) and sold its stake in the Amadeus computer reservation system. Labor relations remained smooth in 2000 as flight attendants ratified a new contract.

Northwest reduced its voting control of Continental to 5% in 2001, but maintained the right to block the sale of Continental to a third party. Also that year Continental announced plans to sell a minority stake in its ExpressJet unit, the parent of Continental Express, to the public.

Chairman and CEO; Chairman, ExpressJet:
Gordon M. Bethune, age 59
President: Lawrence W. Kellner, age 42
EVP and COO: C. D. McLean, age 60
EVP, Corporate: Jeffery A. Smisek, age 46
SVP and Chief Information Officer: Janet P. Wejman
SVP, Airport Services: Mark A. Erwin
SVP, Corporate Development: J. David Grizzle, age 47
SVP, Finance and Treasurer: Gerald Laderman
SVP, Finance: Jeff Misner
SVP, Flight Operations: Deborah L. McCoy, age 46
SVP, Human Resources and Labor Relations:
Michael H. Campbell
SVP, International: Barry P. Simon
SVP, Pricing and Revenue Management: Jim Compton,
age 45
SVP, Purchasing and Materials Services: Kuniaki Tsuruta
SVP, Sales and Distribution: Bonnie S. Reitz
SVP, Scheduling: Glen Hauenstein, age 40
SVP, Technical Operations: George L. Mason
SVP, Worldwide Corporate Communications:
John E. Walker
VP, General Counsel, and Assistant Secretary:
Jennifer Vogel
**Staff VP, Sales and Marketing, Latin America and the
Caribbean:** Pete C. Garcia
Auditors: Ernst & Young LLP

LOCATIONS

HQ: 1600 Smith St., Dept. HQSEO, Houston, TX 77002
Phone: 713-324-5000   **Fax:** 713-324-2637
Web: www.continental.com

2000 Sales

	$ mil.	% of total
US	6,835	69
Atlantic	1,370	14
Latin America	1,022	10
Pacific	672	7
Total	**9,899**	**100**

PRODUCTS/OPERATIONS

2000 Sales

	$ mil.	% of total
Passenger	9,308	94
Cargo & mail	360	4
Other	231	2
Total	**9,899**	**100**

Major Subsidiaries
Continental Micronesia, Inc. (air service in the Pacific)
ExpressJet Holdings, Inc.
   Continental Express (regional airline)

COMPETITORS

Air Canada	Northwest Airlines
AirTran Holdings	Qantas
All Nippon Airways	SAS
AMR	Singapore Airlines
British Airways	Southwest Airlines
Cathay Pacific	Swissair Group
Delta	TWA
JAL	UAL
Lufthansa	US Airways

HISTORICAL FINANCIALS & EMPLOYEES

NYSE: CAL FYE: December 31	Annual Growth	12/91	12/92	12/93	12/94	12/95	12/96	12/97	12/98	12/99	12/00
Sales ($ mil.)	6.8%	5,487	5,575	3,907	5,670	5,825	6,360	7,213	7,951	8,639	9,899
Net income ($ mil.)	—	(306)	(125)	(39)	(613)	224	319	385	383	485	342
Income as % of sales	—	—	—	—	—	3.8%	5.0%	5.3%	4.8%	5.6%	3.5%
Earnings per share ($)	—	—	—	(1.17)	(23.76)	6.29	4.11	4.99	5.02	6.20	5.45
Stock price - FY high ($)	—	—	—	15.25	13.63	23.75	31.44	50.19	65.13	48.00	54.81
Stock price - FY low ($)	—	—	—	6.50	3.75	3.25	19.44	27.00	28.88	30.00	29.00
Stock price - FY close ($)	26.0%	—	—	10.25	4.63	21.75	28.25	48.13	33.50	44.38	51.63
P/E - high	—	—	—	—	—	3	6	7	10	7	10
P/E - low	—	—	—	—	—	0	4	4	5	4	5
Dividends per share ($)	—	—	—	0.00	0.00	0.00	0.00	0.00	0.00	0.00	0.00
Book value per share ($)	20.8%	—	—	5.29	2.93	6.25	10.96	15.55	18.53	24.33	19.85
Employees	4.6%	36,300	38,300	43,100	37,800	32,300	35,400	39,300	43,900	51,275	54,300

STOCK PRICE HISTORY

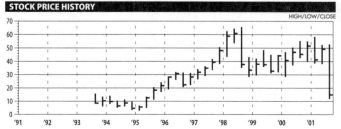

HIGH/LOW/CLOSE

2000 FISCAL YEAR-END

Debt ratio: 75.7%
Return on equity: 24.8%
Cash ($ mil.): 1,371
Current ratio: 0.83
Long-term debt ($ mil.): 3,616
No. of shares (mil.): 58
Dividends
   Yield: —
   Payout: —
Market value ($ mil.): 3,018

COOPER INDUSTRIES, INC.

OVERVIEW

Cooper Industries can light up your life. The Houston-based company's electrical division (about 80% of sales) makes electrical and circuit-protection products and lighting for residential and industrial use, as well as electrical power and distribution products for use by utilities. Its tools and hardware division stocks Apex sockets, Crescent wrenches, Plumb hammers, and Weller soldering equipment. It also produces power tools sold under the Airetool and Buckeye brands and metal support products under the B-Line name.

On its shopping sprees, Cooper typically focuses on firms that fit within its core operations, generate enough cash to cover the capital investment, and have potential to add to its earnings within a year. Hurt by the slow economy, Cooper Industries is cutting jobs, moving more production to Mexico, and having components made by Asian joint-venture partners. For the second time in two years, tool maker Danaher offered to acquire Cooper and was rejected. Cooper is mulling other options.

HISTORY

In 1833 Charles Cooper sold a horse for $50 and borrowed additional money to open a foundry with his brother Elias in Mount Vernon, Ohio. Known as C. & E. Cooper, the company made plows, hog troughs, maple syrup kettles, stoves, and wagon boxes.

C. & E. Cooper began making steam engines in the 1840s for mill and farm use; it later adapted its engines for wood-burning locomotives. In 1868 the company built its first Corliss steam engine, and in 1875 it introduced the first steam-powered farm tractor. By 1900 C. & E. Cooper sold its steam engines in the US and overseas. The company debuted an internal combustion engine-compressor in 1909 for natural gas pipelines.

In the 1920s the company became the #1 seller of compression engines for oil and gas pipelines. A 1929 merger with Bessemer (small engines) created Cooper-Bessemer, which made diesel engines for power boats.

Diversification began in 1959 with the purchase of Rotor Tools. Cooper adopted its current name in 1965 and moved its headquarters to Houston in 1967. It went on to buy other firms, including Lufkin Rule (measuring tapes, 1967), Crescent (wrenches, 1968), and Weller (soldering tools, 1970).

Cooper's 1979 purchase of Gardner-Denver gave it a strong footing in oil-drilling and mining equipment, and the addition of Crouse-Hinds in 1981 was key to its diversification into electrical materials. The decline in oil prices in the early 1980s caused sales to drop, but Cooper stayed profitable due to its tools and electrical products.

Cooper's electrical segment expanded with the 1985 purchase of McGraw-Edison, maker of consumer products (Buss fuses) and heavy transmission gear for electrical utilities. Growth continued as it added RTE (electrical equipment, 1988), Cameron Iron Works (oil-

drilling equipment, 1989), and Ferramentas Belzer do Brasil (hand-tool maker, 1992).

Expanding into auto parts, Cooper bought Champion Spark Plug (1989) and Moog (auto replacement parts, 1992). From 1991 to 1993, the company divested 11 businesses and bought 13. In 1994 it spun off Gardner-Denver Industrial Machinery, sold Cameron Forged Products, and added Abex Friction Products (brake materials) and Zanxx (lighting components) to its auto parts line.

Cooper spun off Cooper Cameron (petroleum equipment) in 1995. The next year Cooper bought electrical fuse supplier Karp Electric, tool manufacturer Master Power, and electrical hub maker Myers Electric Products. Company veteran John Riley took over as chairman that year. Cooper added eight acquisitions in 1997, and some, such as Menvier-Swain Group (emergency lights and alarms, UK), helped to bolster its electrical segment. Despite its growth, the company trimmed its workforce by 30% that year.

Cooper completed 11 acquisitions in 1998 and 10 in 1999; among them were the tool business of Global Industrial Technologies (Quackenbush and Rotor Tool brands), Apparatebau Hundsbach (electronic sensors) and Metronix Elektronik (power tool controls), and several lighting firms. In the meantime, the company sold its automotive operations to Federal-Mogul.

In 2000 Cooper acquired B-Line Systems from Sigma-Aldrich for around $425 million. Early in 2001 the company announced plans to cut about 1,000 jobs by year end. In August tool maker Danaher offered to acquire Cooper in a deal worth about $5.5 billion. Cooper rejected the offer within days and stated that it would explore other options, including "a merger, sale, a strategic alliance, or even an acquisition."

Chairman, President, and CEO: H. John Riley Jr.,
age 60, $1,842,500 pay
COO: Ralph E. Jackson Jr., age 59, $823,463 pay
SVP and CFO: D. Bradley McWilliams, age 59,
$604,200 pay
SVP, General Counsel, and Secretary:
Diane K. Schumacher, age 47, $515,300 pay
SVP, Human Resources: David R. Sheil Jr., age 44,
$481,717 pay
**SVP, Strategic Planning and New Venture Development
Officer:** David A. White Jr., age 59
**SVP, Strategic Sourcing and Chief Information
Technology Officer:** Terry A. Klebe, age 46
VP and Controller: Jeffrey B. Levos, age 40
VP and Treasurer: Alan J. Hill, age 56
VP, Environmental Affairs and Risk Management:
Robert W. Teets, age 50
VP, Information Systems: Terrance M. Smith, age 51
VP, Investor Relations: Richard J. Bajenski, age 48
VP, Marketing: John J. Peterson
Auditors: Ernst & Young LLP

LOCATIONS

HQ: 600 Travis, Ste. 5800, Houston, TX 77002
Phone: 713-209-8400   **Fax:** 713-209-8995
Web: www.cooperindustries.com

2000 Sales

	$ mil.	% of total
US	3,500	78
UK	233	5
Germany	180	4
Canada	159	4
Other countries	388	9
Total	**4,460**	**100**

PRODUCTS/OPERATIONS

2000 Sales

	$ mil.	% of total
Electrical products	3,659	82
Tools & hardware	801	18
Total	**4,460**	**100**

Selected Products and Brands

Electrical Products
Architectural and landscape lighting (Lumiere)
Aviation lighting products (Crouse-Hinds)
Electric fuses (B&S, Edison, Karp, Mercury)
Electrical construction materials (CEAG, Crouse-Hinds)
Emergency lighting and fire-detection systems (JSB,
Luminox, Menvier)
Fire-detection systems (Fulleon, Nugelec, Transmould)
Fluorescent lighting (Metalux)
Fuses (Buss, Kearney)
Indoor and outdoor HID lighting (McGraw-Edison)
Lighting systems (Iris)
Recessed and track-lighting fixtures (Halo)
Security equipment (Menvier, Scantronic)
Wiring devices (Arrow Hart)

COMPETITORS

ABB	Illinois Tool	Siemens
Black & Decker	Works	SL Industries
Danaher	Ingersoll-Rand	Snap-on
Eaton	Newell	Stanley Works
Emerson	Rubbermaid	Waxman
GE	Philips	
	Electronics	

HISTORICAL FINANCIALS & EMPLOYEES

NYSE: CBE FYE: December 31	Annual Growth	12/91	12/92	12/93	12/94	12/95	12/96	12/97	12/98	12/99	12/00
Sales ($ mil.)	(3.5%)	6,163	6,159	6,274	4,588	4,886	5,284	5,289	3,651	3,869	4,460
Net income ($ mil.)	(1.1%)	393	(229)	367	(20)	94	315	395	423	332	357
Income as % of sales	—	6.4%	—	5.9%	—	1.9%	6.0%	7.5%	11.6%	8.6%	8.0%
Earnings per share ($)	10.1%	1.60	(3.55)	2.15	(0.64)	0.84	2.77	3.26	3.69	3.50	3.80
Stock price - FY high ($)	—	58.00	59.38	54.75	52.25	40.50	44.63	59.69	70.38	56.75	47.00
Stock price - FY low ($)	—	38.50	41.75	45.63	31.63	32.88	34.13	40.00	36.88	39.63	29.38
Stock price - FY close ($)	(2.4%)	57.25	47.38	49.25	34.00	36.75	42.13	49.00	47.69	40.44	45.94
P/E - high	—	19	—	20	—	48	15	18	19	16	12
P/E - low	—	13	—	17	—	39	12	12	10	11	8
Dividends per share ($)	2.1%	1.14	1.22	1.30	1.32	1.65	0.99	1.32	1.32	1.32	1.38
Book value per share ($)	(4.3%)	30.26	25.28	26.13	23.44	15.90	17.50	21.44	16.60	18.50	20.39
Employees	(4.9%)	53,900	52,900	49,500	40,800	40,400	42,000	41,200	28,100	30,100	34,250

STOCK PRICE HISTORY

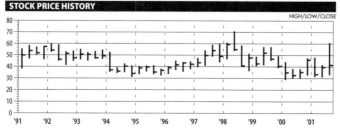

HIGH/LOW/CLOSE

2000 FISCAL YEAR-END

Debt ratio: 40.6%
Return on equity: 19.6%
Cash ($ mil.): 26
Current ratio: 1.48
Long-term debt ($ mil.): 1,301
No. of shares (mil.): 93
Dividends
  Yield: 3.0%
  Payout: 36.3%
Market value ($ mil.): 4,291

DAVE & BUSTER'S, INC.

Food, fun, and foamy heads all come together at Dave & Buster's (D&B).

The Dallas-based company owns and operates about 30 entertainment centers in more than a dozen states that combine casual dining, full bar service, and an adult game center under one roof.

D&B is best known for its immense game rooms that include video games and motion simulators, traditional parlor games (such as billiards and shuffleboard), and games of skill in which patrons can receive coupons redeemable for merchandise.

Its food menu includes such fare as burgers, pasta, seafood, and steak, as well as appetizers, salads, and soups, while its bar menu offers a variety of beer and cocktails. (Alcoholic drinks account for almost 20% of sales.) Its locations draw some 16 million patrons each year.

After declining results in 1999, the company pulled back on its expansion efforts to focus on customer service, cost management, and enhancing its existing locations. In addition to continuing to concentrate on those areas, D&B launched Internet versions of its redemption games on its Web site as part of an effort to strengthen its customer relationships.

Texas investor Lacy Harber owns about 10% of the company, and UK billionaire Joseph Lewis has an 8% stake through his investment vehicle Mandarin. Investor Jeffrey Feinberg owns about 5% of Dave & Buster's. Co-founders and co-chairmen David Corriveau and James "Buster" Corley each own about 4%.

Late in the 1970s David Corriveau and James "Buster" Corley were running two businesses located next to each other in Little Rock, Arkansas. Corriveau operated a billiards and game parlor called Slick Willie's, and Corley ran Buster's, a restaurant that Corriveau helped finance. The two neighbors noticed a large amount of traffic between the two locales, and the idea of Dave & Buster's was formed.

The first D&B opened in a converted Dallas warehouse in 1982; the second opened six years later.

Eager for expansion, Corriveau and Corley sold an 80% stake in the business to Dallas retailer Edison Brothers in 1990. Edison grew weary of the cash drain, however, and divested its stake in 1995. D&B went public that year.

The company picked up its expansion pace in 1996, opening three more locations. The next year the first West Coast D&B opened in Ontario, California, and Bass (now Six Continents) opened the first international D&B in the UK (a second UK location opened in 1998).

In 1998 D&B signed a franchise agreement with TaiMall Development to open seven locations across the Pacific Rim (the first of which opened that year in Taiwan) and an agreement with SVAG Development to open several stores in Germany, Switzerland, and Austria.

New stores opened in Atlanta; Austin and San Antonio, Texas; St. Louis; and Jacksonville in 1999.

D&B also inked an agreement with Canadian firm Funtime Hospitality to open 10 locations in Canada (the first of which opened mid-2000 in Toronto).

Results for FY 1999 were disappointing, however, causing the company to slow its expansion plans in 2000. That year Bass terminated its license agreement and closed the UK locations. SVAG cancelled its development deal as well the next year.

Despite these setbacks Dave & Buster's continued to open locations, although at a slower pace.

The company opened stores in Milpitas, California (a suburb of San Jose); Westminster, Colorado (north of Denver); Pittsburgh; and San Diego in 2000.

In 2001 the company opened stores in Cleveland; Frisco, Texas; Honolulu; and Miami. Also that year the company teamed with online game company Arcade Planet (which is co-owned by Oracle CEO Larry Ellison) to offer skill-based games via the Dave & Buster's Web site.

The Web site allows players to buy virtual tokens to play such games as solitaire and trivia and then to redeem coupons won playing the games to buy prizes, including apparel, toys, and electronics, online or at company stores.

OFFICERS

Co-Chairman, Co-CEO, and President:
David O. Corriveau, age 49, $391,346 pay
Co-Chairman, Co-CEO, and COO: James W. Corley,
age 50, $391,346 pay
VP, CFO, and Secretary: Charles Michel, age 47,
$186,977 pay
VP Accounting and Controller: Jeffrey A. Jahnke, age 46
VP Amusements: Reginald M. Moultrie, age 45
VP Business Development: Vicki Johnson
VP Human Resources: Nancy J. Duricic, age 46
VP Information Technology: Barbara G. Core, age 42
VP International Operations and Beverage Operations:
Cory J. Haynes, age 40
VP Kitchen Operations: J. Michael Plunkett, age 50
VP Marketing: Stuart A. Myers, age 40
VP Operations: Sterling R. Smith, age 48, $187,115 pay
VP Purchasing and Store Support: Barry N. Carter,
age 53
VP Real Estate: Bryan L. Spain, age 53, $140,988 pay
VP Training and New Store Openings: R. Lee Pitts,
age 36
Treasurer: Craig C. Rawls, age 32
Auditors: Ernst & Young LLP

LOCATIONS

HQ: 2481 Manana Dr., Dallas, TX 75220
Phone: 214-357-9588   **Fax:** 214-350-0941
Web: www.daveandbusters.com

2001 Locations

	No.
California	5
Texas	5
Colorado	2
Florida	2
Georgia	2
Illinois	2
Ohio	2
Pennsylvania	2
Maryland	1
Michigan	1
Missouri	1
New York	1
Rhode Island	1
Total	**27**

PRODUCTS/OPERATIONS

2001 Sales

	$ mil.	% of total
Food & beverage		
Food & non-alcoholic drinks	111	33
Alcoholic beverages	57	17
Amusement & other	164	50
Total	**332**	**100**

COMPETITORS

AMF Bowling	Jillian's Entertainment
Champps Entertainment	Planet Hollywood
Hard Rock Cafe	Total Entertainment
HOB Entertainment	Restaurant
Hooters	Walt Disney

HISTORICAL FINANCIALS & EMPLOYEES

NYSE: DAB FYE: Sunday nearest February 1	Annual Growth	1/92	1/93	1/94	1/95	1/96	1/97	1/98	1/99	1/00	1/01
Sales ($ mil.)	33.0%	26	33	49	49	53	89	129	182	247	332
Net income ($ mil.)	39.8%	1	1	2	3	3	6	9	14	5	12
Income as % of sales	—	2.4%	3.6%	4.9%	5.1%	5.5%	7.1%	6.9%	7.5%	2.1%	3.7%
Earnings per share ($)	22.6%	—	—	—	—	0.34	0.58	0.76	1.03	0.39	0.94
Stock price - FY high ($)	—	—	—	—	—	14.84	19.26	27.63	27.75	29.38	12.25
Stock price - FY low ($)	—	—	—	—	—	7.42	9.34	12.67	10.50	5.06	6.00
Stock price - FY close ($)	0.5%	—	—	—	—	9.50	14.09	21.19	22.00	6.75	9.75
P/E - high	—	—	—	—	—	44	33	36	27	39	13
P/E - low	—	—	—	—	—	22	16	16	10	7	6
Dividends per share ($)	—	—	—	—	—	0.00	0.00	0.00	0.00	0.00	0.00
Book value per share ($)	14.6%	—	—	—	—	6.33	6.92	10.25	11.13	11.57	12.54
Employees	32.0%	—	—	—	1,250	2,800	2,800	3,100	5,000	5,900	6,600

STOCK PRICE HISTORY

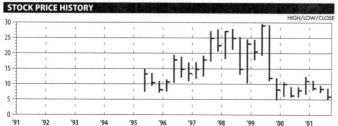

HIGH/LOW/CLOSE

2001 FISCAL YEAR-END

Debt ratio: 39.0%
Return on equity: 7.8%
Cash ($ mil.): 3
Current ratio: 1.20
Long-term debt ($ mil.): 104
No. of shares (mil.): 13
Dividends
  Yield: —
  Payout: —
Market value ($ mil.): 126

DELL COMPUTER CORPORATION

OVERVIEW

The road to Dell is paved with a good invention. Round Rock, Texas-based Dell Computer makes desktop PCs (almost half of sales), notebooks, network servers, and storage devices that it sells to customers ranging from home users to large corporations. It also sells refurbished computers, markets third-party peripherals and software, and offers consulting and support services. With the industry-standard Wintel platform (Microsoft Windows operating system and Intel microprocessor) as its foundation, Dell competes with rival Compaq Computer (which is being acquired by Hewlett-Packard) to be the leading PC maker worldwide.

Entrepreneurial wunderkind Michael Dell pioneered the direct sales model for computers and took the company from his dorm room to the top of the PC heap by keeping it focused on a simple formula: eliminate the middleman

and sell for less. Dell's built-to-order boxes allow for lower inventories, lower costs, and higher profit margins — elements that leave Dell well-armed for price wars that characterize the volatile computer sector. But an industry slide in PC sales has Dell cutting more than prices. After enjoying average annual sales increases of almost 60% during the 1990s, Dell's revenue growth has slowed considerably and for the first time in the company's history it is laying off workers.

To soften the blow of PC swings, Dell has put increasing emphasis on server computers and storage devices for enterprises. The company also is looking to international revenue to supplant sales in the PC-saturated US market.

Founder and chairman Dell, who is the longest-tenured CEO at any major US computer company, owns 12% of the company.

HISTORY

At age 13 Michael Dell was already a successful businessman. From his parents' home in Houston, Dell ran a mail-order stamp trading business that, within a few months, grossed more than $2,000. At 16 he sold newspaper subscriptions and at 17 Dell bought his first BMW. When he enrolled at the University of Texas in 1983, he was thoroughly bitten by the entrepreneurial bug.

Dell started college as a pre-med student but found time to establish a business selling random-access memory (RAM) chips and disk drives for IBM PCs. He bought products at cost from IBM dealers, who were required at the time to order from IBM large monthly quotas of PCs, which frequently exceeded demand. Dell resold his stock through newspapers and computer magazines at 10%-15% below retail.

By April 1984 Dell's dorm room computer components business was grossing about $80,000 a month — enough to persuade him to drop out of college. Soon he started making and selling IBM clones under the brand name PC's Limited. Dell sold his machines directly to consumers rather than through retail outlets, as most manufacturers did. By eliminating the retail markup, Dell could sell PCs at about 40% of the price of an IBM.

The company was plagued by management changes during the mid-1980s. Renamed Dell Computer, it added international sales offices in 1987. In 1988 the company started selling to larger customers, including government agencies. That year Dell went public.

The company tripped in 1990, reporting a

64% drop in profits. Sales were growing — but so were costs, mostly because of efforts to design a PC using proprietary components and reduced instruction set computer (RISC) chips. Also, the company's warehouses were oversupplied. Within a year Dell turned itself around by cutting inventories and introducing new products.

Dell entered the retail arena by letting Soft Warehouse (now CompUSA) in 1990 and office supply chain Staples in 1991 sell its PCs at mail-order prices. Also that year Dell opened a plant in Ireland. In 1992 Xerox agreed to sell Dell machines in Latin America. Dell opened subsidiaries in Japan and Australia in 1993. The computer maker abandoned retail stores in 1994 to refocus on its mail-order origins. It also retooled its troubled notebook computer line and introduced servers.

In 1996 the company started selling PCs through its Web site. In 1998 the company stepped up manufacturing in the Americas and Europe and added a production and customer facility in China. In 1999 the company made its first acquisition — storage area network equipment maker ConvergeNet. Dell broadened its high-end network servers and Internet-related services offerings, and formed a division for its storage operations in 2000.

Faced with slumping PC sales in early 2001, the company eliminated 1,700 jobs — about 4% of its workforce. Soon after it announced it would cut as many as 4,000 additional positions.

OFFICERS

Chairman and CEO: Michael S. Dell, age 36, $2,560,770 pay
Counselor to the CEO and Director: Morton L. Topfer, $872,500 pay
Vice Chairman, President, and COO: Kevin B. Rollins, age 48, $1,847,385 pay
Vice Chairman: James T. Vanderslice, age 60, $1,780,327 pay (prior to title change)
SVP and CFO: James M. Schneider, age 48
SVP and Chief Information Officer: Randall D. Mott, age 44
SVP; President, Europe, Middle East, and Africa; Co-General Manager, Worldwide Home and Small Business Group: Paul D. Bell, age 40
SVP; Co-President, Asia-Pacific/Japan: Charles H. Saunders, age 57
SVP; General Manager, US Relationship Group: Joseph A. Marengi, age 47, $923,701 pay
SVP; Co-General Manager, Small and Medium Business Group: Frank Muehleman, age 43
SVP, Enterprise Systems Group: Michael D. Lambert, age 54
SVP, Home and Small Business Group: Rosendo G. Parra, age 41
SVP, Human Resources: Paul D. McKinnon, age 50
SVP, Law and Administration and Secretary: Thomas B. Green, age 46
SVP, Relationship Group: William J. Amelio, age 43
SVP, Strategy and Business Development; Co-Managing Director, Dell Ventures: Thomas J. Meredith, age 50, $435,000 pay (prior to title change)
VP; General Manager, Americas International: Lawrence A. Pentland, age 42
VP, Development, Server Products: Randall D. Groves, age 44
Auditors: PricewaterhouseCoopers LLP

LOCATIONS

HQ: 1 Dell Way, Round Rock, TX 78682
Phone: 512-338-4400   **Fax:** 512-728-3653
Web: www.dell.com

Dell Computer has offices in more than 30 countries, with manufacturing facilities in Brazil, China, Ireland, Malaysia, and the US.

2001 Sales

	$ mil.	% of total
Americas	22,871	72
Europe	6,399	20
Asia/Pacific	2,618	8
Total	**31,888**	**100**

PRODUCTS/OPERATIONS

2001 Sales

	$ mil.	% of total
Desktop computers	15,452	49
Notebooks	8,572	27
Enterprise systems	5,511	17
Other	2,353	7
Total	**31,888**	**100**

COMPETITORS

Acer	Hewlett-Packard	SGI
Apple Computer	Hitachi	Sony
Bull	IBM	StorageTek
Compaq	Legend Holdings	Sun
EMC	Matsushita	Microsystems
Fujitsu	NEC	Toshiba
Gateway	SANYO	Unisys

HISTORICAL FINANCIALS & EMPLOYEES

Nasdaq: DELL FYE: Sunday nearest January 31	Annual Growth	1/92	1/93	1/94	1/95	1/96	1/97	1/98	1/99	1/00	1/01
Sales ($ mil.)	48.8%	890	2,014	2,873	3,475	5,296	7,759	12,327	18,243	25,265	31,888
Net income ($ mil.)	51.8%	51	102	(36)	149	272	518	944	1,460	1,666	2,177
Income as % of sales	—	5.7%	5.0%	—	4.3%	5.1%	6.7%	7.7%	8.0%	6.6%	6.8%
Earnings per share ($)	43.8%	0.03	0.05	(0.02)	0.05	0.09	0.17	0.32	0.53	0.61	0.79
Stock price - FY high ($)	—	0.38	0.78	0.77	0.75	1.54	4.52	12.98	50.19	55.00	59.69
Stock price - FY low ($)	—	0.21	0.23	0.22	0.30	0.62	0.84	3.74	12.61	31.38	16.25
Stock price - FY close ($)	62.5%	0.33	0.72	0.34	0.67	0.86	4.13	12.43	50.00	38.44	26.13
P/E - high	—	13	16	—	13	17	24	36	87	83	69
P/E - low	—	7	5	—	5	7	4	10	22	48	19
Dividends per share ($)	—	0.00	0.00	0.00	0.00	0.00	0.00	0.00	0.00	0.00	0.00
Book value per share ($)	37.9%	0.12	0.16	0.19	0.26	0.33	0.29	0.50	0.91	2.06	2.16
Employees	33.5%	2,970	4,650	5,980	6,400	8,400	10,350	16,000	24,400	36,500	40,000

STOCK PRICE HISTORY

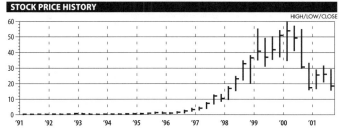

HIGH/LOW/CLOSE

2001 FISCAL YEAR-END

Debt ratio: 8.3%
Return on equity: 39.8%
Cash ($ mil.): 4,910
Current ratio: 1.45
Long-term debt ($ mil.): 509
No. of shares (mil.): 2,601
Dividends
 Yield: —
 Payout: —
Market value ($ mil.): 67,964

D.R. HORTON, INC.

OVERVIEW

D.R. Horton rarely hears a "Who?" anymore. The rapidly growing Arlington, Texas-based home builder is among the largest in the US and will stand even taller with its planned acquisition of Schuler Homes. Through its 46 divisions, the company builds in nearly 40 markets in more than 20 states. Although D.R. Horton sells mostly entry-level and move-up homes, it also builds luxury models costing up to $800,000. Its homes range in size from 1,000 sq. ft. to 5,000 sq. ft., and the average price is about $182,600. The company also provides mortgage financing and title services, and is also building a small number of condominium projects.

Even though the company has been experiencing a major growth spurt (its sales have more than tripled since 1997), D.R. Horton still sticks to its original strategy: letting buyers customize their homes. The company also gives a great amount of leeway to its divisional managers, allowing them to run their businesses with minimal interference from the home office, and counting on them to understand local tastes and build strong relationships with local contractors.

D.R. Horton is also investing in cyberspace. It has joined with several other major homebuilders to create Builder Homesite, an e-commerce site for the homebuilding industry. And it has invested in other online companies, including Primis, a provider of services to mortgage bankers. Founder Donald Horton owns about 13% of the company; his brother Terrill Horton has a 6% stake.

HISTORY

Donald R. Horton was selling homes in Fort Worth, Texas, when he hit upon a strategy for increasing sales — add options to a basic floor plan. In 1978 he borrowed $33,000 to build his first home, added a bay window for an additional charge, and sold the home for $44,000. Donald soon added floor plans and options that appealed to regional preferences. By the end of 1979 the company had built an additional 19 homes.

The company concentrated on building homes in the Dallas/Fort Worth area in the early and mid-1980s. However, the depressed Texas market drove it to expand beyond DFW in 1987, when it entered the then-hot Phoenix market. It continued to expand into the Southeast, Mid-Atlantic, Midwest, and West in the late 1980s and early 1990s. By 1991 Horton and his family owned more than 25 companies that were combined as D.R. Horton, which went public in 1992.

D.R. Horton acquired six geographically diverse construction firms in 1994 and 1995. In 1996 the company started a mortgage services joint venture, expanded its title operations, and added three more firms.

In 1998 the company bought four builders, including Scottsdale, Arizona-based Continental Homes for $583 million. Continental had been expanding beyond its Arizona and Southern California base and had entered the lucrative retirement community market. After the Continental purchase, Donald Horton stepped down as president, remaining chairman. Richard Beckwitt took over as president, and Donald Tomnitz became CEO. In 1999 the company acquired Century Title and Midwest builder Cambridge Properties, the largest homebuilder in the Chicago area, for $55 million in stock and $103 million in assumed debt.

In 2000 D.R. Horton teamed with several of the nation's largest homebuilders, including Kaufman and Broad, Pulte, and Centex to create Builder Homesite, a business-to-business Web site serving the homebuilding industry. The site allows users, including contractors, distributors, wholesalers, and manufacturers, to buy and sell building materials, and find subcontractors and other labor.

Also in 2000 D.R. Horton sold its St. Louis assets to McBride & Son Enterprises after spending five years trying to break into the St. Louis home building market. That year Tomnitz took over the duties of president when Beckwitt retired.

The next year the company gained home building operations in Houston and Phoenix when it bought Emerald Builders. Also in 2001 D.R. Horton acquired Fortress-Florida, the leading homebuilder in Jacksonville.

In late 2001 D.R. Horton announced plans to buy Schuler Homes for $1.2 billion, including debt. The deal will make D.R. Horton the #2 residential builder in the US, after Pulte Homes.

Chairman: Donald R. Horton, age 50, $1,170,367 pay
Vice Chairman, President, and CEO: Donald J. Tomnitz, age 52, $930,292 pay
EVP, CFO, and Treasurer: Samuel R. Fuller, age 57, $300,583 pay
EVP Investor Relations: Stacey H. Dwyer, age 34, $112,000 pay
VP and Assistant Controller: Steve Lovett
President, Financial Services: Randy Present
President, Northeast Region: George Seagraves
President, South Region: Bruce Dickson
President, Southwest Region: Timothy C. Westfall
President, West Region: Thomas F. Noon
Chief Information Officer: Felix Vasquez
Manager Human Resources: Paula Hunter-Perkins
Auditors: Ernst & Young LLP

LOCATIONS

HQ: 1901 Ascension Blvd., Ste. 100, Arlington, TX 76006
Phone: 817-856-8200   **Fax:** 817-856-8249
Web: www.drhorton.com

D.R. Horton operates in 22 states and in the District of Columbia.

2000 Sales

	% of total
Southwest	33
West	24
Mid-Atlantic	17
Southeast	14
Midwest	12
Total	**100**

PRODUCTS/OPERATIONS

2000 Sales

	% of total
Home sales	96
Land/lots sales	3
Financial services	1
Total	**100**

Selected Subsidiaries
Century Title Agency, Inc.
CH Mortgage Company
Continental Homes, Inc.
DHI Ranch, Ltd.
DRH Mortgage LLC
DRH Realty Company, Inc.
DRH Southwest Construction, Inc.
Encore II, Inc.
GP-Encore, Inc.
Grand Realty Incorporated
KDB Homes, Inc.
Metro Title, LLC
Missouri Meadows, Ltd.
Travis County Title Company

Operating Divisions
Arappco Homes
Cambridge Homes
Continental Homes
Dobson Builders
Milburn Homes
Regency Homes
SGS Communities
Torrey Homes
Trimark Communities

COMPETITORS

Beazer Homes
Centex
Century Builders
Del Webb
George Wimpey
Hovnanian Enterprises
J. F. Shea
KB Home
Lennar
M.D.C. Holdings
M I Schottenstein Homes
NVR
Pulte Homes
Ryland
Toll Brothers

HISTORICAL FINANCIALS & EMPLOYEES

NYSE: DHI FYE: September 30	Annual Growth	12/91	12/92	*9/93	9/94	9/95	9/96	9/97	9/98	9/99	9/00
Sales ($ mil.)	45.6%	124	183	190	393	437	547	837	2,177	3,156	3,654
Net income ($ mil.)	47.0%	6	9	9	18	21	27	36	93	160	192
Income as % of sales	—	4.7%	5.0%	4.7%	4.5%	4.7%	5.0%	4.3%	4.3%	5.1%	5.2%
Earnings per share ($)	28.0%	—	0.39	0.32	0.64	0.69	0.93	1.15	1.56	2.50	2.81
Stock price - FY high ($)	—	—	6.18	9.53	11.40	10.50	11.92	17.25	24.94	23.00	21.00
Stock price - FY low ($)	—	—	3.85	3.85	5.82	5.36	7.50	8.63	15.00	10.63	10.00
Stock price - FY close ($)	15.7%	—	5.36	9.09	7.73	9.95	9.75	15.75	16.00	12.94	17.19
P/E - high	—	—	16	30	18	15	10	13	14	9	7
P/E - low	—	—	10	12	9	8	7	7	9	4	4
Dividends per share ($)	—	—	0.00	0.00	0.00	0.00	0.00	0.04	0.09	0.11	0.15
Book value per share ($)	26.5%	—	2.11	2.39	3.13	3.58	5.49	7.04	9.84	12.70	13.84
Employees	41.1%	—	—	326	461	—	—	—	—	3,355	3,631

* Fiscal year change

STOCK PRICE HISTORY

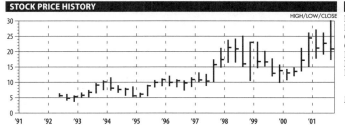

HIGH/LOW/CLOSE

2000 FISCAL YEAR-END
Debt ratio: 58.1%
Return on equity: 21.7%
Cash ($ mil.): 73
Current ratio: 6.03
Long-term debt ($ mil.): 1,344
No. of shares (mil.): 70
Dividends
  Yield: 0.9%
  Payout: 5.3%
Market value ($ mil.): 1,205

DYNEGY INC.

Houston-based Dynegy (short for "dynamic energy" and pronounced DIE-negy) has evolved from a natural gas marketer into a multidimensional energy provider. The company's businesses include energy trading, marketing, and generation; natural gas liquids production; electricity and natural gas transmission and distribution; and telecommunications.

A deal to acquire troubled rival Enron, which would have made Dynegy the world's largest energy trader, fell through in late 2001.

Dynegy's Marketing and Trade unit engages in "energy convergence" — its marketing operations are backed by Dynegy's ownership of energy-related assets. The unit buys and sells electricity, natural gas, and coal in the US, Canada, the UK, and continental Europe. It has a substantial portfolio of 1,500 power plants (with a combined generating capacity of 15,000 MW), located mostly in the US. The company has formed alliances with regional utilities to get a jump on full retail competition in the electricity marketplace. Dynegy plans to replicate its convergence strategy in Europe and Canada, and hopes to make key acquisitions in these regions, as well as in the US.

Dynegy Midstream Services gathers and processes natural gas and produces natural gas liquids in the US. The company has sold its Canadian and midcontinent assets to concentrate on its activities in the Gulf Coast region.

Dynegy is building an 18-city fiber-optic network in the US through new subsidiary Dynegy Global Communications, which also has a 22-city European network.

Chevron owns nearly 27% of Dynegy, and CEO Chuck Watson owns 5%.

Originally Natural Gas Clearinghouse (NGC), Dynegy emerged from the deregulation of the natural gas industry. In 1978 the Natural Gas Policy Act reduced interstate pipeline companies' control over the marketplace. Federal Energy Regulatory Commission (FERC) Order 380 (1984) made gas prices on the open market competitive with those of pipeline companies. NGC was founded in late 1984 to match gas buyers and sellers, without taking title. Chuck Watson became president and CEO in 1985. The company grew dramatically as deregulation secured larger volumes of gas for independent marketers.

The company developed financial instruments (such as natural gas futures) to provide customers with a hedge against wide fluctuations in natural gas prices. By 1990 NGC was trading natural gas futures on NYMEX. It also branched out by buying gas gathering and processing facilities, and it formed NGC Oil Trading and Transportation to market crude oil.

FERC Order 636 (1992) required most interstate pipeline companies to offer merchant sales, transportation, and storage as separate services on the same terms that their own affiliates received. With the low-price advantage taken away from pipeline companies, NGC began selling more to local gas utilities.

In 1994 NGC set up partnerships with Canada's NOVA and British Gas and set up an electric power marketing unit, Electric Clearinghouse. NGC went public in 1995 (making NGC is official name) after it bought Trident NGL, an integrated natural gas liquids company.

In 1996 NGC bought Chevron's natural gas business, giving Chevron a stake in NGC.

In 1997 NGC acquired Destec Energy. Taking the name Dynegy in 1998, the company allied with Florida Power to market wholesale electricity and gas. In 2000 Dynegy paid $4 billion for utility holding company Illinova. (Dynegy had to sell assets to get the merger approved.)

Also in 2000 Dynegy bought telecom software developer Extant, after which it formed Dynegy Global Communications to develop a US broadband network; it also acquired a European network through the purchase of London-based iaxis Limited. In 2001 Dynergy expanded its power generation operations into the Northeast, buying two New York facilities (1,700 MW total capacity) from CH Energy Group for $903 million. It also agreed to purchase two Arizona plants (1,300 MW) from Sierra Pacific Resources for $634 million.

In November 2001 Dynegy announced an agreement to buy energy trading giant Enron for about $9 billion in stock and $13 billion in assumed debt. Enron had seen its stock price driven down because of controversy over the accounting for some financial transactions. As Enron's stock price continued to plunge, Dynegy cancelled the deal and announced that it would exercise its option to buy Enron's Northern Natural Gas pipeline for $1.5 billion. Enron filed for Chapter 11 bankruptcy protection and then sued Dynegy alleging that it had breached the merger agreement and also contesting the Northern Natural Gas sale. Dynegy countersued.

Chairman and CEO: Charles L. Watson, age 51, $6,160,314 pay
President and COO; CEO, Illinois Power: Stephen W. Bergstrom, age 43
EVP; President and CEO, Dynegy Global Communications: Lawrence A. McLernon, age 62
SVP, General Counsel, and Secretary: Kenneth E. Randolph, age 43, $881,417 pay
SVP and CFO, Dynegy and Illinois Power: Robert D. Doty Jr., age 43, $746,125 pay
SVP and Chief Administrative Officer: Milton L. Scott, age 44
SVP and Chief Communications Officer: Deborah Fiorito, age 51
SVP and Chief Information Officer; President, Global Technology: R. Blake Young, age 42, $760,000 pay
SVP and Corporate Controller: Michael R. Mott
SVP Corporate Technology: Maria Anzilotti

VP Human Resources: Andrea Lang
Auditors: Arthur Andersen LLP

LOCATIONS

HQ: 1000 Louisiana, Ste. 5800, Houston, TX 77002
Phone: 713-507-6400   **Fax:** 713-507-3871
Web: www.dynegy.com

2000 Sales

	$ mil.	$ of total
US	26,961	84
Canada	3,686	12
Europe & other regions	1,268	4
Adjustments	(2,470)	—
Total	**29,445**	**100**

PRODUCTS/OPERATIONS

2000 Sales

	$ mil.	% of total
Marketing & trading	22,967	72
Transmission & midstream services	7,338	23
Distribution	1,608	5
Communications	2	—
Adjustments	(2,470)	—
Total	**29,445**	**100**

Major Operations and Subsidiaries
Dynegy Global Communications (telecommunications services)
 DynegyCONNECT (80%, venture with Australian telecom Telstra to develop US network)
 Dynegy Europe Communications (operates European network)
Dynegy Marketing and Trade (electric power and natural gas marketing)
Dynegy Midstream Services (natural gas liquids)
Illinois Power

COMPETITORS

AES	El Paso	TVA
AEP	Enron	Tractebel
Avista	Entergy	TXU
BP	Koch	UtiliCorp
Cinergy	Mirant	Western Gas
Constellation	Mitchell Energy	Williams
Energy Group	& Development	Companies
Duke Energy	PG&E	
Edison	Reliant Energy	
International	Sempra Energy	

HISTORICAL FINANCIALS & EMPLOYEES

NYSE: DYN FYE: December 31	Annual Growth	12/91	12/92	12/93	12/94	12/95	12/96	12/97	12/98	12/99	12/00
Sales ($ mil.)	34.1%	2,099	2,493	2,791	3,238	3,666	7,260	13,378	14,258	15,430	29,445
Net income ($ mil.)	32.8%	39	44	46	42	45	113	(103)	108	152	501
Income as % of sales	—	—	1.9%	1.8%	1.6%	1.3%	1.2%	1.6%	—	0.8%	1.0%	1.7%
Earnings per share ($)	54.2%	—	—	—	0.11	0.41	0.42	0.68	0.33	0.46	1.48
Stock price - FY high ($)	—	—	—	—	8.87	8.51	17.93	17.48	12.68	17.93	59.88
Stock price - FY low ($)	—	—	—	—	5.79	6.07	6.25	10.68	6.79	7.33	17.11
Stock price - FY close ($)	39.5%	—	—	—	7.61	6.43	16.84	12.68	7.92	17.61	56.06
P/E - high	—	—	—	—	81	21	43	—	35	37	39
P/E - low	—	—	—	—	53	15	15	—	19	15	11
Dividends per share ($)	42.4%	—	—	—	0.03	0.02	0.03	0.03	0.03	0.03	0.25
Book value per share ($)	60.7%	—	—	—	0.65	2.50	3.73	3.37	3.71	4.19	11.15
Employees	32.5%	—	—	—	1,070	1,055	1,893	2,572	2,434	2,571	5,778

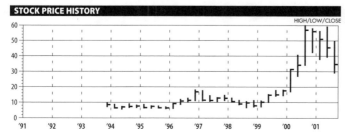

STOCK PRICE HISTORY
HIGH/LOW/CLOSE

2000 FISCAL YEAR-END
Debt ratio: 44.0%
Return on equity: 20.7%
Cash ($ mil.): 86
Current ratio: 1.08
Long-term debt ($ mil.): 2,828
No. of shares (mil.): 323
Dividends
 Yield: 0.4%
 Payout: 16.9%
Market value ($ mil.): 18,092

EL PASO CORPORATION

OVERVIEW

El Paso provides safe passage for natural gas all around del Norte: The Houston-based company, formerly known as El Paso Energy, owns the largest gas pipeline system in the US. The company also gathers and processes natural gas, produces and markets energy, and engages in oil and gas exploration and production. El Paso has expanded by buying diversified energy group Coastal. The $24 billion acquisition (completed in 2001) helped boost the company's proved reserves to more than 6 trillion cu. ft. of natural gas equivalent.

With interests in about 58,000 miles of pipeline in the US, El Paso transports gas from the Gulf Coast to the Northeast; its pipes also reach the West Coast and Southeast. Its major interstate pipelines include Tennessee Gas, Southern Natural Gas, and El Paso Natural Gas. In addition, the company transports gas from the Gulf of Mexico, where it is taking advantage of the region's deepwater production trend.

El Paso explores for and produces oil and gas in the US and Canada. The company's El Paso Field service unit is a leading natural gas gatherer and processor. Its energy marketing arm, El Paso Merchant Energy, sells and trades gas and electricity in North America and operates power plants. Internationally, this unit has plowed millions of dollars into buying and building pipelines and power plants in the Asia/Pacific region, Europe, and South America. The company also has moved into telecommunications bandwidth trading through El Paso Global Networks.

HISTORY

In 1928 Paul Kayser, a Houston attorney, started the El Paso Natural Gas Company and got the rights to sell natural gas to that West Texas town a year later. Despite the 1929 stock market crash, the company built a 200-mile pipeline, first connecting El Paso, Texas, with natural gas wells in Jal, New Mexico. In 1931 it laid pipe again to reach the copper mines of Arizona and Mexico, and three years later expanded to Phoenix and Tucson.

After WWII the company began a 700-mile pipeline to bring natural gas from Texas' Permian Basin to California. As the Golden State's population exploded, sales soared. El Paso also ventured into new business areas; first, chemicals, then textiles, mining, land development, and insurance.

In 1974 the Supreme Court ruled that El Paso had to divest its pipeline holdings north of New Mexico and Arizona. Federal regulators had granted the company the right to buy the holdings two decades earlier, but later rescinded. El Paso received a boost in 1978 when the Natural Gas Policy Act allowed it more freedom to purchase its own reserves. However, by 1982 weak demand, coupled with oversupply brought on by the 1970s spike in energy prices, cut into the company's business.

Conglomerate Burlington Northern acquired El Paso Natural Gas in 1983. Many of El Paso's operations were spun off when federal regulations required pipeline companies to unbundle their sales and transportation businesses and open up interstate pipelines to third parties. El Paso became mainly a gas transportation company.

The company became independent again when Burlington spun it off in 1992. It entered the big leagues in 1996 by buying Tenneco Energy for $4 billion. With more than 16,000 miles of pipeline, Tenneco more than doubled El Paso's transportation capacity and gave it the only coast-to-coast natural gas pipeline in the US. El Paso Natural Gas began using the name El Paso Energy, and moved from its namesake town to Houston, Tenneco's headquarters. In 1997 it sold Tenneco's oil and gas exploration unit to help pay off debt and bought a 29% stake in Capsa, an Argentine energy concern.

Refocusing on Gulf Coast assets, El Paso sold its Anadarko pipeline gas-gathering system in Oklahoma and Texas in 1998, then bought DeepTech International and its stake in the Leviathan Gas Pipeline.

In 1999 El Paso bought Sonat, in a $6 billion deal as well as a natural gas transportation and marketing firm. Sonat was composed of an exploration and production unit. To gain regulators' approval of the Sonat deal, El Paso sold three pipeline systems in 2000, including East Tennessee Natural Gas (to Duke Energy for $386 million) and Sea Robin Pipeline (to CMS Energy for $72 million).

El Paso bought PG&E's natural gas and natural gas liquids businesses for about $900 million in 2000. Also that year the company agreed to buy diversified energy company Coastal in a $24 billion deal, which closed early in 2001.

In 2001 the company changed its name from El Paso Energy to El Paso Corporation. It also expanded its oil and gas operations in Canada by buying Velvet Exploration.

OFFICERS

Chairman, President and CEO; Chairman, El Paso Energy Partners: William A. Wise, age 55, $3,838,338 pay
Vice Chairman: David A. Arledge, age 56
EVP and CFO; EVP, El Paso Energy Partners: H. Brent Austin, age 46, $1,334,167 pay
EVP Human Resources and Administration: Joel Richards III, age 54
EVP Legal and Governmental Affairs and General Counsel: Britton White Jr., age 57, $1,154,175 pay
EVP; President, Merchant Energy Group: Ralph Eads, age 41, $1,423,129 pay
EVP; President, Pipeline Group: John W. Somerhalder II, age 45, $1,334,167 pay
President, ANR Pipeline: James J. Cleary
President, El Paso Energy International: Byron R. Kelley, age 53
Auditors: PricewaterhouseCoopers LLP

LOCATIONS

HQ: 1001 Louisiana St., Houston, TX 77002
Phone: 713-420-2131   **Fax:** 713-420-6030
Web: www.epenergy.com

El Paso gathers natural gas in major producing areas of the US, including South and East Texas, North Louisiana, the Permian Basin in Texas and New Mexico, the San Juan Basin in New Mexico, and both onshore and offshore along the Gulf Coast. The company also has exploration and production operations in Canada. It operates gas pipeline systems in the eastern and western US and in northern Mexico. It has interests in power plant and pipeline systems in Argentina, Australia, Bangladesh, Bolivia, Brazil, Chile, China, the Czech Republic, Hungary, India, Indonesia, Mexico, Pakistan, Peru, the Philippines, and the UK.

PRODUCTS/OPERATIONS

Primary Business Units
El Paso Field Services (natural gas gathering and processing)
El Paso Global Networks Company (telecommunications bandwidth trading)
El Paso Merchant Energy Group (energy marketing and trading, power generation)
El Paso Pipeline Group
  ANR
  Colorado Interstate Gas
  El Paso Natural Gas Company
  Southern Natural Gas Company
  Tennessee Gas Pipeline Company
El Paso Production (oil and gas exploration and production)

COMPETITORS

AES	Equitable	PG&E
AEP	Resources	Reliant Energy
Avista	Imperial Oil	Sempra Energy
Constellation	International	Southern
Energy Group	Power	Company
Duke Energy	Kinder Morgan,	Statoil Energy
Dynegy	Inc.	Tractebel
Edison	MidAmerican	TransCanada
International	Energy	PipeLines
Enron	Mitchell Energy	UtiliCorp
Entergy	& Development	Western Gas
Enterprise	NRG Energy	Williams
	Peabody Energy	Companies

HISTORICAL FINANCIALS & EMPLOYEES

NYSE: EPG FYE: December 31	Annual Growth	12/91	12/92	12/93	12/94	12/95	12/96	12/97	12/98	12/99	12/00
Sales ($ mil.)	45.8%	735	803	909	870	1,038	3,010	5,638	5,782	10,581	21,950
Net income ($ mil.)	18.4%	143	76	92	90	85	38	186	225	(255)	652
Income as % of sales	—	19.4%	9.5%	10.1%	10.3%	8.2%	1.3%	3.3%	3.9%	—	3.0%
Earnings per share ($)	12.6%	—	1.06	1.23	1.23	1.24	0.52	1.59	1.84	(1.12)	2.73
Stock price - FY high ($)	—	—	15.75	20.19	20.94	16.25	26.63	33.75	38.94	43.44	74.25
Stock price - FY low ($)	—	—	10.13	15.13	14.81	12.38	14.31	24.44	24.69	30.69	30.31
Stock price - FY close ($)	21.1%	—	15.50	18.00	15.25	14.38	25.25	33.25	34.81	38.81	71.63
P/E - high	—	—	15	16	17	13	50	21	20	—	29
P/E - low	—	—	10	12	12	10	27	15	13	—	12
Dividends per share ($)	16.0%	—	0.25	0.54	0.59	0.65	0.69	0.72	0.76	0.79	0.82
Book value per share ($)	6.8%	—	9.01	9.60	9.98	10.40	13.93	16.37	17.53	12.84	15.20
Employees	20.9%	2,710	2,499	2,460	2,403	2,393	4,300	3,500	3,600	4,700	15,000

STOCK PRICE HISTORY

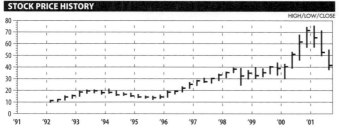

HIGH/LOW/CLOSE

2000 FISCAL YEAR-END

Debt ratio: 62.5%
Return on equity: 20.0%
Cash ($ mil.): 688
Current ratio: 0.96
Long-term debt ($ mil.): 5,949
No. of shares (mil.): 235
Dividends
  Yield: 1.1%
  Payout: 30.0%
Market value ($ mil.): 16,817

ELECTRONIC DATA SYSTEMS

OVERVIEW

With big hair and fresh makeup, Electronic Data Systems (EDS) is undergoing a Texas-style makeover. Plano, Texas-based EDS is the largest independent computer management and services company in the US (IBM is #1 overall). About 75% of sales come from developing and managing complex computer and telecommunications systems for major government and corporate clients, including Chevron, BellSouth, and the US Navy. A broad 1999 deal that included EDS swapping assets, employees, and services with telecom giant MCI WorldCom (now WorldCom) got EDS into electronic business consulting, now a core component offered through the company's E.Solutions division. EDS also offers management consulting through its A.T. Kearney subsidiary. About 60% of sales come from the US.

For more than a decade, EDS was a General Motors (GM) subsidiary; GM still accounts for about 20% of sales. After its 1996 spinoff from GM, EDS's profits and stock slumped. So CEO Richard Brown restructured the company, trimming jobs and building a global marketing campaign to revive and recast EDS's image.

EDS is relying on its specialty in providing traditional systems integration and computer outsourcing services to large clients. It thrives in difficult market conditions that have seen smaller, Web-focused consultancies fall by the wayside.

HISTORY

After 10 years with IBM, disgruntled salesman Ross Perot founded Electronic Data Systems (EDS) in 1962. IBM executives had dismissed Perot's idea of providing electronic data processing management that would relieve clients' data management worries.

Perot took five months to find his first customer, Collins Radio of Cedar Rapids, Iowa. In 1963 EDS pioneered the long-term, fixed-price contract with snack food maker Frito-Lay by writing a five-year contract instead of the 60- to 90-day contracts usually offered by service companies. EDS then got into Medicare and Medicaid claims processing (mid-1960s), data processing for insurance providers (1963), and data management for banks (1968). These moves eventually made it the #1 provider of data management services in these markets.

EDS went public in 1968. It established regional data centers and central data processing stations in the early 1970s to pioneer the notion of distributed processing. In 1976 EDS signed a contract with Iran, one of its first offshore contracts. But by 1978 Iran was behind in its payments, and EDS halted operations there. When two EDS employees were later arrested amid the disorder of the Islamic revolution, Perot assembled a rescue team that spirited them out of the country.

On EDS's 22nd anniversary in 1984, General Motors (GM) bought the company for $2.5 billion. While EDS prospered, Perot and GM chairman Roger Smith's managerial styles differed, resulting in an uneasy alliance and, ultimately, divorce. GM bought Perot's EDS shares in 1986 for more than $700 million. Perot formed competitor Perot Systems in 1988.

In 1993 EDS launched its management consulting service. Two years later it acquired management consulting firm A.T. Kearney and securities industry consultant FCI.

The company won independence from GM in mid-1996. The spinoff involved paying $500 million to GM and agreeing to extend the automaker more favorable computer services contracts. In 1998 CEO Lester Alberthal resigned and was replaced by Cable & Wireless executive Richard Brown, who became chairman and CEO in 1999. Brown cut thousands of jobs (including a third of the sales force), and launched a $100 million global ad campaign to present a reinvented, more nimble EDS.

In 1999 the company exchanged assets and services from its networking business for communications management services and employees from MCI WorldCom (now WorldCom) in a $17 billion alliance. As one part of that deal, EDS paid $1.65 billion to buy MCI Systemhouse. This move thrust EDS into the electronic commerce arena.

In 2001 EDS announced a 10-year service contract valued at $2.2 billion with Sabre Holdings. EDS continued to expand its territory that year, purchasing Structural Dynamics Research Corporation (SDRC) and announcing plans to reacquire the publicly traded shares of Unigraphics Solutions (UGS) it had spun off in 1998. EDS then merged SDRC's operations with those of UGS to create a design and engineering software division with annual sales of more than $1 billion.

That year the company also expanded its relationship with Sun, forging an alliance that combined Sun's hardware and software products with EDS's information technology expertise.

OFFICERS

Chairman and CEO: Richard H. Brown, age 54, $4,912,800 pay
Vice Chairman, President, and COO: Jeffrey M. Heller, age 61, $2,028,306 pay
EVP and CFO: James E. Daley, age 59, $1,464,830 pay
EVP; President, Information Solutions: Douglas L. Frederick, age 51
EVP, Leadership and Change Management (HR): Troy W. Todd, age 72, $1,201,840 pay
EVP, Operations: Paul J. Chiapparone, age 61, $1,460,284 pay
SVP, Chief Information Officer, and Chief Technology Officer: Terence V. Milholland
SVP, General Counsel, and Secretary: D. Gilbert Friedlander, age 54
SVP; President, E.solutions: John W. McCain, age 41
SVP, Financial and Transportation: J. Coley Clark
SVP, Global Marketing and Communications: Donald R. Uzzi
SVP, General Motors: Douglas W. Hoover
VP and Director, Investor Relations: Myrna B. Vance
VP and Treasurer: Scott Krenz
VP, Government Global Industry Group: Albert J. Edmonds
VP, Manufacturing and Retail Global Industry Group: Richard O. King
Auditors: KPMG LLP

LOCATIONS

HQ: Electronic Data Systems Corporation
5400 Legacy Dr., Plano, TX 75024
Phone: 972-604-6000   **Fax:** 972-605-2643
Web: www.eds.com

Electronic Data Systems has operations in more than 40 countries.

2000 Sales

	$ mil.	% of total
US	11,216	58
UK	2,380	12
Other countries	5,631	30
Total	**19,227**	**100**

PRODUCTS/OPERATIONS

2000 Sales

	$ mil.	% of total
Information solutions	14,774	75
Business process management	2,704	14
Consulting	2,297	11
Other	(548)	—
Total	**19,227**	**100**

COMPETITORS

Accenture	Cap Gemini	Keane
Affiliated	Compaq	KPMG
Computer	Computer	Consulting
American	Sciences	McKinsey &
Management	Deloitte Touche	Company
Atos Origin	Tohmatsu	Perot Systems
ADP	Ernst & Young	Pricewaterhouse
Bain & Company	First Data	Coopers
Booz-Allen	Fiserv	Sapient
Boston	Getronics	SAIC
Consulting	Hewlett-Packard	Siemens
BT	IBM	Unisys
Bull	ICL	

HISTORICAL FINANCIALS & EMPLOYEES

NYSE: EDS FYE: December 31	Annual Growth	12/91	12/92	12/93	12/94	12/95	12/96	12/97	12/98	12/99	12/00
Sales ($ mil.)	11.8%	7,029	8,155	8,507	10,052	12,422	14,441	15,236	16,891	18,534	19,227
Net income ($ mil.)	8.5%	548	636	724	822	939	432	731	743	421	1,143
Income as % of sales	—	7.8%	7.8%	8.5%	8.2%	7.6%	3.0%	4.8%	4.4%	2.3%	5.9%
Earnings per share ($)	8.6%	1.14	1.33	1.50	1.69	1.94	0.88	1.48	1.50	0.85	2.40
Stock price - FY high ($)	—	33.06	34.00	35.88	39.50	52.63	63.38	49.63	51.31	70.00	76.69
Stock price - FY low ($)	—	17.50	25.25	26.00	27.50	36.88	40.75	29.56	30.44	44.13	38.38
Stock price - FY close ($)	7.0%	31.50	32.88	29.25	38.38	52.00	43.25	43.94	50.19	66.94	57.75
P/E - high	—	28	26	24	23	27	71	33	34	80	31
P/E - low	—	15	19	17	16	19	46	20	20	51	16
Dividends per share ($)	7.2%	0.32	0.36	0.40	0.48	0.52	0.60	0.60	0.60	0.60	0.60
Book value per share ($)	8.1%	5.46	6.39	7.52	8.79	10.29	9.82	10.80	12.00	9.73	11.04
Employees	7.1%	65,800	70,500	70,000	70,000	96,000	100,000	110,000	120,000	121,000	122,000

STOCK PRICE HISTORY

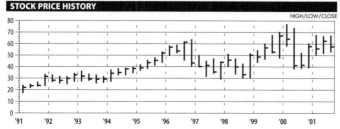

HIGH/LOW/CLOSE

2000 FISCAL YEAR-END

Debt ratio: 33.5%
Return on equity: 23.6%
Cash ($ mil.): 393
Current ratio: 1.43
Long-term debt ($ mil.): 2,586
No. of shares (mil.): 465
Dividends
  Yield: 1.0%
  Payout: 25.0%
Market value ($ mil.): 26,871

ENCOMPASS SERVICES

OVERVIEW

Here's a company that really tries to cover it all. Formerly Group Maintenance America Corp. (GroupMAC), Houston-based Encompass Services is the largest facilities services company in the US, offering a broad range of outsourced electrical, mechanical, janitorial, and maintenance management services throughout the US. The company offers its services in more than 200 locations, including the 100 largest US cities. Its corporate clients include General Motors, WorldCom, and Wal-Mart.

Accounting for almost 75% of sales, Encompass' electrical technologies and mechanical services groups design, install, and maintain physical plant facilities (heating and cooling systems, process piping, and plumbing and electrical systems) for manufacturing plants, power generating stations, hospitals, hotels, and commercial office buildings.

The electrical technologies group also provides and maintains high-speed data networks and voice and data systems. The company's residential services group installs and maintains heating and cooling systems for homes, apartments, and condominiums. Encompass' cleaning systems group provides janitorial services for retail stores, banks, office buildings, and airport terminals.

Formed in 2000 through the merger of GroupMAC and Building One Services, the company immediately eclipsed its rivals in both size and scope. Though it will continue to keep an eye open for future acquisitions, Encompass plans to focus on leveraging its economies of scale to improve margins and expand into new territories. Apollo Management controls 23% of the company.

HISTORY

Houston investor Gordon Cain (founder of the buyout firm Sterling Group) teamed up with Richard Reiling, formerly of Republic Industries (now AutoNation) and Patrick Millinor to form Group Maintenance America Corp. (GroupMAC) in 1996. The group's aim was to consolidate the highly fragmented electrical and mechanical services industry — a sector dominated by more than 100,000 small, owner-operated companies offering limited service in small geographic areas. Its consolidation efforts sought to maximize group buying power, create training programs, and pursue national accounts for its services.

GroupMAC made its first acquisition in early 1997, buying Dayton, Ohio-based Airtron. Airtron was the first of 20 companies with combined sales of about $329 million to be swallowed that year. GroupMAC went public at the end of 1997, using the money for acquisition-related expenses. With most of its revenue coming from low-margin residential contracts, the company began to focus its acquisitions on firms doing more lucrative commercial and industrial work.

In 1998 GroupMAC gobbled up another 39 companies (with combined revenue of more than $700 million), including Texas-based Trinity Contractors. This move put the growing conglomerate past $1 billion in revenue, second only to Washington, DC-based Building One Services. In 1999, 13 more acquisitions (totaling more than $350 million in revenue) followed.

In 2000 GroupMAC merged with Building One to create the country's largest facilities services conglomerate. Founded in 1997, Building One Services Corporation focused on mechanical and electrical systems installation and maintenance services and janitorial and maintenance management services.

Renamed Encompass Services Corporation, the company sold more than $250 million in preferred stock to an affiliate of Apollo Management to help fund the deal, giving the investment firm 23% of Encompass. Following the merger the company organized into Mechanical, Electrical/Communications, Industrial, Residential, Janitorial and Maintenance Management, and National Accounts Group business units.

Following the merger, Encompass continued to expand. The company signed a services sharing agreement with Service Resources, a leading provider of facilities management for the retail industry. Encompass also made a minority investment in OAKLEAF Waste Management, a provider of waste management and other services to retail outlets.

In 2001 Encompass added several major new contracts, including services for Dow Chemical, Newport News Shipbuilding, Nissan, and the US Air Force and Navy. Also in 2001 the company launched its Encompass Edge campaign designed to introduce its new, unified brand to residential customers while allowing the local services companies to keep the names that were familiar to their customers.

Chairman: J. Patrick Millinor Jr., age 55, $406,831 pay
President, CEO, and Director: Joseph M. Ivey Jr.,
  age 42, $316,961 pay
SVP and CFO: Darren B. Miller
SVP Corporate Planning and Development:
  Chester J. Jachimiec, $232,900 pay
**SVP, Chief Information Officer, and Administrative
  Officer:** Daniel W. Kipp
VP Purchasing: Keith B. Kirk
VP Human Resources: Steven C. Ronilo
President, Electrical Technologies Group:
  William P. Love, $259,153 pay
President, Industrial Group: Pat McMahon
President, Cleaning Services: Michael Sullivan
President, Global Technologies Group:
  Thomas P. Rosato, $309,466 pay
President, Mechanical Services Group: Robert Tyler,
  $350,607 pay
Auditors: KPMG LLP

LOCATIONS

HQ: Encompass Services Corporation
  3 Greenway Plaza, Ste. 2000, Houston, TX 77046
Phone: 713-860-0100   **Fax:** 713-626-4766
Web: www.encompserv.com

Encompass Services Corporation operates through more
than 200 locations in 50 states.

PRODUCTS/OPERATIONS

2000 Sales

	$ mil.	% of total
Electrical Technologies	1,857	45
Mechanical Services	1,195	29
Industrial Services	405	10
Residential Services	294	7
Cleaning Systems	265	6
Global Technologies	129	3
Adjustments	(46)	—
Total	**4,099**	**100**

Selected Corporate Clients

Beazer Homes USA
Centex Corporation
DaimlerChrysler
Dow Chemical Company
General Motors
IBM
Kmart
Microsoft
Nextel Communications

Phillip Morris
Pulte Homes
Safeway
Target
United Parcel Service
Wachovia Banks
Wal-Mart Stores
WorldCom

COMPETITORS

ABM Industries
Chemed
Comfort Systems USA
EMCOR
Lennox
Rentokil Initial
ServiceMaster

HISTORICAL FINANCIALS & EMPLOYEES

NYSE: ESR FYE: December 31	Annual Growth	12/91	12/92	12/93	12/94	12/95	12/96	12/97	12/98	12/99	12/00
Sales ($ mil.)	209.3%	—	—	—	—	—	—	139	762	1,548	4,099
Net income ($ mil.)	—	—	—	—	—	—	—	(4)	26	42	55
Income as % of sales	—	—	—	—	—	—	—	—	3.4%	2.7%	1.3%
Earnings per share ($)	—	—	—	—	—	—	—	(0.34)	0.93	1.11	0.63
Stock price - FY high ($)	—	—	—	—	—	—	—	17.19	20.63	15.44	10.63
Stock price - FY low ($)	—	—	—	—	—	—	—	13.00	10.31	7.00	3.25
Stock price - FY close ($)	(33.0%)	—	—	—	—	—	—	16.81	12.13	10.69	5.06
P/E - high	—	—	—	—	—	—	—	—	22	14	13
P/E - low	—	—	—	—	—	—	—	—	11	6	4
Dividends per share ($)	—	—	—	—	—	—	—	0.00	0.00	0.00	0.00
Book value per share ($)	34.9%	—	—	—	—	—	—	6.63	9.53	11.03	16.27
Employees	129.8%	—	—	—	—	—	—	2,800	9,000	30,000	34,000

STOCK PRICE HISTORY

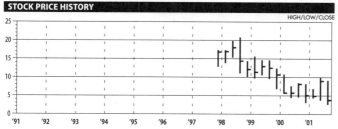

HIGH/LOW/CLOSE

2000 FISCAL YEAR-END

Debt ratio: 48.2%
Return on equity: 9.3%
Cash ($ mil.): 10
Current ratio: 1.73
Long-term debt ($ mil.): 962
No. of shares (mil.): 64
Dividends
  Yield: —
  Payout: —
Market value ($ mil.): 321

ENRON CORP.

OVERVIEW

Houston-based Enron's end run around its energy rivals may be at an end. The company, which transformed itself from a gas pipeline company into the world's largest energy trader, has filed for Chapter 11 bankruptcy protection.

Controversy over how the company accounted for financial transactions with entities controlled by a former CFO and other company officers has driven down Enron's stock price and its credit rating. Enron had agreed to be acquired by smaller rival Dynegy; however, Dynegy backed out of the deal in late 2001 as Enron's financial situation worsened.

The largest buyer and seller of natural gas in the US, Enron operates a 25,000-mile gas pipeline system that spans from Texas to the Canadian border and from California to Florida. The company is also the top wholesale electricity marketer in the US, and it markets

and trades a number of other commodities, including metals, coal, chemicals, paper, and fiber-optic bandwidth.

Enron also provides risk management services, energy project financing, and engineering and construction services around the world. It owns interests in utilities, power plants, and other energy projects in Africa, Asia, Australia, Europe, and the Americas.

Enron has announced plans to sell noncore assets, including its broadband telecommunications unit, its remaining water utility interests, and overseas investments such as its Brazilian and Indian assets. The company has agreed to sell regulated utility Portland General Electric to Oregon utility Northwest Natural Gas. Enron's financial troubles have prompted it to lay off about 4,000 employees.

HISTORY

Enron traces its history through two well-established natural gas companies: InterNorth and Houston Natural Gas (HNG).

InterNorth began in 1930 as Northern Natural Gas, a Nebraska-based gas pipeline company. By 1950 it had doubled capacity, and in 1960 it started processing and transporting natural gas liquids. The company was renamed InterNorth in 1980 and bought Belco Petroleum three years later.

HNG, formed in 1925 as a South Texas gas distributor, started developing oil and gas properties in 1953. It bought Houston Pipe Line Company in 1956 and Valley Gas Production in 1963. HNG sold its original distribution properties to Entex in 1976. In 1984 HNG, faced with a hostile takeover attempt by Coastal, brought in former Exxon executive Kenneth Lay as CEO. He refocused HNG on natural gas and added Transwestern Pipeline (California) and Florida Gas Transmission. By 1985 HNG operated the only transcontinental gas pipeline.

In 1985 InterNorth bought HNG for $2.4 billion, creating the US's largest natural gas pipeline system. Lay became CEO of the new company, called Enron, and the company moved its headquarters from Omaha to Houston. Laden with debt, Enron sold off portions of Citrus Corp. (owner of Florida Gas Transmission, 1986), Enron Cogeneration (1988), and Enron Oil & Gas (1989).

The company bought Tenneco's natural gas liquids and petrochemical operations in 1991. Enron bought several gas businesses from gas giant Williams in 1993 and, as electricity mar-

kets worldwide began deregulating, began its power marketing business.

In 1998 Enron began power trading in Australia. The company continued to build its US portfolio in 1998, buying interests in power plants near New York City. In 1998 it formed Azurix, a global water business, to own and operate its water and wastewater assets and took Azurix public in 1999, retaining a 69% stake.

In 2000 Enron sold its 4,400-mile Houston Pipe Line to American Electric Power; however, the western US energy crisis caused the sale of PGE to Sierra Pacific Resources to fall through.

Transactions between Enron and investment partnerships controlled by CFO Andrew Fastow and other officers drew scrutiny from the SEC in 2001, and Fastow was placed on leave of absence. Enron later restated its net income from 1997 through the first half of 2001 to reflect an overall 20% reduction, and in November it agreed to be acquired by smaller rival Dynegy for about $9 billion in stock and $13 billion in assumed debt.

However, later that year Dynegy cancelled the deal as Enron's credit rating and stock price continued to drop. Dynegy also announced that it would exercise an option to purchase Enron's 16,500-mile Northern Natural Gas pipeline for $1.5 billion. Days after the agreement collapsed, Enron filed for Chapter 11 bankruptcy protection and filed a lawsuit alleging that Dynegy breached the merger agreement and contesting the Northern Natural Gas sale. Dynegy countersued.

Chairman and CEO: Kenneth L. Lay, age 59, $8,300,000 pay
Vice Chairman: Mark A. Frevert, age 46, $2,520,000 pay (prior to promotion)
President and COO: Greg Whalley, age 39
CFO; President and CEO, Enron Industrial Markets: Jeffery McMahon
EVP and Chief Accounting Officer: Richard A. Causey, age 41
EVP and Chief of Staff: Steven J. Kean, age 39
EVP and Chief Risk Officer: Richard B. Buy, age 49
EVP and General Counsel: James V. Derrick Jr., age 56
EVP Corporate Development: J. Mark Metts, age 42
EVP Human Resources and Community Relations: Cindy K. Olson
EVP Investor Relations: Mark E. Koenig, age 45
SVP Board Communications and Secretary: Rebecca C. Carter
Chairman and CEO, Enron Accelerator: Lou L. Pai, age 53
Chairman and CEO, Enron Energy Services: Dave Delainey, age 35
Chairman and CEO, Enron Transportation Services: Stanley C. Horton, age 51, $1,720,000 pay
Vice Chairman, Enron Energy Services: Thomas E. White, age 57
President and CEO, Enron Global Exploration and Production: Jeff Sherrick, age 46
Auditors: Arthur Andersen LLP

LOCATIONS

HQ: 1400 Smith St., Houston, TX 77002
Phone: 713-853-6161   **Fax:** 713-853-3129
Web: www.enron.com

Enron operates in Africa, Asia, Australia, Europe, and North and South America.

2000 Sales

	$ mil.	% of total
US	77,891	77
Other countries	22,898	23
Total	**100,789**	**100**

PRODUCTS/OPERATIONS

2000 Sales

	$ mil.	% of total
Wholesale	93,278	93
Retail energy	3,824	4
Transportation & distribution	2,742	3
Broadband	408	—
Other	537	—
Total	**100,789**	**100**

COMPETITORS

AEP	Iberdrola	Tractebel
Avista	Mirant	TransTexas Gas
Black & Veatch	Peabody Energy	TXU
Cinergy	PG&E	UtiliCorp
Constellation	Reliant Energy	Vivendi
Energy Group	Sempra Energy	Environnement
Duke Energy	Southern	Western Gas
Dynegy	Company	Williams
El Paso	Statoil Energy	Companies
Entergy	Suez	

HISTORICAL FINANCIALS & EMPLOYEES

NYSE: ENE FYE: December 31	Annual Growth	12/91	12/92	12/93	12/94	12/95	12/96	12/97	12/98	12/99	12/00
Sales ($ mil.)	25.0%	13,520	6,325	7,973	8,984	9,189	13,289	20,273	31,260	40,112	100,789
Net income* ($ mil.)	16.8%	242	306	333	453	520	584	105	703	893	979
Income as % of sales	—	1.8%	4.8%	4.2%	5.0%	5.7%	4.4%	0.5%	2.2%	2.2%	1.0%
Earnings per share ($)	9.1%	0.51	0.60	0.63	0.85	0.97	1.08	0.16	1.01	1.10	1.12
Stock price - FY high ($)	—	9.61	12.53	18.50	17.31	19.69	23.75	22.56	29.38	44.88	90.75
Stock price - FY low ($)	—	6.20	7.66	11.09	13.38	14.00	17.31	17.50	19.06	28.75	41.38
Stock price - FY close ($)	28.4%	8.75	11.59	14.50	15.25	19.06	21.56	20.78	28.53	44.38	83.13
P/E - high	—	18	18	28	19	19	20	141	27	33	74
P/E - low	—	11	11	17	15	13	15	109	18	21	34
Dividends per share ($)	5.1%	0.32	0.34	0.36	0.38	0.41	0.43	0.46	0.48	0.50	0.50
Book value per share ($)	13.8%	4.76	5.37	5.27	5.72	6.30	7.30	9.03	10.65	13.37	15.26
Employees	12.0%	7,400	7,780	7,100	6,955	6,700	11,700	15,500	17,800	17,900	20,600

*Prior to restatement

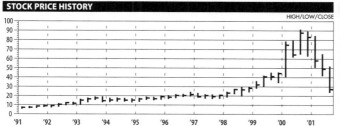

STOCK PRICE HISTORY

HIGH/LOW/CLOSE

2000 FISCAL YEAR-END

Debt ratio: 42.7%
Return on equity: 10.4%
Cash ($ mil.): 1,374
Current ratio: 1.07
Long-term debt ($ mil.): 8,550
No. of shares (mil.): 752
Dividends
  Yield: 0.6%
  Payout: 44.6%
Market value ($ mil.): 62,483

EOTT ENERGY PARTNERS, L.P.

OVERVIEW

Crude oil is dirty stuff, but EOTT Energy Partners is willing to get it together and spread it around. The Houston-based public limited partnership is one of the largest independent gatherers and marketers of crude oil in North America. EOTT purchases about 420,000 barrels per day of crude oil, produced from about 33,000 leases in 18 US states and Canada. It buys mainly from independent producers (91%).

EOTT operates principally in the US's Gulf Coast, Southwest, Rocky Mountains, and midcontinent regions, but it also has businesses on the West Coast and in Canada. Acting as an intermediary between supplier and buyer, it transports oil to refineries and other customers via 8,200 miles of pipelines and a fleet of about 285 trucks. It markets refined oil products (fuels and unleaded gasoline) on the West Coast.

The company's former parent, power giant Enron, effectively owns 37% of EOTT. This includes a 25% stake controlled by Enron's wholly owned subsidiary. EOTT Energy Core is also EOTT's general partner.

HISTORY

EOTT Energy Partners was originally a part of Enron, which emerged from the combination of Houston Natural Gas (HNG, 1925), and InterNorth (1930).

HNG, once a South Texas natural gas distributor, started developing oil and gas fields in 1953. In 1984 Coastal Corp. tried to take over HNG. HNG brought in former Exxon executive Kenneth Lay as CEO to help fend off the bid. Lay shifted HNG's direction to natural gas production and exploration.

Over in Omaha, Nebraska, Northern Natural Gas was a gas pipeline company that started processing and transporting natural gas liquids in 1960. It changed its name to InterNorth in 1980. Three years later it bought Belco Petroleum, giving it considerable natural gas and oil reserves.

When InterNorth bought HNG for $2.4 billion in 1985, the US's largest natural gas system (38,000 miles) was created. The next year Lay became CEO of the newly named Enron, and company headquarters moved from Omaha to Houston.

Under Lay's direction, Enron bought crude oil terminals and gathering and transportation systems. In 1987 it purchased a terminal and transportation facility from Fairway Crude. A year later, it bought Tesoro's gathering and transportation businesses.

But Enron had bigger fish to fry, planning to become the first natural gas major; it wanted to exit the volatile commodity and trading side of the business. In 1992 it announced the spin-off of Enron Oil Trading & Transportation Company, which brought in high revenues but few profits. In 1993, Enron acquired Shell's eastern New Mexico oil pipeline system.

Finally, in 1994 Enron combined Enron Oil Trading & Transportation (renamed EOTT Energy) and Enron Products Marketing Company to create EOTT Energy Partners. With this public partnership, the IPO raised about $200 million. Philip Hawk took charge of the firm, which was one of the largest independent gatherers and marketers of crude oil in North America.

EOTT had troubles from the start; through the first half of 1995, it suffered through the worst industry refining margins in a decade. To stem the losses from its West Coast operation, EOTT renegotiated its contract with its key processor, Paramount Petroleum, agreeing to sell crude to Paramount and then market the fuel in exchange for a share of the revenues.

EOTT also made several acquisitions. These include 600 miles of pipeline in Mississippi and Alabama from oil giant Amerada Hess in 1996 and the 1997 purchase of 400 miles of pipeline in Louisiana and Texas from CITGO.

The company lost money in 1997, and Hawk resigned the next year. He was replaced by venture capital consultant Michael Burke, who guided EOTT toward upgrading its communications and streamlining its business processes. EOTT almost tripled its pipeline mileage with the 1998 acquisition of crude oil marketing and gathering operations from Koch Industries. In 1999 EOTT bought 2,000 miles of pipeline and other assets from the Texas-New Mexico Pipe Line. The next year the company reported a $6.2 million loss resulting from an internal theft of natural gas liquids.

Chairman Stanley Horton, the CEO of the Enron Gas Pipeline Group, took over as EOTT's CEO in 2000 after Burke stepped down.

OFFICERS

Chairman and CEO: Stanley C. Horton, age 51, $80,126 pay
President, COO, and Director: Dana R. Gibbs, age 41, $475,004 pay
VP and Controller: Lori L. Maddox, age 36, $200,000 pay
VP and General Counsel: Molly M. Sample, age 45, $194,272 pay
VP Business Transformation: David R. Hultsman
VP Human Resources and Administration: Mary Ellen Coombe, age 50, $220,000 pay
Treasurer: Susan C. Ralph
Director Investor Relations: Scott D. Vonderheide
Auditors: Arthur Andersen LLP

LOCATIONS

HQ: 2000 W. Sam Houston Pkwy. S., Ste. 400, Houston, TX 77042
Phone: 713-993-5200   **Fax:** 713-993-5821
Web: www.eott.com

EOTT Energy Partners operates in Canada and the US states of Alabama, Arkansas, California, Colorado, Florida, Kansas, Louisiana, Mississippi, Missouri, Montana, Nebraska, New Mexico, North Dakota, Oklahoma, South Dakota, Texas, Utah, and Wyoming.

PRODUCTS/OPERATIONS

2000 Sales

	$ mil.	% of total
North American crude oil (east of the Rockies)	10,710	91
West Coast operations	893	8
Pipeline operations	140	1
Adjustments	(129)	—
Total	**11,614**	**100**

Selected Limited Partnerships and Subsidiaries
EOTT Energy Canada Limited Partnership
EOTT Energy Financing Corp.
EOTT Energy Operating Limited Partnership
EOTT Energy Pipeline Limited Partnership

COMPETITORS

Amerada Hess	Phillips Petroleum
BP	Plains All American
Chevron	Pipeline
Conoco	Royal Dutch/Shell
Devon Energy	Sunoco
Exxon Mobil	TEPPCO Partners
Genesis Energy	Texaco
Imperial Oil	Ultramar Diamond
Kerr-McGee	Shamrock
Koch	Unocal
Occidental	USX-Marathon
PDVSA	Williams Companies
PEMEX	

HISTORICAL FINANCIALS & EMPLOYEES

NYSE: EOT FYE: December 31	Annual Growth	12/91	12/92	12/93	12/94	12/95	12/96	12/97	12/98	12/99	12/00
Sales ($ mil.)	3.9%	8,236	7,697	6,359	4,557	5,088	7,470	7,646	5,295	8,664	11,614
Net income ($ mil.)	(7.6%)	28	(19)	20	12	(61)	29	(14)	(4)	(1)	14
Income as % of sales	—	0.3%	—	0.3%	0.3%	—	0.4%	—	—	—	0.1%
Earnings per share ($)	(6.0%)	—	—	—	0.71	(3.54)	1.50	(0.75)	(0.21)	(0.02)	0.49
Stock price - FY high ($)	—	—	—	—	20.13	18.50	22.00	22.38	20.00	19.25	17.00
Stock price - FY low ($)	—	—	—	—	14.75	12.75	16.13	14.75	11.25	12.25	11.13
Stock price - FY close ($)	1.2%	—	—	—	15.25	18.25	21.88	17.13	15.75	13.00	16.38
P/E - high	—	—	—	—	28	—	15	—	—	—	35
P/E - low	—	—	—	—	21	—	11	—	—	—	23
Dividends per share ($)	13.7%	—	—	—	0.88	1.80	1.90	1.90	1.90	1.90	1.90
Book value per share ($)	(15.0%)	—	—	—	9.33	4.46	5.64	3.30	3.15	5.01	3.51
Employees	5.0%	—	—	850	900	800	828	966	1,500	—	1,200

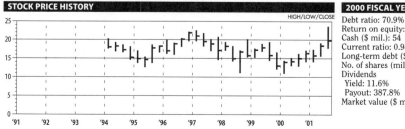

STOCK PRICE HISTORY — HIGH/LOW/CLOSE

2000 FISCAL YEAR-END
Debt ratio: 70.9%
Return on equity: 12.7%
Cash ($ mil.): 54
Current ratio: 0.94
Long-term debt ($ mil.): 235
No. of shares (mil.): 27
Dividends
  Yield: 11.6%
  Payout: 387.8%
Market value ($ mil.): 450

EXXON MOBIL CORPORATION

OVERVIEW

Two Big Oil names have become one to make Exxon Mobil the world's #1 oil company, ahead of Royal Dutch/Shell and BP. Irving, Texas-based Exxon Mobil is engaged in oil and gas exploration, production, supply, transportation, and marketing. With major oil and gas holdings in Europe, the US, and eastern Canada, the company has proved reserves of almost 21 billion barrels of oil equivalent. It is looking for new opportunities in West Africa, both onshore and off; in the former Soviet Union; and in South America.

Exxon Mobil's refining capacity exceeds 6 million barrels per day, and the company sells refined products under the Exxon, Esso, and Mobil brands at more than 40,000 service stations in 118 countries. The company has more than 16,000 gas stations in the US. Exxon Mobil produces and sells petrochemicals (including ethylene, olefin, polyolefin, and paraxylene) and mines coal and other minerals. It also has stakes in electric power plants in China.

Still sorting out the logistical and cost-saving ramifications of the 1999 acquisition of Mobil by Exxon, Exxon Mobil has announced plans to cut 14,000 jobs — about 12% of its workforce — by 2002.

HISTORY

Exxon's 1999 acquisition of Mobil reunited two descendants of John D. Rockefeller's Standard Oil Company. Rockefeller, a commodity trader, started his first oil refinery in 1863 in Cleveland. Realizing that the price of oil at the well would shrink with each new strike, Rockefeller chose to monopolize oil refining and transportation. In 1870 he formed Standard Oil, and in 1882 he created the Standard Oil Trust, which allowed him to set up new, ostensibly independent, companies, including the Standard Oil Company of New Jersey (Jersey Standard); Rochester, New York-based Vacuum Oil; and Standard Oil of New York (nicknamed Socony).

The Standard Oil Trust controlled 90% of the petroleum industry. In 1911, after two decades of political and legal wrangling, the Supreme Court broke up the trust into 34 companies, the largest of which was Jersey Standard.

Walter Teagle, who became president of Jersey Standard in 1917, secretly bought half of Humble Oil of Texas (1919) and expanded operations into South America. In 1928 Jersey Standard joined in the Red Line Agreement, which reserved most Middle East oil for a few companies. Teagle resigned in 1942 after the company was criticized for a prewar research pact with German chemical giant I.G. Farben. The 1948 purchase of a 30% stake in Arabian American Oil Company, combined with a 7% share of Iranian production bought in 1954, made Jersey Standard the world's #1 oil company at that time.

Meanwhile, Vacuum Oil and Socony reunited in 1931 as Socony-Vacuum and adopted the Flying Red Horse (Pegasus — representing speed and power) as a trademark. The fast-growing company changed its name to Socony Mobil Oil in 1955 and became Mobil in 1976.

Other US companies, still using the Standard Oil name, objected to Jersey Standard's marketing in their territories as Esso (derived from the initials for Standard Oil). To end the confusion, in 1972 Jersey Standard became Exxon.

Nationalization of oil assets by producing countries reduced Exxon's access to oil during the 1970s. Though it increased exploration that decade and the next, Exxon's reserves shrank.

Oil tanker *Exxon Valdez* spilled some 11 million gallons of oil into Alaska's Prince William Sound in 1989. Exxon spent billions on the cleanup, and in 1994 a federal jury in Alaska slapped Exxon with a $5 billion fine. (Exxon appealed in 1997.)

With the oil industry consolidating, Exxon merged its worldwide oil and fuel additives business with that of Royal Dutch/Shell in 1996. The next year, under FTC pressure, Exxon agreed to run ads refuting claims that its premium gas enabled car engines to run more efficiently. Another PR disaster followed in 1998: CEO Lee Raymond upset environmentalists by publicly questioning the global warming theory.

Still, Exxon was unstoppable. It acquired Mobil for $81 billion in 1999; the new company had Raymond at the helm and Mobil's Lucio Noto as VC. (Noto retired in 2001.) To get the deal done, Exxon Mobil had to divest $4 billion in assets. It agreed to end its European gasoline and lubricants joint venture with BP and to sell more than 2,400 gas stations in the US.

In 2000 Exxon Mobil sold 1,740 East Coast gas stations to Tosco. It also sold its refinery in Benicia, California, plus 340 gas stations, to Valero Energy. In 2001 Exxon Mobil joined the California Fuel Cell Partnership, a group studying possible alternatives to, and supplements for, gasoline in fuel-burning engines.

Chairman and CEO: Lee R. Raymond, age 63, $5,200,000 pay
EVP and Director: Eugene A. Renna, age 56, $1,963,000 pay (prior to promotion)
EVP and Director: Harry J. Longwell, age 60, $1,963,000 pay (prior to promotion)
EVP and Director: René Dahan, age 59, $1,960,000 pay (prior to promotion)
SVP: Edward G. Galante, age 50
SVP: Rex W. Tillerson, age 49
VP and General Counsel: Charles W. Matthews Jr., age 56
VP and Treasurer: Frank A. Risch, age 58
VP Human Resources: Timothy J. Hearn
VP Public Affairs: Kenneth P. Cohen
VP; President, Exxon Coal and Minerals: Joe T. McMillan, age 64
VP; President, ExxonMobil Chemical: Daniel S. Sanders, age 61
VP; President, ExxonMobil Exploration: Jon L. Thompson, age 61
Auditors: PricewaterhouseCoopers LLP

LOCATIONS

HQ: 5959 Las Colinas Blvd., Irving, TX 75039
Phone: 972-444-1000 **Fax:** 972-444-1350
Web: www.exxon.mobil.com

2000 Sales

	$ mil.	% of total
US	70,036	31
Japan	24,520	11
UK	19,904	9
Canada	16,059	7
Other countries	97,920	42
Total	**228,439**	**100**

PRODUCTS/OPERATIONS

2000 Sales

	$ mil.	% of total
Petroleum & natural gas		
Downstream	188,563	83
Upstream	21,443	9
Chemicals	17,501	8
Other	932	—
Total	**228,439**	**100**

Selected Subsidiaries and Affiliates
Aera Energy, LLC (48%)
Esso Deutschland GmbH
Esso Petroleum Company, Limited (UK)
Esso (Thailand) Public Company, Limited (88%)
ExxonMobil Chemical Company
Imperial Oil Limited (70%, Canada)
Mobil Oil Corporation
General Sekiyu K.K. (50%, Japan)

COMPETITORS

7-Eleven	Huntsman	Royal
Amerada Hess	ICI	Dutch/Shell
Ashland	Kerr-McGee	Saudi Aramco
BHP Billiton	Koch	Sunoco
BP	Lyondell	Texaco
Caltex	Chemical	Tosco
Celanese	Norsk Hydro	TOTAL FINA
Chevron	Occidental	ELF
Costco	PDVSA	Ultramar
Wholesale	PEMEX	Diamond
Dow Chemical	PETROBRAS	Shamrock
DuPont	Phillips	Union Carbide
Eastman	Petroleum	Unocal
Chemical	Racetrac	USX-Marathon
Eni	Petroleum	
Enron	Repsol YPF	

HISTORICAL FINANCIALS & EMPLOYEES

NYSE: XOM FYE: December 31	Annual Growth	12/91	12/92	12/93	12/94	12/95	12/96	12/97	12/98	12/99	12/00
Sales ($ mil.)	9.3%	102,847	103,160	97,825	99,683	107,893	116,728	120,279	100,697	160,883	228,439
Net income ($ mil.)	13.7%	5,600	4,770	5,280	5,100	6,470	7,510	8,460	6,433	7,910	17,720
Income as % of sales	—	5.4%	4.6%	5.4%	5.1%	6.0%	6.4%	7.0%	6.4%	4.9%	7.8%
Earnings per share ($)	9.5%	1.12	0.95	1.05	1.02	1.29	1.50	1.69	1.29	1.13	2.53
Stock price - FY high ($)	—	15.47	16.38	17.25	16.84	21.50	25.31	33.63	38.66	43.63	47.72
Stock price - FY low ($)	—	12.41	13.44	14.44	14.03	15.03	19.41	24.13	28.31	32.16	34.94
Stock price - FY close ($)	12.4%	15.22	15.28	15.78	15.19	20.28	24.50	30.59	36.56	40.28	43.47
P/E - high	—	14	17	16	17	17	17	20	30	38	21
P/E - low	—	11	14	14	14	12	13	14	22	28	15
Dividends per share ($)	3.1%	0.67	0.71	0.72	0.73	0.75	0.98	0.82	0.82	0.84	0.88
Book value per share ($)	2.7%	7.03	6.80	7.00	7.53	8.14	8.76	8.88	9.01	9.13	8.95
Employees	2.2%	101,000	95,000	91,000	86,000	82,000	79,000	80,000	79,000	123,000	123,000

STOCK PRICE HISTORY

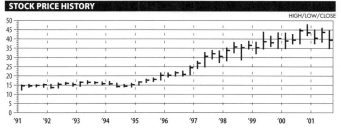

HIGH/LOW/CLOSE

2000 FISCAL YEAR-END

Debt ratio: 9.3%
Return on equity: 26.4%
Cash ($ mil.): 7,080
Current ratio: 1.06
Long-term debt ($ mil.): 7,280
No. of shares (mil.): 7,910
Dividends
  Yield: 2.0%
  Payout: 34.8%
Market value ($ mil.): 343,848

FLEMING COMPANIES, INC.

OVERVIEW

Fleming Companies weighs in as the nation's #2 wholesale food distributor (behind SUPERVALU), but it's been trimming some fat. Based in Lewisville, Texas, Fleming supplies brand-name and private-label food and general merchandise to about 7,000 US retailers, including mass merchandisers (Kmart), independent retailers, franchised stores (under its Piggly Wiggly banner), limited assortment stores, and convenience stores. It also owns more than 90 stores that operate

under the Food 4 Less, Rainbow Foods, and Yes!Less banners. Fleming also offers an array of marketing, consulting, and insurance services to food retailers.

After losing several of its largest customers (Randall's Food Markets, Furrs Supermarkets), the company initiated a restructuring effort to make itself more efficient. It shed unprofitable company-owned retail chains and consolidating distribution facilities. The Yucaipa Companies owns almost 9% of Fleming.

HISTORY

Lux Mercantile, a Topeka, Kansas, wholesale grocery founded by O. A. Fleming, Gene Wilson, and Sam Lux, was incorporated in 1915. Three years later the company became Fleming-Wilson Mercantile.

Facing competition from chains, independent wholesalers and grocers banded together to provide competitive mass merchandising, advertising, and efficient store operations. Fleming's son Ned helped establish Fleming-Wilson as the first voluntary wholesaler west of the Mississippi (1927). The enterprise was renamed the Fleming Company (1941), and Ned became president (1945-64) and then chairman and CEO (1964-81). The company went public in 1959 and adopted the name Fleming Companies in 1972.

Fleming has grown by acquisitions since the 1930s, primarily of midwestern wholesale food distributors and supermarkets such as Grainger Brothers (1962, renamed the Fleming Co. of Nebraska); Associated Grocers of Arizona (1985); and Godfrey, with 32 Sentry supermarkets and four Sun warehouse markets (1987). The company also acquired a coffee company, a bakery, a wholesale drug firm, and several distribution centers.

The 1988 purchase of Malone & Hyde, the sixth-largest wholesale food distributor in the US (and owner of the Piggly Wiggly franchise), made Fleming the largest in that field for several years. Later that year the company sold Malone & Hyde's 99-store retail pharmacy subsidiary, M&A Drugs.

Fleming lost important customers when Albertson's began self-distributing in 1990 and when Alpha Beta stores merged with Lucky. As the company saw its supermarkets losing market share to superstores and warehouses in 1993, it began a major restructuring that year (which encountered so much resistance it was delayed until 1998).

In 1994 Fleming added nearly 3,000 stores,

including 175 company-owned outlets, with its $1.1 billion purchase of Scrivner, the US's #3 food wholesaler at the time, from German company Franz Haniel & Cie. That year Fleming sold off underperforming units such as the 28-unit Brooks convenience store chain and cut its workforce again.

With its performance flagging in 1998, Fleming ousted chairman and CEO Robert Stauth and eventually replaced him with Mark Hansen, former CEO of Wal-Mart's Sam's Club. Hansen announced a five-year program to improve profit margins by selling or closing seven supply centers and weaker stores.

To that end, in 1999 the company sold its struggling Boogaarts Food Stores, Hyde Park Market, and Consumers Food & Drug chains. Fleming also began converting SuPeRSaVeR stores to its Sentry Foods banner in Wisconsin to streamline marketing efforts in that area.

Fleming signed a three-year deal to supply Kmart stores in 1999. In another move signaling the company might be focusing on mass merchandisers and deepening relationships with other large customers such as Kroger, Fleming announced in 2000 it would sell various chains, including ABCO Desert Markets, Sentry, and Baker's Supermarkets.

In 2001 Fleming beat out rival supplier SUPERVALU and secured a deal worth $4.5 billion to be the sole provider of food and consumable products to all Kmart and Super Kmart stores. The deal caught the eye of investment firm The Yucaipa Companies, which bought almost 9% of the company. Also in 2001 Fleming bid on the bankrupt Furrs Supermarket chain in New Mexico and Texas and bought 36 of the 71 Furrs stores. Fleming then sold most of the stores to major retail chains and independent grocers, with about half of the new store owners naming Fleming as their supplier. Furrs closed 35 stores for which Fleming was unable to find buyers.

OFFICERS

Chairman and CEO: Mark S. Hansen, age 46,
$2,547,115 pay
EVP and CFO: Neal J. Rider, age 39, $1,191,735 pay
EVP and President, Retail: Dennis C. Lucas, age 53,
$1,007,692 pay
EVP and President, Retail and Corporate Marketing:
Tom Dahlen
EVP and President, Wholesale: E. Stephen Davis,
$993,654 pay
**EVP, Business Development and Chief Knowledge
Officer:** William H. Marquard, age 41, $1,007,692 pay
EVP, Human Resources: Scott M. Northcutt, age 39
SVP, Convenience Store and E-Commerce Fulfillment:
John F. Baldi, age 48
SVP, Finance: Mark D. Shapiro, age 40 ·
SVP, Finance and Treasurer: Matt Hildreth
SVP, General Counsel, and Secretary:
Carlos M. Hernandez, age 46
SVP, Logistics: William Merrigan
SVP, Procurement: Philip B. Murphy
SVP, Real Estate and Store Development:
Charles L. Hall, age 50
Auditors: Deloitte & Touche LLP

LOCATIONS

HQ: 1945 Lakepointe Dr., Box 299013,
Lewisville, TX 75057
Phone: 972-906-8000   **Fax:** 972-906-7810
Web: www.fleming.com

Fleming Companies serves about 7,000 retailers
(supermarkets, convenience stores, drug stores, discount
stores, limited assortment stores, and specialty stores) in
41 states, including about 90 company-owned stores,
predominantly in the Midwest and the South. It has
more than 30 distribution centers across the US.

PRODUCTS/OPERATIONS

Business Operations

Fleming Brands	Fleming Retail Services
BestYet	Advertising
IGA	Category management
Living Well	Cerespan (electronic
Marquee	communications
Nature's Finest	network)
Piggly Wiggly	Finance
Rainbow	Insurance
SuperTru	Marketing
	Pricing
Fleming Retail Group	Promotions
Food 4 Less	Store development
Rainbow Foods (Minnesota	Store operations
and Wisconsin)	Technology
Yes!Less	

COMPETITORS

A&P	Meijer
Albertson's	Nash Finch
Associated Food	Publix
AWG	Roundy's
C&S Wholesale	Royal Ahold
Di Giorgio	Safeway
H-E-B	Spartan Stores
Homeland Holding	SUPERVALU
Hy-Vee	Wakefern Food
Kroger	Wal-Mart
McLane	Winn-Dixie

HISTORICAL FINANCIALS & EMPLOYEES

NYSE: FLM FYE: Last Sat. nearest Dec. 31	Annual Growth	12/91	12/92	12/93	12/94	12/95	12/96	12/97	12/98	12/99	12/00
Sales ($ mil.)	1.3%	12,902	12,938	13,092	15,754	17,502	16,487	15,373	15,069	14,646	14,444
Net income ($ mil.)	—	63	113	35	56	42	27	25	(511)	(45)	(122)
Income as % of sales	—	0.5%	0.9%	0.3%	0.4%	0.2%	0.2%	0.2%	—	—	—
Earnings per share ($)	—	1.50	3.06	0.96	1.51	1.12	0.71	0.67	(13.48)	(1.17)	(3.15)
Stock price - FY high ($)	—	40.63	35.13	34.38	30.00	29.88	20.88	20.38	20.75	13.44	17.63
Stock price - FY low ($)	—	29.88	27.25	23.75	22.63	19.13	11.50	13.44	8.63	7.19	8.69
Stock price - FY close ($)	(11.2%)	34.38	31.50	24.75	23.25	20.63	17.25	13.44	10.38	10.25	11.81
P/E - high	—	23	11	34	20	27	29	20	—	—	—
P/E - low	—	17	8	23	15	17	16	13	—	—	—
Dividends per share ($)	(25.6%)	1.14	1.20	1.20	1.20	1.20	0.36	0.08	0.08	0.08	0.08
Book value per share ($)	(9.7%)	27.01	28.90	28.90	28.78	28.72	28.47	28.48	14.79	14.43	10.78
Employees	2.9%	22,800	22,800	23,300	42,400	44,000	41,200	39,700	38,900	36,300	29,567

STOCK PRICE HISTORY

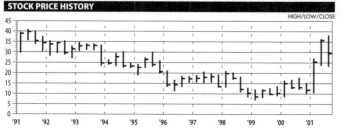

HIGH/LOW/CLOSE

2000 FISCAL YEAR-END

Debt ratio: 79.0%
Return on equity: —
Cash ($ mil.): 30
Current ratio: 1.32
Long-term debt ($ mil.): 1,610
No. of shares (mil.): 40
Dividends
 Yield: 0.7%
 Payout: —
Market value ($ mil.): 468

FOSSIL, INC.

OVERVIEW

Fossil puts a new wrinkle on time. The Richardson, Texas-based company is one of the leading makers of midpriced fashion watches. Like rivals Guess? and Swatch, Fossil targets those in their teens, 20s, and 30s — i.e., those hip to the latest trends. Many of Fossil's funky timepieces have a retro 1950s look, a trend the company continues in its Relic (less-expensive watches) brand. Building on the Fossil brand name, the company also markets wallets, handbags, belts, sunglasses, and apparel, and has recently added jewelry to its product line.

In addition to selling its merchandise through about 70 of its own retail and outlet stores in the US and eight foreign countries, Fossil sells through department stores, specialty stores, and other retail outlets in more than 80 countries.

The company added a technological twist to its product line when it introduced its Wrist PDA and Wrist PDA/PC watches in 2001, which offer an interface with most popular personal digital assistants.

Founder and CEO Tom Kartsotis and his brother, president Kosta Kartsotis, own 49% of the company.

HISTORY

Tom Kartsotis founded a Dallas area import-export company, originally called Overseas Products International, in 1984. He was only 24, and Swatch was the hot watch brand. His brother, Kosta Kartsotis, a department store executive, had told him about the high profits that Asian imports could offer. With Lynne Stafford (whom Tom later married) as designer, the company gave its Asian-made Fossil watches a retro image, and sales took off. In 1988 Kosta joined the firm to woo department stores.

Between 1987 and 1989 sales rose from $2 million to $20 million. In 1990 a less-expensive line of watches, Relic, was created for stores such as JCPenney and Sears. Tom renamed the company Fossil in 1992 and took it public in 1993. Its product line then included women's accessories (such as belts) and small leather goods for men. Two years later Fossil introduced sunglasses.

The company opened its first US retail outlets in 1996. The next year Fossil signed licensing agreements with Giorgio Armani for the Emporio Armani Orologi watch line and with London Fog to make Fossil outerwear. Through a joint venture with Netherlands-based Capstan Bay, the firm opened its first European store in 1998 in Amsterdam.

In 1999 Fossil entered a joint venture with the American subsidiary of Japanese watchmaker Seiko to produce and market Lorus and Disney character watches. Also that year it signed a licensing agreement with Donna Karan International to produce a line of watches under the Donna Karan New York, DKNY, and DKNY Active brand names. The company in 1999 also signed a deal with Italian design firm Diesel to produce a line of Diesel branded watches.

The following year Fossil launched its own Fossil-brand jeans and apparel line to be sold at its approximately 12 new Fossil apparel stores. Also in 2000 the company announced plans to launch a line of women's jewelry, including rings, earrings, necklaces, and bracelets.

Fossil acquired UK-based The Avia Watch Company, maker of Avia-brand watches, in mid-2001 to grow its business in the UK. The company strengthened its European presence even further that year when it acquired its French distributor, Vedette Industries. Also in 2001 Fossil bought an 80% stake in its Australian distributor FSLA.

Later that year Fossil put down roots in the watchmaking fatherland when it acquired three separate Swiss watch companies. The company also acquired the worldwide rights to 120-year-old Zodiac brand name.

Late in 2001 Fossil introduced a line of high-tech watches that work with personal digital assistants (PDAs) such as the Palm Pilot and the Compaq iPaq. The first two products, the Wrist PDA and Wrist PDA/PC, allow users to download up to 190 kb of information from their PDAs to their watches through an infrared interface. While the data is read-only (the user can't add to it or change it), the watch can store things like contacts, appointments, and to-do lists.

OFFICERS

Chairman: Tom Kartsotis, age 41, $262,500 pay
President, CEO, and Director: Kosta N. Kartsotis, age 48, $255,000 pay
EVP: Randy S. Kercho, age 44
EVP, Chief Legal Officer, and Secretary: T. R. Tunnell, age 47
SVP, Product Development: Dairmuid Bland, age 45
SVP, Donna Karan Division: Gary A. Bollinger, age 53
SVP and Image Director: Timothy G. Hale, age 40
SVP, RELIC, Private Label and Special Markets: David Heath, age 47
SVP, CFO, and Treasurer: Mike Kovar, age 39
SVP, Global Marketing: Enrico Margaretelli, age 41
SVP, Stores and Real Estate: Tom Olt, age 54
SVP, International: Franz Scheurl, age 49
SVP, RELIC and Private Label: Daniel M. Smith, age 63
VP, Product Development: Suzanne Amundsen, age 43
VP, Process Engineering: Heath Carr, age 34
VP, Midwest Region: Robert V. Fiore, age 56
VP, Northeast Region: Cheri J. Friedman, age 44
VP, e-Commerce: Kurt Hagen, age 32
VP, Human Resources and Organizational Development: Lisa Lapiska, age 45
VP, Eyewear: David R. Moore, age 40
Auditors: Deloitte & Touche LLP

LOCATIONS

HQ: 2280 N. Greenville Ave., Richardson, TX 75082
Phone: 972-234-2525   **Fax:** 972-234-4669
Web: www.fossil.com

2000 Sales

	$ mil.	% of total
US	352	70
Europe	99	20
Far East		
Japan	6	1
Other countries	47	9
Total	**504**	**100**

PRODUCTS/OPERATIONS

Selected Products
Apparel
Belts
DKNY watches
Donna Karan New York watches
Emporio Armani watches
Fossil Blue sports watches
Fossil watches (including collectors' watches featuring sports team logos, characters from movies, and other images)
Leather goods (handbags, minibags, coin purses, key chains, wallets)
Private-label/licensed products
Relic watches
Sunglasses

COMPETITORS

Abercrombie & Fitch
Calvin Klein
Casio Computer
Citizen Watch
E. Gluck
The Gap
Gucci
Guess?
Jones Apparel
Kenneth Cole
Liz Claiborne
Loews
Movado Group
Seiko
Swank
Swatch
Swiss Army Brands
Timex
Tommy Hilfiger

HISTORICAL FINANCIALS & EMPLOYEES

Nasdaq: FOSL FYE: Sat. nearest Dec. 31	Annual Growth	12/91	12/92	12/93	12/94	12/95	12/96	12/97	12/98	12/99	12/00
Sales ($ mil.)	27.4%	57	74	105	162	181	206	245	305	419	504
Net income ($ mil.)	26.2%	7	7	12	15	12	14	19	32	52	56
Income as % of sales	—	12.0%	9.5%	10.9%	9.5%	6.7%	6.6%	7.7%	10.6%	12.4%	11.1%
Earnings per share ($)	22.6%	—	—	0.41	0.51	0.27	0.30	0.61	0.99	1.55	1.71
Stock price – FY high ($)	—	—	—	9.34	13.12	11.68	7.29	11.79	20.43	36.60	26.75
Stock price – FY low ($)	—	—	—	3.34	5.45	3.11	2.89	4.67	8.67	17.26	10.50
Stock price – FY close ($)	8.0%	—	—	8.45	5.84	3.73	6.01	11.12	19.18	23.13	14.48
P/E – high	—	—	—	23	26	43	24	19	20	22	16
P/E – low	—	—	—	8	11	12	9	7	8	11	6
Dividends per share ($)	—	—	—	0.00	0.00	0.00	0.00	0.00	0.00	0.00	0.00
Book value per share ($)	30.8%	—	—	1.12	1.65	2.07	2.51	3.13	4.32	5.97	7.32
Employees	35.8%	130	234	370	555	430	668	722	828	1,217	2,044

STOCK PRICE HISTORY

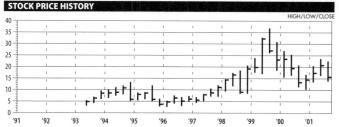

HIGH/LOW/CLOSE

2000 FISCAL YEAR-END

Debt ratio: 0.0%
Return on equity: 27.1%
Cash ($ mil.): 80
Current ratio: 3.05
Long-term debt ($ mil.): 0
No. of shares (mil.): 30
Dividends
  Yield: —
  Payout: —
Market value ($ mil.): 436

HAGGAR CORP.

OVERVIEW

Haggar is hooked on classics. Dallas-based Haggar is a leading maker of men's dress and casual pants, sport coats, and suits. The bulk of its lines consist of basic styles that (the company hopes) are less susceptible to the vagaries of fashion. The Haggar brand, which accounts for nearly two-thirds of the company's sales, is sold in about 10,000 US stores, including department stores such as JCPenney and Kohls (its largest customers) and more than 65 Haggar outlet stores.

The company moved into womenswear with its purchase of Jerell, which makes the Stonebridge and Selena lines. Haggar has also begun test marketing a line of its own branded womenswear, hoping to use the strong brand awareness it has in menswear (consumer awareness of the Haggar brand name exceeds 90%) to diversify its product lines. The company is looking to expand its reach through a series of licensing agreements with designers, including Donna Karan and Liz Claiborne. It is also seeking to acquire additional men's brands to add to its stable.

Haggar also makes lower priced products for mass merchants and private-label clothing. Independent firms in Asia and Latin America make about three-fourths of Haggar's apparel. Hurt by the general weakness in the retail industry, the company has been restructuring its manufacturing operations to lower costs.

Chairman and CEO J. M. Haggar III, the grandson of the company's founder, owns about 8% of Haggar.

HISTORY

J. M. Haggar Sr., an immigrant from Lebanon, started his clothing business near Dallas in 1926. His son E. R. became president in 1948 and helped popularize the word "slacks" to describe pants worn after work. Haggar pioneered finished-bottom pants (ending the need for alterations) in the 1950s and was a big promoter of permanent-press pants in the 1960s. The company introduced its lower-priced Reed St. James brand in 1983.

Joseph Haggar III, E. R.'s nephew, became CEO in 1990, just as the popularity of Levi's Dockers was shrinking the dress pants market. Haggar launched the immediately popular Wrinkle-Free cotton pants (no ironing or dry cleaning needed) in 1992, the year it went public. Riding the fashion trend of natural fibers and casual clothing, its cotton products soon racked up almost a third of sales.

In 1995 the company introduced Wrinkle-Free cotton shirts and opened the first Haggar retail store. Storm damage of $40 million at its Dallas distribution center and a $14 million restructuring charge to consolidate its US operations and shift more production to other countries caused a $2 million loss the next year.

In the late 1990s Haggar introduced the Ultimate Pant for the casual market, its more upscale Black Label line, and Cotton Flex fabric, a wrinkle-free, stretchable cotton. In 1997 and 1998 Haggar opened its subsidiaries in the UK and Japan.

In 1999 Haggar diversified its product line when it purchased women's apparel maker Jerell. The acquisition gave Haggar a major womenswear company with national accounts in a number of major department stores, including Coldwater Creek, Dillard's, Federated Stores, Foley's, JCPenney, Sears, and Nordstrom's.

Also that year it established a Canadian subsidiary, Haggar Canada. And in 1999 the company launched a Web site, haggar.com.

In 2000 the company formed an alliance with Donna Karan International to make the fashion company's DKNY brand of men's pants. Also that year the company launched a line of women's clothing, and it introduced a new line of men's clothing in Japan. The company also launched a major advertising campaign to promote its popular Micromattique line of micro-fiber pants.

In 2001 the company signed a licensing deal with fashion design company Liz Claiborne to market Claiborne brand casual and dress pants. Also that year Haggar announced a major reorganization of its manufacturing operations designed to lower expenses and improve efficiency as the retail market tightened. Costs related to the reorganization coupled with the weakening retail environment led to a loss in fiscal 2001.

OFFICERS

Chairman and CEO: J. M. Haggar III, age 49, $1,070,000 pay
President and COO: Frank D. Bracken, age 60, $927,000 pay
EVP and CFO: David M. Tehle, age 44, $402,000 pay
EVP and Chief Marketing Officer: Alan C. Burks, age 46, $462,000 pay
EVP Operations: David G. Roy, age 46, $278,000 pay
SVP Haggar Direct: Lou Spagna
SVP Human Resources: Billy Langston
SVP Sales: David Condo
VP Retail Marketing: Karen Rambo
Auditors: Arthur Andersen LLP

LOCATIONS

HQ: 6113 Lemmon Ave., Dallas, TX 75209
Phone: 214-352-8481   **Fax:** 214-956-4367
Web: www.haggarcorp.com

Haggar markets in Canada, Europe, Japan, and the US; it has plants in the Dominican Republic and Mexico and uses contract manufacturers in Asia and Latin America.

PRODUCTS/OPERATIONS

2000 Sales

	% of total
Haggar label	63
Other	37
Total	**100**

Selected Products

Custom-fit suits (separately sized pants and matching jackets purchased together)
Dresses
Pants
Shirts
Shorts
Skirts
Sport coats
Sweaters
Vests

Selected Brands

Menswear
Black Label
City Casuals
Collections
Generations
Haggar Golf
Haggar Heritage (basics line)
Haggar Wrinkle-Free Cottons

Womenswear
Haggar
Selena
Stonebridge

COMPETITORS

Benetton
Fruit of the Loom
The Gap
Hampton Industries
Hartmarx
J. Crew
Kellwood
Lands' End
Levi Strauss
Liz Claiborne
L.L. Bean
Nautica Enterprises
Oxford Industries
Perry Ellis International
Phillips-Van Heusen
Polo
Spiegel
Tommy Hilfiger
Tropical Sportswear
VF
Warnaco Group

HISTORICAL FINANCIALS & EMPLOYEES

Nasdaq: HGGR FYE: September 30	Annual Growth	9/91	9/92	9/93	9/94	9/95	9/96	9/97	9/98	9/99	9/00
Sales ($ mil.)	2.2%	355	381	394	491	449	438	406	403	434	433
Net income ($ mil.)	6.7%	5	12	15	26	10	(2)	4	8	9	9
Income as % of sales	—	1.4%	3.3%	3.8%	5.2%	2.2%	—	0.9%	2.0%	2.2%	2.1%
Earnings per share ($)	(4.4%)	—	—	1.88	2.95	1.14	(0.28)	0.44	0.94	1.26	1.37
Stock price - FY high ($)	—	—	—	22.50	40.50	27.75	19.00	18.75	18.00	15.13	15.00
Stock price - FY low ($)	—	—	—	15.50	17.75	17.75	11.50	11.50	10.19	9.56	10.31
Stock price - FY close ($)	(5.5%)	—	—	18.63	27.75	18.63	14.50	14.88	11.00	12.63	12.50
P/E - high	—	—	—	12	14	24	—	43	19	12	11
P/E - low	—	—	—	8	6	16	—	26	11	8	7
Dividends per share ($)	10.4%	—	—	0.10	0.20	0.20	0.20	0.20	0.20	0.20	0.20
Book value per share ($)	6.9%	—	—	15.70	18.51	19.46	19.00	19.24	20.55	22.88	25.05
Employees	(3.4%)	—	5,100	6,100	6,400	6,500	6,000	4,300	3,979	4,250	3,856

STOCK PRICE HISTORY

HIGH/LOW/CLOSE

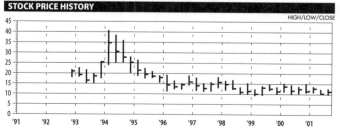

2000 FISCAL YEAR-END

Debt ratio: 22.0%
Return on equity: 5.7%
Cash ($ mil.): 6
Current ratio: 2.89
Long-term debt ($ mil.): 46
No. of shares (mil.): 7
Dividends
  Yield: 1.6%
  Payout: 14.6%
Market value ($ mil.): 82

HALLIBURTON COMPANY

OVERVIEW

No matter where you are in the oil field of dreams, if you need it built, Halliburton will come. The world's largest oil field services provider (followed by Schlumberger), the Dallas-based company also makes oil field equipment and offers construction, engineering, and maintenance services, particularly for the petroleum industry, in more than 120 countries.

The company's Energy Services Group accounts for two-thirds of Halliburton's sales. It includes Brown & Root Energy Services, which constructs offshore production facilities and land-based plants and pipelines. Halliburton Energy Services offers well evaluation, drilling, and maintenance services for oil companies; Landmark Graphics develops exploration-related software and provides information technology services. The group also manufactures drill bits and field processing equipment.

Part of the company's Engineering and Construction Group, Kellogg Brown & Root builds facilities primarily for energy, petrochemical, and refinery clients. Its Brown & Root Services provides engineering, construction, management, and technology services for non-energy businesses and government institutions.

Halliburton is spending big bucks on technology in an effort to develop more efficient oil field products and processes. As part of its strategy of refocusing on core businesses, Halliburton sold its Dresser Equipment Group, a manufacturer of energy-related meters, engines, and automated controls.

HISTORY

Erle Halliburton began his oil career in 1916 at Perkins Oil Well Cementing. He moved to oil boomtown Burkburnett, Texas, to start his Better Method Oil Well Cementing Company in 1919. Halliburton used cement to hold a steel pipe in a well, which kept oil out of the water table, strengthened well walls, and reduced the risk of explosions. Though the contribution would later be praised, his technique was considered useless at the time.

In 1920 Halliburton moved to Oklahoma. Incorporating Halliburton Oil Well Cementing Company in 1924, he patented its products and services, forcing oil companies to employ his firm if they wanted to cement wells.

Erle died in 1957, but his company grew through acquisitions between the 1950s and the 1970s. In 1962 the company bought Houston construction giant Brown & Root, an expert in offshore platforms. After the 1973 Arab oil embargo, Halliburton benefited from the surge in global oil exploration, and later, as drilling costs surged, it became a leader in well stimulation.

When the oil industry slumped in 1982, the firm halved its workforce. Three years later a suffering Brown & Root coughed up $750 million to settle charges of mismanagement at the South Texas Nuclear Project.

In the 1990s Halliburton expanded abroad, entering Russia in 1991 and China in 1993. The next year Brown & Root was named contractor for a pipeline stretching from Qatar to Pakistan. Halliburton drilled the world's deepest horizontal well (18,860 ft.) in Germany in 1995.

Also in 1995 Dick Cheney, a former US defense secretary, became CEO. Brown & Root began providing engineering and logistics services to US Army peacekeeping troops in the Balkans in 1995, and won a major contract to develop an offshore Canadian oil field the next year.

In 1997 Halliburton completed a major reorganization started in 1993, uniting 10 businesses under the Halliburton Energy Services umbrella. The company nearly doubled in size in 1998 with its $7.7 billion acquisition of oil field equipment manufacturer Dresser Industries. The purchase, coupled with falling oil prices in 1998 and 1999, prompted Halliburton to ax more than 9,000 workers. (Even after oil prices rebounded in 2000, Halliburton had to wait for the effects of the upturn to reach the oil field services sector.)

Brown & Root Energy Services won a contract to provide logistics support for the US Army in Albania in 1999. Halliburton also invested in oil field emergency-response firm Boots & Coots and took a stake in Japanese engineering firm Chiyoda.

The company began to sell off portions of its Dresser acquisition in 1999. Partner Ingersoll-Rand bought Halliburton's stake in Ingersoll-Dresser Pump for $515 million and bought Halliburton's stake in Dresser-Rand (industrial compressors) for $579 million in 2000. Cheney resigned as chairman and CEO that year after he was chosen as George W. Bush's vice presidential running mate. President and COO David Lesar succeeded him.

In 2001 a group of two investment firms, First Reserve and Odyssey Investment Partners, and Dresser managers paid $1.55 billion for Dresser Equipment Group.

Chairman, President, and CEO: David J. Lesar, age 47, $2,971,042 pay
Vice Chairman: Donald C. Vaughn, age 65, $1,908,178 pay
EVP and CFO: Douglas L. Foshee, age 42
EVP and General Counsel: Lester L. Coleman, age 58, $973,808 pay
EVP, Global Business Development: John W. Kennedy, age 50
EVP: Gary V. Morris, age 47, $973,808 pay (prior to title change)
SVP: David A. Reamer, age 48, $717,543 pay
VP and Chief Technology Officer: Robert F. Heinemann, age 47
VP, Secretary, and Corporate Counsel: Susan S. Keith
VP and Treasurer: Jerry H. Blurton, age 56
VP and Controller: R. Charles Muchmore Jr., age 47
VP, Human Resources: Margaret Carriere, age 49
VP, Investor Relations: Guy T. Marcus
Chairman, Kellogg Brown & Root: A. Jack Stanley
President and CEO, Kellogg Brown & Root: R. Randall Harl
President, Energy Services Group: Edgar Ortiz, age 58
Auditors: Arthur Andersen LLP

LOCATIONS

HQ: 3600 Lincoln Plaza, 500 N. Akard St., Dallas, TX 75201
Phone: 214-978-2600   **Fax:** 214-978-2611
Web: www.halliburton.com

Halliburton has operations in more than 120 countries.

PRODUCTS/OPERATIONS

2000 Sales

	% of total
Energy Services Group	66
Engineering & Construction Group	34
Total	**100**

Selected Operations

Brown & Root Energy Services (oil and gas, offshore and subsea construction and engineering)
Halliburton Energy Services (contract development, drilling, production, and operation of oil fields)
Landmark Graphics Corporation (exploration and production software, information systems)

COMPETITORS

ABB	Fluor	Perini
Baker Hughes	FMC	Peter Kiewit
Bechtel	Foster Wheeler	Sons'
BJ Services	Global Marine	Petroleum Geo-
Black & Veatch	Ishikawajima-	Services
Bouygues	Harima	Pride
Caterpillar	McDermott	International
Coflexip	Mitsubishi	Raytheon
Compagnie	Nabors Industries	Schlumberger
Générale de	National-Oilwell	Smith
Géophysique	Noble Drilling	International
Cooper Cameron	Nuovo Pignone	Varco
Diamond	Industrie	International
Offshore	Meccaniche	Weatherford
ENSCO	Parsons	International

HISTORICAL FINANCIALS & EMPLOYEES

NYSE: HAL FYE: December 31	Annual Growth	12/91	12/92	12/93	12/94	12/95	12/96	12/97	12/98	12/99	12/00
Sales ($ mil.)	6.0%	7,019	6,525	6,351	5,741	5,699	7,385	8,819	17,353	14,898	11,856
Net income ($ mil.)	38.6%	27	(137)	(161)	178	168	300	454	(15)	438	501
Income as % of sales	—	0.4%	—	—	3.1%	3.0%	4.1%	5.2%	—	2.9%	4.2%
Earnings per share ($)	23.4%	0.17	(0.63)	(0.61)	0.73	0.74	1.19	1.75	(0.03)	0.99	1.13
Stock price - FY high ($)	—	27.63	18.44	22.00	18.63	25.44	31.81	63.25	57.25	51.75	55.19
Stock price - FY low ($)	—	12.75	10.88	12.88	13.94	16.44	22.38	29.69	25.00	28.13	32.25
Stock price - FY close ($)	10.9%	14.25	14.38	15.94	16.56	25.31	30.13	51.88	29.63	40.25	36.25
P/E - high	—	276	—	—	26	34	27	36	—	76	86
P/E - low	—	128	—	—	20	22	19	17	—	41	50
Dividends per share ($)	0.0%	0.50	0.50	0.50	0.50	0.50	0.50	0.50	0.50	0.50	0.50
Book value per share ($)	(1.0%)	10.11	8.90	8.27	8.51	7.64	8.62	9.85	9.23	9.70	9.20
Employees	2.7%	73,400	69,200	64,700	57,200	57,300	60,000	70,750	107,800	103,000	93,000

STOCK PRICE HISTORY

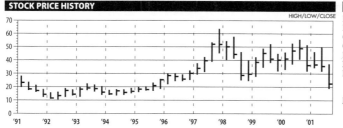

HIGH/LOW/CLOSE

2000 FISCAL YEAR-END

Debt ratio: 21.1%
Return on equity: 7.0%
Cash ($ mil.): 231
Current ratio: 1.46
Long-term debt ($ mil.): 1,049
No. of shares (mil.): 427
Dividends
  Yield: 1.4%
  Payout: 78.1%
Market value ($ mil.): 15,479

HARTE-HANKS, INC.

OVERVIEW

Harte-Hanks helps its customers stay on target. The San Antonio-based company generates almost 70% of its sales through direct marketing services including response management, database marketing, printing, fulfillment, transportation logistics, and interactive marketing tasks such as Web site development and e-commerce services. Harte-Hanks is also the nation's largest publisher of advertising shoppers (coupons and advertising circulars sent by mail), delivering them to nearly 10 million homes in California and Florida each week.

Harte-Hank's clients include retail, financial services, high-tech, healthcare, pharmaceuticals, and telecommunications companies. It has operations in North America, Europe, South America, and the Pacific Rim. The company is focusing on building its customer relationship management business (CRM); it recently split its direct marketing operations into two units, CRM and Marketing Services, as part of that initiative.

The family of co-founder Houston Harte (including vice chairman Houston H. Harte) owns about 16% of the company; director David Copeland owns about 12%; and chairman and CEO Larry Franklin, 16%.

HISTORY

Harte-Hanks Newspapers was founded by publishers Houston Harte and Bernard Hanks in 1924. The firm bought Texas newspapers — including papers in Corpus Christi (1928), Wichita Falls (1948), and San Antonio (1960) — and added a San Antonio TV station (1962). The firm went public in 1972, the year Harte died. Harte's son, Houston H. Harte, became chairman.

Over the next decade the company diversified into shoppers (ad circulars) and expanded beyond Texas (it sold the San Antonio papers in 1973), changing its name to Harte-Hanks Communications in 1977. In 1984 five executives took the company private again, adding $700 million in debt in the process. In 1986, when it had 70 newspapers, Harte-Hanks began consolidating operations to reduce its debt and focus on fewer, larger markets. By 1988 it had sold off half its holdings and bought others in California, Dallas, and Boston.

In 1991 twenty-year company veteran Larry Franklin was named CEO. (He added the chairman title in 1999.) Two years later the company went public a second time, but suffered a hefty loss attributable to its 14 suburban Boston newspapers (sold 1994). In 1994 Harte-Hanks acquired Select Marketing, which serves the high-tech industry.

The firm bought marketing group Steinert & Associates in 1995. The next year Harte-Hanks acquired marketing agency DiMark, and database-marketing services firm Marketing Communications. In 1997 Harte-Hanks bought ABC Shoppers, which reaches 2.4 million homes, from Walt Disney for $104 million. The company also added London-based Information For Marketing Ltd. to its portfolio of international database marketing firms.

Believing that marketing was moving away from traditional mass media toward targeted groups, the company sold its newspaper and broadcast operations (25% of revenues) to E.W. Scripps for $775 million in 1997. To reflect the divestiture, the company dropped "Communications" from its name the next year. Also in 1998 the company bought Cornerstone Integrated Services, which offers technology support and marketing services to the high-tech industry.

In 1999 Harte-Hanks established the Harte-Hanks Interactive division to focus on e-commerce, Web site development, and other Internet-related operations. It then bought Ziff-Davis' ZD Market Intelligence unit (database products for the high-tech and communications industries) for $106 million.

In 2000 the company expanded its European operations with acquisition of the UK's Hi-Tech Marketing Limited and the construction of a new direct marketing facility in Belgium. Harte-Hanks strengthened its business-to-business data management operations when it purchased database marketing provider Information Resource Group in late 2000.

In 2001 Harte-Hanks introduced Retail Daily Sales Builder, a marketing tool that analyzes point-of-sales and Web transactions in either real-time or at night. Retailers can use the tool to follow up on sales transactions or customer communication.

Also in 2001 the company introduced its Allink, a customer data management product that includes software tools and services from Harte-Hank consultants. The system takes large amounts of customer data and builds a database. This database helps the business get a better understanding of its customers.

Chairman and CEO: Larry Franklin, age 59
Vice Chairman: Houston H. Harte, age 74
President and COO: Richard M. Hochhauser, age 56
SVP; President, Harte-Hanks Shoppers:
Peter E. Gorman, age 52
SVP, Finance and CFO: Jacques Kerrest, age 53
SVP, Legal and Secretary: Donald R. Crews, age 57
SVP, Direct Marketing: Craig Combest
SVP, Direct Marketing: Charles Dall'Acqua
SVP, Direct Marketing: Gary J. Skidmore
VP, Legal and Secretary: Dean H. Blythe, age 43
VP, Tax: Fredrico Ortiz
Group President, Harte-Hanks Market Intelligence:
Terry Olson
General Manager, Harte-Hanks Market Intelligence:
Paul Kamman
Controller and Chief Accounting Officer:
Jessica M. Huff
Director Human Resources: Carolyn Oatman
Auditors: KPMG LLP

LOCATIONS

HQ: 200 Concord Plaza Dr., San Antonio, TX 78216
Phone: 210-829-9000   **Fax:** 210-829-9403
Web: www.harte-hanks.com

Harte-Hanks has operations in Australia, Belgium, Brazil, Canada, France, Germany, Ireland, Singapore, Spain, the UK, and the US.

2000 Sales

	$ mil.	% of total
US	917	95
Other countries	44	5
Total	**961**	**100**

PRODUCTS/OPERATIONS

2000 Sales

	$ mil.	% of total
Direct marketing	662	69
Shoppers	299	31
Total	**961**	**100**

Direct Marketing Services
Database marketing (creation of customized customer lists)
Interactive marketing (Web site development, e-commerce, and other Internet-based and interactive services)
Marketing services (development and mailing of advertising)
Response management (evaluation and tracking of customer inquiries)

Advertising Shoppers
The Flyer (South Florida)
PennySaver/Bargain Bulletin/El Informador (Greater San Diego)
PennySaver/Magic Ads (Northern California)
PennySaver/South Coast Shopper (Greater Los Angeles)

COMPETITORS

Acxiom	Copley Press	Omnicom
Advanstar	Digitas	Panoramic
ADVO	Freedom	R. R. Donnelley
Berlin Industries	Communications	SOFTBANK
Cadmus	Hearst	Valassis
Communications	Interpublic	Vertis
Catalina	Group	WPP Group
Marketing	Knight Ridder	
CMGI	MediaNews	

HISTORICAL FINANCIALS & EMPLOYEES

NYSE: HHS FYE: December 31	Annual Growth	12/91	12/92	12/93	12/94	12/95	12/96	12/97	12/98	12/99	12/00
Sales ($ mil.)	10.8%	—	423	464	514	533	666	638	749	830	961
Net income ($ mil.)	56.3%	—	2	(53)	24	34	41	336	68	73	82
Income as % of sales	—	—	0.5%	—	4.6%	6.4%	6.1%	52.6%	9.1%	8.8%	8.5%
Earnings per share ($)	—	—	—	(1.36)	0.40	0.53	0.53	4.36	0.90	1.01	1.18
Stock price - FY high ($)	—	—	—	6.50	7.21	11.30	14.25	19.34	28.50	29.25	28.44
Stock price - FY low ($)	—	—	—	5.04	5.88	6.21	9.81	12.69	17.34	19.06	19.63
Stock price - FY close ($)	20.3%	—	—	6.50	6.50	9.88	13.88	18.50	28.50	21.75	23.69
P/E - high	—	—	—	—	18	20	25	4	30	28	24
P/E - low	—	—	—	—	15	11	18	3	18	18	16
Dividends per share ($)	—	—	—	0.00	0.00	0.04	0.04	0.04	0.06	0.08	0.10
Book value per share ($)	25.4%	—	—	1.75	1.96	2.75	3.43	7.74	8.10	8.48	8.52
Employees	5.4%	—	5,825	6,150	6,225	5,627	7,510	6,896	7,098	8,145	8,849

STOCK PRICE HISTORY

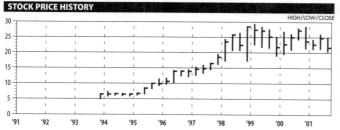

HIGH/LOW/CLOSE

2000 FISCAL YEAR-END

Debt ratio: 10.6%
Return on equity: 14.5%
Cash ($ mil.): 23
Current ratio: 1.57
Long-term debt ($ mil.): 65
No. of shares (mil.): 65
Dividends
  Yield: 0.4%
  Payout: 8.5%
Market value ($ mil.): 1,532

H. E. BUTT GROCERY COMPANY

H. E. Butt Grocery Company (H-E-B) is the real "king of the hill" of the Texas Hill Country. The #1 food retailer in Austin, home-base San Antonio, and Corpus Christi, H-E-B is by far the largest private company in Texas, and one of the nation's largest regional supermarket chains. The company runs more than 280 supermarkets, mostly in South and Central Texas. Among these stores are about 90 small-sized H-E-B stores (sometimes under the Pantry banner) that serve mostly rural towns in Southeast Texas and Southwest Louisiana. In addition to a full line of groceries, some of its stores have Gas 'N Go outlets. H-E-B also operates facilities for processing milk, meat,

ice cream, and baked goods, as well as bread and tortillas. The founding Butt family owns the chain.

H-E-B is familiar with the tastes of Latinos (about half of its market is Hispanic). It has made greater inroads in Mexico than it has in North Texas. (H-E-B's headquarters is actually closer to Mexico than it is to Dallas.) The company has moved into Monterrey's more affluent neighborhoods, with stores operating under the H-E-B banner and the Economax name (a discount supermarket format). The company has a dozen stores in Mexico and plans to have about 40 by 2004.

In 1905 Charles C. Butt and his wife, Florence, moved to Kerrville, in the Texas Hill Country, hoping the climate would help Charles' tuberculosis. Since Charles was unable to work, Florence began peddling groceries door-to-door for A&P. Later that year she opened a grocery store, C. C. Butt Grocery. Florence, a dyed-in-the-wool Baptist, refused to carry such articles of vice as tobacco. The family lived over the store, and all three of the Butt children worked there. The youngest son, Howard, began working in the business full-time in his teens, and took over the business after WWI.

By adopting modern marketing methods such as price tagging (and deciding to sell tobacco), the Butts earned enough to begin expanding. In 1927 Howard opened a second store in Del Rio in West Texas, and over the next few years he opened other stores in the Rio Grande Valley. The company gained patron loyalty by making minimal markups on staples. It moved from Kerrville to Harlingen, Texas, in 1928, then on to Corpus Christi, Texas, in 1940 and to San Antonio in 1985.

The company began manufacturing foods in the 1930s, and it invested in farms and orchards. In 1935 Howard (who had adopted the middle name Edward) rechristened the chain the H. E. Butt Grocery Company (H-E-B). He put his three children to work for the company, grooming son Charles for the top spot after Howard Jr. took over the H. E. Butt Foundation from his mother.

While other chains updated their stores during the 1960s, H-E-B plodded. Howard Sr. resigned in 1971 and Charles took over, bringing in fresh management. But this was not enough. Studies showed that the reasons for

H-E-B's lagging market share were its refusal to stock alcohol and its policy of Sunday closing. H-E-B abandoned these policies in 1976. It also drastically undercut competitors, driving many independents out of business. Winning the price wars, H-E-B emerged the dominant player in its major markets.

H-E-B's first superstore, a 56,000-sq.-ft. facility offering general merchandise, photo-finishing, and a pharmacy, opened in Austin, Texas, in 1979. H-E-B concentrated on building more superstores over the next decade. It also installed in-store video rentals and added 35 freestanding Video Central locations (sold to Hollywood Entertainment in 1993).

In 1988 H-E-B launched its H-E-B Pantry division, which remodeled and built smaller supermarkets mostly in rural Texas towns. Three years later it launched another format, the 93,000-sq.-ft. H-E-B Marketplace in San Antonio, which included a restaurant. H-E-B also opened the upscale Central Market in Austin in 1994, with extensive cheese, produce, and wine departments.

Chairman and CEO Charles retired as president in 1996, and James Clingman became the first non-family member to assume the office. That year H-E-B opened its first non-Texas store, in Lake Charles, Louisiana. In 1997 it opened its first Mexican store in an affluent area of Monterrey, followed the next year by a discount supermarket there under the Economax banner. As supermarket giant Safeway re-entered the Texas market in 1999, H-E-B unveiled aspirations to expand further in Mexico with six to eight new stores per year.

In 2000 H-E-B announced plans to sell on-line; those plans were halted in early 2001.

OFFICERS

Chairman and CEO: Charles C. Butt
President and COO: James F. Clingman
CFO and Chief Administrative Officer:
  Jack C. Brouillard
SVP, Human Resources: Susan Allford

LOCATIONS

HQ: 646 S. Main Ave., San Antonio, TX 78204
Phone: 210-938-8000   **Fax:** 210-938-8169
Web: www.heb.com

H. E. Butt Grocery Company operates grocery stores and gas stations in Central and South Texas, Louisiana, and Mexico. The company also operates bakeries, a photo processing lab, and meat, milk, and ice cream plants.

PRODUCTS/OPERATIONS

Private Labels
H-E-B
Hill Country Fare

Store Formats
Central Market (upscale supermarket with expanded
  organic and gourmet foods)
Economax (discount supermarkets, Mexico)
Gas 'N Go (gas stations)
H-E-B (large supermarkets)
H-E-B Marketplace (large supermarkets with specialty
  departments)
H-E-B Pantry (small, rural supermarkets)

COMPETITORS

7-Eleven	IGA
Albertson's	Kmart
Brookshire Brothers	Kroger
Chedraui	Randall's
Comerci	Rice Food Markets
Costco Wholesale	Soriana
Eckerd	Walgreen
Fiesta Mart	Wal-Mart
Fleming Companies	Wal-Mart de México
Gigante	Whole Foods
Grupo Corvi	Winn-Dixie

HISTORICAL FINANCIALS & EMPLOYEES

Private FYE: October 31	Annual Growth	10/91	10/92	10/93	10/94	10/95	10/96	10/97	10/98	10/99	10/00
Sales ($ mil.)	11.2%	3,162	3,204	4,500	4,844	5,137	5,800	6,500	7,000	7,500	8,200
Employees	17.2%	12,000	12,000	19,772	25,000	25,000	42,000	45,000	45,000	45,000	50,000

SALES HISTORY

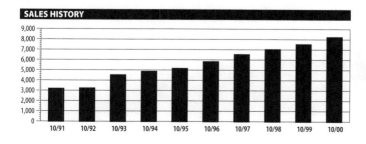

HICKS, MUSE, TATE & FURST

OVERVIEW

These Texas Hicks know an investment pool ain't no cement pond. Dallas-based Hicks, Muse, Tate & Furst creates investment pools in the form of limited partnerships. Investors are mostly pension funds, but also include financial institutions and wealthy private investors such as Texas' Hunt family. The firm targets underperforming niche companies and builds them up through add-on investments.

As its target industries consolidate — making US acquisitions scarce — Hicks, Muse has increasingly turned to foreign markets. The firm (which sold its AMFM to Clear Channel Communications to create the US's largest radio, television, and outdoor advertising group) is exporting its media mogul strategy through investments in Latin America and Europe. Hicks, Muse, along with US-based Liberty Media International, owns CableVision SA, Argentina's largest cable operator.

Hicks, Muse has had its share of disappointments as the US economy cools. It abandoned plans to buy out manufacturing firm Johns Manville with Bear Stearns when its stock took a dive. Hicks, Muse, along with New York-based Kohlberg Kravis Roberts & Co., lost a battle with Philip Anschutz for control of Regal Cinemas. The firm also closed down offices in Argentina and New York. Hicks, Muse, along with UK-based Apax Partners & Co., has agreed to buy British Telecommunication's yellow pages firm Yell.

HISTORY

The son of a Texas radio station owner, Thomas Hicks became interested in leveraged buyouts as a member of First National Bank's venture capital group. Hicks and Robert Haas formed Hicks & Haas in 1984; the next year the firm bought Hicks Communications, a radio outfit run by Hicks' brother Steven. (This would be the first of many media companies bought or created by the buyout firm, often with Steven Hicks' involvement.)

Hicks & Haas' biggest coup was its mid-1980s buy of several soft drink makers, including Dr Pepper and Seven-Up. The firm took Dr Pepper/Seven-Up public just 18 months after merging the two companies. In all, Hicks & Haas turned $88 million of investor funding into $1.3 billion. The pair split up in 1989; Hicks wanted to raise a large pool to invest, but Haas preferred to work deal by deal.

Hicks raised $250 million in 1989 and teamed with former Prudential Securities banker John Muse. Early investments included Life Partners Group (life insurance, 1990; sold 1996). In 1991 Morgan Stanley's Charles Tate and First Boston's Jack Furst became partners.

As part of its buy-and-build strategy, Hicks, Muse bought DuPont's connector systems unit in 1993, renamed it Berg Electronics, added six more companies to it, and doubled its earnings before selling it in 1998. Not every move was a star in the Hicks, Muse crown, though. Less-than-successful purchases included bankrupt brewer G. Heileman, bought in 1994 and sold two years later for an almost $100 million loss.

The buyout firm's Chancellor Media radio company went public in 1996. That year Hicks, Muse gained entry into Latin America with its purchases of cash-starved Mexican companies, including Seguros Commercial America, one of the country's largest insurers. That year also brought International Home Foods (Jiffy Pop, Chef Boyardee) into the Hicks, Muse fold.

In 1997 Chancellor and Evergreen Media merged to form Chancellor Media (renamed AMFM in 1999). The next year Hicks, Muse continued buying US and Latin American media companies. Hicks, Muse and Kohlberg Kravis Roberts' merged their cinema operations to form the US's largest theater chain. That year the company also moved into the depressed energy field (Triton Energy) and formed a $1.5 billion European fund.

Buys in 1999 included UK food group Hillsdown Holdings, one-third of Mexican flour maker Grupo Minsa, and popular champagne brands Mumm and Perrier-Jouet. (The company quadrupled its investment when it sold the champagne houses in late 2000.)

Amid assorted media and other buys in 2000, the firm helped put together several joint deals. With investment bank Bear Stearns, it planned to buy construction-materials manufacturer Johns Manville; the deal soured later that year as the economy cooled. After vying with another buyout group for UK food concern United Biscuits, the two competitors teamed up to complete the deal.

Hicks, Muse sold International Home Foods to food giant ConAgra in 2000. The next year Hicks, Muse bought bankrupt Vlasic Foods International Inc.'s North American assets, including Vlasic pickles, Open Pit barbecue sauces, and Swanson frozen dinners. Also in 2001 Hick, Muse, along with US-based Liberty Media International, bought CableVision SA, the largest cable operator in Argentina.

Chairman and CEO: Thomas O. Hicks, age 55
President: Charles W. Tate
COO: John R. Muse, age 50
CFO: Darron Ash
General Counsel: Michael Salem
Human Resources Manager: Lynita Jessen

LOCATIONS

HQ: Hicks, Muse, Tate & Furst Incorporated
   200 Crescent Ct., Ste. 1600, Dallas, TX 75201
Phone: 214-740-7300   **Fax:** 214-720-7888

Hicks, Muse, Tate & Furst has offices in Dallas and London.

PRODUCTS/OPERATIONS

Selected Holdings
CEI Citicorp Holding (40%, telecommunications and publishing)
Glass Group (automotive information services software)
Grupo Minsa, S.A. de C.V. (32%, corn flour producer, Mexico)
Grupo MVS SA (23%, pay-TV provider and radio station owner, Mexico)
Grupo Vidrio Formas (69%, glass container supplier, Mexico)
Hedstrom Corp. (playground equipment)
Hillsdown Holdings PLC (food production, office furniture)
Home Interiors & Gifts, Inc. (80%, direct-selling of decorative accessories and gift items)
Ibero-American Media Partners (50%, Latin American media buyout fund)
International Outdoor Advertising (97%; billboards in Argentina, Chile, and Uruguay)
International Wire Holdings Corp. (60%; wire, wire harnesses, and cable)
LIN Holdings (69%, television stations)
Metrocall Inc. (paging systems)
OmniAmerica Wireless LP (45%, broadcast towers)
Pan-American Sports Network (80%, regional cable sports network)
RCN Corp. (fiber-optic telecommunications networks)
Rhythms NetConnections (8%, high-speed Internet access)
Sunrise Television Corp. (87%, small-market television stations)
Traffic (49%; broadcasting, Brazil)
United Biscuits (Holdings) plc (87%, with Finalrealm; food products, UK)
Viasystems Group (printed circuit boards)

COMPETITORS

Bain Capital	Equity Group	Texas Pacific
Berkshire	Investments	Group
Hathaway	Haas Wheat	Thomas Lee
Boston Ventures	Heico	Vestar Capital
Clayton,	Investcorp	Partners
Dubilier	Jordan Company	Vulcan
CVC Capital	KKR	Northwest
Partners	Leonard Green	Wingate
Equitex	Maseca	Partners

HISPANIC BROADCASTING

OVERVIEW

Hola, radio fans! Dallas-based Hispanic Broadcasting (formerly Heftel Broadcasting) is the largest Spanish-language radio broadcaster in the US, with some 50 radio stations in more than a dozen markets. Its stations include KLVE, KSCA, and KTNQ in Los Angeles (where the company generates a substantial portion of its revenue); Miami's WAMR; and New York City's WCAA. Hispanic Broadcasting's stations offer a variety of formats, including contemporary, news and talk, regional Mexican, Tejano, and tropical. The company also operates the HBC Radio Network, which links its radio stations and lets advertisers reach multiple markets. It also runs HBCi, which operates the company's radio station Web sites.

Hispanic Broadcasting plans to maintain its top spot in Spanish-language radio by adding more stations to its collection. The company has purchased four Phoenix-area radio stations from Big City Radio for about $34 million. Radio behemoth Clear Channel Communications owns 26% of the company; the family of chairman and CEO McHenry Tichenor Jr. controls about 17%.

HISTORY

Cecil Heftel, a US Congressman from Hawaii from 1976 until 1986, founded Hispanic Broadcasting in 1974. An industry veteran, Heftel had been involved in radio station ownership since the 1950s. After he left Congress in 1986, Heftel focused on Spanish-language radio. He combined his company with Statewide Broadcasting in 1987 to form H&G Communications, but the partnership fizzled a year later. Heftel struck out on his own as Heftel Broadcasting, taking four radio stations with him. His company teamed with Mambisa Broadcasting in 1989 to form national Hispanic network Viva America Media. (Heftel Broadcasting bought Mambisa's interest in the network in 1995.)

Heftel Broadcasting went public in 1994. The acquisitions that followed helped the company's radio-station holdings grow to 16 by 1996. That year Clear Channel Communications bought a stake in the company and combined it with Tichenor Media System, a Spanish-language radio group with 18 radio stations.

McHenry Tichenor got his start in radio in 1949 when he acquired KGBS and KGBT in Harlingen, Texas. KGBT signal covered most of Mexico, and at night the station broadcast in Spanish. By 1962 Tichenor Media Systems (TMS) had switched KGBT to all-Spanish programming. In 1967 McHenry Tichenor II took over the company from his father.

In 1975 TMS bought San Antonio's KCOR (which in 1955 had become the first all-Spanish programming radio station in the US). Tichenor II's son, McHenry T. Tichenor, Jr. became president of the company in 1982, and he led an expansion into major markets. In 1984 the company acquired KLAT in Houston, and in 1986 it made its biggest purchase to date when it bought Chicago's WOJO. The company bought interests in stations in New York and Miami in 1991, but sold them

two years later. In 1993 the company bought several stations in San Antonio, including KXTN-FM, the first Spanish-language station to be the highest-rated station in a major market. The company merged with Heftel in 1996.

Cecil Heftel left the company in 1996, and McHenry Tichenor Jr. became CEO in 1997. Heftel Broadcasting purchased stations in New York, Houston, and San Diego the next year.

In 1999 the company changed its name to Hispanic Broadcasting and unveiled its HBC Radio Network. Also that year the company bought KHOT-FM in Phoenix and KISF-FM in Las Vegas. It also acquired the broadcast license for 94.1 FM in Dallas, which it used to create KLNO-FM, its full-market signal station covering Dallas/Ft. Worth. Hispanic Broadcasting continued growing in 2000 with agreements to buy radio stations in Denver, Phoenix, and Austin from Clear Channel.

In 2001 Hispanic Broadcasting purchased four Phoenix stations from Big City Radio and bought a station in Indian Springs, Nevada, which served the Las Vegas market. Later in 2001 the company signed a content-sharing agreement with MSNBC.com to incorporate Spanish language local news into MSNBC.com affiliate network Web sites. The agreement was MSNBC.com's first with a Spanish language partner.

OFFICERS

Chairman, President, and CEO:
McHenry T. Tichenor Jr., age 45
EVP of Corporate Affairs: David D. Lykes, $551,331 pay
(prior to title change)
SVP and COO: Gary Stone, age 49
SVP, CFO, and Treasurer: Jeffrey T. Hinson, age 46
VP, Human Resources: Ellen Fox
Auditors: KPMG LLP

LOCATIONS

HQ: Hispanic Broadcasting Corporation
3102 Oak Lawn, Ste. 215, Dallas, TX 75219
Phone: 214-525-7700   **Fax:** 214-525-7750
Web: www.hispanicbroadcasting.com

Hispanic Broadcasting has radio stations in Arizona,
California, Florida, Illinois, Nevada, New York,
and Texas.

PRODUCTS/OPERATIONS

Selected Radio Stations
KAMA(AM) (El Paso, TX)
KBZR(FM) (Phoenix)
KCOR(AM) (San Antonio)
KDDJ(FM) (Phoenix)
KDXX(FM) (Dallas/Ft. Worth)
KEDJ(FM) (Phoenix)
KESS(AM) (Dallas/Ft. Worth)
KGBT(FM) (McAllen/Brownsville/Harlingen, TX)
KHOT(FM) (Phoenix)
KISF(FM) (Las Vegas)
KIWW(FM) (McAllen/Brownsville/Harlingen, TX)
KLAT(AM) (Houston)
KLNO(FM) (Dallas/Ft. Worth)
KLNV(FM) (San Diego)
KLTO(FM) (Houston)
KLVE(FM) (Los Angeles)
KOVA(FM) (Houston)
KSCA(FM) (Los Angeles)
KSOL(FM) (San Francisco/San Jose, CA)
KSSL(FM) (Phoenix)
KTNQ(AM) (Los Angeles)
WADO(AM) (New York City)
WAMR(FM) (Miami)
WAQI(AM) (Miami)
WCAA(FM) (New York City)
WOJO(FM) (Chicago)
WQBA(AM) (Miami)
WRTO(FM) (Miami)

COMPETITORS

Cox Radio	Infinity	Spanish
Cumulus Media	Broadcasting	Broadcasting
Entercom	Radio Unica	Telemundo
Entravision		Univision

HISTORICAL FINANCIALS & EMPLOYEES

NYSE: HSP FYE: December 31	Annual Growth	9/91	9/92	9/93	9/94	9/95	9/96	*12/97	12/98	12/99	12/00
Sales ($ mil.)	42.9%	—	—	—	28	68	72	137	164	198	238
Net income ($ mil.)	—	—	—	—	1	4	(47)	19	27	34	42
Income as % of sales	—	—	—	—	1.8%	5.4%	—	13.8%	16.4%	17.3%	17.5%
Earnings per share ($)	—	—	—	—	(0.01)	0.08	(1.14)	0.23	0.27	0.33	0.38
Stock price - FY high ($)	—	—	—	—	3.53	5.44	10.94	23.75	25.88	49.81	67.50
Stock price - FY low ($)	—	—	—	—	2.44	2.38	3.50	7.81	13.84	20.28	18.50
Stock price - FY close ($)	40.5%	—	—	—	3.31	4.81	10.91	23.38	24.63	46.11	25.50
P/E - high	—	—	—	—	—	60	—	103	92	147	178
P/E - low	—	—	—	—	—	26	—	34	49	60	49
Dividends per share ($)	—	—	—	—	0.00	0.00	0.00	0.00	0.00	0.00	0.00
Book value per share ($)	43.6%	—	—	—	1.12	1.00	0.28	4.42	6.31	9.43	9.83
Employees	14.0%	—	—	—	—	—	—	609	652	828	903

* Fiscal year change

STOCK PRICE HISTORY

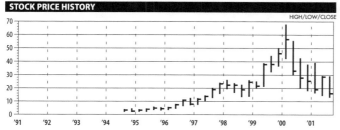

HIGH/LOW/CLOSE

2000 FISCAL YEAR-END

Debt ratio: 0.1%
Return on equity: 4.0%
Cash ($ mil.): 116
Current ratio: 8.18
Long-term debt ($ mil.): 1
No. of shares (mil.): 109
Dividends
  Yield: —
  Payout: —
Market value ($ mil.): 2,778

i2 TECHNOLOGIES, INC.

OVERVIEW

i2 is enjoying the view from atop the supply chain software world. The Dallas, Texas-based company is a leading provider of supply chain management software used by manufacturers to boost operating efficiency, schedule production and the delivery of raw materials, and collaborate with customers and suppliers. i2's software suites include applications for supply chain management, as well as related functions such as procurement, content management, customer relationship management, and the integration and administration of public and private electronic marketplaces.

The company's clients span numerous markets, including the automotive, pharmaceutical, metal, pulp and paper, retail, and telecommunications industries. i2 also offers services such as consulting and maintenance, which account for more than one-third of its sales.

An early leader in supply chain management software, the company has used acquisitions to expand past that core expertise into related fields, including procurement and customer relationship management. While i2 continues to expand its product lines (targeting private electronic marketplaces for future growth), the company has been unable to escape the effects of a slumping economy. The company first trimmed its staff by about 25%, then it announced plans for additional reductions of about 1,000 jobs.

Founder and chairman Sanjiv Sidhu owns about 35% of i2.

HISTORY

Sanjiv Sidhu, the son of a chemist who oversaw India's national laboratories, turned a chemical engineering degree and a tenure with Texas Instruments' artificial intelligence operations into i2 Technologies. Sidhu, who used his apartment as a base of operations for two years to develop the supply chain technology, founded the company in 1988. He chose not to have venture capitalists back him, deciding instead to let the industry's need for the product do the talking.

RHYTHM supply chain software began shipping in 1992. i2 opened offices in Australia, Germany, Japan, and the UK in 1995, and in Singapore in 1996 (the year i2 went public). The following year it acquired custom manufacturing capacity specialist Optimax Systems, and product demand change software company Think Systems.

In 1998 the company signed a $17.5 million, three-year deal to supply RHYTHM to Motorola's semiconductor manufacturing operations. It also bought Canada-based Inter-Trans Logistics, a developer of software that manages the transportation of raw materials and finished products. i2 also formed an alliance with information management software leader Oracle to develop supply chain products for the Japanese market.

As the Internet grew, i2 developed needed electronic applications, improved its marketing, and beefed-up its sales force, all of which boosted sales and profits for 1998. The following year i2 bought customer relationship software maker SMART Technologies for $68 million. Later in 1999 the company launched TradeMatrix, software used to build online business-to-business marketplaces.

In 2000 i2 expanded its online marketplace business through alliances with Ariba and IBM. It also purchased supply-chain management software maker Aspect Development in a $9.3 billion stock deal. Also in 2000 the company's i2 Foundation announced plans to create aidmatrix, a non-profit e-marketplace designed to link businesses and charities together, giving not-for-profits improved access to aid items such as food and clothing and building supplies. Late in 2000 i2 teamed with Trade-Ranger to create a content management system for an online energy and petrochemical marketplace. Sales eclipsed the $1 billion mark for the first time in fiscal 2000.

At the beginning of 2001 i2 signed a deal with Neoforma.com, a provider of health care supply chain products, to develop Internet supply chain software for the health care industry. The company's alliance with Ariba and IBM crumbled early in 2001 when i2 purchased RightWorks, a provider of procurement software (Ariba's core field of expertise). Later that year Sidhu stepped down as CEO (he remains chairman); he was replaced by president Greg Brady.

A slowing economy resulted in job cuts totaling about 25% of the company's workforce; in late 2001 the company announced plans for cutting an additional 1,000 jobs. i2 also signed an agreement with Hewlett-Packard to market solutions for private marketplaces based on i2 Supply Chain Collaboration software solution running on HP hardware.

Chairman: Sanjiv S. Sidhu, age 43
Vice Chairman: Romesh Wadhwani, age 53
President and CEO: Gregory A. Brady, age 40
EVP and CFO: William M. Beecher, age 44
EVP: Pallab K. Chatterjee, age 50
EVP, Business Development: Tom Cooper
EVP, Global Business Solutions: Hiten D. Varia, age 44
President, Asia-Pacific: Raymond Teh
President; Europe, Middle East, and Africa:
  Philip Crawford
President, Japan: Sam Nakane
Director, Human Resources: Lucy Contreras
Auditors: Arthur Andersen LLP

LOCATIONS

HQ: 1 i2 Place, 11701 Luna Rd., Dallas, TX 75234
Phone: 214-357-1000   **Fax:** 214-860-6060
Web: www.i2.com

i2 Technologies has offices in Australia, Belgium, Brazil, Canada, China, Denmark, Finland, France, Germany, India, Italy, Japan, Mexico, the Netherlands, Singapore, South Africa, South Korea, Sweden, Switzerland, Taiwan, the UK, and the US.

2000 Sales

	$ mil.	% of total
US	733	65
Europe	224	20
Asia	128	11
Other regions	41	4
Total	**1,126**	**100**

PRODUCTS/OPERATIONS

2000 Sales

	$ mil.	% of total
Software licenses	709	63
Services	271	24
Maintenance	146	13
Total	**1,126**	**100**

Services
Application hosting
Consulting
Implementation
Maintenance

Software
Content management (i2 Content)
Customer relationship management (i2 Customer
  Relationship Management suite)
Electronic marketplace creation and management (the
  i2 TradeMatrix family)
Procurement (i2 Supplier Relationship
  Management suite)
Supply chain management (i2 Supply Chain
  Management suite)

COMPETITORS

Adexa	J.D. Edwards
Agile Software	Kewill Systems
Ariba	Lawson Software
Aspen Technology	Manugistics Group
Baan	MAPICS
Commerce One	Oracle
Epicor Software	PeopleSoft
EXE Technologies	QAD
Frontstep	SAP
Intentia	Vignette
IBM	

HISTORICAL FINANCIALS & EMPLOYEES

Nasdaq: ITWO FYE: December 31	Annual Growth	12/91	12/92	12/93	12/94	12/95	12/96	12/97	12/98	12/99	12/00
Sales ($ mil.)	121.8%	—	2	5	11	26	76	201	362	571	1,126
Net income ($ mil.)	—	—	0	1	2	4	6	7	20	24	(1,752)
Income as % of sales	—	—	2.9%	17.5%	19.0%	14.7%	8.0%	3.6%	5.5%	4.1%	—
Earnings per share ($)	—	—	—	—	—	—	0.02	0.03	0.07	0.07	(4.83)
Stock price - FY high ($)	—	—	—	—	—	—	7.31	7.00	10.56	54.50	111.75
Stock price - FY low ($)	—	—	—	—	—	—	2.97	3.22	2.31	4.44	34.50
Stock price - FY close ($)	83.7%	—	—	—	—	—	4.78	6.59	7.59	48.75	54.38
P/E - high	—	—	—	—	—	—	244	233	132	681	—
P/E - low	—	—	—	—	—	—	99	107	29	56	—
Dividends per share ($)	—	—	—	—	—	—	0.00	0.00	0.00	0.00	0.00
Book value per share ($)	186.0%	—	—	—	—	—	0.31	0.70	0.82	1.07	20.83
Employees	92.3%	—	—	—	—	228	426	1,006	2,244	2,800	6,000

STOCK PRICE HISTORY

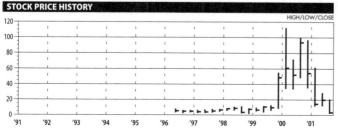

HIGH/LOW/CLOSE

2000 FISCAL YEAR-END

Debt ratio: 4.0%
Return on equity: —
Cash ($ mil.): 739
Current ratio: 2.84
Long-term debt ($ mil.): 350
No. of shares (mil.): 406
Dividends
  Yield: —
  Payout: —
Market value ($ mil.): 22,070

J. C. PENNEY COMPANY, INC.

OVERVIEW

J. C. Penney Company is cleaning out its closets. The debt-ridden Plano, Texas-based company is closing some failing JCPenney department stores and some Eckerd drugstores. To boost sales at its 1,100 or so JCPenney department stores, the company is expanding upon and re-emphasizing what made it popular in the early 1990s: private-label clothing.

To do this, J. C. Penney is creating stores-within-stores to feature its eight key private-label brands, including the popular Arizona Jean Co. line, which is expanding into new categories. The company hopes to lure back customers from discount stores such as Target and hot specialty retailers such as The Gap.

Although the department stores have struggled, the company still boasts one of the largest catalog operations in the US and the Eckerd chain, with 2,600 stores. (Eckerd accounts for about 40% of sales.)

HISTORY

In 1902 James Cash Penney and two former employers opened the Golden Rule, a dry goods store, in Kemmerer, Wyoming. Penney bought out his partners in 1907 and opened stores that sold soft goods in small towns. Basing his customer service policy on his Baptist heritage, he held employees (called "associates") to a high moral code.

The firm incorporated in Utah in 1913 as the J. C. Penney Company, with headquarters in Salt Lake City, but it moved to New York City the next year to improve buying and financial operations. It expanded to nearly 1,400 stores in the 1920s and went public in 1929. The company grew during the Depression with its reputation for high quality and low prices.

J. C. Penney rode the postwar boom, and by 1951 sales had surpassed $1 billion. It introduced credit plans in 1958 and entered catalog retailing in 1962 with its purchase of General Merchandise Co. The next year JCPenney added hard goods, allowing it to compete with Sears and Montgomery Ward.

The company formed JCPenney Insurance in the mid-1960s and bought Thrift Drug in 1969. The chain continued to grow, and in 1973, two years after Penney's death, there were 2,053 stores. Also in the 1970s J. C. Penney began its ill-fated foray overseas by buying chains in Belgium and Italy in hopes of duplicating its US formula — giant department stores.

It bought Delaware-based First National Bank in 1983 (renamed JCPenney National Bank in 1984) to issue MasterCard and Visa cards. JCPenney stores refocused on soft goods during the 1980s and stopped selling automotive services, appliances, paint, hardware, and fabrics in 1983. It discontinued sporting goods, consumer electronics, and photographic equipment in 1987.

The next year JCPenney Telemarketing was formed to take catalog phone orders and provide telemarketing services for other companies. Also in 1988 the company moved its headquarters to Plano, Texas. JCPenney tried to move upmarket in the 1980s, enlisting fashion designer Halston. The line failed, however, so the company developed its own brands.

James Oesterreicher was named CEO in 1995. J. C. Penney opened its first Mexican department store in Monterrey that year. Facing a slow-growing department store business back home, it then bought 272 drugstores from Fay's Inc. and 200 more from Rite Aid. In 1997 it acquired Eckerd (nearly 1,750 stores) for $3.3 billion, converting its other drugstores to the Eckerd name. The company also sold its $740 million credit card portfolio of JCPenney National Bank to Associates First Capital, and dealt its bank branches to First National Bank of Wyoming in 1997.

The retailer struggled in 1998, swallowing slumps in sales and a $70 million charge for consolidating its drugstore operations. J. C. Penney also closed 75 underperforming department stores that year. In late 1998 the company bought a controlling stake in Brazilian department store chain Lojas Renner.

With its stock value falling, J. C. Penney announced in 1999 it would sell 20% of Eckerd in the form of a tracking stock, but it has postponed the IPO three times since. Also in 1999 it sold its private-label credit card operations to GE Capital and sold its store in Chile to department store chain Almacenas Paris.

In 2000 the company closed about 50 department stores and 300 Eckerd drugstores. Also in 2000 CEO Oesterreicher retired and was replaced by Allen Questrom; the company hired Questrom because of the work he did turning around Federated Department Stores and Barneys New York.

In January 2001 the company announced plans to shutter about 50 more department stores and drugstores. In June, Dutch insurer AEGON acquired J. C. Penney's Direct Marketing Services (DMS) unit, including its life insurance subsidiaries, for $1.3 billion.

Chairman and CEO: Allen I. Questrom, age 61
EVP, President, and COO, JCPenney Stores,
  Merchandising and Catalog: Vanessa Castagna, age 50,
  $1,761,520 pay
EVP and CFO: Robert B. Cavanaugh, age 49
EVP and Chief Human Resources and Administration
  Officer: Gary L. Davis, age 57
EVP and Chief Information Officer: Stephen F. Raish,
  age 50
EVP, Secretary, and General Counsel: Charles R. Lotter,
  age 63, $719,713 pay
SVP and Chief Marketing Officer, JCPenney Stores and
  Catalog: John Budd
SVP; President, Catalog and Internet: John Irvin
SVP and General Merchandise Manager, Home and Fine
  Jewelry: Charles Chinni
SVP and General Merchandise Manager, Fine Jewelry:
  Beryl B. Raff, age 50
SVP and General Merchandise Manager, Men's and
  Children's: William Cappiello
VP and Director Merchandising, Family Footwear:
  Edward Mawyer
Chairman and CEO, Eckerd: J. Wayne Harris
Auditors: KPMG LLP

LOCATIONS

HQ: 6501 Legacy Dr., Plano, TX 75024
Phone: 972-431-1000   **Fax:** 972-431-1362
Web: www.jcpenney.net

J. C. Penney Company operates about 1,100 JCPenney
retail stores in Mexico, Puerto Rico, and the US; some
46 Brazilian department stores under the name Renner;
and approximately 2,600 Eckerd drugstores in the
American northeastern, southeastern, and Sunbelt
regions. It has six catalog distribution centers.

PRODUCTS/OPERATIONS

2001 Sales

	% of total
Department store & catalog	56
Eckerd	40
Direct Marketing Services	4
Total	**100**

Selected Private Labels

Arizona Jean Co.	JCPenney Home
Crazy Horse by Liz	Collection
Claiborne (exclusive	St. John's Bay
third-party brand)	Stafford
Delicates	USA Olympic
Hunt Club	Worthington
Jacqueline Ferrar	

COMPETITORS

American Retail	Federated	Otto Versand
Ames	Fred Meyer	Rite Aid
Bed Bath &	The Gap	Ross Stores
Beyond	Heilig-Meyers	Saks Inc.
Belk	J. Crew	Sears
BJs Wholesale	J. Jill Group	Signet
Club	Kmart	Spiegel
Brown Shoe	Kohl's	Stage Stores
Comerci	Lands' End	Target
Costco	The Limited	TJX
Wholesale	Longs	Venator Group
CVS	May	Walgreen
Dillard's	Nine West	Wal-Mart
Dress Barn	Nordstrom	Zale

HISTORICAL FINANCIALS & EMPLOYEES

NYSE: JCP FYE: Last Saturday in January	Annual Growth	1/92	1/93	1/94	1/95	1/96	1/97	1/98	1/99	1/00	1/01
Sales ($ mil.)	7.8%	16,201	18,009	18,983	20,380	21,419	23,649	29,618	30,678	32,510	31,846
Net income ($ mil.)	—	448	777	940	1,057	838	565	566	594	336	(705)
Income as % of sales	—	2.8%	4.3%	5.0%	5.2%	3.9%	2.4%	1.9%	1.9%	1.0%	—
Earnings per share ($)	—	0.20	2.95	3.53	4.05	3.33	2.25	2.10	2.19	1.16	(2.81)
Stock price - FY high ($)	—	29.13	40.19	56.38	59.00	50.00	57.00	68.25	78.75	54.44	19.69
Stock price - FY low ($)	—	23.56	27.06	36.00	39.88	41.13	46.25	44.88	38.13	17.69	8.63
Stock price - FY close ($)	(7.2%)	27.38	35.81	52.38	41.50	48.88	47.38	67.38	39.00	19.63	13.97
P/E - high	—	29	13	15	14	14	25	32	36	47	—
P/E - low	—	24	9	9	9	12	20	21	17	15	—
Dividends per share ($)	(3.1%)	1.32	1.32	1.41	1.62	1.86	2.04	2.13	2.17	2.18	0.99
Book value per share ($)	3.2%	17.95	20.04	22.72	24.74	26.27	26.57	29.17	28.68	27.69	23.80
Employees	4.2%	185,000	192,000	193,000	202,000	205,000	252,000	260,000	262,000	291,000	267,000

STOCK PRICE HISTORY

HIGH/LOW/CLOSE

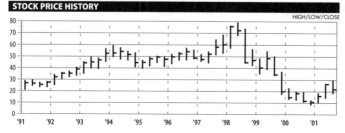

2001 FISCAL YEAR-END

Debt ratio: 46.5%
Return on equity: —
Cash ($ mil.): 944
Current ratio: 1.71
Long-term debt ($ mil.): 5,448
No. of shares (mil.): 263
Dividends
  Yield: 7.1%
  Payout: —
Market value ($ mil.): 3,674

KIMBERLY-CLARK CORPORATION

OVERVIEW

In good times or bad, Kimberly-Clark is on a roll. The Irving, Texas-based company generates about half of its sales from tissue products (it's the world leader), including Cottonelle toilet paper, Scott toilet paper and paper towels, Kleenex facial tissues, and Classic Crest writing papers. The company also makes personal care products such as Huggies disposable diapers and baby wipes, Depend undergarments, and Kotex feminine pads. New products, such as Huggies Little Swimmers disposable swimpants, help fuel the company's sales growth.

Kimberly-Clark has been adding products for the health care market through acquisitions. It has become the market leader in sterilization wrap, face masks, surgical drapes and gowns, and closed-suction respiratory products. The company's purchase of Safeskin made it the #1 US manufacturer of examination gloves.

Kimberly-Clark also produces business papers, as well as specialty and technical papers and newsprint for many leading US newspapers.

HISTORY

John Kimberly, Charles Clark, Havilah Babcock, and Frank Shattuck founded Kimberly, Clark & Company in Neenah, Wisconsin, in 1872 to manufacture newsprint from rags. The company incorporated as Kimberly & Clark Company in 1880 and built a pulp and paper plant on the Fox River in 1889.

In 1914 the company developed cellu-cotton, a cotton substitute used by the US Army as surgical cotton during WWI. Army nurses began using cellu-cotton pads as disposable sanitary napkins, and six years later the company introduced Kotex, the first disposable feminine hygiene product. Kleenex, the first throwaway handkerchief, followed in 1924, and soon many Americans were referring to all sanitary napkins as Kotex and facial tissues as Kleenex. Kimberly & Clark joined with The New York Times Company in 1926 to build a newsprint mill (Spruce Falls Power and Paper) in Ontario, Canada. Two years later the company went public as Kimberly-Clark.

The firm expanded internationally during the 1950s, opening plants in Mexico, Germany, and the UK. It began operations in 17 more foreign locations in the 1960s.

Before retiring in 1971, CEO Guy Minard sold the four mills that handled Kimberly-Clark's unprofitable coated-paper business and entered the paper towel and disposable diaper markets. Minard's successor, Darwin Smith, introduced Kimbies diapers in 1968, but they leaked and were withdrawn from the market. An improved version came out in 1976, followed by Huggies, a premium-priced diaper with elastic leg bands, two years later.

The company formed Midwest Express Airlines from its corporate flight department in 1984 (a business it exited in 1996). Smith moved Kimberly-Clark's headquarters from Neenah to Irving, Texas, the following year.

In 1991 Kimberly-Clark and The New York Times Company sold Spruce Falls Power and Paper. Smith retired as chairman in 1992 and was succeeded by Wayne Sanders, who was largely responsible for designing Huggies Pull-Ups (introduced in 1989).

Kimberly-Clark bought Scott Paper in 1995 for $9.4 billion. This boosted its market share in bathroom tissue from 5% to 31% and its share in paper towels from 6% to 18%, but led to some headaches as the company absorbed Scott's operations.

Two years later Kimberly-Clark sold its 50% stake in Canada's Scott Paper to forest products company Kruger. Also in 1997 it bought diaper operations in Spain and Portugal and disposable surgical face masks maker Tecnol Medical Products. A tissue price war in Europe bruised the company's bottom line that year. As a result, the company began massive job cuts.

In part to focus on its health care business, which it entered in 1997, the company in 1999 sold some of its timber interests and its timber fleet (19 tugboats and 120 barges) to Cooper/T. Smith Corp, a maritime company. Augmenting its presence in Germany, Switzerland, and Austria, in 1999 the company bought the tissue business of Swiss-based Attisholz Holding. Adding to its lineup of medical products, the company bought Ballard Medical Products in 1999 for $744 million and examination glove maker Safeskin in 2000 for about $800 million.

Also in 2000 the company bought virtually all of Taiwan's S-K Corporation; the move made Kimberly-Clark one of the largest manufacturers of consumer packaged goods in Taiwan and set the stage for expanded distribution in the Asia/Pacific region. It later purchased Taiwan Scott Paper Corporation and merged the two companies together, forming Kimberly-Clark Taiwan. In 2001 Kimberly-Clark said it would buy Italian diaper maker Linostar, which makes the country's #2 diaper brand, Lines.

OFFICERS

Chairman and CEO: Wayne R. Sanders, age 54, $2,060,304 pay
President and COO: Thomas J. Falk, age 42, $1,199,584 pay
EVP: Kathi P. Seifert, age 51, $844,012 pay
Group President: Robert E. Abernathy
Group President: Juan Ernesto de Bedout, age 56
Group President: Paul S. Geisler
Group President; Chairman and Managing Director, Kimberly-Clark de México: Claudio X. Gonzalez, age 66
Group President: Steven R. Kalmanson
Group President: W. Dudley Lehman
Group President: Russell C. Taylor
Group President: Robert P. van der Merwe
SVP, and CFO: John W. Donehower, age 55, $724,792 pay
SVP, Law and Government Affairs: O. George Everbach, age 62, $739,792 pay
Auditors: Deloitte & Touche LLP

LOCATIONS

HQ: 351 Phelps Dr., Irving, TX 75038
Phone: 972-281-1200 **Fax:** 972-281-1490
Web: www.kimberly-clark.com

2000 Sales

	$ mil.	% of total
US	9,059	60
Europe	2,475	16
Asia, Latin America & Africa	2,681	18
Canada	990	6
Adjustments	(1,223)	—
Total	**13,982**	**100**

PRODUCTS/OPERATIONS

2000 Sales

	$ mil.	% of total
Tissue-based products	7,303	52
Personal care products	5,438	39
Health care & other	1,291	9
Adjustments	(50)	—
Total	**13,982**	**100**

Selected Products and Brands

Medical Products
Examination gloves (Safeshield)
Face masks
Infection-control products
Scrub suits and apparel
Surgical drapes and gowns

Personal Care Products
Disposable diapers (Huggies, Pull-Ups)
Feminine hygiene products (Kotex, Lightdays)
Incontinence products (Depend, Poise)
Swimpants (Little Swimmers)

Tissue-Based Products
Bathroom tissue (Cottonelle, Scott)
Commercial wipes (Kimwipes, WypAll)
Facial tissue (Kleenex)
Paper napkins (Scott)
Paper towels (Kleenex, Scott, Viva)

COMPETITORS

3M	Bristol-Myers	Molnlycke
Akorn	Squibb	Paragon
Alba-Waldensian	DSG	Playtex
Allegiance	Georgia-Pacific	Potlatch
Becton	Johnson &	Procter &
Dickinson	Johnson	Gamble
	Medline	SSI Surgical

HISTORICAL FINANCIALS & EMPLOYEES

NYSE: KMB FYE: December 31	Annual Growth	12/91	12/92	12/93	12/94	12/95	12/96	12/97	12/98	12/99	12/00
Sales ($ mil.)	8.4%	6,777	7,091	6,973	7,364	13,789	13,149	12,547	12,298	13,007	13,982
Net income ($ mil.)	15.1%	508	135	511	535	33	1,404	902	1,166	1,668	1,801
Income as % of sales	—	7.5%	1.9%	7.3%	7.3%	0.2%	10.7%	7.2%	9.5%	12.8%	12.9%
Earnings per share ($)	8.5%	1.59	0.42	0.41	1.34	0.06	2.48	1.61	2.11	3.09	3.31
Stock price - FY high ($)	—	26.13	31.63	31.00	30.00	41.50	49.81	56.88	59.44	69.56	73.25
Stock price - FY low ($)	—	19.00	23.13	22.31	23.50	23.63	34.31	43.25	35.88	44.81	42.00
Stock price - FY close ($)	12.1%	25.34	29.50	25.94	25.19	41.38	47.63	49.31	54.50	65.44	70.69
P/E - high	—	16	29	60	22	692	20	36	28	22	22
P/E - low	—	12	21	43	17	394	14	27	17	14	13
Dividends per share ($)	4.3%	0.73	0.82	0.85	0.88	0.90	0.92	0.95	0.99	1.03	1.07
Book value per share ($)	3.6%	7.87	6.81	7.63	8.10	11.39	8.01	7.42	7.22	9.42	10.81
Employees	5.4%	41,286	42,902	42,131	42,707	55,341	54,800	57,000	54,700	54,800	66,300

STOCK PRICE HISTORY

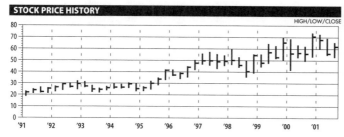

HIGH/LOW/CLOSE

2000 FISCAL YEAR-END

Debt ratio: 25.8%
Return on equity: 33.2%
Cash ($ mil.): 207
Current ratio: 0.83
Long-term debt ($ mil.): 2,001
No. of shares (mil.): 533
Dividends
  Yield: 1.5%
  Payout: 32.3%
Market value ($ mil.): 37,706

KING RANCH, INC.

OVERVIEW

King Ranch's property is Texas-sized (not really, but it is larger than all of Rhode Island). The company's 825,000-acre namesake ranch still conducts the farming and ranching that made it famous, but the dwindling demand for beef has made it more dependent on oil and gas royalties, fruit and sugar cane farming in Florida, and tourist dollars (from sightseers, hunters, and birdwatchers). The operations are managed from its Houston corporate headquarters.

Considered the birthplace of the American ranching industry, King Ranch also has introduced the new highly fertile breed of beef cattle:

the King Ranch Santa Cruz, which is one-fourth Gelbvieh, one-fourth Red Angus, and one-half Santa Gertrudis. About 60,000 cattle still roam the land, but raising animals isn't the only thing King Ranch cottons to; this sprawl of four noncontiguous ranches is also one of the US's largest cotton producers.

Like a good western movie, some things ride into the sunset at King Ranch. The company sold its 670-acre Kentucky Thoroughbred breeding and racing farm, as well as most of its foreign ranches and its primary oil and gas subsidiary. About 85 descendants of the company's founder, Richard King, own King Ranch.

HISTORY

King Ranch was founded in 1853 by former steamboat captain Richard King and his wife Henrietta, the daughter of a Brownsville, Texas, missionary. On the advice of his friend Robert E. Lee, King used his steamboating profits and occasional strong-arm tactics to buy land — miles of flat, brush-filled, coastal plain and desert south of Corpus Christi, Texas, valued at pennies an acre.

The next year King relocated the residents of an entire drought-ravaged village to the ranch and employed them as ranch hands, known ever after as *kinenos* ("King's men"). The Kings built their homestead in 1858 at a site recommended by Lee.

King Ranch endured attacks from Union guerrillas during the Civil War and Mexican bandits after the war. Times were tough, but King was up to the challenge, always traveling armed and with outriders.

In 1867 the ranch used its famed Running W brand for the first time. After King's death in 1885, Robert Kleberg, who married King's daughter Alice, managed the 1.2 million-acre ranch for his mother-in-law. Henrietta died in 1925 and left three-fourths of the ranch to Alice. Before Robert's death in 1932, control of the ranch passed to sons Richard and Bob. In 1933 Bob negotiated an exclusive oil and gas lease with Houston-based Humble Oil, which later became part of Exxon.

While Richard served in Congress, Bob ran the ranch. He developed the Santa Gertrudis, the first breed of cattle ever created in the US, by crossing British shorthorn cattle with Indian Brahmas. The new breed was better suited to the hot, dry South Texas climate.

Bob made King Ranch a leading breeder of quarter horses that worked cattle, and Thoroughbreds, which he raced. He bought

Kentucky Derby winner Bold Venture in 1936 and a Kentucky breeding farm in 1946; that year a King Ranch horse, Assault, won racing's Triple Crown.

When Bob died in 1974, the family asked James Clement, husband of one of the founders' great-granddaughters, to become CEO. They bypassed Robert Shelton, a King relative and orphan whom Bob had raised as his own son. Shelton severed ties with the ranch in 1977 over a lawsuit he filed (and partially won) against Exxon, which alleged underpayment of royalties.

Under Clement, King Ranch became a multinational corporation. In 1980 it formed King Ranch Oil and Gas (also called King Ranch Energy) to explore for and produce oil and gas in five states and the Gulf of Mexico. In 1988 Clement retired, and Kimberly-Clark executive Darwin Smith became the first CEO not related to the founders. Smith left after one year, and the reins passed to petroleum geologist Roger Jarvis, then to Jack Hunt in 1995.

With the help of scientists, in the early 1990s the company developed a leaner, more fertile breed of the Santa Gertrudis called Santa Cruz.

In 1998 Stephen "Tio" Kleberg, the only King descendant still actively working the ranch, was pushed from the saddle of daily operations to a seat on the board. King Ranch sold its Kentucky horse farm in 1998, then teamed up with Collier Enterprises to purchase citrus grower Turner Foods from utility holding company FPL Group. In 2000 the company sold King Ranch Energy to St. Mary Land and Exploration Co. for $60 million.

OFFICERS

Chairman: James H. Clement
President and CEO: Jack Hunt
CFO: Bill Gardiner
VP, Livestock: Paul Genho
VP, Audit: Richard Nilles
Secretary and General Counsel: Frank Perrone
Director of Human Resources: Martha Breit

LOCATIONS

HQ: 3 River Way, Ste. 1600, Houston, TX 77056
Phone: 832-681-5700 **Fax:** 832-681-5759
Web: www.king-ranch.com

King Ranch operates ranching and farming interests in South Texas and Florida.

Selected Agricultural Operations
Florida
  3,100 acres (St. Augustine sod)
  12,000 acres (sugar cane)
  40,000 acres (orange and grapefruit groves)
Texas
  60,000 acres (cotton and grain)

PRODUCTS/OPERATIONS

Selected Operations
Consolidated Citrus Limited
  Partnership (southern Florida citrus groves)
King Ranch Museum
King Ranch Nature Tour Program
King Ranch Saddle Shop (leather products)

COMPETITORS

Alico
AZTX Cattle
Cactus Feeders
Calcot
Devon Energy
Koch
Southern States
Southwestern Irrigated Cotton
Tejon Ranch

HISTORICAL FINANCIALS & EMPLOYEES

Private FYE: December 31	Annual Growth	12/91	12/92	12/93	12/94	12/95	12/96	12/97	12/98	12/99	12/00
Estimated sales ($ mil.)	6.9%	165	330	250	250	250	250	300	300	300	300
Employees	8.0%	350	700	700	700	700	700	700	700	700	700

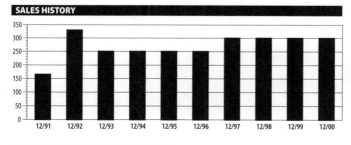

SALES HISTORY

LA QUINTA CORPORATION

OVERVIEW

La Quinta Corp. wants to be your mid-priced hotel hacienda. Based in Irving, Texas, La Quinta Corp. is the lodging division of real estate investment trust The La Quinta Companies. La Quinta Corp. operates about 300 hotels across 30 states: about 230 La Quinta Inns and 70 La Quinta Inn & Suites hotels. La Quinta Inns eschews typical hotel features such as restaurants and cocktail lounges, opting instead for clean, reasonably priced rooms with amenities including in-room coffee makers and complimentary breakfasts. La Quinta Inn & Suites offers guests two-room suites, as well as fitness centers, courtyards, and spas.

In order to expand its geographic reach, La Quinta Corp. plans to open about 15 new hotels in the next year through its new franchising program. The company is expanding north of the border, signing a franchise agreement with Toronto-based AFM Hospitality to open more than 30 hotels in Canada. Parent company The La Quinta Companies is also looking to streamline its operations. It plans to turn La Quinta Properties, its REIT operating division that actually owns the hotels, into a subsidiary of La Quinta Corp.

Fort Worth's Bass family owns about 8.5% of La Quinta Corporation's stock.

HISTORY

La Quinta (Spanish for "the country estate") was founded by Sam Barshop and his brother, Phil, who launched the chain to provide accommodations for San Antonio's HemisFair (the World's Fair) in 1968. La Quinta went public in 1972. It continued building new hotels during the 1970s and emphasized the purchase of existing hotels during the 1980s. In 1988 the company celebrated the opening of its 200th hotel.

By the early 1990s La Quinta was viewed as undervalued and inefficient. In 1991 billionaire Texas investors Sid and Lee Bass led a group of dissident La Quinta shareholders (which together owned more than 50% of the company) in ousting half of La Quinta's board of directors.

The following year they brought in Motel 6 veteran Gary Mead to replace Sam Barshop as CEO. (Barshop continued as chairman for two more years.) Under Mead's leadership, the company bought La Quinta hotels held by partnerships and joint ventures and implemented a massive capital improvement campaign.

La Quinta introduced its first La Quinta Inn & Suites in 1996 and began building new hotels for the first time since the 1980s. Two years later real estate investment trust (REIT) The Meditrust Companies bought the company. (Meditrust changed its name to The La Quinta Companies following the purchase.) Immediately after the acquisition, Mead departed, and Ezzat Coutry became CEO of La Quinta Corp. (the operating subsidiary of the new The La Quinta Companies).

La Quinta Corp. moved its headquarters from San Antonio to Irving, Texas, in 1999, and Coutry resigned as CEO. (Francis "Butch" Cash, a former Red Roof Inns chairman, took

over the following year.) Also in 2000 the company announced that it would begin franchising its hotels.

In 2001 La Quinta signed up its first franchisee under its new franchise program with Atlanta-based Diplomat Hotel. The program's plan was to develop La Quinta Inn & Suites, beginning with one near Atlanta's Hartsfield International Airport. Later that year the company opened its first hotel in Oregon through newly signed franchisor Pacific Inns.

Also in 2001 The La Quinta Companies announced plans to streamline its operations, turning La Quinta Properties, its REIT operating subsidiary that actually owns the hotels, into a subsidiary of La Quinta Corp.

La Quinta made its first move to expand outside the US late in 2001 when it signed a master franchise agreement with AFM Hospitality, the leading multi-brand franchisor in Canada. AFM plans to open more than 30 La Quinta properties across Canada over the next five years.

Like its competitors in the lodging industry, La Quinta's revenues were hurt as businesses and consumers cut back on travel following the September 11 terrorist attacks.

OFFICERS

President and CEO: Francis Cash
EVP and CFO: David L. Rea
EVP and Chief Development Officer: Allan L. Tallis
SVP, Human Resources: Vito J. Stellato
SVP, Sales and Marketing: Stephen T. Parker
Group VP, Operations: Wayne Goldberg
Group VP, Operations: Brent Spaeth
VP, Finance: Steven J. Flowers
VP, Franchise Operations: Rajiv Trivedi
VP, Internal Audit: Robert G. Colbert

LOCATIONS

HQ: 909 Hidden Ridge, Ste. 600, Irving, TX 75038
Phone: 214-492-6600   **Fax:** 214-492-6971
Web: www.laquinta.com

2000 Hotels

Location	No.
Texas	98
Florida	34
California	17
Georgia	17
Colorado	15
Louisiana	15
Arizona	12
Tennessee	11
North Carolina	10
Alabama	8
Oklahoma	8
Illinois	7
New Mexico	7
South Carolina	6
Arkansas	5
Nevada	4
Utah	4
Virginia	4
Indiana	3
Washington	3
Kansas	2
Missouri	2
Mississippi	2
Kentucky	1
Nebraska	1
Ohio	1
Pennsylvania	1
Wyoming	1
Total	**299**

PRODUCTS/OPERATIONS

Selected Hotel Features
La Quinta Inn
  Complimentary breakfast
  Dataport telephones
  Free local calls
  In-room coffee makers
  Swimming pool
La Quinta Inn & Suites
  Courtyards
  Fitness center
  Microwave
  Refrigerator
  Spas
  Two-room suites

COMPETITORS

Accor
Best Western
Cendant
Choice Hotels
Hilton
Marriott International
Prime Hospitality
ShoLodge
Six Continents
Sunburst Hospitality

HISTORICAL FINANCIALS & EMPLOYEES

Business segment FYE: December 31	Annual Growth	12/91	12/92	12/93	12/94	12/95	12/96	12/97	12/98	12/99	12/00
Sales ($ mil.)	10.5%	243	256	272	362	414	443	503	543	602	595
Employees	2.7%	5,900	6,000	6,100	5,800	6,600	6,800	7,400	7,600	8,000	7,500

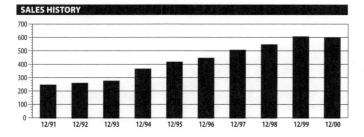

SALES HISTORY

La Quinta
Inns · Inn & Suites

LENNOX INTERNATIONAL INC.

OVERVIEW

Feeling hot, hot, hot? Lennox International might have what it takes to cool you down. The Richardson-based heating and cooling giant makes residential and commercial air conditioners and furnaces, chillers, industrial air handlers, and compressors. Other products include prefabricated fireplaces and condenser coils. Its brand names include Armstrong Air, Bohn, Lennox, Ducane, and Heatcraft. Lennox sells products through more than 200 company-owned dealerships, as well as some 1,500 independent dealers.

In part to protect its market share, Lennox has acquired retail outlets throughout North America. The company is also strengthening its ties with independent dealers by offering retirement and other benefits to those who agree to purchase a minimum of 75% of their HVAC products from Lennox.

The company is looking for growth in countries such as Asia, Europe, and Latin America, where demand for heating and cooling technology (primarily for improved food distribution) is increasing.

Heirs of D.W. Norris, including chairman John Norris and director David Anderson, own more than half of the company.

HISTORY

Inventors Ernest Bryant and Ezra Smith developed and patented a riveted-steel sheet metal coal furnace in Marshalltown, Iowa, in the 1890s. The cast iron furnaces in use at the time tended to warp with usage; their sheet metal furnace did not. The inventors hired machine shop operator Dave Lennox to build the manufacturing equipment necessary to produce the new furnace. They were underfunded, however, so Lennox took over the patents in lieu of payment and redesigned the furnace. Lennox didn't warm to the furnace business and sold out to D. W. Norris, the local newspaper publisher, and three other people for $40,000 in 1904.

Norris, the company's first president, incorporated the business as Lennox Furnace Company and sold about 600 units the first year. Norris soon established the company's method of selling and delivering directly to authorized dealers.

Lennox built a manufacturing plant in New York in 1925 and acquired Armstrong Furnace, a steel coal furnace plant in Ohio, in 1927. That year John Norris, D. W.'s son, joined the company after graduating from MIT. The younger Norris pushed for new innovations such as oil burners, gas furnaces, and blowers. He set up a research department in the 1930s and soon developed a line of gas- and oil-burning furnaces. The company opened another Ohio plant in 1940 and bought a machine shop there in 1942 to make bomb and aircraft parts for WWII. John Norris became president after the death of his father in 1949.

The company established Lennox Industries (Canada) Ltd. in 1952. Norris began developing an air conditioner the same year, after shopping the idea around to his dealers. Soon the company was turning out residential, commercial, and industrial air conditioners and compressors. In 1955 the company's name was changed to Lennox Industries to reflect its broader product range. The international division was created in 1962. Soon manufacturing facilities were established outside London and other offices were opened in the Netherlands and West Germany.

Lennox acquired Heatcraft, a maker of heating and cooling components, in 1973. Headquarters were moved to Dallas in 1978; in 1980 John Norris Jr. was named CEO. Lennox International was formed as the parent company for Heatcraft and Lennox Industries in 1986. The company reacquired Armstrong Air Conditioning (which it had owned in the 1920s and sold in the mid-1950s) in 1988. Armstrong produced residential and commercial heating and cooling products.

Lennox underwent restructuring in 1989 and 1991, leading to the consolidation of production to four locations and the grouping of the sales, management, product ordering, and marketing teams at the new headquarters in Dallas. In 1995 the company formed Lennox Global and rededicated itself to international expansion through joint ventures with foreign companies. Lennox formed HCF-Lennox, a joint venture with France's Brancher group, in 1996. The company agreed in 1998 to pay $6.2 million to settle an age bias lawsuit filed by 11 former employees. Lennox went public in 1999 and began buying HVAC dealers.

In 2000 the company more than doubled its number of owned retail outlets with the $300 million acquisition of Service Experts, a HVAC installation and sales business with 120 locations in 36 states. COO Robert E. Schjerven succeeded John W. Norris, Jr. as CEO in early 2001; Norris remained as chairman.

OFFICERS

Chairman: John W. Norris Jr., age 65, $800,004 pay
CEO and Director: Robert E. Schjerven, age 58,
$670,295 pay
EVP and CFO: Richard A. Smith, age 55
EVP and Chief Administration Officer:
Harry J. Ashenhurst, age 52, $492,703 pay
EVP, Chief Legal Officer, and Secretary:
Carl E. Edwards Jr., age 59
EVP; President, Lennox Industries, Inc.: Scott J. Boxer,
age 50
EVP; President, North American Distributed Products:
Michael G. Schwartz, age 42
EVP; President, Service Experts, Inc.:
James L. Mishler, age 46
**EVP; President, Worldwide Heat Transfer and
Asia/Pacific Operations:** W. Lane Pennington, age 45
Chief Technology Officer: Linda Goodspeed
**President, Worldwide Commercial Refrigeration and
European and Latin American Operations:**
Bob McDonough, age 42
Human Resources: Jackie McClanahan
Auditors: Arthur Andersen LLP

LOCATIONS

HQ: 2140 Lake Park Blvd., Richardson, TX 75080
Phone: 972-497-5000   **Fax:** 972-497-5299
Web: www.lennoxinternational.com

2000 Sales

	$ mil.	% of total
US	2,560	79
Canada	286	9
Other countries	401	12
Total	**3,247**	**100**

PRODUCTS/OPERATIONS

2000 Sales

	$ mil.	% of total
North American residential	1,222	37
North American retail	1,053	31
Commercial air conditioning	469	14
Commercial refrigeration	358	11
Heat transfer	247	7
Adjustments	(102)	—
Total	**3,247**	**100**

Selected Products

North American Residential
Air conditioners
Furnaces
Heat pumps

North American Retail
Sales, installation, and
servicing

Commercial Air Conditioning
Unitary air conditioning
and applied systems

Commercial Refrigeration
Air-cooled condensers
Chillers
Fluid coolers

Heat Transfer
Heat transfer coils
Heat transfer equipment
and tooling to
manufacture coils

COMPETITORS

AAON
American Standard
CFM Majestic
Electrolux AB
Emerson
Fireplace Manufacturers
Goodman Manufacturing
HON INDUSTRIES
Hong Leong Asia
Hussmann International
Linde
Mestek
Modine Manufacturing
Tecumseh Products
United Technologies
Watsco
Whirlpool
York International

HISTORICAL FINANCIALS & EMPLOYEES

NYSE: LII FYE: December 31	Annual Growth	12/91	12/92	12/93	12/94	12/95	12/96	12/97	12/98	12/99	12/00
Sales ($ mil.)	18.6%	—	—	—	1,168	1,307	1,365	1,444	1,822	2,362	3,247
Net income ($ mil.)	11.5%	—	—	—	31	34	55	(34)	53	73	59
Income as % of sales		—	—	—	2.6%	2.6%	4.0%	—	2.9%	3.1%	1.8%
Earnings per share ($)	(42.0%)	—	—	—	—	—	—	—	—	1.81	1.05
Stock price - FY high ($)	—	—	—	—	—	—	—	—	—	19.88	15.13
Stock price - FY low ($)	—	—	—	—	—	—	—	—	—	8.88	6.81
Stock price - FY close ($)	(15.7%)	—	—	—	—	—	—	—	—	9.19	7.75
P/E - high	—	—	—	—	—	—	—	—	—	11	14
P/E - low	—	—	—	—	—	—	—	—	—	5	6
Dividends per share ($)	61.1%	—	—	—	—	—	—	—	—	0.18	0.29
Book value per share ($)	(2.0%)	—	—	—	—	—	—	—	—	13.29	13.03
Employees	43.2%	—	—	—	—	—	—	—	11,700	22,650	24,000

STOCK PRICE HISTORY

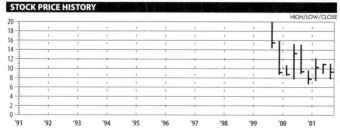

2000 FISCAL YEAR-END

Debt ratio: 45.8%
Return on equity: 8.8%
Cash ($ mil.): 41
Current ratio: 1.53
Long-term debt ($ mil.): 628
No. of shares (mil.): 57
Dividends
  Yield: 3.7%
  Payout: 27.6%
Market value ($ mil.): 442

LUBY'S, INC.

OVERVIEW

Ever wonder what happened to the cafeteria lady? You'll be happy to know she's alive and well and up to her elbows in fried okra at Luby's. Home of the legendary Lu Ann platter, San Antonio-based Luby's (formerly Luby's Cafeterias) has about 220 cafeteria-style restaurants across 10 Southern and Southwestern states (about three-quarters are in Texas). If you're not interested in walking the line, Luby's restaurants also provide a take-out service that has grown to generate about 13% of the company's sales.

Luby's menu includes such comfort foods as mashed potatoes, macaroni and cheese, roast beef, and fried chicken. After experiments with drive-through service at various locations showed promise, the company is expanding its to-go offerings. About 65 Luby's now house drive-throughs.

On the verge of bankruptcy, the company has taken a major step in 2001 to cope with its escalating financial problems. Brothers Christopher (president and CEO) and Harris Pappas (COO), founders of the successful Pappadeaux seafood and Pappasito's Mexican food chains, have been named to the top posts. The Pappas brothers have quietly bought about 6% of ailing Luby's, and have also agreed to buy $10 million of the company's debt.

Luby's hopes the Pappas boys can stem the company's recent decline, which includes millions of dollars in losses, a 75% decline in its stock price over three years, the default of its credit agreements, and a high executive turnover rate.

HISTORY

Bob Luby grew up working in his father's cafeterias, founded his own cafeteria chain in San Antonio in 1947, and opened the first Luby's the following year. Luby's continued opening new cafeterias and branched beyond Texas in 1966 to open a unit in New Mexico. The company went public in 1973. In 1981 it changed its name from Cafeterias, Inc., to Luby's Cafeterias.

During the 1980s and 1990s the company continued expanding across other states. Tragedy struck in 1991 when a gunman killed more than 20 diners at a Luby's in Killeen, Texas; the event prompted the passage of a state concealed-weapons law. In 1996 Luby's entered into an agreement to operate seafood restaurants with Corpus Christi, Texas-based Water Street. Also that year the company acquired 22 Wyatt's Cafeterias in Arkansas, Kansas, Missouri, and Texas from parent Triangle Foodservice for almost $14 million.

CEO John Curtis committed suicide in 1997, and Barry Parker, former chairman and CEO of County Seat Stores, was appointed to replace him. The following year the company launched an effort to improve its operations, with particular emphasis on building restaurants in smaller Texas markets and expanding its take-out business. Bob Luby died that year.

Believing the word "cafeteria" no longer adequately described its business, Luby's Cafeterias shortened its name to Luby's in 1999. The company also debuted prototypes for its redesigned restaurant and its smaller community restaurant. In 2000 Luby's exited the seafood restaurant business by selling its interests in its joint venture to partner Water Street. During the same year the company expanded its food-to-go operations. In late 2000 it closed down 12 underperforming locations.

In 2001 Luby's shook up management by electing brothers Christopher (president and CEO) and Harris Pappas (COO), creators of the successful Pappadeaux and Pappasito's restaurant chains, to run the company. Luby's is hoping the brothers — who are buying its debt and investing much needed capital — can turn around the ailing company's fortunes. It has suffered for years due to stock and sales declines, as well as high management turnover.

The company posted a net loss and decreased sales in fiscal 2001. It also announced plans to close 17 stores: 11 at the end of 2001, and another 6 by August 2002.

Luby's also made plans to dive back into the seafood business, saying it would turn a Huntsville, Texas, Luby's into a new casual seafood restaurant.

Chairman: Robert T. Herres
President and CEO: Christopher J. Pappas
COO: Harris J. Pappas, age 56
SVP and CFO: Ernest Pekmezaris
SVP, Development: Alan M. Davis, $184,167 pay
SVP, Head of Field Operations: S. Darrell Wood
SVP, Operations: Raymond C. Gabrysch, $184,167 pay
SVP, Operations: Clyde C. Hays III, age 48, $204,500 pay
VP, Corporate Human Resources: Wayne R. Shirley
VP, Facilities Management: Thomas B. Van Buskirk
VP, Financial Planning: Paula Y. Gold-Williams
VP, Information Systems: Steven G. Barrow
VP, Purchasing and Product Development:
  Janet L. Duckham
Auditors: Ernst & Young LLP

LOCATIONS

HQ: 2211 NE Loop 410, San Antonio, TX 78265
Phone: 210-654-9000   **Fax:** 210-599-8407
Web: www.lubys.com

Luby's has restaurants in Arizona, Arkansas, Florida, Louisiana, Mississippi, Missouri, New Mexico, Oklahoma, Tennessee, and Texas.

PRODUCTS/OPERATIONS

Selected Menu Items
Baked whitefish
Breaded beef cutlet
Breads
Broiled or baked chicken
Enchiladas
Fried chicken
Fried fillet of fish
Fried okra
Fried salmon croquette
Grilled beef liver
Grilled chopped steak
Macaroni and cheese
Mashed potatoes
Pastries
Roast beef
Salads
Vegetables

COMPETITORS

Advantica Restaurant
  Group
Applebee's
Bob Evans
Boston Market
Brinker
Buffets
CBRL Group
Darden Restaurants
Furr's
Garden Fresh Restaurants
McDonald's
Metromedia
Pancho's Mexican Buffet
Piccadilly Cafeterias
Prandium
The Restaurant Company
Ryan's Family Steak
  Houses
Sbarro
Shoney's
Worldwide Restaurant
  Concepts

HISTORICAL FINANCIALS & EMPLOYEES

NYSE: LUB FYE: August 31	Annual Growth	8/91	8/92	8/93	8/94	8/95	8/96	8/97	8/98	8/99	8/00
Sales ($ mil.)	4.6%	328	346	368	391	419	450	495	509	502	493
Net income ($ mil.)	(13.1%)	32	33	36	39	37	39	28	5	29	9
Income as % of sales	—	9.8%	9.4%	9.7%	10.1%	8.8%	8.7%	5.7%	1.0%	5.7%	1.8%
Earnings per share ($)	(11.1%)	1.18	1.19	1.31	1.51	1.55	1.64	1.21	0.22	1.26	0.41
Stock price - FY high ($)	—	20.75	18.38	25.88	25.75	24.63	25.25	24.38	21.38	18.63	14.13
Stock price - FY low ($)	—	16.00	12.00	15.50	20.88	18.50	19.88	17.63	15.25	13.31	5.50
Stock price - FY close ($)	(12.5%)	18.25	16.00	25.75	23.50	19.88	23.63	19.69	15.25	13.38	5.50
P/E - high	—	18	15	20	18	16	15	20	97	15	34
P/E - low	—	14	10	12	14	12	12	14	69	10	13
Dividends per share ($)	6.3%	0.46	0.50	0.54	0.60	0.66	0.72	0.80	0.80	0.80	0.80
Book value per share ($)	1.9%	7.40	8.01	8.77	8.50	8.27	9.41	9.40	8.83	9.06	8.77
Employees	5.0%	9,000	9,200	9,600	10,100	10,950	11,680	13,000	12,800	14,000	14,000

STOCK PRICE HISTORY

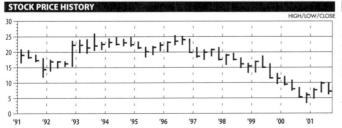

2000 FISCAL YEAR-END
Debt ratio: 37.1%
Return on equity: 4.6%
Cash ($ mil.): 1
Current ratio: 0.26
Long-term debt ($ mil.): 116
No. of shares (mil.): 22
Dividends
  Yield: 14.5%
  Payout: 195.1%
Market value ($ mil.): 123

LYONDELL CHEMICAL COMPANY

OVERVIEW

Lyondell Chemical got mixed up with a good crowd. The Houston-based company is one of the largest North American producers of the petrochemicals ethylene, propylene, and derivative polymer polyethylene, primarily through its 41% stake in Equistar Chemicals. Its polymers (including polypropylene) are used in synthetic and plastic grocery and trash bags, sports equipment, containers, and packaging. It also produces aromatics (benzene, toluene), fuel additives, and specialty chemicals (resin oil, hydrogen), which are made into intermediates and sold to product makers. Through its ARCO Chemical acquisition, Lyondell has become one of the world's top makers of intermediate chemicals and specialty products.

The company conducts refining through 59%-owned LYONDELL-CITGO Refining (LCR), a joint venture with CITGO Petroleum (a subsidiary of Petróleos de Venezuela). LCR refines low-cost, very heavy crude oil from Venezuela into jet fuel, gasoline, low-sulphur diesel fuel, aromatics, lube oils, and other high-margin distillates. Its 75%-owned Lyondell Methanol Company produces methanol.

Lyondell plans to increase its European operations with a focus on butanediol and propylene oxide production. The company is reorganizing operations as it consolidates its Equistar operations. To pay down debt, Lyondell sold its global polyols business to Bayer AG.

HISTORY

It wasn't exactly a model of efficiency. Some 16 miles apart on the Texas Gulf Coast, Atlantic Richfield's Houston refinery and its Channelview petrochemical complex were run by offices in Los Angeles and Philadelphia, respectively.

Sinclair Oil & Refining built the refining facility in 1919. (Sinclair became a subsidiary of Richfield Oil in 1936.) In 1955 Texas Butadiene and Chemical built the complex that would become Lyondell's petrochemical complex on the site of the Lyondell Country Club in Channelview. A Richfield Oil subsidiary bought the plant in 1962. Four years later Richfield and Atlantic Refining merged. The refinery became part of ARCO Products, and the plant joined ARCO Chemical.

The operations were losing ground in the Gulf Coast market, and ARCO Chemical considered selling the petrochemical complex. SVP Bob Gower convinced the company that it could exploit synergies between the refinery and the plant, and in 1985 ARCO set up Lyondell Petrochemical, with Gower as CEO.

By the fourth quarter of its first year, Lyondell was profitable. It upgraded its refinery to handle any kind of crude oil. Through voluntary layoffs in 1985 Gower reduced Lyondell's workforce by more than 1,000 (including 75% of its executive staff). With profits up more than 340% from 1987 to 1988, ARCO decided to take the company public. In 1989 ARCO sold 50.1% of Lyondell in a $1.4 billion IPO. Before the sale, ARCO had Lyondell pay it $500 million, leaving the new company in debt.

Lyondell persevered and increased petrochemical capacities in 1989. It became the first major US refiner to recycle used motor oil into gasoline in 1992.

In 1995 Lyondell bought Occidental Petroleum's high-density polyethylene business Alathon for $356 million. The firm joined petrochemical rivals Eastman Chemical, Quantum Chemical, and Union Carbide the next year to explore building a jointly owned $900-million plant to produce ethylene for use in products such as antifreeze, cosmetics, and plastics. Lyondell also partnered with MCN Corporation, which bought a 25% interest in Lyondell's methanol plant. Lyondell president Dan Smith replaced Gower as CEO in 1996.

ARCO sold its stake in Lyondell in 1997. The company's LYONDELL-CITGO Refining partnership completed upgrading its Pasadena, Texas, oil refinery, enabling it to process very heavy crude oil from its Venezuelan supplier. Also that year, Lyondell and Millennium Chemicals formed Equistar Chemicals, a joint venture that combined their olefins and polymers businesses.

In 1998 Occidental Petroleum added its petrochemical business to Equistar, increasing the size of the venture by a third. That year Lyondell Petrochemical shortened its name to Lyondell Chemical and paid $5.6 billion for ARCO Chemical.

In 1999 Lyondell sold Equistar's concentrates and compounds business, including two facilities in Ohio and Texas, to New York-based Ampacet. It also announced plans to build a butanediol plant in the Netherlands (to begin production in 2002). To alleviate the debt associated with its 1998 purchase of ARCO Chemical, Lyondell sold its polyols business in 2000 to Germany's Bayer for $2.45 billion.

Chairman: William T. Butler, age 68
President, CEO, and Director: Dan F. Smith, age 54, $2,564,556 pay
EVP and CFO: Robert T. Blakely, age 59, $1,058,085 pay
EVP and COO: Morris Gelb, age 54, $983,950 pay
EVP; President and CEO, Equistar Chemicals, LP: Eugene R. Allspach, age 54, $893,388 pay
SVP, Manufacturing: James W. Bayer
SVP, Organizational and Process Change: Debra L. Starnes
SVP, Petrochemicals: Brian A. Gittings, age 54
SVP, Polymers: W. Norman Phillips
SVP, Intermediates and Performance Chemicals: Edward J. Dineen, age 46, $805,140 pay
President, Lyondell Asia Pacific: Charles C. Yang
President, Lyondell Europe: John R. Beard, age 48
VP, General Counsel, and Secretary: Kerry A. Galvin, age 40
VP, Human Resources: John A. Hollinshead
Auditors: PricewaterhouseCoopers LLP

LOCATIONS

HQ: 1221 McKinney St., Ste. 700, Houston, TX 77010
Phone: 713-652-7200   **Fax:** 713-309-2074
Web: www.lyondell.com

Lyondell Chemical has operations in China (Hong Kong), France, Japan, the Netherlands, the UK, and the US (including California, Illinois, Iowa, Louisiana, New Jersey, Ohio, Pennsylvania, and Texas).

2000 Sales

	$ mil.	% of total
US	2,101	52
Other contries	1,935	48
Total	**4,036**	**100**

PRODUCTS/OPERATIONS

Selected Products

Petrochemicals
Aromatics (benzene, toluene)
Olefins (ethylene, propylene, butadiene)
Oxygenated products (MTBE fuel additive)
Specialty chemicals (isoprene, resin oil, hydrogen, ethyl alcohol)

Polymers
Polyethylene
Polyolefins
Polypropylene
Wire and cable resin

Refining
Gasoline
Jet fuel
Low-sulfur diesel fuel
Lubricants

COMPETITORS

Amerada Hess	Huntsman	TransCanada
Ashland	Koch	PipeLines
BASF AG	Methanex	Ultramar
BP	Norsk Hydro	Diamond
Chevron	PETROBRAS	Shamrock
Dow Chemical	PEMEX	Union Carbide
DuPont	Phillips	Unocal
Eastman	Petroleum	USX-Marathon
Chemical	Royal	
Exxon Mobil	Dutch/Shell	
Formosa Plastics	Texaco	

HISTORICAL FINANCIALS & EMPLOYEES

NYSE: LYO FYE: December 31	Annual Growth	12/91	12/92	12/93	12/94	12/95	12/96	12/97	12/98	12/99	12/00
Sales ($ mil.)	(3.8%)	5,729	4,805	3,850	3,857	4,936	5,052	2,878	1,447	3,693	4,036
Net income ($ mil.)	7.8%	222	16	26	223	389	126	286	52	(115)	437
Income as % of sales	—	3.9%	0.3%	0.7%	5.8%	7.9%	2.5%	9.9%	3.6%	—	10.8%
Earnings per share ($)	3.3%	2.78	0.20	0.33	2.78	4.86	1.58	3.58	0.67	(1.10)	3.71
Stock price - FY high ($)	—	26.13	25.88	29.50	33.00	29.13	32.25	27.38	38.13	22.50	19.50
Stock price - FY low ($)	—	14.63	21.13	16.75	20.63	21.13	20.38	18.38	15.00	11.25	8.44
Stock price - FY close ($)	(4.2%)	22.63	24.63	21.25	25.88	22.88	22.13	26.50	18.00	12.75	15.31
P/E - high	—	9	81	492	12	6	20	8	57	—	5
P/E - low	—	5	66	279	7	4	13	5	22	—	2
Dividends per share ($)	(7.1%)	1.75	1.80	1.35	0.90	0.90	0.90	0.90	0.90	0.90	0.90
Book value per share ($)	22.9%	1.53	(0.08)	(1.10)	0.79	4.75	5.39	7.84	7.45	8.57	9.74
Employees	16.4%	2,270	2,312	2,283	2,775	2,732	2,500	400	10,400	9,300	8,900

STOCK PRICE HISTORY

HIGH/LOW/CLOSE

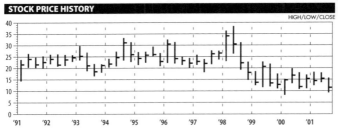

2000 FISCAL YEAR-END

Debt ratio: 77.0%
Return on equity: 40.6%
Cash ($ mil.): 260
Current ratio: 1.83
Long-term debt ($ mil.): 3,844
No. of shares (mil.): 118
Dividends
  Yield: 5.9%
  Payout: 24.3%
Market value ($ mil.): 1,800

MARY KAY INC.

OVERVIEW

Mary Kay promoted Girl Power before any of the Spice Girls were even born. The Dallas-based company, the US's #2 direct seller of beauty products (after Avon), aims to empower its primarily female employees through careers that allow them ample time for their families. Mary Kay sells more than 200 products in eight product categories: facial skin care, cosmetics, body care, nail care, men's skin care, fragrances, nutritional supplements, and sun protection. Some 800,000 direct-sales consultants demonstrate Mary Kay products in small group settings in the US and about 35 other countries. The US accounts for about 80% of sales.

Founded by a woman — Mary Kay Ash — for women, Mary Kay has an overwhelmingly female workforce. Although Ash stands by her original goal of providing financial and career opportunities for women, men exert quite a bit of power at the company: Mary Kay's chairman/CEO and CFO are both men.

The company gives bonuses each year, ranging from jewelry to the company's trademark pink Cadillacs. Ash is known for her religious nature as well as generosity. She suffered a debilitating stroke in 1996, and she died on Thanksgiving Day 2001. Ash's family owns most of the company; her son is chairman and CEO.

HISTORY

Before founding her own company in 1963, Mary Kay Ash worked as a Stanley Home Products sales representative. Impressed with the alligator handbag awarded the top saleswoman at a Stanley convention, Ash was determined to win the next year's prize — and she did. Despite that accomplishment and her 11 years of experience, a male assistant she had trained was made her boss after less than a year at Stanley. Tired of not receiving recognition, Ash started a business with her second husband using their life savings of $5,000. Although her husband died of a heart attack shortly before the business opened, Ash forged ahead with the help of her two grown sons.

First she bought a cosmetics formula invented years earlier by a hide tanner. (The mixture was originally used to soften leather, but the tanner noticed how the formula made his hands look younger, and he began applying the mixture to his face, with great results.) Ash kept her first line simple — 10 products — and packaged her wares in pink to contrast with the typical black and red toiletry cases of the day. Ash also enlisted consultants, who held "beauty shows" with five or six women in attendance. Mary Kay grossed $198,000 in its first year.

The company introduced men's skin care products in 1965. Ash bought a pink Cadillac the following year and began awarding the cars as prizes three years later. (By 1981 orders were so large — almost 500 — that GM dubbed the color "Mary Kay Pink.")

Ash became a millionaire when her firm went public in 1968. Mary Kay grew steadily through the 1970s. Foreign operations began in 1971 in Australia, and over the next 25 years the company entered 24 more countries,

including nations in Asia, Europe, Central and South America, and the Pacific Rim.

Sales plunged in the early 1980s, along with the company's stock prices (from $40 to $9 between 1983 and 1985). Ash and her family reacquired Mary Kay in 1985 through a $375 million LBO. Burdened with debt, the firm lost money in the late 1980s. Mary Kay took a number of steps to boost sales and income, doing a makeover on the cosmetics line and advertising in women's magazines again (after a five-year hiatus) to counter its old-fashioned image. The company also introduced recyclable packaging. In 1989 Avon rebuffed a buyout offer by Mary Kay, and both companies halted animal testing.

Mary Kay introduced a bath and body product line in 1991, and its Skin Revival System, launched in 1993, raked in $80 million in its first six months on the market. It began operations in Russia that year; sales there reached $25 million by 1995. Mary Kay Ash suffered a debilitating stroke in 1996. (The company continues to avoid discussing her health.)

In 1998 the company began selling through retail outlets in China because of a government ban on direct selling. Changing with the times, Mary Kay also added a white sport utility vehicle and new shades of pink to its fleet of 10,000 GM cars in 1998.

Chairman John Rochon was named CEO in 1999. Also in 1999 Mary Kay launched *Women & Success* (a magazine for consultants) and Atlas (its electronic ordering system).

In 2001 Richard Rogers, the company chairman and son of Mary Kay Ash, replaced Rochon as CEO. Mary Kay Ash died on Thanksgiving Day 2001.

OFFICERS

Chairman and CEO: Richard Rogers, age 58
CFO: David Holl
EVP, Global Communications and Public Affairs: Russell Mack
EVP, Global Product Technology: Dennis Greaney
EVP and Chief Scientific Officer: Myra O. Barker
SVP, Global Human Resources and US Branch Operations: Darrell Overcash
SVP and Chief Information Officer: Kregg Jodie
President, US Sales: Tom Whatley
General Counsel: Brad Glendening

LOCATIONS

HQ: 16251 Dallas Pkwy., Addison, TX 75001
Phone: 972-687-6300   **Fax:** 972-687-1609
Web: www.marykay.com

Mary Kay employs about 800,000 direct-sales consultants who sell the company's merchandise in 35 countries in Asia, Australia, Europe, North America, and South America.

PRODUCTS/OPERATIONS

Selected Product Lines
Body care
Cosmetics
Facial skin care
Fragrances
Men's skin care
Nail care
Nutritional supplements for men
Nutritional supplements for women
Sun protection

COMPETITORS

Alberto-Culver	L'Oréal
Allou	Merle Norman
Alticor	New Dana Perfumes
Avon	Nu Skin
BeautiControl Cosmetics	Perrigo
Body Shop	Procter & Gamble
Clarins	Reliv
Colgate-Palmolive	Revlon
Coty	Schwarzkopf & DEP
Del Labs	Scott's Liquid Gold
Dial	Shaklee
Estée Lauder	Shiseido
Helen of Troy	Sunrider
Herbalife	Unilever
Intimate Brands	Wella
Johnson & Johnson	

HISTORICAL FINANCIALS & EMPLOYEES

Private FYE: December 31	Annual Growth	12/91	12/92	12/93	12/94	12/95	12/96	12/97	12/98	12/99	12/00
Sales ($ mil.)	9.7%	520	613	737	850	950	1,000	1,050	1,000	1,000	1,200
Employees	7.4%	1,900	2,100	2,400	2,400	2,800	3,000	3,500	3,500	3,250	3,600

SALES HISTORY

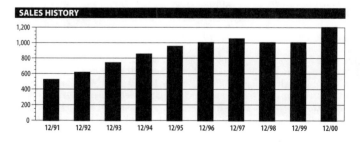

MARY KAY

MAXXAM INC.

OVERVIEW

With a reputation for taking it to the max, corporate raider Charles Hurwitz operates MAXXAM, an eclectic mix of businesses ranging from aluminum and timber products to real estate and horse racing.

The Houston-based holding company gets about 90% of its revenues from its 63% stake in Kaiser Aluminum, one of the world's top aluminum producers. Kaiser operates bauxite mines, aluminum smelters, and refining operations in 10 US states and five other countries. Weakened from higher energy prices, Kaiser is selling some assets.

MAXXAM's Pacific Lumber subsidiary owns about 220,000 acres of timberland in Northern California. The subsidiary has been the target of environmentalists who claim it has harvested ancient California redwoods. Pacific Lumber has sold 10,000 acres of woodlands — including the Headwaters and Elk Head Springs forests — to the US and California governments to end an environmental standoff.

Among MAXXAM's real estate interests are commercial and residential properties in Arizona, California, and Texas, and the Puerto Rican resort, Palmas del Mar. The company also owns about 99% of Sam Houston Race Park, a horse-racing facility near Houston. Hurwitz controls about 73% of MAXXAM.

HISTORY

Robert McCulloch, an oil wildcatter and the developer of the chain saw, founded the Cuban American Oil Company in 1955. In 1960 the company became McCulloch Oil Corp. of California. The founder drilled numerous wells, but made no big strikes.

McCulloch began investing in real estate developments during the 1960s, starting with Lake Havasu City, an Arizona resort. Lake Havasu City was put on the map in 1968 when McCulloch bought the London Bridge and had it reassembled in the Arizona desert. During the late 1960s and 1970s McCulloch Oil continued to diversify by acquiring coal, gas, oil, real estate, and silver mining operations. With Lake Havasu City a success, the company also started developments in Fountain Hills, Arizona; Pueblo West, Colorado; and Spring Creek, Nevada.

With the real estate industry in recession, McCulloch took a $60 million writeoff in 1976. The following year McCulloch died of drug and alcohol abuse, and his son Robert Jr. pleaded guilty to fraud charges related to the company's real estate sales in Colorado.

Charles Hurwitz, a former Bache & Company stockbroker, had established himself as a wheeler-dealer in insurance, investments, and real estate ventures. In 1978 Hurwitz bought 13% of McCulloch's stock. By 1980 he was chairman and CEO and had filled top management with his allies. That year the company became MCO Holdings.

Through MCO, Hurwitz created a puzzle of interlocking holdings. The company purchased 37% of the Maxxam Group, one of Hurwitz's investment partnerships, in 1982. A year later MCO began investing in United Financial Group, which included United Savings Association of Texas. (In 1998 the FDIC sued Hurwitz, alleging he allowed the S&L to fail.) MCO, through Maxxam, also acquired Pacific Lumber in 1986 in a takeover engineered with Michael Milken and Ivan Boesky. To cover acquisition costs, MCO doubled Pacific Lumber's logging output of California redwood, angering environmentalists. In 1988 MCO purchased the outstanding shares of Maxxam and the companies merged as MAXXAM Inc. That year MAXXAM paid $930 million (raised by selling junk bonds) to acquire a majority interest in Kaiser Aluminum Corporation.

Environmental issues during the 1990s threatened Pacific Lumber operations. The spotted owl and marbled murrelet (a small sea bird) were named to the endangered species list; both nest in Pacific Lumber's timberlands and have restricted its ability to harvest old-growth timber. In the 1996 Headwaters Agreement the government offered to pay MAXXAM about $300 million for about 7,500 acres of mostly old-growth timberlands. That year MAXXAM experienced a sharp decline in income (more than 50%) from aluminum operations; the company cited depressed market prices as the chief culprit.

Pacific Lumber and government officials agreed in 1998 to more than double the area of redwood forest protected by the Headwaters deal, in exchange for the company being allowed to log 1,250 acres of old-growth timber. Later that year California officials suspended Pacific's logging permit because of numerous violations. In 1999 the US and California governments paid $480 million for 10,000 acres of old-growth redwoods, including the Headwaters property.

In 2000 MAXXAM acquired Valley Race Park, a greyhound racing venue in Harlingen, Texas.

OFFICERS

Chairman and CEO: Charles E. Hurwitz, age 60, $1,360,102 pay
Vice Chairman and General Counsel: J. Kent Friedman, age 57, $810,000 pay
President, CFO, and Director: Paul N. Schwartz, age 54, $973,440 pay
SVP: John T. La Duc, age 58, $807,493 pay
VP and Chief Personnel Officer: Diane M. Dudley, age 60
VP, Federal Government Affairs: Robert E. Cole, age 54
VP, Special Initiatives, Kaiser and KACC: Ronald L. Reman, age 43, $374,052 pay
VP, Communications: Joshua A. Reiss, age 33
Secretary: Bernard L. Birkel, age 50
Controller: Elizabeth D. Brumley, age 42
Auditors: Arthur Andersen LLP

LOCATIONS

HQ: 5847 San Felipe, Ste. 2600, Houston, TX 77057
Phone: 713-975-7600 **Fax:** 713-267-3701

MAXXAM has bauxite and aluminum production operations in Australia, Ghana, Jamaica, the UK, and the US; timber production in Northern California; and real estate interests in Arizona, California, and Puerto Rico.

2000 Sales

	$ mil.	% of total
US	1,628	66
Jamaica	299	12
Ghana	237	10
Other regions	284	12
Total	**2,448**	**100**

PRODUCTS/OPERATIONS

2000 Sales

	$ mil.	% of total
Aluminum operations	2,170	89
Forest products	200	8
Real estate	47	2
Racing operations	31	1
Total	**2,448**	**100**

Selected Subsidiaries
Britt Lumber Co., Inc. (wood fencing products)
Fountain Hills (a 12,100-acre single-family residential development property in Arizona)
Kaiser Aluminum & Chemical Corporation
Kaiser Aluminum Corporation (63%; alumina/bauxite, aluminum, and fabricated aluminum products)
The Pacific Lumber Co. (redwood and Douglas-fir lumber)
Salmon Creek
Scotia Pacific Timberlands
Palmas del Mar Properties, Inc. (resort, time-sharing, and land development and sales in Puerto Rico)
Sam Houston Race Park, Ltd. (98%, thoroughbred and quarter-horse racing facility near Houston)
Valley Race Park, Inc.

COMPETITORS

Alcan	North Pacific Group
Alcoa	Ormet
Commonwealth Industries	Plum Creek Timber
Connell Limited	Sierra Pacific Industries
Partnership	Simpson Investment
Earle M. Jorgensen	Universal Corporation
Georgia-Pacific Group	Weyerhaeuser
International Paper	Willamette
Louisiana-Pacific	

HISTORICAL FINANCIALS & EMPLOYEES

AMEX: MXM FYE: December 31	Annual Growth	12/91	12/92	12/93	12/94	12/95	12/96	12/97	12/98	12/99	12/00
Sales ($ mil.)	0.9%	2,255	2,203	2,031	2,116	2,565	2,543	2,729	2,573	2,311	2,448
Net income ($ mil.)	(5.7%)	58	(7)	(600)	(122)	58	23	65	(57)	74	34
Income as % of sales	—	2.6%	—	—	—	2.2%	0.9%	2.4%	—	3.2%	1.4%
Earnings per share ($)	(3.4%)	6.08	(0.77)	(69.00)	(14.04)	6.08	2.42	7.14	(8.17)	9.49	4.47
Stock price - FY high ($)	—	54.75	43.50	38.88	44.50	67.63	50.88	62.38	65.25	64.75	43.38
Stock price - FY low ($)	—	26.00	22.25	21.75	29.50	27.25	35.38	41.00	41.50	41.38	13.94
Stock price - FY close ($)	(7.1%)	29.38	27.50	36.75	30.88	35.25	47.63	43.63	57.38	42.88	15.19
P/E - high	—	9	—	—	—	10	19	8	—	6	10
P/E - low	—	4	—	—	—	4	13	5	—	4	3
Dividends per share ($)	—	0.00	0.00	0.00	0.00	0.00	0.00	0.00	0.00	0.00	0.00
Book value per share ($)	(19.8%)	52.98	51.05	(17.77)	(31.61)	(9.62)	(5.86)	(0.41)	(8.11)	3.83	7.28
Employees	1.7%	9,967	12,379	13,795	13,860	12,000	13,400	9,600	9,200	10,800	11,560

STOCK PRICE HISTORY

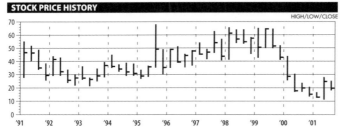

HIGH/LOW/CLOSE

2000 FISCAL YEAR-END

Debt ratio: 97.5%
Return on equity: 88.9%
Cash ($ mil.): 353
Current ratio: 1.52
Long-term debt ($ mil.): 1,883
No. of shares (mil.): 7
Dividends
  Yield: —
  Payout: —
Market value ($ mil.): 103

THE MEN'S WEARHOUSE, INC.

OVERVIEW

With a business strategy tailored for growth, Houston-based The Men's Wearhouse has made alterations even a haberdasher would be hard-pressed to follow. One of the largest discount retailers of men's business attire in the US, the company has grown quickly through a series of acquisitions, and now operates more than 650 stores in 42 states and Canada.

Its more than 470 Men's Wearhouse stores sell name-brand and private-label suits discounted 20% to 30%. The company also has two chains that operate only on the weekends and sell at even cheaper prices: subsidiary K&G Men's Center, with about 60 superstores, and Suit Warehouse, with five stores.

The Men's Wearhouse also owns the Moores menswear chain, which has more than 110 stores in Canada and a manufacturing facility that produces about half of that chain's tailored apparel. Men's Wearhouse has also begun renting tuxedoes at some of its stores.

Tailored clothing accounts for about 65% of sales, although the firm is selling more casual apparel, shoes, and accessories. The Men's Wearhouse stresses attentive, low-pressure customer service to attract the man with little knowledge of buying suits.

The founding Zimmer family owns about 16% of the company.

HISTORY

George Zimmer got his start in the apparel business working as a salesman for his father's coat manufacturing company. An apparel industry veteran at 23, he founded The Men's Wearhouse in fast-growing Houston in 1973 with his father, Robert Zimmer, and college buddy Harry Levy.

By 1981 the company had expanded to 12 stores, all in Texas. That year the company opened its first store outside the state, in San Jose, California.

By the time George debuted on TV in 1986 with his now popular "I guarantee it" motto, the company had 25 stores. During the late 1980s the company continued to add stores in the Southwest, Midwest, and Pacific Northwest. When The Men's Wearhouse went public in 1992 it had 113 stores and sales of nearly $170 million. The company continued to grow at a slower but more sustainable pace than its competitors, some of which went bankrupt as a result of overexpansion.

The Men's Wearhouse entered the Los Angeles market in 1993; during the mid-1990s the company was opening an average of one store a week.

In 1997, through its newly formed Value Price Clothing division, The Men's Wearhouse bought C & R Clothiers, adding 17 stores and a new, lower-priced segment to its operations. The division added four Suit Warehouse stores in the Detroit area the next year. The company entered the New York market in 1998. Also that year the company passed $1 billion in sales.

An on-again-off-again deal to grow into Canada was back on (for good) in early 1999 when The Men's Wearhouse paid $127 million for the Montreal-based Moores Retail Group. In a second acquisition that year, The Men's Wearhouse bought K&G Men's Center, the operator of 34 superstores in 16 states. Also in 1999 the company began testing tuxedo rentals at some of its Men's Wearhouse stores.

As "Friday Casual" became a daily event at many companies, The Men's Wearhouse began to adjust, relaxing its image with more lines of casual clothing. The company focused on providing "dressy casual" clothes for men over 25.

In 2000 it combined its other discount operations with K&G, renaming most of the stores K&G Men's Center. Also in 2000 the company began a major image makeover of Moores Retail Group to emphasize quality over bargains. That same year the company was named to Fortune's list of "100 Best Companies to Work For."

During 2001 the company's sales and income were hurt by the general weakening in the US retail industry. Also in 2001 The Men's Wearhouse began renting tuxedoes at selected locations, with a goal of being the US's largest renter and seller of formal wear. The company hopes to capture 25% of the $1-billion tuxedo rental market.

OFFICERS

Chairman and CEO: George Zimmer, age 52, $465,576 pay
Vice Chairman: David H. Edwab, age 46
President and COO: Eric J. Lane, age 41, $392,885 pay
SVP, Merchandising; Director: James E. Zimmer, age 49, $389,423 pay
EVP, Planning and Systems; Director: Harry M. Levy, age 52
EVP and Director: Richard E. Goldman, age 50, $290,192 pay
EVP: Charles Bresler, age 52, $334,269 pay
EVP: Bruce Hampton, age 46
SVP, CFO, and Treasurer: Neill P. Davis, age 44
SVP and Principal Accounting Officer: Gary G. Ckodre, age 51
SVP, Manufacturing: Will Silveira, age 42
SVP, Real Estate; Director: Robert E. Zimmer, age 77
SVP, Stores: Theodore T. Biele, age 50
VP and Assistant Treasurer: Claudia Pruitt, age 49
VP and Chief Information Officer: Jeffery Marshall, age 48
CEO, K&G Men's Company: Ron Covin, age 53
EVP and COO, K&G Men's Company: Douglas S. Ewert, age 38
General Merchandise Manager: Scott Norris, age 38
Human Resources Manager: Joe Vera
Auditors: Deloitte & Touche LLP

LOCATIONS

HQ: 5803 Glenmont Dr., Houston, TX 77081
Phone: 713-592-7200   **Fax:** 713-664-1957
Web: www.menswearhouse.com

Men's Wearhouse has more than 500 stores in 42 US states and more than 100 stores are in Canada.

PRODUCTS/OPERATIONS

2001 Stores

	No.
Men's Wearhouse	473
Moores	113
K&G	65
Total	**651**

Merchandise
Accessories
Dress shirts
Formal wear (at select locations)
Outerwear
Shoes
Slacks
Sport coats
Sport shirts
Suits
Sweaters

Store Names
K&G Men's Center
Men's Wearhouse
Moores
Suit Warehouse

COMPETITORS

Brooks Brothers	J. C. Penney	S&K Famous
Burlington Coat	Jos. A. Bank	Brands
Factory	Kohl's	Sears
Casual Male	May	Spiegel
Dillard's	Neiman Marcus	Syms
Dylex	Nordstrom	Target
Federated	Ross Stores	TJX
Hudson's Bay	Saks Inc.	Today's Man
J. Crew		

HISTORICAL FINANCIALS & EMPLOYEES

NYSE: MW FYE: Saturday nearest Jan. 31	Annual Growth	1/92	1/93	1/94	1/95	1/96	1/97	1/98	1/99	1/00	1/01
Sales ($ mil.)	29.1%	133	170	240	317	406	484	631	768	1,187	1,334
Net income ($ mil.)	39.6%	4	6	9	12	17	21	29	40	53	85
Income as % of sales	—	3.1%	3.5%	3.6%	3.8%	4.1%	4.4%	4.6%	5.2%	4.5%	6.4%
Earnings per share ($)	31.0%	—	0.23	0.32	0.42	0.55	0.67	0.87	1.15	1.27	2.00
Stock price - FY high ($)	—	—	5.64	14.57	15.46	20.18	25.68	27.51	36.88	34.94	34.88
Stock price - FY low ($)	—	—	2.52	5.04	7.01	8.56	10.84	15.34	14.00	19.50	17.25
Stock price - FY close ($)	24.5%	—	5.49	12.01	9.79	17.84	17.76	23.93	29.63	23.88	31.68
P/E - high	—	—	25	44	36	37	38	31	30	26	17
P/E - low	—	—	11	15	16	16	16	17	12	15	8
Dividends per share ($)	—	—	0.00	0.00	0.00	0.00	0.00	0.00	0.00	0.00	0.00
Book value per share ($)	29.0%	—	1.54	2.13	2.98	4.39	5.08	6.65	8.55	9.76	11.80
Employees	28.3%	1,277	1,766	2,545	3,190	4,100	4,900	6,000	6,800	10,700	12,000

STOCK PRICE HISTORY

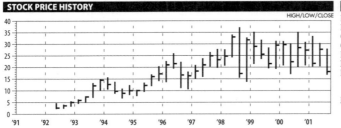

HIGH/LOW/CLOSE

2001 FISCAL YEAR-END

Debt ratio: 7.9%
Return on equity: 18.7%
Cash ($ mil.): 84
Current ratio: 3.12
Long-term debt ($ mil.): 43
No. of shares (mil.): 42
Dividends
  Yield: —
  Payout: —
Market value ($ mil.): 1,329

METALS USA, INC.

OVERVIEW

Metals USA never met a metals processor it didn't like — once, it acquired 26 companies in one six-month span. The Houston-based consolidator buys steel and aluminum from mills and specialty metals from foundries, then provides customized processing services such as shearing and cutting to length, precision blanking, slitting, pickling, tee-splitting, and laser, flame, and plasma cutting.

Metals USA concentrates on four product groups: heavy carbon steel, flat-rolled steel, specialty metals, and aluminum building products. Additional services include just-in-time delivery and inventory management. Metals USA also makes finished products such as pump parts and hydraulic cylinders.

Though the company's diverse roster of more than 65,000 customers in 11 industries has helped protect it from economic downturns, the company's sales and income have been hurt by the overall drop in demand across the metals industry. Faced with the troubled metals market and a recessionary manufacturing economy, Metals USA filed a voluntary petition for reorganization under Chapter 11.

Metals USA believes in decentralized management, and as a result, acquired companies maintain their names and local management.

Director Toby Jeffreys owns about 7% of the company; chairman Arnold Bradburd owns about 5%.

HISTORY

Metals USA was founded in 1996 with an eye toward consolidating the fragmented $75 billion metals-processing industry, which at the time consisted of 3,500 small and mid-sized firms. Metals USA went public in 1997.

That year the company acquired eight small metals processors: Interstate Steel, Affiliated Metals, Queensboro Steel, Uni-Steel, Steel Service Systems, Williams Steel & Supply, Southern Alloy of America, and Texas Aluminum/Cornerstone. Metals USA's so-called founding companies, the group cut a broad swath geographically and provided a diversity of offerings, as well. Metals USA quickly became a leader in the metals processing and distribution industry.

Led by chairman and CEO Arthur French, Metals USA continued to acquire. In the first six months of 1998 it bought businesses with more than $700 million in annual sales, including Pittsburgh-based Levinson Steel (distributor and processor of plate and other structural products), Baltimore's Seaboard Steel and Iron (steel service center), Springfield, Ohio-based Krohn Steel Service Center (flat-rolled steel), and Carlsbad, California-based Metalmart, Inc. (specialty light-metals fabrication). The firm also bought aluminum building-products makers Western Awning Company and National Manufacturing, Inc. Late in 1998 the company acquired Intsel Steel, a leading distributor of heavy carbon steel products, from Philip Services.

The acquisitions continued in 1999 with the purchase of three companies with combined sales of $125 million, including Shreveport, Louisiana-based Premier Steel

(heavy carbon steel products). That year French retired and SVP and CFO Michael Kirksey replaced him as CEO; VC Arnold W. Bradburd became chairman. Also in 1999 Metals USA signed a $29-million supply agreement with the US Department of Defense. Late in 1999 the company acquired commercial and residential aluminum and steel construction-products maker Allmet Building Products, which has locations in the southern, southwestern, and western US.

In 2000 the company created a new business unit, i-Solutions, for providing online ordering and procurement specifically for non-government customers. Also that year the company acquired Gibraltar Steel's flat-rolled steel processing operations in Chattanooga, Tennessee. In fiscal 2001, the company's sales rose, yet net income dropped as Metals USA worked to compete in a tightening steel market and weakening economy.

In early spring of 2001 CEO Michael Kirksey announced that there would be organizational and managerial changes to improve operating margins and sales growth. That year Arnold Bradburd retired as chairman, succeeded by Kirksey, and Richard Singer, president of the company's Plates and Shapes Group, was named president and COO. With sales dropping and losses mounting, Metals USA laid off 850 workers, about 18% of its workforce, during 2001. It also announced plans to sell some units and merge the operations of several others (among the businesses slated for sale were the company's specialty metals and aerospace businesses). Later in the year the company filed for reorganization under Chapter 11 protection.

OFFICERS

Chairman and CEO: J. Michael Kirksey, age 45,
$340,500 pay
President and COO: Richard A. Singer, age 55,
$325,094 pay
SVP: Craig R. Doveala, $291,221 pay
SVP and General Counsel: John A. Hageman, age 46,
$223,000 pay
SVP; President, Building Products:
Edward L. Thompson
SVP: Lester G. Patterson, age 60, $213,546 pay
VP, Corporate Controller, and Chief Accounting Officer:
Terry L. Freeman
VP, Human Resources; Assistant General Counsel:
Jon P. McNaught
VP, Safety and Environmental: Randy Sartain
VP, Sales and Marketing, Flat-Rolled Steel Group:
Nancy Brakers
Auditors: Arthur Andersen LLP

LOCATIONS

HQ: 3 Riverway, Ste. 600, Houston, TX 77056
Phone: 713-965-0990   **Fax:** 713-965-0067
Web: www.metalsusa.com

Metals USA operates metals-processing facilities in 34
US states.

PRODUCTS/OPERATIONS

2000 Sales

	$ mil.	% of total
Plates and Shapes	965	47
Flat-rolled steel	937	45
Building products	170	8
Adjustments	(50)	—
Total	**2,022**	**100**

Selected Products and Services

**Aluminum Building
Products**
Aluminum extruded
Aluminum roll-formed
Awnings and wall systems

Flat-Rolled Steel Products
Cold-rolled
Electro-galvanized
Galvanneal
Hot-dipped galvanized
Hot-rolled P & O
Pre-painted

**Metals Aerospace
International**
Aluminum extrusions
High-temperature alloys
Stainless steel
Titanium

Plates and Shapes Group
Bar grating
Bar, tube, and pipe
Carbon-alloy plate
Carbon plate
Carbon structurals
Diamond grip
Expanded metal
Sheets
Wide-flange beams

Specialty Metal Products
Aluminum
Beryllium copper
Brass/bronze
Copper
Ductile iron
Stainless steel
Titanium
Tool steel

COMPETITORS

A.M. Castle
Commercial Metals
Earle M. Jorgensen
Kreher Steel
Metals USA
Reliance Steel
Ryerson Tull
Steel Technologies
Worthington Industries

HISTORICAL FINANCIALS & EMPLOYEES

NYSE: MUI FYE: December 31	Annual Growth	12/91	12/92	12/93	12/94	12/95	12/96	12/97	12/98	12/99	12/00
Sales ($ mil.)	47.0%	—	—	136	212	235	240	508	1,499	1,745	2,022
Net income ($ mil.)	12.3%	—	—	5	7	7	3	6	40	40	12
Income as % of sales		—	—	3.8%	3.4%	2.9%	1.4%	1.2%	2.7%	2.3%	0.6%
Earnings per share ($)	4.6%	—	—	—	—	—	—	0.28	1.07	1.04	0.32
Stock price - FY high ($)	—	—	—	—	—	—	—	16.50	20.13	13.50	9.94
Stock price - FY low ($)		—	—	—	—	—	—	10.00	6.56	7.44	1.94
Stock price - FY close ($)	(43.1%)	—	—	—	—	—	—	15.25	9.75	8.50	2.81
P/E - high		—	—	—	—	—	—	59	18	13	31
P/E - low		—	—	—	—	—	—	36	6	7	6
Dividends per share ($)	—	—	—	—	—	—	—	0.00	0.00	0.00	0.09
Book value per share ($)	14.2%	—	—	—	—	—	—	6.90	8.95	9.97	10.27
Employees	44.7%	—	—	—	—	—	1,071	2,700	4,000	4,600	4,700

STOCK PRICE HISTORY

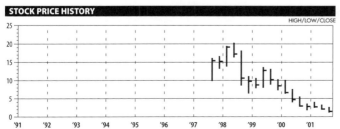

HIGH/LOW/CLOSE

2000 FISCAL YEAR-END

Debt ratio: 56.6%
Return on equity: 3.1%
Cash ($ mil.): 4
Current ratio: 2.70
Long-term debt ($ mil.): 490
No. of shares (mil.): 37
Dividends
  Yield: 3.2%
  Payout: 28.1%
Market value ($ mil.): 103

MICHAELS STORES, INC.

OVERVIEW

Wannabe artists cut and shape their Renoir goatees; working artists cut and shape their merchandise from Michaels Stores. The Irving, Texas-based company operates more than 650 Michaels arts and crafts stores in the US, Canada, and Puerto Rico. Michaels also operates about 125 Aaron Brothers framing and art supply stores, primarily on the West Coast; a frame manufacturing division; and a warehouse business.

The nation's top retailer dedicated to arts, crafts, and decorative items, Michaels sells silk and dried plants and flowers, art and hobby supplies, picture framing materials, decorating knickknacks, party supplies, and seasonal products. To aid sales and create new customers, employees teach craft classes. Customers can order prints and posters, buy arts and crafts supplies, and find arts and crafts tips on the Michaels Web site.

A national chain in an industry where local shops and regional chains are typical, the company is quickly expanding, opening some 75 Michaels Stores and 25 or more Aaron Brothers stores each year.

HISTORY

Michael Dupey founded Michaels arts and crafts store in 1973 by converting a Ben Franklin variety store in Dallas that was owned by his father. With dad footing the bill, Dupey opened several other stores in Texas. By the early 1980s Michaels operated 11 stores.

Dupey wanted to buy the company from his father; the two could not agree on a price, however, so dad sold the chain in 1983 to Peoples Restaurants, which operated the Bonanza Steakhouse chain and was run by brothers Sam and Charles Wyly (now VC and chairman, respectively). As part of the deal, Dupey was paid $1.2 million and was given ownership of two Dallas stores, plus royalty-free licensing rights to Michaels stores in North Texas.

With 16 stores mostly in Texas, Peoples Restaurants spun off Michaels in 1984 to its shareholders. Michaels then acquired Montiel, a Colorado-based retailer with 13 stores. The next year the company acquired six retailers. In 1987 Michaels acquired Moskatel's, a 28-store chain based in California. By 1988 the company operated nearly 100 stores in 14 states.

Michaels had achieved the mass to attract the attention of big investors, and in 1989 it agreed to a $225 million LBO engineered in part by Acadia Partners, an investment group headed by Robert Bass. The group was unable to raise the junk-bond debt financing needed to acquire the company, so the deal fell apart in early 1990; Michaels took a $4 million charge for its effort.

That year the company hired Dupey, who had built his own Michaels-MJ Designs chain in the meantime, to assist in selecting and marketing merchandise; it fired him in 1991, beginning a stormy relationship that played out in court. The company continued to open new stores and had 140 outlets by the end of 1991.

In 1992 Michaels began a drive to become the first national arts and crafts chain. It opened stores in new markets, including Iowa, Ohio, Oklahoma, Virginia, and Washington, and made its debut in Toronto.

Two years later Michaels acquired several chains in the West, including Oregon Craft & Supply, H&H Craft & Floral Company, and Treasure House. Its biggest acquisition that year, however, was its $92 million purchase of 101-store Leewards Creative Crafts, which gave it a total of 360 stores in 38 states. In 1995 Michaels acquired 71 Aaron Brothers specialty framing and art supply stores.

Ironically, the company's far-reaching expansion did not include its birthplace. After a three-year court battle proving even the crafts business has an ugly side, in 1996 Michaels was awarded the right to operate stores in its home market, the Dallas-Fort Worth area. Dupey's Michael's-MJDesigns stores removed the Michaels name from its signs. (Dupey, in turn, was permitted to sell his assets without first getting right of approval from Michaels.)

Lowe's veteran Michael Rouleau became CEO of Michaels in 1996. Struggling to knit together its acquisitions, Michaels lost $31 million in fiscal 1997, its second straight loss. Rouleau refined the chain's merchandise (reducing noncore items like party supplies) and expanded its distribution system.

The company opened 50 Michaels stores and relocated 14 in 1998. Michaels bought 16 stores (mainly in Maryland and Virginia) from bankrupt MJDesigns in 1999. In May 2000 Michaels acquired Star Wholesale Florist.

The company plans to add about 70 Michaels Stores and 20 Aaron Brothers stores by the end of 2001.

OFFICERS

Chairman: Charles J. Wyly Jr., age 67, $225,000 pay
(prior to title change)
Vice Chairman: Sam Wyly, age 66, $450,000 pay
(prior to title change)
President, CEO, and COO: R. Michael Rouleau, age 62,
$899,808 pay (prior to title change)
EVP and CFO: Bryan M. DeCordova, age 44
EVP and Chief Information Officer: James F. Tucker,
age 56
EVP, Development: Douglas B. Sullivan, age 50,
$420,290 pay
EVP, Merchandising: Robert M. Spencer, age 60
EVP, Michaels.com: Stephen W. Davis, age 33
EVP, Store Operations: Edward F. Sadler, age 56,
$385,000 pay
SVP, Advertising and Marketing: James C. Neustadt,
age 53
SVP, Human Resources: Sue Elliott, age 50
SVP, Merchandise Planning and Control:
Thomas C. DeCaro, age 46
SVP, New Business Development: Duane E. Hiemenz,
age 47
Auditors: Ernst & Young LLP

LOCATIONS

HQ: 8000 Bent Branch Dr., Irving, TX 75063
Phone: 972-409-1300   **Fax:** 972-409-1556
Web: www.michaels.com

PRODUCTS/OPERATIONS

2001 Sales

	% of total
General crafts	27
Picture framing	18
Fine art materials	17
Silk & dried floral	17
Seasonal	11
Hobby, party, and candles	10
Total	**100**

Selected Merchandise

Fine art materials
  Brushes
  Canvases
  Easels
  Paints
  Sketch pads
General craft materials
  Apparel crafts
  Doll-making items
  Jewelry-making supplies
  Needlecraft items
  Wall décor
Hobby items
  Paint-by-number kits
  Party supplies

Plastic model kits
Picture framing materials
  and services
Seasonal items
  Artificial trees
  Candles
  Christmas crafts
  Lights and ornaments
  Wreaths
Silk and dried flowers and
  artificial plants
Other products
  Home décor items
  Party supplies
  Wedding supplies

COMPETITORS

A.C. Moore
Albecca
Cost Plus
FNC Holdings
Garden Ridge
Hancock Fabrics
Hobby Lobby

Home Interiors
  & Gifts
Jo-Ann Stores
Kirkland's
Kmart
Martha Stewart
  Living

MJDesigns
National Picture
  & Frame
Pier 1 Imports
Rag Shops
Target
Wal-Mart

HISTORICAL FINANCIALS & EMPLOYEES

Nasdaq: MIKE FYE: Saturday nearest Jan. 31	Annual Growth	1/92	1/93	1/94	1/95	1/96	1/97	1/98	1/99	1/00	1/01
Sales ($ mil.)	20.8%	411	493	620	995	1,295	1,378	1,457	1,574	1,883	2,249
Net income ($ mil.)	31.0%	7	20	26	36	(20)	(31)	30	44	62	79
Income as % of sales	—	1.7%	4.1%	4.2%	3.6%	—	—	2.1%	2.8%	3.3%	3.5%
Earnings per share ($)	16.9%	0.56	1.21	1.52	1.76	(0.96)	(1.35)	1.05	1.43	2.01	2.29
Stock price - FY high ($)	—	24.00	34.75	39.00	46.50	37.00	19.88	37.00	39.92	35.88	49.63
Stock price - FY low ($)	—	4.50	16.50	25.25	29.50	11.00	8.06	11.63	15.50	16.00	18.00
Stock price - FY close ($)	8.0%	20.13	33.75	32.25	33.00	12.75	13.13	30.75	18.75	26.75	40.13
P/E - high	—	27	28	25	26	—	—	33	27	17	21
P/E - low	—	5	14	17	17	—	—	10	10	7	7
Dividends per share ($)	—	0.00	0.00	0.00	0.00	0.00	0.00	0.00	0.00	0.00	0.00
Book value per share ($)	11.4%	8.39	9.43	11.10	16.67	15.63	14.05	15.22	16.84	18.85	22.13
Employees	22.1%	5,490	7,114	10,040	17,440	19,330	16,500	17,900	22,200	26,500	33,000

STOCK PRICE HISTORY

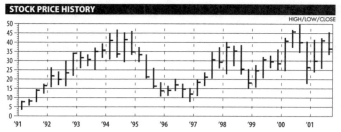

HIGH/LOW/CLOSE

2001 FISCAL YEAR-END

Debt ratio: 15.1%
Return on equity: 12.3%
Cash ($ mil.): 28
Current ratio: 2.53
Long-term debt ($ mil.): 125
No. of shares (mil.): 32
Dividends
  Yield: —
  Payout: —
Market value ($ mil.): 1,278

MITCHELL ENERGY

OVERVIEW

CEO George Mitchell, a rags-to-oil-riches story, brings a lot of energy to Mitchell Energy & Development, an independent oil and gas exploration and production company. Based in The Woodlands, Texas, the firm produces natural gas and oil and gathers, processes, and markets natural gas and natural gas liquids (NGLs). It has agreed to be acquired by Devon Energy in a deal that will form one of the largest natural gas producers in the US.

Mitchell Energy, whose exploration efforts take place mainly in Texas, has proved reserves of 1.5 trillion cu. ft. of natural gas equivalent. It produces 305.5 million cu. ft. of natural gas and 49,800 barrels of NGLs each day. Mitchell Energy also owns or has interests in 9,100 miles of gas gathering pipelines and six gas processing plants.

To survive the late-1990s slump in oil prices, Mitchell Energy trimmed operations and reduced its personnel by about 20%. Its efforts have paid off, and the company has emerged as one of the US's largest producers of NGLs.

George Mitchell owns 56% of the company.

HISTORY

George Mitchell's father, a Greek immigrant railwayman named Savva Paraskivopoulis, renamed himself Mike Mitchell (after a paymaster who complained about the length of the last name). George worked his way through Texas A&M University's petroleum engineering school selling stationery, and after leaving the army in 1946, he bought out the interests of one of the partners in H. Merlyn Christie's Oil Drilling (formerly Roxoil Drilling).

In 1952 Mitchell went against conventional wisdom and purchased a 3,000-acre tract in North Texas based on a tip from a Chicago bookie. After drilling 11 successful wells, he bought leases on 400,000 acres in the area. Mitchell and his brother Johnny continued to buy out shareholders in Oil Drilling and in 1953 joined Christie to form Christie, Mitchell & Mitchell.

The Mitchells bought out Christie's share in 1962 and changed the company's name to Mitchell & Mitchell Gas & Oil. By 1966 it was Texas's largest independent gas producer and the US's #3 independent interstate gas marketer. The firm acquired several assets in the 1960s, including R. E. Smith's oil and gas leases in Canada, Louisiana, and Texas.

The company went public in 1972 as Mitchell Energy & Development. It also expanded its gas operations, acquiring a 25% stake in Ohio's Ken-Ohio pipeline (1973) and moving into natural gas processing (1974). In 1974 Mitchell hired Bruce Withers, a former Tenneco engineer, who helped Mitchell Energy pioneer gas processing plants with cryogenics.

Mitchell Energy ventured into real estate in 1974 with the opening of The Woodlands, a 25,000-acre planned community north of Houston. Although it ate up $60 million in infrastructure costs, The Woodlands, home to several biomedical research and development firms, broke even in 1978. Mitchell Energy relocated its headquarters from downtown Houston to The Woodlands in 1980.

Energy and real estate slumps hit Mitchell Energy hard in the 1980s. Gas prices fell from their 1982 highs, and lot sales at The Woodlands fell by two-thirds. However, the company remained profitable by cutting costs and relying on the strength of natural gas liquid prices. Mitchell Energy teamed with Conoco in 1992 to acquire Oryx Energy's stake in 14 processing plants in Texas and Oklahoma.

In the mid-1990s the company withdrew from the contract drilling business and sold 16 land rigs (1994); it also sold some 22,000 acres of Texas timberland (1995) and its San Luis Resort properties in Galveston, Texas (1996). In 1996 the company was slapped with a $204 million fine by a jury that found it guilty of contaminating the drinking water of homes near its wells in Wise County in North Texas, but an appeals court later overturned the judgment.

Mitchell Energy sold The Woodlands in 1997, and in 1998 it sold the last of its real estate properties (resort holdings in Galveston, Texas). That year, as oil prices plunged, the company slashed its budget and operating costs by laying off staff and closing two gas processing plants.

As natural gas prices rebounded in 1999, Mitchell Energy stepped up drilling. Its stock price rose, and the company emerged as a leader in NGL production. It also bought Conoco's 50% interest in another NGL processing plant. In 2000 the firm agreed to swap assets in Oklahoma for Duke Energy's gas-gathering and processing assets in Texas.

As part of Mitchell Energy's accelerated drilling program, the company announced plans to drill 364 wells in 2001, up from 233 wells in 2000. Also in 2001 Mitchell Energy agreed to be acquired by rival Devon Energy for $3.1 billion in cash and stock and $400 million in assumed debt.

Chairman and CEO: George P. Mitchell, age 81, $2,323,333 pay
Vice Chairman: Bernard F. Clark, age 79
President, COO, and Director; President, Exploration and Production Division: W. D. Stevens, age 66, $1,825,000 pay
SVP and CFO; President, Administration and Financial Division: Philip S. Smith, age 64, $918,000 pay
SVP, Gas Services; President, Gas Services Division: Allen J. Tarbutton Jr., age 64, $822,333 pay
SVP, Human Resources: Clyde Black
SVP, Legal and Governmental Affairs; General Counsel; and Secretary: Thomas P. Battle, age 58, $475,000 pay
Auditors: Arthur Andersen LLP

LOCATIONS

HQ: Mitchell Energy & Development Corp.
2001 Timberloch Place, The Woodlands, TX 77380
Phone: 713-377-5500   **Fax:** 713-377-5680
Web: www.mitchellenergy.com

Mitchell Energy & Development explores for and produces natural gas and oil mainly in Texas, but it also has holdings in Alabama, Colorado, Louisiana, Michigan, Mississippi, New Mexico, Oklahoma, and Utah.

PRODUCTS/OPERATIONS

2000 Sales

	$ mil.	% of total
Gas services	1,141	68
Exploration & production	531	32
Total	**1,672**	**100**

COMPETITORS

BP	Koch
Cabot Oil & Gas	Occidental
Chesapeake Energy	Phillips Petroleum
Chevron	Pioneer Natural Resources
Dynegy	Texaco
El Paso	TransTexas Gas
Enron	UtiliCorp
Exxon Mobil	Western Gas

HISTORICAL FINANCIALS & EMPLOYEES

NYSE: MND FYE: December 31	Annual Growth	1/92	1/93	1/94	1/95	1/96	1/97	1/98	1/99	1/00	*12/00
Sales ($ mil.)	7.5%	874	903	953	895	1,072	1,105	791	701	934	1,672
Net income ($ mil.)	21.6%	44	18	20	46	37	103	(35)	(50)	97	257
Income as % of sales		5.1%	2.0%	2.1%	5.1%	3.5%	9.3%	—	—	10.4%	15.4%
Earnings per share ($)	20.6%	0.95	0.39	0.45	0.84	0.69	1.96	(0.67)	(1.04)	1.95	5.13
Stock price - FY high ($)	—	20.75	19.63	29.63	22.88	19.38	23.63	29.75	28.25	25.25	64.00
Stock price - FY low ($)	—	13.63	13.63	17.00	14.50	15.38	15.50	18.25	9.63	10.50	20.25
Stock price - FY close ($)	17.1%	14.75	16.88	21.25	16.38	18.00	23.50	26.63	11.75	22.50	61.25
P/E - high	—	22	25	46	27	28	12	—	—	13	12
P/E - low	—	14	18	27	17	22	8	—	—	5	4
Dividends per share ($)	5.4%	0.40	0.42	0.48	0.48	0.48	0.48	0.72	0.48	0.48	0.64
Book value per share ($)	(0.8%)	13.59	13.55	14.26	9.09	9.26	10.71	8.42	6.61	8.11	12.63
Employees	(12.5%)	2,900	2,825	2,900	2,600	2,200	1,950	1,123	875	875	875

* Fiscal year change

STOCK PRICE HISTORY

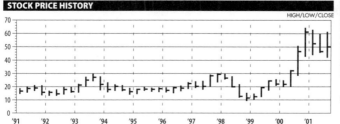

HIGH/LOW/CLOSE

2000 FISCAL YEAR-END

Debt ratio: 32.6%
Return on equity: 50.5%
Cash ($ mil.): 24
Current ratio: 0.88
Long-term debt ($ mil.): 300
No. of shares (mil.): 49
Dividends
　Yield: 1.0%
　Payout: 12.5%
Market value ($ mil.): 3,008

MOTIVA ENTERPRISES LLC

OVERVIEW

Volatile oil prices and stiff competition provided the motivation to create Motiva Enterprises. The Houston-based company was created to combine the East Coast and Gulf Coast refining and marketing operations of Texaco, Shell Oil, and Saudi Aramco. Motiva and Equilon, a sister joint venture formed by Shell and Texaco that operates in the West and Midwest, together form the largest gasoline retailer in the US.

With a long-term agreement with Saudi Aramco for crude oil supply, Motiva has holdings in almost 50 product terminals. It also operates three refineries on the Gulf Coast and one in Delaware, with a total capacity of 825,000 barrels a day. Motiva operates about 13,000 Shell and Texaco gas stations.

ChevronTexaco and Saudi Aramco each own 35% of Motiva, and Shell owns 30%. In 2001 Texaco agreed to sell its stakes in Motiva (to Shell and Saudi Aramco) and Equilon (to Shell) to gain regulatory clearance to be acquired by Chevron. When the deals are completed, Shell and Saudi Aramco will each own 50% of Motiva, and Shell will take full ownership of Equilon.

HISTORY

Although Motiva was not created until 1998, two of its key players, Texaco and Saudi Aramco, had been doing business together in various ventures since 1936. But they had never tried anything on the scale of the Star Enterprise joint venture approved by Texaco CEO James Kinnear and Saudi Oil Minister Hisham Nazer in late 1988. The deal, valued at nearly $2 billion, was the largest joint venture of its kind in the US.

The agreement to create Star Enterprise sprang, in part, from Texaco's tumultuous ride following its purchase of Getty Oil in 1983. Texaco was sued by Pennzoil for pre-empting Pennzoil's bid for Getty, and Pennzoil won a $10.5 billion judgment in 1985. Texaco filed for bankruptcy in 1987, and eventually settled with Pennzoil for $3 billion.

In 1988 Texaco emerged from bankruptcy after announcing a deal with Saudi Aramco at a stockholder meeting. Texaco got a much-needed injection of cash, and Saudi Aramco gained a steady US outlet for its supply of crude. The Saudis had been at odds with their OPEC partners for several years, and in late 1985 then-Saudi Oil Minister Sheikh Yamani and Saudi Aramco began increasing production, leading to an oil price crash in 1986. Nazer replaced Yamani and changed Saudi Aramco's strategy. To secure market share, the Saudis started signing long-term supply contracts.

The deal with Texaco gave Saudi Aramco a 50% interest in Texaco's refining and marketing operations in the East and on the Gulf Coast — about two-thirds of Texaco's US downstream operations — including three refineries and its Texaco-brand stations. In return, the Saudis paid $812 million cash and provided three-fourths of Star's initial inventory, about 30 million barrels of oil. They also agreed to a 20-year, 600,000-barrel-a-day commitment of crude. Each company named three representatives to Star's management.

The new company soon initiated a modernization and expansion program: It acquired 65 stations, built 30 new outlets, and remodeled another 172 during 1989. In 1994 the company began franchising its Texaco-brand Star Mart convenience stores. By mid-1995 it had sold 30 franchises.

Facing a more competitive oil-marketing environment in the US, Shell Oil approached Texaco in 1996 with the possibility of merging some of their operations. In 1998 Shell and Texaco formed Equilon Enterprises, a joint venture that combined their western and midwestern refining and marketing activities.

Later that year Shell and Texaco/Saudi Aramco (Star Enterprises) formed Motiva to merge the companies' refining and marketing businesses on the East Coast and Gulf Coast. Shell and Texaco also formed two more Houston companies as satellite firms for Motiva and Equilon: Equiva Trading Company, a general partnership that provide supplies and trading services; and Equiva Services, which provides support services. L. Wilson Berry, the former president of Texaco Refining and Marketing, took over as CEO of Motiva.

In 1999 Motiva and Equilon together bought 15 product terminals from Premcor. To boost profits, the Motiva board appointed Texaco downstream veteran Roger Ebert as its new CEO in 2000, replacing Berry.

US government regulators in 2001 required that Texaco sell its Motiva and Equilon stakes in order to be acquired by Chevron. Shell and Saudi Aramco agreed to buy Texaco's stake in Motiva, and Shell agreed to buy Texaco's stake in Equilon.

OFFICERS

President and CEO: Roger L. Ebert
CFO: William M. Kaparich
VP, Commercial Marketing and Distribution:
  Ralph Grimmer
VP, Human Resources and Corporate Services, Motiva
  Enterprises and Equilon Enterprises:
  Bruce Culpepper
VP, Refining, Motiva Enterprises and Equilon
  Enterprises: Carmine Falcone
VP, Sales and Marketing: Larry Burch
VP, Sales and Marketing: Hugh Cooley
Chief Diversity Officer, Motiva Enterprises and Equilon
  Enterprises: John Jefferson
General Counsel: Rick Frazier

COMPETITORS

7-Eleven
BP
CITGO
Cumberland Farms
Dairy Mart
Exxon Mobil
Gulf Oil
Marathon Ashland
  Petroleum
Phillips Petroleum
Racetrac Petroleum
Sunoco
Ultramar Diamond
  Shamrock
Valero Energy
Wawa

LOCATIONS

HQ: 1100 Louisiana St., Houston, TX 77002
Phone: 713-277-8000   **Fax:** 713-277-7856
Web: www.equilonmotivaequiva.com

Motiva operates Shell and Texaco gas stations in the
northeastern and southeastern US. It has refineries in
Convent and Norco, Louisiana; Delaware City, Delaware;
and Port Arthur, Texas.

Major Operations
Alabama
Arkansas
Connecticut
Delaware
Florida
Georgia
Louisiana
Maryland
Massachusetts
Mississippi
New Hampshire
New Jersey
New York
North Carolina
Pennsylvania
Rhode Island
Tennessee
Texas
Vermont
Virginia

HISTORICAL FINANCIALS & EMPLOYEES

Joint venture FYE: December 31	Annual Growth	12/91	12/92	12/93	12/94	12/95	12/96	12/97	12/98	12/99	12/00
Sales ($ mil.)	90.3%	—	—	—	—	—	—	—	5,371	12,196	19,446
Net income ($ mil.)	143.1%	—	—	—	—	—	—	—	78	(69)	461
Income as % of sales	—	—	—	—	—	—	—	—	1.5%	—	2.4%
Employees	—	—	—	—	—	—	—	—	—	—	8,000

NET INCOME HISTORY

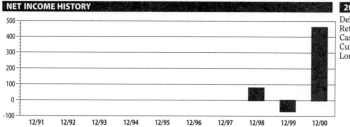

2000 FISCAL YEAR-END

Debt ratio: 30.1%
Return on equity: 14.1%
Cash ($ mil.): 9
Current ratio: 1.20
Long-term debt ($ mil.): 1,429

NATIONAL INSTRUMENTS

OVERVIEW

National Instruments' tools could measure its own success. The Austin, Texas-based company makes hardware and graphical software that convert PCs into industrial automation and test and measurement systems used by scientists and engineers. Its "virtual instruments" are more flexible and less expensive than oscilloscopes and other traditional equipment used to analyze electrical signals and physical attributes such as voltage and speed. A diverse customer base — DeBeers uses National Instruments' systems to sort diamonds, Honeywell-Measurex to produce paper, and Motorola to test telecommunications equipment — buffers the company from fluctuations in any one market. Customers outside North America account for nearly half of sales.

National Instruments has relied on product development — the company holds more than 120 patents and has nearly 120 pending — to give it 24 years of double-digit growth. The company, which has never laid off an employee, continues to incorporate Internet, wireless, and other emerging technologies into its systems.

Co-founder and CEO James Truchard owns 26% of the company. Co-founder and VP Jeffrey Kodosky and his wife Gail own 9%; director Wayne Ashby, 5%.

HISTORY

In the 1970s James Truchard, working at the University of Texas' Applied Research Laboratory, was frustrated by the lack of connectivity between the lab's computers and testing equipment. Truchard, who as a kid built homemade radios, founded National Instruments in 1976 with fellow lab employees Jeffrey Kodosky and William Nowlin. The trio raised $13,000 and used part of Truchard's teacher retirement fund savings to set up camp in a room behind Truchard's garage.

Using Hewlett-Packard's technology for collecting test and measurement data from its own machines, the trio created the general-purpose interface bus (GPIB), a device that links computers to scientific instruments. The device eliminated the practice of using paper, pencils, and rulers to track instruments. The company sold its first GPIB unit in 1977 to Kelly Air Force Base in San Antonio. The colleagues' vigor kept the company small but busy. Truchard designed hardware and wrote press releases. Kodosky developed programs and handled customer support.

National Instruments thrived as PCs became popular. LabVIEW, introduced in 1986, used graphics to simulate the dials of an engineering instrument's control panel. Users worked the controls simply by moving the mouse. The company expanded internationally in 1987, opening an office in Tokyo. It suffered a loss in 1989 after expanding into Europe.

In 1990 NASA used one of the company's programs to trace fuel system leaks affecting space shuttle launches. With too many shareholders to continue privately, National Instruments went public in 1995, and Truchard intensified product development.

The company began acquiring small businesses to expand its technology base, buying industrial automation specialist Georgetown Systems (1996) and motion control equipment maker nuLogic (1997).

Also in 1997 National Instruments signed an agreement with Jet Propulsion Laboratory (JPL) to jointly develop an embedded version of the company's LabVIEW graphical instrumentation software for use onboard space shuttle and space station missions.

In 1998 National Instruments bought two German makers of data acquisition tools, DATALOG and DASYtec. The next year the company joined forces with computer maker Dell to market a scientific measuring and testing workstation. Also in 1999 the company acquired German software company GfS Systemtechnik, a leading provider of software products for the German automotive industry.

National Instruments launched an online store in 1999, then followed that in 2000 with the NI Developer Zone (zone.ni.com), a resource for information on automation and measurement systems. Also in 2000 the company signed a major licensing deal with Lockheed Martin Missiles & Space, giving the aerospace giant the rights to use National Instruments's LabVIEW in Lockheed's spacecraft design and development.

In 2001 National Instruments introduced Fieldpoint 2000, a new, more rugged hardware platform for its LabVIEW software. The new hardware line is designed for use in the extreme temperatures and harsh environments on factory floors.

OFFICERS

Chairman and President: James J. Truchard, age 57
CFO, Chief Information Officer, and Treasurer:
  Alexander M. Davern, age 34, $204,771 pay
VP, Corporate Development: Mihir Ravel, age 41
VP, Engineering: Timothy R. Dehne, age 35,
  $214,103 pay
VP, Human Resources: Mark A. Finger, age 43
VP, Manufacturing: Ruben Reynoso-Mangin, age 53,
  $183,993 pay
VP, Marketing: John M. Graff, age 36
VP, Product Strategy: Ray Almgren
VP, Sales: Peter Zogas Jr., age 40, $247,544 pay
Secretary and General Counsel: David G. Hugley, age 37
Controller: John Roiko
Auditors: PricewaterhouseCoopers LLP

LOCATIONS

HQ: National Instruments Corporation
  11500 N. Mopac Expwy., Austin, TX 78759
Phone: 512-338-9119   **Fax:** 512-794-5794
Web: www.ni.com

National Instruments has offices in more than 35
countries.

2000 Sales

	$ mil.	% of total
North America	216	53
Europe	134	33
Asia/Pacific	60	14
Total	**410**	**100**

PRODUCTS/OPERATIONS

Products
Data acquisition and signal conditioning hardware
General-purpose interface bus cards and other
  PC-instrument connectivity tools
Industrial networks (PC-based interface boards and
  modular instrumentation)
Machine vision and motion control
Software
  DASYlab (instrumentation programming)
  DIAdem (instrumentation programming)
  LabVIEW (graphical programming environment)
  Lookout (human machine interface/supervisory
    control and data acquisition)
  Measurement Studio (text-based programming
    environment)
  TestStand (test measurement)
  Virtual Bench

COMPETITORS

ABB	Invensys
Agilent Technologies	Keithley Instruments
Cognex	LeCroy
Danaher	Rheometrics
Data Translation	Siemens
Emerson	Tektronix
Fisher Scientific	Thermo Electron
IFR Systems	Varian

HISTORICAL FINANCIALS & EMPLOYEES

Nasdaq: NATI FYE: December 31	Annual Growth	12/91	12/92	12/93	12/94	12/95	12/96	12/97	12/98	12/99	12/00
Sales ($ mil.)	22.1%	—	83	106	127	165	201	241	274	330	410
Net income ($ mil.)	48.8%	—	2	10	13	17	26	34	37	45	55
Income as % of sales	—	—	2.8%	9.6%	10.2%	10.6%	12.7%	13.9%	13.6%	13.7%	13.5%
Earnings per share ($)	22.7%	—	—	—	—	0.37	0.51	0.67	0.73	0.87	1.03
Stock price - FY high ($)	—	—	—	—	—	10.12	14.24	22.36	24.35	39.13	59.50
Stock price - FY low ($)	—	—	—	—	—	7.45	7.34	11.57	11.67	17.18	31.88
Stock price - FY close ($)	40.1%	—	—	—	—	9.01	14.24	19.34	22.76	38.25	48.56
P/E - high	—	—	—	—	—	27	27	32	32	43	54
P/E - low	—	—	—	—	—	20	14	17	15	19	29
Dividends per share ($)	—	—	—	—	—	0.00	0.00	0.00	0.00	0.00	0.00
Book value per share ($)	25.4%	—	—	—	—	2.05	2.61	3.30	4.13	5.08	6.34
Employees	18.8%	—	—	—	892	1,062	1,142	1,465	1,658	1,955	2,511

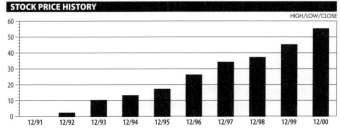

STOCK PRICE HISTORY
HIGH/LOW/CLOSE

2000 FISCAL YEAR-END
Debt ratio: 0.0%
Return on equity: 19.2%
Cash ($ mil.): 75
Current ratio: 4.42
Long-term debt ($ mil.): 0
No. of shares (mil.): 51
Dividends
  Yield: —
  Payout: —
Market value ($ mil.): 2,459

THE NEIMAN MARCUS GROUP, INC.

OVERVIEW

If you're looking for a cheap Mother's Day gift, steer clear of Neiman Marcus. Based in Dallas, Texas, The Neiman Marcus Group operates upscale department stores in 20 states. The company's chain of 31 full-line Neiman Marcus stores offers high-fashion, high-quality merchandise from such labels as Moschino and Versace. The merchandise selection at the company's two Bergdorf Goodman stores in Manhattan includes men's clothing and precious jewelry.

Neiman Marcus also operates about 10 clearance centers that sell marked-down merchandise. NM Direct, the firm's mail-order business, distributes catalogs under the Neiman Marcus, Horchow, and Chef's Catalog names. Like rival Saks, Inc., the company is building smaller stores (called Galleries of Neiman Marcus) to reach new markets.

Though fondly known as "Needless Markup," Neiman Marcus' success can be attributed in part to its customer service. Customers (who tend to be older, affluent women prepared to purchase the best at any price) are often known by name and their needs are fastidiously attended to.

Chairman Richard Smith and his family own 23% of Neiman Marcus.

HISTORY

When Herbert Marcus, his sister Carrie Marcus Neiman, and her husband, A. L. Neiman, sold their sales promotion business in Atlanta, they chose to take $25,000 in cash instead of the Missouri or Kansas franchise rights for a new drink called Coca-Cola (which later prompted family members to joke that their company was founded on poor business judgment since no one recognized the drink's potential). In 1907 the three moved back to Dallas, a city of 84,000 people and used their cash and the contributions of other relatives to open Neiman Marcus, a store for "fashionable women."

The three owners were determined to have a specialty store unlike any in the entire South — one that sold ladies' millinery and outergarments that were stylish, high quality, and ready-to-wear (a new concept). Neiman Marcus was an immediate success that showed a profit its very first year.

In 1928 Herbert bought out the Neimans. Also that year the store added men's fashions. Herbert's son Stanley, who started the extravagant Neiman Marcus Christmas catalog and oversaw the company's expansion into new markets, ran the stores from 1952 to 1979.

Retailer Carter Hawley Hale bought the chain in 1969 but did not maintain the stores in the customary manner. As a result, sales and the chain's reputation as upscale and unique suffered throughout the 1970s and into the 1980s. In 1979 Stanley's son Richard continued the family's reign, becoming the company's chairman and CEO.

As part of its 1987 restructuring, Carter Hawley Hale spun off the Neiman Marcus stores. At that time General Cinema traded its interest in Carter Hawley Hale for a controlling 44% of The Neiman Marcus Group. In addition to the Neiman Marcus stores, The Neiman Marcus Group included New York City's exclusive Bergdorf Goodman and the mainstream chain Contempo Casuals. Tailor Herman Bergdorf and his partner, Edwin Goodman, founded Bergdorf Goodman in New York in 1901. Carter Hawley Hale bought the high-end retailer in 1972.

The Neiman Marcus Group bought Horchow Mail Order of Dallas, a retailer of personal and home upscale decorative items, in 1988. That year Richard resigned as CEO and ended 81 years of family management of the 22-store chain.

An offer in 1990 by General Cinema (renamed Harcourt General in 1993) to buy the rest of The Neiman Marcus Group was rejected. The company sold Contempo Casuals, its money-losing 247-store retail chain for young women, to Wet Seal in 1995. It bought Chef's Catalog, which sells high-dollar cookware, in 1998. The company also began testing the Galleries of Neiman Marcus, a new, smaller store format selling fine jewelry and gifts.

Also in 1998 the company acquired 51% of Gurwitch Bristow Products, makers of Laura Mercier cosmetics. That year Robert Smith was promoted to CEO of The Neiman Marcus Group; his father, Richard, remained chairman. (The two also head up Harcourt General.) In 1999 Neiman Marcus bought 56% of luxury handbag maker Kate Spade. In May of that year Richard's son-in-law, Brian Knez, was named co-CEO. In October 1999 Harcourt General spun off most of its Neiman Marcus stake to its own shareholders, who are led by the Smith family. The company named co-CEOs Robert and Knez co-vice chairman in February 2001 and appointed president and COO Burton Tansky CEO.

OFFICERS

Chairman: Richard A. Smith, age 75
Co-Vice Chairman: Brian J. Knez, age 43
Co-CEO and Co-Vice Chairman: Robert A. Smith, age 41
Co-CEO: Burton M. Tansky, age 63, $2,116,000 pay
SVP and CFO: James E. Skinner, age 47
SVP, General Counsel, and Secretary: Nelson A. Bangs, age 48
Chairman and CEO, Bergdorf Goodman: Ronald L. Frasch, age 52
President, Bergdorf Goodman: Peter J. Rizzo
President and CEO of NM Direct: Karen W. Katz, age 44, $589,000 pay
President and COO of Neiman Marcus Stores: Gerald A. Sampson, age 59, $949,000 pay
VP and Controller: Catherine N. Janowski, age 39
VP and Treasurer: Paul F. Gibbons, age 49
VP, Corporate Relations: Peter Farwell, age 57
VP, Human Resources; SVP, Human Resources, Neiman Marcus Stores: Marita O'Dea, age 52
VP, Strategy and Business Development: Paul J. Robershotte, age 46
Auditors: Deloitte & Touche LLP

LOCATIONS

HQ: 1618 Main St., Dallas, TX 75201
Phone: 214-741-6911   **Fax:** 214-573-6142
Web: www.neimanmarcus.com

2001 Neiman Marcus Stores

	No.
Texas	6
California	5
Florida	4
Illinois	3
New Jersey	2
Other states	13
Total	**33**

PRODUCTS/OPERATIONS

2001 Sales

	% of total
Stores	85
NM Direct	13
Other	2
Total	**100**

Selected Operations
Catalogs (Horchow, Neiman Marcus, Chef's Catalog)
Cosmetics (51% stake in Gurwitch Bristow Products, makes Laura Mercier)
Handbags (56% stake in Kate Spade)
Retail stores (Bergdorf Goodman, Last Call Clearance Centers, Galleries of Neiman Marcus, Neiman Marcus)

COMPETITORS

AnnTaylor	Lands' End
Barneys	The Limited
Brooks Brothers	May
Cache	Nordstrom
DFS Group	Saks Inc.
Dillard's	Spiegel
Federated	Tiffany
J. Crew	Williams-Sonoma

HISTORICAL FINANCIALS & EMPLOYEES

NYSE: NMG FYE: Saturday nearest July 31	Annual Growth	7/92	7/93	7/94	7/95	7/96	7/97	7/98	7/99	7/00	7/01
Sales ($ mil.)	5.8%	1,808	2,017	2,093	1,888	2,075	2,210	2,373	2,553	2,855	3,015
Net income ($ mil.)	19.2%	22	47	16	56	77	91	106	94	134	107
Income as % of sales	—	1.2%	2.4%	0.8%	2.9%	3.7%	4.1%	4.5%	3.7%	4.7%	3.6%
Earnings per share ($)	—	(0.21)	0.48	(0.35)	0.70	1.26	1.32	2.13	1.90	2.75	2.30
Stock price - FY high ($)	—	16.63	19.88	19.25	15.88	30.63	36.25	43.44	34.00	33.44	41.01
Stock price - FY low ($)	—	10.38	11.13	13.88	13.00	14.63	22.38	27.50	15.00	19.38	27.06
Stock price - FY close ($)	10.4%	13.50	14.50	15.25	15.38	26.88	28.50	33.00	25.00	33.00	33.02
P/E - high	—	—	25	—	23	24	27	20	18	12	18
P/E - low	—	—	14	—	19	12	17	13	8	7	12
Dividends per share ($)	—	0.20	0.20	0.20	0.10	0.00	0.00	0.00	0.00	0.00	0.00
Book value per share ($)	7.0%	10.76	11.23	10.73	11.38	12.72	11.12	13.20	15.01	17.39	19.76
Employees	(1.0%)	16,851	16,700	15,400	10,000	11,000	11,300	11,800	14,800	15,150	15,400

STOCK PRICE HISTORY

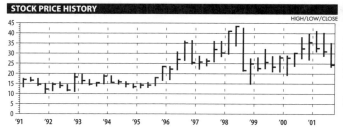

HIGH/LOW/CLOSE

2001 FISCAL YEAR-END

Debt ratio: 20.9%
Return on equity: 12.2%
Cash ($ mil.): 97
Current ratio: 2.14
Long-term debt ($ mil.): 250
No. of shares (mil.): 48
Dividends
  Yield: —
  Payout: —
Market value ($ mil.): 1,575

PALM HARBOR HOMES, INC.

OVERVIEW

You won't see a lot of Palm Harbor homes featuring a 1979 Trans Am on blocks in the driveway. True to its flashy home town, Palm Harbor Homes of Dallas, Texas, offers upscale manufactured homes as an alternative to the stereotypical "double-wide trailer."

A leading maker of such multi-section homes, the company offers more than 150 standard floor plans under brands that include Keystone, Masterpiece, Palm Harbor, River Bend, and Windsor Homes. Ranging from two to five bedrooms with luxury add-ons, the average retail price for a home is about $58,000.

Palm Harbor builds more than 90% of its homes according to customer specifications; manufacturing takes place in about 15 US factories (primarily in the South and Southwest), and the homes are sold through a network of more than 135 company-owned superstores

and 300 independent retailers across the US. Subsidiaries CountryPlace Mortgage and Standard Casualty Company handle Palm Harbor's financing and insurance businesses.

Palm Harbor ranks among the top seven in the more than $30 billion manufactured home market, which is growing to include conventional builders such as Pulte and Centex. The company keeps costs low by buying materials in bulk and through factory construction (as opposed to on-site building). Palm Harbor is increasing its high-end features (whirlpool baths, stone fireplaces, skylights) to broaden its customer base.

Through the Capital Southwest Corporation and Capital Southwest Venture Corporation, company directors William Thomas and John Wilson control about 35% of Palm Harbor.

HISTORY

On the last day of 1977, chairman Lee Posey founded Palm Harbor Homes to take advantage of a new niche in the old-fashioned trailer market — creating a larger trailer home by joining two halves together (the so-called double-wide). Up until that time, even mobile-home builders referred to their customers as "the newly wed or nearly dead." Double-wides offered larger homes and began to upscale the entire industry.

Over the years Posey further refined Palm Harbor's niche by offering customized homes: adding bay windows, enlarging bedrooms, or moving walls to create an image the company calls the "Mercedes of mobile homes."

The company went public in 1995. Soon after, it began a series of acquisitions to build market share, which included the 1996 purchases of retailers Energy Efficient Housing (North Carolina) and Newco Homes (Texas), followed by the 1997 purchase of Sun City Homes (Las Vegas).

Helped by more available financing and growing consumer acceptance, the mobile home industry in general and Palm Harbor in particular experienced strong growth.

In 1997 Posey relinquished his CEO title to Larry Keener, but retained his position as chairman. After six consecutive years of solid sales and profit increases, the company declared a 5-for-4 stock split that year. The firm also continued to increase its number of company-owned stores, adding 40 in 1997.

Palm Harbor expanded into Georgia in 1998 by buying Atlanta-based retailer Cannon

Group. Despite restrictive zoning laws in some US communities, the demand for manufactured homes has grown from one out of every four single-family homes sold a decade ago to one in three in 1998.

Palm Harbor beefed-up its number of company-owned retail superstores by 28% in 1999. Also in 1999 a Dallas woman won a Palm Harbor home valued at $60,000 in the company's "Grand Slam Inning" contest; when her name was drawn, then-Texas Ranger Rafael Palmeiro hit a grand slam home run in a game against Anaheim.

In 2000 Palm Harbor launched a Spanish version of its company Web site to tap into the Latino market. The company's sales growth was flat and net income dropped in fiscal 2000, hurt by a weakening economy.

Palm Harbor's financial troubles continued in 2001 as the overall housing market experienced a downturn. Also in 2001 the company opened 12 new superstores, continuing to shift its emphasis from independent to company-owned stores.

Chairman: Lee Posey, age 65, $400,000 pay
President and CEO: Larry H. Keener, age 50,
$200,000 pay
EVP: Scott W. Chaney, age 42, $175,000 pay
CFO, VP Finance, and Secretary: Kelly Tacke, age 42,
$100,000 pay
Director of Human Resources: Jennifer Burkhart
Auditors: Ernst & Young LLP

LOCATIONS

HQ: 15303 Dallas Pkwy., Ste. 800, Addison, TX 75001
Phone: 972-991-2422   **Fax:** 972-991-5949
Web: www.palmharbor.com

Palm Harbor Homes has 15 active manufacturing plants
in Alabama, Arizona, Florida, Georgia, North Carolina,
Ohio, Oregon, and Texas. It has more than 135 retail
superstores in some 30 states.

2001 Sales

	% of total
Central	38
Southeast	33
West	24
Midwest	5
Total	**100**

PRODUCTS/OPERATIONS

2001 Sales

	$ mil.	% of total
Retail	556	58
Manufacturing	379	40
Financial services	24	2
Adjustments	(308)	—
Total	**651**	**100**

Selected Subsidiaries
Better Homes Systems, Inc.
CountryPlace Mortgage, Ltd.
First Home Mortgage Corporation
Magic Living, Inc.
Palm Harbor Finance Corporation
Palm Harbor G.P., Inc.
Palm Harbor Holding, Inc.
Palm Harbor Homes I, LP
Palm Harbor Insurance Agency, Inc.
Palm Harbor Investments, Inc.
Standard Casualty Corp.
Standard Insurance Agency, Inc.

COMPETITORS

American Homestar	Fleetwood Enterprises
Cavalier Homes	Nobility Homes
Centex	Oakwood Homes
Champion Enterprises	Pulte Homes
Clayton Homes	Skyline
D.R. Horton	Southern Energy Homes
Fairmont Homes	

HISTORICAL FINANCIALS & EMPLOYEES

Nasdaq: PHHM FYE: Last Friday in March	Annual Growth	3/92	3/93	3/94	3/95	3/96	3/97	3/98	3/99	3/00	3/01
Sales ($ mil.)	20.7%	119	163	232	331	417	563	637	761	778	651
Net income ($ mil.)	32.3%	2	4	6	11	15	25	32	40	39	20
Income as % of sales	—	1.3%	2.4%	2.6%	3.4%	3.6%	4.4%	5.0%	5.3%	5.0%	3.1%
Earnings per share ($)	3.0%	—	—	—	—	0.75	1.07	1.35	1.69	1.66	0.87
Stock price - FY high ($)	—	—	—	—	—	13.18	20.16	30.70	38.10	25.38	20.88
Stock price - FY low ($)	—	—	—	—	—	5.63	12.29	13.76	19.00	12.00	11.50
Stock price - FY close ($)	2.9%	—	—	—	—	13.18	13.72	29.50	21.75	15.38	15.19
P/E - high	—	—	—	—	—	18	19	23	23	15	24
P/E - low	—	—	—	—	—	8	11	10	11	7	13
Dividends per share ($)	—	—	—	—	—	0.00	0.00	0.00	0.00	0.00	0.00
Book value per share ($)	25.9%	—	—	—	—	3.26	5.08	6.60	8.21	9.12	10.32
Employees	11.9%	—	1,700	2,887	3,200	3,400	4,010	4,700	5,400	4,700	4,180

STOCK PRICE HISTORY

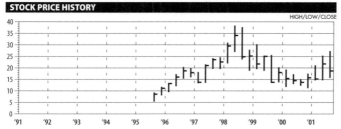

HIGH/LOW/CLOSE

2001 FISCAL YEAR-END
Debt ratio: 1.1%
Return on equity: 8.8%
Cash ($ mil.): 61
Current ratio: 1.35
Long-term debt ($ mil.): 3
No. of shares (mil.): 23
Dividends
  Yield: —
  Payout: —
Market value ($ mil.): 347

PENNZOIL-QUAKER STATE

OVERVIEW

If you think that changing oil is all that Pennzoil-Quaker State does, think again. The Houston-based company, the US's top seller of motor oil (Pennzoil and Quaker State) and provider of oil changes (through its Jiffy Lube chain), also sells about 1,300 automotive consumer products.

Jiffy Lube International has more than 2,140 Jiffy Lubes in North America, including more than 600 former Q Lube oil-change centers that the company has rebranded. About three-quarters of the Jiffy Lubes are franchised.

The company was formed by the 1998 merger of motor-oil moguls Pennzoil and Quaker State. The Procter & Gamble of the auto world, Pennzoil-Quaker State has a stable of well-known products: Gumout, Snap, and Outlaw fuel additives; Classic Car Wax; Fix-A-Flat tire inflators; Slick 50 engine and fuel treatments; Blue Coral car wash; Rain-X window rain repellent; Medo air fresheners; and Axius sunshade products and car accessories. It is exiting the refining and specialty industrial products businesses to focus on its core operations.

HISTORY

T. G. Phinny of Oil City, Pennsylvania, named his motor oil Quaker State in 1912. Two years later Franklin Automobile began putting Quaker State oil cans under its cars' front seats, and by 1915 it was a national brand. About a decade down the road, Eastern Refining bought the name and renamed itself Quaker State Oil Refining. Stockbroker Charles Pape merged 19 small oil companies in 1931, including Quaker State Oil Refining, to form Quaker State Corporation. In 1936 the company went public just as Standard Oil began selling Quaker State products in gas stations.

WWII energy demand pushed Quaker State to buy drilling assets and produce some of its own oil. It began selling oil products in mass retail outlets and doubled its North American motor-oil market share to 20% by the mid-1980s. The company took a drive into insurance in 1984 and then into the fast oil-change market by taking shares in the Minit-Lube chain (later Q Lube) in 1985.

Meanwhile, Pennzoil's predecessor was founded during the post-WWII West Texas oil boom. Brothers J. Hugh and Bill Liedtke and a young George H. W. Bush formed Zapata Petroleum and soon hit it big in the Jameson Field. Zapata added a Gulf of Mexico drilling unit, which Bush bought in 1958. Bush then moved to Houston; he later took a house on Pennsylvania Avenue as the 41st President of the United States. The Liedtkes also set their sights on Pennsylvania — Oil City. With J. Paul Getty's help, they took control of South Penn in 1963, merged it with Zapata, renamed the company Pennzoil in honor of the lubricant, and moved it to Houston.

In 1965 Hugh Liedtke engineered the takeover of United Gas Pipeline, five times the size of Pennzoil. Breaking ground for a generation of corporate raiders, Hugh invited United shareholders to sell their shares for more than

the market price, and the Liedtkes gained 42% of United stock. They spun off a scaled-down United in 1974.

Hugh wanted to buy Getty Oil, and in 1983 he thought he had a deal. When Texaco got Getty instead, Pennzoil sued and in 1985 was awarded $10.5 billion in damages. Bankrupt, Texaco settled with Pennzoil for $3 billion. Hugh stepped down as CEO in 1988. In 1989 Pennzoil bought 8.8% of Chevron. A Chevron suit to keep Pennzoil at bay was dismissed in 1990, the year James Pate became Pennzoil's CEO, and Pennzoil upped its stake to 9.4%. Two years later Pennzoil swapped $1.2 billion of Chevron stock for 260 petroleum properties.

Back in Oil City, Quaker State was hit hard by the 1980s oil slump, and in 1990 it spun off Quaker State Oil Refining. By 1993, when former Campbell Soup head Herbert Baum took over as CEO, Quaker State motor oil was no longer #1 (Pennzoil was). After moving to Dallas in 1995, Quaker State began buying brand-name auto products, and dumped insurance and other unpromising businesses.

Pennzoil's 1995 bid for Union Pacific Resources (UPR) was rebuffed. UPR made a hostile offer to buy Pennzoil in 1997, sparking bitter accusations and litigation; UPR withdrew. The next year Pennzoil merged motor oil and Jiffy Lube operations with Quaker State, forming Pennzoil-Quaker State. Pate took charge of the new company; Baum left to head Hasbro.

Pennzoil-Quaker State completed the rebranding of its Q Lubes centers as Jiffy Lubes in 1999. In 2000 Jim Postl became CEO (Pate remained chairman). Pennzoil also left its Pennsylvania roots behind, selling its refinery there to Calumet Lubricants. In 2001 Calumet agreed to buy the company's refinery in Shreveport, Louisiana. In another cost-cutting move, Pennzoil agreed to sell a San Antonio-based blending and packaging plant.

OFFICERS

Chairman: James L. Pate, age 65, $1,214,800 pay
President, CEO, and Director: James J. Postl, age 55, $894,400 pay
Group VP and CFO: Thomas P. Kellagher, age 44
SVP and Chief Technology Officer: Ahmed Alim, age 53
SVP, Human Resources: Mark S. Esselman, age 44
SVP, Marketing: Anne E. Tawney
SVP, Supply Chain Development: Rob Falivene, age 41
VP and Corporate Secretary: Linda F. Condit, age 53
VP and Treasurer: Laurie K. Stewart, age 41
VP and Controller: Michael J. Maratea, age 56
VP, Administration: Michael P. Schieffer, age 49
VP: Paul B. Siegel, age 55
President, Consumer Products: Rudolph R Wrabel, age 44
President, International Operations: Carlos T. Alcantara, age 50
President, Jiffy Lube: Marc C. Graham, age 48, $389,200 pay
President, Lubricants: Douglas S. Boyle, age 43
General Counsel: James W. Shaddix, age 54, $438,800 pay
Auditors: Arthur Andersen LLP

LOCATIONS

HQ: Pennzoil-Quaker State Company
Pennzoil Place, 700 Milam, Houston, TX 77002
Phone: 713-546-4000   **Fax:** 713-546-8043
Web: www.pennzoil-quakerstate.com

Pennzoil-Quaker State sells its products in more than 90 countries.

PRODUCTS/OPERATIONS

2000 Sales

	$ mil.	% of total
Lubricants & consumer products	1,999	80
Fast lube operations (Jiffy Lube)	332	13
Supply chain investments	167	7
Adjustments	(227)	—
Total	**2,271**	**100**

Selected Brands

Car Care Products	Snap
Autoshade	Westley's
Black Magic	
Blue Coral	**Fast Lube and**
Classic Car Wax	**Oil-Change Centers**
Fix-a-Flat	Jiffy Lube
Gumout	**Motor Oil**
Medo	Pennzoil
Rain-X	Quaker State
Slick 50	Wolf's Head

COMPETITORS

Amerada Hess	Petro-Canada
Ashland	Phillips Petroleum
BP	Sears
Chevron	Shell
Conoco	Sunoco
Exxon Mobil	Texaco
Flying J	Ultramar Diamond
Lubrizol	Shamrock
Lyondell Chemical	Wal-Mart
Pep Boys	

HISTORICAL FINANCIALS & EMPLOYEES

NYSE: PZL FYE: December 31	Annual Growth	12/91	12/92	12/93	12/94	12/95	12/96	12/97	12/98	12/99	12/00
Sales ($ mil.)	4.1%	—	—	1,711	1,748	1,808	1,968	2,013	1,802	2,951	2,271
Net income ($ mil.)	—	—	—	3	(16)	(53)	(9)	(1)	(46)	(321)	(86)
Income as % of sales	—	—	—	0.2%	—	—	—	—	—	—	—
Earnings per share ($)	—	—	—	—	—	—	—	—	(0.96)	(4.12)	(1.10)
Stock price - FY high ($)	—	—	—	—	—	—	—	—	18.00	16.50	13.25
Stock price - FY low ($)	—	—	—	—	—	—	—	—	13.38	8.50	8.38
Stock price - FY close ($)	(6.6%)	—	—	—	—	—	—	—	14.75	10.19	12.88
P/E - high	—	—	—	—	—	—	—	—	—	—	—
P/E - low	—	—	—	—	—	—	—	—	—	—	—
Dividends per share ($)	—	—	—	—	—	—	—	—	0.00	0.75	0.75
Book value per share ($)	(22.5%)	—	—	—	—	—	—	—	17.40	12.13	10.45
Employees	(2.1%)	—	—	—	—	—	—	8,970	13,200	8,198	8,428

STOCK PRICE HISTORY

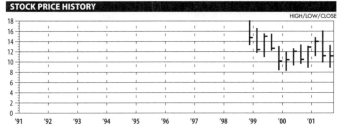

HIGH/LOW/CLOSE

2000 FISCAL YEAR-END

Debt ratio: 60.4%
Return on equity: —
Cash ($ mil.): 38
Current ratio: 1.95
Long-term debt ($ mil.): 1,256
No. of shares (mil.): 79
Dividends
 Yield: 5.8%
 Payout: —
Market value ($ mil.): 1,015

PEROT SYSTEMS CORPORATION

OVERVIEW

Its maverick founder, billionaire Ross Perot, twice set his sights on the Oval Office, but Perot Systems is more interested in your desk. The Dallas-based information technology firm helps businesses create and manage their technology networks, offering services such as consulting, systems integration, data center management, and digital marketplace design. Perot Systems focuses its support on specific markets, including energy, financial services, health care, and travel. Clients include Swiss bank UBS (24% of sales), medical supplies distributor Owens & Minor, and Bank of Ireland.

The departure of chairman and old friend Morton Meyerson — in the wake of cost jumps and earnings drops — prompted the gung-ho Perot to return as CEO in 1998. He quickly revoked health benefits for same-sex partners (a policy instituted in his absence) and reinstated drug tests. Perot's decision to transfer back-office operations onto the Web cut costs and significantly improved net income. Perot passed the CEO torch to son Ross Perot Jr. in 2000.

Hoping to streamline its widespread operations, the company is consolidating around its core expertise in the health care, financial services, and manufacturing industries, which represent about two-thirds of sales.

Ross Perot Sr. owns 33% of the company.

HISTORY

Ross Perot sold Electronic Data Systems (EDS), the data and computer services firm he founded in 1962, to General Motors for $2.5 billion in 1984. It wasn't long before he became irritated with GM; the feeling was mutual. By 1986, neither party could stand the other, and the company paid Perot $700 million for his GM stock on the condition that he go away and not hire any EDS workers for a year and a half.

In June 1988 Perot founded Perot Systems and hired eight EDS veterans. The new firm quickly scored a 10-year contract to cut costs at the US Postal Service. Perot's separation agreement with GM, however, prohibited him from competing with EDS for profit until December 1989, so Perot Systems worked for free until then. Pressure from GM eventually killed the Postal Service contract, but the publicity generated for Perot Systems led to a long list of customers who saw the nonprofit clause as a chance to undertake massive service and support efforts without paying high prices.

The company, however, soon began to founder — in part, some said, because it had promised more than it could deliver. Perot also alienated Hispanics with anti-NAFTA political rhetoric just as his company was working to strike deals with Volkswagen de Mexico and Multibanco Mercantil Probursa. In 1992 Perot stepped down to concentrate on his bid for the US presidency. Former Perot aide and EDS executive Morton Meyerson became CEO and began leading the company away from computer outsourcing and toward higher-margin consulting services.

Perot Systems bought a division of financial software company Platinum Software (now Epicor Software) in 1994. In 1995 James Cannavino, who shared a past at IBM with Perot, became president. (Perot had been a top Big Blue salesman; Cannavino was a strategist who left after he was denied the IBM chairmanship.) A seven-year deal with Tenet Healthcare marked one of the first times that computer operations for that industry were outsourced.

An aggressive emphasis on risk sharing alliances, in which a company is compensated based on its customers' results instead of through consultants' fees, spurred Perot Systems' growth. Perot Systems bought four firms in 1996, including Technical Resource Connection (object-oriented programming). Also that year Perot Systems won a services contract with Swiss Bank (now UBS AG) by offering stock options in exchange for running the bank's computers and networks.

In 1997 the company bought Nets Inc., Lotus founder Jim Manzi's failed e-commerce company (sold soon after to IHS Group). Rising costs and falling earnings that year preceded the resignation of Cannavino. In 1998 Meyerson resigned as chairman, and Perot retook the helm, waiving his own pay, pushing recruitment from the military, and making other changes to control costs.

In 1999 Perot Systems went public, raising $109 million. Also that year it signed a pact with French technology services specialist Atos (now Atos Origin) to jointly provide services to multinational clients. In 2000 the company formed a joint venture (BillingZone) with PNC Bank to provide electronic bill presentment and payment for e-commerce companies. Perot Systems also acquired health care software maker Health Systems Design.

Ross Perot Jr., company director and son of founder Perot, was named CEO in 2000. Ross Perot Sr. remains chairman.

OFFICERS

Chairman: Ross Perot Sr., age 70, $166,667 pay
President, CEO, and Director: Ross Perot Jr., age 42
CFO: Russell Freeman, age 37
Chief Technology Officer: Richard Schroth
VP, Chief Strategy Officer, and Director:
James A. Champy, age 59, $520,000 pay
VP, Secretary, and General Counsel: Peter Altabef,
age 41
VP, European Sales and Operations: Donald E. Drobny,
age 58, $393,208 pay
VP, Global Financial Services Group: John E. King,
age 54
VP, Healthcare Services Group: Randall Booth, age 38
VP, North American Sales: John Vonesh, age 44
VP, North American Sales and Operations:
Joseph E. Boyd, age 41, $325,050 pay
VP; Manager, Perot Systems' Emerging Industries:
Ken Scott, age 58, $355,883 pay
Director, Human Resources: Ross Hansen
Auditors: PricewaterhouseCoopers LLP

LOCATIONS

HQ: 12404 Park Central Dr., Dallas, TX 75251
Phone: 972-340-5000   **Fax:** 972-340-6100
Web: www.perotsystems.com

Perot Systems has operations in France, Germany, Hong
Kong, India, Japan, Luxembourg, the Netherlands,
Singapore, Switzerland, the UK, and the US.

2000 Sales

	$ mil.	% of total
US	803	73
UK	153	14
Other regions	150	13
Total	**1,106**	**100**

PRODUCTS/OPERATIONS

Selected Services
Analysis and consulting
Application development
Back-office applications integration
Business transformation
Call center development and management
Customer relationship management integration
Data warehousing design
Digital marketplace design and deployment
Electronic bill presentment and payment
Health care payor
Internet hosting
Intranet design
Merger and post-merger integration
Network management
Object-oriented technology development
Process automation
Project management
Security
Supply chain management and consulting
Systems integration

COMPETITORS

Accenture	Ernst & Young
Affiliated Computer	Getronics
American Management	Hewlett-Packard
Boston Consulting	IBM
Bull	ICL
Cambridge Technology	Keane
Cap Gemini	KPMG Consulting
CIBER	Logica
Compaq	McKinsey & Company
Computer Horizons	PricewaterhouseCoopers
Computer Sciences	Renaissance Worldwide
Deloitte Touche Tohmatsu	Technology Solutions
EDS	Unisys

HISTORICAL FINANCIALS & EMPLOYEES

NYSE: PER FYE: December 31	Annual Growth	12/91	12/92	12/93	12/94	12/95	12/96	12/97	12/98	12/99	12/00
Sales ($ mil.)	20.6%	—	247	292	292	342	599	782	994	1,152	1,106
Net income ($ mil.)	22.8%	—	11	(15)	6	11	20	11	41	76	56
Income as % of sales		—	4.3%	—	2.2%	3.2%	3.4%	1.4%	4.1%	6.6%	5.0%
Earnings per share ($)	(26.9%)	—	—	—	—	—	—	—	—	0.67	0.49
Stock price - FY high ($)	—	—	—	—	—	—	—	—	—	85.75	27.94
Stock price - FY low ($)	—	—	—	—	—	—	—	—	—	15.31	7.81
Stock price - FY close ($)	(51.3%)	—	—	—	—	—	—	—	—	18.88	9.19
P/E - high		—	—	—	—	—	—	—	—	101	48
P/E - low		—	—	—	—	—	—	—	—	18	13
Dividends per share ($)	—	—	—	—	—	—	—	—	—	0.00	0.00
Book value per share ($)	21.1%	—	—	—	—	—	—	—	—	4.22	5.11
Employees	22.9%	—	1,500	1,800	2,300	2,400	4,788	5,500	6,000	7,000	7,800

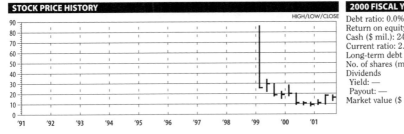

STOCK PRICE HISTORY   HIGH/LOW/CLOSE

2000 FISCAL YEAR-END

Debt ratio: 0.0%
Return on equity: 12.4%
Cash ($ mil.): 240
Current ratio: 2.79
Long-term debt ($ mil.): 0
No. of shares (mil.): 98
Dividends
  Yield: —
  Payout: —
Market value ($ mil.): 901

PIER 1 IMPORTS, INC.

OVERVIEW

Wicker World? Rattans 'R' Us? How about Pier 1 Imports? The Fort Worth, Texas-based company sells about 5,000 home furnishings items imported from more than 50 countries — mostly Asia — in almost 800 US stores. In addition to its growing US operations, Pier 1 has about 35 stores in Canada, and it also operates about 25 The Pier stores in the UK.

Pier 1 gradually has changed its merchandise from the exotic knickknacks the baby boomers used to decorate their dorm rooms to the more upscale, but still exotic, household furnishings they buy today. The product line favors natural materials (rattan, wood) and handcrafted goods. Furniture accounts

for more than a third of sales, and decorative items such as lamps, vases, and baskets account for another quarter. The stores also sell bed and bath products, housewares, and seasonal items. With more than a million active holders, Pier 1's private-label credit card is used to charge almost 30% of sales.

Pier 1 started selling online in 2000 and has hinted that it might create or buy high-end and low-end home furnishings chains (à la The Gap's upscale Banana Republic and lower-priced Old Navy chains). In 2001 Pier 1 acquired the Cargo Furniture chain from home furnishings manufacturer Tandycrafts.

HISTORY

Attracted by a Fisherman's Wharf import outlet called Cost Plus, marketing guru Charles Tandy (founder of RadioShack) made a loan to its owner and obtained the right to open other Cost Plus stores. Opening his first Cost Plus store in 1962 in San Francisco, Tandy leveraged the strength of the US dollar against weaker foreign currencies. He bought inexpensive wicker furniture, brass candlesticks, and other items from countries like India, Mexico, and Thailand, and gave them healthy markups, yet still managed to price them attractively for US customers.

The store was a hit with the peace and free-love generation of the 1960s, who dug its beads, incense, and wicker furniture. In 1965, with 16 locations, the company changed its name to Pier 1 Imports. Pressed by Radio-Shack, Tandy sold Pier 1 the next year. In 1969, with 42 stores, including its first store in Canada, the company went public on the American Stock Exchange.

By 1971 Pier 1 had 123 stores and was celebrating 100% sales gains for four consecutive years. It expanded its international presence, adding locations in Australia and Europe, and moved to the NYSE the next year. The chain experimented with alternative retail formats, including art supply, rug outlets, and fabric stores, but had abandoned them, as well as its foreign stores, by the mid-1970s. Pier 1 boasted nearly 270 locations by 1975.

Baby boomers, key to the chain's success, grew up and acquired different tastes, however. The dollar had also weakened, increasing costs. Performance faltered, and in 1980 the company brought in Robert Camp, successful operator of his own Pier 1 stores in Canada, to give it a makeover. Camp closed poorly performing

stores, opened larger stores in more profitable areas, and began changing the merchandise mix from novelties to higher-quality goods.

In 1983 investment group Intermark bought more than a third of the company. The next year Pier 1 acquired 36 Nurseryland Garden Centers from Intermark (boosting Intermark's stake in Pier 1 to about 50%) and merged the stores with its Wolfe's Nursery to form Sunbelt Nursery Group, which was spun off in 1985. That year Pier 1 named Clark Johnson its CEO. At the time it operated nearly 265 locations, showing little growth in store count in a decade.

Johnson initiated an ambitious plan to double the number of Pier 1 stores, which reached 500 in early 1989. With Intermark struggling, Pier 1 bought back Sunbelt (including a 50% stake in Sunbelt from Intermark) in 1990. The following year Intermark sold its stake in Pier 1 to pay back debt. That year Pier 1 took Sunbelt public, keeping a 57% stake. (Sunbelt has since been dissolved.) In 1993 the company launched The Pier, a chain of stores in the UK, and opened boutiques in Sears stores in Mexico.

Having spruced up stores, the chain continued to adjust the merchandise mix, dumping apparel in 1997 in favor of higher-margin goods. Also in 1997 Pier 1 purchased a national bank charter from Texaco to standardize the interest rates and fees on its private-label credit card. Marvin Girouard replaced Johnson as CEO in 1998 and as chairman in 1999. Pier 1 began selling online with the launch of its Web site in June 2000.

In February 2001 the company acquired the 21-store Cargo Furniture chain from home furnishings manufacturer Tandycrafts.

OFFICERS

Chairman and CEO: Marvin J. Girouard, age 61,
$2,132,000 pay
SVP of Finance, CFO, and Treasurer:
Charles H. Turner, age 44, $580,250 pay
SVP of Stores: Robert A. Arlauskas, age 46
SVP of Merchandising: Jay R. Jacobs, age 46,
$580,250 pay
SVP of Legal Affairs: J. Rodney Lawrence, age 55,
$424,000 pay
SVP of Marketing: Phil E. Schneider, age 49
SVP of Logistics and Allocations: David A. Walker,
age 50
SVP of Human Resources: E. Mitchell Weatherly,
age 53, $404,000 pay
Auditors: Ernst & Young LLP

LOCATIONS

HQ: 301 Commerce St., Ste. 600, Fort Worth, TX 76102
Phone: 817-252-8000   **Fax:** 817-252-8028
Web: www.pier1.com

Pier 1 Imports has about 800 stores in 48 states, plus 35
in Canada. It owns 23 The Pier stores in the UK and 21
Cargo Furniture stores in the US. It also owns or franchises about 30 stores in Japan, Mexico, and Puerto Rico.

PRODUCTS/OPERATIONS

2001 North American Sales

	% of sales
Furniture	40
Decorative accessories	22
Bed & bath	17
Housewares	12
Seasonal	9
Total	**100**

Selected Merchandise
Baskets
Bed and bath accessories
Candles
Ceramics
Dinnerware
Dried and silk flowers
Fragrance products
Furniture
Lamps
Seasonal products
Vases
Wall decor

COMPETITORS

Bed Bath & Beyond
Bombay Company
Container Store
Cost Plus
Euromarket Designs
Garden Ridge
IKEA

Lechters
Linens 'n Things
Michaels Stores
MJDesigns
Spiegel
Williams-Sonoma

HISTORICAL FINANCIALS & EMPLOYEES

NYSE: PIR FYE: Sat. nearest last day in Feb.	Annual Growth	2/92	2/93	2/94	2/95	2/96	2/97	2/98	2/99	2/00	2/01
Sales ($ mil.)	10.2%	587	629	685	712	811	947	1,075	1,139	1,231	1,412
Net income ($ mil.)	15.3%	26	23	6	25	10	44	78	78	75	95
Income as % of sales	—	4.5%	3.7%	0.9%	3.5%	1.2%	4.7%	7.3%	7.1%	6.1%	6.7%
Earnings per share ($)	13.9%	0.30	0.26	0.07	0.27	0.11	0.43	0.72	0.77	0.75	0.97
Stock price - FY high ($)	—	5.14	5.56	5.19	4.29	5.95	8.31	18.84	20.76	12.38	14.50
Stock price - FY low ($)	—	1.91	2.81	3.49	3.02	3.45	5.28	7.23	6.06	5.25	7.94
Stock price - FY close ($)	13.3%	4.24	4.92	3.71	4.18	5.84	7.73	17.84	8.63	8.75	13.00
P/E - high	—	17	21	74	16	54	17	24	25	16	15
P/E - low	—	6	11	50	11	31	11	9	7	7	8
Dividends per share ($)	—	0.00	0.03	0.05	0.05	0.06	0.07	0.07	0.12	0.12	0.15
Book value per share ($)	11.7%	2.04	2.27	2.27	2.53	2.56	3.19	3.87	4.14	4.70	5.53
Employees	7.5%	7,600	7,500	7,850	8,671	9,399	11,255	12,571	12,600	13,600	14,600

STOCK PRICE HISTORY

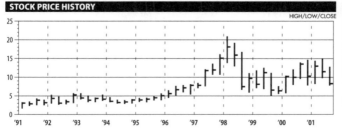

HIGH/LOW/CLOSE

2001 FISCAL YEAR-END
Debt ratio: 4.5%
Return on equity: 19.5%
Cash ($ mil.): 47
Current ratio: 3.31
Long-term debt ($ mil.): 25
No. of shares (mil.): 96
Dividends
  Yield: 1.2%
  Payout: 15.5%
Market value ($ mil.): 1,250

PILGRIM'S PRIDE CORPORATION

OVERVIEW

The pilgrim fathers shunned pride. Not the case with Pittsburg, Texas-based Pilgrim's Pride. The second-largest chicken processor in the US (Tyson Foods is #1) and Mexico (after Industrias Bachoco), the company breeds, hatches, raises, processes, distributes, and markets poultry. It also produces table eggs, animal feeds, and feed ingredients.

Pilgrim's focuses on prepared foods; its frozen fillets, tenderloins, strips, and nuggets sold to food service and retail outlets account for 43% of sales. The company is the biggest chicken supplier to Jack in the Box and Wendy's restaurants and Stouffer's frozen entrees. Pilgrim's also sells whole and cut-up fresh chicken.

Not chicken to grow, the company has acquired WLR Foods, which has served to broaden distribution and bring turkey to the table. The company sells its Pilgrim's and Wampler Foods brands through retailers and restaurants in the central, Mid-Atlantic, southwestern, and western US, and northern and central Mexico.

Chairman Lonnie "Bo" Pilgrim and his family own about 61% of the company.

HISTORY

Aubrey Pilgrim formed Pilgrim's Pride as Farmer's Feed and Seed Co. in 1946, with $1,000 in cash and a $2,500 note. Aubrey and brother Lonnie "Bo" Pilgrim (who joined the business in 1947) sold their first chicken from a pen behind their farm supply store and began to give away 100 baby chicks with each feed sack purchase. The Pilgrims bought back some of the grown birds to resell at a profit.

As demand for chickens grew, Farmer's Feed and Seed took its first steps toward creating a vertically integrated chicken company. It opened its first processing plant in 1957 and entered the distribution business three years later, delivering chicken to restaurants and grocery stores in northeastern Texas. Aubrey died in 1966, and Bo took over the business.

The company was renamed Pilgrim's Industries in 1968 (and Pilgrim's Pride in 1985). Eggs became part of the product mix in 1969. That year Pilgrim's acquired Market Produce Co., a food distributor with facilities in Arlington, Odessa, and El Paso, Texas. By 1979 the company was selling 1 million birds every week.

In the 1970s and 1980s, Pilgrim's grew through acquisitions and by using TV advertising to build a national brand. Its first TV commercial, "The President Speaks," was a humorous 1983 spot featuring Bo in a wide-brimmed Pilgrim's hat, addressing his TV audience. To offset the wide swings in prices and profits in the highly cyclical commodity chicken industry, Pilgrim's moved into prepared foods in 1986, the year it went public. The firm expanded into the Mexican consumer market in 1988 through the purchase of several chicken producers.

Bo caused an uproar the next year when he handed out campaign checks to Texas lawmakers during a senate session (a practice that is now illegal). The activity brought Bo before a grand jury, although he was not indicted.

Between 1987 and 1991 Pilgrim's tripled the size of its Mexican operations and expanded its frozen retail and export businesses. Excess poultry production and low prices led to the company's $30 million loss in 1992. Debt restructuring that year forced it to seek outside capital. Pilgrim's persuaded agricultural titan Archer Daniels Midland (ADM) to buy into the company, limiting ADM's stake to 20%.

In 1993 the company took major steps toward arranging for a successor for the aging Bo by appointing his nephew Lindy "Buddy" Pilgrim as president. (Buddy, formerly a marketing executive with Pilgrim's, had left the company in 1990 to lead a food industry consulting firm.)

Pilgrim's bought Mexican chicken processor Union de Queretaro in 1995. Costs related to acquisitions nudged the company into the red that year and the next. Pilgrim's expanded its US processing capacity with the 1997 purchase of Green Acres Foods of Nacogdoches, Texas.

It also introduced EggsPlus, an egg line with six times the vitamin E content of ordinary eggs, in 1997. Hens that are fed a natural grain diet (consisting of flaxseed and other nutrients) lay EggsPlus eggs, which contain high levels of high-density lipoprotein, the "good" cholesterol.

ADM reduced its stake in Pilgrim's from 20% to 4% in 1997 (and sold the rest in 1999). In 1998 Buddy resigned, Bo took the title of senior chairman, and David Van Hoose, who had ruled the roost in the company's Mexican operations, became CEO.

Pilgrim's opened a plant in Dallas in 1998 and bought a plant in Waco, Texas, from Cargill the next year. Pilgrim's bought poultry processor WLR Foods for about $280 million in 2001.

OFFICERS

Chairman: Lonnie Pilgrim, age 72, $1,603,521 pay
Vice Chairman: Clifford E. Butler, age 58, $509,362 pay
President, CEO, and COO: David Van Hoose, age 59, $922,154 pay
EVP, CFO, Secretary, and Treasurer: Richard A. Cogdill, age 40, $534,114 pay
EVP Sales, Marketing, and Distribution: Michael J. Murray
SVP, Human Resources: Ray Gameson
Auditors: Ernst & Young LLP

LOCATIONS

HQ: 110 S. Texas St., Pittsburg, TX 75686
Phone: 903-855-1000   **Fax:** 903-856-7505
Web: www.pilgrimspride.com

Pilgrim's Pride has operations in Arizona, Arkansas, North Carolina, Oklahoma, Pennsylvania, Texas, Virginia, West Virginia, and Mexico and sells its products in Canada, Eastern Europe, the Far East, Mexico, and the US.

PRODUCTS/OPERATIONS

2000 Sales

	$ mil.	% of total
US		
Prepared foods	641	43
Fresh chicken	253	17
Export & other	156	10
Mexico		
Chicken	307	21
Other	142	9
Total	**1,499**	**100**

Subsidiaries

Avicola Pilgrim's Pride de Mexico, S.A. DE C.V.
Gallina Pesada S.A. DE C.V.
Inmobiliaria Avicola Pilgrim's Pride, S. DE R.L. DE C.V.
Pilgrim's Pride Affordable Housing Corporation
Pilgrim's Pride Corporation of Virginia, Inc.
Pilgrim's Pride Funding Corporation
Pilgrim's Pride International, Inc.
Pilgrim's Pride, S.A. DE C.V.
PPC Marketing, LTD.
PPC of Delaware Business Trust

COMPETITORS

Bachoco	Keystone Foods
Cagle's	Perdue
ConAgra Foods	Sanderson Farms
ContiGroup	Smithfield Foods
Foster Farms	Tyson Foods
Gold Kist	Univasa
Hormel	Zacky Farms

HISTORICAL FINANCIALS & EMPLOYEES

NYSE: CHX FYE: Saturday nearest Sept. 30	Annual Growth	9/91	9/92	9/93	9/94	9/95	9/96	9/97	9/98	9/99	9/00
Sales ($ mil.)	7.4%	787	817	888	923	932	1,139	1,278	1,332	1,357	1,499
Net income ($ mil.)	17.4%	12	(30)	21	31	(8)	(7)	41	50	65	52
Income as % of sales	—	1.6%	—	2.4%	3.4%	—	—	3.2%	3.8%	4.8%	3.5%
Earnings per share ($)	10.0%	0.54	(1.24)	0.76	1.13	(0.29)	(0.26)	1.49	1.81	1.58	1.27
Stock price - FY high ($)	—	8.75	8.13	9.50	9.75	10.50	9.13	15.63	24.38	30.00	9.38
Stock price - FY low ($)	—	4.88	5.00	5.25	6.38	7.50	6.63	7.75	10.69	8.38	6.06
Stock price - FY close ($)	0.2%	6.75	6.38	8.25	9.63	7.88	8.63	14.88	20.81	8.69	6.88
P/E - high	—	16	—	12	9	—	—	10	13	19	7
P/E - low	—	9	—	6	6	—	—	5	6	5	5
Dividends per share ($)	0.0%	0.06	0.06	0.02	0.08	0.06	0.06	0.06	0.06	0.06	0.06
Book value per share ($)	5.9%	4.98	4.06	4.80	5.86	5.51	5.19	6.61	8.37	7.11	8.33
Employees	4.6%	10,300	10,300	10,700	10,300	11,750	11,500	13,000	13,000	15,150	15,400

STOCK PRICE HISTORY

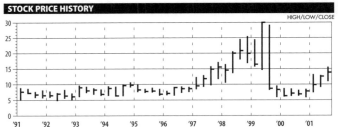

HIGH/LOW/CLOSE

2000 FISCAL YEAR-END

Debt ratio: 32.5%
Return on equity: 16.4%
Cash ($ mil.): 28
Current ratio: 1.86
Long-term debt ($ mil.): 165
No. of shares (mil.): 41
Dividends
 Yield: 0.9%
 Payout: 4.7%
Market value ($ mil.): 283

PILLOWTEX CORPORATION

OVERVIEW

This isn't just a fluff piece, and Pillowtex didn't just sleep its way to the top of the home textiles industry. The Dallas-based company has used a combination of internal growth and acquisitions to become the top producer of blankets, pillows, down comforters, and towels in North America. Overall, Pillowtex is the #3 home textile manufacturer, behind #1 Springs Industries and #2 WestPoint Stevens. Former chairman and CEO Chuck Hansen slashed jobs and consolidated operations after buyouts, but 1999 witnessed the company's first ever annual loss (partially due to snags in modernizing factories). In 2000, under the weight of heavy debt, the company filed for Chapter 11 bankruptcy protection. Hansen owns about 18% of the company's stock; Mary Silverthorne, widow of the founder, owns about 20%.

Aiming to be a single source for domestic textiles, Pillowtex sells mattress pads, sheets, and kitchen accessories under brands such as Fieldcrest, Cannon, Royal Velvet, Touch of Class, and St. Mary's. The company makes private-label and licensed lines such as Martha Stewart Everyday (for Kmart).

Pillowtex sells to mass merchants, department stores, and specialty retail stores, in addition to supplying wholesale clubs, catalog merchants, and institutional distributors. The company also owns 38 outlet stores. Wal-Mart accounts for more than 20% of sales.

HISTORY

John Silverthorne founded Pillowtex in 1954 to manufacture bed pillows in Dallas. He soon formed a national manufacturing network, buying plants in Atlanta, Chicago, Connecticut, and Los Angeles. Silverthorne ran the company until handing the reins over to Texan Charles Hansen, who had started as a salesman at Pillowtex in 1965 and became president in 1973.

After winning the pillow fight for market share in the 1970s and early 1980s by buying Perl Pillow, Synthetic Pillows, and Globe Feather & Down, Hansen stretched out into the mattress pad market, purchasing Acme Quilting and Bed Covers in 1983.

Pillowtex's growth quickly drew the industry's attention. One competitor unsuccessfully charged Pillowtex with violating antitrust laws after the 1987 purchase of Sumergrade, which made Pillowtex the #1 producer of down comforters and gave it the valuable Ralph Lauren Home Furnishings license. The 1991 purchase of Nettle Creek increased its holdings in the decorative home furnishings business. Hansen became chairman and CEO in 1992, following Silverthorne's death.

Looking north, Pillowtex bought two Canadian companies: Torfeaco, a century-old maker of fashion and synthetic bedding (1993) and Imperial Feather, a bedding products manufacturer (1994).

The company went public in 1993. That year it began covering the blanket industry, buying Manetta Mills and Tennessee Woolen Mills; it acquired Beacon Manufacturing, the leading US blanket supplier at the time, in 1994. The following year Pillowtex bought a cotton-yarn spinning plant in North Carolina to reduce raw material costs and to become more vertically integrated.

Pillowtex started 1997 as the third-largest home textile company, but later that year it acquired Fieldcrest Cannon, whose sales more than doubled those of Pillowtex; the purchase moved the company into sheets and bath linens and briefly made it the textile industry's frontrunner. In keeping with Hansen's history of fat trimming, shortly after the buyout about 20% of Fieldcrest Cannon's salaried employees were laid off, just six days before Christmas.

Further narrowing its focus in 1998, Pillowtex sold two Fieldcrest Cannon plants that made home furnishing fabrics and closed another that made decorative bedding, consolidating its operations into an existing Pillowtex plant. Then the company launched a $335 million modernization program to upgrade machinery at both its sheet and towel businesses.

Also in 1998 Pillowtex acquired The Leshner Corporation, expanding its terry products business into the kitchen and institutional markets. In 1999 employees at six Fieldcrest Cannon plants stunned the industry by voting to unionize. (Workers at the plants had resisted union efforts for nearly 100 years.) Also in 1999, in what Hansen called personally embarrassing, Pillowtex took a $6.9 million charge.

In June 2000 Pillowtex lost the lucrative Polo Ralph Lauren license to competitor WestPoint Stevens. In October Hansen resigned and former J. C. Penney executive Ralph La Rovere was named chairman. A month later, still without a CEO, Pillowtex filed to reorganize under Chapter 11 due to a heavy debt load. In 2001 Pillowtex announced it would close plants in Georgia and North Carolina.

Chairman: Ralph LaRovere, age 65
President, COO, and Director: Anthony T. Williams, age 54
EVP and CFO: Michael R. Harmon, age 53
EVP, Manufacturing and Director: A. Allen Oakley, age 47, $300,000 pay
EVP, Sales and Marketing and Director: Scott E. Shimizu, age 47, $375,000 pay
SVP, Marketing: Richard A. Grissinger, age 57, $275,000 pay
SVP, Purchasing and Logistics: Richard L. Dennard, age 52, $275,000 pay
VP and Chief Information Officer: Deborah G. Poole, age 46
VP and General Counsel,: John F. Sterling, age 37
VP, Human Resources: Donald Mallo, age 51
VP and Treasurer: Henry T. Pollock, age 60
Corporate Secretary: Brenda A. Sanders, age 50
Executive Director, Operations: Robert F. Hasse, age 57
Auditors: KPMG LLP

LOCATIONS

HQ: 4111 Mint Way, Dallas, TX 75237
Phone: 214-333-3225   **Fax:** 214-330-6016
Web: www.pillowtex.com

Pillowtex has manufacturing and distribution plants in Canada and the US.

2000 Sales

	% of Sales
US	95
Other countries	5
Total	**100**

PRODUCTS/OPERATIONS

Selected Brands	Selected Products
Beacon	Bath rugs
Caldwell	Bed pillows
Cannon	Bed skirts
Charisma	Bedding accessories
Classic Pooh	Blankets
Comforel (licensed)	Down comforters
Dacron	Kitchen towels, dishcloths,
Fieldcrest	and oven mitts
Healthy Horizons	Mattress pads
Healthy Living	Sheets
Martha Stewart Everyday	Shower curtains
by Kmart (licensed)	Towels
Nettle Creek	Window treatments
Postmark Originals	
Royal Family	**Subsidiaries**
Royal Velvet	Beacon Manufacturing
Royal Velvet Big & Soft	Company
Serene	Encee, Inc.
St. Mary's	Fieldcrest Cannon, Inc.
Terry	The Leshner Corporation
Touch of Class	Opelika Industries, Inc.
Trevira	Pillowtex Canada, Inc.
	Pillowtex Management
	Services

COMPETITORS

Burlington Industries	Mohawk Industries
Croscill	Pacific Coast Feather Co.
Crown Crafts	Springs Industries
Dakotah, Incorporated	Thomaston Mills
Dan River	WestPoint Stevens
Hollander Home Fashions	

HISTORICAL FINANCIALS & EMPLOYEES

OTC: PTEXQ FYE: Saturday nearest Dec. 31	Annual Growth	12/91	12/92	12/93	12/94	12/95	12/96	12/97	12/98	12/99	12/00
Sales ($ mil.)	22.1%	—	274	292	352	475	491	580	1,510	1,552	1,350
Net income ($ mil.)	—	—	8	13	8	12	14	7	43	(20)	(271)
Income as % of sales	—	—	2.8%	4.4%	2.2%	2.4%	2.9%	1.3%	2.8%	—	—
Earnings per share ($)	—	—	—	1.32	0.72	1.08	1.33	0.66	2.52	(2.25)	(19.04)
Stock price – FY high ($)	—	—	—	20.63	21.25	13.13	18.50	35.25	52.00	28.38	6.44
Stock price – FY low ($)	—	—	—	9.00	8.88	8.00	10.38	15.88	23.13	2.75	0.05
Stock price – FY close ($)	(46.6%)	—	—	20.25	9.75	11.63	18.00	34.88	26.75	6.19	0.28
P/E – high	—	—	—	16	29	12	13	47	18	—	—
P/E – low	—	—	—	7	12	7	7	21	8	—	—
Dividends per share ($)	—	—	—	0.00	0.00	0.05	0.20	0.24	0.24	0.18	0.00
Book value per share ($)	—	—	—	6.54	7.22	8.29	9.42	18.58	21.31	19.72	(4.45)
Employees	27.3%	—	1,811	2,636	3,770	3,850	3,900	14,150	14,000	14,000	12,500

STOCK PRICE HISTORY

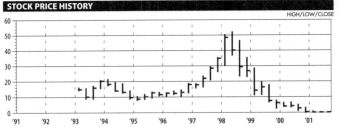

HIGH/LOW/CLOSE

2000 FISCAL YEAR-END

Debt ratio: 0.0%
Return on equity: —
Cash ($ mil.): 32
Current ratio: 0.69
Long-term debt ($ mil.): 0
No. of shares (mil.): 14
Dividends
  Yield: —
  Payout: —
Market value ($ mil.): 4

PLAINS RESOURCES INC.

OVERVIEW

Plains Resources' resources are plain and simple — oil and gas. The Houston-based independent energy company markets, transports, and stores crude oil and develops and produces crude oil and natural gas.

Nearly all of the company's sales come from its 39% stake — reduced from 54% in 2001 — in Plains All American Pipeline LP. The partnership, operating mainly in California, Louisiana, Oklahoma, and Texas, buys and sells crude oil and transports it by pipeline or truck. It owns about 2,800 miles of pipelines and storage facilities with a 9.8 million barrel capacity. The partnership has sold a 1,088-mile section of its namesake All American Pipeline, a 30-inch pipeline that connects California and Texas. It retains a 140-mile stretch in California. Chevron accounts for about 43% of the company's sales.

Plains Resources' other subsidiaries, which handle its oil- and gas-producing activities, include Arguello, which operates its offshore California properties; Calumet Florida, which operates its Sunniland Trend properties in Florida; Plains Illinois, which operates its Illinois Basin properties; and Stocker Resources, which operates its onshore California properties.

Plains Resources' oil- and gas-producing activities are concentrated in California, Florida, and Illinois, where it exploits older fields. The company has proved oil and natural gas reserves of 238.7 million barrels of oil equivalent. Plains Resources is seeking to expand its Canadian pipeline operations through acquisitions.

HISTORY

The company was founded in 1976 in Oklahoma as Alifin, but changed its name to Plains Resources the same year. In the 1980s Plains Resources invested in a number of older producing properties, but in the 1990s the company hit pay dirt by acquiring oil properties in the Los Angeles Basin from Chevron. Although these fields were relatively underdeveloped, Plains Resources boosted their proved oil reserves from 18 million barrels to 74 million. It repeated this strategy — low investment in older properties, high investment in new drilling — by acquiring oil and gas properties in South Florida from Exxon in 1993 and 1994.

In 1996 Plains Resources took over management of a 90-year-old Marathon oil and gas property in Illinois. The next year it paid about $25 million to acquire Chevron's interests in the Los Angeles Basin's Montebello Field, dating from 1917. In 1998 it purchased Goodyear's All American Pipeline. Plains Resources then created Plains All American Pipeline LP to buy and operate the pipeline and spun off a 43% stake in an IPO. In 1999 Plains Resources bought Chevron's 26% stake in the Point Arguello field off the California coast. That year the limited partnership acquired Scurlock Permian (2,300 miles of pipeline) from Marathon Ashland Petroleum.

Shareholders sued Plains All American Pipeline in 1999 after it reported that an employee's unauthorized crude-oil trading would cost the company about $160 million. The company agreed the next year to pay

$29.5 million, plus interest, to settle the cases. Also in 2000 Plains All American Pipeline sold the majority of its All American Pipeline to El Paso Energy for $129 million.

Plains All American Pipeline acquired about 450 miles of oil pipeline and other midstream assets in Canada from Murphy Oil in 2001. The company also bought CANPET Energy, a Calgary-based crude oil and LPG marketing firm.

In 2001 Plains Resources sold a portion of its stake in Plains All American Pipeline to an investor group that included oil industry veteran James Flores, who took over as chairman and CEO of Plains Resources. Greg Armstrong, formerly CEO of both Plains Resources and Plains All American, remained CEO of Plains All American.

Also in 2001, as the company continued its restructuring, John Raymond, formerly of investment firm Kinder Morgan was named COO and Jere Overdyke, formerly an executive with energy giant Enron, was named CFO of Plains Resources.

OFFICERS

Chairman and CEO: James C. Flores, age 41
EVP and COO: John T. Raymond, age 30
EVP and CFO: Jere C. Overdyke Jr., age 49
EVP, Administration; Secretary; General Counsel:
Timothy T. Stephens, age 49
SVP, Engineering: William C. Egg Jr., $470,000 pay
SVP, Operations: Jim G. Hester, age 41
VP, Accounting and Assistant Treasurer:
Cynthia A. Feeback, age 43, $290,000 pay
VP, Administration and Human Resources:
Mary O. Peters, age 52
Administrator, Investor Relations: Carolyn F. Tice
Auditors: PricewaterhouseCoopers LLP

LOCATIONS

HQ: 500 Dallas St., Ste. 700, Houston, TX 77002
Phone: 713-654-1414   **Fax:** 713-654-1523
Web: www.plainsresources.com

Plains Resources' reserves are concentrated in
California, Florida, and Illinois.

PRODUCTS/OPERATIONS

2000 Sales

	$ mil.	% of total
Marketing, transportation & storage	6,426	98
Oil & natural gas	149	2
Total	**6,575**	**100**

Selected Subsidiaries and Affiliates

Arguello Inc. (operates offshore California properties)
Calumet Florida, Inc. (operates Sunniland Trend
properties in Florida)
Plains Illinois Inc. (operates Illinois Basin properties)
Stocker Resources, Inc. (operates onshore California
properties)

COMPETITORS

Adams Resources
Black Hills Power
BP
Chesapeake Energy
Corrpro
Enbridge
Enron
EOTT Energy Partners
Evergreen Resources
Exxon Mobil
GPU
Greka Energy
Helmerich & Payne
Koch
Mission Resources
Mitchell Energy & Development
Nuevo Energy
Pioneer Natural Resources
Royal Dutch/Shell
TC PipeLines
TEPPCO Partners
Texaco
TransMontaigne
Western Gas
Williams Companies

HISTORICAL FINANCIALS & EMPLOYEES

AMEX: PLX FYE: December 31	Annual Growth	12/91	12/92	12/93	12/94	12/95	12/96	12/97	12/98	12/99	12/00
Sales ($ mil.)	63.4%	79	132	186	257	404	630	862	1,293	4,817	6,575
Net income ($ mil.)	—	(13)	(3)	(20)	1	3	17	14	(59)	(25)	41
Income as % of sales	—	—	—	—	0.2%	0.7%	2.6%	1.7%	—	—	0.6%
Earnings per share ($)	—	(1.39)	(0.33)	(1.77)	0.04	0.16	1.23	0.77	(3.77)	(2.05)	1.39
Stock price - FY high ($)	—	30.75	21.75	13.13	8.00	11.00	17.00	20.75	21.00	20.19	21.75
Stock price - FY low ($)	—	4.88	7.50	6.38	5.38	5.50	7.44	11.88	13.44	8.13	10.50
Stock price - FY close ($)	4.7%	14.00	9.25	6.50	5.38	9.00	15.63	17.19	14.06	12.50	21.13
P/E - high	—	—	—	—	200	69	17	24	—	—	12
P/E - low	—	—	—	—	135	34	7	14	—	—	6
Dividends per share ($)	—	0.00	0.00	0.00	0.00	0.00	0.00	0.00	0.00	0.00	0.00
Book value per share ($)	11.4%	3.77	5.65	3.89	5.81	4.76	5.79	7.97	4.32	10.01	9.99
Employees	30.5%	100	140	209	217	202	201	230	370	1,080	1,100

STOCK PRICE HISTORY

HIGH/LOW/CLOSE

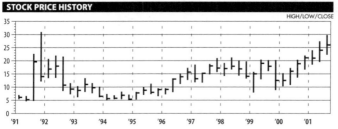

2000 FISCAL YEAR-END

Debt ratio: 77.0%
Return on equity: 175.9%
Cash ($ mil.): 5
Current ratio: 1.05
Long-term debt ($ mil.): 626
No. of shares (mil.): 19
Dividends
  Yield: —
  Payout: —
Market value ($ mil.): 396

RADIOSHACK CORPORATION

OVERVIEW

RadioShack (formerly Tandy) should know about being on the same wavelength as American consumers. The Fort Worth, Texas-based company owns or franchises about 7,200 RadioShack stores throughout the US. Best known for their electronics parts, the stores also offer wireless phones and services, audio and video equipment, satellite TV equipment, computers, and repair services.

The company has boosted sales by opening "store-within-a-store" units with RCA, Sprint, Compaq, Verizon, and Microsoft. To get these exclusive deals, the partners agree to refurbish parts of RadioShack stores — saving the company millions. As part of RadioShack's plan to be "America's Home Connectivity Store," it bought cable installer AmeriLink, and began selling DSL and satellite Internet services.

HISTORY

During the 1950s Charles Tandy expanded his family's small Fort Worth, Texas, leather business (founded 1919) into a nationwide chain of leather craft and hobby stores. By 1960 Tandy stock was being traded on the NYSE. In the early 1960s Tandy began to expand into other retail areas, buying Leonard's, a Fort Worth department store.

In 1963 Tandy purchased RadioShack, a nearly bankrupt electronics parts supplier with a mail-order business and nine retail stores in the Boston area. Tandy collected part of the $800,000 owed the company and started expanding. Between 1961 and 1969 Tandy's sales grew from $16 million to $180 million; the bulk of growth was due to the expansion of Radio-Shack. Between 1968 and 1973 Tandy grew from 172 to 2,294 stores; RadioShack provided over 50% of sales and 80% of earnings in 1973.

Tandy sold its department store operations to Dillard's in 1974. The next year Tandy spun off its leather products business to shareholders as Tandy Brands, and its hobby and handicraft business as Tandycrafts, focusing Tandy on the consumer electronics business. During 1976 the boom in CB radio sales pushed income up 125% as Tandy opened 1,200 stores. The following year it introduced the first mass-marketed PC. In 1979, the year after Charles died, there were 5,530 McDonald's, 6,805 7-Elevens, and 7,353 RadioShacks.

In 1984 the company introduced the Tandy 1000, the first IBM-compatible PC priced under $1,000. Then came acquisitions — electronics equipment chain stores Scott/McDuff and VideoConcepts (1985), laptop specialist GRiD Systems (1988), and microcomputer makers Victor Microcomputer and Micronic (1989, later merged as Victor Technologies).

In 1987 Tandy spun off its foreign retail operations as InterTAN. Realizing that Radio-Shack had nearly exhausted its expansion possibilities, the company focused on alternate retail formats such as GRiD Systems Centers, and in 1991 opened Computer City and the Edge in Electronics. Also that year it introduced name-brand products into RadioShack stores.

Tandy sold Memtek Products (magnetic tape), LIKA (printed circuit boards), and its computer manufacturing and marketing operations in 1993 and spun off O'Sullivan Industries (ready-to-assemble furniture) to the public in 1994. A year later the company announced that it would close all of its VideoConcepts mall stores and half its McDuff electronics stores. Also in 1995 it sold its credit card business.

In 1996 and 1997 Tandy closed down its 19-store Incredible Universe "gigastores" chain, shuttered the 53-store McDuff chain, and closed about 20 Computer City stores, selling others in Europe. It later sold a 20% stake in the ailing chain to a group of former CompUSA and CompuCom executives, who took over the management of the stores.

Longtime CEO John Roach stepped down in 1998, and president Leonard Roberts replaced him. Tandy then bought back the stake it had sold in the Computer City chain and sold the whole 100-store chain to CompUSA for $211 million. In a savvy move to reduce the cost of revamping RadioShack stores, Roberts gave companies exclusive "store within a store" rights to sell their products in exchange for paying for some of the refurbishments.

In 1999 Tandy and Microsoft formed a joint venture, RadioShack.com, LLC, to sell electronics online. The joint company then bought Amerilink installation services. (It has since bought the 25% of RadioShack.com that it did not own.)

In 2000 it changed its name to RadioShack. The company also opened RadioShack.com store/fulfillment centers outside of Denver, Atlanta, and Ft.Worth, offering about 18,000 products (six times the number of products at its usual stores), but pulled the plug on this concept soon after. In 2001 RadioShack announced plans to sell products in about 5,000 Blockbuster video stores; the plan includes kiosks and store-within-a-store setups.

Chairman and CEO: Leonard H. Roberts, age 52, $2,705,547 pay
President and COO: David J. Edmondson, age 41, $967,782 pay
EVP; President, RadioShack International Procurement: David Christopher, age 58, $720,055 pay
SVP and CFO: Michael D. Newman, age 44
SVP and Chief Information Officer: Evelyn Follit, age 54
SVP, Corporate Secretary, and General Counsel: Mark C. Hill, age 49, $611,057 pay
SVP, People: Francesca M. Spinelli, age 47
SVP, Public Relations and Corporate Communications: Laura K. Moore, age 39
VP and Assistant Corporate Secretary: Carolyn Hoopes
VP, Corporate Real Estate: Nina B. Petty
VP, Creative: Barry King
VP, Dealer/Franchise Operations: Paul Rickels
VP, Dealer/Franchise Sales Channel: Tom Cobb
VP, Finance and Corporate Development: Loren K. Jensen, age 40
VP, Human Resources: Jeff Bland
VP, Law: David Goldberg
VP, Organizational Development: Rich Pendergast
Executive Division Vice President, Sales Channels: Louis W. Provost
Senior Division Vice President and General Manager, Connecting People: Stewart F. Asimus Jr.
Senior Division Vice President and General Manager, Connecting Places: Mark E. Stanley
Auditors: PricewaterhouseCoopers LLP

LOCATIONS

HQ: 100 Throckmorton St., Ste. 1800, Fort Worth, TX 76102
Phone: 817-415-3700   **Fax:** 817-415-2647
Web: www.tandy.com

RadioShack owns or franchises about 7,200 RadioShack stores in the US, and it has seven manufacturing plants in the US and one manufacturing plant in China.

PRODUCTS/OPERATIONS

2000 Stores

	No.
Company-owned	5,109
Dealer/franchise	2,090
Total	**7,199**

COMPETITORS

Best Buy	Kmart
Cablevision Electronics Investments	Let's Talk Cellular & Wireless
CDW Computer Centers	Micro Warehouse
Circuit City	Office Depot
CompUSA	OfficeMax
Costco Wholesale	PC Connection
Dell Computer	PC Mall
Egghead	Sears
Fred Meyer	Sharper Image
Fry's Electronics	Staples
GameStop	Target
Gateway	Ultimate Electronics
Good Guys	Wal-Mart
Home Depot	

HISTORICAL FINANCIALS & EMPLOYEES

NYSE: RSH FYE: December 31	Annual Growth	6/92	*12/92	12/93	12/94	12/95	12/96	12/97	12/98	12/99	12/00
Sales ($ mil.)	0.3%	4,680	2,228	4,103	4,944	5,839	6,286	5,372	4,788	4,126	4,795
Net income ($ mil.)	8.0%	184	4	97	224	212	(92)	187	61	308	368
Income as % of sales	—	3.9%	0.2%	2.4%	4.5%	3.6%	—	3.5%	1.3%	7.2%	7.7%
Earnings per share ($)	14.1%	0.56	0.01	0.30	0.72	0.79	(0.41)	0.82	0.27	1.43	1.84
Stock price - FY high ($)	—	7.81	7.94	12.69	12.66	16.09	14.78	23.00	31.94	79.50	72.94
Stock price - FY low ($)	—	5.84	5.56	6.16	7.69	9.13	8.53	10.16	15.19	20.59	35.06
Stock price - FY close ($)	24.1%	6.13	7.44	12.38	12.50	10.38	11.00	19.28	20.59	49.19	42.81
P/E - high	—	14	794	51	17	20	—	27	114	53	38
P/E - low	—	10	556	25	11	11	—	12	54	14	18
Dividends per share ($)	4.3%	0.15	0.08	0.15	0.15	0.18	0.20	0.25	0.20	0.15	0.22
Book value per share ($)	(5.2%)	7.64	7.47	7.63	7.94	6.49	5.53	5.17	4.35	4.36	4.74
Employees	2.1%	—	37,000	42,000	45,800	49,300	48,400	44,000	38,200	40,800	43,600

* Fiscal year change

STOCK PRICE HISTORY

HIGH/LOW/CLOSE

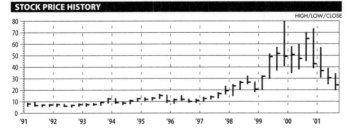

2000 FISCAL YEAR-END

Debt ratio: 25.6%
Return on equity: 46.9%
Cash ($ mil.): 131
Current ratio: 1.48
Long-term debt ($ mil.): 303
No. of shares (mil.): 186
Dividends
  Yield: 0.5%
  Payout: 12.0%
Market value ($ mil.): 7,953

RELIANT ENERGY, INCORPORATED

OVERVIEW

Reliant Energy is becoming much more than a reliable local utility. The Houston-based utility holding company is evolving from a Texas electricity provider into a power broker with expanding energy interests throughout the US and in Western Europe.

Subsidiary Reliant Energy HL&P generates 14,000 MW of electricity that it distributes to 1.7 million residential, commercial, and industrial customers in its hometown and along much of the Texas Gulf Coast. The company's natural gas distribution subsidiaries serve about 3 million customers (nearly one million are also electricity customers of HL&P) in the south-central US and Minnesota and operate 8,200 miles of pipeline.

Majority-owned Reliant Resources has taken over all of its parent's nonregulated activities in preparation for Texas' energy deregulation in 2002. It operates independent power plants with a generating capacity of 12,700 MW in the US and the Netherlands, and markets and trades energy in the US and Western Europe. Other nonregulated operations include telecommunications and Internet business services, which the company is considering selling.

Reliant Energy continues to expand its generation and marketing operations in the US and Europe, but is selling its Latin American operations.

HISTORY

Reliant Energy's earliest predecessor, Houston Electric Lighting and Power, was formed in 1882 by a group including Emanuel Raphael, cashier at Houston Savings Bank, and Mayor William Baker. In 1901 General Electric's financial arm, United Electric Securities Company, took control of the utility, which became Houston Lighting & Power (HL&P). United Electric sold HL&P five years later; by 1922 HL&P ended up in the arms of National Power & Light Company (NP&L), a subsidiary of Electric Bond & Share (a public utility holding company that had been spun off by General Electric).

In 1942 NP&L was forced to sell HL&P in order to comply with the 1935 Public Utility Holding Company Act. As the oil industry boomed in Houston after WWII, so did HL&P.

HL&P became the managing partner in a venture to build a nuclear plant on the Texas Gulf Coast in 1973. Construction on the South Texas Project, with partners Central Power and Light and the Cities of Austin and San Antonio, began in 1975. In 1976, Houston Industries (HI) was formed as the holding company for HL&P.

By 1980 the nuke was four years behind schedule and over budget. HL&P and its partners sued construction firm Brown & Root in 1982 and received a $700 million settlement in 1985. (The City of Austin also sued HL&P for damages, but lost.) The nuke was finally brought online in 1988, with the final cost estimated at $5.8 billion.

Meanwhile, HI diversified into cable TV in 1986 by creating Enrcom (later Paragon Communications) through a venture with Time Inc. Two years later it bought the US cable interests of Canada's Rogers Communications. HI

left the cable business in 1995, selling out to Time Warner.

Developing Latin fever, HI joined a consortium that bought 51% of Argentinean electric company EDELAP in 1992. (However, in 1998 HI sold its stake to AES.) On a roll, HI acquired 90% of Argentina's electric utility EDESE (1995); joined a consortium that won a controlling stake in Light, a Brazilian electric utility (1996); bought a stake in Colombian electric utility EPSA (1997); and interests in three electric utilities in El Salvador (1998).

Back in the US, HI acquired gas dealer NorAm for $2.5 billion in 1997. The next year it bought five generating plants in California from Edison International and laid plans to build merchant plants in Arizona (near Phoenix); Illinois; Nevada (near Las Vegas, in partnership with Sempra Energy); and Rhode Island. Overseas, HI finished a power plant in India in 1998. It also bought a 65% interest in Colombian electric utilities Electricaribe and Electrocosta; EPSA bought about 55% of CET in Colombia, and Light bought about 75% of Metropolitana (Sao Paulo, Brazil).

In 1999 HI became Reliant Energy. That year the company bought a 52% stake in Dutch power generation firm UNA; it bought the remaining 48% the next year. Also in 2000 Reliant Energy paid Sithe Energies $2.1 billion for 21 power plants in the mid-Atlantic states. It sold its operations in Brazil, Colombia, and El Salvador that year, and transferred all of its nonregulated operations to subsidiary Reliant Resources.

Reliant Energy netted about $1.7 billion in 2001 from the sale to the public of a 20% stake in Reliant Resources.

OFFICERS

Chairman, President, and CEO, Reliant Energy and Reliant Resources: R. Steve Letbetter, age 52, $3,015,370 pay
Vice Chairman: Robert W. Harvey, age 45, $1,290,000 pay
Vice Chairman and CFO, Reliant Energy and Reliant Resources: Stephen W. Naeve, age 53, $1,290,000 pay
Vice Chairman, President, and COO, Reliant Energy Delivery Group: David M. McClanahan, age 51, $850,500 pay
EVP, General Counsel, and Corporate Secretary, Reliant Energy and Reliant Resources: Hugh Rice Kelly, age 58
SVP and Chief Accounting Officer: Mary P. Ricciardello, age 45
SVP, Communications: Robert L. Waldrop, age 54
SVP, Human Resources: Preston R. Johnson Jr., age 45
SVP, Regulatory: Stephen G. Schaeffer, age 53
President and COO, Reliant Energy Arkla/Entex: Constantine S. Liollio, age 42
President and COO, Reliant Energy Europe: Ito van Lanschot, age 51
President and COO, Reliant Energy HL&P/Entex: Thomas R. Standish, age 51
President and COO, Reliant Energy Minnegasco: Gary M. Cerny, age 45
Auditors: Deloitte & Touche LLP

LOCATIONS

HQ: 1111 Louisiana St., Houston, TX 77002
Phone: 713-207-3000   **Fax:** 713-207-3169
Web: www.reliantenergy.com

Reliant Energy distributes electricity in Texas and natural gas in Arkansas, Louisiana, Minnesota, Mississippi, Oklahoma, and Texas.

PRODUCTS/OPERATIONS

2000 Sales

	$ mil.	% of total
Wholesale energy	19,290	66
Retail electricity	5,494	18
Retail gas	4,291	14
Gas transport	122	1
Energy products & services	142	1
Total	**29,339**	**100**

Selected Operations

Electric
Reliant Energy HL&P (regulated electricity generation and distribution; formerly Houston Lighting & Power)

Interstate Pipelines
Mississippi River Transmission Corporation
Reliant Energy Gas Transmission Company

Natural Gas Distribution
Reliant Energy Arkla (formerly Arkla)
Reliant Energy Entex (formerly Entex)
Reliant Energy Minnegasco (formerly Minnegasco)

Nonregulated
Reliant Resources, Inc. (80%, independent power projects, energy marketing and trading, telecommunications, e-commerce)

COMPETITORS

Ameren	El Paso	Southern
Avista	Enron	Company
Cinergy	Entergy	Statoil Energy
Constellation	Iberdrola	Tractebel
Energy Group	Koch	TXU
Dominion	Peabody Energy	UtiliCorp
Duke Energy	PG&E	Williams
Dynegy	Sempra Energy	Companies

HISTORICAL FINANCIALS & EMPLOYEES

NYSE: REI FYE: December 31	Annual Growth	12/91	12/92	12/93	12/94	12/95	12/96	12/97	12/98	12/99	12/00
Sales ($ mil.)	23.3%	4,444	4,596	4,324	4,002	3,730	4,095	6,873	11,489	15,303	29,339
Net income ($ mil.)	0.8%	417	435	416	399	1,106	405	421	(141)	1,849	447
Income as % of sales	—	9.4%	9.5%	9.6%	10.0%	29.6%	9.9%	6.1%	—	12.1%	1.5%
Earnings per share ($)	(0.6%)	1.64	1.69	1.60	1.62	4.46	1.66	1.66	(0.50)	5.18	1.56
Stock price - FY high ($)	—	22.19	23.44	24.88	23.88	24.50	25.63	27.25	33.38	32.50	49.00
Stock price - FY low ($)	—	17.31	20.06	21.25	15.00	17.69	20.50	18.88	24.44	22.75	19.75
Stock price - FY close ($)	7.7%	22.13	22.94	23.81	17.81	24.25	22.63	26.75	32.06	22.88	43.31
P/E - high	—	14	18	16	14	5	15	16	—	6	32
P/E - low	—	11	15	13	9	4	12	11	—	4	13
Dividends per share ($)	0.1%	1.48	1.49	1.50	1.50	1.50	1.50	1.50	1.50	1.50	1.50
Book value per share ($)	2.3%	15.09	14.84	14.64	15.57	17.23	16.06	16.58	14.59	18.05	18.58
Employees	1.8%	13,289	11,576	11,350	11,498	8,891	8,100	12,711	12,916	14,256	15,633

STOCK PRICE HISTORY

HIGH/LOW/CLOSE

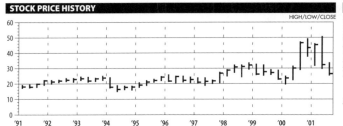

2000 FISCAL YEAR-END

Debt ratio: 47.7%
Return on equity: 8.3%
Cash ($ mil.): 176
Current ratio: 0.64
Long-term debt ($ mil.): 4,996
No. of shares (mil.): 295
Dividends
  Yield: 3.5%
  Payout: 96.2%
Market value ($ mil.): 12,781

RENT-A-CENTER, INC.

OVERVIEW

Customers might rent-to-own, but Rent-A-Center prefers to buy outright. Plano, Texas-based Rent-A-Center (formerly Renters Choice) climbed to the top of the US rent-to-own industry through no less than 60 acquisitions since 1987, including leader Thorn's 1,400 Rent-A-Center, Remco, and U-Can-Rent stores in 1998. It owns and operates more than 2,100 stores throughout the US; an additional 360 locations are franchised through subsidiary ColorTyme.

Items to rent include home electronics, furniture, and accessories, which together account for more than 70% of sales; the company also rents appliances and computers and offers Internet access. Customers can take possession of a rented item after a specified number of payments, but only about 25% ever do.

The company has been the target of several lawsuits, including charges of racial and sexual discrimination and deceptive trade practices.

Rent-A-Center took a break from expansion in 1999, focusing on integrating banners, management, and marketing efforts. However, the company plans to continue adding stores through new store openings and acquisitions. The company is also expanding its offering of upscale brands (Sony electronics, Ashley furniture) to attract more customers.

Founder, chairman, and CEO Ernest Talley retired in 2001. He was succeeded by former COO and VC Mark Speese. Tally owns about 13% and Speese owns about 7% of Rent-A-Center. Los Angeles investment firm Apollo owns about 29% of the company.

HISTORY

Ernest Talley is a pioneer in the rent-to-own industry, having founded one of the first rent-to-own chains in 1963. He sold that business in 1974 and went into commercial real estate in Dallas. In 1987, after the Texas real estate crash, Talley and his son Michael started Talley Leasing, which rented appliances to apartment complex owners.

Talley bought Vista Rent To Own, a chain of 22 stores in New Jersey and Puerto Rico, in 1989. He upgraded merchandise, increased selection, updated information and data systems, and improved store management. In 1993 the company acquired DEF, an 84-store chain, and repeated the upgrading process. That year the company changed its name to Renters Choice. It went public in 1995 and used the proceeds to make more acquisitions.

The purchases of Crown Leasing and Pro Rental (parent of Magic Rent-to-Own) moved Renters Choice into the southern US and increased its store count from just over 100 to 322. In 1996 the company acquired Texas-based competitor ColorTyme, adding another 320 stores (most of them franchises). Renters Choice acquired Trans Texas Capital, another rental purchase enterprise, the following year.

In 1998 the company bought Central Rents, owner of about 180 stores, for $103 million. It also paid $900 million (most of it borrowed) for Thorn Americas, the US subsidiary of Thorn, then changed its name to Rent-A-Center. Also that year it settled a class-action lawsuit with 20,000 customers for $12 million; the suit alleged that the company had misled consumers about actual finance costs.

Rent-A-Center lost an appeal of another lawsuit in 1999 and was ordered to pay $30 million to 30,000 consumers for charging interest rates as high as 750%.

After making no acquisitions in 1999, Rent-A-Center announced in 2000 that it would be adding 100-plus stores annually. The company also began offering Internet service, originally for $5.95 per week through BellSouth; then, in 2001, offering free service through NetZero.

Late in 2001 Talley retired as chairman and CEO. He was succeeded by Mark Speese, a director and former president, COO, and VC of Rent-A-Center. As part of Talley's retirement package, the company bought out part of his stake in the company, reducing his share from 20% to approximately 13%.

In November 2001 Rent-A-Center agreed to settle a sex-bias class-action lawsuit filed in federal court in Kansas City for about $12 million. The suit alleged that the company discriminated against pregnant employees. In other legal news, the company was charged by the New York City Department of Consumer Affairs with 310 violations of the New York City's Consumer Protection Law (including one violation for deceptive trade practices).

Chairman and CEO: Mark E. Speese, age 44
President and Director: Mitchell E. Fadel, age 43,
$391,600 pay
EVP of Operations and COO: Dana F. Goble, age 35,
$250,370 pay
EVP, Growth and Director: L. Dowell Arnette, age 53,
$282,370 pay
SVP of Finance, CFO, and Treasurer: Robert D. Davis,
age 29
SVP and General Counsel: Bradley W. Denison, age 40,
$252,370 pay
SVP: David G. Ewbank, age 44
SVP: Mark S. Connelly, age 38
SVP: Anthony M. Doll, age 32
SVP: Claude E. Ford III, age 34
SVP: David A. Kraemer, age 39
SVP: William C. Nutt, age 44
SVP: Timothy J. Stough, age 45
SVP: John H. Whitehead, age 51
Corporate Secretary: David M. Glasgow, age 31
Director of Human Resources: Marc Tuckey
Auditors: Grant Thornton LLP

LOCATIONS

HQ: 5700 Tennyson Pkwy., 3rd Fl., Plano, TX 75024
Phone: 972-801-1100   **Fax:** 972-943-0113
Web: www.rentacenter.com

Rent-A-Center has more than 2,000 stores in all 50 states and in Puerto Rico.

PRODUCTS/OPERATIONS

2000 Sales

	$ mil.	% of total
Rentals & fees	1,460	91
Merchandise sales	81	5
Franchise revenues	58	4
Other	3	—
Total	**1,602**	**100**

Merchandise

Appliances	Home accessories
Computers	Home electronics
Furniture	Internet access

Selected Brand Names

Ashley	La-Z-Boy
Benchcraft	Magnavox
Compaq	Mitsubishi
Dell	Philips
England-Corsair	Sealy
Hewlett-Packard	Sony
JVC	Whirlpool

Store Names
ColorTyme
Rent-A-Center

COMPETITORS

Aaron Rents	First Cash Financial
Best Buy	Services
Bestway	Rainbow Rentals
Brook Furniture	Rent-Way
Cash America	Sears
Circuit City	Wal-Mart
EZCORP	

HISTORICAL FINANCIALS & EMPLOYEES

Nasdaq: RCII FYE: December 31	Annual Growth	12/91	12/92	12/93	12/94	12/95	12/96	12/97	12/98	12/99	12/00
Sales ($ mil.)	67.1%	16	20	53	74	133	238	328	810	1,417	1,602
Net income ($ mil.)	56.8%	2	4	(1)	6	11	18	26	25	59	103
Income as % of sales	—	—	11.4%	20.2%	—	7.4%	8.0%	7.6%	7.9%	3.1%	4.2%	6.4%
Earnings per share ($)	41.6%	—	—	—	—	0.52	0.72	1.03	0.83	1.74	2.96
Stock price - FY high ($)	—	—	—	—	—	18.25	28.75	24.25	32.50	34.25	36.19
Stock price - FY low ($)	—	—	—	—	—	3.34	12.75	11.75	18.00	15.25	13.63
Stock price - FY close ($)	20.2%	—	—	—	—	13.75	14.50	20.50	31.75	19.81	34.50
P/E - high	—	—	—	—	—	35	39	23	39	17	10
P/E - low	—	—	—	—	—	6	17	11	21	7	4
Dividends per share ($)	—	—	—	—	—	0.00	0.00	0.00	0.00	0.00	0.00
Book value per share ($)	44.4%	—	—	—	—	3.80	5.06	6.14	17.21	19.65	23.90
Employees	51.9%	—	—	672	668	1,700	2,250	2,540	10,550	11,000	12,554

STOCK PRICE HISTORY

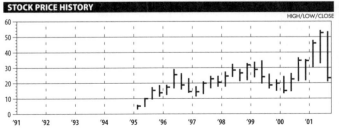

HIGH/LOW/CLOSE

2000 FISCAL YEAR-END

Debt ratio: 48.9%
Return on equity: 39.9%
Cash ($ mil.): 37
Current ratio: 1.99
Long-term debt ($ mil.): 566
No. of shares (mil.): 25
Dividends
   Yield: —
   Payout: —
Market value ($ mil.): 852

RIVIANA FOODS INC.

OVERVIEW

Whether it's short, long, white, brown, or wild, rice is nice. With its Carolina, Mahatma, and Success brands, Riviana Foods is the #1 seller of rice in the US by volume (although it doesn't own the top brand, Uncle Ben's — Mars does). Houston-based Riviana buys rough rice (as well as some rice already milled) from independent suppliers, then processes and packages it for retail sale as plain-old white enriched rice, instant rice, prepared rice mixes, and brown rice. It also supplies food service products, private-label rices for grocery chains, and bulk rice for use in processed foods.

The company has several joint ventures with Riceland Foods. Riviana markets the co-op's consumer rice products, and their Rivland Partnership is the #1 producer of rice flour in the US. In Europe its UK subsidiary, Stevens & Brotherton, markets and distributes branded and private label rice, dried fruit, and other foods. Riviana's Belgian subsidiary N&C Boost operates several joint ventures that mill and market rice products and rice cakes in Belgium and Germany; N&C Boost also sells rice products to major retail and industrial customers throughout Europe.

Riviana's Central American subsidiaries, Alimentos Kern and Pozuelo, make processed fruits and vegetables, cookies, and fruit drinks. In addition to steady growth due to an increased demand for rice, the company has expanded through acquisitions both domestically and abroad.

Chairman Frank Godchaux III and his brother, VC Charles Godchaux, own nearly 45% of Riviana.

HISTORY

Riviana's roots reach back to 1911, when Frank A. Godchaux consolidated 25 rice mills in southwestern Louisiana to form the Louisiana State Rice Milling Company, headquartered in Abbeville, Louisiana. Riviana quickly became one of the largest rice milling companies in the world and a major force in the US rice industry. In 1926 Lousiana State Rice introduced rice for sale in consumer packaging, an industry first. In 1928 the company introduced its Carolina and River brand rice, and in 1932 it launched its best-selling Mahatma brand.

Godchaux's family controlled the company until 1965, when Texas-based River Brand Rice Mills purchased it and changed its name to Riviana Foods. In its early days, Riviana was tied to the commodities market, but it changed its focus to domestic retail in the late 1960s. In 1979 the company moved into Central America when it acquired Pozuelo in Costa Rica and Alimentos Kern de Guatemala. Riviana entered the European market in the 1970s with the acquisitions of N & C Boost (Belgium) in 1973 and Stevens & Brotherton (UK) in 1976.

Godchaux's descendants stuck with the company even when it was sold to a subsidiary of Colgate-Palmolive in 1976. In 1977 Riviana introduced Success boil-in-a-bag rice. Joe Hafner was named CEO in 1984, and Godchaux's grandsons led a management buyout of Riviana two years later.

Riviana and grain cooperative Riceland Foods formed Rivland Partnership in 1989 to produce rice flour. In 1995 Riviana went public.

Riviana teamed up with Tiger Oats to market rice products in South Africa in 1997, and began distributing Riceland's consumer products in the US and the Bahamas the next year.

In 1999 Riviana took over the marketing and distribution of S&W brand rice from longtime customer Tri Valley Growers. That year it also acquired its longtime wild rice supplier, Gourmet House.

Also in 1999 Riviana expanded its product line when it licensed technology to produce crisped rice used in products such as candies, toppings, and health-food bars. The company built a facility in Carlisle, Arkansas, to produce the new product.

Through Belgian subsidiary N&C Boost, Riviana purchased Euryza Reis GmbH, one of Germany's largest rice milling operations, in 2000. Also in 2000 the company launched its corporate Web site. Riviana's sales and profits fell in fiscal 2001, hurt by weakened market conditions. Also in 2001 the company restructured operations at its UK subsidiary, Stevens & Brotherton, after disappointing sales for the year.

OFFICERS

Chairman: Frank A. Godchaux III, age 74
Vice Chairman: Charles R. Godchaux, age 69
President and CEO: Joseph A. Hafner Jr., age 55,
$573,300 pay
EVP and Assistant Secretary: W. David Hanks, age 55,
$125,700 pay
VP, CFO, and Treasurer: E. Wayne Ray Jr., age 59,
$236,600 pay
VP: Alfonso Bocaletti, age 57
VP: Ian W. Boyle, age 64
VP: Bastiaan G. de Zeeuw, age 42
VP, Sales: Thomas M. Forshee, age 54
VP, Marketing: Christopher L. Haines, age 55,
$192,900 pay
VP, Technical Services: Ranvir B. Mohindra, age 51,
$198,550 pay
VP, Industrial Relations: Jack M. Nolingberg, age 67
VP: Paul R. Stevens, age 47
VP, Commodity & International: David E. Van Oss,
age 51
VP, Manufacturing Operations: Richard F. Vincent,
age 63
VP, General Counsel, and Secretary:
Elizabeth B. Woodard, age 47
Personnel Manager: Lucille Pagel
Auditors: Arthur Andersen LLP

LOCATIONS

HQ: 2777 Allen Pkwy., Houston, TX 77019
Phone: 713-529-3251   **Fax:** 713-529-1661

Riviana Foods has facilities in Arkansas, Louisiana,
Minnesota, New Jersey, Tennessee, and Texas. Its
subsidiaries operate in Belgium, Costa Rica, Guatemala,
and the UK.

2001 Sales

	$ mil.	% of total
US	245	64
Central America	84	22
Europe	53	14
Total	**382**	**100**

PRODUCTS/OPERATIONS

Selected Brands
Bosto (rice, Belgium)
Carolina (rice, US)
El Mago (rice, Puerto Rico)
Familia (cookies, Central America)
Gourmet House (wild rice products, US)
Kern's (canned fruit juices and vegetables,
    Central America)
Mahatma (rice, US)
Phoenix (rice, UK)
River (rice, US)
Riviana Pozuelo (crackers, Central America)
S&W (rice, US)
Sello Rojo (rice, Puerto Rico)
Success (rice, US)
WaterMaid (rice, US)

Subsidiaries
Alimentos Kern de Guatemala, SA
Euryza Reis GmbH (Germany)
N&C Boost NV (Belgium)
Pozuelo, SA (Costa Rica)
Stevens & Brotherton Ltd. (UK)

COMPETITORS

American Rice	Kraft Foods
Connell Company	Mars
Goya	Quaker Oats

HISTORICAL FINANCIALS & EMPLOYEES

Nasdaq: RVFD FYE: Sunday nearest June 30	Annual Growth	6/92	6/93	6/94	6/95	6/96	6/97	6/98	6/99	6/00	6/01
Sales ($ mil.)	1.3%	340	379	419	427	441	460	454	463	436	382
Net income ($ mil.)	6.4%	11	13	11	19	18	20	23	24	25	19
Income as % of sales	—	3.2%	3.5%	2.7%	4.5%	4.2%	4.3%	5.0%	5.3%	5.8%	5.0%
Earnings per share ($)	1.7%	—	—	—	1.23	1.16	1.27	1.42	1.60	1.73	1.36
Stock price - FY high ($)	—	—	—	—	14.88	19.00	21.88	25.00	25.75	21.00	19.88
Stock price - FY low ($)	—	—	—	—	11.75	11.63	14.38	17.00	17.63	15.00	15.13
Stock price - FY close ($)	5.3%	—	—	—	13.31	15.13	20.00	23.06	18.75	17.44	18.15
P/E - high	—	—	—	—	12	16	17	17	16	12	15
P/E - low	—	—	—	—	10	10	11	12	11	9	11
Dividends per share ($)	39.9%	—	—	—	0.08	0.35	0.38	0.42	0.47	0.53	0.60
Book value per share ($)	7.6%	—	—	—	6.45	7.34	8.07	8.81	8.90	9.55	10.03
Employees	1.7%	—	2,400	2,645	2,575	2,426	2,751	2,656	2,767	2,784	2,745

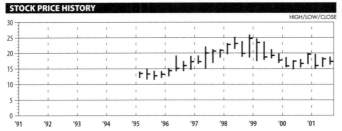

STOCK PRICE HISTORY
HIGH/LOW/CLOSE

2001 FISCAL YEAR-END
Debt ratio: 1.1%
Return on equity: 13.9%
Cash ($ mil.): 15
Current ratio: 2.04
Long-term debt ($ mil.): 2
No. of shares (mil.): 14
Dividends
  Yield: 3.3%
  Payout: 44.1%
Market value ($ mil.): 255

SABRE INC.

OVERVIEW

Sabre has cut away a huge slice of the travel reservations industry. The Fort Worth, Texas-based company is the world's #1 computerized travel reservation system. About 40% of reservations worldwide are made through the Sabre system (Sabre is an acronym for Semi-Automated Business Research Environment). Sabre is used by travel agencies and corporate travel departments to book airline tickets and rental car and hotel reservations. Individual consumers can use Sabre's 70%-owned Travelocity.com, the #1 online travel site.

Travelocity merged with Preview Travel in 2000 as part of Sabre's battle with Microsoft's Expedia and others for control of the online travel market. Sabre also bought Internet travel marketplace GetThere.

While its travel reservation services generate 60% of the company's revenue, Sabre engaged in other activities such as providing information technology services to numerous clients (AeroMexico, Air India, Gulf Air), but the company sold those operations to EDS in 2001.

HISTORY

The original reservation system of American Airlines, inaugurated during the 1930s, used a telephone-based "request and reply" system. Agents would phone a central office where operators kept track of flight seating information by making pencil marks on color-coded cards held in revolving trays.

In 1946 American developed the industry's first electromechanical reservation recording device, which was dubbed the Availability Reservisor. It used basic computer technology to track flights and seating. In 1952 American added memory and mathematical capabilities to the Reservisor to create the Magnetronic Reservisor. With the new machine, agents had immediate access to seating information and could use the computer to sell tickets and cancel reservations.

The next year American president C. R. Smith met IBM senior sales representative Blair Smith on a flight from Los Angeles to New York. The chance encounter sparked collaboration by the two companies that resulted in the SABRE system. The first system was installed in 1963 and could process 84,000 calls each day. By 1964 SABRE reached coast-to-coast and included connections in Canada and Mexico.

The first SABRE terminal was installed in a travel agency in 1976. Initially the system booked American flights, but soon other services joined the network, with each airline, hotel, and car rental agency paying AMR (the holding company for American Airlines formed in 1982) a percentage for each booking. Services grew to include flowers and event tickets. The company's easySABRE PC-based consumer service debuted in 1985.

In 1993 The SABRE Group became a separate division of AMR. SABRE in 1996 made its global data network available to SITA, operator of a private international telecommunications

network for airlines. The company also launched online consumer reservations service Travelocity that year. AMR spun off its SABRE unit as a public company (THE SABRE Group Holdings) in 1996. SABRE expanded into the Asia/Pacific region in 1998 with a joint venture with Singapore-based reservation systems provider ABACUS International Holdings. A nearly six-hour SABRE system outage in 1998 delayed 200 flights.

The company in 1999 executed a restructuring plan to unify a number of functions (sales, marketing, technology) for its IT services and electronic travel activities. The company also shortened its moniker to Sabre Inc. (and ceased styling it in all capitals). CEO Michael Durham resigned that year amid tensions between Sabre and AMR. He was replaced by Southwestern Bell executive William Hannigan.

Early in 2000 AMR completed the spinoff of its interest in Sabre to AMR shareholders. Also that year the company partnered with Ariba to create Sabre e-Marketplace, a business-to-business Internet marketplace for the travel industry; another e-marketplace for the aerospace industry resulted from a partnership with Skyfish.com. Sabre also merged Travelocity with competitor Preview Travel. Later that year the company split into separate business units to focus on three activities: travel marketing, technology solutions and outsourcing, and investing in emerging businesses. It also acquired Internet travel marketplace GetThere. Sabre announced in 2000 that it would lay off about 1,200 employees as part of a cost-cutting initiative.

In 2001 Sabre sold its airline and IT infrastructure outsourcing business to EDS.

OFFICERS

Chairman, President, and CEO; Chairman, Travelocity.com: William Hannigan, $1,200,000 pay
President, Emerging Business: Thomas Klein
EVP and President, Travel Marketing and Distribution: Eric J. Speck, age 44, $450,313 pay
EVP, CFO, and Treasurer: Jeffery M. Jackson, age 44, $496,146 pay
EVP and General Counsel: David A. Schwarte, age 50
SVP and Chief Information Officer: Carol A. Kelly
SVP and Chief of Staff: Joan C. Kuehl
SVP and General Manager, Electronic Travel Distribution: John S. Stow
SVP, Human Resources: Michael E. Haefner
SVP Sales, Account Management, and Customer Care: Joseph I. Saliba, $361,153 pay
VP, e-commerce: Michael Sites
Chairman, President, and CEO, GetThere: Gadi Maier
President and CEO, Travelocity.com: Terrell B. Jones, $468,750 pay
Chief Technology Officer: R. Craig Murphy
Chief Marketing Officer: Sam Gilliland
Corporate Secretary: James F. Brashear
Auditors: Ernst & Young LLP

LOCATIONS

HQ: 4255 Amon Carter Blvd., Fort Worth, TX 76155
Phone: 817-963-6400   **Fax:** 817-931-5582
Web: www.sabre.com

Sabre has operations in 45 countries.

2000 Sales

	$ mil.	% of total
US	2,037	78
Other countries	580	22
Total	**2,617**	**100**

PRODUCTS/OPERATIONS

2000 Sales

	$ mil.	% of total
Travel marketing & distribution	1,626	60
Outsourcing & software	858	32
Travelocity.com	192	7
GetThere	12	1
Adjustments	(71)	—
Total	**2,617**	**100**

Selected Travel Reservations Products and Services

GetThere (Internet travel marketplace)
Planet Sabre (customizable travel booking tool for travel agencies)
Sabre Business Travel Solutions (corporate travel management software)
Travelocity (70%, online travel reservation service for individual consumers)
Turbo Sabre (advanced travel booking tool for travel agencies)
Virtually There destination guide
Virtually There.com (personalized travel site)

COMPETITORS

Amadeus
American Express
Carlson
Cheap Tickets
Expedia
Galileo International
Lowestfare.com
Pegasus Solutions
priceline.com
Worldspan
XTRA On-Line

HISTORICAL FINANCIALS & EMPLOYEES

NYSE: TSG FYE: December 31	Annual Growth	12/91	12/92	12/93	12/94	12/95	12/96	12/97	12/98	12/99	12/00
Sales ($ mil.)	10.1%	1,097	1,174	1,258	1,407	1,530	1,622	1,784	2,306	2,435	2,617
Net income ($ mil.)	0.7%	135	32	100	197	226	187	200	232	332	144
Income as % of sales	—	12.3%	2.8%	7.9%	14.0%	14.8%	11.5%	11.2%	10.1%	13.6%	5.5%
Earnings per share ($)	(6.1%)	—	—	—	—	—	1.43	1.53	1.78	2.54	1.11
Stock price - FY high ($)	—	—	—	—	—	—	33.38	37.00	44.88	72.00	53.50
Stock price - FY low ($)	—	—	—	—	—	—	25.63	23.25	23.00	38.25	22.31
Stock price - FY close ($)	11.5%	—	—	—	—	—	27.88	28.88	44.50	51.25	43.13
P/E - high	—	—	—	—	—	—	23	24	25	28	48
P/E - low	—	—	—	—	—	—	18	15	13	15	20
Dividends per share ($)	—	—	—	—	—	—	0.00	0.00	0.00	0.00	0.00
Book value per share ($)	8.7%	—	—	—	—	—	4.36	5.79	7.35	9.72	6.08
Employees	6.1%	—	—	—	—	—	7,900	8,500	10,800	10,500	10,000

STOCK PRICE HISTORY

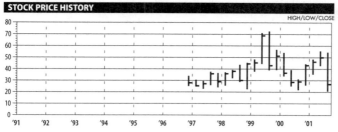

HIGH/LOW/CLOSE

2000 FISCAL YEAR-END

Debt ratio: 15.9%
Return on equity: 14.0%
Cash ($ mil.): 8
Current ratio: 0.55
Long-term debt ($ mil.): 149
No. of shares (mil.): 130
Dividends
  Yield: —
  Payout: —
Market value ($ mil.): 5,607

SBC COMMUNICATIONS INC.

OVERVIEW

The Baby Bell from the Lone Star State is no longer king of the hill, but it still qualifies as telecommunications royalty. San Antonio-based SBC Communications is the #2 local-service phone company in the US, having been dethroned in 2000 by Verizon Communications.

SBC's realm encompasses a host of well-known subsidiaries, including Ameritech, Nevada Bell, Pacific Bell, SNET, and Southwestern Bell. With 61 million network access lines, SBC operates a local phone empire that includes 13 US states (California, Illinois, and Texas account for 60% of its lines), and it is planning to become a competitive local-exchange carrier in 30 new US markets. SBC provides long-distance service in Connecticut, Kansas, Oklahoma, and Texas.

In the court of wireless carriers, SBC has combined its US mobile phone operations with those of BellSouth to form Cingular Wireless, the #2 mobile phone operator in the US, behind Verizon Wireless. The joint venture, 60%-owned by SBC, has more than 21 million customers in 38 states.

However, SBC sees its biggest growth opportunity in data communications. The company is spending a princely sum of $6 billion in an effort to have 80% of its wireline customers broadband-ready in three years, and it has made a deal with Covad Communications to resell Covad digital subscriber line (DSL) connections. SBC's consumer and small-business Internet access operations have been folded into 43%-owned Prodigy Communications.

SBC also has telecom stakes in more than 20 countries outside the US.

HISTORY

In 1878 a dozen customers signed up for the first telephone exchange in St. Louis (later Bell Telephone Company of Missouri). That exchange and the Missouri and Kansas Telephone Company later merged into Southwestern Bell, which became a regional arm of the AT&T monopoly in 1917.

AT&T was broken up in 1984, and Southwestern Bell emerged as a regional Bell operating company (RBOC) with local service rights in five states, a cellular company, a directory business, and a stake in R&D arm Bellcore (later sold). In 1987 the company bought paging and cellular franchises from Metromedia.

Edward Whitacre, a Texan who had worked his way from phone technician to executive at Southwestern Bell, became CEO in 1990. That year the RBOC joined with France Telecom and Mexican conglomerate Grupo Carso to purchase 20% of Teléfonos de México (Telmex), the former state monopoly.

Renamed SBC Communications in 1994, the company hired lobbyists the next year to persuade the Texas Legislature to pass a bill that would deter local phone competitors. It worked: New entrants had to build a phone network to serve every house in a 27-mile square.

The federal Telecommunications Act passed in 1996, and in early 1997 SBC acquired Pacific Telesis, the parent of Pacific Bell and Nevada Bell. That year the FCC denied SBC's request to enter Oklahoma's long-distance market. Undeterred, SBC launched a legal assault on the Telecom Act itself, which proved to be unsuccessful.

SBC bought Southern New England Telecommunications (SNET) in 1998, gaining a foothold on the East Coast. The next year the company bought Comcast's cellular operations and took a minority stake in Williams Communications — the first significant investment in a long-distance carrier by a Baby Bell.

SBC then completed the $62 billion purchase of Ameritech. The acquisition extended SBC's local access dominance into five midwestern states, but about half of Ameritech's wireless business was sold as a condition of the deal. SBC also agreed to provide competitive local phone service in 30 cities outside its home territory by 2002 to win regulatory approval. It then announced plans to spend $6 billion over three years to make its networks capable of delivering high-speed DSL service to 80% of its customers.

In 2000 SBC combined its US wireless operations with those of BellSouth to form Cingular Wireless, a carrier with operations in 38 US states. SBC also combined its consumer and small-business Internet access operations with those of Prodigy Communications, gaining an initial 40% stake in Prodigy.

That year the FCC approved SBC's application to sell long-distance service in Texas, and the company racked up more than a million long-distance customers in less than six months. In 2001 SBC won FCC approval to offer long-distance in Kansas and Oklahoma. Also that year the company was fined by the FCC — it paid $69 million between December 2000 and August 2001 — for failing to meet standards for opening its local networks to competitors.

OFFICERS

Chairman and CEO: Edward E. Whitacre Jr., age 59, $6,386,667 pay
SEVP and CFO: Donald E. Kiernan, age 60, $1,166,167 pay
SEVP and General Counsel: James D. Ellis, age 57, $1,166,167 pay
SEVP, Corporate Communications: Linda S. Mills, age 49
SEVP, Corporate Development: James S. Kahan, age 53
SEVP, External Affairs: Cassandra C. Carr, age 56
SEVP, Human Resources: Karen E. Jennings, age 50
SEVP, Services: Ross K. Ireland, age 54
EVP and Chief Information Officer: Edward L. Glotzbach, age 52
SVP and General Counsel, Human Resources: Michael A. Rodriguez, age 50
SVP, Consumer Marketing: Randall L. Stephenson, age 40
SVP, Corporate Finance: Robert B. Pickering, age 42
SVP, HR Services: Margaret M. Cerrudo, age 52
Auditors: Ernst & Young LLP

LOCATIONS

HQ: 175 E. Houston, San Antonio, TX 78205
Phone: 210-821-4105   **Fax:** 210-351-2071
Web: www.sbc.com

SBC Communications provides incumbent local phone services in Arkansas, California, Connecticut, Illinois, Indiana, Kansas, Michigan, Missouri, Nevada, Ohio, Oklahoma, Texas, and Wisconsin. The company offers long-distance services in Connecticut, Kansas, Oklahoma, and Texas, and has holdings in telecom operations in more than 20 countries in Africa, Asia, Europe, Latin America, the Middle East, and North America.

PRODUCTS/OPERATIONS

2000 Sales

	$ mil.	% of total
Wireline	39,789	77
Wireless	7,941	15
Directory	4,251	8
International	320	—
Other	1,034	—
Adjustments	(1,859)	—
Total	**51,476**	**100**

Selected Subsidiaries and Affiliates
Ameritech Corporation (incumbent local-exchange carrier)
Bell Canada (20%, telecommunications provider)
Cingular Wireless (60%, joint venture with BellSouth)
Pacific Telesis Group (Pacific Bell, incumbent local-exchange carrier)
Nevada Bell (incumbent local-exchange carrier)
Pacific Bell (incumbent local-exchange carrier)
Prodigy Communications (43%, Internet access)
Southern New England Telecommunications Corporation (SNET, incumbent local-exchange carrier)
Southwestern Bell Telephone Company (incumbent local-exchange carrier)
Sterling Commerce, Inc. (e-business integrations)

COMPETITORS

ALLTEL	Intermedia	Telephone &
AT&T	Communications	Data Systems
BellSouth	McLeodUSA	Time Warner
Birch	Nextel	Telecom
Broadwing	Qwest	United States
CenturyTel	Sprint FON	Cellular
France Telecom	Telefónica	Verizon
		WorldCom

HISTORICAL FINANCIALS & EMPLOYEES

NYSE: SBC FYE: December 31	Annual Growth	12/91	12/92	12/93	12/94	12/95	12/96	12/97	12/98	12/99	12/00
Sales ($ mil.)	20.9%	9,332	10,015	10,690	11,619	12,670	13,898	24,856	28,777	49,489	51,476
Net income ($ mil.)	24.9%	1,076	1,302	(845)	1,649	(930)	2,101	1,474	4,023	8,159	7,967
Income as % of sales	—	11.5%	13.0%	—	14.2%	—	15.1%	5.9%	14.0%	16.5%	15.5%
Earnings per share ($)	11.1%	0.90	1.09	(1.37)	1.53	(1.66)	1.77	0.80	2.06	2.36	2.32
Stock price - FY high ($)	—	16.47	18.69	23.50	22.19	29.25	30.13	38.06	54.88	59.94	59.00
Stock price - FY low ($)	—	12.25	14.16	17.09	18.38	19.81	23.00	24.63	35.00	44.06	34.81
Stock price - FY close ($)	12.8%	16.16	18.50	20.75	20.19	28.63	25.94	36.63	53.63	48.75	47.75
P/E - high	—	17	17	—	15	—	17	47	26	31	25
P/E - low	—	13	13	—	12	—	13	30	17	23	15
Dividends per share ($)	4.0%	0.71	0.73	0.75	0.78	0.82	0.85	0.89	0.69	0.97	1.01
Book value per share ($)	2.2%	7.38	7.76	6.34	6.86	5.13	5.70	5.38	6.52	7.87	8.99
Employees	15.0%	61,218	59,500	58,400	58,750	59,300	61,450	118,340	129,850	204,530	215,088

STOCK PRICE HISTORY

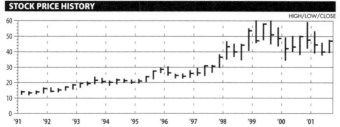

HIGH/LOW/CLOSE

2000 FISCAL YEAR-END

Debt ratio: 33.7%
Return on equity: 27.9%
Cash ($ mil.): 643
Current ratio: 0.76
Long-term debt ($ mil.): 15,492
No. of shares (mil.): 3,387
Dividends
  Yield: 2.1%
  Payout: 43.5%
Market value ($ mil.): 161,715

SERVICE CORPORATION

OVERVIEW

The services of Service Corporation International (SCI) are to die for. The Houston-based company is the world's #1 operator of funeral homes, cemeteries, and crematoria. SCI owns about 4,400 such facilities, primarily in North America, Australia, France, and the UK.

SCI provides such "death services" as embalmment, burial, and cremation. It sells caskets, burial vaults, cremation receptacles, flowers, burial garments, and prearranged funeral services. (Call it unburied treasure: SCI has some $4 billion worth of unperformed funeral contracts.)

SCI operates clusters of homes in the same area, allowing them to share personnel, vehicles, and preparation services, thereby lowering operating costs. The company grows mainly through acquisitions, though it maintains the local identity of each home, allowing it to handle services for different ethnic and religious groups. In Manhattan, for example, SCI owns the top Christian funeral home, Campbell, as well as the leading Jewish home, Riverside.

There are more octogenarians than ever before, and the baby boomers aren't getting any younger, so SCI is banking on the long-term prospects of the funeral services industry. But even though SCI will most likely outlive critics who blame it for the rising costs of funerals, the company has nonetheless taken offense. It even sued — unsuccessfully — an author who repeated SCI founder Robert Waltrip's 1986 comment that the company wanted to be the "the True Value hardware of the funeral service industry."

SCI has been selling operations, including a French insurance subsidiary and other funeral locations and cemeteries, to reduce debt.

HISTORY

When Robert Waltrip was just 20, in the early 1950s, he inherited Houston's Heights Funeral Home, which his father and aunt had founded in 1926. Waltrip acquired several other funeral homes, modeling his operations on other popular service chains such as Holiday Inn and McDonald's. In 1962 Waltrip incorporated Service Corporation International (SCI) and began expanding across the country. SCI went public in 1969.

SCI acquired Kinney Services, which operated 28 funeral homes in New York City and Miami, from Warner Communications in 1971. SCI was the US's largest provider of funeral services by 1975. However, that year the FTC accused the company of overcharging customers for flowers, cremation, and other services. SCI was ordered to refund overcharges it made to cremation customers (it had charged them for caskets), and the FTC issued industry guidelines to prevent deceptive practices.

Two years later SCI began offering advance sales of funeral services so clients could avoid the effects of inflation by reserving future services and caskets at current prices. While it was barred from using the prepaid funds until funerals were performed, some states allowed the use of investment profits from those funds.

The company moved into flower shops in 1982, and two years later SCI bought Amedco, a top casket maker and a major supplier of embalming fluid, burial clothing, and mortuary furniture. (Amedco was later sold.)

SCI spun off 71 rural funeral homes as Equity Corporation International (ECI) in 1991.

The company continued its rapid pace of acquisitions, buying 342 homes and 57 cemeteries from 1991 to 1993. It made its first acquisition outside North America in 1993 with the purchase of Pine Grove Funeral Group, the largest funeral and cremations provider in Australia. SCI entered the European market by acquiring Great Southern Group and Plantsbrook of the UK in 1994, as well as the funeral operations of Lyonnaise des Eaux of France a year later. In 1996 SCI sold its remaining 40% stake in ECI.

In 1997 and 1998 SCI swallowed up 602 funeral homes, 98 cemeteries, and 37 crematoria. SCI bought American Annuity Group's prearranged funeral services division for $164 million in 1998. In early 1999 it bought back all of Equity Corporation International (about 440 US funeral homes and cemeteries) for $867 million.

With SCI's earnings slumping — which the company attributed in part to declining mortality rates — president and COO William Heiligbrodt resigned in 1999. Also that year SCI deep-sixed about 2,000 jobs and consolidated its funeral home and cemetery groups in the US down to 87 (from 200). The company also began offering a low-price service called the Dignity Memorial Plan, which offers customers inexpensive funeral packages.

To help pay down its debt, SCI sold its French insurance subsidiary and its Northern Irish funeral operations. In January 2001 the company said it would further attempt to combat debt through the sale of about 400 funeral locations and more than 100 cemeteries.

OFFICERS

Chairman and CEO: R. L. Waltrip, age 70,
$1,713,500 pay
Vice Chairman: B. D. Hunter, age 70, $731,000 pay
President and COO: Jerald L. Pullins, age 59,
$892,500 pay
SVP and CFO: Jeffrey E. Curtiss, age 52, $680,000 pay
SVP, General Counsel, and Secretary: James M. Shelger,
age 51, $595,000 pay
VP and CIO: Stephen J. Uthoff, age 49
VP, Corporate Development: Michael R. Webb, age 43
VP and Controller: W. Cardon Gerner, age 46
VP, International Operations: Thomas L. Ryan, age 35
**VP, Investor Relations and Assistant Corporate
  Controller:** Eric D. Tanzberger, age 32
VP, Operational Management Systems:
  Lowell A. Kirkpatrick Jr., age 42
VP, North American Cemetery Operations:
  J. Daniel Garrison, age 49
VP, North American Funeral Operations:
  Stephen M. Mack, age 49
VP, Prearranged Sales: W. Mark Hamilton, age 36
VP and Treasurer: Frank T. Hundley, age 41
Director, Human Resources: Helen Dugand
Auditors: PricewaterhouseCoopers LLP

LOCATIONS

HQ: Service Corporation International
  1929 Allen Pkwy., Houston, TX 77019
Phone: 713-522-5141   **Fax:** 713-525-5586
Web: www.sci-corp.com

Service Corporation International operates in 18
countries on five continents.

2000 Sales

	$ mil.	% of total
North America	1,737	68
Europe	686	27
Other regions	142	5
Total	**2,565**	**100**

PRODUCTS/OPERATIONS

2000 Sales & Gross Profit

	$ mil.	% of total
Funeral	1,912	75
Cemetery	641	25
Financial services	12	—
Total	**2,565**	**100**

Facilities	Mausoleum spaces
Cemeteries	Stone and bronze
Crematoria	memorials
Flower shops	
Funeral homes	**Services**
	Cremation
Merchandise	Development loans
Burial garments	Floral arrangements
Burial vaults	Interment
Caskets	Perpetual care
Coffins	Prearranged funeral
Cremation receptacles	services
Flowers	Transportation
Lawn crypts	

COMPETITORS

Carriage Services, Inc.
Hillenbrand
Loewen
Neptune Society
Stewart Enterprises
York Group

HISTORICAL FINANCIALS & EMPLOYEES

NYSE: SRV FYE: December 31	Annual Growth	12/91	12/92	12/93	12/94	12/95	12/96	12/97	12/98	12/99	12/00
Sales ($ mil.)	16.6%	643	773	899	1,117	1,652	2,294	2,468	2,875	3,322	2,565
Net income ($ mil.)	—	73	87	101	131	184	265	334	342	(32)	(1,343)
Income as % of sales	—	11.4%	11.2%	11.2%	11.7%	11.1%	11.6%	13.5%	11.9%	—	—
Earnings per share ($)	—	0.52	0.54	0.58	0.71	0.86	1.08	1.31	1.31	(0.10)	(4.93)
Stock price - FY high ($)	—	9.17	9.38	13.19	14.00	22.00	31.75	38.00	47.13	38.88	7.44
Stock price - FY low ($)	—	6.75	7.84	8.94	11.25	13.13	19.44	26.88	29.50	6.19	1.69
Stock price - FY close ($)	(16.6%)	9.00	9.13	13.13	13.88	22.00	28.00	36.75	38.06	6.94	1.75
P/E - high	—	18	16	21	18	24	28	25	35	—	—
P/E - low	—	13	14	14	15	14	17	18	22	—	—
Dividends per share ($)	—	0.19	0.20	0.20	0.21	0.22	0.24	0.29	0.35	0.36	0.00
Book value per share ($)	6.7%	4.05	4.44	5.21	6.24	9.16	9.46	10.78	12.17	12.85	7.25
Employees	10.9%	11,577	11,818	12,716	18,756	19,824	22,607	24,072	27,618	30,693	29,326

STOCK PRICE HISTORY

HIGH/LOW/CLOSE

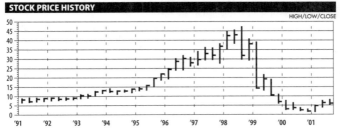

2000 FISCAL YEAR-END

Debt ratio: 61.2%
Return on equity: —
Cash ($ mil.): 48
Current ratio: 1.33
Long-term debt ($ mil.): 3,115
No. of shares (mil.): 273
Dividends
  Yield: —
  Payout: —
Market value ($ mil.): 477

SHELL OIL COMPANY

OVERVIEW

To avoid becoming a shell of its former self, Shell Oil is shelling out $1.3 billion a year to find and develop new oil and gas properties, mainly in the deepwater Gulf of Mexico. The Houston-based company, with proved reserves of 1.2 billion barrels of oil and 1.9 trillion cu. ft. of natural gas, is a member of the Royal Dutch/Shell Group, the world's second-largest oil and gas entity behind Exxon Mobil. Shell Oil is owned by Shell Petroleum, which in turn is owned by Royal Dutch Petroleum (60%) and "Shell" Transport and Trading (40%).

Shell produces and markets oil, natural gas, and chemical products. Most of its US oil production takes place off the California coast and in the Gulf; its natural gas production is focused in South Texas and along the Gulf Coast.

Motiva, Shell's 39%-owned venture with Texaco and Saudi Aramco, combines much of the companies' US refining and marketing (or downstream) operations along the Gulf Coast and the East Coast. Shell and Texaco also jointly operate downstream businesses in the West and Midwest as Equilon (56%-owned by Shell). Together Motiva and Equilon have 22,000 Shell- and Texaco-branded gas stations, eight refineries, more than 100 product terminals, and interests in more than 29,000 miles of pipelines. Shell partners with Exxon Mobil in Aera Energy, a California exploration and production joint venture.

Shell is ramping up its wholesale marketing of electricity through Coral Energy and is selling off noncore operations of Shell Chemical.

HISTORY

The Royal Dutch/Shell Group began importing gasoline from Sumatra to the US in 1912 to take advantage of the expanding automobile industry and the breakup of Standard Oil. That year it formed American Gasoline in Seattle and Roxana Petroleum in Oklahoma. Refineries were established in New Orleans in 1916 and Wood River, Illinois, in 1918.

In 1922 Royal Dutch/Shell placed all of its US operations into a 65%-owned holding company, Shell Union Oil, and soon Shell products were available nationwide. Shell Oil took its present name in 1949.

Shell moved to Houston in 1970. It substantially boosted its oil reserves in 1979 by acquiring Belridge Oil, and was itself fully acquired by Royal Dutch/Shell in 1985. However, unhappy shareholders sued, claiming that Shell's assets were undervalued in the deal. (In 1990 claimants were awarded $110 million.)

When other oil companies abandoned the Gulf of Mexico, finding it unproductive, Shell focused on exploration there. In 1989 it hit pay dirt by discovering the massive Mars field.

Stricter US environmental regulations caused Shell to reduce US activities in the 1990s and look overseas for new sources of oil. The company also exchanged its coal mining unit for a 25% stake in the buyer, Zeigler Coal, in 1992 (sold in 1994).

Though part of the Royal Dutch/Shell Group, Shell had traditionally operated as an independent company. In 1997, like other Royal Dutch/Shell companies, it began integrating its operations with the rest of the group. Meanwhile, it partnered with rivals in search of cost efficiencies. Shell first hooked up with Amoco (which later merged with BP) to form Altura Energy, an exploration and production venture in the Permian Basin, then with Mobil (later acquired by Exxon) to form the Aera venture in California.

When competition at the US gas pumps grew fiercer, in 1998 Shell and Texaco formed Equilon, a venture that combined their West and Midwest refining and (downstream) marketing activities; later Shell, Texaco, and Saudi Aramco formed Motiva to merge downstream businesses on the East Coast and Gulf Coast.

In 1998 Shell bought Tejas Gas (renamed Tejas Energy). Tejas, which gathered, transported, and stored natural gas, had been the company's partner in gas marketing venture Coral Energy. Shell also formed Shell Energy Services to sell natural gas and electricity in deregulated markets.

But as its parent group cut costs, Shell was forced to clean house in 1999, selling Tejas' Oklahoma operations and $745 million of Gulf oil and gas fields to Apache. It also cut Gulf of Mexico production by 10%. On the bright side, the company set a record for deepwater drilling — 4,000 feet below sea level — when its Ursa tension-leg platform began production in the Gulf of Mexico.

In 2000 Shell and BP sold Altura Energy to Occidental Petroleum for $3.6 billion. Shell also agreed to sell its Wood River, Illinois, refinery to Tosco to cut costs. The next year parent Royal Dutch/Shell involved the company in a hostile bid to buy Denver-based natural gas producer Barrett Resources, but the offer was withdrawn when Barrett accepted a higher bid from Williams.

OFFICERS

Chairman, President, and CEO: Steven L. Miller
**President and CEO, Shell Chemical Company (USA);
EVP, Americas, Shell Chemicals, Ltd.:**
Jerry L. Golden
**President and CEO, Shell Exploration & Production
Company:** Raoul Restucci
**VP, Business Development and Technology, Shell
Exploration & Production Company:**
Gaurdie E. Banister
VP, Corporate Affairs: Susan M. Borches
VP, Finance and CFO: Nick J. Caruso
VP, Government Affairs: S. E. Ward
VP, Human Resources: David Ohle
VP, and General Tax Counsel: Steven C. Stryker
VP, General Counsel, and Secretary:
Catherine A. Lamboley
President, Shell Gas Transmission: Doug Krenz
Treasurer: Ronald W. Leftwich
Controller and General Auditor: Greg R. Hullinger
Auditors: PricewaterhouseCoopers LLP

LOCATIONS

HQ: 1 Shell Plaza, Houston, TX 77002
Phone: 713-241-6161   **Fax:** 713-241-4044
Web: www.shellus.com

In the US, Shell Oil explores and produces mainly in the
Gulf of Mexico, off the coast of California, and in
Louisiana, Michigan, and Texas.

PRODUCTS/OPERATIONS

Major Operations

Chemicals
Shell Chemical Company

Downstream Gas and Power Generation
Coral Energy, L.P.
InterGen N.V. (joint venture with Bechtel)
Shell Energy Services Co.

Exploration and Production
Aera Energy LLC (52%)
Shell Exploration & Production Company

Oil Products
Deer Park Refining Limited Partnership (50%)
Equilon Enterprises LLC (56%)
Equiva Services LLC
Equiva Trading Company
Motiva Enterprises LLC (39%)
Shell Global Accounts
Shell Global Solutions
Shell Hydrogen U.S.
Shell Industrial Services

COMPETITORS

7-Eleven	Lyondell Chemical
Amerada Hess	Occidental
Ashland	PDVSA
BP	PEMEX
Chevron	PETROBRAS
Conoco	Phillips Petroleum
Dow Chemical	Racetrac Petroleum
DuPont	Sunoco
Enron	Texaco
Exxon Mobil	TOTAL FINA ELF
Huntsman	Ultramar Diamond
Imperial Oil	Shamrock
Kerr-McGee	Unocal
Koch	USX-Marathon

HISTORICAL FINANCIALS & EMPLOYEES

Subsidiary FYE: December 31	Annual Growth	12/91	12/92	12/93	12/94	12/95	12/96	12/97	12/98	12/99	12/00
Sales ($ mil.)	3.2%	22,411	21,702	21,092	21,581	24,650	29,151	28,959	15,451	19,277	29,671
Net income ($ mil.)	74.5%	20	445	781	508	1,520	2,021	2,104	(1,727)	1,903	3,007
Income as % of sales	—	0.1%	2.1%	3.7%	2.4%	6.2%	6.9%	7.3%	—	9.9%	10.1%
Employees	(10.2%)	29,437	25,308	22,212	21,496	21,050	20,463	19,904	19,800	12,750	11,140

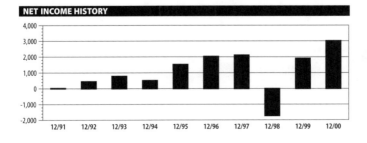

NET INCOME HISTORY

SOUTHERN UNION COMPANY

OVERVIEW

Southern Union has taken its hospitality north. The Austin, Texas-based utility holding company distributes natural gas to some 1.5 million customers in Florida, Massachusetts, Missouri, Pennsylvania, Rhode Island, Texas, and Mexico. Its gas utilities include Atlantic Utilities (doing business as South Florida Natural Gas, or SFNG), Missouri Gas Energy, PG Energy, and Southern Union Gas. It has a 43% stake in a gas distributor that serves 25,000 customers in Piedras Negras, Mexico.

The company's three propane units (Atlantic Gas, SUPro Energy, and PG Energy Services) distribute propane in Florida, New Mexico, Pennsylvania, and Texas. Additionally, Southern Union owns gas transmission pipelines in Texas and Mexico, sells gas appliances, and provides consulting services.

Deregulation in the energy industry has opened up new opportunities for Southern Union. Its Mercado Gas Services markets natural gas to commercial and industrial customers throughout North America. Southern Union is also involved in generating and selling electrical power in the northeastern US. The company is investing in microturbines, which run on natural gas, propane, and other fuels. Southern Union has also jumped on the broadband bandwagon by investing in several high-tech companies.

Southern Union has begun divesting some noncore assets to focus on natural gas distribution and electricity generation operations.

Chairman and CEO George Lindemann and his family own 28% of Southern Union.

HISTORY

Southern Union's earliest predecessor was the Wink Gas Co., formed in 1929 in Wink, Texas, during the West Texas oil boom. Although its first customer had to lay his own pipeline, the company grew, and in 1932 it became the Southern Union Company. In 1949 Southern Union won the Austin gas franchise by merging with Texas Public Service Co.

The energy crisis of the 1970s led Southern Union to diversify into unrelated areas (such as real estate) that turned sour by the 1980s. Shortly after the natural gas industry was deregulated in the 1980s, the company formed Mercado Gas Services in 1986 to market gas to commercial and industrial customers.

Four years later New York entrepreneur George Lindemann acquired Southern Union and installed Peter Kelley as president. Kelley wasted no time in shifting the corporate culture from a lethargic, top-heavy bureaucracy to an efficient sales organization.

Southern Union bought several Texas natural gas companies in 1993, and nearly doubled its customer base in 1994 with the purchase of Gas Service of Kansas City (now Missouri Gas Energy, or MGE). Moving into Florida in 1997, Southern Union acquired gas distributor Atlantic Utilities.

Continuing to look for acquisitions, Southern Union submitted a bid in 1999 to buy Las Vegas-based Southwest Gas, which instead accepted a lower offer from ONEOK. Southern Union sued Southwest Gas to block the ONEOK deal, and ONEOK terminated the agreement in 2000.

Putting aside the Southwest Gas controversy, Southern Union decided to move north in 1999 when it bought natural gas distributor Pennsylvania Enterprises (150,000 customers). The next year Southern Union gained nearly 300,000 customers in New England by buying two Rhode Island gas utilities, Valley Resources and Providence Energy, and Massachusetts-based Fall River Gas.

Kelley resigned for health reasons in 2001, and Thomas Karam moved from the company's Pennsylvania operations to replace him. In a cost-cutting effort, in 2001 Southern Union offered early retirement programs to 400 employees and laid off 48 workers in a reorganization of corporate management functions.

The company also began selling noncore assets, including the gas marketing business of PG Energy Services, its Keystone Pipeline Services unit, two small propane/heating oil distribution units, and a plumbing and heating services unit (Morris Merchants).

In late 2001 Southern Union said it would shift some of its headquarter operations from Austin to Wilkes-Barre, Pennsylvania, creating essentially two headquarters: one in Texas and one in Pennsylvania. As part of that move the company sold its Austin headquarters building.

Chairman Emeritus: Frank W. Denius, age 76
Chairman and CEO: George L. Lindemann, age 65,
$310,619 pay
Vice Chairman and Assistant Secretary:
John E. Brennan, age 55
President, COO, and Director: Thomas F. Karam,
age 42, $1,067,576 pay
EVP and CFO: David J. Kvapil, age 46
EVP, Administration; General Counsel; and Secretary:
Dennis K. Morgan, age 53, $258,908 pay
EVP, Utility Operations: David W. Stevens, age 42,
$385,174 pay
SVP, Human Resources: Nancy M. Capezzuti
President and COO, New England Division:
Thomas B. Robillard, age 56
President and COO, PG Energy: Harry E. Dowling,
age 52
President, Missouri Gas Energy: Steven W. Cattron
Auditors: PricewaterhouseCoopers LLP

LOCATIONS

HQ: 504 Lavaca St., Ste. 800, Austin, TX 78701
Phone: 512-477-5852   **Fax:** 512-370-8380
Web: www.southernunionco.com

2001 Customers

	% of total
Texas	35
Missouri	32
Massachusetts & Rhode Island	19
Pennsylvania	11
Other areas	3
Total	**100**

PRODUCTS/OPERATIONS

Selected Subsidiaries
Alternate Energy Corporation (energy consulting)
Atlantic Gas Corporation (propane sales)
Atlantic Utilities (utility holding company)
  South Florida Natural Gas (SFNG, natural gas utility)
Energía Estrella del Sur, S.A. de C.V. (gas distribution,
  Mexico)
Lavaca Realty Company (real estate investment)
Mercado Gas Services Inc. (natural gas marketing)
Missouri Gas Energy (natural gas utility)
Norteño Pipeline Company (international pipelines)
PEI Power Corporation (cogeneration plant)
PG Energy (natural gas utility)
PG Energy Services (propane sales, energy products,
  and services)
Southern Transmission Company (intrastate pipelines)
Southern Union Energy International, Inc.
  (overseas energy projects)
Southern Union Gas (natural gas utility)
Southern Union International Investments, Inc.
  (overseas energy projects)

COMPETITORS

Ameren	Florida Public Utilities
AmeriGas Partners	Great Plains Energy
Atmos Energy	Laclede Group
Cap Rock Energy	National Fuel Gas
Chesapeake Utilities	NiSource
Cornerstone Propane	NUI
Dominion	ONEOK
El Paso Electric	Reliant Energy
Empire District Electric	Southwestern Energy
Enron	Suburban Propane
Entergy	TNP Enterprises
Exelon	TXU
Ferrellgas Partners	UtiliCorp

HISTORICAL FINANCIALS & EMPLOYEES

NYSE: SUG FYE: June 30	Annual Growth	12/92	12/93	*6/94	6/95	6/96	6/97	6/98	6/99	6/00	6/01
Sales ($ mil.)	29.3%	192	209	375	480	620	717	669	605	832	1,933
Net income ($ mil.)	34.3%	4	8	8	16	21	19	12	10	11	57
Income as % of sales	—	2.1%	3.7%	2.2%	3.4%	3.4%	2.6%	1.8%	1.7%	1.3%	3.0%
Earnings per share ($)	35.0%	0.07	0.31	0.33	0.53	0.69	0.62	0.39	0.30	0.24	1.04
Stock price - FY high ($)	—	3.84	7.48	8.69	7.17	13.30	14.47	18.78	22.20	20.65	27.94
Stock price - FY low ($)	—	3.25	3.34	4.43	5.77	6.42	10.50	11.92	13.48	12.61	16.00
Stock price - FY close ($)	21.7%	3.49	6.27	6.56	6.75	11.47	12.53	18.56	19.71	15.81	20.40
P/E - high	—	55	24	26	13	19	22	47	69	83	26
P/E - low	—	46	11	13	11	9	16	30	42	50	15
Dividends per share ($)	—	0.00	0.00	0.00	0.00	0.00	0.00	0.00	0.00	0.00	0.00
Book value per share ($)	7.2%	8.20	6.91	7.14	11.06	11.68	12.35	12.75	12.84	16.88	15.36
Employees	14.8%	900	900	1,811	1,743	1,623	1,595	1,586	1,563	2,296	3,105

* Fiscal year change

STOCK PRICE HISTORY

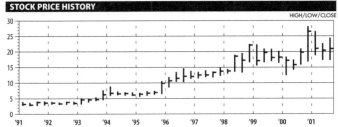

HIGH/LOW/CLOSE

2001 FISCAL YEAR-END

Debt ratio: 61.8%
Return on equity: 7.9%
Cash ($ mil.): 1
Current ratio: 0.99
Long-term debt ($ mil.): 1,330
No. of shares (mil.): 54
Dividends
  Yield: —
  Payout: —
Market value ($ mil.): 1,092

SOUTHWEST AIRLINES CO.

OVERVIEW

Southwest Airlines is veering eastward. The Dallas-based low-fare carrier, which offers some 2,700 daily flights to more than 55 cities in 29 states, has built on its western heritage by boosting service in the eastern US. A top-10 US airline, flights are typically short-haul (about an hour), and the airline usually lands at small airports to avoid the congestion at competitors' larger hubs; in Dallas, Southwest is the big dog at little Love Field, its birthplace.

In an era of airline deregulation, Southwest stands as the inspiration for scrappy low-fare upstarts the world over. This airline keeps it simple: It offers a single class, open seating, and no meals. Its fleet of about 345 aircraft consists only of one type — the Boeing 737 — to minimize training and maintenance costs. Southwest offers a ticketless travel system to trim travel agents' commissions, runs its own reservation system, and sells a significant portion of reservations through its Web site.

By sticking to its formula, which also emphasizes customer service and a sense of fun, Southwest has enjoyed 28 consecutive years of profits. Flamboyant chairman Herb Kelleher, who stepped down as CEO in 2001, has created a highly participative corporate culture; the airline, nearly 85% unionized, has had only one strike in its history. Employees own about 13% of the company.

HISTORY

Texas businessman Rollin King and lawyer Herb Kelleher founded Air Southwest in 1967 as an intrastate airline linking Dallas, Houston, and San Antonio. The now-defunct Braniff and Texas International sued, questioning whether the region needed another airline, but the Texas Supreme Court ruled in Southwest's favor. In 1971 the company, renamed Southwest Airlines, made its first scheduled flight.

Operating out of Love Field in Dallas, Southwest adopted love as the theme of its early ad campaigns, serving love potions (drinks) and love bites (peanuts). When other airlines moved to the new Dallas-Fort Worth Airport (DFW) in 1974, Kelleher insisted on staying at Love Field, gaining a virtual monopoly there.

When Kelleher decided to fly outside Texas, Congress passed the Wright Amendment in 1979. Designed to protect DFW, the law restricted the states served directly from Love Field to Arkansas, Louisiana, New Mexico, and Oklahoma. (A 1997 amendment added Alabama, Kansas, and Mississippi. In 2000, a federal court removed the restrictions for planes with 56 or fewer seats.)

When Lamar Muse, Southwest's president, resigned in 1978 because of differences with King, Kelleher assumed control. (Muse later took over his son Michael's nearly bankrupt airline, Muse Air, which was sold in 1985 to Southwest. The airline was liquidated in 1987.)

An industry maverick, Kelleher introduced advance-purchase Fun Fares in 1986 and a frequent-flier program in 1987 based on the number of flights taken, instead of mileage. He gained attention in 1992 for starring in Southwest's TV commercials and for arm wrestling Stevens Aviation chairman Kurt Herwald for the rights to the "Just Plane Smart"

slogan. When Southwest became the official airline of Sea World in Texas, Kelleher had a 737 painted as a killer whale.

Southwest took on the East Coast with service to Baltimore in 1993, and bought Salt Lake City-based Morris Air in 1994. That year it launched a ticketless system and adopted its own passenger reservation system to cut costs.

The airline expanded into Florida in 1996, and that year Southwest began selling tickets through its Web site. Agreements with Icelandair in 1996 and 1997 allowed Southwest passengers to connect from four US cities to Europe through Icelandair's Baltimore hub. In 1998 Southwest flew its first nonstop transcontinental flight, from Oakland, California, to Baltimore. For the first time since DFW opened, the carrier had to share Love Field with rivals, including AMR.

Southwest added more routes in the East during 1999. In 2000 the airline had its first major accident when a 737 overran the end of a runway in Burbank, California, and ground to a halt in a busy street — a mishap that caused only minor injuries. Later that year Southwest placed its biggest aircraft order ever, calling for delivery of another 94 Boeing 737s between 2002 and 2007. Also in 2000 Southwest experienced a rare labor dispute when stalled contract negotiations led to picketing by the airline's ground crew union.

Kelleher stepped down as president and CEO in 2001. General counsel Jim Parker took over as CEO, and EVP Colleen Barrett — who first worked for Kelleher as his secretary and is given much of the credit for maintaining Southwest's corporate spirit — was named president and COO.

OFFICERS

Chairman: Herbert D. Kelleher, age 70
Vice Chairman and CEO: James F. Parker, age 54
President and COO: Colleen C. Barrett, age 56
EVP and Chief Operations Officer: James C. Wimberly
EVP, Corporate Services: John G. Denison
VP, Finance and CFO: Gary C. Kelly
VP, Customer Relations: James A. Ruppel
VP, Governmental Affairs: Ron Ricks
VP, Ground Operations: Dave Ridley
VP, Flight Operations: Gregory N. Crum
VP, Fuel Management: Roger W. Saari
VP, Inflight Service and Provisioning: Donna D. Conover
VP, Interactive Marketing: Kevin Krone, age 32
VP, Internal Audit and Special Projects: Alan S. Davis
VP, Maintenance and Engineering: Jim Sokol
VP, Marketing: Joyce C. Rogge
VP, Public Relations and Corporate Communications: Ginger C. Hardage
VP, Purchasing: Michael P. Golden
VP, Reservations: Ellen Torbert
VP, Revenue Management: Keith L. Taylor
Auditors: Ernst & Young LLP

LOCATIONS

HQ: 2702 Love Field Drive, Dallas, TX 75235
Phone: 214-792-4000   **Fax:** 214-792-5015
Web: www.southwest.com

PRODUCTS/OPERATIONS

2000 Sales

	$ mil.	% of total
Passengers	5,468	97
Freight	111	2
Other	71	1
Total	**5,650**	**100**

Selected Service
Rapid Rewards (frequent-flier program based on trips rather than mileage)

COMPETITORS

Alaska Air	Mesa Air
America West	Midwest Express
AMR	Northwest Airlines
Continental Airlines	TWA
Delta	UAL
Frontier Airlines	US Airways

HISTORICAL FINANCIALS & EMPLOYEES

NYSE: LUV FYE: December 31	Annual Growth	12/91	12/92	12/93	12/94	12/95	12/96	12/97	12/98	12/99	12/00
Sales ($ mil.)	17.6%	1,314	1,685	2,297	2,592	2,873	3,406	3,817	4,164	4,736	5,650
Net income ($ mil.)	41.3%	27	104	170	179	183	207	318	433	474	603
Income as % of sales	—	2.0%	6.1%	7.4%	6.9%	6.4%	6.1%	8.3%	10.4%	10.0%	10.7%
Earnings per share ($)	38.7%	0.04	0.15	0.23	0.24	0.25	0.27	0.41	0.55	0.59	0.76
Stock price - FY high ($)	—	2.31	3.94	7.45	7.72	5.91	6.58	7.79	10.57	15.74	23.34
Stock price - FY low ($)	—	1.08	2.14	3.60	3.07	3.24	4.08	4.21	6.83	9.59	10.01
Stock price - FY close ($)	29.1%	2.25	3.89	7.40	3.32	4.55	4.35	7.31	10.09	10.76	22.36
P/E - high	—	58	30	35	32	24	24	18	18	25	28
P/E - low	—	27	16	17	13	13	15	10	12	15	12
Dividends per share ($)	0.0%	0.01	0.01	0.01	0.01	0.01	0.01	0.01	0.01	0.01	0.01
Book value per share ($)	18.6%	0.98	1.22	1.46	1.71	1.96	2.25	2.69	3.21	3.75	4.57
Employees	13.0%	9,778	11,397	15,175	16,818	19,933	22,944	23,974	25,844	27,653	29,274

STOCK PRICE HISTORY

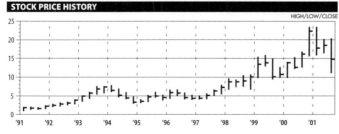

HIGH/LOW/CLOSE

2000 FISCAL YEAR-END

Debt ratio: 18.1%
Return on equity: 19.2%
Cash ($ mil.): 523
Current ratio: 0.64
Long-term debt ($ mil.): 761
No. of shares (mil.): 756
Dividends
  Yield: 0.0%
  Payout: 1.3%
Market value ($ mil.): 16,901

SUIZA FOODS CORPORATION

OVERVIEW

Suiza Foods has got milk and is looking for more. The Dallas-based company has quickly become the leading producer of fluid milk and other dairy products by herding up regional dairies — it has acquired more than 80 plants since entering the business in 1993.

About two-thirds of Suiza Foods' retail and food-service dairy products are made under national brand names (International Delight coffee creamers, Second Nature egg substitute); regional brands (Country Fresh, Suiza); and licensed brands (Lactaid). Suiza Foods makes dairy products under private labels for sale in the US and Puerto Rico. It also makes and distributes fruit juices, flavored drinks, coffee, and bottled water. The company owns 43% of Consolidated Containers (plastic packaging for milk and other beverages).

The company's strategy is to buy the leading dairy in a region, add other dairies in the same area, consolidate operations, and increase efficiency (and profits). To that end, it has formed a milk processing joint venture, Suiza Dairy Group, with Dairy Farmers of America. Suiza is also looking to Europe; it has secured a majority interest in Leche Celta, Spain's fourth-largest dairy.

Suiza Foods is buying rival Dean Foods and is expected to assume that company's name.

HISTORY

Investment banker Gregg Engles formed a holding company in 1988 with other investors, including dairy industry veteran Cletes Beshears, to buy the Reddy Ice unit of Dallas-based Southland (operator of the 7-Eleven chain). The company also bought Circle K's Sparkle Ice and combined it with Reddy Ice. By 1990 it had acquired about 15 ice plants.

The company changed its name to Suiza Foods when it bought Suiza Dairy in 1993 for $99 million. The Puerto Rican dairy was formed in 1942 by Hector Nevares Sr. and named for the Spanish word for "Swiss." By 1993 it was Puerto Rico's largest dairy, controlling about 60% of the island's milk market.

Suiza Foods bought Florida's Velda Farms, manufacturer and distributor of milk and dairy products, in 1994. The company went public in 1996. That year it bought Swiss Dairy, a manufacturer of milk and related products in California and Nevada, for about $54 million. Also in 1996 Suiza Foods bought Garrido y Compania, a Puerto Rican processor of coffee and related products, for about $35 million.

The company became one of the largest players in the North American dairy industry through its acquisitions in 1997. It paid $960 million for Morningstar (Lactaid lactose-free milk, Second Nature egg substitute), which — like Suiza Foods itself — was a Dallas-based company formed in 1988 through a Southland divestiture. The company entered the Midwest with its $98 million purchase of Country Fresh, a milk and dairy products processor formed in the 1940s. Also in 1998 Suiza Foods bought the Bernon family's Massachusetts-based group of dairy and packaging companies, including Garelick Farms and Franklin Plastics (packaging).

Suiza Foods strengthened its presence in the southeastern US in 1998 with its $287 million acquisition of Land-O-Sun Dairies, operator of 13 fluid dairy and ice-cream processing facilities. Also that year Suiza Foods purchased Continental Can (plastic packaging) for about $345 million and sold Reddy Ice to Packaged Ice for $172 million. Expanding its influence in the northeastern US in late 1998, the company formed a joint venture with Dairy Farmers of America. Suiza Foods' deal with the nation's largest dairy cooperative combined each company's dairy operations in the region.

After settling an antitrust lawsuit brought by the US Department of Justice, in June 1999 Suiza Foods bought Ohio milk processor Broughton Foods for $86 million. Suiza Foods then agreed to buy Valley of Virginia Milk Producers Association and bought Colorado's Robinson Dairy.

Also in 1999 Suiza Foods combined its US packaging operations with Reid Plastics to form Consolidated Containers, retaining 43% of the new company. In early 2000 Suiza acquired Southern Foods Group, creating a joint venture with its former 50%-owner, Dairy Farmers of America, called Suiza Dairy Group. Suiza also sold off metal packaging subsidiary Ferembal and bought a majority interest in Spanish dairy processor Leche Celta in 2000.

In April 2001 Suiza Foods announced it had agreed to purchase rival Dean Foods for $1.5 billion and would assume $1 billion worth of debt. Pending antitrust approval, the company will likely take on the Dean Foods name.

OFFICERS

Chairman and CEO: Gregg L. Engles, age 43, $1,825,384 pay
Vice Chairman: Hector M. Nevares Jr., age 50
Vice Chairman; President, Suiza Dairy Group: Pete Schenkel, age 64, $1,237,895 pay
EVP and CFO: Barry A. Fromberg, age 45
EVP, Chief Administrative Officer, General Counsel, and Corporate Secretary: Michelle P. Goolsby, age 43
EVP; President, International: Miguel Calado, age 45
President, Morningstar Foods: Herman L. Graffunder, age 55, $780,538 pay
VP, Human Resources: Robby Dunn
Director; COO, Northeast Region, Suiza Dairy Group: Alan J. Bernon, age 46, $709,803 pay
COO, Southeast Region, Suiza Dairy Group: Rick Fehr, age 49, $741,511 pay
COO, Southwest Region, Suiza Dairy Group: Rick Beaman, age 43
Auditors: Deloitte & Touche LLP

LOCATIONS

HQ: 2515 McKinney Ave., Ste. 1200, Dallas, TX 75201
Phone: 214-303-3400   **Fax:** 214-303-3499
Web: www.suizafoods.com

Suiza Foods has dairy operations in 33 states, Puerto Rico, and Spain.

2000 Sales

	$ mil.	% of total
US	5,364	93
Puerto Rico	227	4
Europe	165	3
Total	**5,756**	**100**

PRODUCTS/OPERATIONS

Selected Products
Cottage cheese
Dairy and nondairy coffee creamers
Dairy and nondairy frozen whipped toppings
Half-and-half
Ice cream
Milk
Sour cream
Soy milk
Whipping cream
Yogurt

Selected Brands
Brown's Dairy
Country Fresh
International Delight coffee creamers (pints, quarts, and singles)
Lactaid (lactose-free milk, licensed)
Meadow Gold
Mocha Mix (liquid, nondairy creamer)
Natural by Garelick Farms
Oak Farms
Schepps
Second Nature (fat-free, cholesterol-free egg product)
West Lynn Creamery

COMPETITORS

Blistex
California Dairies Inc.
Danone
Dean Foods
Foremost Farms
Kraft Foods
Land O'Lakes
Parmalat Finanziaria
Prairie Farms Dairy
Wessanen
White Wave

HISTORICAL FINANCIALS & EMPLOYEES

NYSE: SZA FYE: December 31	Annual Growth	12/91	12/92	12/93	12/94	12/95	12/96	12/97	12/98	12/99	12/00
Sales ($ mil.)	83.6%	—	45	52	341	431	521	1,795	3,321	4,482	5,756
Net income ($ mil.)	—	—	(2)	1	4	(10)	26	29	132	110	119
Income as % of sales	—	—	—	2.7%	1.2%	—	4.9%	1.6%	4.0%	2.4%	2.1%
Earnings per share ($)	18.9%	—	—	—	—	—	1.91	0.91	3.58	3.13	3.82
Stock price - FY high ($)	—	—	—	—	—	—	20.75	62.50	67.00	50.25	52.44
Stock price - FY low ($)	—	—	—	—	—	—	14.00	19.50	25.69	29.63	36.00
Stock price - FY close ($)	24.1%	—	—	—	—	—	20.25	59.56	50.94	39.63	48.00
P/E - high	—	—	—	—	—	—	10	47	22	15	13
P/E - low	—	—	—	—	—	—	7	15	9	9	9
Dividends per share ($)	—	—	—	—	—	—	0.00	0.00	0.00	0.00	0.00
Book value per share ($)	26.0%	—	—	—	—	—	8.70	11.79	19.52	19.94	21.95
Employees	39.6%	—	—	1,740	1,800	1,929	2,450	7,050	16,716	18,000	18,000

STOCK PRICE HISTORY

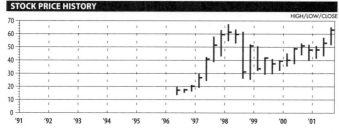

HIGH/LOW/CLOSE

2000 FISCAL YEAR-END
Debt ratio: 67.2%
Return on equity: 20.1%
Cash ($ mil.): 31
Current ratio: 1.17
Long-term debt ($ mil.): 1,225
No. of shares (mil.): 27
Dividends
  Yield: —
  Payout: —
Market value ($ mil.): 1,310

SYSCO CORPORATION

OVERVIEW

Capitalizing on the trend of eating out, Houston-based SYSCO has become the largest food service distributor in North America, providing some 275,000 nationally branded and private-label products to about 356,000 customers. Restaurants account for about two-thirds of its sales. The company's SYGMA Network subsidiary focuses on chain restaurants such as Wendy's International. SYSCO also supplies hotels, schools, hospitals, and industrial caterers with frozen foods, canned and dry goods, fresh meat and produce, medical supplies, and cleaning supplies. The company distributes its products to clients across the US and in Canada from more than 115 distribution facilities and self-serve centers.

SYSCO's "fold-out" expansion program, whereby the company establishes stand-alone companies from profitable distribution centers to serve new markets, has helped it grow more than twice as fast as the food service industry. The company also continues to rapidly expand by acquiring local distributors that specialize in items such as premium steaks and produce. With Cargill, McDonald's, and Tyson Foods, SYSCO has formed Foodservice Network, a system for online sales and purchases in the food industry.

HISTORY

SYSCO was founded in 1969 when John Baugh, a Houston wholesale food distributor, formed a national distribution company with the owners of eight other US wholesalers. Joining Baugh's Zero Foods of Houston to form SYSCO were Frost-Pack Distributing (Grand Rapids, Michigan), Louisville Grocery (Louisville, Kentucky), Plantation Foods (Miami), Thomas Foods and its Justrite subsidiary (Cincinnati), Wicker (Dallas), Food Service Company (Houston), Global Frozen Foods (New York), and Texas Wholesale Grocery (Dallas). The company went public in 1970. SYSCO, which derives its name from Systems and Services Company, benefited from Baugh's recognition of the trend toward dining out. Until SYSCO was formed, small, independent operators almost exclusively provided food distribution to restaurants, hotels, and other non-grocers.

The company expanded through internal growth and the acquisition of strong local distributors, benefiting through buyout agreements requiring the seller to continue managing its own operation while earning a portion of the sale price with future profits.

In 1988, when SYSCO was already the largest North American food service distributor, it acquired CFS Continental, the third-largest North American food distributor. The CFS acquisition added a large truck fleet and increased the company's penetration along the West Coast of the US and Canada. SYSCO also purchased Olewine's, a Pennsylvania-based distributor, that year. In 1990 the company bought Oklahoma City-based Scrivner, later renamed SYSCO Food Services of Oklahoma.

In 1992 SYSCO acquired Collins Foodservice (serving the Northwest) and Benjamin Polakoff & Son and Perloff Brothers (both serving the Northeast). SYSCO sold its only remaining retail business, consumer-size frozen food distributor Global Sysco, that year.

The company acquired St. Louis-based Clark Foodservice and New Jersey's Ritter Food in 1993. The next year it bought Woodhaven Foods, a distributor owned by ARA (now ARAMARK), one of the nation's largest cafeteria and concession operators.

In 1996 it acquired Strano Foodservice, extending SYSCO's market into central Canada. In 1997 the company formed an alliance with National Healthcare Logistics to improve distribution to hospitals and integrated health care systems. Baugh, at age 81, retired from his senior chairman post later that year.

Eager to expand its operations in Florida, SYSCO bought Beaver Street Fisheries' food service distribution division in 1998. The company also bought Maine-based Jordan's Meats.

The company made a number of large acquisitions in 1999, including Atlanta-based Buckhead Beef Company; Newport Meat Company of southern California; and Virginia-based Doughtie's Foods (renamed Sysco Food Services of Hampton Roads). It also bought Watson Foodservice, which distributes food in Texas, New Mexico, and Oklahoma.

SYSCO president Charles Cotros succeeded Bill Lindig as CEO in 2000. That year SYSCO bought Dallas-based produce distributor FreshPoint Holdings. It also purchased Canadian food service distributor North Douglas Distributors, and in 2001 SYSCO acquired specialty meat supplier The Freedman Companies. Later that year SYSCO bought Guest Supply, which distributes personal care amenities and housekeeping supplies to the lodging industry, for about $238 million.

OFFICERS

Senior Chairman: John F. Woodhouse, age 69
Chairman and CEO: Charles H. Cotros, age 63, $1,993,003 pay (prior to promotion)
President and COO: Richard J. Schnieders, age 53, $1,181,193 pay
EVP Finance and Administration and CFO: John K. Stubblefield Jr., age 54, $895,874 pay
EVP Foodservice Operations: Thomas E. Lankford, age 53, $959,938 pay
EVP Merchandising: Larry J. Accardi, age 51
SVP Administration: Kenneth J. Carrig, age 43
SVP; Chairman and CEO, The SYGMA Network: Gregory K. Marshall, age 53
SVP; CEO, FreshPoint: Mitt Parker, age 50
SVP Operations, Midwest Region: James D. Wickus, age 57
SVP Operations, Southeast Region: O. Wayne Duncan, age 62
SVP Operations, Southwest Region: James C. Graham, age 50
SVP Operations, Western Region: Arthur J. Swenka, age 63
VP and Chief Information Officer: Kirk G. Drummond
VP and General Counsel: Michael C. Nichols, age 48
VP and Treasurer: Diane Day Sanders, age 51
VP Healthcare Sales and Marketing: Barry Robinson, age 57
VP Marketing: John S. Carlson
Assistant VP, Human Resources: K. Susan Billiot
Auditors: Arthur Andersen LLP

LOCATIONS

HQ: 1390 Enclave Pkwy., Houston, TX 77077
Phone: 281-584-1390 **Fax:** 281-584-2721
Web: www.syscosmart.com

Sysco has operations in 42 states and in Canada.

PRODUCTS/OPERATIONS

2001 Sales

	% of total
Restaurants	64
Hospitals & nursing homes	11
Schools & colleges	6
Hotels & motels	5
Other	14
Total	**100**

COMPETITORS

Alex Lee
Alliant Exchange
Ben E. Keith
Cagle's
Gordon Food Service
International Multifoods
Keystone Foods
MBM
McLane Foodservice
Performance Food
PYA/Monarch
Services Group
U.S. Foodservice

HISTORICAL FINANCIALS & EMPLOYEES

NYSE: SYY FYE: Saturday nearest June 30	Annual Growth	6/92	6/93	6/94	6/95	6/96	6/97	6/98	6/99	6/00	6/01
Sales ($ mil.)	10.5%	8,893	10,022	10,943	12,118	13,395	14,455	15,328	17,423	19,303	21,785
Net income ($ mil.)	14.8%	172	202	217	252	277	303	297	362	446	597
Income as % of sales	—	1.9%	2.0%	2.0%	2.1%	2.1%	2.1%	1.9%	2.1%	2.3%	2.7%
Earnings per share ($)	15.5%	0.24	0.27	0.29	0.34	0.38	0.43	0.44	0.54	0.67	0.88
Stock price - FY high ($)	—	6.50	6.94	7.75	7.47	8.81	9.56	13.38	15.94	21.69	30.44
Stock price - FY low ($)	—	4.73	5.56	5.66	5.28	6.69	6.91	8.55	9.97	13.06	19.38
Stock price - FY close ($)	17.9%	6.19	6.28	5.66	7.38	8.56	9.13	12.81	14.91	21.06	27.15
P/E - high	—	27	26	26	21	23	22	28	29	31	35
P/E - low	—	20	21	19	15	18	16	18	18	19	22
Dividends per share ($)	20.1%	0.05	0.07	0.08	0.10	0.12	0.14	0.21	0.19	0.21	0.26
Book value per share ($)	9.6%	1.42	1.54	1.69	1.92	2.04	2.03	2.03	2.16	2.66	3.23
Employees	7.5%	22,500	24,200	26,200	28,100	30,600	32,000	33,400	35,100	40,400	43,000

STOCK PRICE HISTORY

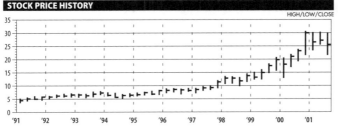

HIGH/LOW/CLOSE

2001 FISCAL YEAR-END

Debt ratio: 30.9%
Return on equity: 30.5%
Cash ($ mil.): 136
Current ratio: 1.43
Long-term debt ($ mil.): 961
No. of shares (mil.): 665
Dividends
  Yield: 1.0%
  Payout: 29.5%
Market value ($ mil.): 18,059

TEMPLE-INLAND INC.

OVERVIEW

There's truly no place like home for Temple-Inland, producer of lumber to build houses and provider of loans to buy them. Through subsidiaries, the Austin, Texas-based company has interests in paper packaging, building materials, and financial services. Temple-Inland's woodsy operations include Inland Paperboard and Packaging (about half of sales), which makes corrugated packaging products, and Temple-Inland Forest Products, which turns out building products such as lumber, particleboard, gypsum wallboard, plywood, and medium-density fiberboard. The company also operates 2.2 million acres of timberland in Alabama, Georgia, Louisiana, and Texas.

Out of the forest, Temple-Inland's Financial Services Group operates about 155 Guaranty Federal Bank branches in Texas and California. The group also provides home mortgage loans, operates insurance agencies, and develops commercial and residential real estate in several states.

Temple-Inland has taken steps to solve supply and demand problems in the paper industry by taking downtimes from production. The company is also facing oversupply problems in its building products business.

HISTORY

Temple-Inland dates back to 1893, when Thomas Temple, a native Virginian, purchased 7,000 acres of Texas timberland from J. C. Diboll. Temple founded the Southern Pine Lumber and built his mill in the town of Diboll, Texas. In 1894 he opened his first sawmill. The company set up a second sawmill in 1903 and a hardwood mill in 1907. Temple formed the Temple Lumber Company three years later. When Temple died in 1934, his son, Arthur, inherited a company heavily in debt. In 1937 a fire destroyed the company's sawmill in Hemphill, Texas.

The Temple family's Southern Pine business fared better, producing basic hardwood and pine lumber items for the construction and furniture industries during the housing boom following WWII. By the early 1950s the company had begun converting chips, sawdust, and shavings into panel products. The company subsequently pioneered southern pine plywood production and branched into making particleboard, gypsum wallboard, and other building materials. Temple Lumber merged with Southern Pine Lumber in 1956 under the Southern Pine name. In 1962 Southern Pine moved into finance with the purchase of the controlling interest of Lumbermen's Investment.

The company changed its name to Temple Industries in 1964. It expanded in the early 1970s by opening a particleboard mill in Diboll in 1971 and acquiring AFCO, a manufacturer of do-it-yourself products, in 1972. The next year Time Inc. acquired Temple Industries and merged it with Eastex Pulp and Paper, creating Temple-Eastex. Time bought Inland Container, a fully integrated packaging company, in 1978 for $272 million.

Inland traces its roots back to 1918, when Herman Krannert started Anderson Box Company in Indiana to make ventilated corrugated products for baby chicks. It had grown into a major manufacturer of packaging materials for the agricultural, horticultural, and poultry industries.

Time spun off the Temple and Inland operations as Temple-Inland in 1983. The company expanded its financial businesses in the late 1980s by acquiring a Kansas insurance company (1985) and three insolvent Texas S&Ls (1988).

Following the retirement of Arthur Temple Jr., Temple-Inland appointed Clifford Grum as chairman and CEO (the first nonfamily chairman) in 1991. Temple-Inland grew by adding plants and resources. In 1994 it bought Rand-Whitney Packaging. It expanded its Latin American production capacity in 1995 with the opening of a box plant in Chile and a corrugated container sheet facility in Mexico. In 1996 it bought a wallboard plant and gypsum quarry in Texas with joint venture partner Caraustar Industries (building products).

Temple-Inland acquired California Financial Holding and Knutson Mortgage in 1997. Acquisitions in 1998 included two medium-density fiberboard plants from MacMillan Bloedel. In 1999 the company paid $120 million for HF Bancorp (parent of California's 18-branch Hemet Federal Savings and Loan), which became part of Guaranty Federal Bank. Temple-Inland also began renovating its mills, modernizing its Diboll, Texas, plant, and converting its Pineland, Texas, sawmill to produce lumber instead of plywood. The company also sold its bleached-paperboard mill in Evadale, Texas, to forestry product company Westvaco.

CFO Kenneth Jastrow became CEO in 2000. The next year Temple-Inland acquired the corrugated packaging assets of Chesapeake Corp.

OFFICERS

Chairman and CEO: Kenneth M. Jastrow II, age 53, $1,352,308 pay
CFO: Randall D. Levy, age 49
EVP, Director, and Chairman and CEO, Inland Paperboard and Packaging: William B. Howes, age 63, $767,016 pay
EVP; Chairman and CEO, Temple-Inland Forest Products: Harold C. Maxwell, age 60
Group VP and EVP, Forest/Solid Wood: Jack C. Sweeny, age 54
Group VP and EVP, Packaging: Bart J. Doney, age 51
Group VP and EVP, Paperboard: James C. Foxworthy, age 49
Group VP; President and CEO, Temple-Inland Financial Services: Kenneth R. Dubuque, age 52, $810,000 pay
Group VP; President and COO, Inland Paperboard and Packaging: Dale E. Stahl, age 53
VP, Chief Administration Officer, and General Counsel: M. Richard Warner, age 49, $650,000 pay
Auditors: Ernst & Young LLP

LOCATIONS

HQ: 1300 S. Mopac Expwy., Austin, TX 78746
Phone: 512-434-8000   **Fax:** 512-434-3750
Web: www.templeinland.com

Temple-Inland has operations in the US (including Puerto Rico) as well as Brazil, Canada, and Mexico.

2000 Sales

	$ mil.	% of total
US	4,122	96
Mexico	106	2
Canada	33	1
South America	25	1
Total	**4,286**	**100**

PRODUCTS/OPERATIONS

2000 Sales

	$ mil.	% of total
Paper	2,089	49
Financial services	1,369	32
Building products	828	19
Total	**4,286**	**100**

Selected Operations and Products

Guaranty Financial Services
Asset-based lending
Checking
Consumer loans
Credit services
Savings bank

Inland Paperboard and Packaging
Consumer packaging and display
Containerboard
Corrugated containers

Temple-Inland Forest Products
Fiberboard
Gypsum wallboard
Laminated panels
Lumber
Medium-density fiberboard
Particleboard
Plywood

COMPETITORS

BANK ONE	Mead
Boise Cascade	Smurfit-Stone Container
ClubCorp	Westvaco
Cullen/Frost Bankers	Weyerhaeuser
Georgia-Pacific Group	Willamette
International Paper	

HISTORICAL FINANCIALS & EMPLOYEES

NYSE: TIN FYE: Sat. nearest December 31	Annual Growth	12/91	12/92	12/93	12/94	12/95	12/96	12/97	12/98	12/99	12/00
Sales ($ mil.)	6.1%	2,507	2,713	2,736	2,938	3,460	3,460	3,625	3,740	3,682	4,286
Net income ($ mil.)	3.9%	138	147	117	131	281	133	51	64	99	195
Income as % of sales	—	5.5%	5.4%	4.3%	4.5%	8.1%	3.8%	1.4%	1.7%	2.7%	4.5%
Earnings per share ($)	4.8%	2.51	2.65	3.01	2.35	5.01	2.39	0.90	1.15	1.78	3.83
Stock price - FY high ($)	—	51.50	57.50	52.50	56.75	55.75	55.38	69.44	67.25	77.50	67.69
Stock price - FY low ($)	—	28.50	43.88	37.25	43.00	41.50	39.75	49.63	42.69	53.63	34.63
Stock price - FY close ($)	0.5%	51.50	51.50	50.38	45.13	43.88	54.13	52.31	59.31	65.94	53.63
P/E - high	—	20	22	25	24	11	23	76	55	43	18
P/E - low	—	11	16	18	18	8	17	55	35	30	9
Dividends per share ($)	4.3%	0.88	0.96	1.00	1.02	1.14	1.24	1.28	1.28	1.28	1.28
Book value per share ($)	3.3%	27.89	29.55	30.64	31.83	35.48	36.34	36.31	35.93	35.55	37.28
Employees	0.2%	14,500	14,500	15,000	15,000	15,400	15,600	15,000	15,700	14,400	14,800

STOCK PRICE HISTORY

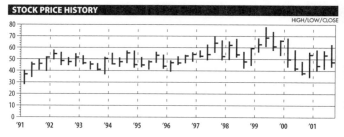

HIGH/LOW/CLOSE

2000 FISCAL YEAR-END

Debt ratio: 46.5%
Return on equity: 10.4%
Cash ($ mil.): 322
Current ratio: 1.06
Long-term debt ($ mil.): 1,591
No. of shares (mil.): 49
Dividends
  Yield: 2.4%
  Payout: 33.4%
Market value ($ mil.): 2,637

TESORO PETROLEUM CORPORATION

OVERVIEW

Tesoro means "treasure" in Spanish, and like all good treasure hunters, independent oil refiner and marketer Tesoro Petroleum travels far and wide. The San Antonio-based company operates refineries in Alaska, Hawaii, North Dakota, Utah, and Washington.

Tesoro's refineries, which have a combined capacity of more than 390,000 barrels per day, make gasoline, diesel fuel, and fuel oil, liquid asphalt, and other fuel products. The company also provides jet and marine fuels, primarily for western-based transporation companies linking North America and Asia via trans-Pacific routes.

Tesoro sells its gasoline on both a wholesale and retail basis; it markets fuel to about 600 branded stations (more than 160 of these stations are company-owned) in Alaska,

Hawaii, and several western US states. As part of a strategy to step up its marketing efforts on the US West Coast, Tesoro has signed an agreement with Wal-Mart to build and operate up to 200 Mirastar-branded gas stations at Wal-Mart locations in 17 states.

Tesoro has sold its exploration and production operations, which had led it to venture as far south as Bolivia, to concentrate on its core downstream businesses. The company announced in 2001 that it would explore "strategic, value-creating opportunities" for its marine services business, which could include a sale of part or all of the unit. Marine services supplies fuels and lubricants to the marine and offshore petroleum industries, primarily along the US Gulf Coast.

HISTORY

Founded by Robert West in 1964 as a spin-off of petroleum producer Texstar, Tesoro Petroleum was hamstrung by debt from the get-go. In 1968 West merged Tesoro with Intex Oil and Sioux Oil to invigorate its financial standing.

Reborn, the company constructed an Alaska refinery and began a 10-year stretch of petroleum-related acquisitions, usually at bargain prices, including almost half of the oil operations of British Petroleum (BP) in Trinidad, which became Trinidad-Tesoro Petroleum. By 1973 earnings had quintupled.

In 1975 Tesoro paid $83 million for about a third of Commonwealth Oil Refining Company (Corco), a troubled Puerto Rican oil refiner one-and-a-half times its size. Debt soon was troubling Tesoro again, and the company divested many of its holdings, including refineries in Montana and Wyoming. Corco declared bankruptcy in 1978. That year Tesoro was hit with tax penalties and revealed it had bribed officials in foreign countries.

The company fought takeover attempts and bankruptcy in the 1980s and sold its stake in Trinidad-Tesoro in 1985. In the 1990s it expanded natural gas operations and returned to profitability.

In 1998 Tesoro bought a refinery and 32 retail outlets in Hawaii from an affiliate of BHP Billiton, and a refinery in Washington from an affiliate of Shell. To concentrate on its downstream businesses, the company in 1999 sold its exploration and production operations in the US (to EEX Corporation for $215 million) and in Bolivia (to BG Group plc

for about $100 million). Also that year subsidiary Tesoro Marine Services acquired BP Marine's US West Coast marine fuels operations, including facilities in Portland, Oregon; Los Angeles, and Seattle. Also in 1999 the company upgraded its Anacortes, Washington refinery to allow production of low-sulfur diesel and jet fuels.

Tesoro West Coast Co., a Tesoro subsidiary, entered into a lease agreement with Wal-Mart in 2000 to build and operate retail fueling facilities at Wal-Mart locations in 11 Western states. (That deal was later expanded to 17 states). That same year the company reviewed the possibility of closing part or all of its Alaska properties, including its underperforming refinery there. However, boosted by higher crude prices and its new deal with Wal-Mart, Tesoro decided to leave its Alaska operations untouched.

In 2001 Tesoro bought refineries in North Dakota and Utah, plus 45 gas stations and contracts to supply 300 others, from BP for about $675 million. Also that year the company acquired 46 gas stations in Idaho, Oregon, and Washington from Gull Industries.

Chairman, President, and CEO: Bruce A. Smith, age 57, $1,855,700 pay
Vice Chairman: Steven H. Grapstein, age 43
EVP and COO: William T. Van Kleef, age 49, $1,044,340 pay
EVP, Secretary, and General Counsel: James C. Reed Jr., age 56, $776,000 pay
EVP Corporate Resources: Thomas E. Reardon, age 54, $531,685 pay
SVP Financial Resources and CFO: Gregory A. Wright, age 51
SVP and Controller: Don M. Heep, age 51
SVP Planning and Risk Management: Everett D. Lewis
VP and Treasurer: Sharon L. Layman, age 47
VP and Controller: Sharlene S. Fey
VP Commercial Marketing: Robert Mills
VP Communications: Susan Pirotina
President, Tesoro Alaska: Eugene Burden, age 52
President, Tesoro Hawaii: Faye W. Kurren, age 50
President, Tesoro Marine Services: Donald A. Nyberg, age 49
President, Tesoro West Coast: Joseph E. Sparano, age 53
EVP and COO, Tesoro Refining, Marketing & Supply: Stephen L. Wormington, age 56, $662,272 pay
EVP Marketing, Tesoro Refining, Marketing & Supply: Jerry H. Mouser
SVP Manufacturing, Tesoro Petroleum Companies Inc.: James L. Taylor
VP Retail, Tesoro West Coast: Richard M. Parry, age 47
Auditors: Deloitte & Touche LLP

LOCATIONS

HQ: 300 Concord Plaza Dr., San Antonio, TX 78216
Phone: 210-828-8484   **Fax:** 210-283-2045
Web: www.tesoropetroleum.com

Tesoro Petroleum operates refineries in Alaska, Hawaii, North Dakota, Utah, and Washington and sells gasoline in Alaska, Arizona, California, Colorado, Hawaii, Idaho, Kansas, Nevada, New Mexico, Oregon, South Dakota, Utah, Washington, and Wyoming. The company distributes refined products from terminals along the Gulf Coast and the West Coast of the US.

PRODUCTS/OPERATIONS

2000 Sales

	$ mil.	% of total
Refining & marketing		
Refined products	4,536	89
Crude oil resales & other	382	7
Marine services	186	4
Total	**5,104**	**100**

Major Subsidiaries
Tesoro Alaska Company
Tesoro Hawaii Corporation
Tesoro Marine Services Holding Company
  Tesoro Marine Services, Inc.
Tesoro Petroleum Companies, Inc.
Tesoro Refining, Marketing & Supply Company
Tesoro West Coast Company

COMPETITORS

ASRC	Exxon Mobil
BP	Ultramar Diamond
Chevron	Shamrock
Equilon Enterprises	Valero Energy

HISTORICAL FINANCIALS & EMPLOYEES

NYSE: TSO FYE: December 31	Annual Growth	12/91	12/92	12/93	12/94	12/95	12/96	12/97	12/98	12/99	12/00
Sales ($ mil.)	18.8%	1,085	946	831	871	970	975	938	1,469	3,000	5,104
Net income ($ mil.)	38.5%	4	(66)	17	16	55	75	31	(19)	75	73
Income as % of sales	—	0.4%	—	2.0%	1.8%	5.6%	7.6%	3.3%	—	2.5%	1.4%
Earnings per share ($)	—	(0.37)	(5.34)	0.54	0.56	2.18	2.81	1.14	(1.03)	1.92	1.75
Stock price - FY high ($)	—	9.38	6.63	7.75	12.38	12.00	15.50	18.19	21.38	18.81	13.00
Stock price - FY low ($)	—	5.75	2.50	3.00	5.25	7.25	8.00	10.25	9.56	7.44	8.94
Stock price - FY close ($)	6.0%	6.88	3.00	5.50	9.25	8.63	14.00	15.50	12.13	11.56	11.63
P/E - high	—	—	—	14	16	5	5	16	—	10	7
P/E - low	—	—	—	5	7	3	3	9	—	4	5
Dividends per share ($)	—	0.00	0.00	0.00	0.00	0.00	0.00	0.00	0.00	0.00	0.00
Book value per share ($)	9.4%	9.66	8.70	9.70	6.59	8.74	11.51	12.67	17.29	19.22	21.74
Employees	1.7%	1,800	900	900	857	840	1,000	1,100	2,140	2,020	2,100

STOCK PRICE HISTORY

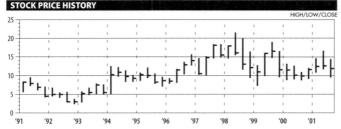

HIGH/LOW/CLOSE

2000 FISCAL YEAR-END

Debt ratio: 31.4%
Return on equity: 15.2%
Cash ($ mil.): 14
Current ratio: 1.65
Long-term debt ($ mil.): 307
No. of shares (mil.): 31
Dividends
  Yield: —
  Payout: —
Market value ($ mil.): 358

TEXAS A&M UNIVERSITY

OVERVIEW

Don't even think about trying to douse the Aggie school spirit. Renowned for their enthusiasm and school traditions, students at the namesake school of The Texas A&M University System don't mind standing for an entire football game or saluting the school mascot (a pooch named Reveille). But behind the fervor is solid education: College Station, Texas-based Texas A&M University System teaches more than 90,000 students at nine universities. Texas A&M in College Station is the largest campus, with an enrollment exceeding 44,000.

A&M's schools are well regarded for engineering and agricultural studies, as well as business administration and veterinary medicine. The system also operates eight state agri-

cultural and engineering extension agencies and a health sciences center (including Baylor College of Dentistry in Dallas). The system (along with the University of Texas) is endowed by the state's Permanent University Fund, valued at about $7.7 billion.

In the wake of a bonfire collapse which took the lives of 12 students in 1999, A&M has been charged by outsiders with trying to conceal the university's involvement in the accident. Still others have called on A&M to loosen some of its traditions. However, the school, students, and alumni have all stood fast against the tide. A&M has also embarked on a mission to renovate its facilities, announcing a $2 billion capital spending campaign in 2000.

HISTORY

The Texas Constitution of 1876 created an agricultural and mechanical college and stated that "separate schools shall be provided for the white and colored children, and impartial provisions shall be made for both." The white school, the Agricultural and Mechanical College of Texas (later Texas A&M), began instruction that year. Texas A&M was a men's school at first, and membership in its Corps of Cadets was mandatory. The Agricultural and Mechanical College of Texas for Colored Youth (later Prairie View A&M) opened in 1878.

To help fund the agricultural colleges and The University of Texas, the Legislature established the Permanent University Fund in 1876 to hold more than one million acres of land in West Texas as an endowment. An additional one million acres was added in 1883. The Santa Rita well on the university land struck oil in 1923 and money flowed into the Permanent University Fund's coffers. Under the provisions of the constitution, The University of Texas got two-thirds of the income, and A&M got the rest.

In 1948 The Texas A&M College System was established to oversee Texas A&M, Prairie View A&M, Tarleton State, and Arlington State (which left the system in 1965 and is now The University of Texas at Arlington). By 1963 enrollment system-wide had reached 8,000. That year the system changed its name to The Texas A&M University System, the same year that Texas A&M went coed.

By the mid-1980s enrollment had surpassed 35,000 students. The system grew quickly in 1989 when it added Texas A&I University (now Texas A&M University-Kingsville), Corpus Christi State (now Texas A&M University-Corpus Christi), and Laredo State University

(now Texas A&M International). West Texas State College in Canyon joined the system in 1990 and became West Texas A&M University in 1993.

The 91-year-old Baylor College of Dentistry (in Dallas) and East Texas State University, well-known for training future teachers, joined the A&M system in 1996 (East Texas State was divided into Texas A&M University-Commerce and Texas A&M-Texarkana). In 1997 the system opened the first portion of the $82 million George Bush Presidential Library and Museum.

In early 1998 the system signed an alliance with the private South Texas College of Law in Houston, which was opposed by the Texas Higher Education Coordinating Board. (In 1999 a judge ruled that the two schools had to discontinue their affiliation.) That year Texas Instruments donated $5.1 million to the system (one of the largest donations in the institution's history) for the creation of an analog technology program. Chancellor Barry Thompson announced he would retire in 1999. The system appointed former Army general Howard Graves as the new chancellor.

Tragedy struck the College Station campus later in 1999 when logs being stacked for the annual bonfire celebrating the University of Texas/Texas A&M football game collapsed and killed 12 people. Clinging to the 90-year tradition, many Aggies past and present insisted the bonfire go on in future years. In 2000 Graves announced a $2 billion, five-year capital improvement plan.

Chairman, Board of Regents: Don Powell
Vice Chairman, Board of Regents: Fredrick D. McClure
Chancellor: Howard D. Graves
Vice Chancellor of Academic and Student Affairs:
  Leo Sayavedra
Vice Chancellor of Agriculture and Life Sciences:
  Edward A. Hiler
Vice Chancellor of Business Services (CFO):
  Tom D. Kale
Vice Chancellor of Engineering: C. Roland Haden,
  age 60
**Vice Chancellor of Facilities Planning and
  Construction:** Wesley E. Peel
Vice Chancellor of Governmental Affairs:
  Stanton C. Calvert
**Vice Chancellor of Health Affairs; President, The Texas
  A&M University System Health Science Center:**
  Jay Noren
Vice Chancellor of Planning and System Integration:
  Walter V. Wendler
Deputy Chancellor: Jerry Gatson
Associate Vice Chancelllor of Human Resources:
  Patti Couger
President, Prairie View A&M University:
  Charles A. Hines
President, Tarleton State University: Dennis P. McCabe
President, Texas A&M International University:
  J. Charles Jennett
President, Texas A&M University: Ray M. Bowen
President, Texas A&M University-Commerce:
  Keith McFarland
President, Texas A&M University-Corpus Christi:
  Robert R. Furgason, age 65
President, Texas A&M University-Kingsville:
  Marc Cisneros
Auditors: Texas State Auditor

LOCATIONS

HQ: The Texas A&M Unversity System
  John B. Connally Bldg., 301 Tarrow, 3rd Fl.,
  College Station, TX 77843
Phone: 979-845-3211   **Fax:** 979-845-5406
Web: tamusystem.tamu.edu

PRODUCTS/OPERATIONS

2000 Revenues

	% of total
Federal & state appropriations	38
Grants & contracts	
Federal	15
State	4
Other	3
Tuition & fees	17
Sales & services	11
Investment & endowment income	6
Gifts	3
Other income & fees	3
Total	**100**

Selected Texas A&M University System Components
Health Science Center
  Baylor College of Dentistry
  College of Medicine
  Graduate School of Biomedical Sciences
  Institute of Biosciences and Technology
  School of Rural Public Health
Universities
  Prairie View A&M University
  Tarleton State University
  Texas A&M International University
  Texas A&M University
  Texas A&M University-Commerce
  Texas A&M University-Corpus Christi
  Texas A&M University-Kingsville
  Texas A&M University-Texarkana
  West Texas A&M University
State agencies
  Texas Agricultural Experiment Station
  Texas Agricultural Extension Service
  Texas Engineering Experiment Station
  Texas Engineering Extension Service
  Texas Forest Service
  Texas Transportation Institute
  Texas Veterinary Medical Diagnostic Laboratory
  Texas Wildlife Damage Management Service

HISTORICAL FINANCIALS & EMPLOYEES

School FYE: August 31	Annual Growth	8/91	8/92	8/93	8/94	8/95	8/96	8/97	8/98	8/99	8/00
Sales ($ mil.)	10.4%	1,073	1,172	1,212	1,287	1,299	1,425	1,550	1,695	1,792	2,620
Employees	4.7%	15,228	15,670	15,966	16,367	20,000	22,600	22,800	23,300	23,000	23,000

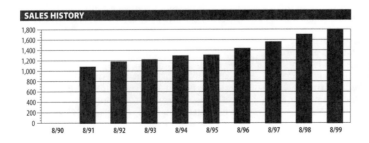

SALES HISTORY

TEXAS INDUSTRIES, INC.

OVERVIEW

Texas Industries, Inc. (TXI), has built a billion-dollar business on rocks and crushed cars. The Dallas-based company has two business segments: cement, aggregates, and concrete (CAC); and steel. More than half of TXI's sales come from the CAC operations, which produce portland and other cements, aggregates, ready-mix concrete, concrete pipe, block, and brick. The company's CAC products include well cements, cement-treated materials used with paving material, shale and clay, limestone, and pea-gravel, which it produces and sells throughout the south and southwestern US.

TXI's steel division, Chaparral Steel, makes structural steel, specialty bar products, reinforcing bar, merchant bar-quality rounds, and channels from recycled steel (mostly from crushed cars). TXI sells its steel products primarily in North America to steel service centers and fabricators (for use in the construction industry), forgers, cold finishers, and OEMs for use in the automotive, defense, energy, mobile home, and railroad industries.

TXI has been both saving and making money with its patented CemStar process, which uses a by-product of steelmaking to increase cement production and reduce emmissions. The company is licensing CemStar to other cement makers. To achieve greater flexibility in its steel operations, TXI uses the market mill concept, which entails producing a wide range of steel products at low cost and allows the company to rapidly shift its product mix and output to match changing prices and market conditions.

HISTORY

Ralph Rogers delivered newspapers as a boy in Boston. There he attended Boston Latin, a prep school that counts among its alumni Ben Franklin, Samuel Adams, and John Hancock. In 1926 he turned down a scholarship to Harvard to support his family. Rogers had become a successful distributor of diesel engines when, in 1942, he contracted rheumatic fever at the age of 33. After he recovered, he headed a project to find a cure for the disease; a link between strep throat and rheumatic fever was discovered, and by use of newly developed penicillin and sulfa drugs, the disease was effectively eliminated.

Rogers retired, moved to Dallas, and formed an investment company with a friend. They invested in Texas Lightweight Aggregate, a small concrete-materials company with assets of about $350,000. In 1951 its successor, Texas Industries (TXI), was incorporated. TXI was fueled by sales of Haydite, its expanded shale and clay aggregate, and had 28 plants by 1954. The company continued to grow throughout the 1950s and 1960s, both internally and through acquisitions. It became vertically integrated with the completion of its own cement plants in Midlothian, Texas, in 1960.

In 1964 TXI launched its first European venture via a French cement distributor. Three years later the company acquired a limestone deposit in southern California and Athens Brick Company and plants in Texas and Louisiana. Also in 1967 Midlothian became the largest cement plant in Texas with the completion of its third kiln.

Ralph Rogers stepped aside for his son Robert to take over around 1970, and TXI diversified into modular buildings and paperboard (sold 1974). The company got into steel in 1973 through Chaparral Steel, a joint venture with Co-Steel International. The Chaparral plant, located near Midlothian, made rolled steel products, such as reinforcing bars, from scrap, and by 1979 it accounted for 23% of TXI's profit. In 1985 TXI bought Co-Steel's interest in Chaparral Steel.

The economic bust at the end of the 1980s hurt TXI, which sold assets to remain profitable. By 1992 things had turned around, and Chaparral accounted for about two-thirds of sales. TXI patented its CemStar process in 1995, and in 1997 it increased its cement capacity by some 60% with the acquisition of Riverside Cement Company (portland and white cement, California).

Cement shortages in 1998 boosted prices in North America between 10% and 20%. However, steel prices shrank from an influx of imports from Asia, Russia, and South America, and contributed to a dip in profits for TXI in fiscal 1999. That year cement product sales, which had been gaining on steel, accounted for the majority of TXI's revenues. TXI purchased Collier Sand & Gravel of Marble Falls, Texas, in 2000, adding about 500 million tons to the company's aggregate capacity. The next year the company completed construction that more than doubled the capacity of its Midlothian, Texas, cement plant. A slow market for concrete and aggregates, the result of wet weather, and competition from imported steel depressed TXI's fiscal 2001 sales.

OFFICERS

Chairman: Gerald R. Heffernan, age 82
President, CEO, and Director: Robert D. Rogers, age 65, $949,636 pay
EVP, Cement, Aggregates, and Concrete: Melvin G. Brekhus, age 52, $340,500 pay
EVP, Finance: Richard M. Fowler, age 58, $312,125 pay
EVP, Steel: Tommy A. Valenta, age 52, $340,500 pay
VP, Accounting and Information Services: James R. McCraw
VP, Aggregates: Stephen D. Mayfield
VP, Bar Product Sales: Peter H. Wright
VP, Cement Production: J. Lynn Davis
VP, Communications and Government Affairs: D. Randall Jones
VP, Concrete: Michael E. Perkins
VP, Controller, Cement, Aggregate, and Concrete: J. Michael Link
VP, Development: Carlos E. Fonts, age 61, $227,000 pay
VP, Environmental Affairs: E. Leo Faciane
VP, Expanded Shale and Clay: George E. Eure
VP, General Counsel, and Secretary: Robert C. Moore, age 67
VP, Human Resources: William J. Durbin, age 56
VP, Marketing, Cement, Aggregates, and Concrete: J. Barrett Reese
Auditors: Ernst & Young LLP

LOCATIONS

HQ: 1341 W. Mockingbird Ln., Dallas, TX 75247
Phone: 972-647-6700   **Fax:** 972-647-3878
Web: www.txi.com

Texas Industries has cement, aggregate, and concrete plants in Arkansas, California, Colorado, Louisiana, Oklahoma, and Texas, and steel plants in Texas and Virginia.

PRODUCTS/OPERATIONS

2001 Sales

	$ mil.	% of total
Cement, aggregate & concrete		
Cement	326	26
Ready-mix concrete	235	19
Stone, sand & gravel	114	9
Steel		
Structural	452	36
Bar mill	105	8
Other	20	2
Total	**1,252**	**100**

Selected Products and Operations

Aggregates	Professional
Cement	groundskeeping
Clay brick	products
Concrete block and pipe	Ready-mix concrete
Development of business	Reinforcing bar
parks	Specialty steel bar
Oil well cements, lost	products
circulation materials	Steel beams
	Steel channels
	Structural steel

COMPETITORS

Algoma Steel	Centex	Lafarge North
AmeriSteel	Construction	America
Bayou Steel	Products	Martin Marietta
Bethlehem Steel	Commercial	Materials
Birmingham	Metals	National Steel
Steel	CSR Limited	Nucor
Cementos de	Earle	U.S. Aggregates
Chihuahua	M. Jorgensen	USX-U.S. Steel
Cemex	Holnam	Vulcan Materials
	Justin Industries	

HISTORICAL FINANCIALS & EMPLOYEES

NYSE: TXI FYE: May 31	Annual Growth	5/92	5/93	5/94	5/95	5/96	5/97	5/98	5/99	5/00	5/01
Sales ($ mil.)	8.5%	601	614	707	831	967	974	1,196	1,127	1,306	1,252
Net income ($ mil.)	33.8%	2	1	26	48	80	76	102	89	70	26
Income as % of sales	—	0.3%	0.2%	3.6%	5.8%	8.3%	7.8%	8.5%	7.9%	5.3%	2.1%
Earnings per share ($)	32.3%	0.10	0.06	1.10	1.94	3.53	3.42	4.69	3.92	3.15	1.24
Stock price - FY high ($)	—	12.63	14.38	19.88	19.75	34.63	34.31	68.25	59.75	43.38	34.94
Stock price - FY low ($)	—	9.00	9.63	10.94	14.75	17.81	20.88	23.63	19.56	28.69	20.88
Stock price - FY close ($)	11.7%	12.06	11.50	16.25	18.81	31.31	24.00	59.38	36.38	28.69	32.75
P/E - high	—	126	240	17	10	10	10	14	14	13	28
P/E - low	—	90	161	10	8	5	6	5	5	9	17
Dividends per share ($)	13.0%	0.10	0.10	0.10	0.15	0.20	0.25	0.30	0.30	0.30	0.30
Book value per share ($)	11.4%	12.91	12.74	14.75	15.55	18.33	21.66	26.08	30.14	33.13	34.19
Employees	5.6%	2,700	2,700	2,700	2,800	3,000	3,400	4,100	4,200	4,500	4,400

STOCK PRICE HISTORY

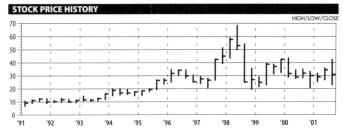

HIGH/LOW/CLOSE

2001 FISCAL YEAR-END

Debt ratio: 46.3%
Return on equity: 3.7%
Cash ($ mil.): 9
Current ratio: 2.01
Long-term debt ($ mil.): 614
No. of shares (mil.): 21
Dividends
  Yield: 0.9%
  Payout: 24.2%
Market value ($ mil.): 682

TEXAS INSTRUMENTS

Do Texans do everything bigger? For analog chips and DSPs, it's no brag, just fact — Texas Instruments is the biggest of all. Dallas-based Texas Instruments (TI) is the world's leading maker of digital signal processors (DSPs), with nearly half of the market. Its DSPs are found in more than half of all wireless phones and in many other devices, including automotive systems, video cameras, modems, and VCRs. The company is banking on even larger markets for its DSPs in the future, as their use becomes more widespread in areas such as wireline communications and medical equipment.

TI is also the world's leading maker of analog chips, which translate real-world analog data such as sound, light, and pressure into digital signals that can be manipulated by computers. TI's semiconductor business — about 85% of sales — also includes logic chips, microprocessors, and microcontrollers. TI's non-chip products include electronic and electrical controls, connectors, and sensors, as well as handheld calculators.

To focus on its analog and DSP businesses, TI has sold off noncore businesses and beefed up core offerings through acquisitions — including the $7.6 billion purchase of analog and mixed-signal chip maker Burr-Brown. It has also announced that it will lay off about 2,500 people (6% of its workforce) in the face of slumping industry demand.

Clarence "Doc" Karcher and Eugene McDermott founded Geophysical Service Inc. (GSI) in Newark, New Jersey, in 1930 to develop reflective seismology, a new technology for oil and gas exploration. In 1934 GSI moved to Dallas. The company produced military electronics during WWII, including submarine detectors for the US Navy. GSI changed its name to Texas Instruments (TI) in 1951.

TI began making transistors in 1952 after buying a license from Western Electric. In 1954 it introduced the Regency Radio, the first pocket-sized transistor radio. (That year TI produced the first commercial silicon transistor.) Impressed by TI's transistor radio, IBM president Thomas Watson made TI a major supplier to IBM in 1957. That year the company opened a plant in the UK — its first foreign operation.

TI engineer Jack Kilby invented the integrated circuit (IC) in 1958. (Working independently, Intel founder Robert Noyce developed an IC at the same time; the two men are credited as co-inventors. In 2000 Kilby was awarded the Nobel Prize in physics for his work; Noyce could not be awarded the Prize, since he had died 10 years earlier.)

Other breakthroughs included terrain-following airborne radar (1958), handheld calculators (1967), and single-chip microcomputers (1971). During the 1970s TI introduced innovative calculators, digital watches, home computers, and educational toys such as the popular Speak & Spell — TI's first use of digital signal processors (DSPs), which decades later would become a major driver of TI's growth.

Low-cost foreign competition led TI to abandon its digital watch and PC businesses. Price competition in the chip market contributed to its first loss, in 1983. In 1988 the company sold most of its remaining oil and gas operations to Halliburton. TI's patent for the IC was upheld in Japan in 1989, and all major Japanese electronics firms except Fujitsu agreed to pay royalties to the company.

As the chip market toughened, TI leveraged its dynamic random-access memory (DRAM) chip know-how through strategic alliances.

When company head Jerry Junkins, who built TI into a semiconductor force, died unexpectedly in 1996, he was replaced by company veteran Thomas Engibous as president and CEO. (Engibous became chairman in 1998.)

Engibous refocused TI, which in 1996 sold its custom manufacturing business to Solectron and acquired Silicon Systems (chips for mass storage devices). In 1997 TI sold its notebook computer business to Acer, its defense electronics operation to Raytheon, and its enterprise applications software unit to Sterling Software (now part of Computer Associates).

In 1998 TI bought networking products maker Amati Communications. It sold its slumping memory chip operations to Micron Technology; the complex deal gave TI about a 15% stake in Micron (some of that stake was sold in 2000). A global chip slump and the loss of the memory chip business lowered TI's results in 1998 and led to the layoff of 3,500 employees.

TI in 2000 paid $7.6 billion to acquire Burr-Brown, an Arizona-based maker of analog and mixed-signal chips. That year it sold its specialty materials unit to Blue Point Capital Partners. In 2001 TI announced that it would lay off about 2,500 workers in reaction to a softening market for its chips.

OFFICERS

Chairman, President, and CEO: Thomas J. Engibous, age 48, $2,096,200 pay
EVP and COO; President, Semiconductor: Richard K. Templeton, age 42, $1,397,200 pay
SVP: Michael J. Hames, age 42, $693,000 pay
SVP: Keh-Shew Lu, age 54, $796,000 pay
SVP, CFO, and Treasurer: William A. Aylesworth, age 58, $665,400 pay
SVP, Secretary, and General Counsel: Joseph F. Hubach, age 43
SVP and Manager, Worldwide Human Resources: Stephen H. Leven, age 49
SVP; President, Educational and Productivity Solutions: Richard J. Schaar, age 55
SVP; President, Sensors & Controls: Thomas Wroe Jr., age 50
Auditors: Ernst & Young LLP

LOCATIONS

HQ: Texas Instruments Incorporated
  12500 TI Boulevard, Dallas, TX 75266
Phone: 972-995-3773   **Fax:** 972-995-4360
Web: www.ti.com

Texas Instruments has operations in more than 25 countries, including major design and manufacturing facilities in France, Germany, Japan, Malaysia, Mexico, the Philippines, Taiwan, and the US.

2000 Sales

	$ mil.	% of total
US	3,209	27
Japan	2,119	18
Other countries	6,547	55
Total	**11,875**	**100**

PRODUCTS/OPERATIONS

2000 Sales

	$ mil.	% of total
Semiconductors	10,284	86
Sensors & controls	1,030	9
Educational & productivity	446	4
Other	115	1
Total	**11,875**	**100**

Selected Products
Analog and mixed-signal
Application-specific integrated circuits (ASICs)
Calculators
Digital light processors (DLPs)
Digital signal processors (DSPs)
Electrical and electronic controls
Electronic connectors
Microcontrollers
Personal organizers
Radio-frequency identification systems
Reduced instruction set computer (RISC) microprocessors
Standard logic

COMPETITORS

Agere Systems
Analog Devices
Atmel
Broadcom
Canon
Casio Computer
Conexant Systems
Cypress Semiconductor
Fairchild Semiconductor
Hitachi
Infineon Technologies
Integrated Device Technology
Intel
IBM
LSI Logic
Maxim Integrated Products
Motorola
National Semiconductor
NEC
ON Semiconductor
Philips Electronics
QUALCOMM
STMicroelectronics
Toshiba

HISTORICAL FINANCIALS & EMPLOYEES

NYSE: TXN FYE: December 31	Annual Growth	12/91	12/92	12/93	12/94	12/95	12/96	12/97	12/98	12/99	12/00
Sales ($ mil.)	6.4%	6,784	7,440	8,523	10,315	13,128	9,940	9,750	8,460	9,468	11,875
Net income ($ mil.)	—	(409)	247	472	691	1,088	63	1,805	407	1,406	3,058
Income as % of sales	—	—	3.3%	5.5%	6.7%	8.3%	0.6%	18.5%	4.8%	14.9%	25.8%
Earnings per share ($)	—	(0.34)	0.16	0.23	0.39	0.71	0.05	1.13	0.26	0.84	1.71
Stock price - FY high ($)	—	2.98	3.27	5.27	5.59	10.47	8.55	17.81	22.61	55.75	99.78
Stock price - FY low ($)	—	1.63	1.88	2.86	3.81	4.30	5.00	7.77	10.06	21.50	35.00
Stock price - FY close ($)	42.8%	1.92	2.91	3.97	4.68	6.44	7.97	11.25	21.41	48.31	47.38
P/E - high	—	—	20	21	14	14	171	15	87	63	55
P/E - low	—	—	12	11	9	6	100	7	39	24	19
Dividends per share ($)	6.7%	0.05	0.05	0.05	0.06	0.06	0.09	0.11	0.09	0.09	0.09
Book value per share ($)	15.0%	1.49	1.47	1.59	2.05	2.70	2.69	3.80	4.18	5.69	5.25
Employees	(4.3%)	62,939	60,557	59,048	56,333	59,574	59,927	44,140	35,948	38,000	42,400

STOCK PRICE HISTORY

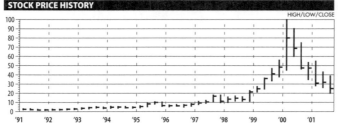

HIGH/LOW/CLOSE

2000 FISCAL YEAR-END

Debt ratio: 8.8%
Return on equity: 28.0%
Cash ($ mil.): 745
Current ratio: 2.88
Long-term debt ($ mil.): 1,216
No. of shares (mil.): 2,399
Dividends
  Yield: 0.2%
  Payout: 5.3%
Market value ($ mil.): 113,656

TEXAS LOTTERY COMMISSION

OVERVIEW

Everything is big in Texas, including the size of its lottery payoffs and the odds against becoming a Texas-sized millionaire. The Austin-based Texas Lottery Commission oversees one of the largest state-run lotteries in the US. Created in 1991, it has generated more than $7 billion for the state's coffers. The lottery offers four numbers games — Lotto Texas, Pick 3, Cash 5, and Texas Two Step — as well as an ever-changing variety of "scratchers," the instant-win tickets sold through retailers and vending machines leased from Cincinnati-based Interlott Technologies. More than 55% of ticket sales is paid out in prizes, while the state's Foundation School Fund gets about 30%. The remaining money goes to cover administration costs and to pay commissions to retailers.

The Lone Star lottery seems to be rebounding, with rising sales after three years of losses. The company is discontinuing its slumping Texas Million lottery game. It also changed its Texas Lotto game so that customers must match six numbers out of 54 numbers instead of 50. The extra four numbers changed the odds of winning from about one in 16 million to one in 26 million.

HISTORY

A state lottery had been an issue in Texas for years before it was discussed in earnest in the mid-1980s. Falling oil and gas revenue had plunged the state into a recession, raising the specter of tax increases. In 1985 the state budget had a shortfall of $1 billion; that figure tripled by 1987. Adding fuel to the fire, the Texas Supreme Court ruled in 1989 that Texas had to change the way it funded public schools to avoid penalizing poor school districts. The ruling forced the state to seek new sources of revenue. In 1991 Governor Ann Richards called a special session of the legislature to deal with the fiscal crisis, and House Bill 54 was passed, creating the state lottery. The measure was approved by 64% of voters.

In May of 1992, Richards bought the symbolic first ticket at an Austin feed store (it was not a winner). Texans had spent nearly $23 million on tickets — breaking the California Lottery's first-day sales record — and had won $10 million in prizes 14 hours later. More than 102 million tickets were sold the first week. GTECH Holdings was awarded a five-year contract that year for lotto operations. Lotto Texas started in November of 1992 with a winner taking nearly $22 million. By the end of fiscal 1992, lotto sales in Texas had topped $1 billion. In its first 15 months, it contributed $812 million to the state's coffers.

In March 1994 five winners split a record $77 million jackpot. By that autumn sales had surpassed $5 billion. In November a Mansfield, Texas, gas station owner picked up the largest single-winner jackpot, $54 million. By the end of 1994, Texas had the largest state lottery in the US. Cumulative sales topped $8 billion in mid-1995. In its first 37 months of operation, the Texas Lottery contributed $2.5 billion to the state's general fund. Cash 5 debuted that year, and instant ticket vending machines were installed at some sites.

In 1996 lottery director Nora Linares was dismissed following allegations that one of her friends received $30,000 from GTECH as a "hunting consultant." When a GTECH official in New Jersey was convicted of taking kickbacks from a lobbyist, questions were raised concerning payments to GTECH's Texas lobbyist, former Texas Lieutenant Governor Ben Barnes. In 1997 Texas canceled its contract with GTECH to operate the lottery through 2002 and reopened bidding; GTECH filed suit to enforce the contract. Executive director Lawrence Littwin later was dismissed by the commission. Littwin sued GTECH, claiming the company had gotten him fired (the case was settled in 1999). Linda Cloud, his replacement, reinstated GTECH's contract. That year the Texas legislature voted to increase the amount going to the state and to reduce prize payouts.

Lottery sales fell sharply in 1998, due in part to the reduced prize money. To combat suffering sales, the legislature reversed itself the next year and restored the level of prize payouts. The commission proposed lengthening the odds of winning to create larger jackpots, but public outcry scuttled the plan. In 2000 the commission agreed to change the wording on its scratch tickets after a San Antonio college professor and his students protested that breaking even is not winning. The following year it introduced its first new lottery game in about three years, Texas Two Step, and discontinued Texas Million following slumping sales.

OFFICERS

Chairman: C. Thomas Clowe
Executive Director: Linda Cloud
Deputy Executive Director: Patsy Henry
Director Communications: Keith Elkins
Director Financial Administration: Bart Sanchez
Director, Human Resources: Jim Richardson
Director Lottery Operations: Gary Grief
Director Marketing: Toni Smith
Director Security: Mike Pitcock
General Counsel: Kimberly Kiplin

LOCATIONS

HQ: 611 E. 6th St., Austin, TX 78701
Phone: 512-344-5000   **Fax:** 512-344-5490
Web: www.txlottery.org

PRODUCTS/OPERATIONS

2000 Sales

	% of Total
Prize money	57
Schools	31
Administrative costs	7
Retailers	5
Total	**100**

Selected Games

Lottery games
Cash 5
Lotto Texas
Pick 3
Texas Two Step

Scratch-off games
$25,000 Diamonds
9's In A Line
Break the Bank
Cupid Cash
Fast Cash
High 5
Jingle Bucks
Masquerade Match Up
Pot O' Gold
Rake in the Cash
Texas Gold Gusher
Triple 3
Triple Blackjack
Weekly Grand

COMPETITORS

Multi-State Lottery
New Mexico Lottery

HISTORICAL FINANCIALS & EMPLOYEES

Government-owned FYE: August 31	Annual Growth	8/91	8/92	8/93	8/94	8/95	8/96	8/97	8/98	8/99	8/00
Sales ($ mil.)	26.7%	—	594	1,863	2,772	3,052	3,449	3,761	3,106	3,156	3,940
Net income ($ mil.)	—	—	250	660	932	1,014	1,101	1,421	1,213	(118)	(116)
Income as % of sales	—	—	42.1%	35.4%	33.6%	33.2%	31.9%	37.8%	39.0%	—	—
Employees	0.4%	—	325	325	325	325	325	304	335	300	335

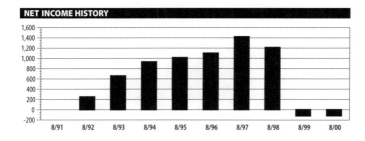

NET INCOME HISTORY

TRAMMELL CROW COMPANY

OVERVIEW

It takes a tough bird to succeed in the real estate business, and Trammell Crow is one of the cocks of the walk.

The Dallas-based firm is a leading real estate manager, overseeing nearly 500 million square feet of office, warehouse, service center, and retail space throughout the US and Canada. Other services include real estate brokerage and investment property advising, development, and construction. Trammell Crow serves multinational companies through 170 offices in Canada and the US, as well as through its Trammell Crow Savills partnership with UK-based real estate service firm Savills. The family of founder Trammell Crow owns nearly 20% of the company; chairman J. McDonald Williams owns about 5%, as does asset management firm T. Rowe Price.

Trammell Crow has reorganized its operations in the hopes of better serving its corporate and institutional customers, integrating its retail property operations into its management services, transaction services, and development and project management services segments. The firm is also integrating the power of the Internet into its operations: it has partnered with such firms as CB Richard Ellis and Simon Property Group to develop online real estate services.

HISTORY

WWII vet Trammell Crow returned to his native Dallas and went to work for a grain wholesaling firm owned by his wife's family. An accountant by training, Crow entered the real estate business by trying to find tenants for some warehouse space the company owned.

When tenant Ray-O-Vac outgrew the grain firm's space in 1948, Crow built a warehouse for the battery company. Believing that if he built it, they would come, Crow built "on speculation," structuring his developments as partnerships and avoiding long leases so as not to get locked into low rents in a rising market.

Crow developed the Dallas Decorative Center (1955), the Dallas Market Center, the Dallas Homefurnishing Mart (1957), and the Trade Mart (1960). He added Market Hall and combined the buildings' operations in 1963.

Other projects in the 1960s and 1970s included Atlanta's Peachtree Center, San Francisco's Embarcadero Center, and a number of residential projects. When Crow planned in 1972 to add the Dallas World Trade Center to the Dallas Market Center, longtime friend and partner John Stemmons balked; Crow bought him out for $7 million.

Then came the recession of the 1970s. High interest rates and heavy debts forced the company to sell $100 million in properties in 1977 to raise money and reorganize.

In the boom of the 1980s, the company began expanding ferociously nationwide. Many of the partners were little more than employees with liability for their projects, so the real estate crash of the late 1980s pushed several deals toward bankruptcy.

Many partners, facing ruin, signed over their interests in the properties to Crow family entities. They then became salaried employees at Trammell Crow, which refocused on property management.

Meanwhile, the Crow family interests, supervised by son Harlan, were so debt-ridden that lenders could not foreclose and had to renegotiate the debt. With some strategic property sales (including the 1996 IPO of Wyndham Hotels, now Wyndham International) and belt-tightening among family members, the Crows came out wealthier than ever. (One Crow's fortune, however, followed a different route: Trammell's only daughter, Lucy, kept her investments separate. In 1996 her husband, Henry Billingsley, head of Crow/Billingsley Investments of Dallas, pleaded guilty to smuggling Libya's finance minister into the US in 1992 in an attempt to sell Texas real estate to the Libyan government. Billingsley was sentenced to six months in a halfway house and fined $5,000.)

In the mid-1990s the real estate market began to recover, and Trammell Crow resumed its development activities — this time on an international scale. In 1997 Trammell Crow International established joint ventures with China Merchants Shekou Port Service and Japan's Nissho Iwai. That year the company bought Doppelt & Company, a retail tenant representation company.

Trammell Crow went public in 1997. It suffered a loss that year from a decrease in the amount of space under management. In the late 1990s the company expanded its operations with such purchases as Fallon Hines & O'Connor (real estate brokerage, 1998) and Phoenix Corporate Services (outsourcing, 1999).

In 2000 it teamed with UK real estate firm Savills to form an outsourcing firm targeting the European Union.

OFFICERS

Chairman: J. McDonald Williams, age 59
President, CEO, and Director: Robert E. Sulentic,
age 44, $575,000 pay
CFO: Derek R. McClain, age 45, $435,000 pay
EVP and Director: Henry J. Faison, age 66
President, Investment and Development, and Director:
H. Pryor Blackwell, age 40, $480,000 pay
President, Global Services, and Director:
William F. Concannon, age 45, $280,000 pay
President, E-Commerce and Corporate Development:
James R. Groch, age 39, $395,000 pay
**Executive Director, Development and Investment,
Western United States:** Charles A. Anderson, age 40
**Executive Director, Development and Investment,
Eastern United States:** T. Christopher Roth, age 48
COO, Global Services: John A. Stirek, age 41
Managing Director, Human Resources: Robert A. James
Auditors: Ernst & Young LLP

LOCATIONS

HQ: 2001 Ross Ave., Ste. 3400, Dallas, TX 75201
Phone: 214-863-3000   **Fax:** 214-863-3138
Web: www.trammellcrow.com

PRODUCTS/OPERATIONS

2000 Sales

	% mil.	% of total
Corporate		
Corporate advisory services	143	19
Facilities management	139	18
Project management services	63	8
Institutional		
Property management	165	22
Brokerage services	154	20
Development		
& investment services	97	13
Total	**761**	**100**

Selected Subsidiaries

Broadview Central Texas, Ltd.
Environmental Asset Services, Inc.
Sixth Street Partners, Ltd.
TC New England Brokerage, Inc.
Tooley & Company, Inc.
Trammell Crow Asset Management, Inc.
Trammell Crow Brokerage Services, Ltd.
Trammell Crow Development, Inc.
Trammell Crow Realty Services, Inc.

COMPETITORS

Cadillac Fairview
CarrAmerica Realty
 Corporation
CB Richard Ellis
Cushman & Wakefield
Equity Group Investments
Forest City Enterprises
Grubb & Ellis
Hines Interests
Inland Group
Insignia Financial Group

Irvine Company
JMB Realty
Jones Lang LaSalle
Lefrak Organization
Lennar
Lincoln Property
Rouse
Simon Property Group
Tishman Realty
TrizecHahn

HISTORICAL FINANCIALS & EMPLOYEES

NYSE: TCC FYE: December 31	Annual Growth	12/91	12/92	12/93	12/94	12/95	12/96	12/97	12/98	12/99	12/00
Sales ($ mil.)	20.6%	—	170	175	201	227	255	293	460	628	761
Net income ($ mil.)	36.8%	—	3	3	4	4	12	(14)	47	54	35
Income as % of sales	—	—	1.7%	1.4%	1.9%	1.9%	4.7%	—	10.1%	8.7%	4.7%
Earnings per share ($)	—	—	—	—	—	—	—	(0.42)	1.28	1.50	0.98
Stock price - FY high ($)	—	—	—	—	—	—	—	25.75	37.56	28.00	15.31
Stock price - FY low ($)	—	—	—	—	—	—	—	20.25	15.00	10.50	10.31
Stock price - FY close ($)	(19.4%)	—	—	—	—	—	—	25.75	28.00	11.63	13.50
P/E - high	—	—	—	—	—	—	—	—	28	18	15
P/E - low	—	—	—	—	—	—	—	—	11	7	10
Dividends per share ($)	—	—	—	—	—	—	—	0.00	0.00	0.00	0.00
Book value per share ($)	26.7%	—	—	—	—	—	—	4.05	5.57	7.24	8.23
Employees	17.2%	—	—	2,400	2,500	2,500	2,900	3,400	5,100	6,500	7,300

STOCK PRICE HISTORY

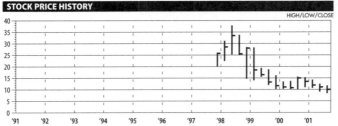

HIGH/LOW/CLOSE

2000 FISCAL YEAR-END

Debt ratio: 21.9%
Return on equity: 13.0%
Cash ($ mil.): 56
Current ratio: 1.55
Long-term debt ($ mil.): 82
No. of shares (mil.): 35
Dividends
 Yield: —
 Payout: —
Market value ($ mil.): 477

TRINITY INDUSTRIES, INC.

OVERVIEW

Dallas-based Trinity Industries operates six business units that serve transportation and construction markets. More than half of sales come from its Railcar Segment, which makes railroad tank cars for hauling products such as liquefied natural gas, liquid fertilizer, and corn syrup. The business also makes hopper, box, intermodal, and gondola cars for transporting everything from cement to lumber.

Other Trinity segments include Industrial Products, which makes metal containers for storing and transporting fertilizer and liquefied petroleum gas; Construction Products, which makes highway guardrails and other roadway barriers; and its Inland Barge Segment, which builds barges used to transport coal, grain, and other commodities. Trinity also makes ready-mix concrete and aggregates, primarily in Texas and Louisiana. The company also has a Parts and Services Segment.

Trinity's railcar business is riding out a declining market as well as the cyclical nature of the business. Anticipating intense competition as a result of this market decline, Trinity agreed to acquire rival Thrall Car Manufacturing, a privately held railcar maker. Trinity's highway construction products group has enjoyed high demand for its products due to increased federal highway spending.

HISTORY

Trinity Industries resulted from the 1958 merger of Trinity Steel, a maker of metal products for the petroleum industry, and Dallas Tank Co. The enterprise was headed by Ray Wallace, a Trinity Steel veteran since the 1940s.

The company (given its current name in 1966) acquired related tank, welding, and steel companies in the 1960s and quickly became the leading manufacturer of metal storage containers for liquefied petroleum gas. During this period it also applied its expertise to containers for another rapidly growing industry — fertilizer — and made custom products for the oil and chemical industries. Other products included railroad hopper bodies and tanks.

During the 1970s Trinity diversified into building seagoing vessels by purchasing Equitable Equipment and its Louisiana shipyards in 1972. The next year the company bought Mosher Steel (steel beams and framing products). By the mid-1970s it was producing highway guardrails and other road construction products. Trinity expanded its railcar parts manufacturing in 1977 to building complete cars and created a railcar-leasing subsidiary.

The company was a leading producer of railcars by the early 1980s, but a change in federal tax laws and a glut of railcars caused demand to plummet; in 1985 Trinity suffered its first loss in 27 years.

Still, Trinity managed to snap up failing competitors, including Pullman Standard, once the US's top freight car maker. It also bought Greenville Steel Car (1986), Ortner Freight (1987), and Standard Forgings (locomotive axles, 1987). Through these purchases Trinity tripled its manufacturing capacity, so that it controlled more than half of the US freight car production capacity in the early 1990s.

The company also expanded its marine division with such acquisitions as Halter Marine (1983) and Bethlehem Steel's manufacturing plant and marine facilities in Beaumont, Texas (1989).

In 1992 Trinity bought railcar maker Beaird Industries (sold in 1999). Trinity also expanded its construction products line with the purchase of Syro Steel (fabricated steel products) and the Texas and Louisiana operations of Lafarge (concrete, 1994).

The company expanded into Mexico in 1995 by acquiring Grupo TATSA (fabricated steel products). Trinity bought railcar services company Transcisco Industries, an acquisition that gave Trinity 23% of SFAT, Russia's largest private service railcar transportation company.

To fund expansion in other segments, Trinity spun off its Halter Marine Group in 1996. In 1997 Trinity acquired two manufacturing facilities from pipe fitting, flange, and valve industry specialist Ladish.

Wallace retired as chairman and CEO in 1999, handing over the company to his son, Timothy. That year Trinity bought McConway and Torley (railcar couplers) and Excell Materials (ready-mix concrete). It also set up a railcar joint venture in Brazil.

Early in 2000 Trinity expanded its equipment manufacturing unit with the purchases of T.L. Smith Machine and Highlands Parts Manufacturer, makers of concrete mixers and parts. Trinity also acquired Wear Products (castings for mining equipment). Less than two years after entering the concrete mixer market, Trinity got out of the struggling business. Also in 2001 Trinity agreed to acquire privately held railcar maker Thrall Car Manufacturing for about $353 million.

Chairman Emeritus: W. Ray Wallace
Chairman, President, and CEO: Timothy R. Wallace, age 47, $1,729,150 pay
EVP: John L. Adams, age 56, $852,750 pay
SVP; Group President, Concrete and Aggregate and Shared Services, Highway Safety: Mark W. Stiles, $743,818 pay
VP and CFO: Jim S. Ivy, $588,588 pay
VP, General Counsel, and Secretary: Michael G. Fortado, $207,295 pay
VP, Human Resources: Michael J. Lintner
VP, Labor Relations: Jack L. Cunningham Jr., $382,950 pay
VP, Mergers and Acquistions; President, Concrete and Aggregate: William A. McWhirter II
Group President, Inland Barge/International: Douglas H. Schneider
Group President, Railcar: John R. Nussrallah, $649,720 pay
Group President, Trinity e-Ventures: R. Stephen Polley, age 48
Group President, Trinity Industries de Mexico and World Wide LPG: Manuel Castro Sr.
President, Highway Safety Division: Rodney A. Boyd
President, TEMCO: Dan Banks
Treasurer: Neil O. Shoop
Auditors: Ernst & Young LLP

LOCATIONS

HQ: 2525 Stemmons Fwy., Dallas, TX 75207
Phone: 214-631-4420   **Fax:** 214-589-8810
Web: www.trin.net

Trinity Industries has 76 manufacturing operations in the US (in 21 states), and in Argentina, Brazil, Mexico, and Romania.

PRODUCTS/OPERATIONS

2001 Sales

	$ mil.	% of total
Railcars	742	36
Construction products	442	22
Parts & services	317	15
Industrial products	230	11
Inland barge	203	10
Other	113	6
Adjustments	(143)	—
Total	**1,904**	**100**

Business Segments and Related Products

Construction Products Segment
Aggregates
Beams and girders
Highway guardrails
Ready-mix concrete

Industrial Products Segment
Fertilizer containers
Heat-transfer equipment
Liquefied petroleum gas containers

Inland Barge Segment
Inland tank barges
River hopper barges

Parts and Services Segment
Railcar leasing, repair, and management

Railcar Segment
Box cars
Freight cars
Intermodal cars
Tank cars

COMPETITORS

ABC-NACO
ACF
Bombardier
Cemex
Conrad Industries
Duchossois Industries
GATX
GE Capital
Greenbrier
Holcim
Johnstown America
Lafarge North America
Nippon Sharyo
Pioneer Railcorp
TTX
Vulcan Materials

HISTORICAL FINANCIALS & EMPLOYEES

NYSE: TRN FYE: March 31	Annual Growth	3/92	3/93	3/94	3/95	3/96	3/97	3/98	3/99	3/00	3/01
Sales ($ mil.)	5.3%	1,192	1,540	1,785	2,315	2,496	2,234	2,473	2,927	2,741	1,904
Net income ($ mil.)	—	22	45	76	89	114	138	104	185	166	(74)
Income as % of sales	—	1.9%	2.9%	4.3%	3.8%	4.6%	6.2%	4.2%	6.3%	6.0%	—
Earnings per share ($)	—	0.69	1.27	1.89	2.20	2.72	3.21	2.36	4.25	4.15	(1.98)
Stock price - FY high ($)	—	21.26	30.85	47.38	40.00	40.38	37.63	55.69	55.13	37.50	26.63
Stock price - FY low ($)	—	15.34	17.68	29.51	30.38	28.13	30.38	24.13	27.56	19.75	18.19
Stock price - FY close ($)	(0.1%)	19.76	30.60	38.00	37.38	34.88	30.38	55.00	29.38	23.69	19.50
P/E - high	—	31	24	28	18	15	12	23	13	9	—
P/E - low	—	22	14	17	14	10	9	10	6	5	—
Dividends per share ($)	3.5%	0.53	0.53	0.61	0.68	0.68	0.68	0.68	0.68	0.72	0.72
Book value per share ($)	9.1%	10.92	12.96	14.37	15.95	17.93	18.83	20.40	23.20	23.18	23.86
Employees	4.3%	10,500	12,600	14,700	16,500	16,300	12,700	17,000	17,450	20,600	15,300

STOCK PRICE HISTORY

HIGH/LOW/CLOSE

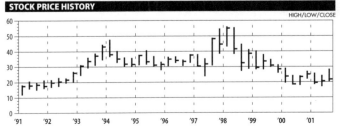

2001 FISCAL YEAR-END

Debt ratio: 4.8%
Return on equity: —
Cash ($ mil.): 14
Current ratio: 0.71
Long-term debt ($ mil.): 44
No. of shares (mil.): 37
Dividends
  Yield: 3.7%
  Payout: —
Market value ($ mil.): 718

THE TURNER CORPORATION

Most years, The Turner Corporation can turn a profit by putting up high-rise buildings. One of the world's leading general builders, Dallas-based Turner — a subsidiary of German construction group HOCHTIEF — has overseen construction of nearly 20 of the world's 100 tallest buildings. Among the landmarks it has erected are the U.S. Steel headquarters in Pittsburgh and the UN Secretariat and Plaza, Madison Square Garden, and Lincoln Center in New York City. Turner is also one of the largest commercial builders within the US, where it has a nationwide network of more than 40 locations.

The company, through Turner Construction and other units, provides construction and project management services, primarily for commercial and multifamily buildings, airports, stadiums, and correctional, entertainment, and manufacturing facilities. Turner plans and schedules construction, buys building materials, enlists subcontractors, and provides management services. It is recognized for its "mega" projects but also works on midsize and smaller projects through its special projects division.

Through subsidiary Turner International the company operates abroad, primarily in Asia and the Middle East, providing design/build, general contracting, and management services.

HISTORY

At the turn of the century, an engineer and devout Quaker named Henry Turner was convinced that a new type of steel-reinforced concrete (called the Ransome system) would change the construction industry. With this conviction and with the help of his partner, D. H. Dixon, Turner bought the rights to the technology for $25,000 and in 1902 founded Turner Construction Company.

One of the company's early projects was building the stairways for New York's first subway stations. As the Ransome method proved to be successful, Turner's reputation grew. Defense contracts during WWI raised Turner's take to $35 million in 1918.

Before the Depression, Turner was building high-rises, hotels, and stadiums. During the economic crash that started in 1929, the company survived by building retail stores, churches, and public buildings, a strategy it would employ successfully in later recessions.

Henry Turner retired in 1941. As WWII raged, more than 80% of the company's work was related to defense. Projects included constructing a submarine base and managing the facilities in Oak Ridge, Tennessee, during the development of the atomic bomb.

In 1947 H. C. Turner Jr., the founder's son, became president, and within four years he had led the company to more than $100 million in sales. By the time he stepped down as chairman in 1970, the firm had built skyscrapers, futuristic airports, and such landmarks as Madison Square Garden and the United Nations Secretariat and Plaza in New York City. Turner went public in 1969.

H. S. Turner (a cousin of H. C. Jr. and the final family member to head the business) led the company during the 1970s. It extended its global presence, opening offices in more countries, including Iran, Pakistan, and the United Arab Emirates. The company also developed construction management services.

In 1984 The Turner Corporation was formed as a holding company for the construction company and the subsidiaries created or acquired as a result of diversification. Property development was one of these activities, but by 1987 Turner had begun to dispose of its real estate holdings. It did not move quickly enough, however, and when the real estate market crashed, Turner was caught with a large portfolio.

As commercial projects slowed, Turner sought more public works and amusement projects. By 1994 these areas accounted for 70% of business. In 1993, as the building slump continued, Turner began a cost-cutting plan, which included laying off workers and closing offices. In 1996 Turner won a contract to build a 10,000-seat arena in Salt Lake City to be used for the 2002 Winter Olympics. In 1997 Turner contracted to renovate 811 schools and build two campuses in California's San Fernando Valley.

In 1999 the company agreed to be acquired by German construction giant HOCHTIEF in a $370 million deal that ended Turner's joint venture with Switzerland's Karl Steiner. The company also relocated its corporate headquarters to Dallas that year to take advantage of the construction boom in the US Southwest.

In 2000 Turner created three new business groups to serve the aviation, pharmaceutical, and sports sectors. By the next year Turner's sports group was working on 17 projects.

OFFICERS

Chairman and CEO; Chairman, Turner Construction:
Thomas C. Leppert
President and COO; President and CEO, Turner Construction: Robert E. Fee
EVP and Chief Technology Officer: Stephen E. Reiter
EVP: Bernhard H. Buerklin
SVP and CFO, Turner Corporation and Turner Construction: Donald G. Sleeman
SVP Research and Planning, Turner Corporation and Turner Construction: Anthony C. Breu
SVP, Turner Corporation and Turner Construction: Ralph W. Johnson
SVP, Turner Corporation and Turner Construction: Roger M. Lang
SVP Human Resources: Saro J. LaScala
VP and General Manager, Turner Aviation (Turner Construction): Jayne M. O'Donnell
VP and General Manager, Turner Pharmaceutical (Turner Construction): Kenneth J. Leach
VP and General Manager, Turner Sports (Turner Construction): Dale K. Koger
VP Human Resources: Bruce Ruthven
VP and Chief Information Officer: Douglas E. Nies
VP and Operations Manager: Richard C. Bach
Auditors: Arthur Andersen LLP

LOCATIONS

HQ: Bank of America Plaza, 901 Main St., Ste. 4900, Dallas, TX 75202
Phone: 214-915-9600 **Fax:** 214-915-9700
Web: www.turnerconstruction.com

The Turner Corporation and its subsidiaries have 41 offices throughout the US. US offices are in Alabama, Arizona, California, Colorado, Connecticut, Florida, Georgia, Illinois, Indiana, Massachusetts, Michigan, Missouri, New Jersey, New York, North Carolina, Ohio, Oregon, Pennsylvania, Tennessee, Texas, Virginia, Washington, and the District of Columbia. Turner International operates primarily in Asia and the Middle East.

PRODUCTS/OPERATIONS

Selected Projects
Arthur Ashe Tennis Stadium for USTA (Flushing Meadows, NY)
Equitable Life Assurance Society Tower (New York City)
Ericsson Stadium (Charlotte, NC)
International Convention Center (Birmingham, UK)
Invesco Field at Mile High for the Denver Broncos (Denver)
John Fitzgerald Kennedy Library (Dorchester, MA)
Kansas International Speedway (Kansas City, KS)
King Faisal Foundation's Al Faisaliah Center (Riyadh, Saudi Arabia)
Lincoln Center for the Performing Arts/Vivian Beaumont Theater and Avery Fisher Hall (New York City)
Long Beach Aquarium of the Pacific (Long Beach, CA)
Montefiore Children's Hospital (Bronx, NY)
Moscone Convention Center and Yerba Buena Gardens (San Francisco)
Motorola Business Campus (Juaguariuila, Brazil)
Mount Sinai Hospital (New York City)
Nationwide Arena (Columbus, OH)
Naval Sea Systems Command Headquarters (Washington, DC)
New Jersey Performing Arts Center (Newark, NJ)
Princeton Stadium (Princeton, NJ)
Rock & Roll Hall of Fame and Museum (Cleveland)
Taipei Financial Center (Taipei, Taiwan)
United Airlines Terminal One/O'Hare International Airport (Chicago)
United Nations Secretariat (New York City)
Washington State Football/Soccer Stadium (Seattle)

COMPETITORS

Austin Industries	Halliburton	Peter Kiewit
Barton Malow	Hensel Phelps	Sons'
Bechtel	Construction	Philipp
Bovis Lend Lease	Hunt	Holzmann
Centex	Construction	Skanska
Clark	Jacobs	Structure Tone
Enterprises	Engineering	Walbridge
Dillingham	MA Mortenson	Aldinger
Construction	McCarthy	Walsh Group
Fluor	Parsons	Washington
Foster Wheeler	PCL	Group
Gilbane	Construction	Whiting-Turner
Granite	Perini	
Construction		

HISTORICAL FINANCIALS & EMPLOYEES

Subsidiary FYE: December 31	Annual Growth	12/91	12/92	12/93	12/94	12/95	12/96	12/97	12/98	12/99	12/00
Sales ($ mil.)	10.4%	2,379	2,201	2,076	2,143	2,727	2,838	3,171	3,699	4,840	5,800
Employees	5.4%	2,620	2,600	2,500	2,499	2,600	2,800	3,000	3,200	3,500	4,200

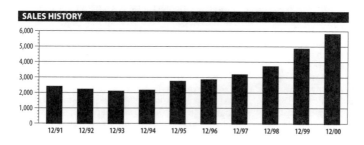

SALES HISTORY

TXU CORP.

OVERVIEW

Texas just wasn't big enough for TXU (formerly Texas Utilities). The Dallas-based holding company, Texas' largest utility, provides energy to more than 11 million customers in Australia, Europe, and, oh yes, Texas. The company, which has changed its name to its ticker symbol to reflect its broadened scope, is also engaged in energy trading, energy marketing, and telecommunications.

TXU Electric and TXU Gas, along with sibling power company TXU SESCO, provide energy to 4 million Texans. TXU's 23 power plants in the state (including one nuclear facility) have a generating capacity of some 21,000 MW. TXU Gas also owns the 7,200-mile long Lone Star Pipeline in Texas.

On the unregulated side of the business, TXU Energy Trading buys and sells wholesale electricity and natural gas throughout the US and in Canada, and TXU Energy Services provides energy-related products and services.

TXU also owns a 50% interest in Pinnacle One, which owns TXU Communications, a local phone company with 181,000 access lines and some 46,000 route miles of fiber-optic cable.

Overseas, TXU's acquisition of Norweb Energi created the largest electricity supplier in the UK. TXU Europe has 5.5 million gas and electricity customers there, as well as 10 power stations with a generating capacity of 6,830 MW. It is adopting TXU Energi as its UK retail brand. The company also generates and markets energy throughout Europe. TXU Australia Holdings' subsidiaries provide electricity and natural gas to about 1 million customers in Victoria.

TXU has been expanding its energy operations throughout the US and continental Europe, focusing on generation, transmission, and merchant trading businesses. It is selling off business units and assets that don't fit into these areas to better compete in deregulated markets and to reduce debt.

HISTORY

The first North Texas electric power company was founded in Dallas in 1883. Another was built in 1885 in Fort Worth. From these and other small power plants, three companies grew to serve most of the state: Texas Power & Light (TP&L, incorporated in 1912), Dallas Power & Light (DP&L, 1917), and Texas Electric Service (TES, 1929). Texas Utilities Company, called TU, was formed in 1945 as a holding company for the three utilities.

In the 1940s, TU began leasing large lignite coal reserves, and in 1952 formed Industrial Generating to mine lignite and operate a coal-fired power plant. TU, after pioneering lignite-burning technology in the 1960s, opened the first of nine large lignite units in 1971. In 1974 it began building the Comanche Peak nuclear plant near Fort Worth.

DP&L, TES, TP&L, and Industrial Generating joined in 1984 as Texas Utilities Electric (TU Electric). The mining company was renamed Texas Utilities Mining.

The Nuclear Regulatory Commission would not license Comanche Peak in 1985, citing design and construction faults, but finally granted the license in 1990. TU bought out its construction partners after much wrangling over multibillion-dollar cost overruns.

In 1993 TU bought Southwestern Electric Service (now TXU SESCO), another Texas electric utility. TU headed down under in 1996, buying Australian electric company Eastern Energy (now part of TXU Electricity). It

purchased gas dealer ENSERCH (now TXU Gas), which brought substantial energy services and trading assets on board, including Texas' largest gas utility, Lone Star Gas.

Despite a windfall tax levied by the UK's Labor Party, TU bought British utility Energy Group (now TXU Europe Group) for about $10 billion in 1998. TU sold Energy Group's Citizens Power, a US power marketer, and Peabody Coal, the #1 US coal producer, to the investment arm of Lehman Brothers.

In 1999 the Texas Legislature approved retail competition for the electric industry, beginning in 2002. That year Texas Utilities restructured its operations and began using the name TXU Corp. It officially changed its name in 2000.

Also in 2000 TXU acquired Norweb Energi, United Utilities' electricity and gas supply business, which added some 1.8 million electricity customers and 400,000 gas customers to TXU's rolls in the UK. TXU also contributed the stock of its telecommunications companies to Pinnacle One Partners in exchange for a 50% stake and about $960 million, which is earmarked for TXU's debt.

After raising its stake in Spanish utility Hidroeléctrica del Cantábrico to 19%, TXU agreed to sell its interest to a consortium led by Electricidade de Portugal and Spanish bank Caja de Ahorro de Asturias in 2001. That year, TXU also acquired a 50% stake in Stadtwerke Kiel, its first utility in Germany, where TXU Europe was already trading energy.

OFFICERS

Chairman and CEO; CEO, TXU Electric and CEO Gas:
Erle Nye, age 63
Vice Chairman, TXU Corp. and TXU Gas:
H. Jarrell Gibbs, age 63
President; Group President TXU Electric and TXU Gas:
David W. Biegler, age 54
COO: Paul Marsh, age 43
EVP; President, TXU Energy: Brian N. Dickie, age 45
EVP and CFO: Michael J. McNally, age 46
EVP Global Human Resources and e-Business:
Barbara B. Curry, age 46
VP Human Resources, TXU Corp.: Richard Wistrand
CEO, 24seven: David Owens
CEO, TXU Australia: Steve Philley
President, Eastern Energy: Roger Partington
President, Electric and Gas Distribution, TXU Electric & Gas: Dan Farell
President, Generation, TXU Energy: W. M. Taylor
President, Transmission and Pipeline, TXU Electric & Gas: M.S. Greene
President, TXU Europe Power and Energy Trading:
Martin Stanley
President, TXU Electric and Gas: Tom Baker
President, TXU Energy Trading: V.J. Horgan
President, TXU Energy Services: Rob McCoy
Auditors: Deloitte & Touche LLP

LOCATIONS

HQ: 1601 Bryan St., 33rd Fl., Dallas, TX 75201
Phone: 214-812-4600   **Fax:** 214-812-7077
Web: www.txu.com

TXU has energy operations in Australia, Bermuda, Canada, China, the Czech Republic, Finland, Germany, India, Italy, Mauritius, Mexico, the Netherlands, Norway, Poland, Spain, Sweden, Switzerland, the US, and the UK.

PRODUCTS/OPERATIONS

2000 Sales

	$ mil.	% of total
Electric	11,132	51
US energy marketing	5,508	25
Europe wholesale energy	3,318	15
Gas	1,658	7
Pipeline transportation	123	1
Other	270	1
Total	**22,009**	**100**

Selected Subsidiaries
TXU Australia Holdings (Partnership) Limited
  Partnership
TXU Electric Company
TXU Energy Industries Company
  TXU Investment Company
    Pinnacle One Partners, L.P. (50%)
TXU Gas Company
TXU International Holdings Limited

COMPETITORS

AEP	Enron	Reliant Energy
AES	Entergy	Royal
Atmos Energy	Exxon Mobil	Dutch/Shell
Avista	International	SBC
BP	Power	Scottish and
Brazos Electric	London	Southern
Power	Electricity	Energy
British Energy	Midlands	Scottish Power
Centrica	Electricity	Southern Union
Dynegy	Northern	TNP Enterprises
East Midlands	Electric	UtiliCorp
Electricity	PG&E	Western Power
Edison	Phillips	Distribution
International	Petroleum	
El Paso Electric	PowerGen	

HISTORICAL FINANCIALS & EMPLOYEES

NYSE: TXU FYE: December 31	Annual Growth	12/91	12/92	12/93	12/94	12/95	12/96	12/97	12/98	12/99	12/00
Sales ($ mil.)	18.2%	4,893	4,908	5,435	5,664	5,639	6,551	7,946	14,736	17,118	22,009
Net income ($ mil.)	—	(410)	700	369	543	(139)	754	661	740	985	916
Income as % of sales	—	—	14.3%	6.8%	9.6%	—	11.5%	8.3%	5.0%	5.8%	4.2%
Earnings per share ($)	—	(1.98)	3.26	1.66	2.40	(0.61)	3.35	2.85	2.79	3.53	3.43
Stock price - FY high ($)	—	43.00	43.75	49.75	43.13	41.25	43.75	42.00	48.06	47.19	45.25
Stock price - FY low ($)	—	34.13	37.00	41.63	29.00	30.13	38.50	31.50	38.38	32.75	25.94
Stock price - FY close ($)	0.7%	41.75	42.50	43.25	32.00	41.00	40.75	41.50	46.69	35.56	44.31
P/E - high	—	—	15	30	18	—	13	15	17	13	13
P/E - low	—	—	13	25	12	—	11	11	14	9	8
Dividends per share ($)	(2.4%)	2.99	3.03	3.07	3.08	3.08	2.00	2.10	2.20	2.30	2.40
Book value per share ($)	(2.1%)	36.63	36.44	35.89	34.31	30.40	31.69	32.80	34.18	30.15	30.13
Employees	0.9%	15,262	10,687	10,859	10,798	11,729	11,451	14,751	22,055	21,934	16,540

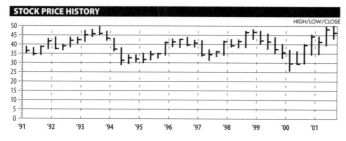

STOCK PRICE HISTORY
HIGH/LOW/CLOSE

2000 FISCAL YEAR-END
Debt ratio: 66.3%
Return on equity: 11.4%
Cash ($ mil.): 1,039
Current ratio: 0.57
Long-term debt ($ mil.): 15,281
No. of shares (mil.): 258
Dividends
  Yield: 5.4%
  Payout: 70.0%
Market value ($ mil.): 11,437

THE UNIVERSITY OF TEXAS SYSTEM

OVERVIEW

Students at The University of Texas System are looking to lock horns with higher education. Based in Austin, Texas, the UT System is one of the largest university systems in the US with more than 153,000 students at its nine campuses throughout the state. (Its flagship university in Austin, with more than 50,000 students, is the largest single campus in the US.) Many of UT's graduate programs rank near the top tiers, including business, education, engineering, and law. It also attracts more than $1 billion in research grants and contracts (mostly from the federal government), making it one of the nation's top research institutes. In addition, the UT System

runs six health institutions and four medical schools. Its $10 billion endowment fund, managed by the University of Texas Investment Management, is the third-largest in the country (behind Harvard and Yale).

With the bulging ranks of Generation Y looming on the horizon, the UT System expects its enrollment to swell to 250,000 by the end of the decade. To accommodate the increase, the system has laid out plans for nearly $3 billion in capital spending for new and improved facilities. It also hopes the improvements will put it on par with research institutions like California State.

HISTORY

The Texas Declaration of Independence (1836) admonished Mexico for having failed to establish a public education system in the territory, but attempts to start a state-sponsored university were stymied until after Texas achieved US statehood and fought in the Civil War. A new constitution in 1876 provided for the establishment of "a university of the first class," and in 1883 The University of Texas (UT) opened in Austin. Eight professors taught 218 students in two curricula: academics and law.

The school's first building opened in 1884, and in 1891 the university's medical school opened in Galveston. By 1894 UT-Austin had 534 students and a football team. UT opened a Graduate School in 1910 and various other colleges over the years. The university added its first academic branch campus when the Texas State School of Mines and Metallurgy (opened in 1914 in El Paso) became part of the system in 1919.

UT's financial future was secured in 1923 when oil was found on West Texas land that had been set aside by the legislature as an education endowment. The income from oil production, as well as the proceeds of surface-use leases, became the Permanent University Fund (PUF), from which only interest and earnings on the revenues can be used: two-thirds by UT and one-third by Texas A&M University. UT continued to grow, thanks to the PUF, which topped $100 million by 1940.

UT suffered the stigma of racial prejudice (as did many other institutions at the time) when it refused to admit Heman Sweatt, a black student, to its law school in 1946. The Supreme Court ordered UT to admit him in 1950, the same year the UT System was officially

organized. In 1966 in one of the nation's most highly publicized crimes, Charles Whitman killed 14 people and wounded 31 others with a high-powered rifle fired from atop the UT-Austin administration tower. The observation deck wasn't closed until 1975, however, after a series of suicides. (It was reopened in 1999.)

In the meantime, UT added a medical center in Dallas and several graduate schools in Austin. The 1960s through the 1980s were a time of geographic expansion for the system as it absorbed other institutions, opened several new campuses, and expanded its network of medical centers. In 1996 the UT System became the first public university to establish a private investment management company (University of Texas Investment Management Co.) to invest PUF money (by that time over $9 billion) and other funds.

The race issue reared its head again in 1996 when a Federal court ruled in the Hopwood decision (named for the plaintiff) that the UT System could no longer use race to determine scholarships and admissions. Minority enrollments declined the following year, prompting the Texas Legislature to enact a law granting admission to the top 10% of graduates from any Texas high school to the state university of their choice. Chancellor William Cunningham announced plans in 2000 to expand the UT System by 100,000 students over the decade. After he resigned that year, R. D. Burck took over as his successor. In 2001 UT received a $50 million donation from Texan and Minnesota Vikings owner Red McCombs, the largest gift in its history. Later that year, Burck announced his intention to step down by 2003.

Chairman, Board of Regents: Tom Loeffler
Vice Chairman, Board of Regents:
  Rita Crocker Clements
Executive Secretary, Board of Regents:
  Francie A. Fredrick
Chancellor: R. D. Burck
Executive Vice Chancellor Academic Affairs:
  Edwin R. Sharpe
Executive Vice Chancellor Business Affairs:
  Kerry L. Kennedy
Executive Vice Chancellor Health Affairs:
  Charles B. Mullins
Vice Chancellor and General Counsel:
  Cullen M. Godfrey
Vice Chancellor Development and External Relations:
  Shirley Bird Perry
Vice Chancellor Federal Relations: Mark Franz
Vice Chancellor Governmental Relations: Tom Scott
President, University of Texas at Arlington:
  Robert E. Witt
President, University of Texas at Austin:
  Larry R. Faulkner
President, University of Texas at Dallas:
  Franklyn G. Jenifer, age 61
President, University of Texas at El Paso:
  Diana S. Natalicio, age 61
President, University of Texas Pan American:
  Miguel A. Nevarez
President, University of Texas of the Permian Basin:
  Charles A. Sorber
President, University of Texas at San Antonio:
  Ricardo Romo
President, University of Texas at Tyler:
  Rodney H. Mabry
Director Human Resources: Gerald Schroeder
Auditors: Texas State Auditor

LOCATIONS

HQ: 601 Colorado St., Austin, TX 78701
Phone: 512-499-4200   **Fax:** 512-499-4218
Web: www.utsystem.edu

The University of Texas System has component institutions in Arlington, Austin, Brownsville, Dallas, Edinburg, El Paso, Galveston, Houston, Odessa, San Antonio, and Tyler, Texas.

PRODUCTS/OPERATIONS

University of Texas System Component Institutions

Academic Institutions
The University of Texas at Arlington (est. 1895; 19,148 students)
The University of Texas at Austin (est. 1883; 50,010 students)
The University of Texas at Brownsville (est. 1991; 9,094 students)
The University of Texas at Dallas (est. 1961; 10,137 students)
The University of Texas at El Paso (est. 1914; 14,695 students)
The University of Texas - Pan American (Edinburg; est. 1927; 12,520 students)
The University of Texas of the Permian Basin (Odessa; est. 1969; 2,222 students)
The University of Texas at San Antonio (est. 1969; 18,607 students)
The University of Texas at Tyler (est. 1971; 3,392 students)

Health Institutions
The University of Texas Health Center at Tyler (est. 1947)
The University of Texas Health Science Center at Houston (est. 1972; 3,170 students)
The University of Texas Health Science Center at San Antonio (est. 1959; 2,557 students)
The University of Texas M.D. Anderson Cancer Center (Houston; est. 1941)
The University of Texas Medical Branch at Galveston (est. 1891; 1,952 students)
The University of Texas Southwestern Medical Center at Dallas (est. 1943; 1,554 students)

HISTORICAL FINANCIALS & EMPLOYEES

School FYE: August 31	Annual Growth	8/91	8/92	8/93	8/94	8/95	8/96	8/97	8/98	8/99	8/00
Sales ($ mil.)	2.4%	4,796	3,433	3,744	4,030	4,300	4,624	4,803	5,244	4,131	5,943
Employees	2.6%	63,271	67,210	67,985	70,000	72,395	74,364	75,517	77,112	—	79,430

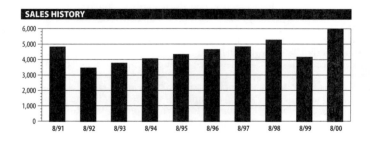

SALES HISTORY

USAA

OVERVIEW

Whether the country is at war or at peace, USAA's relationship with the US military stands firm. With more than 4 million customers, the San Antonio-based mutual company primarily serves military personnel and their families.

In addition to property/casualty (available only to military personnel) and life insurance, USAA offers several financial services through more than 85 subsidiaries and affiliates. These services include discount brokerage, investment management, and banking. It uses direct marketing via the telephone and Internet to distribute its products. It also sells merchandise (jewelry, major appliances, electronic and consumer goods) in seasonal catalogs and offers long-distance telephone services.

After dropping in the early 1990s, USAA's claims continue to rise, outpacing premium income. Technology costs have also cut into its bottom line. However, the company is expecting its membership to continue growing, projecting it to nearly double by 2010. In an attempt to increase revenue, the company has entered new markets — including efforts to target people less affluent than military officers. Cutting costs, USAA has streamlined operations by reducing staff and closing down divisions (including mailing, printing, and information technology offices).

HISTORY

In 1922 a group of 26 US Army officers gathered in a San Antonio hotel and formed their own automobile insurance association. The reason? As military officers who were often relocated, they found it difficult to get insurance because they were considered transient. So the officers decided to insure each other. Led by Major William Garrison, who became the first president, they formed the United States Army Automobile Insurance Association.

In 1924, when US Navy and Marine Corps officers were allowed to join, the company changed its name to United Services Automobile Association. By the mid-1950s the company had some 200,000 members. During the 1960s the company formed USAA Life Insurance Company (1963) and USAA Casualty Insurance Company (1968).

In 1969 Robert McDermott, a retired US Air Force brigadier general, became president. He cut employment through attrition, established education and training seminars for employees, and invested in computers and telecommunications (drastically cutting claims-processing time). McDermott added new products and services, such as mutual funds, real estate investments, and banking. Under McDermott, USAA's membership grew from 653,000 in 1969 to more than 3 million in 1993.

During the 1970s, in an effort to go paperless, USAA became one of the insurance industry's first companies to switch from mail to toll-free (800) numbers. In the early 1980s the company introduced its discount purchasing program, USAA Buying Services. In 1985 it opened the USAA Federal Savings Bank. In the late 1980s USAA began installing an optical storage system to automate some customer service operations.

McDermott retired in 1993. The following year USAA Federal Savings Bank began developing a home banking system, offering members information and services over advanced screen telephones provided by IBM.

In the early 1990s USAA's real estate activities increased dramatically. In 1995 USAA restructured its interest in the Fiesta Texas theme park in San Antonio in order to focus on previously developed properties in geographically diverse areas. That year Six Flags Theme Parks (now Six Flags, Inc.) assumed operation and management of Fiesta Texas (it purchased it from USAA in 1998).

In 1997 USAA began including enlisted military personnel as members. In 1998 USAA began offering Choice Ride in Orlando, Florida. For about $1,100 per quarter and a promise not to drive except in emergencies, the pilot program provided 36 round trips and a 90% discount on car insurance, in hopes of keeping older drivers from unnecessarily getting behind the wheel. That year, as part of its new Financial Planning Network, USAA began offering retirement and estate planning assistance aimed at 25- to 55-year-olds for a yearly $250 fee. In 1999 claims doubled largely as a result of the impact of Hurricane Floyd and spring hail storms hitting military communities in North Carolina and Virginia.

That year USAA also moved to consolidate its customers' separate accounts (such as mutual fund holdings, stocks and bonds, and life insurance products) into one main account to strengthen customer relationships and reduce operational costs. The next year, after completing a number of technology projects, it laid off workers for the first time in its history.

OFFICERS

Chairman, President, and CEO: Robert G. Davis
SVP, CFO, and Corporate Treasurer: Joe Robles Jr.
SVP and Chief Communications Officer:
Wendi E. Strong
SVP, Secretary, and General Counsel: Bradford W. Rich
SVP, Human Resources: Elizabeth Conklyn
Auditors: KPMG LLP

LOCATIONS

HQ: 9800 Fredericksburg Rd., USAA Building,
San Antonio, TX 78288
Phone: 210-498-2211   **Fax:** 210-498-9940
Web: www.usaa.com

USAA has major regional offices in California, Colorado,
Florida, Virginia, and Washington. It maintains
international offices in London and Frankfurt.

PRODUCTS/OPERATIONS

Selected Operations
USAA Alliance Services Company (merchandising &
member services)
USAA Federal Savings Bank
USAA Investment Management Company (mutual funds,
investment and brokerage services)
USAA Property & Casualty (including automobile, home,
boat, and flood insurance)
USAA Real Estate Company

COMPETITORS

21st Century	Kemper Insurance
Allstate	Liberty Mutual
American Express	MassMutual
American Financial	MetLife
American General	Morgan Stanley Dean
AXA Financial	Witter
Berkshire Hathaway	Mutual of Omaha
Charles Schwab	Nationwide
Chubb	New York Life
CIGNA	Northwestern Mutual
Citigroup	Pacific Mutual
CNA Financial	Prudential
FMR	St. Paul Companies
Guardian Life	State Farm
The Hartford	T. Rowe Price
John Hancock Financial	UBS PaineWebber
Services	

HISTORICAL FINANCIALS & EMPLOYEES

Mutual company FYE: December 31	Annual Growth	12/91	12/92	12/93	12/94	12/95	12/96	12/97	12/98	12/99	12/00
Assets ($ mil.)	17.1%	14,520	16,235	18,494	19,548	22,244	23,622	25,007	28,831	30,323	60,000
Net income ($ mil.)	8.0%	413	140	676	564	730	855	1,189	980	765	—
Income as % of assets	—	2.8%	0.9%	3.7%	2.9%	3.3%	3.6%	4.8%	3.4%	2.5%	—
Employees	5.0%	14,222	14,667	15,905	15,233	15,677	16,571	17,967	20,120	21,795	22,000

SALES HISTORY

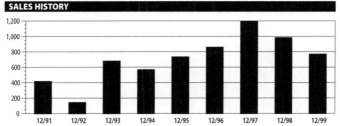

2000 FISCAL YEAR-END

Equity as % of assets: 0.0%
Return on assets: —
Return on equity: —
Long-term debt ($ mil.): —
Sales ($ mil.): 8,550

USX-MARATHON GROUP

In the long-running struggle for profits in the oil and gas industry, USX-Marathon Group is keeping ahead of the game. A business unit of diversified giant USX Corporation, Houston-based Marathon accounts for more than 80% of its parent's revenues; USX-U.S. Steel Group makes up the rest. Marathon explores for and produces oil and natural gas principally in 11 countries, including Angola, the UK, and the US. It has net proved reserves of 1.2 billion barrels of oil equivalent; 57% of reserves are in the US.

In hot pursuit of operating efficiencies, Marathon, an integrated oil company, has combined its downstream operations with those of Ashland. The venture, Marathon Ashland Petroleum (MAP), is 62%-owned by Marathon. MAP

holds stakes in several pipelines, operates asphalt and light-product terminals, and owns seven refineries in the US. It has more than 5,900 US gas stations, which operate under several brand names, including Ashland, Marathon, Speedway, and SuperAmerica.

Marathon is expanding exploration in key areas such as the Gulf of Mexico and the North Sea, as well as Gabon, and the Congo. It has formed an alliance with Russian oil giant Yukos to pursue international ventures. Seeking energy revenues beyond oil and gas, the company is investing in independent electric power generation projects outside North America.

Parent USX has announced plans to abandon its holding company structure and make U.S. Steel and Marathon independent companies.

HISTORY

Marathon was founded in 1887 in Lima, Ohio, as The Ohio Oil Company by 14 independent oil producers to compete with Standard Oil. Within two years Ohio Oil was the largest producer in the state.

This success did not go unnoticed by Standard Oil, which proceeded to buy Ohio Oil in 1889. In 1905 the company moved to Findlay, Ohio, where it remained until it relocated to Houston in 1990.

When the US Supreme Court broke up Standard Oil in 1911, Ohio Oil became independent once again. It expanded exploration activities to Kansas, Louisiana, Texas, and Wyoming.

In a 1924 attempt to drill three wells west of the Pecos River in Texas, it mistakenly drilled three dry holes to the east. The company was on the verge of abandoning the project until a geologist reported the error. Ohio Oil drilled in the right area and the wells flowed. That year the company bought Lincoln Oil Refining — its first venture outside crude oil production.

Ohio Oil continued its expansion into refining and marketing operations in 1927. After WWII the company began international exploration. Through Conorada Petroleum (now Oasis), a partnership with Continental Oil (now Conoco) and Amerada Hess, the company explored in Africa and South and Central America. Conorada's biggest overseas deal came in 1955, when it acquired concessions on more than 60 million acres in Libya.

In 1962 the company acquired Plymouth Oil and changed its name to Marathon Oil Company; it had been using the Marathon name in its marketing activities since the late 1930s. Marathon added a 200,000-barrel-a-day refinery

in Louisiana to its operations in 1976 when it acquired ECOL Ltd.

After a battle with Mobil, U.S. Steel acquired Marathon in 1982 for $6.5 billion. U.S. Steel changed its name to USX in 1986 and acquired Texas Oil & Gas. That year the US government introduced economic sanctions against Libya, putting Marathon's Libyan holdings in suspension.

USX consolidated Texas Oil and Marathon in 1990. After a protracted struggle with corporate raider Carl Icahn, USX split Marathon and U.S. Steel into two separate stock classes in 1991. A third offering, USX-Delhi Group (the pipeline operator division), followed the next year. (Koch Industries bought USX-Delhi in 1997.)

A consortium led by USX-Marathon signed an agreement with the Russian government in 1994 to develop oil and gas fields off Sakhalin Island (although USX-Marathon sold its stake in the project in 2000). In 1996 Marathon formed a venture, ElectroGen International, with East Coast utility DQE to develop power generation projects in the Asia/Pacific region.

In 1998 Marathon and Ashland merged their refining and retail operations, creating Marathon Ashland Petroleum, or MAP, of which USX-Marathon owns 62%.

As part of a restructuring drive, in 1999 MAP sold its crude oil gathering business, Scurlock Permian, to Plains All American Pipeline. Marathon ramped up its oil exploration in 2000, buying more deepwater leases in the Gulf of Mexico and acquiring an interest in an oil and gas play offshore of the Congo. It bought Pennaco Energy, a Colorado-based producer of coalbed methane gas in 2001.

OFFICERS

Chairman and CEO, USX Corporation: Thomas J. Usher, age 59, $3,825,000 pay
Vice Chairman, USX Corporation; President, Marathon Oil Company: Clarence P. Cazalot Jr., age 50, $1,995,652 pay
Vice Chairman and CFO, USX Corporation: Robert M. Hernandez, age 56, $1,600,000 pay
SVP, Human Resources and Public Affairs, General Counsel, and Secretary, USX Corporation: Dan D. Sandman, age 52, $1,145,167 pay
EVP, Marathon Oil Company: J. Louis Frank, age 64
SVP, Business Development, Marathon Oil Company: Steven J. Lowden, age 41
SVP, Production Operations, Marathon Oil Company: Steven B. Hinchman, age 52
SVP, Worldwide Exploration, Marathon Oil Company: Philip G. Behrman, age 50
VP, Human Resources, Marathon Oil Company: Eileen Campbell
Auditors: PricewaterhouseCoopers LLP

LOCATIONS

HQ: 5555 San Felipe Rd., Houston, TX 77056
Phone: 713-629-6600   **Fax:** 713-296-2952
Web: www.marathon.com

USX-Marathon Group conducts exploration and development in Angola, Canada, the Congo, Denmark, Gabon, Ireland, the Netherlands, Norway, UK, and the US.

2000 Sales

	$ mil.	% of total
US	32,239	95
Canada	856	2
UK	567	2
Other countries	197	1
Total	**33,859**	**100**

PRODUCTS/OPERATIONS

2000 Sales

	$ mil.	% of total
Refining, marketing, & transportation	28,693	85
Exploration & production	4,184	12
Other	982	3
Total	**33,859**	**100**

Selected Subsidiaries
Marathon Ashland Petroleum LLC (62%)
  Speedway SuperAmerica LLC
Marathon Canada Limited
Marathon International Oil Company
Marathon International Petroleum Ireland Limited
Marathon Oil Company
Marathon Oil U.K., Ltd
Marathon Petroleum Gabon LDC (Cayman Islands)
Marathon Petroleum Investment, Ltd.
Marathon Sakhalin Limited (Cayman Islands)

COMPETITORS

7-Eleven	Norsk Hydro	Texaco
Amerada Hess	Occidental	TransCanada
BP	PDVSA	PipeLines
Chevron	PEMEX	Ultramar
Enron	Phillips	Diamond
Exxon Mobil	Petroleum	Shamrock
Kerr-McGee	Royal	Unocal
Koch	Dutch/Shell	
Lyondell	Sinclair Oil	
Chemical	Sunoco	

HISTORICAL FINANCIALS & EMPLOYEES

NYSE: MRO FYE: December 31	Annual Growth	12/91	12/92	12/93	12/94	12/95	12/96	12/97	12/98	12/99	12/00
Sales ($ mil.)	10.3%	13,975	12,782	11,962	12,757	13,871	13,564	15,668	21,726	24,212	33,859
Net income ($ mil.)	—	(71)	(222)	(29)	321	(88)	664	456	310	654	432
Income as % of sales	—	—	—	—	2.5%	—	4.9%	2.9%	1.4%	2.7%	1.3%
Earnings per share ($)	—	(0.31)	(0.80)	(0.12)	1.10	(0.33)	2.29	1.58	1.05	2.11	1.39
Stock price - FY high ($)	—	33.13	24.75	20.63	19.13	21.50	25.50	38.88	40.50	33.88	30.38
Stock price - FY low ($)	—	20.88	15.75	16.38	15.63	15.75	17.25	23.75	25.00	19.44	20.69
Stock price - FY close ($)	1.4%	24.50	17.25	16.50	16.38	19.50	23.88	33.75	30.13	24.69	27.75
P/E - high	—	—	—	—	17	—	11	24	38	16	22
P/E - low	—	—	—	—	14	—	7	15	24	9	15
Dividends per share ($)	(5.0%)	1.40	1.22	0.68	0.68	0.68	0.70	0.76	0.84	0.84	0.88
Book value per share ($)	2.2%	12.88	11.65	10.85	11.92	10.63	12.25	12.53	13.98	15.40	15.72
Employees	2.5%	24,762	22,810	21,914	21,005	21,015	20,468	20,310	24,344	33,086	30,892

STOCK PRICE HISTORY

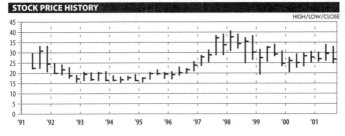

HIGH/LOW/CLOSE

2000 FISCAL YEAR-END

Debt ratio: 28.6%
Return on equity: 9.0%
Cash ($ mil.): 340
Current ratio: 1.24
Long-term debt ($ mil.): 1,937
No. of shares (mil.): 308
Dividends
  Yield: 3.2%
  Payout: 63.3%
Market value ($ mil.): 8,554

VALERO ENERGY CORPORATION

OVERVIEW

Like the Alamo (the Mission San Antonio de Valero) for which it was named, Valero Energy wants to be remembered — for cleaner fuels. The San Antonio-based refiner and marketer specializes in turning lower-cost residual oil and heavy crude into clean-burning, higher-margin products such as reformulated gasoline, oxygenates, and low-sulfur diesel. Valero will become the largest independent refiner in the US by buying Ultramar Diamond Shamrock.

With four refineries in Texas and Louisiana, Valero is the largest independent refiner and marketer on the Gulf Coast; it also has three refineries in California and one in New Jersey. Collectively its refineries have a daily production capacity of 1 million barrels. The company markets petroleum products wholesale in 34 states through 200 terminals.

Valero is banking on the growing worldwide demand for cleaner burning fuels to carry it through the oil industry's ups and downs. By acquiring a refinery in California from Exxon Mobil, the company has entered a market where such clean-burning gasoline brings a higher margin. Valero also gained 340 retail outlets in the deal.

HISTORY

Valero Energy was created as a result of the sins of its father, Houston-based Coastal States Gas Corporation. Led by flamboyant entrepreneur Oscar Wyatt, energy giant Coastal had established Lo-Vaca Gathering Company as a gas marketing subsidiary. Bound by long-term contracts to several Texas cities, Coastal was not able to meet its contractual obligations when gas prices rose in the early 1970s, and major litigation against the company resulted. The Texas Railroad Commission (the energy-regulating authority) ordered Coastal to refund customers $1.6 billion.

To meet the requirements, 55% of Lo-Vaca was spun off to disgruntled former customers as Valero Energy at the end of 1979. The new company was born fully grown — as the largest intrastate pipeline in Texas — with accountant-cum-CEO Bill Greehey, the court-appointed chief of Lo-Vaca, at its head. Greehey relocated the company to San Antonio, where it took its Valero name (from the Alamo, or Mission San Antonio de Valero) and put some distance between itself and its discredited former parent. Under Greehey's direction, Valero developed a squeaky-clean image by giving to charities, stressing a dress code, and keeping facilities clean.

Greehey diversified the company into refining unleaded gasoline. Valero bought residual fuel oil from Saudi Arabian refiners and in 1981 built a refinery in Corpus Christi, Texas, which went on line two years later. But in 1984 a glut of unleaded gasoline on the US market from European refiners undercut Valero's profits. To stay afloat, Valero sold pipeline assets, including 50% of its West Texas Pipeline in 1985 and 51% of its major pipeline operations in 1987. Refining margins finally began to improve in 1988. With one of the most modern refineries in the US, Valero did not have to spend a bundle to upgrade its refining processes to meet the tougher EPA requirements of the 1990s.

In 1992 Valero expanded its refinery's production capacity and acquired two gas processing plants and several hundred miles of gas pipelines from struggling oil firm Oryx Energy (acquired by Kerr-McGee in 1999). That year Valero became the first non-Mexican business engaged in Mexican gasoline production when it signed a deal with oil company Petróleos Mexicanos S.A. to build a gasoline additive plant there.

To expand its natural gas business substantially, Valero bought back the 51% of Valero Natural Gas Partners it didn't own in 1994. Valero also teamed up with regional oil company Swift Energy in a transportation, marketing, and processing agreement. As part of that deal, Valero agreed to build a pipeline linking Swift's Texas gas field with a Valero plant.

In 1997 the company sold Valero Natural Gas to California electric utility PG&E, gaining it $1.5 billion for expansion. It then purchased Salomon's oil refining unit, Basis Petroleum (two refineries in Texas and one in Louisiana) and the next year picked up Mobil's refinery in Paulsboro, New Jersey.

With low crude oil prices hurting its bottom line in 1999, Valero explored partnerships with other refiners as a way to cut operating costs. In 2000 the company bought Exxon Mobil's 130,000 barrel-per-day Benicia, California, refinery, along with 340 retail outlets, for about $1 billion.

In 2001 Valero gained two small refineries when it bought Huntway Refining, a leading supplier of asphalt in California. Also that year the company agreed to buy Ultramar Diamond Shamrock for $4 billion in cash and stock; in addition, Valero will assume about $2.1 billion of debt.

OFFICERS

Chairman, President, and CEO: William E. Greehey, age 64
EVP and COO: Gregory C. King, age 40, $720,833 pay
EVP and CFO: John D. Gibbons, age 47, $650,833 pay
EVP and Chief Administrative Officer: Keith D. Booke, age 42, $611,917 pay
SVP Corporate Communications: Mary Rose Brown
SVP Corporate Development: Michael S. Ciskowski
SVP Planning, Business Development, and Risk Management Division: S. Eugene Edwards, age 44
SVP Refining Operations Division: John F. Hohnholt, age 48, $572,504 pay
SVP and Chief Information Officer: William N. Latham
SVP and Controller: John H. Krueger
VP Investor Relations: Lee Bailey
VP Marketing, Supply, and Transportation Division: Gary L. Arthur Jr., age 44
VP and Treasurer: Donna M. Titzman
Corporate Secretary: Jay D. Browning
Manager Investor Relations: Eric Fisher
Auditors: Arthur Andersen LLP

LOCATIONS

HQ: One Valero Place, San Antonio, TX 78212
Phone: 210-370-2000   **Fax:** 210-370-2646
Web: www.valero.com

Valero Energy operates refineries in California, Louisiana, New Jersey, and Texas.

PRODUCTS/OPERATIONS

2000 Sales

	$ mil.	% of total
Gasoline & blending components	7,831	53
Distillates	3,747	26
Petrochemicals	387	3
Lubes & asphalts	295	2
Other	2,411	16
Total	**14,671**	**100**

Selected Products

Asphalt	Kerosene
Bunker oils	Low-sulfur diesel
CARB Phase II gasoline	Lube oils
Clean-burning oxygenates	Petrochemical feedstocks
Conventional gasoline	Petroleum coke
Crude mineral spirits	Premium reformulated
Customized clean-burning	and conventional
gasoline blends	gasolines
Gasoline blendstocks	Reformulated gasoline
Home heating oil	Sulfur
Jet fuel	

COMPETITORS

Amerada Hess	Marathon Ashland
BP	Petroleum
Chevron	Motiva Enterprises
CITGO	Phillips Petroleum
EOTT Energy Partners	Sunoco
Equilon Enterprises	Texas Petrochemicals
Exxon Mobil	TOTAL FINA ELF
Holly	Ultramar Diamond
Lyondell Chemical	Shamrock

HISTORICAL FINANCIALS & EMPLOYEES

NYSE: VLO FYE: December 31	Annual Growth	12/91	12/92	12/93	12/94	12/95	12/96	12/97	12/98	12/99	12/00
Sales ($ mil.)	34.6%	1,012	1,235	1,222	1,837	3,020	4,991	5,756	5,539	7,961	14,671
Net income ($ mil.)	14.7%	99	84	36	27	60	73	96	(47)	14	339
Income as % of sales	—	9.8%	6.8%	3.0%	1.5%	2.0%	1.5%	1.7%	—	0.2%	2.3%
Earnings per share ($)	10.5%	2.28	1.94	0.82	0.33	1.17	1.42	1.74	(0.84)	0.25	5.60
Stock price - FY high ($)	—	21.11	22.73	17.79	16.43	17.62	20.43	35.13	36.50	25.31	38.63
Stock price - FY low ($)	—	9.70	13.28	13.36	11.24	10.90	13.79	19.49	17.63	16.69	18.50
Stock price - FY close ($)	7.0%	20.26	15.58	14.39	11.49	16.68	19.49	31.44	21.25	19.88	37.19
P/E - high	—	9	12	22	91	16	15	14	—	101	7
P/E - low	—	4	7	16	62	10	10	8	—	67	3
Dividends per share ($)	(0.7%)	0.34	0.42	0.46	0.52	0.52	0.52	0.42	0.32	0.32	0.32
Book value per share ($)	4.2%	17.29	19.44	19.80	23.59	23.80	24.59	20.64	19.40	19.35	25.10
Employees	6.0%	1,890	1,890	1,740	1,666	1,654	1,673	1,855	2,500	2,518	3,180

STOCK PRICE HISTORY

HIGH/LOW/CLOSE

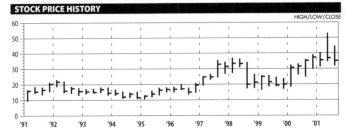

2000 FISCAL YEAR-END

Debt ratio: 40.6%
Return on equity: 26.0%
Cash ($ mil.): 15
Current ratio: 1.24
Long-term debt ($ mil.): 1,042
No. of shares (mil.): 61
Dividends
  Yield: 0.9%
  Payout: 5.7%
Market value ($ mil.): 2,263

VIGNETTE CORPORATION

OVERVIEW

Vignette helps businesses tell their own story. The Austin, Texas-based company has repackaged its flagship StoryServer content management software into a software suite that includes development tools for creating Web-based applications in the areas of content management, customer personalization, integration, and application deployment.

Using Vignette software, companies can distribute updated research, automate customer communication, configure their method of receiving it (via e-mail, fax, phone, pager, Web), and provide workflow, production, and project management. Vignette's clients include American Express, Lands' End, National Semiconductor, AOL Time Warner, and Hoover's (the publisher of this profile).

Vignette has acquired companies to fortify its push into Internet user analysis and site personalization. The company takes a modular approach to its products, which can be used individually or in a full suite or can be implemented with a variety of other third-party software, and they can be used on a wide variety of server platforms. It has tailored its software for both Java and Windows-based development applications, a move emulated by rivals Broadvision and Art Technology Group.

After aggressively expanding through acquisitions, the company has responded to a slumping economy by restructuring, trimming its workforce by about 45%.

HISTORY

Ross Garber and Neil Webber founded Vignette in 1995. The duo, who left executive posts at network software specialist DAZEL to form the venture, wanted to give magazines and newspapers that publish reams of information a way to manage and update the data.

Vignette's break came in 1996 when it allied with CNET (now CNET Networks), which bought a minority stake. Other investors included Austin Ventures, Amerindo, Morgan Stanley Dean Witter, Hambrecht & Quist, Olympus Partners, and Goldman Sachs Private Investment Funds. The company raised more than $36 million in funding — the largest venture investment in an Austin-based software company at the time.

Vignette used CNET's simplified Web publishing technology to form the basis for the development of StoryServer, which was shipped in 1997.

Vignette expanded its software line in 1998 with the purchase of Web site builder Random-Noise. That year Greg Peters, former CEO of software specialist Logic Works (now part of Computer Associates), replaced Garber as chief executive. A lackluster market prompted Vignette to halt its IPO plans for that year, but the company went public in February 1999. In May of that year, Vignette acquired Diffusion, a developer of multi-channel information delivery, including Web, e-mail, fax, telephone, and pager. Also in 1999 Garber resigned as chairman.

Fueled by the post-IPO success of its stock, Vignette in 2000 bought e-marketing software maker DataSage for $600 million. It also acquired e-commerce software maker OnDisplay for $1.7 billion, fueling a transformation away

from pure content management into Web customer relationship analysis. Also in 2000 Vignette bought Engine 5, Ltd, a developer of enterprise-wide Java server technology. Additionally it formed a strategic alliance with Austin-based accelerator venture fund AV Labs to help develop early stage Internet ventures and to give those startups access to Vignette products.

At the beginning of 2001 Vignette signed up its first Japanese customer, Impress Corp. Amid slowing sales the company began restructuring in 2001, cutting about 25% of its workforce. The company spun off its wireless software business into the newly formed venture SoloMio Corp. Vignette also announced plans to partner with IBM and Accenture to upgrade and administer a variety of Web sites for the IRS.

Also in 2001 the company introduced its V6 software suite, offering content management, personalization, integration, and analysis as well as the ability to offer real-time collaboration online. Vignette named Tom Hogan, formerly an executive at Siebel Systems, as president and COO.

With sales still sluggish, later that year the company announced additional job cuts of about 20%.

Chairman and CEO: Gregory A. Peters, age 40,
$239,404 pay
President and COO: Thomas E. Hogan
CFO: Charles W. Sansbury, age 33
SVP and Chief Technology Officer:
Steven W. Manweiler, age 39
**SVP; General Manager, Applications Platform Products
Division:** David J. Shirk, age 34, $265,561 pay
SVP, Global Sales and Operations: Dan J. Lautenbach
SVP, Products: William R. Daniel, age 45
SVP, Professional Services: Phillip C. Powers, age 42
Chief Information Officer: John J. Ciulla
VP, Human Resources: Dee Ann Thompson
Auditors: Ernst & Young LLP

LOCATIONS

HQ: 901 S. Mopac Expwy., Bldg. 3, Austin, TX 78746
Phone: 512-741-4300   **Fax:** 512-741-4500
Web: www.vignette.com

Vignette has offices in Australia, China, France, India,
Malaysia, Singapore, the UK, and the US.

2000 Sales

	% of total
US	74
Other countries	26
Total	**100**

PRODUCTS/OPERATIONS

2000 Sales

	% of total
Licenses	59
Services	41
Total	**100**

Selected Software

Analysis Products
Customer interactions management and personalization
(Vignette Relationship Management Server)

Content Products
Applications development and testing (Vignette
Advanced Deployment Server)
Internet content distribution (Vignette Content
Syndication Server)
Internet content management (Vignette Content
Management Server)
Wireless applications extension (Vignette Mobile
Application Suite)

Integration Products
Business transactions exchange and processing (Vignette
Collaborative Commerce Server)
E-commerce and business application integration
(Vignette Business Integration Studio)
Text, graphics, video, and audio files aggregation
(Vignette Content Aggregation Server)

Selected Services
Consulting
Needs analysis
Project analysis
Software integration
Training
Web site design and deployment

COMPETITORS

Art Technology	Exchange	Microsoft
Group	Applications	Open Market
BroadVision	FileNET	Oracle
Documentum	Gauss Interprise	PeopleSoft
E.piphany	IBM	Siebel Systems
Eprise	Interwoven	

HISTORICAL FINANCIALS & EMPLOYEES

Nasdaq: VIGN FYE: December 31	Annual Growth	12/91	12/92	12/93	12/94	12/95	12/96	12/97	12/98	12/99	12/00
Sales ($ mil.)	—	—	—	—	—	—	0	3	16	89	367
Net income ($ mil.)	—	—	—	—	—	—	(4)	(7)	(26)	(43)	(532)
Income as % of sales	—	—	—	—	—	—	—	—	—	—	—
Earnings per share ($)	—	—	—	—	—	—	—	—	—	(0.31)	(2.59)
Stock price - FY high ($)	—	—	—	—	—	—	—	—	—	56.15	100.57
Stock price - FY low ($)	—	—	—	—	—	—	—	—	—	6.20	14.56
Stock price - FY close ($)	(66.8%)	—	—	—	—	—	—	—	—	54.28	18.00
P/E - high	—	—	—	—	—	—	—	—	—	—	—
P/E - low	—	—	—	—	—	—	—	—	—	—	—
Dividends per share ($)	—	—	—	—	—	—	—	—	—	0.00	0.00
Book value per share ($)	248.3%	—	—	—	—	—	—	—	—	2.44	8.51
Employees	228.5%	—	—	—	—	—	20	156	310	757	2,330

STOCK PRICE HISTORY

HIGH/LOW/CLOSE

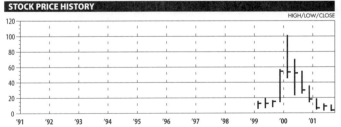

2000 FISCAL YEAR-END

Debt ratio: 0.0%
Return on equity: —
Cash ($ mil.): 436
Current ratio: 3.35
Long-term debt ($ mil.): 1
No. of shares (mil.): 238
Dividends
  Yield: —
  Payout: —
Market value ($ mil.): 4,280

WASTE MANAGEMENT, INC.

OVERVIEW

Waste Management is piling it higher and deeper. The Houston-based company, which provides pickup, transfer, landfill, and other nonhazardous-waste disposal services throughout North America, is #1 in the US solid-waste industry, ahead of Allied Waste. The company serves 27 million commercial, residential, municipal, and industrial customers through a network of some 600 landfills, collection centers, and transfer stations. It also operates waste-to-energy facilities and provides methane gas recovery at select landfills.

The company was formed when USA Waste Services, once the #3 waste management company in the US, acquired Waste Management in 1998, took its name, and climbed to the top spot. The ambitious deal was the culmination of USA Waste's growth strategy — using acquisitions to raise earnings, then using the resulting higher stock price to make more purchases.

But making the transition from industry consolidator to industry leader hasn't been easy. To pay down debt, the company has sold the solid- and hazardous-waste management businesses in Asia, Europe, and South America once operated by Waste Management International, and it is selling some noncore North American assets.

HISTORY

In 1956 Dean Buntrock joined his in-laws' business, Ace Scavenger Service, an Illinois company that Buntrock expanded into Wisconsin. Waste Management, Inc., was formed in 1971 when Buntrock joined forces with his cousin, Wayne Huizenga, who had purchased two waste routes in Florida in 1962. In the 1970s Waste Management bought companies in Michigan, New York, Ohio, Pennsylvania, and Canada. By 1975 it had an international subsidiary.

The company divided into specialty areas by forming Chemical Waste Management (1975) and offering site-cleanup services (ENRAC, 1980) and low-level nuclear-waste disposal (Chem-Nuclear Systems, 1982).

USA Waste was founded in 1987 to run disposal and collection operations in Oklahoma. It went public in 1988, and in 1990 Don Moorehead, a founder and former CEO of Mid-American Waste Systems, bought a controlling interest. Moorehead moved the business to Dallas and began buying companies in the fragmented industry. John Drury, a former president of Browning-Ferris, joined USA Waste in 1994 as CEO.

As USA Waste gathered steam, Waste Management got off track. It diversified, and Buntrock renamed the company WMX Technologies in 1993 to de-emphasize its waste operations. In 1997, however, the company reverted to the Waste Management name and, pressured by disappointed investor George Soros, CEO Phillip Rooney resigned. After more management changes, turnaround specialist Steve Miller became CEO, the fourth one in eight months, and Buntrock retired.

USA Waste picked up market share with large acquisitions, including Envirofill (1994), Chambers Development Corporation (1995), and Western Waste Industries and Sanifill

(1996). In 1996 the company moved to Houston. During the next two years it bought Mid-American Waste, the Canadian operations of Allied Waste and Waste Management, and TransAmerican Waste Industries.

1998 saw the $20-billion merger between USA Waste and Waste Management. The new company, bearing the Waste Management name and led by Drury and other former USA Waste executives, controlled nearly a quarter of North America's waste business. The company finished the year by agreeing to pay shareholders $220 million in a suit over overstated earnings.

The new Waste Management bought Eastern Environmental Services for $1.3 billion in 1999. (A legal battle over negotiations between Eastern and Waste Management executives was settled out of court in 2000.) Drury took leave in 1999 because of an illness that would claim his life, and director Ralph Whitworth, known as a shareholder activist, stepped in as acting chairman.

The company faced shareholder lawsuits after it was reported that executives had sold shares before a second-quarter earnings shortfall was announced. Waste Management said it would investigate the sales; later, so did the SEC. (By 2001 the company had settled with both the SEC and shareholders.) In the fallout, president and COO Rodney Proto, who had sold shares before the earnings announcement, was fired. Later that year the company tapped Maury Myers, CEO of trucking company Yellow Corp., to take over as chairman and CEO.

In 2000, to concentrate on its core business in North America, Waste Management sold operations in Europe, Asia, and South America in a series of transactions that raised about $2.5 billion.

OFFICERS

Chairman, President, and CEO: A. Maurice Myers, age 60
EVP and CFO: William L. Trubeck, age 54
EVP, General Counsel, and Secretary: Lawrence O'Donnell III, age 43
SVP Information Systems and Chief Information Officer: Thomas L. Smith, age 61
SVP People: Robert E. Dees Jr., age 50
SVP Operations: Charles E. Williams, age 51
SVP Sales and Marketing: James E. Trevathan Jr., age 47
SVP, Eastern Area: Richard T. Felago, age 53
VP and Chief Accounting Officer: Bruce E. Snyder, age 45
VP and Treasurer: Ronald H. Jones, age 50
VP and General Counsel, Labor and Employment: Mark Schwartz
VP and Southern Area General Counsel: John Van Gessel
VP and Deputy General Counsel: David P. Steiner
VP and Assistant General Counsel, Regulatory, Health, Environment, and Safety: Steve Morgan
VP Business Ethics and Compliance: William E. Prachar, age 54
VP Corporate Communications: Sarah A. Peterson
VP Customer Service: Paul Marshall
VP Financial Planning and Analysis: Robert C. Huff
VP Fleet Services and Logistics: Thomas F. Derieg
VP Government Affairs: Allan Stalvey
VP Human Resources and Recruiting: Jimmy D. LaValley
Auditors: Arthur Andersen LLP

LOCATIONS

HQ: 1001 Fannin, Ste. 4000, Houston, TX 77002
Phone: 713-512-6200   **Fax:** 713-512-6299
Web: www.wm.com

PRODUCTS/OPERATIONS

2000 Sales

	$ mil.	% of total
North American solid waste		
Collection	7,675	53
Disposal	3,366	23
Transfer	1,394	11
Recycling & other	805	5
Waste Management International	809	5
Nonsolid waste	465	3
Adjustments	(2,022)	—
Total	**12,492**	**100**

Selected Services
Collection
Disposal
Hazardous waste management
Portable sanitation services
Recycling
Transfer stations
Treatment

COMPETITORS

Allied Waste
Casella Waste Systems
Republic Services
Safety-Kleen
Waste Connections

HISTORICAL FINANCIALS & EMPLOYEES

NYSE: WMI FYE: December 31	Annual Growth	12/91	12/92	12/93	12/94	12/95	12/96	12/97	12/98	12/99	12/00
Sales ($ mil.)	106.5%	18	52	78	176	457	1,313	2,614	12,704	13,127	12,492
Net income ($ mil.)	—	3	7	10	14	30	33	267	(771)	(398)	(97)
Income as % of sales	—	16.4%	14.0%	12.3%	7.8%	6.6%	2.5%	10.2%	—	—	—
Earnings per share ($)	—	0.32	0.65	0.32	0.08	0.54	0.37	1.23	(1.32)	(0.65)	(0.16)
Stock price - FY high ($)	—	18.00	18.50	15.00	15.13	22.50	34.25	44.13	58.19	60.00	28.31
Stock price - FY low ($)	—	5.38	10.50	9.75	10.38	10.00	17.25	28.63	34.44	14.00	13.00
Stock price - FY close ($)	5.3%	17.50	14.50	11.38	11.38	18.88	31.88	39.25	46.63	17.19	27.75
P/E - high	—	56	28	47	189	40	88	34	—	—	—
P/E - low	—	17	16	30	130	18	44	22	—	—	—
Dividends per share ($)	—	0.00	0.00	0.00	0.00	0.00	0.00	0.00	0.01	0.02	0.01
Book value per share ($)	10.7%	3.10	3.80	3.98	4.78	6.12	8.28	12.07	7.19	7.02	7.71
Employees	73.2%	406	400	650	1,200	2,500	9,800	17,700	68,000	75,000	57,000

STOCK PRICE HISTORY

HIGH/LOW/CLOSE

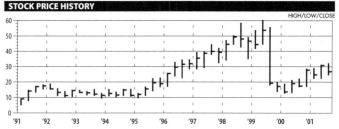

2000 FISCAL YEAR-END

Debt ratio: 63.6%
Return on equity: —
Cash ($ mil.): 94
Current ratio: 0.84
Long-term debt ($ mil.): 8,372
No. of shares (mil.): 623
Dividends
  Yield: 0.0%
  Payout: —
Market value ($ mil.): 17,279

WHOLE FOODS MARKET, INC.

OVERVIEW

How bad can a food fight get when the foods being thrown are all-natural, chemical-free, and good for you? Pretty vicious, even for Whole Foods Market, the nation's largest chain of natural foods stores (by sales). Growing quickly through acquisitions, the Austin, Texas-based company operates about 117 supermarket-sized stores in 22 states and Washington, DC, mostly under the Whole Foods Market banner. It also runs stores under the names Fresh Fields, Bread & Circus, and Wellspring Grocery. The company's merchandise is generally more expensive than similar items found in traditional supermarkets; however, many of its products are organic and free of additives, preservatives, and/or sweeteners.

Since health foods stores don't have as wide of an appeal as mainstream supermarkets, Whole Foods and rival Wild Oats are battling each other for customers city by city. After Wild Oats opened stores in markets dominated by Whole Foods, the company answered back by opening a new store in Wild Oats' hometown of Boulder, Colorado.

To boost profit margins, Whole Foods is expanding its range of private-label items, which includes premium brands Whole Foods and Whole Kids, and the less-expensive 365 brand. It sells some items online through a co-branding agreement with Gaiam.com (Whole Foods owns a minority stake in Gaiam).

HISTORY

With a $10,000 loan from his father, John Mackey started Safer Way Natural Foods in Austin, Texas, in 1978. Despite struggling, Mackey dreamed of opening a larger, supermarket-sized natural foods store. Two years later Safer Way merged with Clarksville Natural Grocery, and Whole Foods Market was born. Led by Mackey, that year it opened an 11,000-sq.-ft. supermarket in a counterculture hotbed of Austin. The store was an instant success, and a second store was added 18 months later in suburban Austin.

The company slowly expanded in Texas, opening or buying stores in Houston in 1984 and Dallas in 1986. Whole Foods expanded into Louisiana in 1988 with the purchase of like-named Whole Food Co., a single New Orleans store owned by Peter Roy (who served as the company's president from 1993 to 1998). Sticking to university towns, Whole Foods added another store in California the following year and acquired Wellspring Grocery (two stores, North Carolina) in 1991. In 1992 it debuted its first private-label products under the Whole Foods name. Seeking capital to expand even more, the company raised $23 million by going public in early 1992 with 12 stores.

Every competitor in the fragmented health foods industry became a potential acquisition, and the chain began growing rapidly. In 1992 Whole Foods bought the six-store Bread & Circus chain in New England. The next year it added Mrs. Gooch's Natural Foods Markets, a seven-store chain in the Los Angeles area. Its biggest acquisition came in 1996, when it bought Fresh Fields, the second-largest US natural foods chain, with 22 stores on the East Coast and in Chicago. Although the purchase

hurt profits in 1996, sales surpassed $1 billion for the first time in fiscal 1997 as Whole Foods neared 70 stores. In 1997 it introduced the less-expensive 365 brand private label and acquired the Granary Market (Monterey, California) and Bread of Life (two stores, South Florida) natural foods supermarkets.

Capitalizing on the growing popularity of nutraceuticals (natural supplements with pharmaceutical-type benefits), late in 1997 the company paid $146 million for Amrion, a maker of nutraceuticals and other nutritional supplements (merged with subsidiary WholePeople.com in 2000). It capped the year by buying coffee roaster Allegro Coffee Company. Both companies are based in Boulder, Colorado, home of its main rival, the smaller Wild Oats. Also in 1997 Whole Foods acquired the six-store Merchant of Vino natural foods and wine shop chain to foster the development of its wine departments.

In 1998 Whole Foods opened its first store in Boulder, a 39,000-sq.-ft. superstore with amenities such as a juice bar and a prepared foods section. At the end of that year, Roy resigned as president and was replaced by Chris Hitt. In 1999 Whole Foods bought four-store Boston-area chain Nature's Heartland for $25 million.

In 2000 Whole Foods merged its online operations (wholefoods.com) with its direct marketing and nutritional supplement unit (Amrion) to form Wholepeople.com. Later that year the company merged Wholepeople.com with lifestyle marketing firm Gaiam; Whole Foods received a minority stake in Gaiam and started selling food online through Gaiam.com.

OFFICERS

Chairman and CEO: John P. Mackey, age 47,
$210,000 pay
President: Chris Hitt, age 51, $266,000 pay
EVP, Operations: Walter Robb, age 47
VP and COO: James P. Sud, age 48, $244,000 pay
VP and CFO: Glenda Flanagan, age 47, $244,000 pay
VP of Human Resources: Cindy Strunk
President, Florida Region: Juan Nunez, age 43
President, Mid-Atlantic Region: Michael Besancon,
age 54, $232,000 pay
President, Midwest Region: Dan Rodenberg, age 45
President, Northeast Region: A. C. Gallo, age 47
President, Southern Pacific Region: Rich Cundiff,
age 43
President, Southwest Region: Lee Valkenaar, age 45
Auditors: KPMG LLP

LOCATIONS

HQ: 601 N. Lamar, Ste. 300, Austin, TX 78703
Phone: 512-477-4455   **Fax:** 512-477-1301
Web: www.wholefoodsmarket.com

2000 Stores

	No.
California	32
Texas	12
Massachusetts	11
Illinois	8
Michigan	8
Virginia	7
Florida	5
Maryland	5
North Carolina	5
Pennsylvania	5
New Jersey	4
District of Columbia	2
Georgia	2
Minnesota	2
Arizona	1
Colorado	1
Connecticut	1
Louisiana	1
New Mexico	1
New York	1
Rhode Island	1
Washington	1
Wisconsin	1
Total	**117**

COMPETITORS

Albertson's
AMCON Distributing
Arden Group
Delhaize America
Fiesta Mart
GNC
H-E-B
Kroger
NBTY
Publix
Rexall Sundown
Safeway
Shaw's
Trader Joe's Co
Wild Oats Markets
Winn-Dixie

HISTORICAL FINANCIALS & EMPLOYEES

Nasdaq: WFMI FYE: Last Sunday in September	Annual Growth	9/91	9/92	9/93	9/94	9/95	9/96	9/97	9/98	9/99	9/00
Sales ($ mil.)	39.4%	93	120	322	402	496	892	1,117	1,390	1,568	1,839
Net income ($ mil.)	—	2	3	4	9	8	(17)	27	45	42	(5)
Income as % of sales	—	1.7%	2.6%	1.2%	2.1%	1.7%	—	2.4%	3.3%	2.7%	—
Earnings per share ($)	—	—	0.22	0.15	0.04	0.09	(0.27)	0.53	0.82	0.77	(0.10)
Stock price - FY high ($)	—	—	8.50	11.69	12.88	8.38	18.56	19.44	35.06	25.38	30.00
Stock price - FY low ($)	—	—	3.63	4.25	6.63	4.75	5.44	8.75	17.31	14.13	15.13
Stock price - FY close ($)	25.0%	—	4.50	9.88	7.50	6.56	13.25	19.31	21.06	16.36	26.84
P/E - high	—	—	39	78	322	93	—	35	40	32	—
P/E - low	—	—	17	28	166	53	—	16	20	18	—
Dividends per share ($)	—	—	0.00	0.00	0.00	0.00	0.00	0.00	0.00	0.00	0.00
Book value per share ($)	11.1%	—	2.49	2.99	3.80	3.84	3.82	4.20	5.23	5.90	5.80
Employees	34.3%	1,300	2,350	4,150	5,300	6,137	9,848	11,268	14,200	16,600	18,500

STOCK PRICE HISTORY

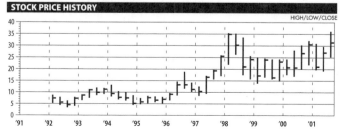

2000 FISCAL YEAR-END

Debt ratio: 49.2%
Return on equity: —
Cash ($ mil.): 0
Current ratio: 1.06
Long-term debt ($ mil.): 298
No. of shares (mil.): 53
Dividends
  Yield: —
  Payout: —
Market value ($ mil.): 1,421

WYNDHAM INTERNATIONAL, INC.

OVERVIEW

Wyndham International has left its real estate investment trust (REIT) status behind and to become a plain-old operator of hotels. In its former life, the Dallas-based company operated as Patriot American Hospitality, a paired-share REIT trading with hotel operator Wyndham International. Struggling to stay afloat, in 1999 Patriot American Hospitality accepted a $1 billion bailout from an investor group, dropped its REIT status, and merged with Wyndham International.

The company left standing when the dust cleared was Wyndham International, an owner or operator of more than 240 hotels across Canada, the Caribbean, Europe, Mexico, and the US. Primarily of the upscale variety, the company's hotels operate under brand names such as Wyndham Hotels & Resorts, Wyndham Luxury Resorts, and Summerfield Suites by Wyndham. Wyndham's Performance Hospitality Management division manages non-proprietary brands such as Hilton, Holiday Inn, and Hyatt.

After leaving the REIT behind, the company is selling off non-core assets to focus on expanding its core Wyndham hotel brand. As part of that strategy in 2001 the company sold its stake in seven Marriott branded hotels to Host Marriott.

Investors include affiliates of Apollo Investment Fund (about 27%), affiliates of Thomas H. Lee Equity Fund (19%), and affiliates of Beacon Capital Partners (about 11%).

HISTORY

Wyndham International traces its roots to Patriot American Group, which was formed by real estate lawyer Paul Nussbaum and other investors in 1991. Patriot American Group's purpose was to buy cut-rate real estate peddled by the Resolution Trust Company in the wake of the 1980s savings and loan crisis. In 1995 it sold an 83% stake in 20 of its hotels in the form of a public company called Patriot American Hospitality. Between 1995 and 1997, Patriot American Hospitality added interests in more than 55 hotels to its portfolio.

Patriot American Hospitality picked up its paired-share real estate investment trust (REIT) status in 1997 when it merged with the California Jockey Club, whose stock was paired with that of Bay Meadows Operating Company (a racetrack). The deal was a reverse merger through which California Jockey Club changed its name to Patriot American Hospitality, and Bay Meadows changed its name to Patriot American Hospitality Operating Company.

In 1998 Patriot American added 217 hotels through its acquisition of Interstate Hotels and another 106 hotels by purchasing Wyndham Hotel Corporation. Following the Wyndham acquisition, Patriot American Hospitality Operating Company changed its name to Wyndham International, and the result was Patriot American Hospitality, a paired-share REIT trading with operating company Wyndham International. That same year Wyndham Hotels acquired the tony Golden Door Spa in Escondido, California.

By 1999 Patriot American Hospitality boasted nearly 475 hotels, but its aggressive acquisition tactics had left it with a heavy debt burden. To settle a lawsuit with Marriott, the company also was forced to spin off the hotel management activities of Interstate Hotels. With its financial health in jeopardy, Patriot American Hospitality accepted a $1 billion bailout from an investor group, dropped its REIT status, became a corporation, and merged with Wyndham International. James Carreker replaced Nussbaum as CEO. The company was recast as a hotelier operating under Wyndham International name.

In 2000 president Fred Kleisner was tapped as CEO (Carreker initially remained chairman, but resigned that position a few months later). The same year, the company sold its Sierra Suites and Clubhouse hotel chains and agreed to sell UK hotel chain Malmaison.

In 2001 the company signed deals to manage several hotels, including sites in New Orleans, San Diego, Vancouver, Martha's Vineyard, and St. Maarten's in the Carribean. The company also announced plans to add a Golden Door Spa to its Dallas Anatole Hotel.

Also in 2001 Wyndham International, pointing to a weakening economy, announced plans to layoff 850 workers. Following the terrorist attacks of September 11, the company said it would cut its workforce by another 1,600 employees as the travel industry saw a drastic slowdown in business.

OFFICERS

Chairman and CEO: Fred J. Kleisner, age 56, $1,544,054 pay
President and COO: Ted Teng, $936,539 pay
EVP and CFO: Richard A. Smith, $717,116 pay
EVP: Michael A. Grossman, $466,154 pay
EVP, Business Development and Chief Investment Officer: Joseph Champ
EVP: David Johnson, $611,405 pay
SVP and Chief Technology Officer: Mark F. Hedley
SVP Diversity and Assistant to the Chairman: Donna DeBerry
SVP Human Resources: Mary Watson
SVP Operations Resources: Curt R. Ewald
SVP Resort Operations: Jay A. Litt, age 54
SVP Sales: James Walters
SVP Vacation Ownership: Robert S. Davis
Auditors: Pricewaterhouse Coopers LLP

LOCATIONS

HQ: 1950 Stemmons Fwy., Ste. 6001, Dallas, TX 75207
Phone: 214-863-1000   **Fax:** 214-863-1527
Web: www.wyndhamintl.com

Wyndham International has hotels in Canada, the Caribbean, Europe, Mexico, and the US.

PRODUCTS/OPERATIONS

2000 Sales

	% of total
Wyndham Hotels & Resorts	48
Non-Proprietary Properties	39
Summerfield Suites	6
Wyndham Luxury Resorts	4
Wyndham Garden Hotels	3
Total	**100**

Selected Hotel Brands
Summerfield Suites by Wyndham (extended-stay upscale suites)
Wyndham Hotels & Resorts (upper-upscale hotels for business, leisure, and resort markets)
Wyndham Luxury Resorts (five-star hotels and resorts)

COMPETITORS

Accor
Carlson
Fairmont Hotels
Granada
Hilton
Hilton Group
Hyatt
Marriott International
MeriStar Hotels & Resorts
Six Continents Hotels
Starwood Hotels & Resorts

HISTORICAL FINANCIALS & EMPLOYEES

NYSE: WYN FYE: December 31	Annual Growth	12/91	12/92	12/93	12/94	12/95	12/96	12/97	12/98	12/99	12/00
Sales ($ mil.)	60.9%	—	54	84	102	11	82	328	1,952	2,484	2,422
Net income ($ mil.)	—	—	1	3	7	6	38	(2)	(158)	(1,072)	(325)
Income as % of sales	—	—	2.6%	3.4%	6.8%	54.5%	46.2%	—	—	—	—
Earnings per share ($)	—	—	—	—	—	—	—	(0.04)	(2.57)	(7.20)	(2.56)
Stock price - FY high ($)	—	—	—	—	—	—	—	34.50	29.50	7.00	2.94
Stock price - FY low ($)	—	—	—	—	—	—	—	23.16	5.31	2.44	1.31
Stock price - FY close ($)	(60.7%)	—	—	—	—	—	—	28.81	6.00	2.94	1.75
P/E - high	—	—	—	—	—	—	—	—	—	—	—
P/E - low	—	—	—	—	—	—	—	—	—	—	—
Dividends per share ($)	—	—	—	—	—	—	—	0.26	1.28	0.00	0.00
Book value per share ($)	—	—	—	—	—	—	—	13.51	12.19	12.79	10.72
Employees	(28.0%)	—	—	—	—	—	—	—	54,000	32,000	28,000

STOCK PRICE HISTORY

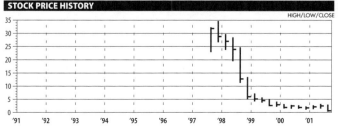

HIGH/LOW/CLOSE

2000 FISCAL YEAR-END

Debt ratio: 60.4%
Return on equity: —
Cash ($ mil.): 53
Current ratio: 0.41
Long-term debt ($ mil.): 2,737
No. of shares (mil.): 167
Dividends
  Yield: —
  Payout: —
Market value ($ mil.): 293

ZALE CORPORATION

OVERVIEW

A trip to the altar often begins with a trip to Zales. Irving, Texas-based Zale is the US's largest specialty jewelry retail chain. It has more than 2,300 stores, primarily in malls, in all 50 states, Canada, and Puerto Rico.

Zale, which lost its luster early in the 1990s and spent time in bankruptcy protection, has repositioned its jewelry chains to reduce the possibility of cannibalizing sales. Zales Jewelers, the largest unit, sells moderately priced jewelry, watches, and gift items. Gordon's Jewelers, which once targeted Zale's customers, has been repositioned in the upper-moderate price range with merchandise that is more contemporary and regional. The Bailey Banks & Biddle Fine Jewelers division offers higher-end jewelry. In Canada, Zale operates about 170 Peoples Jewellers locations.

Further broadening its customer base, the company has opened more than 40 Zale Outlet stores and is selling merchandise by direct mail and through its Web site. It has also purchased about 95% of US kiosk jeweler Piercing Pagoda to target customers shopping for low-priced jewelry.

HISTORY

Russian immigrant Morris Zale opened his first jewelry store in Wichita Falls, Texas, in 1924. The store's most popular items were fountain pens. Zale advertised and offered credit, both of which were novel for the jewelry business of the day, and by 1937 the budding chain had seven stores.

The firm managed to survive the Depression — people were still getting married — and by 1941 it had 12 shops. It added upscale Houston jeweler Corrigan's three years later. Zale established buying offices in the diamond capitals of New York City and Antwerp, Belgium, which allowed it to buy wholesale. Sales were $10 million in 1946, the year the company moved its headquarters to Dallas.

Zale grew rapidly following WWII and had 50 stores by the mid-1950s. During that time the company became a fully integrated jeweler, buying raw goods and manufacturing its jewelry (including cutting and polishing its diamonds). Zale went public in 1957. It acquired Philadelphia-based Bailey Banks & Biddle in 1962 and became the world's largest retailer, with more than 400 stores by the mid-1960s.

Spooked by the introduction of synthetic diamonds, the company began to diversify in 1965. It acquired a drugstore chain (Skillern); a line of airport tobacco/newsstand shops; and retailers of apparel, shoes (Butler), furniture, and sporting goods. By 1974 these operations represented half of Zale's sales.

Morris' son Donald became chairman in 1980, and Zale began selling off its non-jewelry operations. Skillern went to Revco, Butler to Sears, and the sporting goods business to Oshman's.

The stumbling economy of the 1980s and the gold and diamond industries' uncharacteristic weakness rocked Zale. An $80 million restructuring charge contributed to its $60 million loss in 1986. That year Irving Gerstein, head of Canada's People's Jewelers and a 15% owner of Zale, joined with Austrian crystal firm Swarovski to buy Zale. Issuing junk bonds to finance the $650 million deal, each took an equal stake in the company.

Gerstein sold manufacturing operations, liquidated the company's diamond inventory, and cut its advertising budget. Zale looked healthy enough in 1989 to buy the 650-store Gordon's Jewelers chain. But a recession hurt sales in the early 1990s, and debt hindered the company's fiscal health.

Unable to make a junk bond payment in late 1991, Zale filed for bankruptcy protection early the next year. It emerged from bankruptcy in 1993 as a debt-free public company with 700 fewer stores. The following year Zale chose former Bon Marche CEO Robert DiNicola to lead its revival. DiNicola began adding new stores (especially the higher-end Bailey Banks & Biddle shops) and repositioned existing ones. In 1996 Zale bought Karten's Jewelers, a 20-store chain in New England. The next year the company sold its Diamond Park Fine Jewelers division to Finlay Enterprises.

On the heels of a just-completed $40 million stock repurchase, Zale announced in 1998 a plan to repurchase up to $50 million more. The next year the company bought Peoples Jewellers, a 177-store Canadian chain. COO Beryl Raff succeeded DiNicola as CEO that year. In 2000 the company partnered with WeddingChannel.com to offer wedding planning services online. Zale also agreed to sell its private-label credit card business to Associates First Capital Corporation. It bought about 95% of US kiosk jeweler Piercing Pagoda. In 2001 DiNicola once again became chairman and CEO after Raff resigned.

OFFICERS

Chairman and CEO: Robert J. DiNicola
President and COO: Alan P. Shor, age 41, $590,625 pay (prior to promotion)
EVP and CFO: Sue E. Gove, age 42, $393,750 pay
EVP and Chief Merchandise Officer: Mary L. Forté, age 49, $464,625 pay
SVP and Controller: Mark R. Lenz
SVP and Treasurer: Stephen C. Massanelli
SVP, Credit Services: Gary W. Melton
SVP, General Counsel, and Secretary: Susan S. Lanigan
SVP, Human Resources: Gregory Humenesky
SVP; President, Zales Jewelers: Pamela J. Romano
SVP, Real Estate: Thomas A. Carroll
SVP, Support Operations: Ervin G. Polze
SVP: Philip N. Diehl
President, Bailey Banks & Biddle Fine Jewelers: Charles Fieramosca
President, Gordon's Jewelers: Charleen Wuellner
President, Zale.com: Sue H. Davidson
President, Zales Outlet: Steve Strong
Senior Director, Investor Relations: Cynthia Gordon
Director, Corporate Communications: Jan Roberts
Auditors: Arthur Andersen LLP

LOCATIONS

HQ: 901 W. Walnut Hill Ln., Irving, TX 75038
Phone: 972-580-4000   **Fax:** 972-580-5523
Web: www.zalecorp.com

Zale has more than 2,300 locations throughout Canada, Puerto Rico, and the US.

PRODUCTS/OPERATIONS

2001 Sales

	$ mil.	% of total
Zales	919	44
Gordon's	324	16
Bailey Banks & Biddle	324	16
Piercing Pagoda	254	12
Peoples	151	7
Zales Outlet	96	5
Total	**2,068**	**100**

Selected Operations and Merchandise
Bailey Banks & Biddle Fine Jewelers (higher-priced items, including diamond, precious stone, and gold jewelry; watches; giftware)
Gordon's Jewelers (mid-priced items, including regional and contemporary fashion-oriented jewelry)
Peoples Jewellers (Canada)
Piercing Pagoda (mall-based, lower-priced jewelry kiosks)
Zales Jewelers (lower-priced items, including engagement rings, wedding bands, bridal sets, anniversary bands, cocktail rings, earrings, chains, watches, and pearls)
Zales Outlet (discounted new jewelry, pre-owned jewelry)

COMPETITORS

Federated
Fred Meyer
Friedman's
Helzberg Diamonds
J. C. Penney
May
Mayor's Jewelers
QVC
Saks Inc.
Samuels Jewelers
Sears
Service Merchandise
Signet
Tiffany
Wal-Mart
Whitehall Jewellers

HISTORICAL FINANCIALS & EMPLOYEES

NYSE: ZLC FYE: July 31	Annual Growth	3/92	3/93	3/94	*7/95	7/96	7/97	7/98	7/99	7/00	7/01
Sales ($ mil.)	17.6%	—	—	665	1,036	1,137	1,254	1,314	1,429	1,794	2,068
Net income ($ mil.)	17.2%	—	—	27	31	44	51	69	81	112	82
Income as % of sales	—	—	—	4.1%	3.0%	3.9%	4.0%	5.2%	5.7%	6.2%	4.0%
Earnings per share ($)	17.4%	—	—	0.77	0.86	1.20	1.37	1.84	2.21	3.11	2.36
Stock price - FY high ($)	—	—	—	11.63	14.88	20.25	22.13	34.13	44.63	51.75	41.75
Stock price - FY low ($)	—	—	—	8.00	8.38	13.25	15.63	21.00	19.50	32.06	23.38
Stock price - FY close ($)	21.5%	—	—	8.63	14.25	17.38	21.75	31.00	40.00	37.38	33.75
P/E - high	—	—	—	15	17	16	16	17	20	16	18
P/E - low	—	—	—	10	10	11	11	11	9	10	10
Dividends per share ($)	—	—	—	0.00	0.00	0.00	0.00	0.00	0.00	0.00	0.00
Book value per share ($)	13.2%	—	—	10.11	11.20	12.96	15.43	17.80	19.44	22.17	24.14
Employees	14.2%	—	—	—	9,000	10,000	10,000	10,000	12,000	13,000	20,000

* Fiscal year change

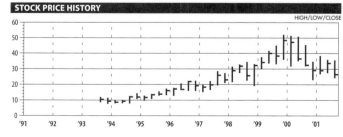

STOCK PRICE HISTORY
HIGH/LOW/CLOSE

2001 FISCAL YEAR-END
Debt ratio: 11.5%
Return on equity: 10.1%
Cash ($ mil.): 29
Current ratio: 2.84
Long-term debt ($ mil.): 110
No. of shares (mil.): 35
Dividends
  Yield: —
  Payout: —
Market value ($ mil.): 1,175

Hoover's
Texas 500

KEY TEXAS COMPANIES

3TEC ENERGY CORPORATION

Nasdaq: TTEN

777 Walker St., Two Shell Plaza, Ste. 2400
Houston, TX 77002
Phone: 713-821-7100
Fax: 713-821-7200
Web: www.3tecenergy.com

CEO: Floyd C. Wilson
CFO: R. A. Walker
HR: Kelly Walker
Type: Public

2000 Sales: $103.2 million
1-Yr. Sales Change: 391.4%
Employees: 50
FYE: December 31

Using 3-D technology, 3TEC Energy explores its possibilities as an oil and gas exploration and production company. Formerly Middle Bay Oil, the company operates primarily in East Texas and the Gulf Coast region. It also has properties in the midcontinent region and the Permian and San Juan basins. The company's acquisitions, including Magellan Exploration, CWR Properties, and Classic Resources, have boosted its reserves substantially. Natural gas accounts for 79% of 3TEC Energy's proved reserves of 302 billion cu. ft. of natural gas equivalent. It has also acquired several drilling prospects covered by a large 3-D seismic database. CEO Floyd Wilson owns 23% of the company.

KEY COMPETITORS
Chesapeake Energy
ChevronTexaco
KCS Energy

7-ELEVEN, INC.

NYSE: SE

2711 N. Haskell Ave.
Dallas, TX 75204
Phone: 214-828-7011
Fax: 214-828-7848
Web: www.7-eleven.com

CEO: James W. Keyes
CFO: Donald E. Thomas
HR: Joe Eulberg
Type: Public

2000 Sales: $9,346.0 million
1-Yr. Sales Change: 13.3%
Employees: 33,400
FYE: December 31

7-Eleven is the Big Gulp of the convenience store business. The company (formerly The Southland Corporation) runs the world's largest chain of convenience stores, including more than 5,600 stores in the US and Canada under the 7-Eleven name (over half are franchised). Slurpees, cigarettes, and Citgo gas account for much of the chain's sales, but it's also ringing up such items as prepaid phone cards and perishable grocery and deli items. Japanese retailer Ito-Yokado owns 51% of licensee Seven-Eleven Japan (with nearly 8,500 stores in Japan and Hawaii) and about 73% of 7-Eleven. Altogether, 7-Eleven operates or franchises about 20,600 stores throughout North America and 16 other countries.

KEY COMPETITORS
Exxon Mobil
Kroger
Royal Dutch/Shell

 See pages 34–35 for a full profile of this company.

ACADEMY SPORTS & OUTDOORS, LTD.

1800 N. Mason Rd.
Katy, TX 77449
Phone: 281-646-5200
Fax: 281-646-5204
Web: www.academy.com

CEO: David Gochman
CFO: Michael Ondruch
HR: Sylvia Barrera
Type: Private

2001 Sales: $720.0 million
1-Yr. Sales Change: 17.6%
Employees: 4,748
FYE: January 31

Academy Sports & Outdoors is near the head of the class among sporting goods retailers. The company is the third-largest full-line sporting goods chain in the US, behind The Sports Authority and Gart Sports. Academy's low-frills stores carry clothing, shoes, and equipment for almost any sport, including hunting, fishing, and boating. Academy has about 50 stores in Alabama, Florida, Louisiana, Mississippi, Oklahoma, Tennessee, and Texas; it plans to add more stores in the Southeast. Academy dates back to a San Antonio tire shop opened by Max Gochman in 1938. The business moved into military surplus items and during the 1980s began focusing on sports and outdoor merchandise. The Gochman family still owns Academy.

KEY COMPETITORS
Gart Sports
Sports Authority
Wal-Mart

ACE CASH EXPRESS, INC.

Nasdaq: AACE

1231 Greenway Dr., Ste. 600
Irving, TX 75038
Phone: 972-550-5000
Fax: 972-550-5150
Web: www.acecashexpress.com

CEO: Donald H. Neustadt
CFO: Joe Conner
HR: T. J. Carter
Type: Public

2001 Sales: $196.8 million
1-Yr. Sales Change: 40.0%
Employees: 2,397
FYE: June 30

Cha-ching! Ace Cash Express (ACE) operates a leading chain of check-cashing stores in the US. In addition to cashing checks for individuals, the company's stores offer a range of other products and services, including money orders, money transfers, bill payment, lottery tickets, and small consumer loans. However, check cashing is the cash cow, bringing in almost two-thirds of the company's revenue. ACE has grown in recent years largely through acquisitions; it owns or franchises more than 1,200 check-cashing stores in nearly 35 states, with the largest concentration in Texas. Approximately 15% of its stores are franchised.

KEY COMPETITORS
Cash America
Check Into Cash
First Cash Financial Services

ACR GROUP, INC.

OTC: ACRG

3200 Wilcrest Dr., Ste. 440
Houston, TX 77042
Phone: 713-780-8532
Fax: 713-780-4067
Web: www.acrgroup.com

CEO: Alex Trevino Jr.
CFO: Anthony R. Maresca
HR: Carol Russell
Type: Public

2001 Sales: $136.4 million
1-Yr. Sales Change: 7.9%
Employees: 400
FYE: February 28

Whether the mercury is rising or it's 10 below, ACR Group is in the cool business of climate control. The company acquires and operates wholesale distributors of heating, ventilating, air conditioning, and refrigeration (HVACR) equipment and supplies, which are sold to contractors and dealers responsible for the installation, repair, and maintenance of HVACR systems. Started in 1990, ACR Group operates more than 45 distribution centers throughout 10 southern and southeastern states, including three of the largest HVACR markets: California, Florida, and Texas. ACR Group plans to continue expansion in the Sun Belt and other high-growth regions. Chairman, president, and CEO Alex Trevino Jr. owns about 20% of the firm.

KEY COMPETITORS
Pameco
Watsco
W.W. Grainger

ACS DATALINE, LP

1826 Kramer Ln., Ste. M
Austin, TX 78758
Phone: 512-837-4400
Fax: 512-837-6767
Web: www.acsdataline.com

CEO: Albert Sawyer III
CFO: Mike Castleberry
HR: Jim Tramel
Type: Private

2000 Sales: $145.0 million
1-Yr. Sales Change: 38.1%
Employees: 1,500
FYE: December 31

The ABCs for ACS Dataline include the design, installation, testing, and maintenance of cable infrastructures primarily for large corporations. A subsidiary of ACS Communications, the company provides data, fiber-optic, and telecom products and services, in addition to network infrastructure hardware and wireless networks. ACS Dataline also provides complete system documentation. Customers include IBM, Compaq, Motorola, and Dell Computer. Founded in 1985, the company has expanded by acquiring ICG Fiber Optic Technologies, an installer of fiber-optic cable systems. Equity firm Behrman Capital owns about 80% of ACS Dataline.

KEY COMPETITORS
Active Link
Dycom
SASCO

ACTIVE POWER, INC.

Nasdaq: ACPW

11525 Stonehollow Dr., Ste. 110
Austin, TX 78758
Phone: 512-836-6464
Fax: 512-836-4511
Web: www.activepower.com

CEO: Joseph F. Pinkerton III
CFO: David S. Gino
HR: Amber Babcock
Type: Public

2000 Sales: $4.9 million
1-Yr. Sales Change: 390.0%
Employees: 167
FYE: December 31

Active Power wants to keep the juices flowing. The company's CleanSource UPS (uninterruptible power supply) is designed to replace conventional UPS products that use lead-acid batteries. The CleanSource UPS uses a flywheel that stores kinetic energy by spinning. When a power quality problem is detected, the CleanSource UPS converts the kinetic energy into electricity. The CleanSource UPS was developed in partnership with heavy equipment manufacturer Caterpillar, which markets the product with its generator sets. The CleanSource UPS is marketed to Internet service providers as well as telecommunications, industrial, and commercial customers. Founder and CEO Joseph F. Pinkerton III owns 15% of Active Power.

KEY COMPETITORS
American Power Conversion
C&D Technologies
Powerware

ADAMS RESOURCES & ENERGY, INC.

AMEX: AE

4400 Post Oak Pkwy., Ste. 2700
Houston, TX 77027
Phone: 713-881-3600
Fax: 713-881-3491

CEO: K. S. "Bud" Adams Jr.
CFO: Richard B. Abshire
HR: Jay Grimes
Type: Public

2000 Sales: $7,022.2 million
1-Yr. Sales Change: 75.8%
Employees: 685
FYE: December 31

Bud Adams may have moved his football team to Tennessee, but his Adams Resources & Energy remains a Houston oiler. Subsidiary GulfMark Energy buys crude oil at the wellhead for transport to refiners and other customers. Subsidiary Ada Resources markets refined petroleum products such as gasoline and diesel fuel, and Service Transport delivers refined petroleum products and liquid chemicals. With exploration and production mainly in Texas, Adams Resources boasts proved reserves of 8.6 billion cu. ft. of natural gas and 626,000 barrels of oil. Chairman and CEO Adams, owner of the NFL's Tennessee Titans, controls about 50% of the company.

KEY COMPETITORS
Exxon Mobil
Mitchell Energy & Development
Royal Dutch/Shell

📖 See pages 36–37 for a full profile of this company.

ADMINISTAFF, INC.

NYSE: ASF

19001 Crescent Springs Dr.
Kingwood, TX 77339
Phone: 281-358-8986
Fax: 281-358-3354
Web: www.administaff.com

CEO: Paul J. Sarvadi
CFO: Richard G. Rawson
HR: Howard G. Buff
Type: Public

2000 Sales: $3,708.5 million
1-Yr. Sales Change: 64.0%
Employees: 62,140
FYE: December 31

Administaff handles the payroll so you don't have to. The company is one of the leading professional employer organizations (PEO) in the country, providing small and midsized companies such services as payroll and benefits administration, health and workers' compensation insurance programs, personnel records management, and employee recruiting. As a PEO it becomes a co-employer of its clients' workers. Administaff also offers Internet-based services through its Administaff Assistant and operates business-to-business e-commerce site bizzport. The company has 35 sales offices serving 19 US markets. About 50% of its revenue comes from Texas. Investor Lang Gerhard has a 21% stake in the company; American Express owns 15%.

KEY COMPETITORS
EPIX
Gevity HR
TeamStaff

📖 See pages 38–39 for a full profile of this company.

ADVANCEPCS, INC.

Nasdaq: ADVP

5215 N. O'Connor Blvd., Ste. 1600
Irving, TX 75039
Phone: 469-420-6000
Fax: 972-830-6168
Web: www.advparadigm.com

CEO: David D. Halbert
CFO: T. Danny Phillips
HR: Steven C. Mizell
Type: Public

2001 Sales: $7,024.3 million
1-Yr. Sales Change: 256.9%
Employees: 4,534
FYE: March 31

Just when you thought the paradigm couldn't get more advanced, Advance Paradigm and PCS Health Systems have come together to form AdvancePCS. The company provides pharmacy and health management services for health plans covering 75 million members (more than one-fourth of all Americans). AdvancePCS offers mail-order pharmacy programs, disease management programs, clinical trials and outcomes research, information management, and prescription drug services. The company has two online health care services: AdvanceRx.com, a Web-based pharmacy; and BuildingBetterHealth.com, a health and wellness information provider.

KEY COMPETITORS
Caremark
Express Scripts
Merck

 See pages 40–41 for a full profile of this company.

AEGIS COMMUNICATIONS GROUP, INC.

OTC: AGIS

7880 Bent Branch Dr., Ste. 150
Irving, TX 75063
Phone: 972-830-1800
Fax: 972-830-1801
Web: www.aegiscomgroup.com

CEO: Herman M. Schwarz
CFO: Michael J. Graham
HR: Thomas P.G. Franklin
Type: Public

2000 Sales: $295.4 million
1-Yr. Sales Change: 19.9%
Employees: 9,500
FYE: December 31

This is not a pre-recorded message. Aegis Communications Group provides outsourced telemarketing and customer care services through 17 call centers in the US and Canada. The company handles both inbound and outbound calling services, order provisioning, and multilingual communications programs, among other services. In addition to teleservices, Aegis offers online customer services such as e-mail responses, real-time chat, and data collection. Through subsidiary Elrick & Lavidge, the company offers market research services (about 10% of sales). AT&T accounts for more than one-third of sales. Investment firms Questor Partners and Thayer Equity Investors own the company.

KEY COMPETITORS
Convergys
SITEL
West Corporation

AFFILIATED COMPUTER SERVICES, INC.

NYSE: ACS

2828 N. Haskell Ave.
Dallas, TX 75204
Phone: 214-841-6111
Fax: 214-821-8315
Web: www.acs-inc.com

CEO: Jeffrey A. Rich
CFO: —
HR: Lora Villarreal
Type: Public

2001 Sales: $2,063.6 million
1-Yr. Sales Change: 5.2%
Employees: 21,000
FYE: June 30

Affiliated Computer Services (ACS) has dispensed with its cash business. The company sold its automated teller machine processing and maintenance operations to focus on its fast-growing information technology business. ACS provides professional, business process, and technology outsourcing to commercial clients (two-thirds of sales) such as Motorola, and to agencies of the US government. ACS's aggressive growth strategy has resulted in its acquisition of nearly 50 companies since its 1988 inception, which combined make it one of the largest information technology services specialists in the US, behind EDS, Computer Sciences, and IBM. ACS has maintained an annual growth rate of about 30% since 1995.

KEY COMPETITORS
Computer Sciences
EDS
IBM

 See pages 42–43 for a full profile of this company.

AFFILIATED FOODS INCORPORATED

1401 Farmers Ln.	CEO: George Lankford	2000 Est. Sales: $700.0 mil.
Amarillo, TX 79118	CFO: Wayne Smith	1-Yr. Sales Change: 4.3%
Phone: 806-372-3851	HR: Merle Voigt	Employees: 1,100
Fax: 806-372-3647	Type: Cooperative	FYE: September 30
Web: www.afiama.com		

Actually, it's the stores — 350 of them — that are affiliated with grocery distributor Affiliated Foods. The cooperative distributes food and nonfood items to its member-owners' stores in Colorado, Kansas, New Mexico, Oklahoma, and Texas. Founded in 1946 as Panhandle Associated Grocers, Affiliated Foods also helps retailers implement computer systems and software. In addition, the co-op operates Tri-State Baking (TenderCrust and Always Fresh brands) and owns the Plains Dairy, which produces 60,000 gallons of milk a day and bottles water, juice, and fruit drinks. It also owns a stake in private-label products supplier Western Family Foods (Western Family and Shurfine brands).

KEY COMPETITORS
AWG
Fleming Companies
SUPERVALU

ALAMO GROUP INC.   NYSE: ALG

1502 E. Walnut	CEO: Ronald A. Robinson	2000 Sales: $215.9 million
Seguin, TX 78155	CFO: Robert H. George	1-Yr. Sales Change: 22.3%
Phone: 830-379-1480	HR: Gabrielle Garcia	Employees: 1,535
Fax: 830-372-9679	Type: Public	FYE: December 31
Web: www.alamo-group.com		

Remember the Alamo Group for tractor-mounted mowing equipment (rotary, flail, and sickle-bar). The company's products include Alamo Industrial and Tiger hydraulically powered tractor-mounted mowers, which it sells to government entities. Its Rhino and M&W Gear Company subsidiaries sell rotary cutters and other equipment to farmers and ranchers for pasture maintenance. Its McConnel, Bomford, and S.M.A. units sell hydraulic boom-mounted hedge and grass cutters. Alamo Group also sells replacement parts (30% of sales). Plants are mainly in the Midwest with five others in Europe. Board member William Thomas owns nearly 30% of Alamo Group through his Capital Southwest Venture Corporation.

KEY COMPETITORS
Deere
Toro

ALAMOSA HOLDINGS, INC.   Nasdaq: APCS

5225 South Loop 289, Ste. 120	CEO: David E. Sharbutt	2000 Sales: $82.7 million
Lubbock, TX 79424	CFO: Kendall W. Cowan	1-Yr. Sales Change: 818.9%
Phone: 806-722-1100	HR: R. Gomez	Employees: 582
Fax: 806-722-1120	Type: Public	FYE: December 31
Web: www.alamosapcs.com		

Alamosa Holdings (formerly Alamosa PCS Holdings) is galloping into town as part of the Sprint PCS posse. The holding company's operating subsidiaries are among a handful of companies that provide mobile phone service under the Sprint PCS brand name and use Sprint's national network. Alamosa is building its own digital CDMA (code division multiple access) network and owns exclusive rights to the Sprint PCS brand in its 15-state territory, mostly in the central and western US. Overall the company serves more than 260,000 subscribers in more than 20 markets where the company has initiated services.

KEY COMPETITORS
AT&T Wireless
Cingular Wireless
Verizon Wireless

ALLEGIANCE TELECOM, INC.

Nasdaq: ALGX

9201 N. Central Expressway	CEO: Royce J. Holland	2000 Sales: $285.2 million
Dallas, TX 75231	CFO: Thomas M. Lord	1-Yr. Sales Change: 187.8%
Phone: 214-261-7100	HR: Jessica Ochoa	Employees: 3,249
Fax: 214-261-7110	Type: Public	FYE: December 31
Web: www.allegiancetele.com		

Allegiance Telecom is pledging its loyalty to small and midsized businesses in large metropolitan areas. The facilities-based CLEC (competitive local-exchange carrier) offers a menu of telecommunications services, including local, long-distance, and international phone service; Internet access; and Web hosting through its subsidiary Hosting.com. Access options include dial-up, DSL (digital subscriber line), and dedicated services. Fast-growing Allegiance has more than 635 equipment colocations and manages more than 840,000 access lines. The company serves 27 US markets, including Boston, Dallas/Fort Worth, Los Angeles, and New York, and plans to expand to a total of 36 cities.

KEY COMPETITORS
Qwest
SBC Communications
Verizon

ALLIANCE DATA SYSTEMS CORPORATION

NYSE: ADS

17655 Waterview Pkwy.	CEO: J. Michael Parks	2000 Sales: $503.3 million
Dallas, TX 75252	CFO: Edward Heffernan	1-Yr. Sales Change: (21.3%)
Phone: 972-348-5100	HR: Dwayne H. Tucker	Employees: 6,500
Fax: 972-348-5555	Type: Public	FYE: December 31
Web: www.alliancedatasystems.com		

Alliance Data Systems wants to get to know you better. The company provides customer relationship management services to retailers, supermarkets, and financial service providers. These services include loyalty programs and data-base marketing, which help clients retain customer loyalty through private-label credit cards; payment authorizations, processing, and other transaction services; and credit services, including underwriting and risk management for clients' credit card receivables. The company resulted from the merger of J. C. Penney's transaction services unit and The Limited's credit card bank, both owned by investment firm Welsh, Carson, Anderson & Stowe, which still owns about 60% of the company.

KEY COMPETITORS
First Data
Metris
Total System Services

AMERICAN GENERAL CORPORATION

2929 Allen Pkwy.	CEO: —	2000 Sales: $11,063.0 million
Houston, TX 77019	CFO: Nicholas R. Rasmussen	1-Yr. Sales Change: 3.6%
Phone: 713-522-1111	HR: Laura Nichol	Employees: 7,500
Fax: 713-523-8531	Type: Subsidiary	FYE: December 31
Web: www.agc.com		

This American General has two stars — one for each of its operating segments. Its asset accumulation business offers retirement services and investment management; the financial services division sells life insurance and provides consumer lending. It also offers fixed income and equity investments, as well as financial advisory services. Clients include individuals, families, businesses, and educational institutions. The company distributes its products and services through branch offices, independent agents, telemarketing, and the Internet. The firm should perhaps get a medal of valor for surviving a bidding war between suitors American International Group (AIG) and UK insurer Prudential; AIG emerged the victor.

KEY COMPETITORS
Citigroup
John Hancock Financial
  Services
Prudential

AMERICAN HOMESTAR CORPORATION

Pink Sheets: HSTRQ

2450 S. Shore Blvd., Ste. 300	CEO: Finis F. "Buck" Teeter	2000 Sales: $574.0 million
League City, TX 77573	CFO: Craig A. Reynolds	1-Yr. Sales Change: (6.2%)
Phone: 281-334-9700	HR: Don Robison	Employees: 3,934
Fax: 281-334-9737	Type: Public	FYE: June 30
Web: www.americanhomestar.com		

American Homestar Corporation is a leading maker and marketer of manufactured housing, producing factory-built single-family residences that are about half the price of comparable site-built homes. Priced from $12,900 to about $253,000, its homes are made in 10 plants and sold from more than 150 company-owned or franchised (Oak Creek Village) retail sales centers and more than 300 independent retail centers in 28 states. American Homestar also offers financing (Homestar 21, LLC), insurance (Western Insurance Agency), and home transportation (Roadmasters Transport and Brilliant Carriers). Chairman and CEO Finis Teeter and former CEO Laurence Dawson together own about 28% of American Homestar, which has filed for bankruptcy.

KEY COMPETITORS
Champion Enterprises
Fleetwood Enterprises
Oakwood Homes

AMERICAN NATIONAL INSURANCE COMPANY

Nasdaq: ANAT

1 Moody Plaza	CEO: Robert L. Moody	2000 Sales: $1,837.5 million
Galveston, TX 77550	CFO: Stephen E. Pavlicek	1-Yr. Sales Change: (3.8%)
Phone: 409-763-4661	HR: Glenn C. Langley	Employees: 4,300
Fax: 409-766-6663	Type: Public	FYE: December 31
Web: www.anico.com		

You can't get much more American than this. Through its subsidiaries (many of which begin with the word "American"), American National Insurance Company offers life, health, personal property/casualty, credit, annuities, and other types of insurance. Key subsidiaries include Standard Life and Accident Insurance and American National Life Insurance Company of Texas. Its Securities Management and Research unit provides investment advisory services and manages and distributes mutual funds. The company operates in the US and western Europe; it also entered the Mexican market with the launching of American National Compañía de Seguros de Vida. The company has acquired life insurance holding company Farm Family Holdings.

KEY COMPETITORS
Allstate
Conseco
Minnesota Mutual

AMERICAN PLUMBING AND MECHANICAL, INC.

1950 Louis Henna Blvd.	CEO: Robert A. Christianson	2000 Sales: $569.0 million
Round Rock, TX 78664	CFO: David C. Baggett	1-Yr. Sales Change: 70.4%
Phone: 512-246-5265	HR: Phil Thompson	Employees: 5,200
Fax: 512-246-5290	Type: Private	FYE: December 31
Web: www.ampam.com		

It would take a lot of Teflon tape to connect the far-flung companies of American Plumbing and Mechanical (AMPAM). AMPAM primarily provides contract plumbing services, as well as HVAC and mechanical services, in more than 20 US states. The company concentrates on single-family and multi-family residential structures, as well as commercial and institutional projects. AMPAM, founded in 1998 to acquire 10 regional contracting companies, began operations in 1999 and has continued to acquire or create similar companies in new service areas. The firm's subsidiaries operate as separate entities, with AMPAM providing financial and accounting support. Management members own more than 80% of the company.

KEY COMPETITORS
American Residential Services
Chemed
Scott Co.

AMERICAN REALTY INVESTORS, INC.

NYSE: ARL

1800 Valley View Ln., Ste. 300
Dallas, TX 75234
Phone: 469-522-4200
Fax: 469-522-4299
Web: www.amrealtytrust.com

CEO: —
CFO: Brent Horak
HR: Michael K. Lane
Type: Public

2000 Sales: $366.0 million
1-Yr. Sales Change: 9.2%
Employees: 867
FYE: December 31

American Realty Investors was formed by the merger of American Realty Trust and National Realty, L.P. The firm owns about 130 apartment complexes, 25 office buildings, shopping centers, and hotels, and 75 undeveloped parcels of land throughout the US, but primarily in the Midwest, Southwest, and Southeast. The company also owns Me-N-Ed's, a chain of more than 50 pizza parlors in California and Texas. Gene Phillips earns management fees from and holds more than a 55% interest in American Realty Investors through Basic Capital Management, Inc. (run as a trust for his children).

KEY COMPETITORS
Cousins Properties
Pennsylvania Real Estate
Walden

AMERICAN RICE, INC.

10700 North Fwy., Ste. 800
Houston, TX 77037
Phone: 281-272-8800
Fax: 281-272-9707
Web: www.amrice.com

CEO: Steven Z. Weinreb
CFO: C. Bronson Schultz
HR: Marsha Donaghe
Type: Private

2000 Sales: $171.2 million
1-Yr. Sales Change: —
Employees: 250
FYE: September 30

American Rice gives new meaning to "converted" rice. The company is one of the largest US rice millers. Formed in 1969 as a marketing cooperative, American Rice produces and markets white, brown, and instant rice under US brands, including Comet, Adolphus, Blue Ribbon, and Sno-Brite. The company's global brands include Abu Bint, aka Golden Chopsticks. It sells rice in more than 50 countries worldwide, including Saudi Arabia, the firm's largest market. The company sold its olive operations (it was the #2 US producer) to US industry leader Musco Olive Products in 1998. Formerly 81%-owned by ERLY Industries, American Rice emerged from bankruptcy in late 1999 owned by its creditors.

KEY COMPETITORS
Goya
Riceland Foods
Riviana Foods

AMERICREDIT CORP.

NYSE: ACF

801 Cherry St., Ste. 3900
Fort Worth, TX 76102
Phone: 817-302-7000
Fax: 817-302-7101
Web: www.americredit.com

CEO: Michael R. Barrington
CFO: Daniel E. Berce
HR: Brett Cohne
Type: Public

2001 Sales: $818.2 million
1-Yr. Sales Change: 60.5%
Employees: 4,392
FYE: June 30

Bad credit is a good risk, according to AmeriCredit. The company makes loans through more than 14,000 franchised and independent car dealers to shoppers buying late-model and new automobiles. (Franchised dealers make up more than 95% of AmeriCredit's loan portfolio.) With almost 200 offices across the US and Canada, AmeriCredit seeks to attract consumers who have credit limitations or past credit trouble. AmeriCredit securitizes most of its loans, retaining the servicing and reinvesting the proceeds in new loans. Through an alliance with J.P. Morgan Chase and Wells Fargo, the company has formed a Web-based auto finance company.

KEY COMPETITORS
Capital One Financial
MFN Financial
WFS Financial

AMR CORPORATION

NYSE: AMR

4333 Amon Carter Blvd.
Fort Worth, TX 76155
Phone: 817-963-1234
Fax: 817-967-9641
Web: www.amrcorp.com

CEO: Donald J. Carty
CFO: Thomas W. Horton
HR: Susan M. Oliver
Type: Public

2000 Sales: $19,703.0 million
1-Yr. Sales Change: 11.1%
Employees: 116,054
FYE: December 31

AMR knows America's spacious skies well — its main subsidiary is American Airlines, the US's #2 air carrier based on revenue passenger miles (behind UAL's United Airlines). With a fleet of nearly 700 jetliners and hubs in Chicago; Dallas-Fort Worth; Miami; and San Juan, Puerto Rico, American Airlines serves about 170 destinations in the Americas, Europe, and the Pacific Rim (some through code-sharing). With British Airways, American leads the Oneworld global marketing alliance. AMR's regional feeder subsidiary, American Eagle, has been aggressive in rolling out regional jet service. AMR has acquired the assets of bankrupt TWA, which are being integrated with those of American Airlines.

KEY COMPETITORS
Delta
Northwest Airlines
UAL

 See pages 44–45 for a full profile of this company.

AMRESCO, INC.

Nasdaq: AMMBQ

700 N. Pearl St., Ste. 2400
Dallas, TX 75201
Phone: 214-953-7700
Fax: 214-969-5478
Web: www.amresco.com

CEO: Randolph E. Brown
CFO: Jonathan S. Pettee
HR: Mary Cranford
Type: Public

2000 Sales: $170.7 million
1-Yr. Sales Change: (60.3%)
Employees: 218
FYE: December 31

AMRESCO is a commercial finance company, but has behaved more like a salvage operation of late, selling off assets to pay down debt. The formerly diverse financial services firm had provided asset management, commercial mortgage, and residential mortgage banking but sold these lines to Lend Lease Corporation. AMRESCO also sold its home equity portfolio to Lehman Brothers in 1998 to salvage its position after the overseas economy went bust. AMRESCO sold all of its European operations to its European management team. To avert a takeover, the company was forced to pay Mortgage Investors Corp. $25 million and sell that company back to its original shareholders.

KEY COMPETITORS
FINOVA
Heller Financial
Tyco Capital

AMX CORPORATION

Nasdaq: AMXC

3000 Research Dr.
Richardson, TX 75082
Phone: 469-624-8000
Fax: 469-624-7153
Web: www.amxcorp.com

CEO: Robert J. Carroll
CFO: Jean Nelson
HR: Steve Byars
Type: Public

2001 Sales: $94.0 million
1-Yr. Sales Change: 20.2%
Employees: 418
FYE: March 31

Like a football fan on Sunday, AMX knows how to work the remote control. Formerly Panja, the company designs and sells systems that control devices such as lights, audio and video equipment, and security cameras from a common remote interface. Its systems are used in corporate, educational, entertainment, industrial, and government settings. AMX also offers systems for residential customers (23% of sales) that control security systems, lighting, and electronic devices in the home. The firm sells its products through manufacturers and distributors. About 30% of AMX's revenues come from outside the US.

KEY COMPETITORS
Crestron Electronics
Universal Electronics
X10

ANADARKO PETROLEUM CORPORATION

NYSE: APC

17001 Northchase Dr.
Houston, TX 77060
Phone: 281-875-1101
Fax: 281-874-3385
Web: www.anadarko.com

CEO: Robert J. Allison Jr.
CFO: Michael E. Rose
HR: Richard A. Lewis
Type: Public

2000 Sales: $5,686.0 million
1-Yr. Sales Change: 711.0%
Employees: 3,500
FYE: December 31

Anadarko Petroleum has ventured beyond its original area of operation — the Anadarko Basin — to explore for, develop, produce, and market oil, natural gas, and related products worldwide. The large independent oil and gas company has expanded significantly with the acquisition of fellow independent Union Pacific Resources, which has boosted Anadarko's proved reserves to more than 2 billion barrels of oil equivalent, evenly divided between crude oil and natural gas. Although more than half of the company's reserves are in the US (Alaska, Louisiana, Texas, the midcontinent and Rocky Mountain regions, and the Gulf of Mexico), Anadarko also has major operations in Algeria, western Canada, Guatemala, and Venezuela.

KEY COMPETITORS
BP
Burlington Resources
Exxon Mobil

 See pages 46–47 for a full profile of this company.

ANCIRA ENTERPRISES

6111 Bandera Rd.
San Antonio, TX 78238
Phone: 210-681-4900
Fax: 210-681-9413
Web: www.ancira.com

CEO: Ernesto Ancira Jr.
CFO: Betty Ferguson
HR: Valerie Tackett
Type: Private

2000 Sales: $589.0 million
1-Yr. Sales Change: 12.2%
Employees: 625
FYE: December 31

Ancira Enterprises wants to help Texans hit the road: It sells cars, trucks, and recreational vehicles exclusively in the Lone Star State. The company's dealerships feature new vehicles under the Buick, Chevrolet, Chrysler, Ford, GMC, Jeep, Kia, Nissan, Pontiac, and Volkswagen brands, as well as used cars and trucks. Ancira Enterprises also sells new and used campers and recreational vehicles under the American Dream, Coachman, Fleetwood, and Winnebago names, among others. The company is one of the nation's top fleet dealers and operates on-site parts and service departments. Ancira Enterprises, which was founded in 1984, is owned by president Ernesto Ancira Jr.

KEY COMPETITORS
AutoNation
David McDavid
Group 1 Automotive

ANGELO STATE UNIVERSITY

2601 West Ave. North
San Angelo, TX 76909
Phone: 915-942-2211
Fax: 915-942-2271
Web: www.angelo.edu

CEO: E. James Hindman
CFO: Robert Krupala
HR: James Ocker
Type: School

2000 Sales: $95.0 million
1-Yr. Sales Change: (12.0%)
Employees: —
FYE: August 31

Out in the West Texas town of San Angelo, some 6,000 students attend ASU. Angelo State University was founded in 1928 as San Angelo College, a two-year school under the city school system of San Angelo, Texas. In 1965 the school became Angelo State College, a moniker it kept until it was upgraded to a state university in 1969. Its undergraduate program features the College of Liberal and Fine Arts (music, history, English, and other humanities disciplines), the School of Education, the College of Business and Professional Studies (accounting, education, computer science), and the College of Science (nursing, biology, mathematics). ASU also has a graduate school that offers a variety of advanced degrees.

APACHE CORPORATION

NYSE: APA

2000 Post Oak Blvd., Ste. 100
Houston, TX 77056
Phone: 713-296-6000
Fax: 713-296-6496
Web: www.apachecorp.com

CEO: Raymond Plank
CFO: Roger B. Plank
HR: Jeffrey M. Bender
Type: Public

2000 Sales: $2,283.9 million
1-Yr. Sales Change: 75.6%
Employees: 1,546
FYE: December 31

There's more than a patch of oil in Apache's portfolio. Apache is an oil and gas exploration and production company with onshore and offshore operations in North America and in Australia, China, Egypt, and Poland. The company has proved reserves of more than 1 billion barrels of oil equivalent, mostly from five North American regions: the Gulf of Mexico, the Gulf Coast of Texas and Louisiana, the Permian Basin in West Texas, the Anadarko Basin in Oklahoma, and western Canada. Some 52% of these reserves are natural gas. The company has been aggressively targeting overseas drilling opportunities, especially in Australia, Canada, Egypt, and Poland.

KEY COMPETITORS
Anadarko Petroleum
BP
Exxon Mobil

 See pages 48–49 for a full profile of this company.

ARENA BRANDS INC.

601 Marion Dr.
Garland, TX 75042
Phone: 972-494-0511
Fax: 972-494-7114

CEO: John R. Tillotson
CFO: Bill Grimsley
HR: Phil Reyna
Type: Private

2001 Sales: $175.0 million
1-Yr. Sales Change: (2.8%)
Employees: 2,200
FYE: June 30

Arena Brands outfits all kinds of cowboys from head to toe. The company makes western hats, including Stetson, Resistol, and Charlie 1 Horse, as well as Dobbs dress hats. With the purchase of Lucchese, Arena Brands added the Acme, Dingo, and Dan Post boot lines. The Lucchese brand is licensed to Circle T Western Wear for apparel and home furnishings. Arena also owns Imperial Headwear (golf and casual hats) and Montana Silversmiths (silver jewelry and western accessories). Arena Brands began at the top as a maker of Resistol hats near Dallas in 1927. Investment firm Hicks, Muse, Tate & Furst has owned the company since 1992.

KEY COMPETITORS
Ashworth
Justin Industries
Texas Boot

ARGONAUT GROUP, INC.

Nasdaq: AGII

10101 Reunion Place, Ste. 800
San Antonio, TX 78216
Phone: 210-321-8400
Fax: 210-337-2637
Web: www.argonautgroup.com

CEO: Mark E. Watson III
CFO: Mark Haushill
HR: Jim Richter
Type: Public

2000 Sales: $209.9 million
1-Yr. Sales Change: 27.8%
Employees: 435
FYE: December 31

This group of Argonauts is on a quest for workers' compensation. Argonaut Group is a holding company with subsidiaries in the insurance and real estate industries. Subsidiary Argonaut Insurance focuses on workers' compensation insurance, which accounts for about 80% of Argonaut Group's premiums, specializing in the construction industry; the division also writes general and automobile lines for commercial clients. Argonaut Great Central sells property, liability, commercial multiple-peril, and workers' compensation policies in some 30 states, specializing in the hospitality industry. Subsidiary AGI Properties conducts real estate leasing in California. Argonaut has acquired specialty insurer Front Royal.

KEY COMPETITORS
AIG
CNA Financial
Liberty Mutual

ARMY AND AIR FORCE EXCHANGE SERVICE

3911 S. Walton Walker Blvd.
Dallas, TX 75236
Phone: 214-312-2011
Fax: 214-312-3000
Web: www.aafes.com

CEO: Maj. Gen. Charles J. Wax, USAF
CFO: Terry B. Corley
HR: James K. Winters
Type: Government-owned

2000 Sales: $6,991.7 million
1-Yr. Sales Change: 3.1%
Employees: 54,000
FYE: January 31

Be all that you can be and buy all that you can buy at the PX (Post Exchange). The Army and Air Force Exchange Service (AAFES) runs more than 10,500 facilities — including PXs and BXs (Base Exchanges) — at US Army and Air Force bases worldwide. Its outlets range from tents to shopping centers that have retail stores, fast-food outlets, movie theaters, beauty shops, and gas stations. AAFES serves active-duty military personnel, reservists, retirees, and their family members. A government agency under the Department of Defense (DoD), it receives no funding from the DoD. More than 70% of profits fund amenities such as libraries and youth programs. Other profits are used to build or refurbish stores.

KEY COMPETITORS
Kmart
Target
Wal-Mart

ASCENT ASSURANCE, INC.
OTC: AASR

110 W. 7th St., Ste. 300
Fort Worth, TX 76102
Phone: 817-878-3300
Fax: 817-878-3430
Web: www.ascentassurance.com

CEO: Patrick J. Mitchell
CFO: Cynthia B. Koenig
HR: Tammy Haggard
Type: Public

2000 Sales: $149.6 million
1-Yr. Sales Change: 41.2%
Employees: 650
FYE: December 31

Ascent Assurance (formerly Westbridge Capital) is an insurance holding company that underwrites medical expense and supplemental health insurance to self-employed individuals and small-business owners. The company's medical expense policies reimburse various medical and hospital costs. It also offers indemnity policies for the treatment of specified diseases and lump sum payments upon the diagnosis of catastrophic illness. The company sells mainly through subsidiaries, which are licensed in some 40 states (Texas accounts for about 20% of premiums); it generates leads via its telemarketing unit. Credit Suisse First Boston owns almost 75% of Ascent, which changed its name after emerging from bankruptcy in 1999.

KEY COMPETITORS
AFLAC
Health Care Service
UICI

ASSOCIATED MATERIALS INCORPORATED
Nasdaq: SIDE

2200 Ross Ave., Ste. 4100 E
Dallas, TX 75201
Phone: 214-220-4600
Fax: 214-220-4607
Web: www.associatedmaterials.com

CEO: William W. Winspear
CFO: Robert L. Winspear
HR: Stephanie Johnson
Type: Public

2000 Sales: $499.4 million
1-Yr. Sales Change: 10.3%
Employees: 2,000
FYE: December 31

Associated Materials is quick to side with its customers. Through its Alside division (almost 90% of sales), the company makes vinyl siding and vinyl windows for the new construction and home remodeling markets. Other Alside products include vinyl fencing, decking, and garage doors. Alside operates through more than 75 supply centers and distributes metal siding and other building products made by other OEMs. Associated Materials' AmerCable unit makes jacketed electrical cable for industrial, mining, marine, and telecommunications industries. Chairman, president, and CEO William Winspear and his family own about 60% of Associated Materials.

KEY COMPETITORS
Nortek
Owens Corning
Royal Group Technologies

ATMOS ENERGY CORPORATION

NYSE: ATO

3 Lincoln Centre, Ste. 1800, 5430 LBJ Fwy.
Dallas, TX 75240
Phone: 972-934-9227
Fax: 972-855-3075
Web: www.atmosenergy.com

CEO: Robert W. Best
CFO: John P. Reddy
HR: Wynn D. McGregor
Type: Public

2001 Sales: $1,442.3 million
1-Yr. Sales Change: 69.6%
Employees: —
FYE: September 30

Atmos Energy looks for greenbacks in Green Acres: The holding company is growing through its acquisitions of natural gas utilities in small towns and rural areas in the US. Atmos distributes and sells natural gas and propane to some 1.4 million customers in 11 midwestern and southern states through its Atmos Energy Louisiana, Energas, Greeley Gas, United Cities Gas, and Western Kentucky Gas operating divisions. The company markets natural gas through its Woodward Marketing unit. In 2001 Atmos more than tripled its customer base in Louisiana by buying Louisiana Gas Service from Citizens Communications.

KEY COMPETITORS
TXU
UtiliCorp
Xcel Energy

ATRIUM COMPANIES, INC.

1341 W. Mockingbird Ln., Ste. 1200W
Dallas, TX 75247
Phone: 214-630-5757
Fax: 214-630-5001
Web: www.atriumcompanies.com

CEO: Jeff L. Hull
CFO: Eric W. Long
HR: Gus Agostinelli
Type: Private

2000 Sales: $496.2 million
1-Yr. Sales Change: (0.4%)
Employees: 4,100
FYE: December 31

Atrium Companies produces aluminum and vinyl windows and patio doors and the company wood not have it any other way. The company, which has sold its wood window and door business, sells to retail centers (Centex, Home Depot, and Lowe's), contractors, lumberyards, and wholesalers. Its windows account for about 80% of sales. The company's products are used in both new construction and remodeling markets. Atrium also offers installation services and operates a vinyl extrusion business. The company operates nearly 55 manufacturing facilities across the US. Atrium Companies is a subsidiary of Atrium Corporation, formerly D & W Holdings. GE Investment Private Placement Partners II owns about 74% of Atrium Corporation.

KEY COMPETITORS
Nortek
Pella

ATWOOD OCEANICS, INC.

NYSE: ATW

15835 Park Ten Place Dr.
Houston, TX 77084
Phone: 281-492-2929
Fax: 281-492-0345
Web: www.atwd.com

CEO: John R. Irwin
CFO: James M. Holland
HR: Bill Sullens
Type: Public

2000 Sales: $134.5 million
1-Yr. Sales Change: (10.3%)
Employees: 850
FYE: September 30

Atwood Oceanics is at work at sea. An offshore oil and gas drilling contractor, the firm owns four semisubmersible rigs, one jack-up, one submersible, one semisubmersible tender assist vessel (which places drilling equipment on permanent platforms), one platform rig, and 50% of another platform rig. About 72% of sales come from overseas operations in the territorial waters of Australia, Egypt, India, Israel, Malaysia, and the Philippines; customers include British-Borneo Petroleum, Esso Production Malaysia, and Shell Philippines Exploration. Atwood Oceanics also operates in the Gulf of Mexico. Fellow drilling contractor Helmerich & Payne owns 22% of Atwood Oceanics.

KEY COMPETITORS
Diamond Offshore
Global Marine
Transocean Sedco Forex

AUSTIN ENERGY

721 Barton Springs Rd.
Austin, TX 78704
Phone: 512-322-9100
Fax: 512-322-6005
Web: www.austinenergy.com

CEO: Charles B. Manning Jr.
CFO: Elaine Kuhlman
HR: Ken Andriessen
Type: Government-owned

2000 Sales: $782.7 million
1-Yr. Sales Change: (7.9%)
Employees: 1,361
FYE: September 30

Despite its laid-back reputation, the capital of Texas has plenty of energy. Austin Energy is a municipally owned electric utility that serves 350,000 residential and commercial customers. It has a generating capacity of 2,600 MW from coal, gas, and nuclear sources. The utility is expanding its renewable energy base through its GreenChoice program, which offers customers the option to use renewable energy sources such as solar power. Austin Energy is constructing a 180 MW natural gas-fired power plant to ease demand caused by the city's booming high-tech industry. A portion of the utility's revenue goes to the City of Austin General Fund, which is used for services such as fire protection, libraries, and parks.

AUSTIN INDUSTRIES INC.

3535 Travis St., Ste. 300
Dallas, TX 75229
Phone: 214-443-5500
Fax: 214-443-5581
Web: www.austin-ind.com

CEO: William T. Solomon
CFO: Paul W. Hill
HR: Linda Bayless
Type: Private

2000 Sales: $1,216.6 million
1-Yr. Sales Change: 45.6%
Employees: 6,000
FYE: December 31

Paving the way for progress, Austin Industries provides civil, commercial, and industrial construction services. Its oldest subsidiary, Austin Bridge & Road, provides road, bridge, and parking lot construction across Texas. Subsidiary Austin Commercial, known for its high-rises, builds corporate headquarters, technology sites, and hospitals throughout the central and southwestern US. Austin Commercial is tackling its first major sports arena, American Airlines Center, in Dallas. Austin Industrial focuses on construction, instrumentation, and electrical services for the chemical, refining, power, and manufacturing industries, mostly in the US South and Southeast. The employee-owned firm was founded in 1918.

KEY COMPETITORS
Beck Group
Granite Construction
Turner Industries

AUSTIN VENTURES, L.P.

114 W. 7th St., Ste. 1300
Austin, TX 78701
Phone: 512-485-1900
Fax: 512-476-3952
Web: www.austinventures.com

CEO: Jeffery C. Garvey
CFO: John Nicholson
HR: Ronnie L. Gerry
Type: Private

Sales: —
1-Yr. Sales Change: —
Employees: —
FYE: December 31

Austin Ventures is helping Texas become a technology mecca. A leading venture capital firm with more than $3.1 billion under management, the company offers seed and early-stage funding mainly to semiconductor, communications, and Web software and services startups. Focused on the Southwest, it has made more than 120 investments in Texas. Investments range from $100,000 to $20 million and are usually held long-term; the firm tends to cash out when an investment merges, is sold, or goes public. The firm formed business incubator AV Labs to invest in earlier stage companies. Austin Ventures' investments have included e-tailer Ashford.com and software firms Tivoli Systems (now part of IBM) and Vignette.

KEY COMPETITORS
Benchmark Capital
Kleiner Perkins
TL Ventures

AVIALL, INC.

NYSE: AVL

2075 Diplomat Dr.	CEO: Paul E. Fulchino	2000 Sales: $485.9 million
Dallas, TX 75234	CFO: Jacqueline K. Collier	1-Yr. Sales Change: 31.9%
Phone: 972-406-2000	HR: Jeffrey J. Murphy	Employees: 817
Fax: 972-406-2071	Type: Public	FYE: December 31
Web: www.aviall.com		

Aviall has it all when it comes to aviation — it is one of the largest independent distributors of commercial and general aftermarket aviation parts. Aviall operates through two main subsidiaries: Aviall Services (over 90% of sales) supplies new aviation parts and aftermarket services to commercial airlines, OEMs, and general aviation markets. A smaller subsidiary, Inventory Locator Service (ILS), provides online inventory and service capabilities information to the aviation, marine, and defense industries. ILS software has about 5,000 customers in over 70 countries, who use their PCs to access a database of over 100 million records of government data. Aviall has operations worldwide.

KEY COMPETITORS
AAR
Fairchild
SPS Technologies

AXIA INCORPORATED

801 Travis, Ste. 1400	CEO: Jeff Gwinnell	2000 Est. Sales: $150.0 mil.
Houston, TX 77002	CFO: Lyle J. Feye	1-Yr. Sales Change: 13.7%
Phone: 713-425-2150	HR: Robert P. Roy	Employees: 1,054
Fax: 713-425-2151	Type: Private	FYE: December 31

AXIA aims to help finish the job. Through its Ames subsidiary, AXIA makes automatic taping and finishing tools (ATF) used by interior contractors to prepare drywall joints for painting. The inventor of the ATF tool sells and rents them in North America through 60 retail and 65 franchise outlets in the US and Canada. AXIA's Nestaway subsidiary makes dishwasher racks, dish drainers, and shower caddies and other formed wire products. The company's Fischbein subsidiary makes industrial sewing heads, heat sealing systems, and other bag closing products. It also makes motorized conveyors and portable storage racks. AXIA is controlled by New York private equity firm, Cortec Group.

KEY COMPETITORS
Molins
Newell Rubbermaid
Q.E.P.

BAKER BOTTS L.L.P.

One Shell Plaza	CEO: Richard C. Johnson	2000 Sales: $311.5 million
Houston, TX 77002	CFO: Lydia Joachim	1-Yr. Sales Change: 19.8%
Phone: 713-229-1234	HR: Sue Robinson	Employees: 1,500
Fax: 713-229-1522	Type: Partnership	FYE: December 31
Web: www.bakerbotts.com		

Baker Botts is a Lone Star legal legend. The law firm's history stretches back to 1840, when Peter Gray first hung his shingle in Houston. The firm eventually became Baker & Botts after Walter Browne Botts and James Addison Baker, great-grandfather of former US Secretary of State and current partner James A. Baker III, joined the partnership. Its more than 540 lawyers specialize in practice areas ranging from banking to litigation to tax, but headquartered deep in the heart of Texas, it's no surprise that Baker Botts has carved a niche in energy as well, representing clients such as Baker Hughes and Conoco. As its energy practice has evolved, the firm has set up offices in London and Baku, Azerbaijan.

KEY COMPETITORS
Fulbright & Jaworski
Jenkens & Gilchrist
Vinson & Elkins

BAKER HUGHES INCORPORATED

NYSE: BHI

3900 Essex Ln., Ste. 1200
Houston, TX 77027
Phone: 713-439-8600
Fax: 713-439-8699
Web: www.bakerhughes.com

CEO: Michael E. Wiley
CFO: George S. Finley
HR: Greg Nakanishi
Type: Public

2000 Sales: $5,233.8 million
1-Yr. Sales Change: 15.1%
Employees: 24,500
FYE: December 31

"Hey, Hughes guys, let's go get us some oil!" Baker Hughes provides products and services for the global petroleum market. Its oil field division makes equipment and specializes in the discovery and recovery of oil and gas. The company tests potential well sites and drills and operates the wells; it also makes bits and produces drilling fluids. The company also makes submersible pumps that deliver oil from the well to the surface. In addition, Baker Hughes makes specialty chemicals used by the petroleum and wastewater-treatment industries. Sales outside the US account for more than 60% of revenues. Baker Hughes is selling Baker Process, its waste-material separation and removal systems business.

KEY COMPETITORS
Halliburton
Schlumberger
Smith International

 See pages 50–51 for a full profile of this company.

BANCTEC, INC.

2701 E. Grauwyler Rd.
Irving, TX 75061
Phone: 972-579-6000
Fax: —
Web: www.banctec.com

CEO: Craig D. Crisman
CFO: Brian R. Stone
HR: James R. Wimberley
Type: Private

2000 Sales: $487.7 million
1-Yr. Sales Change: (8.8%)
Employees: 3,700
FYE: December 31

BancTec keeps tabs on all sorts of financial transactions. The company provides electronic processing systems, software, and services for governments, banks, utility and telecommunications companies, and other organizations that do high-volume financial transactions. BancTec's systems and software capture and process checks, bills, and other documents. Its products include digital archiving systems, workflow software, and scanners. BancTec's services feature cost estimates and contingency planning, resource use, systems integration, and maintenance. Founded in 1972, BancTec is nearly 95%-owned by investment firm Welsh, Carson, Anderson & Stowe, which took the company private in 1999.

KEY COMPETITORS
First Data
Fiserv
Total System Services

BAYLOR HEALTH CARE SYSTEM

3500 Gaston Ave.
Dallas, TX 75246
Phone: 214-820-0111
Fax: 214-820-7499
Web: www.baylordallas.edu

CEO: Joel T. Allison
CFO: John L. Hess
HR: Venita McCellon-Allen
Type: Not-for-profit

2000 Sales: $875.0 million
1-Yr. Sales Change: (4.0%)
Employees: 12,000
FYE: June 30

The Baylor Health Care System (BHCS) offers a bundle of services. Founded in 1981, it was governed by Baylor University until establishing autonomy in 1997. The not-for-profit medical network, which serves seven counties in the Dallas-Fort Worth metroplex, includes the Baylor University Medical Center complex, one of the state's major teaching and referral facilities. Other system members include rehabilitation facilities, primary care centers, senior health centers, family health centers, community hospitals, and medical centers. The system also provides home health care and specialty pediatric services.

KEY COMPETITORS
CHRISTUS Health
HCA
Texas Health Resources

BAYLOR UNIVERSITY

Pat Neff Hall, Rm. 340	CEO: Robert B. Sloan Jr.	2000 Sales: $275.3 million
Waco, TX 76798	CFO: David R. Brooks	1-Yr. Sales Change: 20.2%
Phone: 254-710-1961	HR: Marilyn A. Crone	Employees: 2,318
Fax: 254-710-1490	Type: School	FYE: May 31
Web: www.baylor.edu		

In the heart of Waco, Texas, stands Baylor University, the largest Baptist institution of higher learning in the world. Founded in 1845, Baylor offers more than 150 undergraduate programs, nearly 80 master's programs, and about 15 doctoral programs. The university also offers a law school, as well as Master of Divinity and Doctor of Ministry programs at its George W. Truett Theological Seminary. Baylor's more than 13,000 students are taught by some 750 full- and part-time faculty members. The university also supports several institutes focusing on areas of study such as archeology, biblical and related languages, and gerontology. Baylor University and the Baylor Health Care System severed their ties in 1997.

THE BECK GROUP

1700 Pacific Ave., Ste. 3800	CEO: Lawrence A. Wilson	2000 Sales: $950.0 million
Dallas, TX 75201	CFO: Patricia Priest	1-Yr. Sales Change: 62.7%
Phone: 214-965-1100	HR: Jerry Cooper	Employees: 687
Fax: 214-965-1300	Type: Private	FYE: December 31
Web: www.beckgroup.com		

At the beck and call of commercial developers, The Beck Group has built everything from racetracks to runways, hotels, and hospitals. The firm provides design/build, general contracting, and construction management services in the US and Mexico. It offers facility development, construction financing, and such construction services as scheduling, contract administration, and procurement support. The Beck Group also provides real estate development services. Its projects include Dallas' Cotton Bowl, the Texas Motor Speedway outside Fort Worth, the Museum of Contemporary Art in Los Angeles, and California's Beverly Hills Hotel. Members of the Beck family own the company, which was founded in 1912 by Henry Beck.

KEY COMPETITORS
Austin Industries
Bechtel
Turner Corporation

BELO CORP.

NYSE: BLC

400 S. Record St.	CEO: Robert W. Decherd	2000 Sales: $1,588.8 million
Dallas, TX 75202	CFO: Dunia A. Shive	1-Yr. Sales Change: 10.8%
Phone: 214-977-6606	HR: Marian Spitzberg	Employees: 7,245
Fax: 214-977-7655	Type: Public	FYE: December 31
Web: www.belo.com		

Long before TV's infamous Ewing clan, A. H. Belo was wheeling and dealing in Dallas. The company, now Belo Corp., publishes *The Dallas Morning News* (founded in 1885), one of the nation's largest newspapers, with a daily circulation of about 520,000. It publishes three other dailies, including *The Providence Journal* (Rhode Island) and *The Press-Enterprise* (Riverside, California), as well as a handful of community papers serving the Dallas-Fort Worth area. Belo also owns 17 and manages three TV stations in 10 states, and runs 24-hour local news channels Texas Cable News and Northwest Cable News. Its burgeoning Internet division includes some 35 Web sites.

KEY COMPETITORS
Cox Enterprises
Gannett
Knight Ridder

See pages 52–53 for a full profile of this company.

BEN E. KEITH COMPANY

601 E. 7th St.
Fort Worth, TX 76102
Phone: 817-877-5700
Fax: 817-338-1701
Web: www.benekeith.com/main.html

CEO: Robert Hallam
CFO: Mel Cockrell
HR: Sam Reeves
Type: Private

2000 Sales: $959.0 million
1-Yr. Sales Change: 21.9%
Employees: 2,160
FYE: June 30

Ben E. Keith is your bud if you like eating out and drinking Bud. The company delivers a full line of foods (produce, dry groceries, frozen food, meat), paper goods, equipment, and supplies to more than 12,000 customers in Arkansas, Kansas, Louisiana, New Mexico, Oklahoma, and Texas. It is one of the world's largest Anheuser-Busch distributors, delivering beer in 49 Texas counties. Ben E. Keith's customers include restaurants, hospitals, schools, and other institutional businesses. Founded in 1906 as Harkrider-Morrison, the company assumed its current name in 1931 in honor of Ben E. Keith, who served as the company's president until 1959. Its owners include Robert and Howard Hallam.

KEY COMPETITORS
Alliant Exchange
SYSCO
U.S. Foodservice

BENCHMARK ELECTRONICS, INC.

NYSE: BHE

3000 Technology Dr.
Angleton, TX 77515
Phone: 979-849-6550
Fax: 979-848-5270
Web: www.bench.com

CEO: Donald E. Nigbor
CFO: Gayla J. Delly
HR: Tim Nolen
Type: Public

2000 Sales: $1,704.9 million
1-Yr. Sales Change: 94.2%
Employees: 6,158
FYE: December 31

Streams of electronics gear flow from the workbenches of Benchmark Electronics. The company, which provides contract manufacturing services to electronics makers, produces complex printed circuit boards and other subsystems used in business computers (36% of sales), telecommunications equipment (34%), and medical and testing instruments. Its services include design engineering, prototyping, system assembly, and testing. Sun Microsystems and EMC (data storage products) together account for about a quarter of Benchmark's sales. Over four-fifths of sales come from customers in the Americas. Benchmark, which has facilities in Asia, Europe, and the Americas, is using acquisitions to speed its global expansion.

KEY COMPETITORS
Flextronics
SCI Systems
Solectron

BJ SERVICES COMPANY

NYSE: BJS

5500 NW Central Dr.
Houston, TX 77092
Phone: 713-462-4239
Fax: 713-895-5898
Web: www.bjservices.com

CEO: J. W. Stewart
CFO: Michael McShane
HR: Stephen A. Wright
Type: Public

2001 Sales: $2,233.5 million
1-Yr. Sales Change: 43.6%
Employees: —
FYE: September 30

When it comes to petroleum, BJ Services pumps up the volume. Along with Halliburton and Schlumberger, the company is one of the top providers of pressure-pumping services used to protect the oil formation, wellbore, and casing pipe during drilling and well completion; the company also boosts production from existing wells. BJ Services stimulates production through acidizing, coiled tubing, fracturing, and sand control. It makes the downhole tools for each process. The company operates onshore and offshore in most of the world's major oil and gas producing regions. Besides pressure pumping, BJ Services provides tubular services, pipeline connection inspection, and specialty chemical treatments.

KEY COMPETITORS
Halliburton
Schlumberger
Weatherford International

BLOCKBUSTER INC.

NYSE: BBI

1201 Elm St.
Dallas, TX 75270
Phone: 214-854-3000
Fax: 214-854-4848
Web: www.blockbuster.com

CEO: John F. Antioco
CFO: Larry J. Zine
HR: —
Type: Public

2000 Sales: $4,960.1 million
1-Yr. Sales Change: 11.1%
Employees: 95,800
FYE: December 31

When it comes to renting movies, this company is a Blockbuster. Blockbuster is the world's largest video rental chain, with about 5,000 company-owned or franchised US stores and almost 2,500 stores in 26 other countries. The company rents more than 1 billion videos, DVDs, and video games at its Blockbuster Video outlets each year. It also operates Blockbuster.com and has marketing partnerships with companies such as AOL Time Warner and DIRECTV. Entertainment giant Viacom owns 82% of Blockbuster (96% of voting power) after taking 18% of the company public in 1999. Viacom announced two years later that it had abandoned plans to sell the rest of the company to Viacom shareholders.

KEY COMPETITORS
Best Buy
Hollywood Entertainment
Movie Gallery

 See pages 54–55 for a full profile of this company.

BLUE BELL CREAMERIES L.P.

1101 S. Horton
Brenham, TX 77833
Phone: 979-836-7977
Fax: 979-830-2198
Web: www.bluebell.com

CEO: Howard W. Kruse
CFO: William J. Rankin
HR: Darrell Winkelmann
Type: Private

2000 Est. Sales: $300.0 mil.
1-Yr. Sales Change: 11.1%
Employees: 2,500
FYE: December 31

Despite its bucolic trademark of a barefoot country girl leading a milk cow, ice cream maker Blue Bell Creameries means big business. Although Blue Bell is still a regional brand (with distribution in only 13 states), it is the #3 ice cream brand in the country (after Breyers and Dreyer's). In addition to ice cream, the company sells yogurt, frozen treats, and sherbet. Blue Bell is slowly expanding from its strong regional base surrounding Texas, but it is retaining total control over production and distribution. CEO Howard Kruse and his family maintain control of the creamery, which was started in an abandoned cotton gin in 1907.

KEY COMPETITORS
Dean Foods
Dreyer's
Unilever

BLUE CROSS AND BLUE SHIELD OF TEXAS INC.

901 S. Central Expwy.
Richardson, TX 75080
Phone: 972-766-6900
Fax: 972-766-6234
Web: www.bcbstx.com

CEO: Pat Hemingway Hall
CFO: Sherman M. Wolff
HR: Paulette Smith
Type: Subsidiary

1999 Est. Sales: $2,000.0 mil.
1-Yr. Sales Change: (8.7%)
Employees: —
FYE: December 31

If an apple a day kept the doctor away, Blue Cross and Blue Shield of Texas (BCBST) would play the Serpent to each of its more than 2.8 million customers. A division of Chicago-based Health Care Service Corporation (formerly Blue Cross Blue Shield Illinois), the not-for-profit insurer emphasizes preventive medicine to hold down the costs of operating its HMO, PPO, point-of-service, and indemnity insurance health care plans in Texas. BCBST sold its Medicare administration subsidiary to Blue Cross and Blue Shield of South Carolina; it then bought Aetna's NYLCare Texas HMO (now HMO Blue Texas), making it among the largest health insurers in Texas.

KEY COMPETITORS
Aetna
Prudential
UnitedHealth Group

BMC SOFTWARE, INC.

NYSE: BMC

2101 City West Blvd.	CEO: Robert E. Beauchamp	2001 Sales: $1,504.0 million
Houston, TX 77042	CFO: John W. Cox	1-Yr. Sales Change: (12.5%)
Phone: 713-918-8800	HR: Johnnie Horn	Employees: 7,330
Fax: 713-918-8000	Type: Public	FYE: March 31
Web: www.bmc.com		

BMC hopes making a transition from mainframe sales to corporate networks is easy as A-B-C (or 1-2-3). Although mainframe-related utilities software and services still account for more than two-thirds of sales, BMC Software is moving past a reliance on the larger, mature computers to focus on corporate networked systems. BMC Software's more than 450 software products optimize database performance, eliminate unplanned outages, predict and remove computer bottlenecks, and recover system assets. Its customers include Dow Corning, First Union, and Home Depot. The company, respected for its employee-friendly environment, is growing through acquisitions and expanding into the e-business management realm.

KEY COMPETITORS
Computer Associates
Hewlett-Packard
IBM

📖 See pages 56–57 for a full profile of this company.

THE BOMBAY COMPANY, INC.

NYSE: BBA

550 Bailey Ave.	CEO: Carmie Mehrlander	2001 Sales: $421.5 million
Fort Worth, TX 76107	CFO: Elaine D. Crowley	1-Yr. Sales Change: 7.8%
Phone: 817-347-8200	HR: James D. Johnson	Employees: 5,000
Fax: 817-332-7066	Type: Public	FYE: January 31
Web: www.bombayco.com		

You don't have to visit an 18th-century British colony to get 18th-century, British-styled furniture — just the nearest mall. The Bombay Company operates more than 400 stores, mostly in malls throughout the US and Canada, offering classic and traditional furniture, wall decor, and accessories for the bedroom, dining room, home office, and living room. Furniture accounts for 45% of sales. Bombay is moving beyond its traditional boundaries by including products such as baskets, candles, home fragrances, crystal, and soft goods. It also operates about two dozen outlet stores and a furniture wholesaler, and sells items through catalogs and the Internet.

KEY COMPETITORS
Ethan Allen
Pier 1 Imports
Williams-Sonoma

BOY SCOUTS OF AMERICA

1325 W. Walnut Hill Ln.	CEO: Milton H. Ward	2000 Sales: $242.0 million
Irving, TX 75015	CFO: John C. Cushman III	1-Yr. Sales Change: 4.3%
Phone: 972-580-2000	HR: Robert T. Herres	Employees: 487
Fax: 972-580-2502	Type: Not-for-profit	FYE: December 31
Web: www.bsa.scouting.org		

They enter on tender feet but leave flying like eagles. Boy Scouts of America (BSA) is one of the nation's largest youth organizations, with nearly 5 million members in about 145,000 units. Incorporated by Chicago publisher William Boyce in 1910, BSA offers educational and character-building programs emphasizing leadership, citizenship, personal development, and physical fitness. In addition to traditional scouting programs, it offers the Venturing program for boys and girls ages 14-20. BSA generates revenue through membership and council fees, supply and magazine sales, and contributions. In 2000 the Supreme Court ruled that the organization can bar homosexuals from becoming troop leaders.

BRAZOS ELECTRIC POWER COOPERATIVE, INC.

2404 La Salle Ave.	CEO: John Hargraves	2000 Sales: $290.0 million
Waco, TX 76702	CFO: Bret Fox	1-Yr. Sales Change: (3.3%)
Phone: 254-750-6500	HR: Tom Yows	Employees: 295
Fax: 254-750-6290	Type: Cooperative	FYE: December 31

Brazos means "arms" in Spanish, and the generation and transmission arms of Brazos Electric Power Cooperative reach across 66 Texas counties. Founded in 1941, the utility serves 19 member distribution cooperatives, three cities, and Texas A&M University in an area spanning from north of Houston to the Panhandle. Sources of Brazos Electric Power's 1,651 MW generating capacity include lignite, natural gas, and outside purchases. Preparing for deregulation, the cooperative has an agreement with Southern Company Energy Marketing to market its excess power supply and provide an additional 600 MW as needed. Pipeline subsidiary Brazos Fuel purchases and distributes the cooperative's natural gas supply.

KEY COMPETITORS
Entergy
LCRA
TXU

BRINKER INTERNATIONAL, INC.   NYSE: EAT

6820 LBJ Fwy.	CEO: Ronald A. McDougall	2001 Sales: $2,473.7 million
Dallas, TX 75240	CFO: Charles M. Sonsteby	1-Yr. Sales Change: 14.5%
Phone: 972-980-9917	HR: Stan A. Fletcher	Employees: 78,500
Fax: 972-770-4139	Type: Public	FYE: June 30
Web: www.brinker.com		

Brinker International can satisfy almost any culinary craving. One of the largest casual-dining operations in the US, Brinker runs the popular Chili's Grill & Bar chain, offering southwestern-style dishes and a host of appetizers like boneless chicken wings. Brinker also operates the Italian-themed Romano's Macaroni Grill and Maggiano's Little Italy, as well as the Mexican-flavored On The Border Mexican Grill & Cantina and Cozymel's Coastal Mexican Grill. Other concepts emerging from Brinker include Big Bowl (Asian cuisine), Corner Bakery Cafe (fresh bread and quick foods), and Eatzi's Market & Bakery (upscale home replacement meals and grocery). Brinker has about 1,150 locations in the US and internationally.

KEY COMPETITORS
Carlson Restaurants Worldwide
Darden Restaurants
Outback Steakhouse

 See pages 58–59 for a full profile of this company.

BROOKSHIRE BROTHERS, LTD.

1201 Ellen Trout Dr.	CEO: Tim Hale	2001 Est. Sales: $750.0 mil.
Lufkin, TX 75901	CFO: Donny Johnson	1-Yr. Sales Change: 7.1%
Phone: 936-634-8155	HR: Jerry Johnson	Employees: 6,000
Fax: 936-633-4611	Type: Private	FYE: April 30
Web: www.brookshirebrothers.com		

Offering everything from garden-fresh vegetables to gasoline, Brookshire Brothers is a grocery retailer with about 70 locations, most of which feature Pump & Save outlets selling Conoco gasoline. Dating back to 1921, the firm has supermarkets mostly in East Texas, but also in Louisiana. Most of its stores operate under the Brookshire Brothers banner; its other store names include Budget Chopper, B&B Foods, and Celebrity Foods. Brookshire Brothers is not affiliated with Brookshire Grocery of Tyler, Texas. The companies share a common ancestry, but a split between the founding brothers in the late 1930s resulted in the separate grocery chains. Formerly family-owned, Brookshire Brothers is now 67%-owned by employees.

KEY COMPETITORS
H-E-B
Kroger
Wal-Mart

BROOKSHIRE GROCERY COMPANY

1600 W. South West Loop 323	CEO: Tim Brookshire	2000 Est. Sales: $1,600.0 mil.
Tyler, TX 75701	CFO: Marvin Massey	1-Yr. Sales Change: (3.0%)
Phone: 903-534-3000	HR: Tim Brookshire	Employees: 10,500
Fax: 903-534-2206	Type: Private	FYE: September 30
Web: www.brookshires.com		

By selling staples, specialties, and Southern hospitality, Brookshire Grocery Company has grown into a chain of about 135 Brookshire's and Super 1 Food supermarkets in Texas, Arkansas, and Louisiana. The company also owns two distribution centers, a dairy plant, a fleet of nearly 350 trucks, and bakery, ice cream, drink, and ice manufacturing facilities. Brookshire's stores average about 40,000 sq. ft., while its warehouse-style Super 1 Foods stores average 80,000 sq. ft. More than 40 of Brookshire Grocery's stores sell gasoline. Originally part of the Brookshire Brothers grocery chain (dating back to 1921), the company split from it in 1939. The Brookshire family is still among the company's owners.

KEY COMPETITORS
Albertson's
Kroger
Wal-Mart

BUILDERS FIRSTSOURCE, INC.

2200 Ross Ave., Ste. 4900 West	CEO: Floyd F. Sherman	2000 Sales: $1,580.0 million
Dallas, TX 75201	CFO: Charles L. Horn	1-Yr. Sales Change: 12.9%
Phone: 214-880-3500	HR: —	Employees: 7,335
Fax: 214-880-3599	Type: Private	FYE: December 31
Web: www.buildersfirstsource.com		

Builders FirstSource, like an ambitious weight lifter, is bulking up an already well-built form. It aims to be a leading supplier to professional builders — it sells doors, hardware, windows, lumber, and other building products. It also provides engineering services. Since its founding in 1997 as Stonegate Resources, the company has grown from a $250 million building supplier to one with revenues of almost $2 billion. It operates about 80 distribution centers and 60 manufacturing plants and is growing in the eastern and southern areas of the US through acquisitions and internal development. The company was founded by a management team headed by CEO John Roach and private investment firm Littlejohn & Levy.

KEY COMPETITORS
84 Lumber
CertainTeed
U.S. Industries

BURLINGTON NORTHERN SANTA FE CORPORATION   NYSE: BNI

2650 Lou Menk Dr., 2nd Fl.	CEO: Matthew K. Rose	2000 Sales: $9,205.0 million
Fort Worth, TX 76131	CFO: Thomas N. Hund	1-Yr. Sales Change: 1.2%
Phone: 817-333-2000	HR: Gloria Zamora	Employees: 39,600
Fax: 817-352-7171	Type: Public	FYE: December 31
Web: www.bnsf.com		

Burgeoning Burlington Northern Santa Fe Corporation (BNSF) is the second-largest railroad in the US, behind Union Pacific. The company had planned to get bigger still by merging with Canadian National Railway, but the deal was canceled after US regulators imposed a moratorium on rail mergers. BNSF operates about 33,500 track miles in 28 states, mainly west of the Mississippi, and in Canada. A big revenue generator is its intermodal freight business (shipping by a combination of truck, train, or ship), which accounts for 29% of sales. BNSF's carload business (chemicals, forest products, metals, minerals, machinery, and consumer goods) accounts for 28%.

KEY COMPETITORS
CSX
Schneider National
Union Pacific

See pages 60–61 for a full profile of this company.

BURLINGTON RESOURCES INC.

NYSE: BR

5051 Westheimer, Ste. 1400
Houston, TX 77056
Phone: 713-624-9500
Fax: 713-624-9645
Web: www.br-inc.com

CEO: Bobby S. Shackouls
CFO: Steven J. Shapiro
HR: William Usher
Type: Public

2000 Sales: $3,147.0 million
1-Yr. Sales Change: 52.4%
Employees: 1,783
FYE: December 31

It's big, it's burly, it's Burlington. Burlington Resources is one of the largest independent oil and gas companies in the US (especially in terms of proved reserves) and a top producer of natural gas in North America. It has proved reserves exceeding 7.6 trillion cu. ft. of natural gas equivalent. Most of the company's production comes from North America, where Burlington operates in the San Juan Basin (New Mexico and Colorado), the Gulf of Mexico, the US midcontinent region, and western Canada. The company also has operations in the East Irish Sea and North Sea and in Asia, Latin America, and North and West Africa.

KEY COMPETITORS
Anadarko Petroleum
BP
Devon Energy

 See pages 62–63 for a full profile of this company.

CABOT OIL & GAS CORPORATION

NYSE: COG

1200 Enclave Pkwy.
Houston, TX 77077
Phone: 281-589-4600
Fax: 281-589-4828
Web: www.cabotog.com

CEO: Ray R. Seegmiller
CFO: Scott C. Schroeder
HR: Abraham D. Garza
Type: Public

2000 Sales: $368.7 million
1-Yr. Sales Change: 122.5%
Employees: 323
FYE: December 31

Like a cog on a gear in a well-oiled machine, Cabot Oil & Gas (ticker symbol: COG) has engaged in the oil industry's recovery very efficiently. Cabot explores for and produces natural gas and oil, and it sells gas to industrial customers, local utilities, and gas marketers. It has interests in more than 3,000 wells, operates 2,450 miles of pipeline, and has proved reserves of some 1,018.7 billion cu. ft. of natural gas equivalent. Operations in the Anadarko Basin (Kansas, Oklahoma, and Texas) and the Rocky Mountains (Wyoming) account for 46% of its reserves, and the Appalachian region holds about 40%. To boost its Gulf Coast reserves, Cabot has agreed to acquire Cody Co., parent of Cody Energy.

KEY COMPETITORS
Anadarko Petroleum
ChevronTexaco
Petroleum Development

CACTUS FEEDERS, INC.

2209 W. 7th St.
Amarillo, TX 79106
Phone: 806-373-2333
Fax: 806-371-4767
Web: www.cactusfeeders.com

CEO: Paul F. Engler
CFO: Matt Forrester
HR: Kevin Hazelwood
Type: Private

2000 Est. Sales: $600.0 mil.
1-Yr. Sales Change: 20.0%
Employees: 500
FYE: October 31

Cactus Feeders owner Paul Engler may operate the world's largest cattle feedlot business, but he was no match for Oprah Winfrey. Cactus Feeders has a capacity for about 480,000 head of cattle, which it beefs up and sells to beef packers. The company operates nine feedyards in Texas and Kansas, as well as three cattle ranches under the Spike Box brand in Texas and New Mexico. It also provides market analysis, marketing services, and financing for its rancher/suppliers. Engler and other cattle ranchers unsuccessfully sued Winfrey and a guest after a 1996 show disparaged the beef industry. Employees own 32% of Cactus Feeders, which Engler founded in 1960.

KEY COMPETITORS
AZTX Cattle
ContiGroup
King Ranch

CAL DIVE INTERNATIONAL, INC.

Nasdaq: CDIS

400 N. Sam Houston Pkwy. East, Ste. 400	CEO: Owen Kratz	2000 Sales: $181.0 million
Houston, TX 77060	CFO: A. Wade Pursell	1-Yr. Sales Change: 12.4%
Phone: 281-618-0400	HR: Gena Quintanilla	Employees: 758
Fax: 281-618-0501	Type: Public	FYE: December 31
Web: www.caldive.com		

Cal Dive International plunges head first into the oil and gas services it performs in the Gulf of Mexico. The subsea contractor, with a fleet of 20 vessels, installs, maintains, and inspects offshore platforms, pipelines, and production systems in the Outer Continental Shelf (depths to 1,000 feet) and deepwater areas. Subsidiary Aquatica provides diving services in water up to 300 feet. The company also performs salvage operations on abandoned fields. Subsidiary Energy Resource Technology buys and operates mature gas and oil fields in the Gulf, controlling proved reserves of 28.2 billion cu. ft. of natural gas equivalent. Cal Dive makes alliances with subsea equipment makers and other service providers.

KEY COMPETITORS
Global Industries
Halliburton
Stolt Offshore

CALLOWAY'S NURSERY, INC.

Nasdaq: CLWY

4200 Airport Fwy.	CEO: James C. Estill	2000 Sales: $53.8 million
Fort Worth, TX 76117	CFO: Daniel G. Reynolds	1-Yr. Sales Change: 77.0%
Phone: 817-222-1122	HR: Suzanne Rankin	Employees: 250
Fax: 817-654-2662	Type: Public	FYE: September 30
Web: www.calloways.com		

Plant retailer Calloway's Nursery babies its customers with green-thumb know-how — many of its employees are certified nursery professionals. The company operates about 20 nurseries in Texas — 17 under the Calloway's name in the Dallas-Fort Worth area and three Cornelius locations in Houston. Its stores sell lawn and garden products; plants account for about two-thirds of sales, with the rest coming primarily from plant care products. Calloway's also runs two growing facilities, Miller Plant Farms and Turkey Creek Farms. Its freestanding stores are in high-traffic areas, and most include a greenhouse and outdoor nursery yard. CEO James Estill owns about 13% of Calloway's.

KEY COMPETITORS
Home Depot
Kmart
Wal-Mart

CAMDEN PROPERTY TRUST

NYSE: CPT

3 Greenway Plaza, Ste. 1300	CEO: Richard J. Campo	2000 Sales: $403.5 million
Houston, TX 77046	CFO: G. Steven Dawson	1-Yr. Sales Change: 8.7%
Phone: 713-354-2500	HR: Cindy Scharringhausen	Employees: 1,735
Fax: 713-354-2599	Type: Public	FYE: December 31
Web: www.camdenprop.com		

Camden Property Trust is a real estate investment trust (REIT) that buys, develops, and manages apartment complexes in the southern, midwestern, and western portions of the US (most of its properties are located in Nevada and Texas). The trust owns interests in and operates some 150 multifamily properties with more than 51,300 apartment units. In addition, Camden has about half a dozen properties under development and manages several Las Vegas properties through its joint venture with TMT-Nevada, Sierra-Nevada Multifamily Investments. The company continues to grow through development and acquisitions.

KEY COMPETITORS
Archstone-Smith Trust
Equity Residential
Summit Properties

CAMERON ASHLEY BUILDING PRODUCTS, INC.

11651 Plano Rd.	CEO: Duane Faulkner	1999 Sales: $1,138.4 million
Dallas, TX 75243	CFO: Steve Robin	1-Yr. Sales Change: 26.6%
Phone: 214-860-5100	HR: Melanie Corley	Employees: 2,669
Fax: 214-860-5148	Type: Subsidiary	FYE: December 31
Web: www.cabp.com		

Cameron Ashley Building Products works under the watchful eye of a Guardian angel. The company distributes building supplies through more than 160 distribution centers in nearly 40 states and Canada. It sells roofing (which accounts for about 35% of sales), insulation, millwork, siding, pool and patio enclosures, and other materials, mostly to contractors, building materials dealers, home center chains, and builders. The company, formed in 1991 by the acquisitions of Wm. Cameron & Co. and Ashley Aluminum, has grown by purchasing dozens of building supply firms. Guardian Industries, one of the world's largest glassmakers, owns Cameron Ashley.

KEY COMPETITORS
ABC Supply
Georgia-Pacific Group
Huttig Building Products

CAPSTEAD MORTGAGE CORPORATION   NYSE: CMO

1 Lincoln Park	CEO: Wesley R. Edens	2000 Sales: $519.9 million
Dallas, TX 75225	CFO: Andrew F. Jacobs	1-Yr. Sales Change: (8.6%)
Phone: 214-874-2323	HR: Kezia O'Neil	Employees: 17
Fax: 214-874-2398	Type: Public	FYE: December 31
Web: www.capstead.com		

Capstead Mortgage's best friends just might be Fannie Mae, Freddie Mac, and Ginnie Mae. Capstead, which invests in mortgage-backed securities, operates its mortgage investment business as a real estate investment trust (REIT) and avoids corporate taxes by distributing its earnings to stockholders. After being pummeled by financial crisis in 1998, Capstead Mortgage sold its mortgage servicing and originating operations, along with some of its investments. The company has been rebuilding its portfolio with investments in adjustable-rate securities issued by government mortgage agencies. Entities associated with chairman and CEO Wesley Edens own slightly less than one-third of Capstead Mortgage.

KEY COMPETITORS
Annaly Mortgage Management
Redwood Trust
Thornburg Mortgage

CARBO CERAMICS INC.   NYSE: CRR

6565 MacArthur Blvd.	CEO: C. Mark Pearson	2000 Sales: $93.3 million
Irving, TX 75039	CFO: Paul G. Vitek	1-Yr. Sales Change: 33.9%
Phone: 972-401-0090	HR: Dan Jowers	Employees: 168
Fax: 972-401-0705	Type: Public	FYE: December 31
Web: www.carboceramics.com		

CARBO Ceramics' proppants (tiny ceramic beads) are a welcome release for natural gas and oil well operators. After a well is hydraulically fractured, proppants are used to create a permeable channel through which natural gas and oil flow from the formation to the surface. Some of the company's products compete against sand-based proppants. CARBO Ceramics' customers include pressure-pumping service companies and well owners worldwide. The company's three top customers — BJ Services, Schlumberger, and Halliburton — together account for nearly 80% of sales. The US accounts for more than 60% of sales. Chairman William Morris owns about 28% of CARBO Ceramics.

KEY COMPETITORS
Alcoa
Borden Chemicals
Saint-Gobain

CARLSON RESTAURANTS WORLDWIDE INC.

7540 LBJ Fwy.	CEO: Wallace B. Doolin	2000 Est. Sales: $750.0 mil.
Dallas, TX 75251	CFO: Jeff D. Warne	1-Yr. Sales Change: 8.5%
Phone: 972-450-5400	HR: Anne Verano	Employees: 20,000
Fax: 972-450-3644	Type: Subsidiary	FYE: December 31
Web: www.tgifridays.com		

Carlson Restaurants has a lot of Friday's for which to be thankful. The company is home to the T.G.I. Friday's casual dining chain, which spans about 590 restaurants (one-third are company-owned; the rest are franchised). T.G.I. Friday's eateries are decked out with dark wood, brass rails, and stained glass and offer signature fare such as Jack Daniels Grill items, the Tex-Mex tower of appetizers, and Mocha Mud Pie. Sales of alcohol generate about 22% of the restaurants' revenues. Carlson Restaurants also operates other restaurants under names such as Aquaknox, Italianni's, Mignon, Samba Room, Star Canyon, Taqueria Canonita, and Timpano Italian Chophouse. The company is a subsidiary of Carlson Companies.

KEY COMPETITORS
Darden Restaurants
Metromedia
Ruby Tuesday

CARREKER CORPORATION

Nasdaq: CANI

4055 Valley View Ln., Ste. 1000	CEO: John D. "Denny" Carreker Jr.	2001 Sales: $110.3 million
Dallas, TX 75244	CFO: Terry L. Gage	1-Yr. Sales Change: 45.5%
Phone: 972-458-1981	HR: Roger Bean	Employees: 477
Fax: 972-701-0758	Type: Public	FYE: January 31
Web: www.carreker.com		

Carreker (formerly Carreker-Antinori) wants to e-nsure that e-very bank is e-nabled to maximize its e-finance opportunities. The company provides consulting and software that help banks increase revenue and reduce costs. Its offerings include revenue enhancement, payment systems, and electronic business consulting. Carreker has moved to capitalize on the e-finance revolution, offering a variety of software and services (eFraudLink, eFinancial Services, eTransport, eTrac) that enable banks to leverage existing assets into electronic commerce success. The company's customers include about 70 of the US's 100 largest banks. Chairman and CEO John Carreker owns 24% of the firm.

KEY COMPETITORS
EDS
Misys
SunGard Data Systems

CARRIAGE SERVICES, INC.

NYSE: CSV

1900 Saint James Place, 4th Fl.	CEO: Melvin C. Payne	2000 Sales: $162.6 million
Houston, TX 77056	CFO: Thomas C. Livengood	1-Yr. Sales Change: (3.5%)
Phone: 713-332-8400	HR: Mark Groeneman	Employees: 2,186
Fax: 713-332-8401	Type: Public	FYE: December 31
Web: www.carriageservices.com		

Although it buries its customers, Carriage Services hasn't come close to burying its competition. It's one of the largest US death care companies, but it trails far behind Service Corporation International and other big rivals. Carriage runs more than 170 funeral homes and about 40 cemeteries in 30-plus states, with concentrations in California, Florida, Kentucky, Ohio, and Texas. It removes and prepares remains, sells caskets and memorials, provides transportation services, hosts visitations and ceremonies, performs burials, and maintains cemetery grounds. Carriage is pursuing management deals at municipal cemeteries as a new avenue for growth. CEO Melvin Payne controls 17% of Carriage's voting power.

KEY COMPETITORS
Loewen
Service Corporation
  International
Stewart Enterprises

CASH AMERICA INTERNATIONAL, INC.

NYSE: PWN

Cash America International Building
Fort Worth, TX 76102
Phone: 817-335-1100
Fax: 817-335-1119
Web: www.cashamericaonline.com

CEO: Daniel R. Feehan
CFO: Thomas A. Bessant Jr.
HR: Robert D. Brockman
Type: Public

2000 Sales: $363.7 million
1-Yr. Sales Change: (2.5%)
Employees: 3,035
FYE: December 31

Cash America International, the world's largest pawn lender (EZCORP is #2), has about 470 shops in the US, as well as 42 in the UK and 11 in Sweden. Cash America's customers collateralize high-interest loans with jewelry, electronics, and other items, which the firm sells if the loans aren't repaid. InnoVentry (formerly Cash America's Mr. Payroll subsidiary) is a joint venture with Wells Fargo. InnoVentry provides automated check cashing services to individuals without bank accounts; it uses proprietary facial-recognition technology to verify users' identities. Subsidiary Rent-A-Tire offers rent-to-own programs for automobile tires. Cash America offers franchising to select pawn operators.

KEY COMPETITORS
Ace Cash Express
EZCORP
World Acceptance

📖 See pages 64–65 for a full profile of this company.

CASTLE DENTAL CENTERS, INC.

OTC: CASL

1360 Post Oak Blvd., Ste. 1300
Houston, TX 77056
Phone: 713-479-8000
Fax: 713-513-1401
Web: www.castledental.com

CEO: James M. Usdan
CFO: John M. Slack
HR: Deedee Lubow
Type: Public

2000 Sales: $106.0 million
1-Yr. Sales Change: 3.2%
Employees: 985
FYE: December 31

Castle Dental Centers manages and operates dental practice networks in California, Florida, Tennessee, and Texas; its centers in Texas account for some two-thirds of sales. The company provides nondental management services to some 100 dental centers, which include general, orthodontic, and multi-specialty dental practices. Its administrative management services include marketing and sales, human resources services, equipment supply, insurance services, and financial and accounting reporting and administration. Castle Dental intends to continue to add dental practices to its networks. Chairman Jack Castle Jr. and his parents own almost half of the company.

KEY COMPETITORS
Coast Dental Services
Monarch Dental
Orthodontic Centers of America

CEC ENTERTAINMENT, INC.

NYSE: CEC

4441 W. Airport Fwy.
Irving, TX 75062
Phone: 972-258-8507
Fax: 972-258-8545
Web: www.chuckecheese.com

CEO: Richard M. Frank
CFO: Rodney Carter
HR: Catherine Olivieri
Type: Public

2000 Sales: $505.9 million
1-Yr. Sales Change: 15.6%
Employees: 17,802
FYE: December 31

It has a mouse for a mascot and features robotic song and dance routines, but this entertainment kingdom is founded on the power of pizza. CEC Entertainment operates and franchises nearly 400 Chuck E. Cheese's Pizza restaurants in the US and Canada. (About 330 restaurants are owned by the company.) The chain is best known for its life-sized, computer-controlled mechanical characters and animated props that entertain children. It also offers pizza, salads, sandwiches, beverages, and desserts. The restaurants feature musical and comical entertainment, video and interactive games, rides, and arcades. CEC targets families with children ages two to 12 years old (birthday parties generate about 12% of sales).

KEY COMPETITORS
Jeepers!
LDB Corp
Pizza Hut

CELLSTAR CORPORATION

Nasdaq: CLST

1730 Briercroft Ct.
Carrollton, TX 75006
Phone: 972-466-5000
Fax: 888-896-0576
Web: www.cellstar.com

CEO: Terry S. Parker
CFO: Austin P. Young
HR: Scott Campbell
Type: Public

2000 Sales: $2,475.7 million
1-Yr. Sales Change: 6.1%
Employees: 1,300
FYE: November 30

Mobile phone mover CellStar does not have a wired sense of humor. A leading global wholesale cellular phone distributor (Brightpoint is its main rival), CellStar gets phones to the many people who want to go wireless. The company distributes phones and accessories made by Ericsson, NEC, Nokia, QUALCOMM, and Motorola to retailers, carriers, exporters, and dealers. Its distribution services include inventory, logistics, and e-commerce management plans. Customers outside North America generate 80% of sales. CellStar also operates retail stores in Latin America, Europe, and Asia, and it has sold all but two of its US retail outlets in a round of belt-tightening. Founder Alan Goldfield owns 33% of the company.

KEY COMPETITORS
Audiovox
Brightpoint
SED International

 See pages 66–67 for a full profile of this company.

CENTEX CONSTRUCTION PRODUCTS, INC.

NYSE: CXP

2728 N. Harwood
Dallas, TX 75201
Phone: 214-981-5000
Fax: 214-252-4513
Web: www.centex-cxp.com

CEO: Richard D. Jones Jr.
CFO: Arthur R. Zunker Jr.
HR: Janice Pras
Type: Public

2001 Sales: $441.1 million
1-Yr. Sales Change: 5.3%
Employees: 1,665
FYE: March 31

Centex Construction Products (CXP) mixes it up. The company makes cement, concrete, and gypsum wallboard for residential, commercial, and industrial construction. CXP produces gypsum wallboard (50% of sales) at its plants in New Mexico and Colorado and sells it primarily in those states and in Florida, Illinois, and Texas. It makes cement (about 40% of sales) at plants in Wyoming and Nevada and at joint-venture facilities in Texas and Illinois (Heidelberger Zement AG and RAAM Limited Partnership are 50% partners). Other products include concrete and aggregates sold in Texas and California. CXP is a spinoff of mega-homebuilder Centex Corp., which owns more than 60% of the company.

KEY COMPETITORS
Holnam
USG
Vulcan Materials

CENTEX CORPORATION

NYSE: CTX

2728 N. Harwood
Dallas, TX 75201
Phone: 214-981-5000
Fax: 214-981-6859
Web: www.centex.com

CEO: Laurence E. Hirsch
CFO: Leldon E. Echols
HR: —
Type: Public

2001 Sales: $6,710.7 million
1-Yr. Sales Change: 12.7%
Employees: 13,000
FYE: March 31

Home buyers are making their moves with Centex and its Centex Homes unit, the top home builder in the US. Centex Homes operates in 22 states and Washington, DC, as well as in Latin America and the UK. It builds almost 19,000 homes a year with an average price tag of $190,000 for both first-time and move-up buyers. Other Centex subsidiaries offer home security systems and pest-control services and construction contracting for hospital, school, office building, and hotel projects. The company has interests in land development, mortgage banking, commercial real estate, and construction supply manufacturing (gypsum wallboard, cement, and concrete). Centex also owns Cavco Industries, a manufactured-homes maker.

KEY COMPETITORS
KB Home
Lennar
Pulte Homes

 See pages 68–69 for a full profile of this company.

CENTRAL FREIGHT LINES, INC.

5601 W. Waco Dr.
Waco, TX 76710
Phone: 254-741-5311
Fax: 254-741-5370
Web: www.centralfreight.com

CEO: Ron Moyes
CFO: Vicky O'Brien
HR: David Mueck
Type: Private

2000 Est. Sales: $350.0 mil.
1-Yr. Sales Change: 34.6%
Employees: 5,000
FYE: December 31

Shipping freight is central to Central Freight Lines, a leading regional less-than-truckload (LTL) carrier in the US, with more that 10,000 trucks, trailers, and vans in its fleet. Specializing in next-day and second-day service in 15 states, Central operates more than 90 terminals, stretching from California to Alabama. Founded in 1925, Central was first acquired by trucking firm Roadway (now Caliber System) in 1993, then purchased in a 1997 LBO by a group of managers led by chairman Jerry Moyes. Outside its main service area, Central partners with Oak Harbor Freight in the Pacific Northwest.

KEY COMPETITORS
American Freightways
CNF
Yellow

CHRISTUS HEALTH

6363 N. Hwy. 161, Ste. 450
Irving, TX 75038
Phone: 214-492-8500
Fax: 214-492-8540
Web: www.christushealth.org

CEO: Thomas C. Royer
CFO: Jay Herron
HR: Mary Lynch
Type: Not-for-profit

2001 Sales: $2,200.0 million
1-Yr. Sales Change: 5.8%
Employees: 8,000
FYE: June 30

CHRISTUS is born! CHRISTUS Health was formed in 1999 by a merger of Incarnate Word Health System and Sisters of Charity Health System. The not-for-profit system operates about 30 hospitals and other health care facilities in more than 60 communities, mostly in Texas and Louisiana. Facilities range from acute-care hospitals to outpatient centers and also include nursing homes, hospice services, and long-term acute-care centers. CHRISTUS' predecessor organizations have their roots in the religious order Sisters of Charity of the Incarnate Word, founded when three French nuns arrived in Texas in 1866 to care for the poor and sick.

KEY COMPETITORS
Memorial Hermann Healthcare
Sisters of Mercy
Triad Hospitals

CINEMARK USA, INC.

3900 Dallas Pkwy., Ste. 500
Plano, TX 75093
Phone: 972-665-1000
Fax: 972-665-1004
Web: www.cinemark.com

CEO: Lee Roy Mitchell
CFO: Robert D. Copple
HR: Brad Smith
Type: Private

2000 Sales: $786.3 million
1-Yr. Sales Change: 10.3%
Employees: 8,000
FYE: December 31

Cinemark USA has left its mark on the cinema landscape. The movie exhibitor has more than 2,900 screens in more than 270 theaters in the US and 12 other countries (mostly in Latin America). Cinemark operates multiplex theaters (89% with a minimum of eight screens) in midsized cities and in suburban areas of major metropolitan markets. Some larger theaters operate under the Tinseltown name. About 15% of the company's theaters are discount operations. Cinemark also has online ticketing available at nearly 20% of its theaters. Chairman and CEO Lee Roy Mitchell owns about 24% of the company and controls 100% of the voting shares; Cypress Merchant Banking Partners owns 42%.

KEY COMPETITORS
AMC Entertainment
Loews Cineplex Entertainment
Regal Cinemas

 See pages 70–71 for a full profile of this company.

CIRRUS LOGIC, INC.

Nasdaq: CRUS

4210 S. Industrial Dr.
Austin, TX 78744
Phone: 512-445-7222
Fax: 512-445-7581
Web: www.cirrus.com

CEO: David D. French
CFO: Steven D. Overly
HR: Steven D. Overly
Type: Public

2001 Sales: $778.7 million
1-Yr. Sales Change: 38.0%
Employees: 1,356
FYE: March 31

Cirrus Logic's focus on chips for niche markets has left its skies not cloudy all day. The company, which produces the Cirrus Logic, Maverick, and Crystal microchip brands, offers specialized system-level integrated circuits based on analog and digital technologies. It makes mass storage chips for Fujitsu and Hitachi and precision data acquisition chips for Rockwell and Schlumberger. It also jockeys with Texas Instruments as the dominant maker of chips for Internet audio applications. Its audio customers include Apple, Dell, Nokia, and Sony. Cirrus Logic, which outsources its production, continues to serve a variety of end markets, but is focusing growth efforts on chips for consumer electronic applications.

KEY COMPETITORS
LSI Logic
STMicroelectronics
Texas Instruments

CLARENT HOSPITAL CORPORATION

515 W. Greens Rd., Ste. 500
Houston, TX 77067
Phone: 281-774-5100
Fax: 281-774-5200

CEO: Robert L. Smith
CFO: Lawrence A. Humphrey
HR: Roinne Greer
Type: Private

2000 Sales: $369.2 million
1-Yr. Sales Change: (28.5%)
Employees: 4,670
FYE: December 31

Learned physician Philippus Aureolus Paracelsus might be stunned at today's health care industry. His namesake company, the troubled Paracelsus Healthcare, owns or operates 10 acute care hospitals in about as many states. The firm operates in small and midsized markets (under the radar of major hospital consolidators) primarily in the South. Rising health care costs and declining reimbursement rates aren't the company's only troubles: Accounting errors forced it to restate earnings from 1997 forward. Paracelsus is in Chapter 11 bankruptcy and hopes to recapitalize rather than sell its holdings.

KEY COMPETITORS
Community Health Systems
HMA
Triad Hospitals

CLASSIC COMMUNICATIONS, INC.

Nasdaq: CLSC

6151 Paluxy Rd., Bldg. A
Tyler, TX 75703
Phone: 903-581-2121
Fax: 512-476-5204
Web: www.classic-cable.com

CEO: James A. Kofalt
CFO: Jimmie F. Taylor
HR: Shanna Cagle
Type: Public

2000 Sales: $182.3 million
1-Yr. Sales Change: 63.6%
Employees: 970
FYE: December 31

Growth through acquisitions is a classic business strategy, and Classic Communications is no stranger to it. Classic has acquired more than 20 systems in rural areas of 10 states in the US since its 1992 founding. But the buying spree and the costs of upgrading these smaller systems to provide digital cable and Internet access has taken its toll. These high costs and increased competition from direct-broadcast satellite operators brought Classic close to default, forcing it to undergo management changes, streamline operations, and consider selling some systems. Classic systems pass more than 700,000 households, and it has about 375,000 basic subscribers. Brera Classic holds a 79% voting control of the company.

KEY COMPETITORS
DIRECTV
EchoStar Communications
Pegasus Satellite
Communications

CLAYTON WILLIAMS ENERGY, INC.

Nasdaq: CWEI

6 Desta Dr., Ste. 6500
Midland, TX 79705
Phone: 915-682-6324
Fax: 915-688-3247
Web: www.claytonwilliams.com

CEO: Clayton W. Williams
CFO: Mel G. Riggs
HR: Louann Bolding
Type: Public

2000 Sales: $109.8 million
1-Yr. Sales Change: 128.3%
Employees: 96
FYE: December 31

Former Texas gubernatorial candidate Clayton Williams once devoted his energy to politics. Now he's devoted to the independent oil and gas firm that he founded. Clayton Williams Energy explores for oil and gas deposits in Louisiana, New Mexico, and Texas and exploits those resources. The company has proved reserves of 17.6 million barrels of oil equivalent, 73% of which is oil. Most of those reserves are in East Texas, where the company employs horizontal drilling. Clayton Williams Energy operates about 80% of the 550 working oil and gas wells in which it holds an interest. It also operates 70 miles of gas pipeline and processing plants in Texas and Mississippi. Williams is CEO and controls 48.9% of the firm.

KEY COMPETITORS
Burlington Resources
ChevronTexaco
XTO Energy

CLEAR CHANNEL COMMUNICATIONS, INC.

NYSE: CCU

200 E. Basse
San Antonio, TX 78209
Phone: 210-822-2828
Fax: 210-822-2299
Web: www.clearchannel.com

CEO: L. Lowry Mays
CFO: Randall T. Mays
HR: Demetra Koelling
Type: Public

2000 Sales: $5,345.3 million
1-Yr. Sales Change: 99.6%
Employees: 36,350
FYE: December 31

Much of what you see and hear is brought to you by Clear Channel Communications. The company's acquisitions of rivals Jacor and AMFM made it the #1 radio station owner in the US. Clear Channel owns, programs, or sells airtime for some 1,200 radio stations (including pending transactions) throughout the US; it also has equity interests in more than 240 radio stations internationally. One of the world's largest outdoor advertising companies, Clear Channel has nearly 700,000 outdoor advertising displays worldwide. The company also owns or manages 19 TV stations and is the leader in live entertainment through subsidiary Clear Channel Entertainment (formerly SFX Entertainment).

KEY COMPETITORS
Citadel Communications
Cumulus Media
Infinity Broadcasting

 See pages 72–73 for a full profile of this company.

CLUBCORP, INC.

3030 LBJ Fwy., Ste. 700
Dallas, TX 75234
Phone: 972-243-6191
Fax: 972-888-7338
Web: www.clubcorp.com

CEO: Robert H. Dedman Jr.
CFO: Jeffrey P. Mayer
HR: Albert E. Chew III
Type: Private

2000 Sales: $1,068.8 million
1-Yr. Sales Change: 4.0%
Employees: 24,000
FYE: December 31

ClubCorp makes its green from the green — the golf green, that is. The world's largest operator of golf courses, country clubs, private business clubs, and resorts, the company owns and operates more than 220 properties in nearly a dozen countries. Its holdings include Mission Hills Country Club near Palm Springs, California, and North Carolina's Pinehurst Resort and Country Club (site of the 1999 US Open). The company also owns 25% of ClubLink, a leading Canadian developer and operator of golf courses, and 30% of PGA European Tour Courses, an operator of tournament golf courses across Europe. Founder and chairman Robert Dedman and his family own 75% of ClubCorp.

KEY COMPETITORS
American Golf
Golf Trust of America
National Golf Properties

 See pages 74–75 for a full profile of this company.

CMS OIL AND GAS COMPANY

1021 Main St., Ste. 2800	CEO: Bradley W. Fischer	2000 Sales: $131.0 million
Houston, TX 77002	CFO: Mark E. Stirl	1-Yr. Sales Change: (8.2%)
Phone: 713-651-1700	HR: Lena Richardson	Employees: 170
Fax: 713-651-0611	Type: Subsidiary	FYE: December 31

CMS Oil and Gas, a subsidiary of integrated energy company CMS Energy, is engaged in oil and natural gas acquisition, exploration and development activities primarily in Africa (which holds more than 80% of the company's proved reserves), the US, and South America. Formed in 1967 the independent oil exploration and production company has grown through acquisitions and exploration. CMS Oil and Gas boast proved reserves of 212 million barrels of oil equivalent, including 724 billion cu. ft. of natural gas and 91 million barrels of oil. The company has sold its Michigan and Ecuador properties in order to focus on its core exploration areas.

KEY COMPETITORS
PDVSA
Royal Dutch/Shell
Triton Energy

COASTAL BANCORP, INC.

Nasdaq: CBSA

5718 Westheimer, Ste. 600	CEO: Manuel J. Mehos	2000 Sales: $249.3 million
Houston, TX 77057	CFO: Catherine N. Wylie	1-Yr. Sales Change: 16.9%
Phone: 713-435-5000	HR: Teri Blackwell	Employees: 661
Fax: 713-435-5106	Type: Public	FYE: December 31
Web: www.coastalbanc.com		

Coastal Bancorp is the holding company for Coastal Banc, a Texas state savings bank. The bank serves customers from about 50 branches in and around Austin, Corpus Christi, Houston, the Rio Grande Valley, and other southeast Texas communities. The bank offers traditional deposit products including savings, checking, and money market accounts, as well as CDs. Nearly 45% of its loan portfolio consists of residential mortgages. Coastal Banc also writes multifamily real estate, residential construction, commercial real estate, consumer, and business loans.

KEY COMPETITORS
BANK ONE
BOK Financial
Cullen/Frost Bankers

COMFORT SYSTEMS USA, INC.

NYSE: FIX

777 Post Oak Blvd., Ste. 500	CEO: William F. Murdy	2000 Sales: $1,591.1 million
Houston, TX 77056	CFO: J. Gordon Beittenmiller	1-Yr. Sales Change: 16.1%
Phone: 713-830-9600	HR: Valinda Fladen	Employees: 10,959
Fax: 713-830-9696	Type: Public	FYE: December 31
Web: www.csusafix.com		

One of the largest consolidators in the HVAC industry, Comfort Systems USA is altering ambient temperatures across the US, Puerto Rico, and Mexico. An all-out series of HVAC company acquisitions has boosted the number of climate-controlling companies under the Comfort Systems USA umbrella to more than 125 locations. The company generates about 97% of its revenue from performing work for commercial and industrial customers (manufacturing, office, retail, apartment facilities). It performs installation (nearly 60% of revenue) and other services such as maintenance, repair, and replacement. In late 1999 Comfort Systems USA purchased Outbound Services, a company that provides Web-based customer service and support.

KEY COMPETITORS
American Residential Services
Encompass Services Corp.
Lennox

COMMEMORATIVE BRANDS, INC.

7211 Circle S Rd.
Austin, TX 78745
Phone: 512-444-0571
Fax: 512-443-5213

CEO: David G. Fiore
CFO: Sherice P. Bench
HR: Sharon Brown
Type: Private

2000 Est. Sales: $200.0 mil.
1-Yr. Sales Change: 24.8%
Employees: 3,000
FYE: August 31

Like many a lovestruck high-schooler, Commemorative Brands wants you to wear its ring. Founded in 1996 to buy ArtCarved and Balfour, the company is the #2 US maker of class rings, after Jostens. It also produces diplomas, graduation announcements, and other paper products, and sells caps and gowns, yearbooks, and related items made by third parties. About 90% of the company's sales come from scholastic products, which it sells through retailers and independent sales representatives. It also makes commemorative family jewelry, jewelry for sports fans, employee awards, and Super Bowl and World Series rings. Merchant bank Castle Harlan owns Commemorative Brands as well as yearbook producer Taylor Publishing.

KEY COMPETITORS
Herff Jones
Jostens

COMMERCIAL METALS COMPANY
NYSE: CMC

7800 Stemmons Fwy.
Dallas, TX 75247
Phone: 214-689-4300
Fax: 214-689-5886
Web: www.commercialmetals.com

CEO: Stanley A. Rabin
CFO: William B. Larson
HR: Jesse Barnes
Type: Public

2000 Sales: $2,661.4 million
1-Yr. Sales Change: 18.2%
Employees: 8,378
FYE: August 31

Commercial Metals Company (CMC) wants to steel the limelight. The company's manufacturing segment (50% of sales) operates four steel minimills, 26 steel fabrication plants, and 22 concrete products warehouses. The unit also runs a heat-treating plant and plants for making steel fence posts, castellated steel beams, and steel joists. Subsidiary Howell Metal Company manufactures copper tubing. CMC's recycling unit (17% of sales) operates more than 30 secondary metals-processing plants that shred, shear, and pulverize scrap metal, which is then sold to steel mills, foundries, and nonferrous ingot producers. CMC's marketing and trading segment (33% of sales) brokers metals, chemicals, and other materials worldwide.

KEY COMPETITORS
Nucor
OmniSource
USX-U.S. Steel

 See pages 76–77 for a full profile of this company.

COMPAQ COMPUTER CORPORATION
NYSE: CPQ

20555 State Hwy. 249
Houston, TX 77070
Phone: 281-370-0670
Fax: 281-514-1740
Web: www.compaq.com

CEO: Michael D. Capellas
CFO: Jeff Clarke
HR: Yvonne R. Jackson
Type: Public

2000 Sales: $42,383.0 million
1-Yr. Sales Change: 10.0%
Employees: 94,600
FYE: December 31

The common mispronunciation of its name notwithstanding, Compaq Computer is anything but compact. It vies with Dell to be the world's #1 PC maker and it's the third-largest computer company (behind IBM and Hewlett-Packard). Compaq's computers range from handheld devices to the servers and mainframes that keep companies running and Web sites loading. The company's Global Services unit (about 15% of sales) provides a standard array of consulting, implementation, and support services. Compaq derives most of its sales from business customers, but also markets products to home users, government agencies, schools, and students.

KEY COMPETITORS
Dell Computer
Hewlett-Packard
IBM

See pages 78–79 for a full profile of this company.

COMPAQ GLOBAL SERVICES

20555 State Hwy. 249
Houston, TX 77070
Phone: 281-370-0670
Fax: 281-514-1740
Web: www.compaq.com

CEO: Peter Blackmore
CFO: —
HR: —
Type: Business segment

2000 Sales: $6,993.0 million
1-Yr. Sales Change: (2.4%)
Employees: 30,000
FYE: December 31

While you still can't spell Compaq without "pc", the company hopes its name will become increasingly synonymous with service. Compaq offers a slew of information technology (IT) services through its Global Services division (which employs 40,000 service professionals), including systems integration, applications development, management consulting, support services, and network operations outsourcing, with customers in more than 200 countries. Like the IT service arms of IBM and Hewlett-Packard, Compaq Global Services (which accounts for 15% of Compaq's sales) relies on Compaq's sprawling empire of hardware and software sales to build, integrate, and maintain the technological backbones of companies worldwide.

KEY COMPETITORS
Computer Sciences
EDS
IBM Global Services

COMPUCOM SYSTEMS, INC.

Nasdaq: CMPC

7171 Forest Ln.
Dallas, TX 75230
Phone: 972-856-3600
Fax: 972-856-5395
Web: www.compucom.com

CEO: J. Edward Coleman
CFO: M. Lazane Smith
HR: David A. Loeser
Type: Public

2000 Sales: $2,710.6 million
1-Yr. Sales Change: (6.8%)
Employees: 4,100
FYE: December 31

CompuCom Systems helps businesses keep their digital rivers flowing. The company resells computers, networking equipment, peripherals, and software and provides consulting, distribution, and other information technology services. Its products (90% of sales) are made by tech heavyweights such as Compaq (30% of product sales), IBM (26%), Hewlett-Packard (20%), Microsoft, and Palm. Its services include asset tracking, system configuration, help desk support, and network management. Investment and management firm Safeguard Scientifics owns about 55% of CompuCom.

KEY COMPETITORS
Ingram Micro
IBM
Tech Data

 See pages 80–81 for a full profile of this company.

COMPUSA INC.

14951 N. Dallas Pkwy.
Dallas, TX 75240
Phone: 972-982-4000
Fax: 972-982-4276
Web: www.compusa.com

CEO: Harold F. Compton
CFO: Javier Laraza
HR: Randy Smith
Type: Subsidiary

1999 Sales: $6,321.4 million
1-Yr. Sales Change: 19.6%
Employees: 19,700
FYE: June 30

CompUSA needs to reboot. Computer sales at the nation's leading computer retailer have stalled, and the company has been sold to Mexico-based retailer Grupo Sanborns. CompUSA has about 225 stores that sell hardware (including its own brand of PCs), software, and accessories in more than 40 states. CompUSA also has a direct sales operation targeting corporate, government, and education customers. The retailer has been battered by direct computer sellers (such as Dell Computer and Gateway), PC price wars, and its purchase of rival (and unprofitable) Computer City stores. CompUSA sells online, but has shut down subsidiary cozone.com, an e-tailer that suffered from sluggish sales.

KEY COMPETITORS
Best Buy
Circuit City
Dell Computer

COMPX INTERNATIONAL INC.

NYSE: CIX

5430 LBJ Fwy., Ste. 1700
Dallas, TX 75240
Phone: 972-233-1700
Fax: 972-448-1445
Web: www.compxnet.com

CEO: Brent A. Hagenbuch
CFO: Stuart M. Bitting
HR: —
Type: Public

2000 Sales: $253.3 million
1-Yr. Sales Change: 12.1%
Employees: 2,270
FYE: December 31

CompX International tries to keep the workday from being too much of a pain. CompX makes ergonomic computer support systems, ball bearing slides, and locks, which it sells primarily to office furniture makers. Its ergonomic and ball bearing products are sold under the Waterloo Furniture Components, Thomas Regout, and Dynaslide names and include cabinet and drawer slides, keyboard support arms, and a device for mounting computers under desks. Its locks are sold under the National Cabinet Lock, Fort Lock, Chicago Lock, and Timberline Lock names and include KeSet high-security locks for vending machines and parking meters. Parent Valhi, through its wholly owned Valcor subsidiary, owns about 68% of CompX.

KEY COMPETITORS
Eastern Company
Fellowes
Knape & Vogt

COMSTOCK RESOURCES, INC.

NYSE: CRK

5300 Town and Country Blvd., Ste. 500
Frisco, TX 75244
Phone: 972-668-8800
Fax: 972-668-8812
Web: www.comstockresources.com

CEO: M. Jay Allison
CFO: Roland O. Burns
HR: Roland O. Burns
Type: Public

2000 Sales: $169.4 million
1-Yr. Sales Change: 88.0%
Employees: 48
FYE: December 31

Comstock Resources' stock in trade is producing natural gas and oil. The mid-sized independent oil and gas company has proved reserves of nearly 403 billion cu. ft. of natural gas equivalent (74% is natural gas) on its properties in three areas: the Gulf of Mexico, East Texas and North Louisiana, and Southeast Texas. Comstock Resources owns interests in about 500 producing wells and operates more than half of them. Although the company has grown by making acquisitions in its core areas, Comstock has focused on exploring its undeveloped acreage and exploiting its existing reserves since 1998. El Paso Energy is the company's major natural gas customer; Williams-Gulfmark Energy is the top oil buyer.

KEY COMPETITORS
Apache
BP
Shell

CONCENTRA, INC.

5080 Spectrum Dr.
Addison, TX 75001
Phone: 972-364-8000
Fax: 972-387-1938
Web: www.concentramc.com

CEO: Daniel J. Thomas
CFO: Thomas E. Kiraly
HR: Dana Payne
Type: Private

2000 Sales: $752.2 million
1-Yr. Sales Change: 10.4%
Employees: 8,800
FYE: December 31

Concentra (formerly CONCENTRA Managed Care) concentrates on getting people back to work cheaper. It is the holding company for Concentra Operating Corporation, which provides cost containment and case management services to employers and to occupational, auto, and group health payors throughout the US. Concentra offers specialized cost-containment services for occupational and auto injury cases, preferred provider network management, telephone case management, and medical bill review. The company also operates more than 200 medical centers in about 30 states, providing occupational health care including pre-employment screening, injury care, and loss prevention.

KEY COMPETITORS
CorVel
First Health Group
NDCHealth

CONOCO INC.

NYSE: COC

600 N. Dairy Ashford	CEO: Archie W. Dunham	2000 Sales: $38,737.0 million
Houston, TX 77079	CFO: Robert W. Goldman	1-Yr. Sales Change: 43.3%
Phone: 281-293-1000	HR: Thomas C. Knudson	Employees: 17,600
Fax: 281-293-1440	Type: Public	FYE: December 31
Web: www.conoco.com		

Conoco boasts a cornucopia of energy assets. Formerly a unit of chemical giant DuPont, the integrated oil company explores for oil and gas in 20 countries (proved reserves are more than 2.6 billion barrels of oil equivalent, 38% of which is natural gas) and has production mainly in Norway, the UK, and the US. The company will gain reserves of more than 1 billion barrels of oil equivalent by buying Gulf Canada Resources. Conoco runs about 6,000 miles of US pipeline and owns or has stakes in nine refineries in the US, Europe, and Asia. The company operates more than 7,000 gas stations in the US, Europe, and Thailand. Its power division also markets and trades electricity and gas and develops and builds power plants.

KEY COMPETITORS
BP
Exxon Mobil
Royal Dutch/Shell

 See pages 82–83 for a full profile of this company.

CONSOLIDATED CONTAINER COMPANY LLC

5605 N. MacArthur, Ste. 360	CEO: William L. Estes	2000 Sales: $754.6 million
Irving, TX 75038	CFO: Bryan J. Carey	1-Yr. Sales Change: 59.2%
Phone: 972-518-9150	HR: David M. Stulman	Employees: 4,400
Fax: 972-580-9332	Type: Subsidiary	FYE: December 31

Being flexible allowed Consolidated Container to can its former name (Continental Can). The company is one of the largest manufacturers of rigid plastic containers in the US, selling over 4 billion containers a year. Consolidated markets its products to the consumer, agricultural, and industrial chemical industries. It makes containers for a variety of products including water, milk, ketchup, salsa, soap, motor oil, anti-freeze, insect repellent, fertilizers, and medical supplies. Procter & Gamble is Consolidated's largest customer, accounting for about 15% of total sales. Suiza Foods owns about 43% of the company.

KEY COMPETITORS
Ball Corporation
Crown Cork & Seal
Owens-Illinois

CONSOLIDATED GRAPHICS, INC.

NYSE: CGX

5858 Westheimer, Ste. 200	CEO: Joe R. Davis	2001 Sales: $683.4 million
Houston, TX 77057	CFO: Wayne M. Rose	1-Yr. Sales Change: 9.4%
Phone: 713-787-0977	HR: Michael Barton	Employees: 4,700
Fax: 713-787-5013	Type: Public	FYE: March 31
Web: www.consolidatedgraphics.com		

Consolidated Graphics (CGX) is on a mission to acquire independent commercial printing businesses and exploit economies of scale. The company has bought more than 60 medium-sized printing firms since its 1985 inception. The newly acquired firms operate as subsidiaries of CGX, receive volume discounts on supplies, and benefit from general administrative functions provided by the company. CGX, which is one of the nation's largest commercial printers, generates most of its sales by printing items such as brochures, catalogs, and direct-mail fliers. The company also provides electronic services (online digital asset management, online purchasing) and fulfillment services (assembling, packaging, storing).

KEY COMPETITORS
Bowne
Quebecor World
R. R. Donnelley

THE CONTAINER STORE

2000 Valwood Pkwy.
Dallas, TX 75234
Phone: 214-654-2000
Fax: 214-654-2003
Web: www.containerstore.com

CEO: Kip Tindell
CFO: Stefan Ferm
HR: Nancy Donley
Type: Private

2001 Sales: $260.0 million
1-Yr. Sales Change: 8.3%
Employees: 1,500
FYE: March 31

With its packets, pockets, holders, and boxes, The Container Store has the storage products niche well-contained. Its merchandise ranges from backpacks to recipe holders. The home organization pioneer has more than 20 stores, mostly in major cities in California, Colorado, Florida, Georgia, Illinois, New York, and Texas, and also in Washington, D.C. The stores carry up to 10,000 items; the company's Elfa brand wire shelving accounts for about one-fifth of sales. The company touts a low employee turnover rate, thanks in part to high wages. CEO Garrett Boone and president Kip Tindell own the company. They met in 1969 working in a Montgomery Ward paint department and opened their first store in Dallas in 1978.

KEY COMPETITORS
Bed Bath & Beyond
Linens 'n Things

CONTINENTAL AIRLINES, INC.   NYSE: CAL

1600 Smith St., Dept. HQSEO
Houston, TX 77002
Phone: 713-324-5000
Fax: 713-324-2637
Web: www.continental.com

CEO: Gordon M. Bethune
CFO: Lawrence W. Kellner
HR: Michael H. Campbell
Type: Public

2000 Sales: $9,899.0 million
1-Yr. Sales Change: 14.6%
Employees: 54,300
FYE: December 31

Continental breakfast? It's available on Continental Airlines, which serves more than 135 US cities and more than 95 cities overseas with 2,200 daily flights. The #5 US carrier (trailing United, American, Delta, and Northwest) has hubs in Cleveland, Houston, and Newark, New Jersey. Continental Micronesia serves the western Pacific from Guam, and regional carrier Continental Express serves 70 US cities. Continental code-shares with airlines such as Air France, Alitalia, and Virgin Atlantic. It has a major alliance with Northwest Airlines, which includes code-sharing as well as shared frequent-flyer programs. Continental, Northwest, and KLM have been working to form a global airline alliance called Wings.

KEY COMPETITORS
AMR
Southwest Airlines
UAL

 See pages 84–85 for a full profile of this company.

CONTRAN CORPORATION

5430 LBJ Fwy., Ste. 1700
Dallas, TX 75240
Phone: 972-233-1700
Fax: 972-448-1444

CEO: Harold C. Simmons
CFO: Bob D. O'Brien
HR: Keith A. Johnson
Type: Private

2000 Sales: $1,200.0 million
1-Yr. Sales Change: 3.4%
Employees: 9,000
FYE: December 31

Founded by Texas billionaire Harold Simmons, Contran is a holding company that controls more than 90% of Valhi, Inc., a publicly traded company. Through subsidiaries and affiliations, Valhi conducts diversified operations involved in chemicals (NL Industries), titanium metals (Titanium Metals Corporation), waste management services (Waste Control Specialties), computer support systems, and precision ball bearing slides and locking systems (CompX International). Contran also has a controlling interest in Keystone Consolidated Industries, a maker of fencing and wire products. Trusts benefiting Simmons' daughters and his grandchildren (with Simmons as the sole trustee) own almost all of Contran.

KEY COMPETITORS
RTI International Metals
Steelcase
Waste Management

COOPER CAMERON CORPORATION

NYSE: CAM

515 Post Oak Blvd., Ste. 1200
Houston, TX 77027
Phone: 713-513-3300
Fax: 713-513-3355
Web: www.coopercameron.com

CEO: Sheldon R. Erikson
CFO: Thomas R. Hix
HR: Jane L. Crowder
Type: Public

2000 Sales: $1,386.7 million
1-Yr. Sales Change: (5.3%)
Employees: 7,300
FYE: December 31

Cooper Cameron knows how to work under pressure. A manufacturer, provider, and servicer of oil and gas industry equipment, the company makes products that control pressure at oil and gas wells, including blowout preventers, chokes, wellheads, and valves. It also makes integral and separable reciprocating engines and compressors, turbochargers, and centrifugal compressors used in oil and gas and power-generation applications. Cooper Cameron markets its products under brand names such as Ajax, Demco, Foster, McEvoy, and Willis. The company's products are marketed globally.

KEY COMPETITORS
ABB
Halliburton
Ingersoll-Rand

COOPER INDUSTRIES, INC.

NYSE: CBE

600 Travis, Ste. 5800
Houston, TX 77002
Phone: 713-209-8400
Fax: 713-209-8995
Web: www.cooperindustries.com

CEO: H. John Riley Jr.
CFO: D. Bradley McWilliams
HR: David R. Sheil Jr.
Type: Public

2000 Sales: $4,459.9 million
1-Yr. Sales Change: 15.3%
Employees: 34,250
FYE: December 31

Getting uptight or blowing a fuse is no problem for Cooper Industries, maker of electrical products, tools, hardware, and metal support products. The company's electrical products (about 80% of sales) include electrical and circuit-protection devices and systems, residential and industrial lighting, and electrical power and distribution products for use by utilities. Cooper's tool offerings include such venerable brands as Crescent wrenches and pliers, Apex impact sockets, and Plumb hammers. It's metal support products (B-Line) include conduits and cable trays. Cooper operates about 120 manufacturing plants and 20 warehouse facilities, primarily in North America and Europe. The US accounts for almost 80% of sales.

KEY COMPETITORS
ABB
Black & Decker
GE

 See pages 86–87 for a full profile of this company.

COOPERATIVE COMPUTING HOLDING COMPANY, INC.

804 Las Cimas Parkway, Ste. 200
Austin, TX 78746
Phone: 512-328-2300
Fax: 512-328-6461

CEO: Glenn E. Staats
CFO: Paul D. Stone
HR: Scott Zinnecker
Type: Private

2000 Sales: $223.9 million
1-Yr. Sales Change: (7.1%)
Employees: 1,700
FYE: September 30

Cooperative Computing Holding Company wants all parts of a business holding hands and singing in perfect harmony. The company (which does business as CCI/Triad) provides information management software and systems for the automotive aftermarket and the hardline and lumber industries. Its software automates functions such as inventory management, parts selection, and point-of-sale (POS) analysis. The company also offers automotive databases (which include parts catalogs, pricing updates, and repair information) and hardware systems, including computers, monitors, and POS terminals. Investment firm Hicks, Muse, Tate & Furst owns 55% of the company; CEO Glen Staats holds a 38% stake.

KEY COMPETITORS
Intermec Technologies
JDA Software
Manugistics Group

CORNELL COMPANIES, INC.

NYSE: CRN

1700 W. Loop South, Ste. 1500
Houston, TX 77027
Phone: 713-623-0790
Fax: 713-623-2853
Web: www.cornellcorrections.com

CEO: Steven W. Logan
CFO: John L. Hendrix
HR: Patrick N. Perrin
Type: Public

2000 Sales: $226.1 million
1-Yr. Sales Change: 27.7%
Employees: 3,673
FYE: December 31

Graduating from this Cornell may not impress people as much as earning a degree from the Ivy League university with the same name. Cornell Companies (formerly Cornell Corrections) designs, builds, and operates private detention and maximum and minimum correctional centers. It runs 71 adult and juvenile "slammers" with more than 14,000 beds in 13 states and Washington, DC. The company's pre-release facilities (including halfway houses) provide services such as job training and placement. Its juvenile and adult facilities offer programs such as recreation and leisure activities, health care (including mental health and drug counseling), and life skills training (including personal finance and parenting skills).

KEY COMPETITORS
CSC
Corrections Corporation of America
Wackenhut Corrections

CRESCENT OPERATING, INC.

OTC: COPI

306 W. 7th St., Ste. 1000
Fort Worth, TX 76102
Phone: 817-339-2200
Fax: 817-339-2220
Web: www.crescentoperating.com

CEO: John C. Goff
CFO: Richard P. Knight
HR: Marcia Davee
Type: Public

2000 Sales: $716.8 million
1-Yr. Sales Change: (0.2%)
Employees: 1,851
FYE: December 31

Crescent Operating holds interests in land development firms, hotels, cold-storage facilities, and an equipment leasing company. Formed to manage properties owned by Crescent Real Estate Equities, the company owns more than 50% of Woodlands Operating, which manages The Woodlands, a master-planned residential and commercial community near Houston. Crescent Operating also has stakes in about a half dozen hotels and resorts, as well as firms that develop residential properties in New Mexico and Colorado. The company owns about 40% of AmeriCold Logistics, which operates more than 100 refrigerated storage facilities. Through Crescent Machinery, the firm sells and leases construction equipment in six states.

KEY COMPETITORS
FelCor
Glenborough
Hospitality Properties

CRESCENT REAL ESTATE EQUITIES COMPANY

NYSE: CEI

777 Main St., Ste. 2100
Fort Worth, TX 76102
Phone: 817-321-2100
Fax: 817-321-2000
Web: www.cei-crescent.com

CEO: John C. Goff
CFO: Jerry R. Crenshaw Jr.
HR: Thomas Shaw Jr.
Type: Public

2000 Sales: $923.0 million
1-Yr. Sales Change: 13.3%
Employees: 707
FYE: December 31

Crescent Real Estate Equities, a real estate investment trust (REIT), owns about 80 office properties (about 90% are found in the Dallas and Houston areas) and about 10 scattered upscale hotels and fitness resorts. The company is in the process of selling about 20 buildings that once housed Charter Behavioral Health System, which is in Chapter 11 bankruptcy. The company also has interests in residential developments, primarily in Colorado, and owns 40% of refrigerated warehouse firm AmeriCold Logistics. The REIT has sold off sexy but noncore interests such as its stakes in Station Casinos and the NBA's Dallas Mavericks.

KEY COMPETITORS
HRPT Properties
M.D.C. Holdings
Parkway Properties

CROWN CASTLE INTERNATIONAL CORP.

NYSE: CCI

510 Bering Dr., Ste. 500
Houston, TX 77057
Phone: 713-570-3000
Fax: 713-570-3100
Web: www.crowncomm.net

CEO: John P. Kelly
CFO: W. Benjamin Moreland
HR: Kelli H. Cole
Type: Public

2000 Sales: $649.2 million
1-Yr. Sales Change: 87.7%
Employees: 2,100
FYE: December 31

Crown Castle International's (CCI) crown jewels are its kingdom of radio towers. Its subsidiaries and joint ventures provide broadcast, data, and wireless communications infrastructure services in Australia, Puerto Rico, the UK, and the US. The company has lined up clients such as AT&T Wireless and Sprint PCS; they lease antenna space on Crown Castle's 13,000 owned or managed towers and rooftop sites. Crown Castle provides broadcast transmission services to the BBC (accounting for nearly half of sales in the UK) and other TV and radio networks. It also designs networks, selects and develops sites, and installs antennas.

KEY COMPETITORS
American Tower
NTL
SpectraSite

CROWN GROUP, INC.

Nasdaq: CNGR

4040 N. MacArthur Blvd., Ste. 100
Irving, TX 75038
Phone: 972-717-3423
Fax: 972-719-4466
Web: www.cngr.com

CEO: Edward R. McMurphy
CFO: Mark D. Slusser
HR: —
Type: Public

2001 Sales: $282.5 million
1-Yr. Sales Change: 44.6%
Employees: 1,060
FYE: April 30

Crown Group aims to become king of sub-prime used-car sales. The company owns America's Car-Mart and 70% of Smart Choice Automotive Group, both of which target consumers with poor or limited credit histories. Car-Mart has 29 dealerships in smaller urban markets in Arkansas, Missouri, Oklahoma, and Texas. Smart Choice, including subsidiary Paaco, operates over 20 used-car dealerships in Texas and Florida. Crown Group also owns Precision, which sells and rents bulk containers; 80% of sub-prime mortgage lender Concorde Acceptance; 90% of Salvadoran casino operator CG; and 45% of engine parts manufacturer Atlantic Castings. Revenues have increased by a third, due to acquisitions and higher sales from subsidiaries.

KEY COMPETITORS
AutoNation
CarMax
Ugly Duckling

CULLEN/FROST BANKERS, INC.

NYSE: CFR

100 W. Houston St.
San Antonio, TX 78205
Phone: 210-220-4011
Fax: 210-220-4325
Web: www.frostbank.com

CEO: Richard W. Evans Jr.
CFO: Phillip D. Green
HR: James A. Eckel
Type: Public

2000 Sales: $683.2 million
1-Yr. Sales Change: 13.0%
Employees: 3,394
FYE: December 31

One of the largest independent bank holding companies in Texas, Cullen/Frost Bankers owns Frost National Bank, managed through a second-tier holding company. The bank serves individuals and local businesses with about 80 branches throughout Texas; the company also serves clients in Mexico. Frost National Bank offers a variety of traditional deposit products including checking, savings, and money market accounts, as well as CDs. Lending activities consist mostly of commercial loans (about 40% of all loans), as well as residential mortgage, commercial real estate, and construction loans. Through nonbanking subsidiaries, Cullen/Frost provides insurance products and investment banking services.

KEY COMPETITORS
BANK ONE
Compass Bancshares
Wells Fargo

DAISYTEK INTERNATIONAL CORPORATION

Nasdaq: DZTK

1025 Central Expwy. South, Ste. 200	CEO: James R. Powell	2001 Sales: $1,189.7 million
Allen, TX 75013	CFO: Ralph Mitchell	1-Yr. Sales Change: 12.2%
Phone: 972-881-4700	HR: Deborah D'Atra	Employees: 880
Fax: 972-881-4238	Type: Public	FYE: March 31
Web: www.daisytek.com		

Give a bouquet of Daisytek International Corporation's products to the hardest workers in your office. The firm is a leading wholesaler of non-paper computer supplies and accessories, including laser and ink jet printer, copier, and fax supplies; diskettes; computer tape cartridges; and cleaning kits. Major suppliers include Hewlett-Packard and IBM. Daisytek distributes nearly 20,000 products to about 30,000 customers (retailers and resellers) in more than 50 countries worldwide. The company spun off to the public its subsidiary Priority Fulfillment Services (as PFSweb), which provides call center, distribution, and order-management services. Daisytek also sells recording media for professionals.

KEY COMPETITORS
Buhrmann
Danka
United Stationers

DALLAS COWBOYS FOOTBALL CLUB, LTD.

1 Cowboys Pkwy.	CEO: Jerral W. "Jerry" Jones	2001 Sales: $181.0 million
Irving, TX 75063	CFO: Robert Nunez	1-Yr. Sales Change: 4.1%
Phone: 972-556-9900	HR: Stephen Jones	Employees: 300
Fax: 972-556-9304	Type: Private	FYE: February 28
Web: www.dallascowboys.com		

Texas humor has it that there's a hole in the roof of Texas Stadium so God can watch his favorite team. He may get a better view if Dallas Cowboys owner Jerry Jones has his way: A proposed renovation would make the roof retractable. The Cowboys are the NFL's second-most-valuable team at $713 million (the Washington Redskins are first) and sell more licensed merchandise than any other. "America's Team" has won five Super Bowls, including three in four years (1992-95). The Boys are led by stars such as Emmitt Smith (running back) and Joey Galloway (wide receiver). The Dallas Cowboys Cheerleaders are their own institution. Veteran quarterback Troy Aikman was released and later retired after the 2000-01 season.

KEY COMPETITORS
New York Giants
Philadelphia Eagles
Washington Redskins

DALLAS MAVERICKS

Reunion Arena, 777 Sports St.	CEO: Terdema L. Ussery II	2000 Sales: $59.7 million
Dallas, TX 75207	CFO: Jay McKim	1-Yr. Sales Change: 19.4%
Phone: 214-748-1808	HR: Buddy Pitman	Employees: 85
Fax: 214-748-0510	Type: Private	FYE: June 30
Web: www.dallasmavericks.com		

The Dallas Mavericks want to buck the image of a losing team. Formed in 1980 by millionaire Donald Carter, the franchise has contended only once for a conference title. After struggling with losing seasons through the 1990s, the Mavs returned to playoff contention with the 2000-01 season. It was the first year for principal owner Mark Cuban (co-founder of broadcast.com), who bought the team in 2000 for $280 million from a group headed by Ross Perot Jr. (son of the outspoken Texas billionaire). The team has moved into the $420 million American Airlines Center; built partly with public funds, it is twice the size of the Reunion Arena, the Mavericks' former home.

KEY COMPETITORS
Minnesota Timberwolves
Utah Jazz
San Antonio Spurs

DALLAS SEMICONDUCTOR CORPORATION

4401 S. Beltwood Pkwy.
Dallas, TX 75244
Phone: 972-371-4000
Fax: 972-371-4956
Web: www.dalsemi.com

CEO: Chao C. Mai
CFO: Alan P. Hale
HR: Gay Vencill
Type: Subsidiary

2000 Sales: $517.0 million
1-Yr. Sales Change: 31.8%
Employees: 1,991
FYE: June 30

Dallas Semiconductor has made more than 2,000 variations of its more than 350 computer chips and chip-based subsystems. The company's products are used to enhance broadband telecommunications systems, Internet security, data storage devices, cellular phones and base stations, and various industrial equipment. Its systems provide safety backups, keep computer time, and control product temperature. Its portable iButton, for example, is designed to provide secure electronic commerce. Dallas Semiconductor sells directly and via distributors to more than 15,000 customers worldwide; US clients account for 55% of sales. The company is a subsidiary of analog chip maker Maxim Integrated Products.

KEY COMPETITORS
Analog Devices
STMicroelectronics
Texas Instruments

DALLAS STARS L.P.

211 Cowboys Pkwy.
Irving, TX 75063
Phone: 972-831-2401
Fax: 972-868-2860
Web: www.dallasstars.com

CEO: James R. Lites
CFO: Robert Hudson
HR: Terry Turner
Type: Private

2000 Sales: $72.7 million
1-Yr. Sales Change: 22.4%
Employees: 200
FYE: June 30

The Dallas Stars will have to wish upon the luminaries for another year. The professional hockey team won its first Stanley Cup in 1999, but subsequent runs at the championship title have ended in defeat. A group led by Walter Bush organized the team as the Minnesota North Stars for the 1967 league expansion. In 1978 the team was bought by George and Gordon Gund (now owners of the San Jose Sharks and the Cleveland Cavaliers basketball team), then eventually sold to Norm Green, who moved the team to Dallas in 1993. Tom Hicks, chairman and CEO of Dallas-based private investment firm Hicks, Muse, Tate & Furst, bought the team in 1995. Hicks also owns the Texas Rangers baseball team.

KEY COMPETITORS
Los Angeles Kings
Phoenix Coyotes
San Jose Sharks

DAL-TILE INTERNATIONAL INC.   NYSE: DTL

7834 C. F. Hawn Freeway
Dallas, TX 75217
Phone: 214-398-1411
Fax: 214-309-4835
Web: www.dtile.com

CEO: Jacques R. Sardas
CFO: W. Christopher Wellborn
HR: Andrew D. Hiduke
Type: Public

2000 Sales: $952.2 million
1-Yr. Sales Change: 11.9%
Employees: 7,524
FYE: December 31

Dal-Tile International never fails to floor its customers. As one of the US's largest makers of ceramic tiles, Dal-Tile sells its floor, wall, quarry, and mosaic tiles under the Daltile and American Olean brand names. The company also sells installation materials and tools. It manufactures tiles at plants in the US and Mexico and sells its products through more than 200 North American sales centers, independent distributors, and retailers such as The Home Depot and Lowe's. The tilemaker's customers include architects, builders, developers, and homeowners. AEA Investors owns 51% of Dal-Tile.

KEY COMPETITORS
Armstrong Holdings
Congoleum
Formica

DARLING INTERNATIONAL INC.

AMEX: DAR

251 O'Connor Ridge Blvd., Ste. 300
Irving, TX 75038
Phone: 972-717-0300
Fax: 972-717-1588
Web: www.darlingii.com

CEO: Denis J. Taura
CFO: John O. Muse
HR: Mike Campbell
Type: Public

2000 Sales: $242.8 million
1-Yr. Sales Change: (6.1%)
Employees: 1,242
FYE: December 31

It's not the most darling of businesses — in fact it's messy and stinky — but Darling International, the largest independent rendering operation in the US, is willing to do it. The company collects animal by-products and used cooking grease from some 80,000 restaurants, butcher shops, grocery stores, and independent meat and poultry processors throughout the US. Rendering produces yellow grease, tallow, and meat and bone meal, which Darling sells in the US and internationally to makers of soap, rubber, pet and livestock feed, and chemicals. Competition comes from vegetable oil sources. Director Bruce Waterfall and Edwin Morgens own about 45% of Darling through their MW Group investment firm.

KEY COMPETITORS
ADM
EarthCare
Weststar Environmental

DARR EQUIPMENT COMPANY

2000 E. Airport Fwy.
Irving, TX 75062
Phone: 972-721-2000
Fax: 972-438-2481
Web: darrequipment.cat.com

CEO: Randall R. Engstrom
CFO: Gary Brigham
HR: Michael Shropshire
Type: Private

2000 Est. Sales: $600.0 mil.
1-Yr. Sales Change: —
Employees: 1,450
FYE: December 31

Need a Caterpillar product? Darr Equipment's got it all. Through about 15 locations in Oklahoma and North Texas, Darr rents and sells Caterpillar's full line of construction, material handling, power systems, and truck engine products. Its supply of construction and earthmoving equipment includes air compressors, saws, and water trailers. Darr also supplies power system products (industrial engines, light towers, and loadbanks) and material handling products (industrial loaders, hydraulic cranes, and lift trucks) and is a reseller of Cat's truck engines. The company also offers equipment maintenance. Its Darr Export unit exports Caterpillar parts and other industrial equipment.

KEY COMPETITORS
Hertz
Komatsu America
Stewart & Stevenson

DAVE & BUSTER'S, INC.

NYSE: DAB

2481 Manana Dr.
Dallas, TX 75220
Phone: 214-357-9588
Fax: 214-350-0941
Web: www.daveandbusters.com

CEO: James W. "Buster" Corley
CFO: Charles "Chas" Michel
HR: Nancy J. Duricic
Type: Public

2001 Sales: $332.3 million
1-Yr. Sales Change: 34.5%
Employees: 6,600
FYE: January 31

Part restaurant, part saloon, and part carnival midway, for more than 16 million patrons, Dave & Buster's (D&B) is all fun. The company owns and operates about 30 restaurant and entertainment complexes in more than a dozen states offering casual dining, full bar service, and an adult game center. Its cavernous game rooms feature the latest in video games and motion simulators, as well as games of skill in which players can win coupons redeemable for merchandise. Its menu features traditional America fare such as burgers, seafood, and steak. D&B's games generate almost half the company's revenue; alcoholic beverages account for 17% of sales. The company also has locations operating under license in Canada and Taiwan.

KEY COMPETITORS
Champps Entertainment
Hard Rock Cafe
Jillian's Entertainment

 See pages 88–89 for a full profile of this company.

DAVID MCDAVID AUTO GROUP

3600 W. Airport Fwy.
Irving, TX 75062
Phone: 972-790-6100
Fax: 972-986-5689
Web: www.mcdavid.com

CEO: David McDavid Sr.
CFO: Jay Torda
HR: Amanda Slaughter
Type: Private

2000 Sales: $596.0 million
1-Yr. Sales Change: 9.9%
Employees: 1,100
FYE: December 31

David McDavid Auto Group is one of the largest vehicle vendors in Texas, with about a dozen dealerships in Austin, Houston, and Dallas. The company sells new cars made by Acura, Ford, Honda, General Motors, Kia, Nissan, and Suzuki, as well as used cars. David McDavid Auto Group is named for its founder and CEO, who started his first car dealership in 1962 at age 19; he is a former minority owner of the Dallas Mavericks basketball team. McDavid sold 70% of David McDavid Auto Group to automotive consolidator Asbury Automotive Group in 1997. Asbury Automotive is a joint venture of Ripplewood Holdings (part-owned by Mitsubishi Corporation) and LBO firm Freeman, Spogli & Co.

KEY COMPETITORS
Gulf States Toyota
Sonic Automotive
VT

DAVID WEEKLEY HOMES

1111 N. Post Oak Rd.
Houston, TX 77055
Phone: 713-963-0500
Fax: 713-963-8822
Web: www.davidweekleyhomes.com

CEO: David Weekley
CFO: Jim Alexander
HR: Mike Gentry
Type: Private

2000 Sales: $828.0 million
1-Yr. Sales Change: 16.5%
Employees: 1,010
FYE: December 31

A development home developed to your taste? Founded in 1976, David Weekley Homes builds houses offering hundreds of floor plans and custom upgrades for its customers. Priced from $120,000 to about $650,000, the builder's homes range in size from about 1,500 sq. ft. to more than 4,000 sq. ft. Weekley constructs on home buyers' lots, but it primarily works in its own planned communities in the southeastern US and in Colorado, Oklahoma, and Texas. The company is building a home in Tampa in conjunction with the *Today* show, allowing viewers to vote on and determine every aspect of the home's construction, from the floor plan to the bathroom's color scheme. Founder and chairman David Weekley owns the firm.

KEY COMPETITORS
D.R. Horton
Engle Homes
Town and Country Homes

DELL COMPUTER CORPORATION   Nasdaq: DELL

1 Dell Way
Round Rock, TX 78682
Phone: 512-338-4400
Fax: 512-728-3653
Web: www.dell.com

CEO: Michael S. Dell
CFO: James M. Schneider
HR: Paul D. McKinnon
Type: Public

2001 Sales: $31,888.0 million
1-Yr. Sales Change: 26.2%
Employees: 40,000
FYE: January 31

Dell Computer has taken the direct approach all the way to the top. Touting a sales model that sidesteps middleman markups for lower prices, the world's #1 direct-sale computer vendor gives perennial leader Compaq a run for the worldwide PC title. Led by founder Michael Dell — who owns 12% of his creation and is the longest-tenured CEO of any major US computer company — the company generates about three-quarters of its sales from desktop and notebook PCs. Its enterprise products include network servers, workstations, and storage systems. It also markets third-party software and peripherals. Despite its success in grabbing market share, Dell has felt the effects of a market-wide slump and responded with job cuts.

KEY COMPETITORS
Compaq
Hewlett-Packard
IBM

 See pages 90–91 for a full profile of this company.

DENALI INCORPORATED

OTC: DNLI

1360 Post Oak Blvd., Ste. 2250
Houston, TX 77056
Phone: 713-627-0933
Fax: 713-627-0937
Web: www.denaliincorporated.com

CEO: Richard W. Volk
CFO: R. Kevin Andrews
HR: Janice McCormick
Type: Public

2000 Sales: $189.9 million
1-Yr. Sales Change: 27.6%
Employees: 1,710
FYE: June 30

Denali makes underground and aboveground storage tanks and fiberglass-reinforced composites used to handle hazardous fluids. Formed to buy Owens Corning's operations in fiberglass composite underground storage tanks, Denali makes products for petroleum, chemical, pulp and paper, electric power, and other industrial process plants. Denali's Plasticon Fluid Systems (PFS) unit makes fiberglass reinforced products including metered manholes, gates and flumes used in the water/wastewater industry. Denali operates overseas through Plasticon Europe and Hanwell Europe. The company is restructuring after William Blair Mezzanine Capital Partners backed out of a proposed $23 million investment in Denali.

KEY COMPETITORS
Kingspan
Matrix Service

DENBURY RESOURCES INC.

NYSE: DNR

5100 Tennyson Pkwy., Ste. 3000
Plano, TX 75024
Phone: 972-673-2000
Fax: 972-673-2150
Web: www.denbury.com

CEO: Gareth Roberts
CFO: Phil Rykhoek
HR: Kandy Miller
Type: Public

2000 Sales: $179.4 million
1-Yr. Sales Change: 119.9%
Employees: 242
FYE: December 31

Denbury Resources has long since capped its oil and gas operations in its native Canada to try its luck in the Deep South. The independent exploration and production company has proved reserves of 87.4 million barrels of oil equivalent (81% is oil) and working interests in more than 500 oil and gas wells in Louisiana, Mississippi, and the Gulf of Mexico. In Mississippi the company also owns wells that produce carbon dioxide, which it uses to force oil out of the ground at nearby abandoned wells acquired from other companies. Denbury Resources has expanded into Texas and is seeking reserves on its acquisitions there and in Mississippi. Buyout firm Texas Pacific Group, led by David Bonderman, controls 60% of Denbury.

KEY COMPETITORS
Meridian Resource
Newfield Exploration
Swift Energy

DIAMOND OFFSHORE DRILLING, INC.

NYSE: DO

15415 Katy Fwy.
Houston, TX 77094
Phone: 281-492-5300
Fax: 281-492-5316
Web: www.diamondoffshore.com

CEO: James S. Tisch
CFO: Gary T. Krenek
HR: R. Lynn Charles
Type: Public

2000 Sales: $659.4 million
1-Yr. Sales Change: (19.7%)
Employees: 4,000
FYE: December 31

Diamond is an oiler's best friend. Diamond Offshore Drilling is a contract offshore oil and gas driller capable of descending the deep blue at depths of 7,500 ft. A leading US drilling contractor, Diamond Offshore has 30 semisubmersibles, one drillship, and 14 jack-up rigs (mobile drilling platforms). Operating in waters off six continents, Diamond Offshore contracts with major oil and gas companies, including PETROBRAS (25% of revenues) and BP (20% of revenues). Subsidiary Diamond Offshore Team Solutions provides project management and other drilling-related services. Loews Corp., which spun off Diamond Offshore in 1995, owns about 52% of the company.

KEY COMPETITORS
Global Marine
Noble Drilling
Transocean Sedco Forex

D.R. HORTON, INC.

NYSE: DHI

1901 Ascension Blvd., Ste. 100	CEO: Donald J. Tomnitz	2000 Sales: $3,653.7 million
Arlington, TX 76006	CFO: Samuel R. Fuller	1-Yr. Sales Change: 15.8%
Phone: 817-856-8200	HR: Paula Hunter-Perkins	Employees: 3,631
Fax: 817-856-8249	Type: Public	FYE: September 30
Web: www.drhorton.com		

With little heraldry or hooplah, D.R. Horton has become a head honcho in the hierarchy of the hottest US home builders, taking its place alongside KB Home, Lennar, and Pulte Homes behind industry leader Centex. The company builds and sells single-family homes designed primarily for the entry-level and move-up markets. Homes range in size from 1,000 sq. ft. to 5,000 sq. ft., and the average selling price is about $182,600. D.R. Horton also builds luxury homes that can cost up to $800,000. The company, which provides mortgage financing and title services to home buyers, has 46 divisions operating in more than 20 states and about 40 markets. Founder Donald Horton owns about 13% of the company.

KEY COMPETITORS
Centex
KB Home
Pulte Homes

 See pages 92–93 for a full profile of this company.

DR PEPPER/SEVEN UP BOTTLING GROUP, INC.

Sherry Ln., Ste. 500	CEO: Jim L. Turner	2000 Sales: $1,900.0 million
Dallas, TX 75225	CFO: Holly Loworn	1-Yr. Sales Change: 90.0%
Phone: 214-530-5000	HR: Kellie Defratus	Employees: 8,000
Fax: 214-530-5036	Type: Subsidiary	FYE: December 31

Dr Pepper/Seven Up Bottling Group (DPSUBG) rings up sweet results for Cadbury Schweppes, the world's #3 soft drink firm. It is a leading bottler of soft drinks in the US, distributing in much of California, Texas, and a number of western states from 14 distribution centers. Besides the Dr Pepper and 7 UP brands (owned by Cadbury Schweppes), it also bottles other brands including A&W Root Beer, Canada Dry, Hawaiian Punch, and RC Cola. DPSUBG was formed in 1999 when Dr Pepper Bottling Company of Texas and American Bottling merged. Cadbury Schweppes and The Carlyle Group own 40% and 53% of the company, respectively. CEO Jim Turner joined Dr Pepper Bottling Company of Texas in 1982 and built it by acquiring franchises.

KEY COMPETITORS
Coca-Cola Enterprises
Cott
Pepsi Bottling

DRIL-QUIP, INC.

NYSE: DRQ

13550 Hempstead Hwy.	CEO: J. Mike Walker	2000 Sales: $164.0 million
Houston, TX 77040	CFO: Jerry M. Brooks	1-Yr. Sales Change: 4.9%
Phone: 713-939-7711	HR: Mike Mills	Employees: 1,262
Fax: 713-939-8063	Type: Public	FYE: December 31
Web: www.dril-quip.com		

Dril-Quip equips the oil and gas industry. Its products include drilling and production riser systems, subsea and surface wellheads and production trees, wellhead connectors and diverters, mudline hanger systems, and specialty connectors and pipe. The company, which specializes in deep-water or severe-condition equipment, also provides installation, reconditioning, and tool-rental services. Drill-Quip makes about 35% of its sales outside the US. The company has manufacturing plants in Scotland, Singapore, and the US. Co-chairmen and co-founders Larry Reimert and Gary Smith, along with CEO J. Mike Walker, each control 20% of the company.

KEY COMPETITORS
Cooper Cameron
FMC
Grant Prideco

THE DUNLAP COMPANY

200 Bailey Ave.
Fort Worth, TX 76107
Phone: 817-336-4985
Fax: 817-877-1302
Web: www.dunlaps.com

CEO: Reg Martin
CFO: Craig Peterson
HR: Ret Martin
Type: Private

2001 Est. Sales: $250.0 mil.
1-Yr. Sales Change: 0.0%
Employees: 3,000
FYE: January 31

Small-town department stores soldier on, thanks in part to The Dunlap Company. Dunlap owns about 60 department stores in small to midsized towns in about a dozen states stretching from New Mexico to Maine. The stores operate under 25 names, led by Dunlaps (11 stores, mostly in West Texas), Steketee's, M.M. Cohn, Stripling & Cox, Lintz, Porteous, and Heironimus. Dunlap has grown by acquiring family-owned department store retailers in distress or generational transition, preserving the flow of Estée Lauder, Tommy Hilfiger, and similar brand names into secondary markets. Members of the founding H. G. Dunlap and Retha Martin families still own and manage the company, which was started in 1892.

KEY COMPETITORS
Federated
Goody's Family Clothing
Kohl's

DUPONT PHOTOMASKS, INC.
Nasdaq: DPMI

131 Old Settlers Blvd.
Round Rock, TX 78664
Phone: 512-310-6500
Fax: 512-255-9627
Web: www.photomask.com

CEO: Peter S. Kirlin
CFO: Satish Rishi
HR: Kathy Conway
Type: Public

2001 Sales: $407.9 million
1-Yr. Sales Change: 24.3%
Employees: 1,950
FYE: June 30

DuPont Photomasks, Inc. (DPI) can't mask the fact that it is one of the world's leading suppliers of photomasks. Photomasks are high-purity glass or quartz plates etched with complex circuit patterns; semiconductor makers use them to transfer chip designs onto silicon wafers. DPI — which vies with Photronics in North America and Dai Nippon Printing worldwide for market leadership — supplies major chip makers including Texas Instruments (12% of sales), AMD, Hewlett-Packard, IBM, Philips, and Samsung. DPI has expanded by acquiring the photomask operations of leading chip makers worldwide, then cutting deals to supply them with masks. Chemical giant DuPont — DPI's former parent — owns 35% of DPI.

KEY COMPETITORS
Dai Nippon Printing
Photronics
Taiwan Semiconductor

DXP ENTERPRISES, INC.
Nasdaq (SC): DXPE

7272 Pinemont
Houston, TX 77040
Phone: 713-996-4700
Fax: 713-996-4701
Web: www.dxpe.com

CEO: David R. Little
CFO: Mac McConnell
HR: Tracy Pawlak
Type: Public

2000 Sales: $182.6 million
1-Yr. Sales Change: 1.5%
Employees: 532
FYE: December 31

DXP Enterprises can keep you well-equipped. The company distributes more than 170,000 maintenance, repair, and operating equipment products, primarily to the oil and gas, petrochemical, and wood products industries. DXP manufactures centrifugal pumps, rotary gear pumps, plunger pumps, and other fluid handling equipment. The company also sells bearings and power transmission equipment (stainless steel hoses), general mill (cutting tools) and safety supplies, and electrical products (wire conduit). It provides system design, fabrication, and repair services. DXP has exited the valve business. CEO David Little owns 22% of DXP; VP David Vinson owns 48%.

KEY COMPETITORS
Applied Industrial Technologies
Graco
Roper Industries

DYNACARE INC.

Nasdaq: DNCR

14900 Landmark Blvd.
Dallas, TX 75240
Phone: 972-387-3200
Fax: 972-387-3212
Web: www.dynacare.com

CEO: Harvey A. Shapiro
CFO: Zbig S. Biskup
HR: David Meadows
Type: Public

2000 Sales: $352.9 million
1-Yr. Sales Change: 29.4%
Employees: 5,500
FYE: December 31

Dynacare offers clinical laboratory testing services in about 20 states in the US as well as in Ontario and Alberta in Canada. The company conducts tests on body fluids, tissues, and other subjects, as well as on human cells. Dynacare also handles more difficult testing needs, such as molecular diagnostic services. The firm provides its services directly through its own laboratory facilities as well as through joint-venture partnerships with hospitals. Its clients include clinics, physicians, employers, and managed care companies. Director Albert Latner and his family own about a third of Dynacare, as does investment firm Golder, Thoma, Creesey, Rauner.

KEY COMPETITORS
Canadian Medical Labs
Laboratory Corporation of America
Quest Diagnostics

DYNAMEX INC.

AMEX: DDN

1431 Greenway Dr., Ste. 345
Irving, TX 75038
Phone: 972-756-8180
Fax: 972-756-8199
Web: www.dynamex.com

CEO: Richard K. McClelland
CFO: Jeffrey N. MacDowell
HR: Sam Reeves
Type: Public

2000 Sales: $251.5 million
1-Yr. Sales Change: 5.0%
Employees: 2,800
FYE: July 31

Dynamex is an expert in on-demand delivery of time-sensitive materials. The company uses its on-demand services, which account for nearly 60% of sales, to transport biomedical supplies, confidential materials, and aircraft repair parts. Dynamex provides services in almost 40 US cities and more than 20 Canadian cities; it uses third-party carriers to provide services between cities and countries. The company also provides fleet management services (including dedicated fleets for customer sites) and business services (such as mailroom operations). Dynamex has acquired more than 25 smaller same-day transportation and distribution companies since 1996.

KEY COMPETITORS
CD&L
FedEx
UPS

DYNEGY INC.

NYSE: DYN

1000 Louisiana, Ste. 5800
Houston, TX 77002
Phone: 713-507-6400
Fax: 713-507-3871
Web: www.dynegy.com

CEO: Charles L. Watson
CFO: Robert D. Doty Jr.
HR: Andrea Lang
Type: Public

2000 Sales: $29,445.0 million
1-Yr. Sales Change: 90.8%
Employees: 5,778
FYE: December 31

Power dynamo Dynegy markets and trades electricity, natural gas, coal, and other energy products in North America and Europe. Dynegy controls nearly 15,000 MW of generating capacity through investments in power projects; it sells the energy in wholesale markets and through alliances with utilities in deregulated retail markets. Dynegy Midstream Services gathers and processes natural gas and produces natural gas liquids in the US. Subsidiary Illinois Power distributes electricity and natural gas to 650,000 customers. Dynegy Global Communications builds and operates fiber-optic networks in the US and Europe. ChevronTexaco owns nearly 27% of Dynegy, which has terminated its agreement to acquire troubled rival Enron.

KEY COMPETITORS
Duke Energy
Enron
Reliant Energy

📖 See pages 94–95 for a full profile of this company.

EEX CORPORATION

NYSE: EEX

2500 CityWest Blvd., Ste. 1400	CEO: Thomas M. Hamilton	2000 Sales: $262.4 million
Houston, TX 77042	CFO: Richard S. Langdon	1-Yr. Sales Change: 47.9%
Phone: 713-243-3100	HR: Carol Barnes	Employees: 162
Fax: 713-243-3417	Type: Public	FYE: December 31
Web: www.eex.com		

EEX likes getting its feet wet. The independent natural gas and oil exploration and production company focuses on properties in deepwater Gulf of Mexico, inland and coastal Texas, and onshore and offshore Indonesia. EEX's proved reserves of 533 billion cu. ft. of natural gas equivalent are 72% natural gas; most of the 440 wells in which it holds interests are natural gas and are located on shore. EEX also operates two cogeneration electric power plants in Texas and Washington. The company has sold off nearly all of its shallow-water Gulf of Mexico properties to focus on exploring its high-risk deepwater Gulf and low-risk inland Texas holdings.

KEY COMPETITORS
Meridian Resource
Pioneer Natural Resources
Spinnaker Exploration

EFFICIENT NETWORKS, INC.

4849 Alpha Rd.	CEO: Bruce W. Brown	2000 Sales: $202.2 million
Dallas, TX 75244	CFO: Jill S. Manning	1-Yr. Sales Change: 1,266.2%
Phone: 972-852-1000	HR: Jack Brooks	Employees: 430
Fax: 972-852-1001	Type: Subsidiary	FYE: June 30
Web: www.efficient.com		

Efficient Networks wants to live up to its name. Its digital subscriber line (DSL) equipment provides high-speed Internet connections through copper phone lines for consumers, branch offices of large companies, and small and midsized businesses. Products include modems for single users and high-speed routers for multiple users. DSL equipment accounts for most of sales, but Efficient also sells routers through its FlowPoint subsidiary, which it bought from Cabletron. Newly acquired Network Telesystems develops broadband client services software. Customers include Ameritech, BellSouth, and Covad Communications. Efficient Networks is a subsidiary of electronics and industrial giant Siemens AG.

KEY COMPETITORS
Alcatel
Cisco Systems
Netopia

EGL, INC.

Nasdaq: EAGL

15350 Vickery Dr.	CEO: James R. Crane	2000 Sales: $1,861.2 million
Houston, TX 77032	CFO: Elijio V. Serrano	1-Yr. Sales Change: 189.0%
Phone: 281-618-3100	HR: Gary Abram	Employees: 9,000
Fax: 281-618-3429	Type: Public	FYE: December 31
Web: www.eagleusa.com/IE/Home.asp		

Even without wings this eagle makes shipments fly. Formerly Eagle USA Airfreight, now operating as EGL Eagle Global Logistics, EGL provides international airfreight forwarding and related transport and logistics services. Although its customers' shipments are usually transported by commercial carriers, EGL coordinates all aspects of the shipments (which usually weigh more than 50 pounds). Services include document preparation, packing and handling, insurance, and monitoring. The company also provides same-day local pickup and delivery services, customs brokerage services, and online tracking. EGL has expanded by buying rival Circle International. Founder and CEO James Crane owns about 25% of EGL.

KEY COMPETITORS
BAX Global
CHR
CNF

EL CHICO RESTAURANTS, INC.

12200 Stemmons Fwy., Ste. 100	CEO: Wallace A. Jones	2000 Sales: $148.0 million
Dallas, TX 75234	CFO: Eleana Jones	1-Yr. Sales Change: (1.3%)
Phone: 972-241-5500	HR: Garry Gay	Employees: 3,600
Fax: 972-888-8198	Type: Subsidiary	FYE: December 31
Web: www.elchico.com		

You'll find El Chico, but there's no Groucho, Harpo, or Zeppo in sight — just five good sons who moved their Mama's cafe to Dallas in 1940 and started El Chico Restaurants. Now more than 90 of the Mexican-food restaurants exist in 12 midwestern and southern states. The restaurants feature casual dining and standard Tex-Mex fare such as burritos, enchiladas, fajitas, quesadillas, and tacos. About 30% of the restaurants are franchised, and the rest are company-owned. El Chico Restaurants is now owned by restaurant investment group Consolidated Restaurants Operations, which also owns Good Eats and Spaghetti Warehouse.

KEY COMPETITORS
Avado Brands
Brinker
Mexican Restaurants

EL PASO CORPORATION
NYSE: EPG

1001 Louisiana St.	CEO: William A. Wise	2000 Sales: $21,950.0 million
Houston, TX 77002	CFO: H. Brent Austin	1-Yr. Sales Change: 107.4%
Phone: 713-420-2131	HR: Joel Richards III	Employees: 15,000
Fax: 713-420-6030	Type: Public	FYE: December 31
Web: www.epenergy.com		

Hey, amigo, que pasa? When it comes to natural gas, El Paso. El Paso Corporation, formerly known as El Paso Energy, is engaged in the production, gathering, transporting, processing, and marketing of natural gas. Operator of the largest gas pipeline system in the US, El Paso owns or has interests in 58,000 miles of pipeline in the US and Mexico. The company also has proved reserves of more than 6 trillion cu. ft. of natural gas equivalent. It has grown significantly through the $24 billion acquisition of diversified energy giant Coastal. El Paso is also involved in power generation, energy marketing, and telecommunications bandwidth trading. Internationally, the company operates power plants and pipelines.

KEY COMPETITORS
Duke Energy
Enron
Williams Companies

 See pages 96–97 for a full profile of this company.

EL PASO ELECTRIC COMPANY
AMEX: EE

Kayser Center, 100 N. Stanton	CEO: Gary R. Hedrick	2000 Sales: $701.6 million
El Paso, TX 79901	CFO: Gary R. Hedrick	1-Yr. Sales Change: 23.0%
Phone: 915-543-5711	HR: Leslie Beal	Employees: 1,000
Fax: 915-521-4787	Type: Public	FYE: December 31
Web: www.epelectric.com		

El Paso Electric creates currents in the Rio Grande Valley. The utility generates and distributes electricity to more than 300,000 customers in West Texas and southern New Mexico. More than half of the company's sales come from its namesake city. The firm has 1,500 MW of generating capacity, half of which comes from the Palo Verde nuclear power plant. El Paso Electric also sells wholesale power in the southwestern US and in northern Mexico, and offers energy efficiency services. El Paso Electric will be exempt from Texas deregulation until 2005, and has delayed plans to separate generation operations from transmission and distribution operations due to conflicting restructuring requirements in New Mexico and Texas.

KEY COMPETITORS
Public Service (NM)
Southern Union
TNP Enterprises

EL PASO ENERGY PARTNERS, L.P.

NYSE: EPN

1001 Louisiana St.
Houston, TX 77002
Phone: 713-420-2131
Fax: 713-420-6030
Web: www.epenergy.com/elpasopartners

CEO: Robert G. Phillips
CFO: Keith B. Forman
HR: Joel Richards III
Type: Public

2000 Sales: $112.4 million
1-Yr. Sales Change: 16.5%
Employees: 0
FYE: December 31

El Paso Energy Partners covers the Gulf of Mexico with a network of oil and gas pipelines and platforms. The company has five pipelines that connect offshore producers to onshore distributors and five offshore platforms in the Gulf for pipeline maintenance. It also has a 7.2 billion cu. ft. capacity salt dome storage facility in Mississippi, and a 450-mile coal bed methane gathering system in Alabama. El Paso Energy has no employees because its operations are overseen by general partner and 28%-owner El Paso Corp. After El Paso Corp. bought energy giant Coastal in 2001, El Paso Energy absorbed South Texas transportation and fractionation assets from another El Paso unit and agreed to divest pipelines in the Gulf.

KEY COMPETITORS
Dynegy
EOTT Energy Partners
Williams Companies

ELCOR CORPORATION

NYSE: ELK

Wellington Centre, 14643 Dallas Pkwy., Ste. 1000
Dallas, TX 75240
Phone: 972-851-0500
Fax: 972-851-0543
Web: www.elcor.com

CEO: Harold K. Work
CFO: Harold R. Beattie Jr.
HR: James J. Waibel
Type: Public

2001 Sales: $379.2 million
1-Yr. Sales Change: 8.3%
Employees: 1,163
FYE: June 30

Reindeer are known to prance on rooftops, so Elcor turns to Elk when it's time to repair those roofs. Nearly 90% of Elcor's sales are from its Elk Corporation subsidiary, which makes fiberglass asphalt shingles and nonwoven fiberglass roofing mats. The company's Cybershield unit offers contract electronics manufacturing services such as the application of specialty coatings to control electrical interference. Its Chromium Corporation subsidiary remanufactures liners for diesel engine cylinders for the rail and shipping industries. Elcor also provides consulting and patent services to the oil and gas industry through Ortloff Engineers. Elcor serves US and Latin American markets and is expanding into Europe.

KEY COMPETITORS
CertainTeed
g-i holdings
Owens Corning

ELECTROLUX L.L.C.

5956 Sherry Ln.
Dallas, TX 75225
Phone: 214-378-4000
Fax: 214-378-7561
Web: www.electrolux-usa.com

CEO: Joseph P. Urso
CFO: Warren Bonham
HR: Bob McComas
Type: Private

2000 Sales: $226.0 million
1-Yr. Sales Change: —
Employees: 2,500
FYE: December 31

A pioneer in the vacuum business, Electrolux L.L.C. has been steaming shags and butting baseboards since 1924. The manufacturer sells its Electrolux-brand vacuums and accessories through in-home demonstrations and about 600 Electrolux sales centers in the US and Canada. Salesman Axel Wenner-Gren, instrumental in founding Swedish appliance maker AB Electrolux, started the Electrolux companies in Europe and North and South America in the 1920s. All were later bought by AB Electrolux, except the US company. In 2000 AB Electrolux bought the Electrolux trademark for North America from Electrolux L.L.C. (owned by investment firm Engles Urso Follmer); Electrolux L.L.C. retains the trademark on floor care products until 2007.

KEY COMPETITORS
Kirby
Maytag
Royal Appliance

ELECTRONIC DATA SYSTEMS CORPORATION
NYSE: EDS

5400 Legacy Dr.	CEO: Richard H. Brown	2000 Sales: $19,226.8 million
Plano, TX 75024	CFO: James E. Daley	1-Yr. Sales Change: 3.7%
Phone: 972-604-6000	HR: Troy W. Todd	Employees: 122,000
Fax: 972-605-2643	Type: Public	FYE: December 31
Web: www.eds.com		

Electronic Data Systems Corporation (EDS) hopes that size does indeed matter. The largest independent systems consulting firm in the US (IBM is #1 overall), EDS offers systems integration, network and systems operations, data center management, applications development, field services for companies and government agencies, and management consulting (A.T. Kearney). EDS was spun off in 1996 by General Motors, which still accounts for nearly 20% of EDS's sales. The company, founded by Texas billionaire Ross Perot (now chairman of rival Perot Systems), is expanding its electronic business consulting division, E.Solutions (which was jump-started through the purchase of MCI Systemhouse) and is swapping other assets with WorldCom.

KEY COMPETITORS
Accenture
Computer Sciences
IBM

 See pages 98–99 for a full profile of this company.

EMCARE HOLDINGS INC.

1717 Main St., Ste. 5200	CEO: Leonard M. Riggs Jr.	1999 Sales: $471.0 million
Dallas, TX 75201	CFO: Kent Fannon	1-Yr. Sales Change: —
Phone: 214-712-2000	HR: Barbara Heim	Employees: 5,700
Fax: 214-712-2444	Type: Subsidiary	FYE: August 31
Web: www.emcare.com		

EmCare Holdings provides emergency department management in more than 365 hospitals in almost 40 states. Nearly 4,700 physicians on its employee rolls treat some 5 million patients per year. EmCare manages emergency services for hospitals, including recruiting and hiring medical directors, doctors, and nurses and monitoring their performance. Through subsidiary Reimbursement Technologies, the company also provides such administrative functions as billing, record keeping, and staff scheduling. The firm markets its services directly to hospitals. Parent company Laidlaw, both the largest ambulance company and bus company in North America, is looking to sell EmCare and other health care subsidiaries to focus on its bus business.

KEY COMPETITORS
Med-Emerg International
PhyAmerica
Team Health

ENBRIDGE ENERGY PARTNERS, L.P.
NYSE: EEP

1100 Louisiana	CEO: Dan C. Tutcher	2000 Sales: $305.6 million
Houston, TX 77002	CFO: J. L. Balko	1-Yr. Sales Change: (2.2%)
Phone: 713-650-8900	HR: Don Hoag	Employees: 1
Fax: 713-653-6710	Type: Public	FYE: December 31
Web: www.enbridgepartners.com		

Heading up petroleum transport around the Great Lakes is Enbridge Energy Partners (formerly Lakehead Pipe Line Partners), which owns the 1,880-mile US portion of the world's longest liquid petroleum pipeline. When combined with the Canadian segment (owned and operated by diversified energy company Enbridge, which owns a 15% stake in Enbridge Energy), the pipeline system spans some 3,100 miles across North America. The system delivers an average of 1.4 million barrels a day of crude oil and other liquid hydrocarbons, primarily from western Canada, to refineries in the Great Lakes and Midwest regions of the US.

KEY COMPETITORS
Northern Border Partners
TransCanada PipeLines
Williams Companies

ENCOMPASS SERVICES CORPORATION

NYSE: ESR

3 Greenway Plaza, Ste. 2000	CEO: Joseph M. Ivey Jr.	2000 Sales: $4,099.4 million
Houston, TX 77046	CFO: Darren B. Miller	1-Yr. Sales Change: 164.9%
Phone: 713-860-0100	HR: Steven C. Ronilo	Employees: 34,000
Fax: 713-626-4766	Type: Public	FYE: December 31
Web: www.encompserv.com		

Encompass Services is all about keeping it cool — or hot. Formerly Group Maintenance America Corp. (GroupMAC), Encompass is the largest out-sourced facilities services firm in the country. Its electrical and mechanical service operations (together, almost 75% of revenue) include designing, installing, and maintaining heating and cooling, plumbing, and electrical systems in facilities such as manufacturing plants and office buildings. Encompass also installs and maintains systems for residential customers and home builders and offers janitorial services. Encompass was formed through the merger of GroupMAC and Building One Services in 2000. Investment firm Apollo Management owns 23% of the company.

KEY COMPETITORS
ABM Industries
EMCOR
ServiceMaster

 See pages 100–101 for a full profile of this company.

ENCORE WIRE CORPORATION

Nasdaq: WIRE

1410 Millwood Rd.	CEO: Vincent A. Rego	2000 Sales: $283.7 million
McKinney, TX 75069	CFO: Frank J. Bilban	1-Yr. Sales Change: 23.5%
Phone: 972-562-9473	HR: Brad Rattan	Employees: 474
Fax: 972-542-4744	Type: Public	FYE: December 31
Web: www.encorewire.com		

Encore Wire wants to leave its customers applauding for more. A manufac-turer of copper electrical building wire and cable, Encore produces THHN cable (feeder, circuit, and branch wiring for commercial and industrial build-ings) and NM cable (sheathed cable used to wire homes, apartments, and manufactured housing). It also produces UF cable, an underground feeder cable for outside lighting and other remote uses for residential buildings. The company sells primarily to wholesale electrical distributors across the US and to some retail home-improvement centers. Chairman and CEO Vincent Rego owns about 10% of the company.

KEY COMPETITORS
General Cable
Southwire
Superior TeleCom

ENNIS BUSINESS FORMS, INC.

NYSE: EBF

1510 N. Hampton, Ste. 300	CEO: Keith S. Walters	2001 Sales: $229.2 million
DeSoto, TX 75115	CFO: Robert M. Halowec	1-Yr. Sales Change: 37.7%
Phone: 972-228-7801	HR: Ronald M. Graham	Employees: 2,181
Fax: 972-228-7820	Type: Public	FYE: February 28
Web: www.ennis.com		

Ennis Business Forms is in a sticky business. The company makes a wide range of custom business forms and related products (envelopes, Post-it Notes, labels) in a variety of custom sizes, colors, and quantities (business products account for over 90% of sales). In an industry hurt by the high-tech boom (faster com-puters, better printers, etc.), Ennis has survived by catering to smaller cus-tomers more likely to do business the old-fashioned way — on paper. With 17 manufacturing facilities in 12 states, Ennis sells its products to stationers, print-ers, and the like. Subsidiary Connolly Tool and Machine Company makes tools, dies, and machinery for individual customers on a contract basis.

KEY COMPETITORS
Avery Dennison
Moore Corporation
Wallace Computer

ENRON CORP.

NYSE: ENE

1400 Smith St.	CEO: Kenneth L. Lay	2000 Sales: $100,789.0 million
Houston, TX 77002	CFO: Jeffery McMahon	1-Yr. Sales Change: 151.3%
Phone: 713-853-6161	HR: Cindy K. Olson	Employees: 20,600
Fax: 713-853-3129	Type: Public	FYE: December 31
Web: www.enron.com		

In danger of financial collapse, Enron may lose its spot as the #1 electricity and natural gas trader and marketer in the US. Rival power marketer Dynegy had agreed to purchase Enron after controversy over accounting procedures caused Enron's stock price and credit rating to drop sharply in 2001; however, Dynegy backed out of the deal late in the year as Enron's finances worsened. Besides its energy trading operations, the company buys and sells other commodities, including metals, paper, coal, chemicals, and fiber-optic bandwidth. Enron has a 9,000-MW global power generation portfolio, and it operates a 25,000-mile gas pipeline system in the US. Enron plans to sell its remaining utility and telecommunications interests.

KEY COMPETITORS
AEP
Duke Energy
Reliant Energy

See pages 102–103 for a full profile of this company.

ENSCO INTERNATIONAL INCORPORATED

NYSE: ESV

2700 Fountain Place, 445 Ross Ave.	CEO: Carl F. Thorne	2000 Sales: $533.8 million
Dallas, TX 75202	CFO: C. Christopher Gaut	1-Yr. Sales Change: 46.8%
Phone: 214-922-1500	HR: Brian Gifford	Employees: 3,400
Fax: 214-855-0080	Type: Public	FYE: December 31
Web: www.enscous.com		

ENSCO International is well ensconced as a leading offshore drilling contractor. The company owns 54 offshore rigs, comprising 37 jack-ups, nine barge rigs, seven platform rigs, and one semiubmersible (capable of drilling to 8,000 feet). International operations in Latin America, Europe, and the Asia/Pacific region represent 34% of revenues; most of its US drilling business is in the Gulf of Mexico. ENSCO's marine unit provides support services to oil and gas firms in the Gulf with a fleet of 23 supply vessels and five anchor-handling tugs. To capture its share of the expanding deepwater market, ENSCO has added a jack-up for harsh environments as well as a deepwater semisubmersible.

KEY COMPETITORS
Diamond Offshore
Global Marine
Transocean Sedco Forex

ENTERPRISE PRODUCTS PARTNERS L.P.

NYSE: EPD

2727 North Loop West, Suite 700	CEO: O. S. "Dub" Andras	2000 Sales: $3,049.0 million
Houston, TX 77008	CFO: Michael A. Creel	1-Yr. Sales Change: 126.4%
Phone: 713-880-6500	HR: John Tomerlin	Employees: 782
Fax: 713-880-6668	Type: Public	FYE: December 31
Web: www.epplp.com		

Both enterprising and productive, Enterprise Products Partners is a leading player in the North American natural gas and natural gas liquids (NGL) industry with a range of processing, transportation, and storage services. Operations include natural gas processing, NGL fractionation (separating NGLs into components), isomerization (converting butane to isobutane), and propylene fractionation (extracting high purity propylene). The hub of the company's business is Houston's Mont Belvieu refinery complex. Enterprise, which has grown through such acquisitions as Shell Oil's Tejas Natural Gas Liquids, and Acadian Gas, owns interests in 12 natural gas processing plants and 3,000 miles of pipeline along the Gulf Coast.

KEY COMPETITORS
Duke Energy
Dynegy
El Paso Energy Partners

ENTRUST INC.

Nasdaq: ENTU

4975 Preston Park Blvd., Ste. 400
Plano, TX 75093
Phone: 972-943-7300
Fax: 972-943-7305
Web: www.entrust.com

CEO: F. William Conner
CFO: David L. Thompson
HR: Jeff Bearrows
Type: Public

2000 Sales: $148.4 million
1-Yr. Sales Change: 74.2%
Employees: 1,108
FYE: December 31

Who can you entrust with your network security? Entrust's security software ensures the privacy of electronic communications and transactions across corporate intranets and the Internet. Its Entrust suite of tools automates the management of digital certificates (electronic passports that identify users) and monitors applications such as remote access and e-mail. Entrust (formerly Entrust Technologies) also issues digital certificates through Entrust.net, offers systems integration services, and (through its 2000 purchase of enCommerce) offers software for managing e-business portals. The company sells to customers such as Citibank, FedEx, and NASA. Telecom giant Nortel Networks owns almost 26% of Entrust.

KEY COMPETITORS
Baltimore Technologies
RSA Security
VeriSign

EOG RESOURCES, INC.

NYSE: EOG

1200 Smith St., Ste. 300
Houston, TX 77002
Phone: 713-651-7000
Fax: 713-651-6995
Web: www.eogresources.com

CEO: Mark G. Papa
CFO: —
HR: Patricia L. Edwards
Type: Public

2000 Sales: $1,489.9 million
1-Yr. Sales Change: 85.9%
Employees: 850
FYE: December 31

EOG Resources hogs a resource — natural gas. The independent oil and gas company is engaged in exploring for natural gas and crude oil and developing, producing, and marketing them, EOG has proved reserves of 3.4 trillion cu. ft. of natural gas and 73 million barrels of crude oil, condensate and natural gas liquids. The company operates in major production basins in Canada, offshore Trinidad, and in the US. EOG established its independence by trading its China and India operations to former parent Enron for nearly all of Enron's interest in EOG. The company's strategy is to increase its reserves through exploration, rather than through further large acquisitions.

KEY COMPETITORS
Anadarko Petroleum
BP
Royal Dutch/Shell

EOTT ENERGY PARTNERS, L.P.

NYSE: EOT

2000 W. Sam Houston Pkwy. South
Houston, TX 77042
Phone: 713-993-5200
Fax: 713-993-5821
Web: www.eott.com

CEO: Stanley C. Horton
CFO: Susan C. Ralph
HR: Mary Ellen Coombe
Type: Public

2000 Sales: $11,614.0 million
1-Yr. Sales Change: 34.0%
Employees: 1,200
FYE: December 31

Put that in your pipe or truck it. EOTT Energy Partners is one of the US's largest independent gatherers and marketers of crude oil. The company gathers and markets crude oil from more than 33,000 wells (420,000 barrels per day) in 18 states and Canada, buying mostly from independent producers. With a pipeline network of 8,200 miles and a fleet of some 285 trucks, the company transports the oil. EOTT Energy Partners also has crude oil storage, terminals, and blending operations and processes natural gas liquids. On the West Coast it markets refined petroleum products. Enron subsidiary EOTT Energy Corp. has a 25% stake in EOTT Energy Partners and acts as general partner; Enron also owns a direct 12% stake in the company.

KEY COMPETITORS
BP
ChevronTexaco
Plains All American Pipeline

See pages 104–105 for a full profile of this company.

EQUILON ENTERPRISES LLC

1100 Louisiana Dr.	CEO: Rob J. Routs	2000 Sales: $50,010.0 million
Houston, TX 77210	CFO: Ronald B. Blakely	1-Yr. Sales Change: 70.1%
Phone: 713-277-7000	HR: Bruce Culpepper	Employees: 13,000
Fax: 713-277-7856	Type: Joint venture	FYE: December 31
Web: www.equilonmotivaequiva.com		

For oil refiner and marketer Equilon Enterprises and its sister company, Motiva, East is East and West is West, and never the twain shall meet. Shell Oil (owner of 56% of Equilon) and Texaco (44%) formed Equilon as a joint venture in 1998. Equilon operates four refineries on the West Coast with a total capacity of 480,000 barrels a day, and it owns or has interests in more than 60 crude oil and product terminals. The company markets petroleum products at 9,400 Shell and Texaco outlets throughout the West and Midwest. Motiva does the same in the Northeast and Southeast as a venture of Shell, Texaco, and Saudi Aramco, and Motiva and Equilon together form the #1 US gasoline retailing business.

KEY COMPETITORS
7-Eleven
BP
Exxon Mobil

EQUISTAR CHEMICALS, LP

1221 McKinney St., Ste. 700	CEO: Dan F. Smith	2000 Sales: $7,495.0 million
Houston, TX 77010	CFO: Kelvin R. Collard	1-Yr. Sales Change: 37.9%
Phone: 713-652-7300	HR: John A. Hollinshead	Employees: 3,700
Fax: 713-652-4151	Type: Partnership	FYE: December 31
Web: www.equistarchem.com		

Credit good chemistry, but Equistar Chemical — a partnership of Lyondell (about 40%), Millennium Chemicals, and Occidental Petroleum (about 30% each) — is one of the world's largest producers of ethylene and its derivatives, olefins, and polymers. Equistar's two segments, petrochemicals (75% of sales) and polymers (25%), make products for use in the manufacture of items ranging from food and beverage packaging to carpet facing, paints, wire insulation, and cleaners. Through a joint venture with DuPont, the company also produces ethylene glycol (antifreeze, polyester fibers, resins, and films). Millennium was trying to sell its share of Equistar, but stopped when it received no offers.

KEY COMPETITORS
Dow Chemical
ExxonMobil Chemical
Huntsman

EVERCOM, INC.

8201 Tristar Dr.	CEO: Richard Falcone	2000 Sales: $234.5 million
Irving, TX 75063	CFO: Keith S. Kelson	1-Yr. Sales Change: 155.5%
Phone: 972-988-3737	HR: Julie Hoagland	Employees: 289
Fax: 972-988-3774	Type: Private	FYE: December 31
Web: www.evercom.net		

For prisoners with phone privileges, Evercom is ready with a dial tone. The company provides collect and prepaid phone service to inmates of more than 2,000 city, county, state, and private correctional facilities in 43 states in the US and in Washington, DC. As an exclusive phone provider, Evercom installs and maintains its equipment at no cost to the facility. It also handles billing and collection services for other providers of inmate phone services. The company was formed in 1996 with the acquisitions of AmeriTel Payphones and Talton Telecommunications. Major investors include Julius Talton (13%), a director, and Canadian Imperial Bank of Commerce (41%).

KEY COMPETITORS
AT&T
Science Dynamics
T-NETIX

E. W. BLANCH HOLDINGS, INC.

500 N. Akard, Ste. 4500	CEO: Rod Fox	2000 Sales: $191.3 million
Dallas, TX 75201	CFO: Tim Binek	1-Yr. Sales Change: (18.7%)
Phone: 214-756-7000	HR: Kerry L. Schaughnessy	Employees: 1,154
Fax: 214-756-7001	Type: Subsidiary	FYE: December 31
Web: www.ewb.com		

E. W. Blanch Holdings is the holding company for E. W. Blanch Co., which provides risk management and distribution services through several subsidiaries. As a reinsurance intermediary, the company arranges reinsurance coverage between insurers and reinsurers. The firm also offers technical and analytical consulting services. Most of its foreign business (about a third of sales) is conducted in the UK and includes international risk management and distribution services, design and administration of employee benefits packages, pension fund administration, and a Lloyd's of London insurance and reinsurance brokerage. The company has been acquired by UK-based reinsurance intermediary Benfield Greig.

KEY COMPETITORS
Aon
Marsh & McLennan
Munich Re

EXCEL COMMUNICATIONS, INC.

8750 N. Central Expwy., Ste. 2000	CEO: Christina Gold	2000 Sales: $166.1 million
Dallas, TX 75231	CFO: Jim Timmer	1-Yr. Sales Change: (88.4%)
Phone: 214-863-8000	HR: —	Employees: 3,000
Fax: 214-863-8843	Type: Subsidiary	FYE: December 31
Web: www.excel.com		

Is that ringing telephone a telemarketer, your mom, or both? Excel Communications, a subsidiary of Canada's BCE, uses direct sales with independent representatives and multilevel marketing to sell long-distance through its nationwide facilities-based network. Among the leaders in North America's long-distance market (AT&T is #1), the company is now ringing doorbells in Canada and the UK to compete for long-distance customers there. In addition to long-distance service, Excel representatives offer calling cards, Internet access, paging, and related products and services. The company also resells wireless services through the Sprint PCS network. BCE owns 95% of the company.

KEY COMPETITORS
AT&T
Sprint FON
WorldCom

EXE TECHNOLOGIES, INC.   Nasdaq: EXEE

8787 Stemmons Fwy.	CEO: Raymond R. Hood	2000 Sales: $115.6 million
Dallas, TX 75247	CFO: Michael A. Burstein	1-Yr. Sales Change: 19.4%
Phone: 214-775-6000	HR: Kirk Johansen	Employees: 630
Fax: 214-775-0911	Type: Public	FYE: December 31
Web: www.exe.com		

EXE Technologies can help you ship it, stack it, stock it, and sell it. The company offers inventory and supply chain management software primarily to the e-commerce, logistics, manufacturing, and retail markets. Its EXceed fulfillment software includes a core warehouse management system and components for such applications as quality control, reporting, returns, and transportation management. Its EXceed collaborative software provides modules for tracking orders and sending fulfillment notifications, among other applications. More than 40% of sales come from international clients. Customers include Ford, UPS, and Safeway. General Atlantic Partners owns 29% of the company.

KEY COMPETITORS
Industri-Matematik
Manhattan Associates
SAP

EXPRESS ONE INTERNATIONAL, INC.

1420 Viceroy Dr.	CEO: David Robb	2000 Sales: $115.0 million
Dallas, TX 75235	CFO: Richard J. Pettit	1-Yr. Sales Change: (7.3%)
Phone: 214-902-2500	HR: Dan Menendez	Employees: 500
Fax: 214-350-1399	Type: Private	FYE: December 31
Web: www.express-one.com		

The information economy demands some heavy lifting. Express One International moves cargo with a fleet of 27 Boeing 727s and two Boeing 727-200s out of hubs in Indianapolis, Brussels, and the East Midlands region of the UK. Express One flies nationwide for the US Postal Service and in Europe. The airline has also flown passenger charters for companies but has phased out that line of business. Past customers have included the US Department of Defense (for which it has flown into such conflict areas as Bosnia) and the US Immigration and Naturalization Service. Founded in 1983 as Jet East International, Express One is owned by Orchard Capital Corporation.

KEY COMPETITORS
Airborne
FedEx
UPS

EXXON MOBIL CORPORATION

NYSE: XOM

5959 Las Colinas Blvd.	CEO: Lee R. Raymond	2000 Sales: $228,439.0 million
Irving, TX 75039	CFO: Frank A. Risch	1-Yr. Sales Change: 42.0%
Phone: 972-444-1000	HR: Timothy J. Hearn	Employees: 123,000
Fax: 972-444-1350	Type: Public	FYE: December 31
Web: www.exxon.mobil.com		

It's not necessarily the oil standard, but Exxon Mobil is the world's largest integrated oil company (ahead of Royal Dutch/Shell). Exxon Mobil engages in oil and gas exploration, production, supply, transportation, and marketing around the world. It has proved reserves of just less than 21 billion barrels of oil equivalent. Exxon Mobil's refineries can handle more than 6 million barrels per day, and the company operates more than 40,000 service stations in 118 countries under the Exxon, Esso, and Mobil brands (including more than 16,000 in the US). Exxon Mobil also produces and sells petrochemicals, and it has interests in coal mining, minerals, and electric power generation.

KEY COMPETITORS
BP
ChevronTexaco
Royal Dutch/Shell

 See pages 106–107 for a full profile of this company.

EXXONMOBIL CHEMICAL COMPANY

13501 Katy Fwy.	CEO: —	2000 Sales: $21,503.0 million
Houston, TX 77079	CFO: —	1-Yr. Sales Change: 35.2%
Phone: 281-870-6000	HR: David Clements	Employees: 14,600
Fax: 281-870-6661	Type: Subsidiary	FYE: December 31
Web: www.exxonmobilchemical.com		

If you need to orient your polypropylene or catalyze your zeolites, ExxonMobil Chemical may be able to oblige. The company's facilities around the world turn petroleum into a wide variety of petrochemical products and base stocks, from fuel and lubricant additives to chewing gum and Snickers candy wrappers. Its petrochemical division makes olefins and aromatics, which are used to make ethylene, propylene, and polyethylene. The films division produces oriented polypropylene films for food packaging and other uses. The company's chemical products operation makes fuel additives, synthetic lubricant base stocks, zeolite catalysts, and other products. ExxonMobil Chemical is a subsidiary of Exxon Mobil Corporation.

KEY COMPETITORS
Dow Chemical
CEPSA
OMV

EYE CARE CENTERS OF AMERICA, INC.

11103 West Ave.
San Antonio, TX 78213
Phone: 210-340-3531
Fax: 210-524-6585
Web: www.ecca.com

CEO: David E. McComas
CFO: Alan E. Wiley
HR: Michele M. Benoit
Type: Private

2000 Sales: $338.5 million
1-Yr. Sales Change: 15.2%
Employees: 3,900
FYE: December 31

Eye Care Centers of America hasn't quite mastered the eye-center market, but it is among the top eyewear chains. The company runs about 360 optical stores in about 30 states (primarily in Texas and Florida). Its stores operate under the EyeMasters name and a host of others, including Dr. Bizer's VisionWorld, Hour Eyes, VisionWorks, and Vision World. Its stores, located mostly in malls, sell about 400 styles of eyeglass frames under its own and designer brands. Eye Care Centers' stores offer one-hour service and on-site processing labs; independent optometrists are located inside or adjacent to the stores. Investment firm Thomas H. Lee owns about 90% of Eye Care Centers, which was founded in 1984.

KEY COMPETITORS
Cole National
LensCrafters
National Vision

E-Z MART STORES, INC.

602 Falvey Ave.
Texarkana, TX 75501
Phone: 903-832-6502
Fax: 903-832-7903
Web: www.e-zmart.com

CEO: Sonja Y. Hubbard
CFO: Stacy Y. Floyd
HR: David Roberts
Type: Private

2000 Sales: $641.0 million
1-Yr. Sales Change: 22.1%
Employees: 3,845
FYE: September 30

In 1970, when small-town America closed at 6 p.m., E-Z Mart Stores founder Jim Yates kept his first convenience store in Ashdown, Arkansas, open until 11. The company rode the wave of convenience store growth, adding more than 85 locations in Arkansas and Oklahoma in 1999 alone. It now boasts about 510 outlets across five southern states (Arkansas, Louisiana, Missouri, Oklahoma, and Texas). E-Z Mart prefers to expand through acquisitions, thus eliminating building costs and competitors in one stroke. Yates died in late 1998 when the plane he was piloting crashed, leaving his daughter Sonja Hubbard at the company's helm as CEO.

KEY COMPETITORS
7-Eleven
Ultramar Diamond Shamrock

EZCORP, INC.   Nasdaq: EZPW

1901 Capital Pkwy.
Austin, TX 78746
Phone: 512-314-3400
Fax: 512-314-3404
Web: www.ezcorp.com

CEO: Joseph L. Rotunda
CFO: Daniel N. Tonissen
HR: Matt Campbell
Type: Public

2000 Sales: $197.4 million
1-Yr. Sales Change: (14.9%)
Employees: 2,100
FYE: September 30

No mere pawn in the game, EZCORP's EZ Pawn is the US's second-largest pawnshop chain (after Cash America International), with almost 300 shops; almost two-thirds are in Texas. EZ Pawn sells second-hand jewelry (about half of sales), tools, electronics, and musical instruments — items forfeited by other customers who had used them as collateral and then failed to repay small, short-term, high-interest (12%-300%) loans. About 70% of the company's revenues come from reselling merchandise and about 30% from interest on loans. The company owns a nearly 30% stake in Albemarle & Bond Holdings, a UK pawnshop operator.

KEY COMPETITORS
Cash America
First Cash Financial Services
PawnMart

FAIRCHILD DORNIER CORPORATION

10823 NE Entrance Rd.
San Antonio, TX 78216
Phone: 210-824-9421
Fax: 210-827-9476
Web: www.faidor.com

CEO: Louis F. Harrington
CFO: Rudy Lenz
HR: Paul Granato
Type: Private

2000 Est. Sales: $650.0 mil.
1-Yr. Sales Change: 16.1%
Employees: 3,650
FYE: September 30

The sky's the limit at Fairchild Dornier, a maker of aircraft for commercial, corporate, and government markets. The company formed in 1996 when Fairchild Aerospace bought Dornier Luftfahrt from Daimler-Benz Aerospace (now DaimlerChrysler Aerospace). Fairchild Dornier makes the Dornier 228 and the Dornier 328 for regional airlines. The company's Metro 23 is built and sold to corporate customers, and the Metro 23 is designed for its government customers such as the US Air Force. Fairchield Dornier also produces components and subassemblies for Airbus. The company's majority owners are German insurance company Allianz Capital Partners and US investment group Clayton, Dubilier & Rice.

KEY COMPETITORS
Bombardier
Embraer
Gulfstream Aerospace

FELCOR LODGING TRUST INCORPORATED

NYSE: FCH

545 E. John Carpenter Fwy., Ste. 1300
Irving, TX 75062
Phone: 972-444-4900
Fax: 972-444-4949
Web: www.felcor.com

CEO: Thomas J. Corcoran Jr.
CFO: Richard J. O'Brien
HR: Barbara J. Lacy
Type: Public

2000 Sales: $556.7 million
1-Yr. Sales Change: 10.5%
Employees: 51
FYE: December 31

Its name may not have the cachet of a Waldorf, but FelCor Lodging Trust is still making a name for itself in the hotel business. The real estate investment trust (REIT) owns interests in about 190 hotels with 50,000 rooms in the US and Canada (California, Florida, Georgia, and Texas account for half). FelCor renovates and rebrands its properties, which bear such names as Crowne Plaza, Embassy Suites, Doubletree, Sheraton, and Holiday Inn. Following changes in REIT rules, taxable subsidiaries of FelCor are acquiring most of the hotel leases. The firm is buying MeriStar Hospitality, a purchase that will create the US's largest hotel REIT with nearly 300 hotels in 39 states.

KEY COMPETITORS
Crescent Operating
Host Marriott
Starwood Hotels & Resorts

FFP MARKETING COMPANY, INC.

AMEX: FMM

2801 Glenda Ave.
Fort Worth, TX 76117
Phone: 817-838-4700
Fax: 817-838-4799
Web: www.ffpmarketing.com

CEO: John H. Harvison
CFO: Craig T. Scott
HR: Nicki Banks
Type: Public

2000 Sales: $688.4 million
1-Yr. Sales Change: 36.5%
Employees: 1,622
FYE: December 31

FFP Marketing Company is a roadside respite, operating about 430 convenience stores (under the names Kwik Pantry, Nu-Way, Economy Drive-Ins, and Taylor Food Mart), self-service gas outlets, and truck stops (Drivers). The company's outlets are located primarily in Texas, but also in 10 other central, southern, and southwestern states. In addition, the company runs a fuel-storage terminal that sells wholesale motor fuel and owns a money-order business that operates through its outlets. FFP Marketing was formed when FFP Partners spun off its marketing operations in 1997. CEO John Harvison and his family own about 40% of FFP Marketing; they also own FFP Partners.

KEY COMPETITORS
7-Eleven
ChevronTexaco
TravelCenters of America

FIESTA MART, INC.

5235 Katy Fwy.
Houston, TX 77007
Phone: 713-869-5060
Fax: 713-865-5514
Web: www.fiestamart.com

CEO: Louis Katopodis
CFO: Vicki Baum
HR: Mimi Buderus
Type: Private

2000 Est. Sales: $730.0 mil.
1-Yr. Sales Change: (11.5%)
Employees: 7,500
FYE: May 31

Fiesta Mart celebrates food every day of the year. The company runs about 40 stores in Texas that sell ethnic and mainstream groceries, including items popular with its target customers, Mexican- and Asian-Americans. Its stores are located mainly in Houston, but also in Dallas and Austin; the chain has found inner-city locations to be more successful than suburban sites. At its supermarkets, Fiesta Mart also leases kiosks to vendors who offer such items as jewelry and cellular phones. The company also runs almost 20 Beverage Mart liquor stores. Donald Bonham and O. C. Mendenhall founded Fiesta Mart in 1972. Their families, along with employees, own the company.

KEY COMPETITORS
H-E-B
Minyard Food Stores
Randall's

FIRST CASH FINANCIAL SERVICES, INC.

Nasdaq: FCFS

690 E. Lamar Blvd., Ste. 400
Arlington, TX 76011
Phone: 817-460-3947
Fax: 817-461-7019
Web: www.firstcash.com

CEO: Phillip E. "Rick" Powell
CFO: Rick L. Wessel
HR: Jan Hart
Type: Public

2000 Sales: $105.9 million
1-Yr. Sales Change: 8.3%
Employees: 1,090
FYE: December 31

First Cash Financial Services operates more than 110 pawnshops in six states and Mexico. The company lends money secured by such personal property as jewelry, electronic equipment, tools, firearms (no handguns), sporting goods, and musical equipment; it charges its pawn customers annual interest rates of up to 240%. The company also offers check cashing through some 30 additional stores. More than half of First Cash's sales come from retail sales of merchandise; another 40% comes from its lending activities. First Cash touts its stores as being larger, cleaner, and better lit than traditional mom-and-pop stores.

KEY COMPETITORS
Ace Cash Express
Cash America
EZCORP

FIRST FINANCIAL BANKSHARES, INC.

Nasdaq: FFIN

400 Pine St., 3rd Fl.
Abilene, TX 79601
Phone: 915-627-7155
Fax: 915-627-7393
Web: www.ffin.com

CEO: Kenneth T. Murphy
CFO: Curtis R. Harvey
HR: Pam Mann
Type: Public

2000 Sales: $143.9 million
1-Yr. Sales Change: 7.0%
Employees: 706
FYE: December 31

First Financial Bankshares is a multibank holding company for 10 banks in north central and west Texas: First National Bank of Abilene; Hereford State Bank; First National Bank in Sweetwater; Eastland National Bank; First Financial Bank in Cleburne; Stephenville Bank & Trust; San Angelo National Bank; Weatherford National Bank; Texas National Bank in Southlake, and City National Bank (acquired in 2001). Through about 25 branches, the banks provide individual and commercial clients with trust, asset management, correspondent, leasing, insurance, real estate, and investment services. Commercial and consumer each account for about a third of the banks' loan portfolios; they also write mortgages.

KEY COMPETITORS
Bank of America
BANK ONE
Wells Fargo

FLEMING COMPANIES, INC.

NYSE: FLM

1945 Lakepointe Dr., Box 299013
Lewisville, TX 75057
Phone: 972-906-8000
Fax: 972-906-7810
Web: www.fleming.com

CEO: Mark S. Hansen
CFO: Neal J. Rider
HR: Scott M. Northcutt
Type: Public

2000 Sales: $14,443.8 million
1-Yr. Sales Change: (1.4%)
Employees: 29,567
FYE: December 31

There's nothing secret about Fleming's bond with supermarkets: The company is the #2 US wholesale food distributor (behind SUPERVALU). Fleming Companies supplies branded and private-label grocery and nonfood items to about 7,000 retailers (supermarkets, supercenters, and convenience stores). In addition to serving independent retailers, it also serves mass merchandisers and independents under the company's franchised names (IGA and Piggly Wiggly). Fleming operates more than 90 stores (under the Food 4 Less, Rainbow Foods, and Yes!Less banners) and offers services in advertising, consulting, and information technology. The firm has an agreement to become Kmart's sole foods and consumables supplier.

KEY COMPETITORS
Kroger
SUPERVALU
Wal-Mart

 See pages 108–109 for a full profile of this company.

FLOWSERVE CORPORATION

NYSE: FLS

222 W. Las Colinas Blvd., Ste. 1500
Irving, TX 75039
Phone: 972-443-6500
Fax: 972-443-6800
Web: www.flowserve.com

CEO: C. Scott Greer
CFO: Renee J. Hornbaker
HR: Cheryl D. McNeal
Type: Public

2000 Sales: $1,538.3 million
1-Yr. Sales Change: 44.9%
Employees: 10,000
FYE: December 31

Flowserve is pumped up about fluid-handling equipment. The company makes pumps, valves, and mechanical seals. Flowserve's acquisition of Ingersoll-Dresser Pumps (IDP) from Ingersoll-Rand made it the world's largest provider of pumps for the chemical, petroleum, and power industries. Flowserve's flow solutions division offers mechanical seals and sealing systems, as well as parts and repair services to OEMs that make pumps, compressors, and mixers. The company's flow control division makes valves, actuators, and related equipment that control the flow of liquids and gases. Flowserve sells worldwide through sales representatives, service centers, and distributors.

KEY COMPETITORS
IDEX
ITT Industries
Roper Industries

FOSSIL, INC.

Nasdaq: FOSL

2280 N. Greenville Ave.
Richardson, TX 75082
Phone: 972-234-2525
Fax: 972-234-4669
Web: www.fossil.com

CEO: Kosta N. Kartsotis
CFO: Mike Kovar
HR: Lisa Lapiska
Type: Public

2000 Sales: $504.3 million
1-Yr. Sales Change: 20.4%
Employees: 2,044
FYE: December 31

America's 1950s may be fossils in time, but those times have turned Fossil into a leading maker of fashion watches. The company targets teens to thirty-somethings with Americana-themed Fossil-brand timepieces, which usually have a 1950s retro look. Fossil also has a less-expensive brand (Relic) and a line of sports watches (Fossil Blue). It markets accessory products such as leather goods (handbags, wallets, and belts) and sunglasses, as well as apparel. Fossil also makes private-label watches for companies such as Giorgio Armani and Diesel. The firm sells through department stores, specialty shops, and about 70 company-owned stores in 80 countries. Brothers Tom and Kosta Kartsotis own 49% of Fossil.

KEY COMPETITORS
Guess?
Seiko
Swatch

 See pages 110–111 for a full profile of this company.

FOXWORTH-GALBRAITH LUMBER COMPANY

17111 Waterview Pkwy.	CEO: —	2000 Sales: $540.0 million
Dallas, TX 75252	CFO: Jack Foxworth	1-Yr. Sales Change: 20.0%
Phone: 972-437-6100	HR: R. Lynn Guillory	Employees: 2,500
Fax: 972-454-4251	Type: Private	FYE: December 31
Web: www.foxgal.com		

It might be a mouthful to say, but Foxworth-Galbraith Lumber Company sells more than a handful of building materials to customers in the Southwest. Through more than 70 locations in Arizona, Colorado, New Mexico, and Texas, it sells lumber, paint, plumbing equipment, hardware, and tools. Foxworth-Galbraith's main customers are residential and commercial builders; other clients include do-it-yourselfers, retailers, specialty contractors, and federal and state agencies. The company also owns Brookhart's Building Centers in Colorado. The company is still owned and operated by the families of W. L. Foxworth and H. W. Galbraith, who founded Foxworth-Galbraith in Dalhart, Texas, in 1901.

KEY COMPETITORS
Ace Hardware
Home Depot
Lowe's

THE FREEMAN COMPANIES

1421 W. Mockingbird	CEO: Donald S. Freeman Jr.	2001 Sales: $801.0 million
Dallas, TX 75247	CFO: Joseph V. Popolo Jr.	1-Yr. Sales Change: 6.8%
Phone: 214-670-9000	HR: Dan Camp	Employees: 34,000
Fax: 214-670-9100	Type: Private	FYE: June 30
Web: www.freemanco.com		

There's no business like the trade show business. Having staged thousands of conventions, corporate meetings, expositions, and trade shows annually, The Freeman Companies knows that maxim well. Freeman's operations include AVW Audio Visual (presentation technologies), Freeman Decorating (event design and production services), Freeman Exhibit (exhibit production), and Sullivan Transfer (material handling services). The company's projects have ranged from single trade show exhibits to the Republican National Convention. Founded in 1927 by D.S. "Buck" Freeman, the company is owned by the Freeman family (including chairman and CEO Donald Freeman) and company employees.

KEY COMPETITORS
Key3Media
Viad
VNU

FRESH AMERICA CORP.

OTC: FRES

6600 LBJ Fwy., Ste. 180	CEO: Darren L. Miles	2000 Sales: $554.6 million
Dallas, TX 75240	CFO: Cheryl A. Taylor	1-Yr. Sales Change: (17.2%)
Phone: 972-774-0575	HR: Rose Rush	Employees: 590
Fax: 972-774-0515	Type: Public	FYE: December 31
Web: www.freshamerica.com		

Fresh America is hoping to revive some stale business. The firm distributes about 500 perishable products, including produce and packaged and specialty foods, to over 4,000 customers, such as retailers, restaurants, and distributors, in 42 states and Canada. Fresh America also offers services such as produce ripening and vegetable processing. Its Freshfreight Logisitics division hauls the produce to markets. To further freshen up its bottom line the company has been reducing overhead and divesting underperforming subsidiaries. Larry Martin, executive vice president of Martin Brothers, a Fresh America division, owns nearly 38%.

KEY COMPETITORS
Nash Finch
SUPERVALU
SYSCO

FRESHPOINT, INC.

15305 Dallas Parkway, Ste. 1010
Addison, TX 75001
Phone: 972-392-8100
Fax: 972-392-8130
Web: www.freshpoint.com

CEO: Brian Sturgeon
CFO: Webb Crunk
HR: Vicki Rodgers
Type: Subsidiary

1999 Sales: $732.0 million
1-Yr. Sales Change: —
Employees: 2,500
FYE: June 30

Eating veggies isn't just good for your body, it's good for FreshPoint, too. The company, a subsidiary of food service giant SYSCO, is one of the top fruit and vegetable distributors in the nation. It owns more than 25 distribution facilities in North America. Operations involve food service and retail distribution, wholesale supply, procurement, and transportation to such customers as restaurants, hotels, cruise ships, and grocery stores. FreshPoint gained independence when UK-based Albert Fisher sold its US distribution business to management in 1996. After a planned 1999 merger with rival Fresh America failed, SYSCO bought FreshPoint in 2000.

KEY COMPETITORS
Fresh America
Nash Finch
SUPERVALU

FRIONA INDUSTRIES, L.P.

500 S. Taylor, Ste. 601
Amarillo, TX 79101
Phone: 806-374-1811
Fax: 806-374-1324
Web: www.frionaind.com

CEO: James E. Herring
CFO: Dal C. Reid
HR: Brad Stout
Type: Private

2000 Sales: $300.0 million
1-Yr. Sales Change: 0.0%
Employees: 450
FYE: December 31

Friona Industries puts the beef in the Big Mac. Founded in 1962, Friona owns five feed yards in northwestern Texas with a feeding capacity of 220,000 head of cattle. The company partners with beef packers, livestock traders, and McDonald's in BAP Management, a partnership formed to buy, raise, process and market better beef. Friona's feed division serves horses, livestock, poultry, and pets under the Hi-Pro Feed and Goldbold Feed brands. Its Hi-Pro Animal Health unit distributes pharmaceuticals. Friona Agricultural Credit helps ranchers finance and market feeding programs. Private investment firm Edwin L. Cox Co. controls Friona Industries.

KEY COMPETITORS
AZTX Cattle
Bartlett and Company
Cactus Feeders

FRITO-LAY, INC.

7701 Legacy Dr.
Plano, TX 75024
Phone: 972-334-7000
Fax: 972-334-2019
Web: www.fritolay.com

CEO: Abelardo E. "Al" Bru
CFO: Dave Rader
HR: Ron Parker
Type: Subsidiary

2000 Sales: $12,881.0 million
1-Yr. Sales Change: 10.9%
Employees: 100,000
FYE: December 31

Salty, cheesy, and crunchy best describe the products of Frito-Lay, the largest snack-food maker in the world. The company makes some of the top-selling snack-food brands in the country, including Cheetos, Doritos, Fritos, Lay's, Ruffles, Santitas, SunChips, Rold Gold, and Tostitos. It also makes Grandma's cookies, Funyuns onion-flavored rings, Cracker Jack candy-coated popcorn, and Smartfood popcorn. Frito-Lay's WOW! line of chips are made with the fat substitute olestra. The company holds about 40% of the world's salty-snack market and about 60% of the US market. Its products are sold in about 120 countries. Frito-Lay products ring up about two-thirds of parent PepsiCo's sales and profits.

KEY COMPETITORS
Keebler
Kraft Foods
Procter & Gamble

FRONTIER OIL CORPORATION

NYSE: FTO

10000 Memorial Dr., Ste. 600
Houston, TX 77024
Phone: 713-688-9600
Fax: 713-688-0616
Web: www.frontieroil.com

CEO: James R. Gibbs
CFO: Julie H. Edwards
HR: Penny Newmark
Type: Public

2000 Sales: $2,045.2 million
1-Yr. Sales Change: 306.1%
Employees: 700
FYE: December 31

Frontier Oil's territory covers the old frontier of the Rocky Mountains and the Great Plains. The company refines crude oil and markets petroleum products wholesale, primarily along the eastern slope of the Rockies and in nearby plains states. Frontier's Cheyenne, Wyoming, refinery can handle 41,000 barrels of heavy crude oil per day; products include various grades of gasoline, diesel fuel, and asphalt, which Frontier sells to independent retailers, wholesalers, and major oil companies. The company processes 110,000 barrels of oil per day at its refinery in El Dorado, Kansas. Besides marketing unbranded products, Frontier sells gasoline and diesel under the CITGO brand.

KEY COMPETITORS
Conoco
Sinclair Oil
Ultramar Diamond Shamrock

FROZEN FOOD EXPRESS INDUSTRIES, INC.

Nasdaq: FFEX

1145 Empire Central Place
Dallas, TX 75247
Phone: 214-630-8090
Fax: 214-819-5625
Web: www.ffeinc.com

CEO: Stoney M. "Mit" Stubbs Jr.
CFO: F. Dixon McElwee Jr.
HR: Donna Mecom
Type: Public

2000 Sales: $392.4 million
1-Yr. Sales Change: 5.5%
Employees: 2,647
FYE: December 31

Keeping others' assets frozen means big business for Frozen Food Express Industries (FFEX), the largest temperature-controlled trucking company in North America. FFEX delivers less-than-truckload (between 50 and 20,000 pounds) and truckload (20,000 to 40,000 pounds) shipments to destinations in the US, Canada, and Mexico. The firm specializes in transporting temperature-sensitive products (more than 80% of revenues), including pharmaceuticals, cosmetics, aerospace equipment, and perishable food. FFEX owns and operates a fleet of about 1,200 tractors and contracts with more than 500 independent drivers; its distribution network is made up of 15 US terminals. FFEX uses satellite technology to track its shipments.

KEY COMPETITORS
KLLM Transport Services
Marten Transport
Simon Transportation Services

FULBRIGHT & JAWORSKI L.L.P.

1301 McKinney St., Ste. 5100
Houston, TX 77010
Phone: 713-651-5151
Fax: 713-651-5246
Web: www.fulbright.com

CEO: A. T. Blackshear Jr.
CFO: Kevin Miller
HR: Jane Williams
Type: Partnership

2000 Sales: $343.0 million
1-Yr. Sales Change: 7.7%
Employees: 1,800
FYE: December 31

One of the foremost law firms in Texas, Fulbright & Jaworski takes its moniker from late partner and Watergate special prosecutor Leon Jaworski, but its history can be traced back decades before the infamous summer of 1974. Founded in 1919 by Houston attorneys R. Clarence Fulbright and John Crooker, the firm has grown to include three other Texas offices, as well as offices in Hong Kong, London, Los Angeles, Minneapolis, New York, and Washington, DC. The firm's 750 attorneys specialize in practice areas such as litigation, public finance, environmental law, family law, and labor and employment.

KEY COMPETITORS
Baker Botts
Jenkens & Gilchrist
Vinson & Elkins

FURR'S RESTAURANT GROUP, INC.

AMEX: FRG

3001 E. President George Bush Hwy.
Richardson, TX 75082
Phone: 972-808-2923
Fax: 972-808-5713
Web: www.furrs.net

CEO: Craig S. Miller
CFO: Paul Hargett
HR: Bruce S. Dudley
Type: Public

2000 Sales: $196.0 million
1-Yr. Sales Change: 4.2%
Employees: 5,400
FYE: December 31

Furr's Restaurant Group (formerly Furr's/Bishop's) pleases the palates of those who want inexpensive, good ol' American food, and plenty of it. The company operates about 95 cafeterias under the Furr's and Bishop's names in 12 midwestern, southwestern, and western states. Most customers at the cafeterias, which offer all-you-can-eat service for about $6, are age 45 or older. Dynamic Foods, the company's food preparation, processing, and distribution center in Lubbock, Texas, provides about 85% of the food served at the restaurants and sells food to third parties. Furr's also owns two pay-at-the-door buffets. Rock Finance Group owns 47% of the company; Grace Brothers, 41%.

KEY COMPETITORS
Bob Evans
Luby's
Shoney's

F.Y.I. INCORPORATED

Nasdaq: FYII

3232 McKinney Ave., Ste. 900
Dallas, TX 75204
Phone: 214-953-7555
Fax: 214-953-7556
Web: www.fyii.com

CEO: Ed H. Bowman Jr.
CFO: Barry L. Edwards
HR: Gary R. Patton
Type: Public

2000 Sales: $457.6 million
1-Yr. Sales Change: 29.0%
Employees: 11,000
FYE: December 31

For your information, F.Y.I. Incorporated is one of the leading information management outsourcing companies in the US. The company provides document and information services, including database management, record storage and maintenance, and direct mail and fulfillment to a variety of industries in 45 states. F.Y.I. also has specialized services for legal and health care clients, such as deposition reporting, discovery assistance, and temporary staffing for hospital information departments. In addition to international facilities (the Caribbean, Mexico, and Puerto Rico), F.Y.I. operates almost 140 offices.

KEY COMPETITORS
Iron Mountain
Lason
ProQuest

GADZOOKS, INC.

Nasdaq: GADZ

4121 International Pkwy.
Carrollton, TX 75007
Phone: 972-307-5555
Fax: 972-662-4290
Web: www.gadzooks.com

CEO: Gerald R. Szczepanski
CFO: James A. Motley
HR: Stephen R. Puterbaugh
Type: Public

2001 Sales: $288.4 million
1-Yr. Sales Change: 19.4%
Employees: 4,458
FYE: January 31

Besides being a fine interjection, Gadzooks is a mall-based retailer of casual apparel and accessories for teenagers. Mall-hoppers can visit about 400 Gadzooks stores in midsized and metropolitan markets in 37 states, primarily east of the Rocky Mountains. The stores feature brand names (Billabong, Mudd, Dr. Marten) and private labels on dresses, pants, shoes, watches, sunglasses, costume jewelry, and T-shirts (one of which attracted a lawsuit by showing TV's Mister Rogers holding a gun). Gadzooks also offers its easily bored customers an entertaining environment with such diversions as music videos, neon lighting, and old, sawed-in-half Volkswagen Beetles that serve as clothes racks.

KEY COMPETITORS
Buckle
The Gap
Pacific Sunwear

GAINSCO, INC.

500 Commerce St.	CEO: Glenn W. Anderson	2000 Sales: $164.7 million
Fort Worth, TX 76102	CFO: Daniel J. Coots	1-Yr. Sales Change: 31.2%
Phone: 817-336-2500	HR: Kim Prichard	Employees: 339
Fax: 817-335-1230	Type: Public	FYE: December 31
Web: www.gainsco.com		

Well, you wouldn't call an insurance company LOSSCO, would you? GAINSCO's subsidiaries sell nonstandard auto, commercial, general liability, and property/casualty insurance. The company's commercial auto insurance covers local freight haulers and trucking firms; it also covers the garages in which their fleets are stored. GAINSCO sells general liability and property insurance to small businesses. The firm markets its policies through some 1,200 agency offices. The company has sold its policy management software unit and is exiting the commercial trucking business.

KEY COMPETITORS
The Hartford
Kemper Insurance
St. Paul Companies

THE GAMBRINUS COMPANY

14800 San Pedro Ave.	CEO: Carlos Alvarez	2000 Sales: $425.0 million
San Antonio, TX 78232	CFO: James Bolz	1-Yr. Sales Change: 0.0%
Phone: 210-490-9128	HR: Brad Kohanke	Employees: 300
Fax: 210-490-9984	Type: Private	FYE: December 31

Named after a medieval Belgian duke credited with inventing the toast as a social custom, The Gambrinus Company brews, imports, and distributes beer. Among the brews it distributes are Corona Extra (the #1 imported beer in the US; Heineken is #2), Modelo Especial, Negra-Modelo, Pacifico, and Moosehead Beer. Imports pour in from Mexico and Canada and are sold primarily in the eastern US, Texas, Bermuda, and the Caribbean. Gambrinus also owns the Shiner, Texas, Spoetzl Brewery (Shiner Bock, the #1 selling bock in the US); Oregon's oldest microbrewery, BridgePort Brewing Company; and Pete's Brewing Company (Pete's Wicked Ale). Owner Carlos Alvarez founded Gambrinus in 1986 and serves as its president and CEO.

KEY COMPETITORS
Anheuser-Busch
Boston Beer
Heineken

GAMESTOP, INC.

2250 William D. Tate Ave.	CEO: R. Richard "Dick" Fontaine	2001 Sales: $756.7 million
Grapevine, TX 76051	CFO: David W. Carlson	1-Yr. Sales Change: 36.8%
Phone: 817-424-2000	HR: David Shuart	Employees: 11,000
Fax: 817-424-2002	Type: Subsidiary	FYE: January 31
Web: www.gamestop.com		

In the hands of Leonard Riggio, Babbage's has risen from laggard to leader among video and computer game retailers. Now a subsidiary of bookseller Barnes & Noble (where Riggio is CEO and 25% owner), Babbage's sells video games, software, and accessories through more than 975 Babbage's, Gamestop, Planet X, Software Etc., SuperSoftware, and FuncoLand stores in the US and Puerto Rico. Its June 2000 purchase of rival Funco added 400 FuncoLand stores and boosted Babbage's to the top spot in its retail niche. Barnes & Noble bought Babbage's predecessor in 1986 and spun it off in 1988. Babbage's entered bankruptcy in 1996 and was bought by a group led by Riggio. The group sold Babbage's to Barnes & Noble in 1999.

KEY COMPETITORS
Best Buy
Electronics Boutique
Toys "R" Us

GARDEN RIDGE CORPORATION

19411 Atrium Place, Ste. 170	CEO: Paul Davies	2001 Sales: $365.0 million
Houston, TX 77084	CFO: Jane L. Arbuthnot	1-Yr. Sales Change: 0.1%
Phone: 281-579-7901	HR: Kevin Rutherford	Employees: 1,800
Fax: 281-578-0999	Type: Private	FYE: January 31
Web: www.gardenridge.com		

Megastore retailer Garden Ridge offers decorating accessories for more than just the garden. The company operates 37 stores, each covering almost three acres and located off major highways, in 12 states (Texas has 16 stores). Its stores sell silk and dried flowers, baskets, candles, crafts, home accents, housewares, party supplies, pictures and frames, pottery, and seasonal items. In addition, the stores sell plants and furniture, and some have snack bars. Garden Ridge, which started with a single store outside of San Antonio in 1979, was bought by a group of investors (including chairman Armand Shapiro) led by Three Cities Research in early 2000.

KEY COMPETITORS
Hobby Lobby
Michaels Stores
Wal-Mart

GENESIS ENERGY, L.P.

AMEX: GEL

500 Dallas, Ste. 2500	CEO: Mark J. Gorman	2000 Sales: $4,324.6 million
Houston, TX 77002	CFO: Ross A. Benavides	1-Yr. Sales Change: 100.1%
Phone: 713-860-2500	HR: Joe Mueller	Employees: 260
Fax: 713-860-2640	Type: Public	FYE: December 31
Web: www.genesiscrudeoil.com		

In the beginning was the oil. And on the third day (or thereabouts) there was oil gathering and marketing. Genesis Energy purchases and aggregates crude oil at the wellhead and makes bulk buys at pipeline and terminal facilities for resale. The company transports crude oil — about 84,000 barrels a day — through three common carrier pipeline systems: a 750-mile system in Texas, a 117-mile system between Florida and Alabama, and a 281-mile system between Mississippi and Louisiana. Genesis Energy owns some 1.4 million barrels of storage capacity in association with these pipelines. It also has a fleet of 73 tractor-trailers that carry oil from the wellhead to the pipelines, terminals, or refineries.

KEY COMPETITORS
EOTT Energy Partners
Plains All American Pipeline
TEPPCO Partners

GLAZER'S WHOLESALE DRUG COMPANY INC.

14860 Landmark Blvd.	CEO: Bennett Glazer	2000 Sales: $1,480.0 million
Dallas, TX 75240	CFO: Cary Rossel	1-Yr. Sales Change: 33.3%
Phone: 972-702-0900	HR: Rusty Harmount	Employees: 3,200
Fax: 972-702-8508	Type: Private	FYE: December 31
Web: www.glazers.com		

Glazer's Wholesale Drug, named during Prohibition when only drugstores and drug wholesalers could deal in liquor, is a wholesale distributor of alcoholic beverages. It is the largest distributor of malts, spirits, and wines in Texas and one of the largest US wine and spirits distributors. It also operates in Arizona (Alliance Beverage), Arkansas, Indiana (Olinger Distributing), Iowa, Louisiana, Missouri, and Ohio. The company distributes Robert Mondavi wines and Brown-Forman and Bacardi spirits, among others. Glazer's has been acquiring wholesalers and distributors in the Midwest, including Mid-Continent Distributor (Missouri). CEO Bennett Glazer and family own Glazer's.

KEY COMPETITORS
Gallo
National Wine & Spirits
Southern Wine & Spirits

GLOBAL MARINE INC.

NYSE: GLM

777 N. Eldridge Pkwy.
Houston, TX 77079
Phone: 281-596-5100
Fax: 281-596-5163
Web: www.glm.com

CEO: Robert E. Rose
CFO: W. Matt Ralls
HR: Dave Boutelle
Type: Public

2000 Sales: $1,039.8 million
1-Yr. Sales Change: 31.5%
Employees: 2,700
FYE: December 31

Global Marine mixes oil and water — the company provides offshore contract drilling services through a fleet of 33 mobile rigs. The company uses mostly jack-up rigs (23) but also has six semisubmersibles and three ultra-deepwater drillships that can drill to depths of more than 7,800 ft. Global Marine's fleet is deployed mainly in the Gulf of Mexico, the North Sea, and offshore West Africa. Global Marine also is one of the industry's largest providers of offshore turnkey drilling services. In addition, the company has its own oil and gas exploration activities in the Gulf of Mexico.

KEY COMPETITORS
Diamond Offshore
Noble Drilling
Transocean Sedco Forex

GOLFSMITH INTERNATIONAL, L.P.

11000 N. IH-35
Austin, TX 78753
Phone: 512-837-8810
Fax: 512-837-1245
Web: www.golfsmith.com

CEO: Carl F. Paul
CFO: Mark Osborn
HR: Jan Petty
Type: Private

2000 Sales: $275.0 million
1-Yr. Sales Change: (3.5%)
Employees: 1,800
FYE: December 31

You might not be so quick to wrap that 5-iron around a tree if you'd made it yourself. Golfsmith International began in 1967 as a mail-order seller of custom-made golf clubs, and it still teaches golfers how to craft their own irons, woods, and putters. The company sells its products through its catalog, Web site, and about 30 golf superstores in the US and Canada. The company's stores — averaging about 25,000 sq. ft. — sell private-label and brand-name golf equipment, accessories, and related paraphernalia and offer such services as swing analysis. Golfsmith also operates the Harvey Penick Golf Academy. Founder Carl Paul and his brother, Frank, own the company.

KEY COMPETITORS
Dick's Sporting Goods
Edwin Watts Golf Shops
Sports Authority

GOODMAN MANUFACTURING COMPANY, L.P.

1501 Seamist Dr.
Houston, TX 77008
Phone: 713-861-2500
Fax: 713-861-2176
Web: www.goodmanmfg.com

CEO: John B. Goodman
CFO: Tanya Klepser
HR: Cliff Reilly
Type: Private

2000 Est. Sales: $2,160.0 mil.
1-Yr. Sales Change: 5.4%
Employees: 7,750
FYE: December 31

Goodman knows how to cool off a hot situation. Goodman Manufacturing Company, through its Amana Heating and Air Conditioning, Goodman Manufacturing, and Quietflex divisions, makes air-conditioning, ventilation, and heating equipment for residential and commercial use. Goodman, which sells its products through independent installers and distributors worldwide, is among the top US makers of air conditioners. Its brands include Amana, Caloric, Goodman, GmC, Modern Maid, and Janitrol. The company is selling its Amana Appliance division (washers, dryers, microwaves, and refrigerators) to Maytag for $325 million. Goodman is owned by the family of Harold Goodman, who founded the company in 1977.

KEY COMPETITORS
Carrier
Fedders
GE Appliances

GRANT PRIDECO, INC.

NYSE: GRP

1450 Lake Robbins Dr., Ste. 600
The Woodlands, TX 77380
Phone: 281-297-8500
Fax: 281-297-8699
Web: www.grantprideco.com

CEO: Curtis W. Huff
CFO: Louis A. Raspino
HR: Warren S. Avery
Type: Public

2000 Sales: $498.5 million
1-Yr. Sales Change: 74.1%
Employees: 3,825
FYE: December 31

If Jed Clampett's method for getting "black gold" out of the ground seems a bit haphazard, oilmen may seek help from Grant Prideco. The company, spun off by drilling equipment maker Weatherford International, makes engineered tubular products for oil field exploration and development. They include drill pipe and drill stem products, couplings, large-diameter casings, tubing and connections, and risers for subsea wells. Grant Prideco offers sales and technical support through offices in 20 countries and manufactures its products in North and South America, Asia, and Europe. The company also provides repair and field services worldwide.

KEY COMPETITORS
Lone Star Technologies
LTV
RPC

GREY WOLF, INC.

AMEX: GW

10370 Richmond Ave., Ste. 600
Houston, TX 77042
Phone: 713-435-6100
Fax: 713-435-6170

CEO: Thomas P. Richards
CFO: David W. Wehlmann
HR: Gary D. Lee
Type: Public

2000 Sales: $269.3 million
1-Yr. Sales Change: 82.9%
Employees: 2,300
FYE: December 31

Grey Wolf makes its living hunting down onshore oil and gas drilling contracts. The company owns more than 120 drilling rigs and has operations in five main markets in the US: South Texas; the Gulf Coast; the Ark-La-Tex region; Mississippi and Alabama; and the Rockies. Grey Wolf has suspended its international operations (although it still owns five rigs in Venezuela). Focusing on natural gas production, the company provides rigs, related equipment, and field personnel to customers on either a turnkey or day-work basis. Bouncing back from the market downturn in the late 1990s, Grey Wolf is riding higher oil prices and increased drilling activities by major oil and gas companies to greater revenues.

KEY COMPETITORS
Helmerich & Payne
Nabors Industries
Patterson-UTI Energy

GREYHOUND LINES, INC.

15110 N. Dallas Pkwy., Ste. 600
Dallas, TX 75248
Phone: 972-789-7000
Fax: 972-387-1874
Web: www.greyhound.com

CEO: Craig R. Lentzsch
CFO: Jeffrey W. Sanders
HR: John LaGreca
Type: Subsidiary

2000 Sales: $1,498.2 million
1-Yr. Sales Change: 62.2%
Employees: 24,700
FYE: August 31

The old grey dog is the only one on the track. A subsidiary of #1 North American bus company Laidlaw, Greyhound Lines is the largest bus firm in the US and the only one with a regular intercity schedule. Greyhound carries more than 24 million passengers yearly to more than 3,700 destinations in the US and Canada with a fleet of almost 2,900 buses. Greyhound also provides additional service into Mexico. Passengers are typically low- to middle-income consumers who pay cash for tickets on the day of departure. In addition to its intercity routes, Greyhound offers charter buses, food service at many of its terminals, and express package delivery. Laidlaw announced it will no longer finance Greyhound's long-term debt.

KEY COMPETITORS
AMR
Amtrak
Southwest Airlines

GROCERS SUPPLY CO. INC.

3131 E. Holcombe Blvd.
Houston, TX 77021
Phone: 713-747-5000
Fax: 713-746-5611
Web: www.grocerssupply.com

CEO: Max Levit
CFO: Michael Castleberry
HR: Curtis Hopkins
Type: Private

2000 Est. Sales: $1,400.0 mil.
1-Yr. Sales Change: 0.0%
Employees: 1,200
FYE: May 31

Need crackers in Caracas or vanilla in Manila? Grocers Supply Co. distributes groceries near and far. The company (not to be confused with fellow Texas distributor GSC Enterprises) distributes food, health and beauty items, household products, and school and office supplies to convenience stores and supermarkets. Grocers Supply mainly serves customers throughout Texas and Louisiana. Its Grocers Supply International (GSI) division ships supplies to oil company operations, other commercial customers, and US embassies around the world. GSI boasts that it will buy anything to ship anywhere for anyone, including macaroons in Rangoon, or even oleo in Tokyo. Grocers Supply is owned by the Levit family.

KEY COMPETITORS
C.D. Hartnett
GSC Enterprises
McLane

GROUP 1 AUTOMOTIVE, INC.   NYSE: GPI

950 Echo Ln., Ste. 100
Houston, TX 77024
Phone: 713-647-5700
Fax: 713-647-5800
Web: www.group1auto.com/default.htm

CEO: B. B. "Ben" Hollingsworth Jr.
CFO: Scott L. Thompson
HR: J. Brooks O'Hara
Type: Public

2000 Sales: $3,586.1 million
1-Yr. Sales Change: 43.0%
Employees: 5,830
FYE: December 31

Group 1 Automotive is only one in a group of companies (AutoNation and United Auto Group are the largest) striving to consolidate the US car dealership business. Group 1 owns about 60 dealerships (100 franchises) and about 20 collision service centers in Colorado, Florida, Georgia, Louisiana, Massachusetts, New Mexico, Oklahoma, and Texas; it also sells cars online. Together these dealerships offer new and used cars and light trucks under about 30 different brands. In addition, Group 1 offers financing, provides maintenance and repair services, and sells replacement parts. Robert Howard II, who sold his dealerships to Group 1 in 1997, owns almost 15% of the company.

KEY COMPETITORS
AutoNation
Sonic Automotive
United Auto Group

GSC ENTERPRISES, INC.

130 Hillcrest Dr.
Sulphur Springs, TX 75482
Phone: 903-885-0829
Fax: 903-885-6928
Web: www.grocerysupply.com

CEO: Michael K. McKenzie
CFO: Kerry Law
HR: Theresa Patterson
Type: Private

2000 Sales: $1,111.0 million
1-Yr. Sales Change: 5.8%
Employees: 2,000
FYE: December 31

GSC Enterprises brings the groceries to the grocery store. The wholesale distributor (whose name stands for "Grocery Supply Company," not to be confused with Grocers Supply Co.) supplies independently owned convenience stores, grocers, discounters, and other retailers and wholesalers. It serves a total of some 15,000 stores in about 15 states in the Southwest, Southeast, and Midwest. GSC stocks and distributes tobacco, candy, grocery items, prepared foods (Chicago Style Pizza, Chester Fried Chicken, Deli-Fast Foods), and other items. The firm also owns Fidelity Express, which sells money orders in stores. GSC is owned by the McKenzie family, descendants of two of the men who founded the company in 1947.

KEY COMPETITORS
Eby-Brown
Fleming Companies
SUPERVALU

GULF STATES TOYOTA, INC.

7701 Wilshire Place Dr.	CEO: Toby Hynes	2000 Est. Sales: $3,158.0 mil.
Houston, TX 77040	CFO: Frank Gruen	1-Yr. Sales Change: 17.0%
Phone: 713-580-3300	HR: Dominic Gallo	Employees: 1,650
Fax: 713-744-3332	Type: Private	FYE: December 31

Even good ol' boys buy foreign cars from Gulf States Toyota. One of only two US Toyota distributors not owned by Toyota Motor Sales (the other is JM Family Enterprises' Southeast Toyota Distributors), the company distributes Toyota and Lexus cars, trucks, and sport utility vehicles in Arkansas, Louisiana, Mississippi, Oklahoma, and Texas. Founded in 1969 by Thomas Friedkin and still owned by The Friedkin Companies, Gulf States distributes new Toyotas, parts, and accessories to around 140 dealers in its region. Because Toyota has had success converting Internet leads into actual sales, Gulf States offers customizable Web site packages to its entire dealership network.

KEY COMPETITORS
Ford
General Motors
Nissan

GUNDLE/SLT ENVIRONMENTAL, INC.   NYSE: GSE

19103 Gundle Rd.	CEO: Samir Badawi	2000 Sales: $191.3 million
Houston, TX 77073	CFO: Roger J. Klatt	1-Yr. Sales Change: 7.2%
Phone: 281-443-8564	HR: Rob Johnson	Employees: 901
Fax: 281-875-6010	Type: Public	FYE: December 31
Web: www.gseworld.com		

Oil and water don't mix, and Gundle/SLT Environmental (GSE) plans to keep it that way. The company makes and installs synthetic liners used to prevent groundwater contamination. Waste-management firms, mining companies, and government agencies use the liners at garbage dumps and water-containment facilities. GSE's high-density polyethylene smooth sheet accounts for more than half of sales. The company also makes textured sheets and geosynthetic clay liners. GSE operates plants in Egypt, Germany, Thailand, the UK, and the US. It also has sales offices in Australia, Africa, Europe, the Middle East, and the US. The US accounts for more than 50% of sales. Chairman Samir Badawi owns about 44% of GSE.

KEY COMPETITORS
Baker Hughes
BJ Services
Halliburton

HAGGAR CORP.   Nasdaq: HGGR

6113 Lemmon Ave.	CEO: J. M. Haggar III	2000 Sales: $432.9 million
Dallas, TX 75209	CFO: David M. Tehle	1-Yr. Sales Change: (0.3%)
Phone: 214-352-8481	HR: Billy Langston	Employees: 3,856
Fax: 214-956-4367	Type: Public	FYE: September 30
Web: www.haggarcorp.com		

Haggar's classic men's casual and dress wear puts wrinkles in the competition. A leading maker of men's apparel, the company's clothes include pants, sport coats, suits, shirts, and shorts. Haggar's products (including its "wrinkle-free" shirts and pants) are sold through about 10,000 stores in the US. Its Haggar brand, which accounts for nearly two-thirds of its sales, is sold through department stores such as JCPenney and Kohls (its largest customers) and at more than 65 Haggar outlet stores. The company also makes lower-priced brands for mass merchandisers and offers private-label clothing. It owns women's wear maker Jerell (Selena and Stonebridge brands). Chairman and CEO J. M. Haggar III owns 8% of Haggar.

KEY COMPETITORS
Levi Strauss
Phillips-Van Heusen
VF

See pages 112–113 for a full profile of this company.

HALF PRICE BOOKS

5803 E. Northwest Hwy.
Dallas, TX 75231
Phone: 214-360-0833
Fax: 214-890-0850
Web: www.halfpricebooks.com

CEO: Sharon Anderson Wright
CFO: Nando Arduini
HR: Tim Jernigan
Type: Private

2000 Sales: $80.0 million
1-Yr. Sales Change: 25.0%
Employees: 1,200
FYE: June 30

Half Price Books tries to live up to its name and its hippie roots. The book-store chain sells used and new books, magazines, videos, and recorded music. Only about 50% to 60% of the merchandise it sells is new. Its more than 60 stores are located in 10 states, primarily in Texas. Its wholesale catalog division, Texas Bookman, reprints classics and other public domain works. The company was started by Ken Gjemre and Pat Anderson (late mom of president and CEO Sharon Anderson Wright) in 1972 to save trees by recycling unwanted books. It keeps a small-business look with secondhand and employee-made furnishings. Half Price Books grows slowly, opening a few stores a year. The Anderson family owns most of the company.

KEY COMPETITORS
Amazon.com
Barnes & Noble
Borders

HALLIBURTON COMPANY
NYSE: HAL

3600 Lincoln Plaza
Dallas, TX 75201
Phone: 214-978-2600
Fax: 214-978-2611
Web: www.halliburton.com

CEO: David J. Lesar
CFO: Douglas L. Foshee
HR: Margaret Carriere
Type: Public

2000 Sales: $11,856.0 million
1-Yr. Sales Change: (20.4%)
Employees: 93,000
FYE: December 31

The world's #1 provider of oil field services (ahead of Schlumberger), Halliburton has operations in more than 120 countries. The company's Energy Services Group (66% of sales) provides well evaluation, construction of production facilities, offshore drilling, and well maintenance services for the oil and gas industry. Halliburton's Engineering and Construction Group works on both energy-related and civil infrastructure facilities. Its projects include gas processing facilities and chemical plants, as well as prisons, stadiums, and highways. Halliburton has sold its Dresser Equipment Group, which makes meters, engines, and other equipment primarily for the energy industry.

KEY COMPETITORS
Baker Hughes
Bechtel
Schlumberger

HANOVER COMPRESSOR COMPANY
NYSE: HC

12001 N. Houston Rosslyn
Houston, TX 77086
Phone: 281-447-8787
Fax: 281-447-8781
Web: www.hanover-co.com

CEO: Michael J. McGhan
CFO: William S. Goldberg
HR: Errol Robinson
Type: Public

2000 Sales: $603.8 million
1-Yr. Sales Change: 90.5%
Employees: 2,700
FYE: December 31

Applying pressure is Hanover Compressor's forte — the company rents and repairs compressors and performs natural gas compression services for oil and gas companies. It has a fleet of more than 4,800 mobile compressors ranging from 24 to 5,000 horsepower. The company's Hanover Maintech and Hanover Dresser-Rand subsidiaries make compressor units, while Hanover Smith and Hanover Applied Process Solutions make oil and gas production equipment. Hanover Compressor, which operates throughout the Americas, has expanded by buying rival OEC Compression and Dresser-Rand's compressor services unit, and it has agreed to buy Schlumberger's gas compression business. Investment firm GKH Partners owns 25% of the company.

KEY COMPETITORS
Production Operators
Schlumberger
Universal Compression

HARTE-HANKS, INC.

NYSE: HHS

200 Concord Plaza Dr.
San Antonio, TX 78216
Phone: 210-829-9000
Fax: 210-829-9403
Web: www.harte-hanks.com

CEO: Larry Franklin
CFO: Jacques Kerrest
HR: Carolyn Oatman
Type: Public

2000 Sales: $960.8 million
1-Yr. Sales Change: 15.8%
Employees: 8,849
FYE: December 31

Direct marketing and advertising shoppers are meat and potatoes to Harte-Hanks, one of the largest US producers of shoppers (coupons and advertising circulars sent by mail). Although its shopper circulation is nearly 10 million a week (California and Florida), direct marketing is Harte-Hanks' fastest-growing business, accounting for about two-thirds of sales. Its direct-marketing efforts include response management (dealing with buyer inquiries for its clients), database marketing, printing, and interactive marketing functions such as Web site development. The family of co-founder Houston Harte (including vice chairman Houston H. Harte) owns about 16% of the company.

KEY COMPETITORS
ADVO
Interpublic Group
Omnicom

 See pages 116–117 for a full profile of this company.

HASTINGS ENTERTAINMENT, INC.

Nasdaq: HAST

3601 Plains Blvd.
Amarillo, TX 79102
Phone: 806-351-2300
Fax: 806-351-2424
Web: www.gohastings.com

CEO: John H. Marmaduke
CFO: Dan Crow
HR: Lisa Hallett
Type: Public

2001 Sales: $458.2 million
1-Yr. Sales Change: 2.5%
Employees: 6,245
FYE: January 31

Hastings Entertainment brings books, music, movies, and games to towns where "There's nothing to do" may be more than just a cliched teenage lament. The company operates about 140 multimedia stores in the midwestern and western US, mostly in small and medium-sized towns. It also sells merchandise online. Nearly 20% of Hastings' sales come from videotape, video game, and DVD rentals. Many of its stores — which average about 22,000 sq. ft. — offer such amenities as reading chairs and free coffee. The founding Marmaduke family, including CEO John and director Stephen — owns about 45% of Hastings.

KEY COMPETITORS
Barnes & Noble
Blockbuster
Wal-Mart

H. B. ZACHRY COMPANY

527 Logwood
San Antonio, TX 78221
Phone: 210-475-8000
Fax: 210-475-8060
Web: www.zachry.com

CEO: Henry Bartell Zachry Jr.
CFO: Joe J. Lozano
HR: Barry Lacey
Type: Private

2000 Sales: $1,195.0 million
1-Yr. Sales Change: 70.7%
Employees: 11,000
FYE: December 31

H. B. Zachry began building roads and bridges in 1924, and now his son and grandsons are running the show. The construction and industrial service firm's business today includes building and maintaining power and chemical plants, steel and paper mills, refineries, roadways, dams, airfields, and pipelines. Operating mostly in the southern US, H. B. Zachry has built facilities for companies such as Phillips, DuPont, Samsung, Alcoa, and Shell. It also works internationally, and recently completed the reconstruction of the US Embassy in Moscow. Zachry also holds interests in ranches, oil exploration, cement, hospitality, realty, and entertainment companies, as well as the San Antonio Spurs basketball team.

KEY COMPETITORS
Bechtel
Fluor
Peter Kiewit Sons'

HCC INSURANCE HOLDINGS, INC.

NYSE: HCC

13403 Northwest Fwy.
Houston, TX 77040
Phone: 713-690-7300
Fax: 713-744-9632
Web: www.hcch.com

CEO: Stephen L. Way
CFO: Edward H. Ellis Jr.
HR: Susan Howie
Type: Public

2000 Sales: $466.2 million
1-Yr. Sales Change: 36.4%
Employees: 958
FYE: December 31

Through its subsidiaries, HCC Insurance Holdings sells specialized property/ casualty insurance, underwrites for unaffiliated insurance companies, and provides related services for commercial and individual customers. The company's products include direct and reinsurance policies for the aviation, marine, and offshore energy industries; property/casualty and health policies; medical stop-loss; workers' compensation and occupational accident insurance. HCC Insurance's acquisition of Schanen Consulting added insurance intermediary services to its products.

KEY COMPETITORS
Highlands Insurance
Navigators
NYMAGIC

H.D. VEST, INC.

6333 N. State Hwy. 161, 4th Fl.
Irving, TX 75038
Phone: 972-870-6000
Fax: 972-870-6128
Web: www.hdvest.com

CEO: Herb D. Vest
CFO: W. Ted Sinclair
HR: Tim O'Brien
Type: Subsidiary

2000 Sales: $193.8 million
1-Yr. Sales Change: 30.4%
Employees: 375
FYE: September 30

Financial services firm H.D. Vest, through its brokerage and investment advisory divisions, manages a network of some 6,000 tax professionals that offer asset management services and sell insurance to individuals and businesses. Subsidiary H.D. Vest Investment Securities is a registered broker-dealer in all 50 states, the District of Columbia, and Puerto Rico. Securities offered include mutual funds and unit investment trusts, which together account for more than half of revenues. Fee-based investment consulting services are provided through H.D. Vest Advisory Services. H.D. Vest also offers online income tax filing via its Web site. Wells Fargo bought the company in 2001.

KEY COMPETITORS
Charles Schwab
Citigroup
Vanguard Group

H. E. BUTT GROCERY COMPANY

646 S. Main Ave.
San Antonio, TX 78204
Phone: 210-938-8000
Fax: 210-938-8169
Web: www.heb.com

CEO: Charles C. Butt
CFO: Jack C. Brouillard
HR: Susan Allford
Type: Private

2000 Sales: $8,200.0 million
1-Yr. Sales Change: 9.3%
Employees: 50,000
FYE: October 31

The Muzak bounces between Tejano and country, and the tortillas and ribs are big sellers at H. E. Butt Grocery Company (H-E-B). Texas' largest private company, H-E-B is the #1 food retailer in South and Central Texas, with more than 280 H-E-B supermarkets, including about 90 rural locations and several gourmet Central Markets. Nearly a fourth of the stores also have gas pumps. H-E-B operates facilities for processing meat, dairy products, and bread, and it offers the H-E-B and Hill Country Fare private labels. Already familiar with the tastes of Latinos (who make up about half of its Texas market), it is expanding in Mexico with both upscale and discount stores. The founding Butt family owns the firm.

KEY COMPETITORS
Albertson's
Randall's
Wal-Mart

 See pages 118–119 for a full profile of this company.

HELEN OF TROY LIMITED

Nasdaq: HELE

1 Helen of Troy Plaza	CEO: Gerald J. Rubin	2001 Sales: $361.4 million
El Paso, TX 79912	CFO: Russell G. Gibson	1-Yr. Sales Change: 20.7%
Phone: 915-225-8000	HR: Robert D. Spear	Employees: 558
Fax: 915-225-8004	Type: Public	FYE: February 28
Web: www.hotus.com		

Need help battling your hair? You might call on those warriors who sailed after Helen of Troy. The firm sells licensed personal care products and accessories under the Vidal Sassoon and Revlon brand names, as well its own WIGO, Karina, and Helen of Troy brands. Hair care items include hair dryers, curling irons, brushes, rollers, and mirrors; other products include women's shavers and foot massagers (Dr. Scholl's, Carel, Hotspa). Helen of Troy products are made under contract by manufacturers in Asia and are marketed primarily to retailers such as warehouse clubs and grocery stores, and to salons in the US (its main market) and abroad. Wal-Mart accounts for about 25% of sales.

KEY COMPETITORS
Applica
Conair
Remington Products

HICKS, MUSE, TATE & FURST INCORPORATED

200 Crescent Ct., Ste. 1600	CEO: Thomas O. Hicks	Sales: —
Dallas, TX 75201	CFO: Darron Ash	1-Yr. Sales Change: —
Phone: 214-740-7300	HR: Lynita Jessen	Employees: —
Fax: 214-720-7888	Type: Private	FYE: December 31

Hicks, Muse, Tate & Furst likes to buy, buy, buy & buy. (It sells sometimes, too.) The leveraged buyout firm assembles limited partnership investment pools and targets companies in specific niches that can be used to form a nucleus for other investments. Hicks, Muse (which sold its AMFM broadcast group to rival Clear Channel Communications to form the US's largest radio/TV/outdoor advertising firm) is moving abroad with media and food-company acquisitions, particularly in Latin America and Europe. Hicks, Muse also has holdings in manufacturing, real estate, and other sectors.

KEY COMPETITORS
Clayton, Dubilier
Investcorp
KKR

 See pages 120–121 for a full profile of this company.

HINES INTERESTS L.P.

2800 Post Oak Blvd., Ste. 4800	CEO: Jeffery C. Hines	2000 Est. Sales: $750.0 mil.
Houston, TX 77056	CFO: C. Hastings "Hasty" Johnson	1-Yr. Sales Change: 0.0%
Phone: 713-621-8000	HR: David LeVrier	Employees: 2,800
Fax: 713-966-2051	Type: Private	FYE: December 31
Web: www.hines.com		

Hines Interests, which has nothing to do with ketchup, is a private commercial real estate development company. Founded by Gerald Hines in 1957, the firm handles most aspects of real estate development, including site selection, rezoning, design, construction bidding and management, and financing. Its portfolio includes corporate headquarters, industrial complexes, and master-planned resorts. Hines also manages more than 70 million sq. ft. of real estate in the US and 11 other countries. Management services include public relations, security, tenant relations, and vendor contract-negotiation services. Hines has developed more than 190 million sq. ft. of space worldwide, including Houston's Galleria shopping center.

KEY COMPETITORS
CB Richard Ellis
Jones Lang LaSalle
Trammell Crow

HISPANIC BROADCASTING CORPORATION

NYSE: HSP

3102 Oak Lawn, Ste. 215
Dallas, TX 75219
Phone: 214-525-7700
Fax: 214-525-7750
Web: www.hispanicbroadcasting.com

CEO: McHenry T. Tichenor Jr.
CFO: Jeffrey T. Hinson
HR: Ellen Fox
Type: Public

2000 Sales: $237.6 million
1-Yr. Sales Change: 20.1%
Employees: 903
FYE: December 31

Cumbia! Mariachi! Tejano! Hispanic Broadcasting is *el mejor*. With 47 radio stations in more than a dozen leading markets, Hispanic Broadcasting (formerly Heftel Broadcasting) is the #1 Spanish-language radio broadcaster in the US. The company generates a substantial portion of its sales in Los Angeles, where stations KLVE, KSCA, and KTNQ entertain listeners. Hispanic Broadcasting's portfolio also includes Miami's WAMR and New York City's WCAA. Its stations offer programming in a variety of formats, including contemporary, full service, news and talk, Tejano, and tropical. Radio giant Clear Channel Communications owns 26% of the company; the family of chairman and CEO McHenry Tichenor Jr. controls about 17%.

KEY COMPETITORS
Infinity Broadcasting
Radio Unica
Spanish Broadcasting

 See pages 122–123 for a full profile of this company.

HOLLY CORPORATION

AMEX: HOC

100 Crescent Ct., Ste. 1600
Dallas, TX 75201
Phone: 214-871-3555
Fax: 214-871-3560
Web: www.hollycorp.com

CEO: Lamar Norsworthy
CFO: Stephen J. McDonnell
HR: Pam Reese
Type: Public

2001 Sales: $1,142.1 million
1-Yr. Sales Change: 18.2%
Employees: 521
FYE: July 31

A company for all seasons, this Holly refines petroleum to produce gasoline, diesel fuel, and jet fuel, which it sells primarily in the southwestern US, northern Mexico, and Montana. Subsidiaries Navajo Refining (located in New Mexico) and Montana Refining have a combined capacity of 67,000 barrels a day. Together with its refining operations, Holly operates a product distribution system that includes about 1,700 miles of pipeline. Customers include other refiners (including an affiliate of Mexican energy company PEMEX), wholesalers, convenience store chains, independent marketers, and other retailers. The company also engages in oil and gas exploration and production.

KEY COMPETITORS
Exxon Mobil
Giant Industries
Ultramar Diamond Shamrock

HOLLYWOOD CASINO CORPORATION

AMEX: HWD

2 Galleria Tower, Ste. 2200, 13455 Noel Rd., LB 48
Dallas, TX 75240
Phone: 972-392-7777
Fax: 972-716-3896
Web: www.hollywoodcasino.com

CEO: Edward T. Pratt III
CFO: Paul C. Yates
HR: Kathy Whitney
Type: Public

2000 Sales: $348.2 million
1-Yr. Sales Change: 13.3%
Employees: 4,720
FYE: December 31

Starstruck gamblers are the goal for Hollywood Casino Corporation (HCC). The company owns and operates three casinos with a Tinseltown theme, featuring movie memorabilia, celebrity look-alikes, and movie-themed games, restaurants, and entertainment facilities. Its Aurora, Illinois, casino features over 1,000 slot machines and 45 gaming tables on two multilevel riverboats. The company's Tunica, Mississippi, casino features some 1,500 slot machines, 50 table games, a 500-room hotel, and a 123-space RV park. In 2000 HCC opened its new Hollywood Casino Shreveport in Louisiana with about 1,500 slots, 68 tables, and 400 rooms. The Pratt family (including CEO Jack Pratt) owns about 57% of HCC.

KEY COMPETITORS
Boyd Gaming
Harrah's Entertainment
Isle of Capri Casinos

HOME INTERIORS & GIFTS, INC.

1649 Frankford Road	CEO: Donald J. Carter Jr.	2000 Sales: $460.4 million
Carrollton, TX 75007	CFO: Kenneth J. Cichocki	1-Yr. Sales Change: (8.5%)
Phone: 972-386-1000	HR: Pat Sinclair	Employees: 1,200
Fax: 972-386-1112	Type: Private	FYE: December 31
Web: www.homeinteriors.com		

If silk flowers and sconces are your thing, Home Interiors & Gifts wants in your house. The company makes or purchases decorating accessories, which about 60,000 independent "displayers" then sell through home parties, mainly in the US but also in Mexico and Puerto Rico. Its products (framed artwork, candles, plaques, artificial flowers) are geared toward women on a budget; most items sell for $7-$30. The company was founded in 1957 by Mary Crowley, sister-in-law of makeup maven Mary Kay Ash. Executives led by Joey Carter (Crowley's grandson) and buyout firm Hicks, Muse, Tate & Furst recapitalized Home Interiors & Gifts in 1998 in an intermediate step toward taking it public. Hicks, Muse owns 66% of the firm.

KEY COMPETITORS
Garden Ridge
Interiors, Inc.
Michaels Stores

HORIZON HEALTH CORPORATION
Nasdaq: HORC

1500 Waters Ridge Dr.	CEO: James W. McAtee	2001 Sales: $127.7 million
Lewisville, TX 75057	CFO: Ronald C. Drabik	1-Yr. Sales Change: (4.5%)
Phone: 972-420-8200	HR: Dan Perkins	Employees: —
Fax: 972-420-8252	Type: Public	FYE: August 31
Web: www.horz.com		

Horizon Health sees hope on the horizon for those in need of psychiatric and rehabilitation therapy. The firm manages some 250 mental health and physical rehabilitation programs offered by hospitals in 34 states. It handles administration, clinical protocols, and marketing for its clients. Programs include inpatient hospitalization, day treatment, outpatient treatment, and home health services. Some 70% of its managed programs focus on psychiatric care for the elderly. Other services include rehab management and a mental health database, which provides benchmarks to measure quality of care. The company also offers employee-assistance programs and mental health services to businesses and managed care organizations.

KEY COMPETITORS
Integra
Magellan Health
RehabCare

HORIZON OFFSHORE, INC.
Nasdaq: HOFF

2500 City West Blvd., Ste. 2200	CEO: Bill J. Lam	2000 Sales: $160.5 million
Houston, TX 77042	CFO: David W. Sharp	1-Yr. Sales Change: 80.3%
Phone: 713-361-2600	HR: Allen Bruns	Employees: 467
Fax: 713-361-2690	Type: Public	FYE: December 31
Web: www.horizonoffshore.com		

Scanning the sea for new business horizons is all part of a day's work for Horizon Offshore. Horizon provides offshore marine construction services to oil and gas companies, primarily in the US Gulf of Mexico. Its 11-vessel fleet installs pipelines from production platforms and other subsea sites in shallow and intermediate waters. The company also installs and removes production platforms. Horizon lays deepwater pipeline in the Gulf of Mexico, offshore Mexico, and in Central and South America. It has formed a deepwater reel pipelaying joint venture with Cal Dive to help it expand its operations. PEMEX accounts for 36% of the company's revenues.

KEY COMPETITORS
Global Industries
McDermott
Torch Offshore

HORIZON PHARMACIES, INC.

AMEX: HZP

531 W. Main St.
Denison, TX 75020
Phone: 903-465-2397
Fax: 903-465-8922

CEO: Ricky D. McCord
CFO: Michael F. Loy
HR: Terri Watkins
Type: Public

2000 Sales: $136.3 million
1-Yr. Sales Change: 3.4%
Employees: 903
FYE: December 31

HORIZON Pharmacies has that local apothecary appeal. The company owns about 50 small-town pharmacies in some 16 states, mainly in Texas and New Mexico, but as far away as Montana, Wisconsin, and Virginia. Prescription drugs account for more than 75% of its sales; higher-margin goods and services (over-the-counter drugs, greeting cards, medical equipment) bring in the rest. HORIZON has 16 home medical equipment (HME) locations, one home health care agency, and mail-order/Internet pharmacy HorizonScripts.com. It also has a handful of institutional pharmacies and intravenous operations. HORIZON has reduced its workforce and has shut down underperforming locations in an effort to cut costs.

KEY COMPETITORS
Eckerd
Walgreen
Wal-Mart

HOTEL RESERVATIONS NETWORK, INC.

Nasdaq: ROOM

8140 Walnut Hill Lane, Ste. 800
Dallas, TX 75231
Phone: 214-361-7311
Fax: 214-361-7299
Web: www.hoteldiscount.com

CEO: David Litman
CFO: Mel Robinson
HR: Stephanie Douglas
Type: Public

2000 Sales: $328.0 million
1-Yr. Sales Change: 102.7%
Employees: 360
FYE: December 31

Hotel Reservations Network (HRN) wants to transform the Internet into the inn-ternet. The company sells rooms at more than 2,600 hotels in over a hundred markets in western Europe, North America, the Caribbean, and Asia through its four Web sites (hoteldiscount.com, 180096hotel.com, condosaver.com, travelnow.com). With some 16,000 Internet and call center affiliates, the company offers rooms at discounts of up to 65%. It also accepts reservations through its toll-free call centers. HRN has room supply agreements with hotel chains such as Hilton Hotels, Best Western, Radisson, and Sheraton. Barry Diller's USA Networks owns about 70% of the firm but controls virtually all of its voting power.

KEY COMPETITORS
Expedia
priceline.com
Travelocity

HOUSTON ASTROS BASEBALL CLUB

501 Crawford, Ste. 400
Houston, TX 77002
Phone: 713-259-8000
Fax: 713-259-8025
Web: astros.mlb.com

CEO: Drayton McLane
CFO: Teresa Pelanne
HR: Mike Anders
Type: Private

2000 Sales: $122.2 million
1-Yr. Sales Change: 31.0%
Employees: 100
FYE: December 31

The Astros crashed back down to Earth in 2000 after closing out the 1990s by winning the National League Central (NLC) division for three straight years. The ball club left the Astrodome for the new $248 million Enron Field in 2000 and promptly gave up a rash of home runs and collapsed to fourth place. The team again claimed the NLC title in 2001 with the help of All Star slugger Jeff Bagwell. The Astros, which joined the National League as the Colt .45s in the expansion of 1962, have yet to win the NL pennant. Owner Drayton McLane bought the team for $115 million in 1992 from John McMullen, who also owned the New Jersey Devils at the time.

KEY COMPETITORS
Cincinnati Reds
Milwaukee Brewers
St. Louis Cardinals

THE HOUSTON EXPLORATION COMPANY

NYSE: THX

1100 Louisiana, Ste. 2000
Houston, TX 77002
Phone: 713-830-6800
Fax: 713-830-6885
Web: www.houstonexploration.com

CEO: William G. Hargett
CFO: Thomas W. Powers
HR: Christine Teichelman
Type: Public

2000 Sales: $270.6 million
1-Yr. Sales Change: 79.7%
Employees: 110
FYE: December 31

Houston, we have a platform. Houston Exploration performs some of its gas and oil exploration, development, and production from offshore platforms in the shallow waters of the Gulf of Mexico, although 59% of its reserves are located onshore. The company offsets the risks of its high-potential Gulf operations by holding lower-risk onshore properties and operating 85% of its production from interests in about 1,100 producing wells. Houston Exploration's proved reserves (94% of which are natural gas) total 562 billion cu. ft. of natural gas equivalent. Its biggest customer, Dynegy, accounts for 23% of sales. THEC Holdings, a unit of New York-based utility KeySpan, owns 68% of the company.

KEY COMPETITORS
Exxon Mobil
Newfield Exploration
Royal Dutch/Shell

HOUSTON ROCKETS

Two Greenway Plaza, Ste. 400
Houston, TX 77046
Phone: 713-627-3865
Fax: 713-963-7315
Web: www.nba.com/rockets

CEO: Leslie Alexander
CFO: Marcus Jolibois
HR: Darryl James
Type: Private

2000 Sales: $79.4 million
1-Yr. Sales Change: 79.2%
Employees: 75
FYE: June 30

The Houston Rockets first took to the court in 1967 but never really got off the launching pad as the then-San Diego Rockets, despite the best efforts of center Elvin Hayes. The team moved to Houston after four years, but it wasn't until 1976, when the Rockets picked up center Moses Malone (who bypassed college to play pro ball), that the team became a force in the NBA. Under the leadership of head coach and former Rocket Rudy Tomjanovich, the team won repeat championships in 1994 and 1995. The Rockets squad has lost some star power in recent years: Charles Barkley retired in 2000 and Hakeem "The Dream" Olajuwon was traded to Toronto in 2001. Former Wall Street securities trader Leslie Alexander owns the team.

KEY COMPETITORS
Utah Jazz
Minnesota Timberwolves
San Antonio Spurs

HUGOTON ROYALTY TRUST

NYSE: HGT

901 Main St., 17th Fl.
Dallas, TX 75202
Phone: 877-228-5083
Fax: —

CEO: Ron E. Hooper
CFO: —
HR: —
Type: Public

2000 Sales: $56.9 million
1-Yr. Sales Change: 71.4%
Employees: 1
FYE: December 31

Hugoton Royalty Trust was formed by Cross Timbers Oil Company (now XTO Energy) to pay royalties to shareholders based on the proceeds of sales from its oil and gas holdings. Payouts depend on oil and gas prices, the volume of gas and oil produced, and production and other costs. The trust receives 80% of the net proceeds from XTO's properties, located in the Hugoton fields of Kansas, Oklahoma, and Texas; the Anadarko Basin of Oklahoma; and the Green River Basin of Wyoming. These properties contain approximately 98% natural gas and 2% oil reserves. Hugoton is one of several royalty trusts formed by XTO since 1980. The oil and gas company owns about 55% of the trust.

KEY COMPETITORS
BP Prudhoe Bay
Sabine Royalty Trust
San Juan Basin

HUNT BUILDING CORPORATION

4401 N. Mesa, Ste. 201	CEO: Woody L. Hunt	2000 Est. Sales: $200.0 mil.
El Paso, TX 79912	CFO: William C. Sanders	1-Yr. Sales Change: 0.0%
Phone: 915-533-1122	HR: Patricia Minor	Employees: 170
Fax: 915-545-2631	Type: Private	FYE: December 31
Web: www.huntbuilding.com		

When sailors come home from the sea and airmen come home to roost, many of them seek refuge in Hunt Building's bedrooms and barracks. The firm primarily converts military facilities into private commercial and residential properties and upgrades military housing. The developer is building more than 1,200 such units at places like Keesler, Lackland, and McChord Air Force bases in Mississippi, Texas, and Washington, respectively. It's also active at Camp Pendleton, California, the Schofield Barracks in Hawaii, Navy bases in Virginia, and at two Naval Air Stations in California and Maine. Hunt, which is also developing about 140 private homes in El Paso, is owned and operated by descendants of founder Marion Hunt.

KEY COMPETITORS
Bovis Lend Lease
Landmark Organization
Lincoln Property

HUNT CONSOLIDATED INC.

Fountain Place	CEO: Ray L. Hunt	2000 Sales: $1,200.0 million
Dallas, TX 75202	CFO: Donald Robillard	1-Yr. Sales Change: 60.0%
Phone: 214-978-8000	HR: Charles Mills	Employees: 2,600
Fax: 214-978-8888	Type: Private	FYE: December 31

Hunt Consolidated is a holding company for the oil and real estate businesses of Ray Hunt, son of legendary Texas wildcatter and company founder H.L. Hunt. Founded in 1934 (reportedly with H. L.'s poker winnings), Hunt Oil is an oil and gas production and exploration company with primary interests along the US Gulf Coast and in South America. Hoping to repeat huge discoveries in Yemen, Hunt is exploring in Ghana, Newfoundland, and Madagascar. It has also teamed up with Repsol YPF and the SK Group on a large exploration project in Peru, and it is expanding its Canadian operations through acquisitions. Hunt Realty handles commercial and residential real estate development and investment management activities.

KEY COMPETITORS
BP
Exxon Mobil
Lincoln Property

HYDRIL COMPANY

Nasdaq: HYDL

3300 N. Sam Houston Pkwy. East	CEO: Christopher T. Seaver	2000 Sales: $180.0 million
Houston, TX 77032	CFO: Michael C. Kearney	1-Yr. Sales Change: 12.9%
Phone: 281-449-2000	HR: Mike Danford	Employees: 1,400
Fax: 281-985-3376	Type: Public	FYE: December 31
Web: www.hydril.com		

Hydril Company's connections help oil and gas companies pump profits. The company makes tubular connections and pressure-control products used to drill and produce oil and gas in deepwater, deep-formation, and horizontal well-drilling environments. Its tubular products include tubing, casings, and drill pipe connections; pressure-control products include blowout preventers, control systems, and friction reducers. Hydril also offers field services for operating its connections. Chairman Richard Seaver a nephew of the founder of Hydril, owns 34% of the company, and The Seaver Institute (a charitable organization created by the late founder Frank Seaver) owns 29%.

KEY COMPETITORS
Grant Prideco
Lone Star Technologies
Peerless Manufacturing

I2 TECHNOLOGIES, INC.

Nasdaq: ITWO

1 i2 Place, 11701 Luna Rd.
Dallas, TX 75234
Phone: 469-357-1000
Fax: 214-860-6060
Web: www.i2.com

CEO: Gregory A. Brady
CFO: William M. Beecher
HR: Lucy Contreras
Type: Public

2000 Sales: $1,126.3 million
1-Yr. Sales Change: 97.2%
Employees: 6,000
FYE: December 31

i2 hopes to capitalize on its management potential. The company's software not only helps manufacturers plan and schedule production and related operations such as raw materials procurement and product delivery, but also enables companies to create electronic marketplaces that link employees, customers, suppliers, and trading partners. i2 serves customers (including IBM, General Motors, and 3M) in a variety of industries, including automotive, software, and semiconductors. i2 has used its dominant position in supply chain management software to expand into related fields, including procurement and customer relationship management. Chairman Sanjiv Sidhu, who founded the company, owns about 35% of i2.

KEY COMPETITORS
Oracle
PeopleSoft
SAP

 See pages 124–125 for a full profile of this company.

ICO, INC.

Nasdaq: ICOC

5333 Westheimer, Ste. 600
Houston, TX 77056
Phone: 281-351-4100
Fax: 281-335-2201
Web: www.icoinc.com

CEO: Timothy J. Gollin
CFO: Christopher N. O'Sullivan
HR: Steve Vanburen
Type: Public

2000 Sales: $325.3 million
1-Yr. Sales Change: 24.0%
Employees: 2,199
FYE: September 30

I see, oh, a change in control of ICO, a company that processes petrochemicals and reconditions oil well drilling equipment. The company's subsidiaries grind, blend, and compound petroleum resin pellets into smaller sizes for use in paint and such plastic products as garbage bags and plastic film. In order to focus on its petrochemical businesses (68% of revenues), the company is selling off its oil-field services operations. The change in control? Investor group and 7% owner Travis Street Partners, which has offered to buy ICO, prevailed in a proxy fight in 2001 that led to the ouster of chairman and CFO Al Pacholder and president and CEO Sylvia Pacholder.

KEY COMPETITORS
Baker Hughes
BJ Services
Varco International

ILEX ONCOLOGY, INC.

Nasdaq: ILXO

4545 Horizon Hill Blvd.
San Antonio, TX 78229
Phone: 210-949-8200
Fax: 210-949-8210
Web: www.ilexonc.com

CEO: Richard L. Love
CFO: Gregory L. Weaver
HR: John Barnes
Type: Public

2000 Sales: $27.6 million
1-Yr. Sales Change: 54.2%
Employees: 361
FYE: December 31

ILEX Oncology is waging a war on cancer. The company not only provides oncology contract research services to pharmaceutical firms, but it also develops its own drugs for the treatment of the disease. Contract research services, provided through its ILEX Services division, account for almost 90% of sales. Its ILEX Products unit develops drugs for non-Hodgkin's lymphoma, solid tumors, and other forms of cancer; primary product Campath was co-developed with Millennium Pharmaceuticals as a treatment for leukemia. The company is shifting its focus toward the development of drugs and will no longer take new clients for its contract research services. It plans to use ILEX Services solely for its own products.

KEY COMPETITORS
ImmunoGen
Maxim Pharmaceuticals
SuperGen

IMCO RECYCLING INC.

5215 N. O'Connor Blvd., Ste. 1500
Irving, TX 75039
Phone: 972-401-7200
Fax: 972-401-7342
Web: www.imcorecycling.com

CEO: Don V. Ingram
CFO: Paul V. Dufour
HR: James A. Madden
Type: Public

2000 Sales: $846.9 million
1-Yr. Sales Change: 10.7%
Employees: 1,755
FYE: December 31

"Waste not, want not" could be the motto at IMCO Recycling, a leading aluminum recycler (71% of sales) that also processes zinc. Its main business is recycling customer-owned materials for a processing fee, a transaction called tolling. Customers — aluminum companies Alcoa, Kaiser Aluminum, and Wise Metals — use the recycled aluminum to produce containers, building-construction materials, and automotive products. General Motors agreed in 1999 to buy $1 billion worth of IMCO's recycled aluminum over the next 13 years. IMCO operates more than 20 production facilities in the US and an aluminum-recycling facility in Wales. The company also owns a 50% interest in two recycling and foundry alloy plants in Germany.

KEY COMPETITORS
Connell Limited Partnership
David J. Joseph
Metal Management

IMPERIAL SUGAR COMPANY

OTC: IPRLQ

One Imperial Square
Sugar Land, TX 77487
Phone: 281-491-9181
Fax: 281-490-9879
Web: www.imperialsugar.com

CEO: Robert J. McLaughlin
CFO: —
HR: R. Martin Thompson
Type: Public

2000 Sales: $1,821.2 million
1-Yr. Sales Change: (3.6%)
Employees: 3,800
FYE: September 30

Imperial Sugar occupies the sweetest spot in its field — it's the largest refined sugar supplier in the US. Imperials' brands of sugar include Dixie Crystals, Imperial, Holly, Spreckels, Pioneer, and Wholesome Sweeteners (organic sweetener). Imperial makes sugar in 15 refineries and sells to grocery, food service, and industrial customers. The Kempner family owns more than 15% of Imperial; Irish sugar maker Greencore owns another 15%. Imperial filed for Chapter 11 bankruptcy protection in early 2001 and later sold its Diamond Crystal Brands nutritional products business to Hormel Foods.

KEY COMPETITORS
American Crystal Sugar
SYSCO
Tate & Lyle

INDUSTRIAL HOLDINGS, INC.

Nasdaq: IHII

7135 Ardmore
Houston, TX 77054
Phone: 713-747-1025
Fax: 713-749-9642
Web: www.industrialholdings.com

CEO: Robert E. Cone
CFO: Titus H. Harris III
HR: Larry G. Hodges
Type: Public

2000 Sales: $186.2 million
1-Yr. Sales Change: (23.1%)
Employees: 1,925
FYE: December 31

Industrial Holdings has its grip on numerous subsidiaries operating in three businesses: energy, stud bolts, and heavy fabrication. The energy segment remanufactures and distributes pumps and pipeline valves used in petroleum and chemical refining. The stud bolt segment makes a line of bolts, nuts, gaskets, hoses, and fittings that are used primarily by the oil and gas industry. The company's heavy fabrication unit makes large machine weldments such as gas turbine casings and heat exchangers for the electric power, marine, petrochemical, and medical equipment industries. Industrial Holdings is exiting its cold-formed fasteners and specialty metal components business.

KEY COMPETITORS
Baker Hughes
National-Oilwell
Reunion Industries

INET TECHNOLOGIES, INC.

Nasdaq: INTI

1500 N. Greenville Ave.	CEO: Elie S. Akilian	2000 Sales: $159.0 million
Richardson, TX 75081	CFO: Jeffrey A. Kupp	1-Yr. Sales Change: 44.5%
Phone: 469-330-4000	HR: Cristi Spears	Employees: 640
Fax: 469-330-4001	Type: Public	FYE: December 31
Web: www.inet.com		

Inet Technologies gives telecom networks top billing. The company's software helps telecommunications carriers monitor and manage their networks, receive early warnings of potential problems, and manage billing, sales, fraud prevention, and call routing. The company's primary products are its GeoProbe network monitoring application and its Spectra diagnostic and troubleshooting tool. Inet has more than 500 customers, including British Telecommunications and WorldCom, which collectively account for about 25% of sales; more than half of its sales come from international business. The company's co-founders — chairman Samuel Simonian, CEO Elie Akilian, and director Mark Weinzierl — collectively own nearly 80% of Inet.

KEY COMPETITORS
Agilent Technologies
Orchestream Canada
Telcordia Technologies

INPUT/OUTPUT, INC.

NYSE: IO

12300 C. E. Selecman Dr.	CEO: Timothy J. Probert	2000 Sales: $78.3 million
Stafford, TX 77477	CFO: C. Robert Bunch	1-Yr. Sales Change: (35.6%)
Phone: 281-933-3339	HR: Glenn Weissinger	Employees: 736
Fax: 281-879-3500	Type: Public	FYE: May 31
Web: www.i-o.com		

There's a whole lotta shakin' goin' on at Input/Output (I/O). The seismic data-acquisition systems and software systems company helps seismic contractors and petroleum industry contractors worldwide to identify and measure sub-surface geologic structures that could contain oil and gas. Its core I/O System is land-based with 3-D imaging capabilities. The company's systems include modules for land, marine, and transition areas (such as swamps). Baker Hughes and its affiliates account for 17% of sales; Schlumberger and its affiliates, 12%; Petroleum Geo-Services, 12%; and China Petroleum Technology and Development, 11%. I/O faces an industrywide downturn in exploration — the result, in part, of lowered energy prices.

KEY COMPETITORS
Allegheny Technologies
Compagnie Générale de
  Géophysique
OYO Geospace

INSPIRE INSURANCE SOLUTIONS, INC.

Nasdaq: NSPR

300 Burnett St.	CEO: Richard "Dic" Marxen	2000 Sales: $126.6 million
Fort Worth, TX 76102	CFO: Patrick E. Grady	1-Yr. Sales Change: (10.0%)
Phone: 817-348-3900	HR: Greg Vick	Employees: 1,087
Fax: 817-348-3677	Type: Public	FYE: December 31
Web: www.nspr.com		

INSpire Insurance Solutions provides policy and claims administration out-sourcing and software services to the property/casualty insurance industry. Outsourcing services include marketing support, policy issuance, customer service, applying underwriting and rating standards, accounting, and commis-sion calculation, as well as claims administration and IT outsourcing. The company is discontinuing efforts to increase its proprietary software licenses to focus on its outsourcing business. About one-quarter of the company is owned by Millers Mutual, which founded the company to market its own internal software systems to other insurers.

KEY COMPETITORS
Computer Sciences
Crawford & Company
EDS

INTEGRATED ELECTRICAL SERVICES, INC.

NYSE: IEE

1800 West Loop South	CEO: H. David Ramm	2000 Sales: $1,672.3 million
Houston, TX 77027	CFO: William W. Reynolds	1-Yr. Sales Change: 61.4%
Phone: 713-860-1500	HR: Margery M. Harris	Employees: 15,500
Fax: 713-860-1599	Type: Public	FYE: September 30
Web: www.ielectric.com		

Integrated Electrical Services keeps turning up the juice on its electrical contracting and maintenance business. The fast-growing company has a network of about 125 affiliates across the US. Services include the installation and maintenance of electrical wiring in commercial and industrial businesses such as hospitals, hotels, manufacturing plants, office and retail buildings and schools; customers include WorldCom, Dell Computer, and Wal-Mart. The company also wires new homes and apartments; its communication infrastructure services include installing telecommunications cables, power lines, computer networks, and electrical substations.

KEY COMPETITORS
EMCOR
Encompass Services Corp.
Quanta Services

INTERLOGIX, INC.

Nasdaq: ILXI

114 W. 7th St., Ste. 1300	CEO: Kenneth L. Boyda	2000 Sales: $539.5 million
Austin, TX 78701	CFO: John R. Logan	1-Yr. Sales Change: 343.7%
Phone: 512-381-2760	HR: Jeff Quade	Employees: 3,344
Fax: 512-381-1774	Type: Public	FYE: December 31
Web: www.interlogixinc.com		

Interlogix seems the logical choice to protect your home from burglars or fire. The company provides electronic security systems for residential and commercial use, including intrusion and fire protection systems that use sensors to detect motion, heat, smoke, and other gases. The company also provides electronic and remote-access systems. Interlogix distributes fiber-optic transmission and reception equipment, and surveillance and media storage equipment such as closed-circuit televisions and other video products. Formed from the merger of ITI Technologies and SLC Technologies, Interlogix sells its products worldwide to installation companies, wholesale distributors, systems integrators, and corporate end users.

KEY COMPETITORS
Detection Systems
Honeywell International
Sensormatic

INTERNATIONAL BANCSHARES CORPORATION

Nasdaq (SC): IBOC

1200 San Bernardo Ave.	CEO: Dennis E. Nixon	2000 Sales: $479.1 million
Laredo, TX 78042	CFO: Imelda Navarro	1-Yr. Sales Change: 19.3%
Phone: 956-722-7611	HR: Rosie Ramirez	Employees: 1,634
Fax: 956-726-6647	Type: Public	FYE: December 31
Web: www.iboc.com		

The largest minority-owned bank holding company in the US, International Bancshares Corporation is leading after-NAFTA banking in South Texas. Its International Bank of Commerce and Commerce Bank subsidiaries serve residents and businesses in Texas and Mexico (about 40% of deposits) from about 90 Texas offices. The firm offers banking services to *maquiladoras* (US-owned plants in Mexico that temporarily import materials for assembly and then re-export to the US). About 60% of the company's loan portfolio is made up of business loans. The family of founder Antonio Sanchez owns about 30% of the company, which plans to enter the fast-growing Austin, Texas, market with its purchase of mortgage lender First Equity.

KEY COMPETITORS
BANK ONE
Cullen/Frost Bankers
J.P. Morgan Chase

INTERVOICE-BRITE, INC.

Nasdaq: INTV

17811 Waterview Pkwy.
Dallas, TX 75252
Phone: 972-454-8000
Fax: 972-454-8781
Web: www.intervoice.com

CEO: David W. Brandenburg
CFO: Rob-Roy J. Graham
HR: H. Don Brown
Type: Public

2001 Sales: $274.7 million
1-Yr. Sales Change: (4.0%)
Employees: 1,196
FYE: February 28

InterVoice-Brite is electronic armor for those who go *mano a máquina*. The company develops call automation systems that individuals access when electronically checking their bank balances, making hotel reservations, or ordering catalog merchandise. Its OneVoice product (about 35% of sales) combines hardware and software to allow a company's customers to access databases via Touch-Tone and rotary phones, modems, or credit card terminals. InterVoice-Brite sells direct and through distributors to telcos and other large clients such as British Telecom (16% of sales), J.P. Morgan Chase & Co., Qwest, and Microsoft. The company took its current form following InterVoice's 1999 purchase of rival Brite Voice Systems.

KEY COMPETITORS
Comverse
Lucent
Nortel Networks

J. C. PENNEY COMPANY, INC.

NYSE: JCP

6501 Legacy Dr.
Plano, TX 75024
Phone: 972-431-1000
Fax: 972-431-1362
Web: www.jcpenney.net

CEO: Allen I. Questrom
CFO: Robert B. Cavanaugh
HR: Gary L. Davis
Type: Public

2001 Sales: $31,846.0 million
1-Yr. Sales Change: (2.0%)
Employees: 267,000
FYE: January 31

J. C. Penney Company is pinching the penny, closing stores in both its department and drugstore operations. The retailer's chain of more than 1,100 JCPenney department stores, located mostly in the US, has suffered as the middle child of the market between upscale competitors and major discounters such as Target and Wal-Mart. Its struggling chain of 2,600 Eckerd drugstores has experienced the same squeeze from its competitors. J. C. Penney also runs one of the nation's largest catalog operations, and sells membership services. J. C. Penney hired Allen Questrom as CEO, who helped turn around Federated Department Stores, in September 2000.

KEY COMPETITORS
Sears
Target
Wal-Mart

 See pages 126–127 for a full profile of this company.

JENKENS & GILCHRIST, P.C.

1445 Ross Ave., Ste. 3200
Dallas, TX 75202
Phone: 214-855-4500
Fax: 214-855-4300
Web: www.jenkens.com

CEO: David M. Laney
CFO: Tom Laughlin
HR: David Lopater
Type: Partnership

2000 Sales: $249.0 million
1-Yr. Sales Change: (16.3%)
Employees: 1,050
FYE: December 31

Need a Texas-sized law firm? Look no further than Jenkens & Gilchrist — one of the largest law firms in the Lone Star State. Most of the firm's 600 attorneys work out of its Dallas office; the firm has three additional offices in Texas, as well as offices in Chicago, Los Angeles, New York City, and Washington, DC. A full-service law firm, Jenkens & Gilchrist specializes in areas ranging from First Amendment rights to venture capital. Holman Jenkens and William Bowen founded the firm as Jenkens & Bowen in 1951. Henry Gilchrist joined the practice in 1952, and the firm later adopted its present name.

KEY COMPETITORS
Akin, Gump
Fulbright & Jaworski
Vinson & Elkins

JPI

600 E. Las Colinas Blvd., Ste. 1800
Irving, TX 75039
Phone: 972-556-1700
Fax: 972-556-3784
Web: www.jpi.com

CEO: Frank Miller III
CFO: Frank B. Schubert
HR: John O'Connor
Type: Private

2000 Est. Sales: $1,000.0 mil.
1-Yr. Sales Change: 66.7%
Employees: 1,500
FYE: December 31

JPI can walk your dog or rent you a bike but what it does best is build and manage apartments (its own and other property owners'). One of the largest luxury multifamily housing developers in the US, JPI also manages more than 20,000 units in about a dozen states. The company typically buys down-at-the-heels properties and upgrades them with such features as theaters, putting greens, mail centers, and 24-hour concierge services. JPI's student complexes may include amenities like fitness centers. Founded in 1976 as Jefferson Properties, Inc., JPI was a subsidiary of Southland Financial until the early 1990s when Hunt Realty Corp. invested in it. JPI also operates in partnership with GE Capital.

KEY COMPETITORS
Castle & Cooke
Gables Residential Trust
Trammell Crow Residential

JUSTIN INDUSTRIES, INC.

2821 W. 7th St.
Fort Worth, TX 76101
Phone: 817-336-5125
Fax: 817-390-2477

CEO: Harrold Melton
CFO: Judy B. Hunter
HR: —
Type: Subsidiary

1999 Sales: $509.8 million
1-Yr. Sales Change: 12.1%
Employees: 3,826
FYE: December 31

Justin Industries' business portfolio is built on bricks, boots, and books. Its Acme Building Brands building-materials segment generates about two-thirds of the company's sales and includes the operations of Acme (clay brick), Featherlite Building Products (concrete building products), and American Tile (floor and wall tile distribution). Justin Brands is the company's subsidiary for its footwear lines that include Justin Boot, Nocona Boot, and Tony Lama, makers of western boots and work and sport footwear. Justin also publishes books on western history and art and Native American culture through its Northland Publishing unit. Warren Buffett's Berkshire Hathaway owns the company.

KEY COMPETITORS
Dal-Tile
Lafarge North America
TXI

KAISER ALUMINUM CORPORATION NYSE: KLU

5847 San Felipe, Ste. 2600
Houston, TX 77057
Phone: 713-267-3777
Fax: 713-267-3701
Web: www.kaiseral.com

CEO: Jack A. Hockema
CFO: John T. La Duc
HR: Diane Dudley
Type: Public

2000 Sales: $2,169.8 million
1-Yr. Sales Change: 6.1%
Employees: 7,800
FYE: December 31

Jawohl, kommandant! Kaiser Aluminum wasn't one of Colonel Klink's cronies on *Hogan's Heroes* but it does have a commanding presence in the world of bauxite and aluminum. Through subsidiary Kaiser Aluminum & Chemical Corporation, the company operates two wholly owned and two partially owned aluminum smelting facilties. Major businesses include bauxite and alumina mining; primary aluminum production (for trading intermediaries and metals brokers); flat-rolled sheet and plate aluminum products (used to make beverage cans and specialty coils); and extruded products and forgings (engineered products). Kaiser uses about 25% of the alumina and bauxite it produces and sells the rest. MAXXAM Inc. has a 63% stake in the company.

KEY COMPETITORS
Alcan
Alcoa
Pechiney

KANEB PIPE LINE PARTNERS, L.P.

2435 N. Central Expwy.
Richardson, TX 75080
Phone: 972-699-4000
Fax: 972-699-4025
Web: www.kanebpipeline.com

CEO: Edward D. Doherty II
CFO: Howard C. Wadsworth
HR: William H. Kettler Jr.
Type: Public

2000 Sales: $156.2 million
1-Yr. Sales Change: (1.1%)
Employees: 600
FYE: December 31

Kaneb Pipe Line Partners (KPP) transports refined petroleum products — gasoline, diesel, and propane — primarily in Colorado, Iowa, Kansas, Nebraska, North Dakota, South Dakota, and Wyoming. Its 2,090-mile East Pipeline has 16 product terminals and 22 product tanks with a combined capacity of 3.5 million barrels. The 550-mile West Pipeline has four product terminals and total storage of about 1.7 million barrels. KPP's liquid-related terminal operations include 35 facilities in 19 states, and Washington, DC, with a total capacity of about 23.4 million barrels. The company also owns six terminals in the UK. Kaneb Pipe Line, a subsidiary of Kaneb Services, owns 30% of KPP and serves as its general partner.

KEY COMPETITORS
Phillips Petroleum
Ultramar Diamond Shamrock
Williams Companies

KANEB SERVICES LLC

2435 N. Central Expwy.
Dallas, TX 75080
Phone: 972-699-4000
Fax: 972-644-3524
Web: www.kanebllc.com

CEO: John R. Barnes
CFO: —
HR: —
Type: Public

2000 Sales: $537.4 million
1-Yr. Sales Change: 321.2%
Employees: 1,131
FYE: December 31

Kaneb Services engages in wholesale fuel marketing in the Great Lakes and Rocky Mountain regions and in California. The company's subsidiary Kaneb Pipe Line Company owns 30% of pipeline operator Kaneb Pipe Line Partners (KPP) and serves as its general partner. KPP operates refined products pipelines and terminals for specialty liquids and petroleum products in the midwestern US. Kaneb Services LLC was created in 2001 when KPP parent Kaneb Services, Inc. (now Xanser) spun off its fuel marketing operations and its stake in KPP to Kaneb Services shareholders.

KEY COMPETITORS
Phillips Petroleum
Ultramar Diamond Shamrock
Williams Companies

KCS ENERGY, INC.

5555 San Felipe Rd., Ste. 1200
Houston, TX 77056
Phone: 713-877-8006
Fax: 713-877-1372
Web: www.kcsenergy.com

CEO: James W. Christmas
CFO: Frederick Dwyer
HR: Patti Osborne
Type: Public

2000 Sales: $192.0 million
1-Yr. Sales Change: 40.7%
Employees: 164
FYE: December 31

KCS Energy has been dancing with abandon — abandoning pipelines, properties, and production payments — in a successful effort to appease the banking and investment gods. The independent exploration and production company has reorganized and emerged from bankruptcy protection. After pursuing an aggressive drilling program and benefiting from higher commodity prices, KCS has also reduced its debt significantly. The company has refocused its operations on the midcontinent and Gulf Coast regions, and it also holds interests in Rocky Mountain and West Texas properties. It owns reserves of more than 265.5 billion cu. ft. of gas equivalent. Chairman Stewart Kean owns about 9% of KCS Energy.

KEY COMPETITORS
Anadarko Petroleum
BP

KEVCO, INC.

OTC: KVCOQ

University Center I
Fort Worth, TX 76107
Phone: 817-885-0000
Fax: 817-332-3403

CEO: Frederick B. Hegi Jr.
CFO: Wilford W. Simpson
HR: John Wittig
Type: Public

1999 Sales: $840.3 million
1-Yr. Sales Change: (6.4%)
Employees: 2,238
FYE: December 31

There's trouble at home for Kevco. The company has been forced into bankruptcy due to the industry-wide slowdown for manufactured homes. Kevco distributes its products to more than 500 makers of manufactured homes and RVs in the US. Its 25 distribution centers provide plumbing fixtures and supplies, wood roof trusses and lumber, laminated wallboard, electrical components, hardware, fasteners, and power tools, and other building products. Kevco's two largest customers are Champion Enterprises and Fleetwood Enterprises. The company also is selling some units to raise cash. Chairman and CEO Frederick Hegi owns 46% of Kevco through investment firm KPI, and VC Jerry Kimmel owns 30%.

KEY COMPETITORS
Louisiana-Pacific
Moore-Handley
Patrick Industries

KEY ENERGY SERVICES, INC.

NYSE: KEG

6 Desta Dr.
Midland, TX 79705
Phone: 915-620-0300
Fax: 915-862-7901
Web: www.keyenergy.com

CEO: Francis D. John
CFO: Thomas K. Grundman
HR: Belinda McAnear
Type: Public

2001 Sales: $865.9 million
1-Yr. Sales Change: 35.8%
Employees: 9,300
FYE: June 30

Energy is the key to growth for Key Energy Services, one of the US's largest well-servicing and workover companies. The company provides maintenance, workover, and recompletion of wells, primarily for onshore drilling. It owns about 1,400 well service rigs, 1,200 oil field trucks, and more than 70 drilling rigs. Key Energy is also a contract driller and transports oil field fluids. Its Odessa Exploration subsidiary produces oil and gas in West Texas. Key Energy operates in the major onshore oil- and gas-producing areas of the US, including the Four Corners, Gulf Coast, and midcontinent regions and the Appalachian, Permian, and San Joaquin Basins. It also operates in Argentina and Canada.

KEY COMPETITORS
Nabors Industries
Pride International
Schlumberger

KEYSTONE CONSOLIDATED INDUSTRIES, INC.

NYSE: KES

5430 LBJ Fwy., Ste. 1740, Three Lincoln Centre
Dallas, TX 75240
Phone: 972-458-0028
Fax: 972-448-1408

CEO: Robert W. Singer
CFO: Harold M. Curdy
HR: Kathy Brownlee
Type: Public

2000 Sales: $338.3 million
1-Yr. Sales Change: (4.9%)
Employees: 1,830
FYE: December 31

If you're born to be wired, Keystone Consolidated Industries can rock your world. The company makes fabricated wire products (mainly under the Red Brand name), including fencing, barbed wire, welded wire, and woven wire mesh for the agricultural, construction, and do-it-yourself markets. Keystone also makes industrial wire and carbon steel rod. The company uses industrial wire internally and also sells it to companies that produce items such as coat hangers and nails. Keystone also sells its unused carbon steel rod. Customers include The Home Depot, Lowe's Companies, and Tractor Supply. Through Contran Corporation, a privately owned holding company, Harold Simmons owns almost 50% of Keystone.

KEY COMPETITORS
GS Industries
Insteel

KIMBERLY-CLARK CORPORATION

NYSE: KMB

351 Phelps Dr.
Irving, TX 75038
Phone: 972-281-1200
Fax: 972-281-1490
Web: www.kimberly-clark.com

CEO: Wayne R. Sanders
CFO: John W. Donehower
HR: —
Type: Public

2000 Sales: $13,982.0 million
1-Yr. Sales Change: 7.5%
Employees: 66,300
FYE: December 31

Nobody knows noses better than Kimberly-Clark, the world's top maker of personal paper products. With brand names such as Kleenex and Scott, the company gets about 50% of its sales from making tissue products (facial tissue, bathroom tissue, and paper towels) and business papers. The company also makes personal care items, including Huggies diapers and baby wipes, Kotex feminine hygiene pads, and Depend incontinence items. It makes commercial wipes under the WypAll and Kimwipes names. Since 1997 it has been expanding into medical products: It is a leading US maker of disposable surgical masks, examination gloves, and sterilization wrap.

KEY COMPETITORS
Georgia-Pacific Corporation
Playtex
Procter & Gamble

 See pages 128–129 for a full profile of this company.

KINDER MORGAN ENERGY PARTNERS, L.P.

NYSE: KMP

One Allen Center, Ste. 1000, 500 Dallas St.
Houston, TX 77002
Phone: 713-369-9000
Fax: 713-369-9100
Web: www.kindermorgan.com

CEO: Richard D. Kinder
CFO: C. Park Shaper
HR: James E. Street
Type: Public

2000 Sales: $816.4 million
1-Yr. Sales Change: 90.4%
Employees: 1,600
FYE: December 31

Kinder Morgan Energy Partners (KMP) keeps petroleum on the move throughout the US. The company transports refined petroleum products (gasoline, diesel, and jet fuel) over 10,000 miles of pipelines and stores the products in more than 20 associated terminals. KMP also operates 10,000 miles of natural gas transportation pipelines and natural gas gathering and storage facilities, and it oversees bulk terminal facilities that handle more than 40 million tons of coal, petroleum coke and other products annually. Its Kinder Morgan CO2 unit is the largest transporter and marketer of carbon dioxide in the US. Parent Kinder Morgan, Inc., controls the company through its Kinder Morgan Management unit.

KEY COMPETITORS
Koch
TEPPCO Partners
TransMontaigne

KINDER MORGAN, INC.

NYSE: KMI

One Allen Center, Ste. 1000, 500 Dallas St.
Houston, TX 77002
Phone: 713-369-9000
Fax: —
Web: www.kindermorgan.com

CEO: Richard D. Kinder
CFO: C. Park Shaper
HR: James E. Street
Type: Public

2000 Sales: $2,713.7 million
1-Yr. Sales Change: 55.5%
Employees: 3,801
FYE: December 31

Kinder Morgan pipes in profits by operating more than 30,000 miles of natural gas and product pipelines throughout the US. The company also distributes natural gas to 225,000 customers in the Midwest, and it is adding gas-fired power plants along its pipelines. Through Kinder Morgan Management, it controls Kinder Morgan Energy Partners, which transports refined products and operates more than 29 bulk terminals that handle products such as coal and coke. Kinder Morgan, formed in 1997 when Richard Kinder and William Morgan bought an Enron pipeline unit, expanded dramatically in 1999 through a reverse merger with troubled natural gas pipeline giant K N Energy. Chairman and CEO Kinder owns 21% of the company.

KEY COMPETITORS
TEPPCO Partners
Western Gas
Williams Companies

KINETIC CONCEPTS, INC.

8023 Vantage Dr.
San Antonio, TX 78230
Phone: 210-524-9000
Fax: 210-255-6998
Web: www.kci1.com

CEO: Dennert O. "Denny" Ware
CFO: William M. Brown
HR: Rush E. Cone
Type: Private

2000 Sales: $353.8 million
1-Yr. Sales Change: 10.1%
Employees: 2,400
FYE: December 31

Kinetic Concepts makes its bed and has no problems lying in it. The company makes specialized mattresses and pressure relief and pulmonary care products to treat and prevent complications associated with patient immobility, such as pressure sores and the harmful buildup of fluid in the lungs. Products include the BariKare line of specialized beds, the NuPulse system for treatment of diabetic-related wounds, and the PlexiPulse All In 1 pneumatic compression device. Kinetic Concepts operates through more than 100 service facilities across the US; the company also markets its products abroad, primarily in Australia, Canada, and Europe.

KEY COMPETITORS
Hillenbrand
Invacare
Sunrise Medical

KING RANCH, INC.

3 River Way, Ste. 1600
Houston, TX 77056
Phone: 832-681-5700
Fax: 832-681-5759
Web: www.king-ranch.com

CEO: Jack Hunt
CFO: Bill Gardiner
HR: Martha Breit
Type: Private

2000 Est. Sales: $300.0 mil.
1-Yr. Sales Change: 0.0%
Employees: 700
FYE: December 31

Meanwhile, back at the ranch . . . the sprawling King Ranch, that is. King Ranch, founded in 1853, extends beyond the legendary 825,000 acres in South Texas that are home to about 60,000 cattle and a wide variety of animal species. The business oversees ranching and farming interests in Texas and Florida, but these days it also benefits from oil and gas royalties, farming (cotton, citrus, and sugar), and retail operations (designer saddles, leather goods). In addition, King Ranch also beefs up revenues with tourist dollars from hunters and sightseers. It sold its Kentucky horse farm, once a producer of champion thoroughbreds, and its primary oil and gas subsidiary. About 85 descendants of founder Richard King own King Ranch.

KEY COMPETITORS
AZTX Cattle
Cactus Feeders
Koch

 See pages 130–131 for a full profile of this company.

KIRBY CORPORATION   NYSE: KEX

55 Waugh Drive, Ste. 1000
Houston, TX 77007
Phone: 713-435-1000
Fax: 713-435-1010
Web: www.kmtc.com

CEO: J. H. Pyne
CFO: Norman W. Nolen
HR: Jack M. Sims
Type: Public

2000 Sales: $512.6 million
1-Yr. Sales Change: 40.2%
Employees: 1,850
FYE: December 31

The only curbs on Kirby Corporation's growth are downturns in the transportation market. The largest inland barge operator in the US, Kirby owns a fleet of more than 870 tank barges that ply the inland waterways of the US. The barges, operated by subsidiary Kirby Inland Marine, transport petrochemicals and processed chemicals (60% of transportation revenues), agricultural chemicals, and refined petroleum products. Subsidiary Western Towing operates 215 towing vessels. Three Kirby subsidiaries, Marine Systems, Rail Systems, and Engine Systems, engage in overhaul and repair of marine, rail, and industrial diesel engines. Big customer Dow Chemical accounts for 10% of the company's revenues.

KEY COMPETITORS
American Commercial Lines
Crowley Maritime
Ingram Industries

LA MADELEINE FRENCH BAKERY & CAFE

6060 N. Central Expwy., #138
Dallas, TX 75206
Phone: 214-696-6962
Fax: 214-696-0485
Web: www.lamadeleine.com

CEO: John Corcoran
CFO: Brant Wood
HR: Jennifer Palmer
Type: Private

2001 Sales: $121.4 million
1-Yr. Sales Change: 3.4%
Employees: 2,781
FYE: June 30

La Madeleine French Bakery & Cafe brings its French flair to patrons in Arizona, Georgia, Louisiana, Maryland, Texas, Virginia, and Washington, DC. The company's more than 60 restaurants offer French country cuisine in an atmosphere reminiscent of a French village. Adding to the atmosphere, the staff wears white uniforms complete with large chefs' hats. Serving breakfast, lunch, and dinner, restaurants allow diners to indulge their French food fetishes with a menu offering such items as crème brulée, croissants, quiche, and rosemary chicken. Patrick Esquerre, a native of France, founded the company in Dallas in 1983. Esquerre departed La Madeleine in 1998 after selling his stake in the company to his partners.

KEY COMPETITORS
Brinker
Darden Restaurants
Starbucks

THE LA QUINTA COMPANIES
NYSE: LQI

909 Hidden Ridge, Ste. 600
Irving, TX 75038
Phone: 214-492-6600
Fax: 214-492-6616
Web: www.laquinta.com

CEO: Francis W. Cash
CFO: David L. Rea
HR: Vito J. Stellato
Type: Public

2000 Sales: $822.8 million
1-Yr. Sales Change: (9.8%)
Employees: 7,500
FYE: December 31

Who doesn't favor a continental breakfast over hospital food? The La Quinta Companies (formerly The Meditrust Companies), perennially discouraged by Medicare cutbacks, has sold off the majority of its 300 US health care facilities, including nursing homes, hospitals, and medical offices, in order to focus on its more than 300 La Quinta Inns hotel properties. Enjoying a paired-share structure, the company consists of La Quinta Properties, a real estate investment trust (REIT) that owns the properties, and La Quinta Corp., which operates the properties. The REIT's lodging properties are concentrated in the southern and western US.

KEY COMPETITORS
Equity Inns
Shaner Hotel Group
Starwood Hotels & Resorts

LA QUINTA CORPORATION

909 Hidden Ridge, Ste. 600
Irving, TX 75038
Phone: 214-492-6600
Fax: 214-492-6971
Web: www.laquinta.com

CEO: Francis "Butch" Cash
CFO: David L. Rea
HR: Vito J. Stellato
Type: Business segment

2000 Sales: $595.0 million
1-Yr. Sales Change: (1.2%)
Employees: 7,500
FYE: December 31

Looking for a place to rest your weary traveling bones? La Quinta, the lodging division of paired share real estate investment trust The La Quinta Companies, might be your siesta solution. Scattered across 28 states, La Quinta's holdings include about 230 La Quinta Inns, which offer clean, reasonably priced rooms with amenities such as in-room coffee makers and complimentary breakfast. La Quinta's 70 La Quinta Inn & Suites offer two-room suites, fitness centers, courtyards, and spas. In an effort to expand its geographical base, the company has established a franchising program; it plans to open about 15 of these in the next year.

KEY COMPETITORS
Accor
Cendant
Choice Hotels

 See pages 132–133 for a full profile of this company.

LANCER CORPORATION

AMEX: LAN

6655 Lancer Blvd.
San Antonio, TX 78219
Phone: 210-310-7000
Fax: 210-310-7183
Web: www.lancercorp.com

CEO: George F. Schroeder
CFO: —
HR: Stephanie Eiden
Type: Public

2000 Sales: $113.5 million
1-Yr. Sales Change: (12.6%)
Employees: 1,452
FYE: December 31

"Make it a Coke," is music to Lancer Corporation, maker of fountain soft drink- and other drink-dispensing equipment for the food service and beverage industries. Products include mechanically cooled and ice-cooled soft drink- and citrus-dispensing systems, post-mix dispensing valves (which mix syrup and carbonated water), ice dispensers, beer dispensing systems, and related parts. In an agreement with Coca-Cola, Lancer makes various items specifically for Coke (about 25% of sales). Lancer FBD Partnership, a joint venture with the Frank family, makes frozen beverage dispensers. The US accounts for about 60% of sales. Co-founders and brothers Alfred Schroeder (chairman) and George Schroeder (CEO) own 27% of Lancer.

KEY COMPETITORS
Enodis
IMI
Manitowoc

LANDRY'S RESTAURANTS, INC.

NYSE: LNY

1400 Post Oak Blvd., Ste. 1010
Houston, TX 77056
Phone: 713-850-1010
Fax: 713-963-8194
Web: www.landrysseafood.com

CEO: Tilman J. Fertitta
CFO: Paul S. West
HR: Lisa Moore
Type: Public

2000 Sales: $521.0 million
1-Yr. Sales Change: 18.7%
Employees: 16,000
FYE: December 31

If "Yo ho ho and a gaggle of crabs" is your personal mantra, Landry's Restaurants (formerly Landry's Seafood Restaurants) is the company for you. Landry's operates about 190 restaurants in nearly 35 states. Trailing only Darden Restaurants' Red Lobster, the company is the nation's #2 operator of casual-dining seafood restaurants. Landry's primary restaurant chains include Landry's Seafood House, The Crab House, Joe's Crab Shack, and Rainforest Cafe (which it acquired in late 2000). It also owns a handful of restaurants under the Willie G's Oyster Bar and Cadillac Bar names. Entree prices range from about $10 to $20. Chairman and CEO Tilman Fertitta owns about 28% of the company.

KEY COMPETITORS
Brinker
Darden Restaurants
Metromedia

L.D. BRINKMAN AND CO.

1655 Waters Ridge Dr.
Lewisville, TX 75057
Phone: 972-353-3500
Fax: 972-353-3621
Web: www.ldbrinkman.com

CEO: Jeff Sills
CFO: Jack Wulz
HR: Buffy Upchurch
Type: Business segment

1999 Sales: $378.0 million
1-Yr. Sales Change: 13.2%
Employees: 1,550
FYE: December 31

L.D. Brinkman hopes to floor you. A division of carpet maker Beaulieu of America, Brinkman is a flooring maker and wholesale distributor. Its products include carpeting and wood, vinyl, and ceramic flooring, and it is a leading distributor of Pergo brand flooring. The company operates 39 distribution centers, primarily in the western US. It supports its retail outlet customers with merchandising, advertising, and other sales support services. L.D. Brinkman also sells its products through flooring industry associations such as independently owned Pro Flooring Centers, as well as through its FloorSource program that partners the company with various home builders.

KEY COMPETITORS
Armstrong Holdings
Mohawk Industries
Shaw Industries

LDB CORP.

444 Sidney Baker St. South	CEO: L. D. Brinkman	2000 Est. Sales: $120.0 mil.
Kerrville, TX 78028	CFO: Charlie Thomas	1-Yr. Sales Change: 0.0%
Phone: 830-257-2000	HR: —	Employees: 1,200
Fax: 830-257-2030	Type: Private	FYE: April 30

LDB Corp. wants you to have some family fun along with your pizza. Through its Mr. Gatti's Inc. subsidiary, LDB operates the Mr. Gatti's pizza restaurant chain with more than 200 locations in the US. Most of the units, which offer a variety of pizzas and Italian-style foods served in a family-friendly atmosphere, are franchised. The chain also incorporates a fun-center concept called GattiTown, featuring private meeting rooms, a video game arcade, carousels, and bumper cars. Lt. Col. James Eure opened the first Mr. Gatti's in 1969 in Austin, Texas. LDB, founded by carpet and cattle king L. D. Brinkman, bought the chain in 1978.

KEY COMPETITORS
Domino's Pizza
Papa John's
Pizza Hut

LENNOX INTERNATIONAL INC.

NYSE: LII

2140 Lake Park Blvd.	CEO: Robert E. Schjerven	2000 Sales: $3,247.4 million
Richardson, TX 75080	CFO: Richard A. Smith	1-Yr. Sales Change: 37.5%
Phone: 972-497-5000	HR: Jackie McClanahan	Employees: 24,000
Fax: 972-497-5299	Type: Public	FYE: December 31
Web: www.lennoxinternational.com		

Lennox's products are so cool they're hot — and vice versa. Lennox International makes commercial and residential air conditioning, furnace, and fireplace systems, as well as commercial refrigeration and heat transfer systems. Its brands include Armstrong Air, Ducane, and Lennox. Subsidiary Lennox Industries distributes the company's products in the US and Canada through independent dealers and more than 200 company-owned dealerships. Focused on expanding its retail operations, Lennox International also has interests and facilities in Australia, Europe, and South America. Named after inventor Dave Lennox, the company in 1904 was sold to newspaper publisher D.W. Norris, whose descendants still run and control Lennox.

KEY COMPETITORS
American Standard
United Technologies
York International

 See pages 134–135 for a full profile of this company.

LINCOLN PROPERTY COMPANY

Lincoln Plaza	CEO: Mack Pogue	2000 Sales: $1,251.0 million
Dallas, TX 75201	CFO: Nancy Davis	1-Yr. Sales Change: (14.4%)
Phone: 214-740-3300	HR: Luanne Hudson	Employees: 4,900
Fax: 214-740-3313	Type: Private	FYE: June 30
Web: www.lincolnproperty.com		

Lincoln Property is one of the US's largest diversified real estate companies — honest! Lincoln began by building apartments in the Dallas area, then expanded into commercial and retail projects. It now has residential properties comprising more than 140,000 units, and has developed about 140 million sq. ft. of commercial properties nationwide (still managing 90 million). The firm is divided into commercial and residential divisions, and offers management and investment services. It has a joint venture with Lend Lease to develop commercial property, and with Sam Zell's Equity Residential Properties to build apartments. Mack Pogue cofounded Lincoln in 1965 with Trammell Crow, whose stake Pogue bought out in 1977.

KEY COMPETITORS
JMB Realty
Tishman Realty
Trammell Crow Residential

LONE STAR TECHNOLOGIES, INC.

NYSE: LSS

15660 N. Dallas Pkwy., Ste. 500
Dallas, TX 75248
Phone: 972-770-6401
Fax: 972-770-6471
Web: www.lonestartech.com

CEO: Rhys J. Best
CFO: Charles J. Keszler
HR: James Wilson
Type: Public

2000 Sales: $645.3 million
1-Yr. Sales Change: 82.6%
Employees: 2,358
FYE: December 31

Lone Star Technologies, a holding company, owns Lone Star Steel Company, a maker of oil field, specialty tubing, and other tubular steel products. Oil field products, which account for 56% of sales, include casing (the structural retainer for oil and gas well walls), tubing, and line pipe (used to transfer oil and gas). Specialty tubing is used in high-pressure mechanical applications. Lone Star's Fintube subsidiary makes finned tubes for heat recovery at power generating plants. (The finned tubes convert exhaust heat into steam, which is used to generate additional electricity.) Anne and Robert Bass control 38% of the company.

KEY COMPETITORS
Maverick Tube
NS Group
Oregon Steel Mills

LOWER COLORADO RIVER AUTHORITY

3700 Lake Austin Blvd.
Austin, TX 78703
Phone: 512-473-3200
Fax: 512-473-3298
Web: www.lcra.org

CEO: Joseph J. Beal
CFO: John Meismer
HR: Karen Farabee
Type: Government-owned

2000 Sales: $537.6 million
1-Yr. Sales Change: 18.3%
Employees: 1,724
FYE: June 30

The stars at night are big and bright, but Texans in 58 counties still need electricity from the Lower Colorado River Authority (LCRA). The utility provides electricity to 44 wholesale customers, comprising 10 electric cooperatives and 33 towns, through the use of hydroelectric, gas, coal-fired, and wind-powered generators with a capacity of about 2,390 MW. Its 13 water and wastewater facilities provide services for 86,000 customers in seven counties. LCRA operates six dams and monitors the water quality of the resulting Highland Lakes. LCRA's revenues, about 90% of which are from electricity sales, provide funding for its parks program (40 recreation areas, an archaeological center, and a science laboratory).

KEY COMPETITORS
Austin Energy
Brazos Electric Power
TNP Enterprises

LUBY'S, INC.

NYSE: LUB

2211 NE Loop 410
San Antonio, TX 78265
Phone: 210-654-9000
Fax: 210-599-8407
Web: www.lubys.com

CEO: Christopher J. Pappas
CFO: Ernest Pekmezaris
HR: Wayne R. Shirley
Type: Public

2000 Sales: $493 million
1-Yr. Sales Change: (1.8%)
Employees: 14,000
FYE: August 31

When Mom wants a salad, Dad craves fried chicken, and little Johnny is screaming for enchiladas, what's an all-American family to do? A simple trip to the cafeteria line at Luby's may do the trick. Luby's has about 220 cafeteria-style restaurants across 10 states (about three-quarters are in Texas). Each restaurant serves 12-14 entrees, 15-20 salads, 12-14 vegetable dishes, and 18-20 desserts. The restaurants are expanding their take-out offerings (13% of sales), with about 65 Luby's restaurants now featuring pick-up service. The deeply troubled company has brought in new management with money to invest to try and cope with a major slump in its revenues and stock price, as well as the default on its credit.

KEY COMPETITORS
Buffets
Furr's
Piccadilly Cafeterias

📖 See pages 136–137 for a full profile of this company.

LUFKIN INDUSTRIES, INC.

Nasdaq: LUFK

601 S. Raguet
Lufkin, TX 75901
Phone: 936-634-2211
Fax: 936-637-5474
Web: www.lufkin.com

CEO: Douglas V. Smith
CFO: R. D. Leslie
HR: Paul G. Perez
Type: Public

2000 Sales: $254.6 million
1-Yr. Sales Change: 5.0%
Employees: 2,000
FYE: December 31

Lufkin takes the oil industry to heart. Lufkin Industries makes oil-field pumps (nearly 40% of sales), power-transmission equipment (about 25% of sales), highway trailers, and foundry castings. Its oil-field pumps are its primary export products used primarily for underground pumping. Lufkin's trailer products include vans, platforms, dump trailers, and high-capacity trailers for over-the-road use. Lufkin's power-transmission equipment division provides industrial and manufacturing customers with gears up to 16 feet in diameter and weigh up to 250 tons. The company also makes custom-designed iron castings for OEMs. The US accounts for about 75% of sales.

KEY COMPETITORS
Atchison Casting
Tuthill
Utility Trailer

LUMINANT WORLDWIDE CORPORATION

Nasdaq: LUMT

13737 Noel Rd.
Dallas, TX 75240
Phone: 972-581-7000
Fax: 972-581-7002
Web: www.luminant.com

CEO: James R. Corey
CFO: Thomas G. Bevivino
HR: —
Type: Public

2000 Sales: $134.6 million
1-Yr. Sales Change: 158.3%
Employees: 648
FYE: December 31

Luminant Worldwide is lighting the path to cyberspace. Formerly Clarant Worldwide, the company develops online applications and Web sites for its blue chip clients, including Compaq, Enron, and MasterCard. Luminant also offers consulting and marketing services, as well as ongoing Web site maintenance and data analysis. The company was founded in 1998 and quickly gained size through the acquisition of eight e-services companies, including Brand Dialogue-New York (which had been part of advertising firm Young & Rubicam). Luminant has offices in 10 states and Washington, DC. Young & Rubicam owns about 27% of the company.

KEY COMPETITORS
Digitas
Sapient
Scient

LYONDELL CHEMICAL COMPANY

NYSE: LYO

1221 McKinney St., Ste. 700
Houston, TX 77010
Phone: 713-652-7200
Fax: 713-309-2074
Web: www.lyondell.com

CEO: Dan F. Smith
CFO: Robert T. Blakely
HR: John A. Hollinshead
Type: Public

2000 Sales: $4,036.0 million
1-Yr. Sales Change: 9.3%
Employees: 8,900
FYE: December 31

Quick with a reaction, Lyondell Chemical makes polymers and petrochemicals, mainly through its 41% stake in Equistar Chemicals. Lyondell is a leading producer of polymer polyethylene and petrochemicals ethylene and propylene. Its polymers are used in synthetic and plastic trash bags, containers, and sports equipment. Lyondell also produces aromatics (benzene, toluene), fuel additives, and specialty chemicals. Lyondell Chemical (formerly ARCO Chemical) is the world's top producer of propylene oxide, a coatings and adhesives intermediate. Lyondell refines petroleum products (gasoline, jet fuel, motor oil) through a joint venture with CITGO Petroleum, a subsidiary of Petróleos de Venezuela.

KEY COMPETITORS
BASF AG
Dow Chemical
Royal Dutch/Shell

📖 See pages 138–139 for a full profile of this company.

MAGNUM HUNTER RESOURCES, INC.

AMEX: MHR

600 E. Las Colinas Blvd., Ste. 1100
Irving, TX 75039
Phone: 972-401-0752
Fax: 972-401-3110
Web: www.magnumhunter.com

CEO: Gary C. Evans
CFO: Chris Tong
HR: Annette Martinez
Type: Public

2000 Sales: $127.5 million
1-Yr. Sales Change: 83.2%
Employees: 95
FYE: December 31

It's always open season on oil and gas for Magnum Hunter Resources. The independent exploration and production company has proved reserves of 367 billion cu. ft. of natural gas equivalent (74% is natural gas) in the midcontinent, Permian Basin, and onshore and offshore Gulf of Mexico (where it partners with Remington Oil and Gas and Wiser Oil). It owns interests in 3,000 producing wells. In addition, Magnum Hunter owns more than 480 miles of gas gathering systems and a half interest in three gas processing facilities. The company markets gas in the western US through 30%-owned NGTS and provides oil field services through subsidiary Gruy Petroleum Management. Natural gas distributor ONEOK owns 22% of Magnum Hunter.

KEY COMPETITORS
Anadarko Petroleum
ChevronTexaco
Kerr-McGee

MANNATECH, INCORPORATED

Nasdaq: MTEX

600 S. Royal Ln., Ste. 200
Coppell, TX 75019
Phone: 972-471-7400
Fax: 972-471-8135
Web: www.mannatech.com

CEO: Robert M. Henry
CFO: Stephen D. Fenstermacher
HR: Gwendolyn J. Pennington
Type: Public

2000 Sales: $150.0 million
1-Yr. Sales Change: (16.5%)
Employees: 304
FYE: December 31

Mannatech develops and sells nutritional supplements and topical products in Australia, Canada, Japan, the UK, and the US through a network more than 235,000 independent salespeople. The company's products, made by third-party manufacturers, are based on Ambrotose, a proprietary carbohydrate that improves cell-to-cell communication; products are targeted for dermal care, sports performance, and support of the immune, endocrine, and intestinal systems. Chairman Charles Fioretti owns about 19% of the company; co-founder and "global vision architect" Sam Caster owns almost a fourth. Mannatech has terminated the operations of its Internet Health Group subsidiary.

KEY COMPETITORS
GNC
Twinlab
Weider Nutrition International

MARKETING SPECIALISTS CORPORATION

OTC: MKSP

17855 N. Dallas Pkwy., Ste. 200
Dallas, TX 75287
Phone: 972-349-6200
Fax: 972-349-6400

CEO: Gerald R. Leonard
CFO: Timothy M. Byrd
HR: Brad Kimball
Type: Public

2000 Sales: $380.8 million
1-Yr. Sales Change: 31.0%
Employees: 5,800
FYE: December 31

Marketing Specialists Corporation (MSC) wants to be a vital link in the food chain. The company provides sales, marketing, and merchandising services to food manufacturers, producers, and suppliers. It has 76 offices in 37 US states and earns commissions based upon its sales to traditional and electronic retailers. MSC was formed from the 1999 merger of food brokerage firm Merkert American (which was swimming in debt) and consumer products marketer Richmont Marketing Specialists. Former director James Monroe's lawsuit, for $2.5 million in advisory fees, was settled, and MS Acquisition now owns about 82% of the company. The financially strapped firm has dismissed its staff and filed for Chapter 11 bankruptcy protection.

KEY COMPETITORS
Acosta-PMI
Advantage Sales and Marketing
Crossmark

MARY KAY INC.

16251 Dallas Pkwy.	CEO: Richard Rogers	2000 Sales: $1,200.0 million
Addison, TX 75001	CFO: David Holl	1-Yr. Sales Change: 20.0%
Phone: 972-687-6300	HR: Darrell Overcash	Employees: 3,600
Fax: 972-687-1609	Type: Private	FYE: December 31
Web: www.marykay.com		

Mary Kay is in the pink (and in Avon's shadow) as the US's #2 direct seller of beauty products. It sells more than 200 products in eight product categories: facial skin care, cosmetics, fragrances, nutritional supplements, sun protection, nail care, body care, and men's skin care. Some 800,000 direct-sales consultants demonstrate Mary Kay products in the US (80% of sales) and about 35 other countries. Consultants vie for prizes such as the use of cars (including pink Cadillacs, first given in 1969, and white sport utility vehicles, added in 1998). Mary Kay has a mostly female workforce, although it does employ some men (such as its chairman/CEO and CFO). Founder Mary Kay Ash passed away in November 2001; her family owns most of the company.

KEY COMPETITORS
Alticor
Avon
L'Oréal

 See pages 140–141 for a full profile of this company.

MATTRESS GIANT CORPORATION

14665 Midway Rd., Ste. 100	CEO: Phil Lang	2000 Sales: $178.0 million
Addison, TX 75001	CFO: Pat McColpin	1-Yr. Sales Change: 15.6%
Phone: 972-392-2208	HR: Katrina Tiner	Employees: 900
Fax: 972-392-7308	Type: Private	FYE: December 31
Web: www.mattressgiant.com		

A good bedtime story might include Mattress Giant. The company has more than 200 bedding stores in a dozen states. Most of Mattress Giant's stores are in or around big cities, including Boston, Chicago, Dallas, Houston, Miami, and Philadelphia. Mattress Giant stores sell mattresses, futons, daybeds, headboards, pillows, and other sleep-related products. The company stocks major US brands such as Simmons, Serta, and Spring Air. Mattress Giant also sells mattresses directly through the Internet and by phone (1-800-GIANT-BED). Chairman and CEO Phil Lang founded the company with his brother in 1992; Lang, other officers, and investment firms own Mattress Giant.

KEY COMPETITORS
Dial-A-Mattress
J. C. Penney
Sears

MAXXAM INC.

AMEX: MXM

5847 San Felipe, Ste. 2600	CEO: Charles E. Hurwitz	2000 Sales: $2,448.0 million
Houston, TX 77057	CFO: Paul N. Schwartz	1-Yr. Sales Change: 5.9%
Phone: 713-975-7600	HR: Diane M. Dudley	Employees: 11,560
Fax: 713-267-3701	Type: Public	FYE: December 31

The holding company run by corporate raider Charles Hurwitz, MAXXAM deals in worldwide aluminum mining and production, timber products, real estate investment, and horse racing. MAXXAM's top revenue source is its 63% interest in Kaiser Aluminum, which accounts for about 90% of sales. MAXXAM's timber subsidiary, Pacific Lumber, owns about 220,000 acres of old-growth redwood and Douglas fir timberlands in Humboldt County, California. MAXXAM's real estate interests include commercial and residential properties in Arizona, California, and Texas, and the Puerto Rican resort Palmas del Mar. The company also has a 99% stake in the Sam Houston Race Park, a horse-racing track near Houston. Hurwitz controls about 73% of MAXXAM.

KEY COMPETITORS
Alcan
Alcoa
International Paper

See pages 142–143 for a full profile of this company.

MCCOY CORPORATION

1200 IH-35 North
San Marcos, TX 78666
Phone: 512-353-5400
Fax: 512-395-6608
Web: www.mccoys.com

CEO: Brian McCoy
CFO: Chuck Churchwell
HR: Tammy McCarty
Type: Private

2000 Sales: $467.0 million
1-Yr. Sales Change: (7.3%)
Employees: 2,500
FYE: December 31

Even though it's battling building supply retail leaders The Home Depot and
Lowe's, McCoy still has time for a day off. The company owns and operates
about 100 McCoy's Building Supply Centers located primarily in Texas, but
also in Arkansas, Louisiana, Mississippi, New Mexico, and Oklahoma. McCoy's
locations adhere to the retailer's steadfast tradition of keeping stores closed on
Sundays. In addition, McCoy is an affiliate of the TruServ hardware cooperative. In 2001 Mike McCoy and his sister Brenda sold their interest in the business to their brother Brian. Their grandfather, Frank, founded a roofing
company in 1923, which their father, Emmett, combined with McCoy Supply
to form the current company.

KEY COMPETITORS
Ace Hardware
Home Depot
Lowe's

MCLANE COMPANY, INC.

4747 McLane Pkwy.
Temple, TX 76504
Phone: 254-771-7500
Fax: 254-771-7244
Web: www.mclaneco.com

CEO: W. Grady Rosier
CFO: Kevin J. Koch
HR: Stuart Schoppert
Type: Subsidiary

2001 Sales: $10,542.0 million
1-Yr. Sales Change: 20.3%
Employees: 16,120
FYE: January 31

You'll find McLane driving in about every lane in the US. The wholesale distributor hauls food and nonfood (tobacco, general merchandise, and toys)
products to Wal-Mart stores, and it is the largest supplier to convenience
stores nationwide (including 7-Eleven stores). The company also distributes
merchandise to theaters and drugstores and has expanded its fast-food distribution network to more than 20,000 restaurants since purchasing the US operations of AmeriServe Food Distribution (now McLane Foodservice). McLane
also offers retailers its own line of private-label products and various support
services, and it provides logistics services in Brazil and Taiwan. Wal-Mart
bought McLane, founded in 1894, in 1990.

KEY COMPETITORS
Core-Mark
GSC Enterprises
H.T. Hackney

MEMORIAL HERMANN HEALTHCARE SYSTEM

7737 Southwest Fwy., Ste. 200
Houston, TX 77074
Phone: 713-448-5525
Fax: 713-448-5540
Web: www.mhcs.org

CEO: Dan S. Wilford
CFO: Carrol Aulbaugh
HR: Doug Veckstett
Type: Not-for-profit

1998 Sales: $1,003.2 million
1-Yr. Sales Change: (16.4%)
Employees: 12,000
FYE: June 30

Memorial Hermann Healthcare System is a "munster" of an organization.
Houston's largest not-for-profit health care system includes about a dozen
hospitals (one is a children's hospital), two long-term nursing facilities, and a
retirement community. Through Memorial Hermann Regional Healthcare
Services, the company is also affiliated with 16 community hospitals.
Subsidiaries include home health care agency Memorial Hermann Home
Health and physician practice company Memorial Hermann Health Network
Providers. The company's Memorial Hermann Family Practice Residency
Program is affiliated with the University of Texas-Houston Medical School.
The organization was formed by the 1997 merger of two smaller systems.

KEY COMPETITORS
CHRISTUS Health
HCA
Tenet Healthcare

THE MEN'S WEARHOUSE, INC.

NYSE: MW

5803 Glenmont Dr.	CEO: George Zimmer	2001 Sales: $1,333.5 million
Houston, TX 77081	CFO: Neill P. Davis	1-Yr. Sales Change: 12.4%
Phone: 713-592-7200	HR: Joe Vera	Employees: 12,000
Fax: 713-664-1957	Type: Public	FYE: January 31
Web: www.menswearhouse.com		

CEO George "I guarantee it" Zimmer can afford to loosen his tie — The Men's Wearhouse is one of the largest retailers of men's business attire in the US. The outfit has more than 650 stores, including about 110 Moores outlets in Canada. Its primary operation is Men's Wearhouse, which has about 470 stores (mostly in strip malls) in more than 40 states and Washington, DC. The chain sells tailored suits priced 20% to 30% less than competitors, as well as shoes, formal wear, and casual clothes. The company's K&G Men's Center subsidiary (about 60 superstores) and its Suit Warehouse chain (five stores) sell clothes for even less. The founding Zimmer family owns about 16% of The Men's Wearhouse.

KEY COMPETITORS
Brooks Brothers
Federated
Jos. A. Bank

 See pages 144–145 for a full profile of this company.

THE MERIDIAN RESOURCE CORPORATION

NYSE: TMR

1401 Enclave Pkwy., Ste. 300	CEO: Joseph A. Reeves Jr.	2000 Sales: $223.4 million
Houston, TX 77077	CFO: —	1-Yr. Sales Change: 68.5%
Phone: 281-597-7000	HR: —	Employees: 163
Fax: 281-558-5595	Type: Public	FYE: December 31
Web: www.tmrc.com		

Locating oil and gas requires a little latitude, so Meridian Resource uses 3-D seismic technology to improve its success rate. The exploration and development company focuses on the Gulf Coast and Gulf of Mexico; it has proved reserves of 306 billion cu. ft. of natural gas equivalent, about 56% of which is natural gas. Meridian Resource moved into the Gulf when it bought Cairn Energy USA and has beefed up its Gulf Coast holdings by buying almost all of Shell Oil's southern Louisiana exploration properties. The company bought back shares from Shell in 2001, reducing Shell's stake in Meridian Resource from 40% to about 15%.

KEY COMPETITORS
BP
ChevronTexaco
Exxon Mobil

METALS USA, INC.

NYSE: MUI

3 Riverway, Ste. 600	CEO: J. Michael Kirksey	2000 Sales: $2,021.6 million
Houston, TX 77056	CFO: Terry L. Freeman	1-Yr. Sales Change: 15.8%
Phone: 713-965-0990	HR: Jon P. McNaught	Employees: 4,700
Fax: 713-965-0067	Type: Public	FYE: December 31
Web: www.metalsusa.com		

Metals USA is riveting together the consolidation of the US metals-processing industry. The company operates in four sectors: heavy carbon (wide-flange beams, plate, and structural steel), flat-rolled steel (alloyed steel and steel-processing services), specialty metals (stainless steel, brass, and copper), and aluminum building products (finished products such as awnings). Clients include aerospace manufacturers, furniture makers, and the electrical equipment industry. Metals USA maintains operations primarily in the US mid-Atlantic and Southeast.

KEY COMPETITORS
Commercial Metals
Ryerson Tull
Worthington Industries

 See pages 146–147 for a full profile of this company.

METASOLV, INC.

Nasdaq: MSLV

5560 Tennyson Pkwy.
Plano, TX 75024
Phone: 972-403-8300
Fax: 972-403-8333
Web: www.metasolv.com

CEO: James P. Janicki
CFO: Glenn A. Etherington
HR: Julie Black
Type: Public

2000 Sales: $131.9 million
1-Yr. Sales Change: 80.7%
Employees: 574
FYE: December 31

MetaSolv hopes to provide solutions for all your telecommunication needs. Through its subsidiary MetaSolv Software, the company provides software and services which telephone and Internet service providers use to fulfill customer requests for telecommunications services, including order processing, customer relationship management, network inventory and design, and troubleshooting. MetaSolv's customers include Allegiance Telecom, Cox Communications, Reliant Energy, and Qwest Communications. The company has offices in Europe and the US, and continues to nurture partnerships with systems integrators to expand its global presence. Technology venture capital firm Austin Ventures owns 16% of MetaSolv.

KEY COMPETITORS
Amdocs
Eftia OSS Solutions
Telcordia Technologies

METHODIST HEALTH CARE SYSTEM

6565 Fannin St.
Houston, TX 77030
Phone: 713-790-3333
Fax: 713-790-4885
Web: www.methodisthealth.com

CEO: Peter Butler
CFO: Albert Zimmerli
HR: Donald T. Benson
Type: Not-for-profit

2000 Sales: $795.0 million
1-Yr. Sales Change: 31.3%
Employees: 8,100
FYE: December 31

Methodist Health Care System owns and operates several Houston-area hospitals, including Methodist Hospital, San Jacinto Methodist Hospital, Methodist Diagnostic Hospital, and Methodist Health Center-Sugar Land. Flagship Methodist Hospital is known for innovations in urology and neurosurgery, among other specialties, and is Baylor College of Medicine's teaching facility. Methodist Health Care's health care plan, MethodistCare, offers HMO, PPO, and point-of-service options; its Visiting Nurse Association provides home health services. The not-for-profit system, which was founded in 1919, has about 1,900 beds and also operates in Latin America, Saudi Arabia, and Turkey.

KEY COMPETITORS
Harris County Hospital
Memorial Hermann Healthcare
St. Luke's

MICHAELS STORES, INC.

Nasdaq: MIKE

8000 Bent Branch Dr.
Irving, TX 75063
Phone: 972-409-1300
Fax: 972-409-1556
Web: www.michaels.com

CEO: R. Michael Rouleau
CFO: Bryan M. DeCordova
HR: Sue Elliott
Type: Public

2001 Sales: $2,249.4 million
1-Yr. Sales Change: 19.5%
Employees: 33,000
FYE: January 31

You can always count on Michaels for a good yarn. The nation's #1 arts and crafts retailer operates about 600 Michaels Stores canvassing the US, Canada, and Puerto Rico. Michaels stores sell silk and dried flowers, art and hobby supplies, frames, needlecraft kits — virtually everything an artist, decorator, or hobbyist needs. Employees hold workshops and teach classes on crafts to generate interest and boost sales. Michaels also operates a frame-making division and about 110 Aaron Brothers stores, primarily on the West Coast, that provide framing and art supplies. The company also sells prints and posters on its Web site.

KEY COMPETITORS
Hobby Lobby
Jo-Ann Stores
Wal-Mart

 See pages 148–149 for a full profile of this company.

THE MINUTE MAID COMPANY

2000 St. James Place
Houston, TX 77252
Phone: 713-888-5000
Fax: —
Web: www.minutemaid.com

CEO: Donald R. Knauss
CFO: Tom Hensler
HR: Michelle Beale
Type: Subsidiary

2000 Sales: $2,200.0 million
1-Yr. Sales Change: —
Employees: 2,500
FYE: December 31

In the juice business, The Minute Maid Company comes in second. It makes juice products under the Minute Maid, Hi-C, and FIVE ALIVE names, among others. A unit of The Coca-Cola Company, Minute Maid dominates the frozen juice and ready-to-drink from concentrate markets. The popularity of not-from-concentrate juice (archrival Tropicana Products' forte) has cost it market share: Tropicana (owned by PepsiCo) controls about 43% of the US market, while Minute Maid commands 20%. In response, Minute Maid is forming the Simply Orange Juice Company, which will make not-from-concentrate juice. Purchased by Coca-Cola in 1960, Minute Maid is part of Coca-Cola's joint venture with Procter & Gamble (maker of Sunny Delight).

KEY COMPETITORS
Louis Dreyfus Citrus
Tropicana Products
Vitality Beverages, Inc.

MINYARD FOOD STORES, INC.

777 Freeport Pkwy.
Coppell, TX 75019
Phone: 972-393-8700
Fax: 972-462-9407
Web: www.minyards.com

CEO: Gretchen Minyard Williams
CFO: Mario J. LaForte
HR: Alan Vaughan
Type: Private

2000 Est. Sales: $1,000.0 mil.
1-Yr. Sales Change: (7.0%)
Employees: 7,155
FYE: June 30

Everything's bigger in Texas, including regional grocery chains such as Minyard Food Stores. Its nearly 85 supermarkets are located primarily in the Dallas/Fort Worth area, where it has a 13% market share. Almost half are conventional supermarkets that operate under the Minyard Food Stores name. The rest include Sack 'n Save warehouse stores (low-cost shopping with customers bagging their own groceries), and Carnival Food Stores, which stock more ethnic products. Minyard also owns eight gas stations. The Minyard family started the company in 1932 with one East Dallas neighborhood grocery. It is among the largest US private companies owned and run by women: sisters Elizabeth Minyard and Gretchen Minyard Williams.

KEY COMPETITORS
Albertson's
Kroger
Randall's

MITCHELL ENERGY & DEVELOPMENT CORP.

NYSE: MND

2001 Timberloch Place
The Woodlands, TX 77380
Phone: 713-377-5500
Fax: 713-377-5680
Web: www.mitchellenergy.com

CEO: George P. Mitchell
CFO: Philip S. Smith
HR: Clyde Black
Type: Public

2000 Sales: $1,672.1 million
1-Yr. Sales Change: 79.0%
Employees: 875
FYE: December 31

This former Texas wildcatter now runs with the big dogs. Mitchell Energy & Development explores for and processes oil and gas and gathers, processes, and markets natural gas and natural gas liquids (NGLs). The company, which operates mainly in Texas, has proved reserves of 1.5 trillion cu. ft. of natural gas and 210 million barrels of NGLs. Mitchell Energy also owns or has interests in 8,800 miles of gas gathering pipelines and six gas processing plants, and it's one of the largest US producers of NGLs at more than 50,000 barrels per day. The company is 51%-owned by CEO George Mitchell and his wife.

KEY COMPETITORS
Chesapeake Energy
Enron
Exxon Mobil

See pages 150–151 for a full profile of this company.

MMI PRODUCTS, INC.

515 W. Greens Rd., Ste. 710	CEO: Ronald R. Ross	2000 Sales: $530.4 million
Houston, TX 77067	CFO: Robert N. Tewczar	1-Yr. Sales Change: 10.4%
Phone: 281-876-0080	HR: Gary Hoffpauir	Employees: 2,590
Fax: 281-876-1648	Type: Private	FYE: December 31
Web: www.merchantsmetals.com		

MMI Products wants to fence you in. MMI operates in two segments: fencing products (56% of sales) and concrete construction products (44%). The company's fencing products include residential and commercial chain-link security fencing, aluminum and die-cast galvanized steel fencing fittings, and ornamental iron fence products. MMI sells its fencing products primarily to fence wholesalers and residential and commercial contractors. The company's concrete construction products include wire mesh and other products used to install reinforcing bars and grids. These products have applications in the construction of concrete pipe, bridges, and roads. Chairman Julius Burns controls 26% of MMI; Citicorp Venture Capital, about 38%.

KEY COMPETITORS
Associated Materials
Dayton Superior
Insteel

MONARCH DENTAL CORPORATION
Nasdaq (SC): MDDS

4201 Spring Valley Rd., Ste. 320	CEO: W. Barger Tygart	2000 Sales: $211.3 million
Dallas, TX 75244	CFO: Lisa K. Peterson	1-Yr. Sales Change: 3.5%
Phone: 972-702-7446	HR: Mary Preston	Employees: 2,100
Fax: 972-702-0824	Type: Public	FYE: December 31
Web: www.monarchdental.com		

Open wide and say, "Monarch." Monarch Dental manages almost 200 dental practice offices in 14 states. The practices offer general dentistry and such specialty services as orthodontics, oral surgery, endodontics, periodontics, and pediatric dentistry. The company handles marketing, staff recruiting, scheduling and follow-ups through call centers and individual offices, and bulk purchases of dental and other supplies for its offices. Monarch also maintains patient information, practitioner schedules, insurance information, clinical records, and billing information at the individual offices.

KEY COMPETITORS
Castle Dental
InterDent
Orthodontic Centers of America

MOTIVA ENTERPRISES LLC

1100 Louisiana St.	CEO: Roger L. Ebert	2000 Sales: $19,446.0 million
Houston, TX 77002	CFO: William M. Kaparich	1-Yr. Sales Change: 59.4%
Phone: 713-277-8000	HR: Bruce Culpepper	Employees: 8,000
Fax: 713-277-7856	Type: Joint venture	FYE: December 31
Web: www.equilonmotivaequiva.com		

Motiva Enterprises mainstreams downstream operations for three oil giants. The company was formed in 1998 to combine the eastern and southeastern US refining and marketing businesses of Texaco, Shell Oil, and Saudi Aramco. (Star Enterprise, Texaco and Saudi Aramco's joint venture, was absorbed by the new company.) Motiva, which together with another Texaco-Shell joint venture — Equilon (western US) — forms the #1 US gasoline retailer, operates about 14,600 Shell and Texaco outlets. Motiva operates three refineries on the Gulf Coast and one in Delaware, with a total refining capacity of 850,000 barrels a day. Shell Oil owns 35% of the company, and Texaco and Saudi Aramco's Saudi Refining each own 32.5%.

KEY COMPETITORS
7-Eleven
BP
Exxon Mobil

 See pages 152–153 for a full profile of this company.

MULTIMEDIA GAMES, INC.

Nasdaq: MGAM

8900 Shoal Creek Blvd.
Austin, TX 78757
Phone: 512-371-7100
Fax: 512-371-7114
Web: www.multimediagames.com

CEO: Gordon T. Graves
CFO: Craig Nouis
HR: —
Type: Public

2000 Sales: $96.8 million
1-Yr. Sales Change: 8.9%
Employees: 152
FYE: September 30

B-I-N-G-O spells M-O-N-E-Y for Multimedia Games. The company provides electronic bingo games for the Indian gaming industry in the US. Its MegaMania is a high-speed bingo game transmitted to independently owned reservation bingo halls, allowing bingo players to compete against each other for the same jackpot. Multimedia Games provides bingo games to some 80 reservation bingo halls in seven states and Washington, DC. Other products include MegaBingo and MegaCash (live TV bingo game shows that are transmitted via satellite to players at reservation bingo halls). Multimedia Games also owns a 30% interest in Gamebay.com, an Internet sweepstakes site. Chairman and CEO Gordon Graves owns about 20% of the company.

KEY COMPETITORS
GameTech
Littlefield
Online Gaming Systems

NABORS INDUSTRIES, INC.

AMEX: NBR

515 W. Greens Rd., Ste. 1200
Houston, TX 77067
Phone: 281-874-0035
Fax: 281-872-5205
Web: www.nabors.com

CEO: Anthony G. Petrello
CFO: Bruce P. Koch
HR: Bertha Gonzales
Type: Public

2000 Sales: $1,327.1 million
1-Yr. Sales Change: 106.6%
Employees: 17,980
FYE: December 31

Oil and gas exploration and production companies need a little help in order to ply their trade all around the globe, and like a good neighbor, Nabors Industries, one of the world's largest drilling contractors, is there for them. Overall the company has about 500 land drilling rigs and about 740 land workover rigs. Its offshore equipment includes 43 platform rigs, 15 jack-ups, and three barge drilling rigs; it also operates 30 ships. Besides drilling, Nabors also provides oil field hauling, engineering, and construction services. Key markets for Nabors and its subsidiaries include the US, Canada, Mexico, Oman, and Saudi Arabia.

KEY COMPETITORS
Global Marine
Patterson-UTI Energy
Pride International

NATCO GROUP INC.

NYSE: NTG

2950 North Loop West, Ste. 700
Houston, TX 77092
Phone: 713-683-9292
Fax: 713-683-6768
Web: www.natcogroup.com

CEO: Nathaniel A. Gregory
CFO: J. Michael Mayer
HR: David Walker
Type: Public

2000 Sales: $224.6 million
1-Yr. Sales Change: 32.2%
Employees: 1,411
FYE: December 31

Looking to oil flow for its cash flow, NATCO Group provides the oil and gas industry with wellhead equipment, systems, and services. The company's products are used in onshore and offshore oil and gas fields throughout the world. NATCO Group's products include equipment to separate hydrocarbon streams into oil, gas, and water; dehydration and desalting units; heaters to prevent solids from forming in gas and to reduce the viscosity of oil; gas conditioning equipment; water filtration systems; and production equipment control systems. The company designs, builds, installs, and services its equipment.

KEY COMPETITORS
Baker Hughes
FMC

NATIONAL INSTRUMENTS CORPORATION

Nasdaq: NATI

11500 N. Mopac Expwy.
Austin, TX 78759
Phone: 512-338-9119
Fax: 512-794-5794
Web: www.ni.com

CEO: James J. Truchard
CFO: Alexander M. Davern
HR: Mark A. Finger
Type: Public

2000 Sales: $410.1 million
1-Yr. Sales Change: 24.4%
Employees: 2,511
FYE: December 31

National Instruments turns a PC's mouse into a lab rat. The company's instrumentation hardware and graphical software convert standard PCs into industrial automation and test and measurement systems. The systems, known as "virtual instruments," are used to observe, measure, and control electrical signals and physical attributes such as voltage, temperature, pressure, and speed. Customers outside North America account for nearly half of sales. National Instruments stresses innovation, and continues to increase its research and development budget to expand its product lines. Chairman and CEO James Truchard, one of National Instruments' founders, owns 26% of the company.

KEY COMPETITORS
Agilent Technologies
Danaher
Keithley Instruments

 See pages 154–155 for a full profile of this company.

NATIONAL WESTERN LIFE INSURANCE COMPANY

Nasdaq: NWLIA

850 E. Anderson Ln.
Austin, TX 78752
Phone: 512-836-1010
Fax: 512-835-2729
Web: www.nationalwesternlife.com

CEO: Robert L. Moody
CFO: Robert L. Busby III
HR: Carol Jackson
Type: Public

2000 Sales: $292.7 million
1-Yr. Sales Change: (16.7%)
Employees: 228
FYE: December 31

National Western Life Insurance Company (NWLI) sells annuities as well as individual, whole, universal, and term life insurance. Almost 70% of its direct life insurance premiums come from outside the US, where the company targets wealthy Latin Americans. NWLI also offers real estate management services through its Westcap subsidiary. This unit was formerly a broker/dealer operation which had entered Chapter 11 bankruptcy in response to several large suits over its sale of derivative products hard hit by the 1994 bond crash. Chairman and CEO Robert Moody and his son Ross, members of the wealthy Moody family of Galveston, Texas, own about 35% of the company, and they own an agency that does business with the company.

KEY COMPETITORS
AIG
AmerUs
Hartford

NATIONAL-OILWELL, INC.

NYSE: NOI

10000 Richmond Ave.
Houston, TX 77042
Phone: 713-346-7500
Fax: 713-435-2195
Web: www.natoil.com

CEO: Joel V. Staff
CFO: Steven W. Krablin
HR: Vicky Despeaux
Type: Public

2000 Sales: $1,149.9 million
1-Yr. Sales Change: 54.3%
Employees: 5,000
FYE: December 31

National-Oilwell is the tool man of the oil patch. The company produces and distributes oil and natural gas drilling equipment for both land and offshore drilling rigs. Its mechanical components include drawworks, mud pumps, rotary tables, SCR houses, top drives, and traveling equipment. Other products include masts, derricks, substructures, and pedestal cranes. National-Oilwell operates 130 distribution service centers worldwide that sell National-Oilwell products as well as other companies' fittings, spare parts, tools, and valves. The company also services its oil field equipment. National-Oilwell has acquired oil field equipment maker IRI International, whose brands include Cardwell, Franks, Ideco, and IRI.

KEY COMPETITORS
Bechtel
Halliburton
Schlumberger

NCH CORPORATION

NYSE: NCH

2727 Chemsearch Blvd.	CEO: Irvin L. Levy	2001 Sales: $679.7 million
Irving, TX 75062	CFO: Tom F. Hetzer	1-Yr. Sales Change: (6.7%)
Phone: 972-438-0211	HR: Neil Thomas	Employees: 8,404
Fax: 972-438-0186	Type: Public	FYE: April 30
Web: www.nch.com		

NCH Corporation is a clean, mean, well-oiled machine. The company makes maintenance, repair, and supply products, which it markets through its sales force to customers in more than 60 countries worldwide. Specialty chemicals (56% of sales) include lubricants, cleaning agents, deodorizers, water treatments, and oil field production chemicals. Through its numerous subsidiaries and divisions, NCH also markets direct broadcast satellite equipment, fasteners, welding alloys, plumbing and electrical supplies, and first-aid supplies. Founder Milton Levy's descendants — including his son Irvin (chairman and president) — control NCH.

KEY COMPETITORS
Cintas
Hughes Supply
National Service Industries

NCI BUILDING SYSTEMS, INC.

NYSE: NCS

10943 N. Sam Houston Pkwy. West	CEO: Johnie Schulte Jr.	2000 Sales: $1,018.3 million
Houston, TX 77064	CFO: Robert J. Medlock	1-Yr. Sales Change: 8.7%
Phone: 281-897-7788	HR: Donnie R. Humphries	Employees: 4,250
Fax: 281-477-9647	Type: Public	FYE: October 31
Web: www.ncilp.com		

NCI Building Systems isn't afraid of the big bad wolf. NCI makes engineered metal building systems and metal building components such as overhead doors, roofs, and trim, which it designs for commercial, industrial, agricultural, civic, and residential uses. The company's engineered building systems products include brands A&S Building Systems and Mid-West Steel Building; its brands of metal-building components include DOUBLECOTE and American Building Components. NCI also provides metal-coating and paint products. The company operates about 40 manufacturing and distribution facilities in 18 states in the US and in Mexico.

KEY COMPETITORS
American Buildings
Butler Manufacturing
LTV

THE NEIMAN MARCUS GROUP, INC.

NYSE: NMG

1618 Main St.	CEO: Burton M. Tansky	2001 Sales: $3,015.5 million
Dallas, TX 75201	CFO: James E. Skinner	1-Yr. Sales Change: 5.6%
Phone: 214-741-6911	HR: Marita O'Dea	Employees: 15,400
Fax: 214-573-6142	Type: Public	FYE: July 31
Web: www.neimanmarcus.com		

Not for the faint of finances, Neiman Marcus department stores offer high-fashion, high-quality women's and men's apparel, accessories, fine jewelry, china, crystal, silver, and gourmet foods. The Neiman Marcus Group operates 31 Neiman Marcus stores in 20 states and the District of Columbia, as well as two Bergdorf Goodmans in New York City, and about 10 clearance centers. Its direct-marketing business, NM Direct, distributes catalogs. Neiman Marcus also owns stakes in firms that make cosmetics and handbags. The retailer offers extravagant special events, one-of-a-kind items, and especially attentive salespeople. The Smith family controls about 23% of Neiman Marcus.

KEY COMPETITORS
Federated
Nordstrom
Saks Inc.

📖 See pages 156–157 for a full profile of this company.

NEW CENTURY EQUITY HOLDINGS CORP.

Nasdaq: NCEH

10101 Reunion Place, Ste. 450
San Antonio, TX 78216
Phone: 210-949-7000
Fax: 210-615-0281
Web: www.newcenturyequity.com

CEO: Parris H. Holmes Jr.
CFO: David P. Tusa
HR: Brenda M. Wolfe
Type: Public

2000 Sales: $144.6 million
1-Yr. Sales Change: (20.2%)
Employees: 1,175
FYE: December 31

New Century Equity Holdings (formerly Billing Concepts) has a new name and a new focus for the new millennium. The firm sold business units that provided billing services and software for the telecommunications industry, but held on to subsidiary FIData, which offers an automated Web-based loan approval system used by credit unions, banks, mortgage lenders, and insurance firms. New Century Equity Holdings also owns more than 40% of Princeton eCom, which provides online bill payment and presentment for financial services firms and large corporations. COREintellect (22%-owned) develops and sells Internet-based products that aggregate, sort, and disseminate business information.

KEY COMPETITORS
Fair, Isaac
First Data
NOVA Corporation

NEWFIELD EXPLORATION COMPANY

NYSE: NFX

363 N. Sam Houston Pkwy.
Houston, TX 77060
Phone: 281-847-6000
Fax: 281-847-6006
Web: www.newfld.com

CEO: David A. Trice
CFO: Terry W. Rathert
HR: —
Type: Public

2000 Sales: $526.6 million
1-Yr. Sales Change: 86.7%
Employees: 348
FYE: December 31

Newfield Exploration explores for new fields of oil and gas but is happy with old reserves, too. The independent oil and gas exploration and production company drills in and around the Gulf of Mexico, mostly in the shallow waters off the Louisiana coast. It works onshore, in the Gulf Coast region of Texas and Louisiana. Newfield has also expanded into Oklahoma's Anadarko Basin through the acquisition of Lariat Petroleum. Its international activities include drilling offshore of China and off the coast of northern Australia. Newfield uses 3-D seismic data and other advanced geological analysis technologies in its quest. The company has proved reserves of 940 billion cu. ft. of natural gas equivalent.

KEY COMPETITORS
BP
Houston Exploration
Royal Dutch/Shell

NEWMARK HOMES CORP.

Nasdaq: NHCH

1200 Soldiers Field Dr.
Sugar Land, TX 77479
Phone: 281-243-0100
Fax: 281-243-0123
Web: www.newmarkhomes.com

CEO: Lonnie M. Fedrick
CFO: Terry C. White
HR: Kathy Wistner
Type: Public

2000 Sales: $640.5 million
1-Yr. Sales Change: 30.3%
Employees: 543
FYE: December 31

On its mark, home builder Newmark Homes is targeting move-up buyers relocating primarily in high-growth areas in Florida, North Carolina, Tennessee, and Texas. Marketed under the Newmark and Westbrooke brands, its standard homes cost between $140,000 and $400,000 and range in size from 1,700 sq. ft. to 4,500 sq. ft. In addition, Newmark makes custom homes under the Fedrick, Harris Estate Homes name that cost more than $1 million. To target empty-nest buyers, the company has created Marksman Homes, which builds homes that average at $150,000. Greek construction firm Technical Olympic owns 80% of Newmark Homes, which is considering a combination with Technical Olympic's Engle Homes unit.

KEY COMPETITORS
Centex
D.R. Horton
KB Home

N.F. SMITH & ASSOCIATES, LP

5306 Hollister
Houston, TX 77040
Phone: 713-430-3000
Fax: 713-430-3099
Web: www.smithmart.com

CEO: Robert G. Ackerley
CFO: Douglas C. Kelly
HR: Ester Burton
Type: Private

2000 Est. Sales: $500.0 mil.
1-Yr. Sales Change: 77.3%
Employees: 287
FYE: December 31

New York-born Robert and Leland Ackerley were exiting a Houston rodeo when they decided to take the bull by the horns and start high-tech distribution company N.F. Smith & Associates. The independent distributor of semiconductors and computer components carries active components (microprocessors, memory chips), computer products (CD-ROM drives, motherboards), and passive components (capacitors, inductors). Services include lead inspection, memory testing, and component dry packing. The company, which sells to top manufacturers and technology and computer equipment resellers, also auctions components through its Smithmart.com Web site. President Robert Ackerley and EVP Leland Ackerley own N.F. Smith.

KEY COMPETITORS
Arrow Electronics
Avnet
TTI

NL INDUSTRIES, INC.

NYSE: NL

16825 Northchase Dr., Ste. 1200
Houston, TX 77060
Phone: 281-423-3300
Fax: 281-423-3236
Web: www.nl-ind.com

CEO: J. Landis Martin
CFO: Susan E. Alderton
HR: Ross Buckner
Type: Public

2000 Sales: $922.3 million
1-Yr. Sales Change: 1.5%
Employees: 2,500
FYE: December 31

NL Industries hopes to paint a bright future through its Kronos subsidiary. Kronos is a leading supplier of titanium dioxide pigments, which maximize the whiteness, opacity, and brightness of paints, plastics, paper, fibers, and ceramics. The company produces more than 40 different grades of titanium dioxide, which it sells under the Kronos brand worldwide to manufacturers of paints, plastics, and paper. Europe accounts for about half of sales. Kronos operates six plants in North America and Europe; it has a joint venture with Huntsman Corporation that operates a titanium dioxide plant (Louisiana Pigment). Chairman Harold Simmons owns a controlling stake in NL Industries.

KEY COMPETITORS
DuPont
Kerr-McGee
Millennium Chemicals

NOBLE AFFILIATES, INC.

NYSE: NBL

350 Glenborough Dr., Ste. 100
Houston, TX 77067
Phone: 281-872-3100
Fax: 281-872-3111
Web: www.nobleaff.com

CEO: Charles D. Davidson
CFO: James L. McElvany
HR: Calvin Burton
Type: Public

2000 Sales: $1,381.3 million
1-Yr. Sales Change: 55.8%
Employees: 576
FYE: December 31

Noble prizes petroleum and has the reserves to prove it. Noble Affiliates looks for oil and natural gas and produces and markets them in the US and internationally. US operations are in the West Coast, Rocky Mountain, midcontinent, and Gulf Coast regions. International operations include onshore and offshore activities in the Asia/Pacific region, the Middle East, South America, West Africa, and the North Sea. Noble has estimated proved reserves of 1.5 trillion cu. ft. of natural gas and more than 148 million barrels of oil. Subsidiary Samedan conducts much of the company's exploration and production; other subsidiaries market natural gas and oil from Noble's own wells and for other companies.

KEY COMPETITORS
Anadarko Petroleum
ChevronTexaco
Unocal

NOBLE DRILLING CORPORATION

NYSE: NE

13135 S. Dairy Ashford, Ste. 800
Sugar Land, TX 77478
Phone: 281-276-6100
Fax: 281-491-2092
Web: www.noblecorp.com

CEO: James C. Day
CFO: Mark A. Jackson
HR: Julie J. Robertson
Type: Public

2000 Sales: $882.6 million
1-Yr. Sales Change: 25.0%
Employees: 2,943
FYE: December 31

Noble Drilling may be heir to a fortune as demand increases for deepwater oil and gas contract drilling services. The company owns a fleet of 49 offshore rigs, including three submersibles, three drillships, nine semisubmersibles, and 34 jack-ups. Noble also operates eight drilling units under labor contracts, and subsidiary Triton Engineering Services provides turnkey drilling, engineering, and consulting services. With operations worldwide, Noble is focusing on deepwater drilling and has converted five submersible drilling units into ultra-deepwater semisubmersible rigs capable of drilling at depths of more than 5,000 feet. The company gets about 86% of its revenues from offshore drilling operations.

KEY COMPETITORS
Diamond Offshore
Global Marine
Transocean Sedco Forex

NORTHERN BORDER PARTNERS, L.P.

NYSE: NBP

1400 Smith St.
Houston, TX 77002
Phone: 713-853-6161
Fax: 713-646-4970
Web: www.nbp.enron.com

CEO: WIlliam R. Cordes
CFO: Jerry L. Peters
HR: —
Type: Public

2000 Sales: $339.7 million
1-Yr. Sales Change: 6.5%
Employees: 280
FYE: December 31

Northern Border Partners gasses up and ships its product through two interstate pipelines that run through the Upper Midwest. Its 70%-owned 1,210-mile Northern Border Pipeline (TransCanada owns the rest) carries natural gas from the Montana-Saskatchewan border and from the Dakotas' Williston Basin to connections in the Midwest. Its 350-mile Midwestern Gas Transmission system links Tennessee with Chicago, where it connects to Northern Border Pipeline. The company also owns 3,800 miles of gas-gathering pipe and facilities in the Dakotas, Montana, and Canada and a 273-mile coal slurry pipeline connecting Arizona coal mines to a Nevada power station. The company's general partners are subsidiaries of Enron and Williams.

KEY COMPETITORS
El Paso
Enbridge
Westcoast Energy

NORWOOD PROMOTIONAL PRODUCTS, INC.

106 E. Sixth St., Ste. 300
Austin, TX 78701
Phone: 512-476-7100
Fax: 512-477-8603
Web: www.norwood.com

CEO: Frank P. Krasovec
CFO: Gary S. Kofnovec
HR: Deborah A. Garrett
Type: Private

2000 Sales: $431.0 million
1-Yr. Sales Change: (0.1%)
Employees: 3,500
FYE: December 31

Norwood Promotional Products makes its money off the freebies. The leading supplier of promotional items in the US, Norwood has more than a dozen operating companies that make such trinkets as magnets, caps, mugs, pens, and outerwear imprinted with logos and promotional messages. Norwood makes some 10,000 products from its 18 manufacturing and printing plants in the US and Canada. Norwood sells its wares to about 15,000 independent distributors (mostly domestic), including promotional giants like Cyrk and Ha-Lo. A group including CEO Frank Krasovec and investment firm Liberty Partners owns the company.

KEY COMPETITORS
Equity Marketing
Sherwood Promotions
Simon Worldwide

NUEVO ENERGY COMPANY

NYSE: NEV

1021 Main, Ste. 2100
Houston, TX 77002
Phone: 713-652-0706
Fax: 713-756-1744
Web: www.nuevoenergy.com

CEO: James L. Payne
CFO: Robert M. King
HR: —
Type: Public

2000 Sales: $331.7 million
1-Yr. Sales Change: 36.9%
Employees: 67
FYE: December 31

Nuevo Energy applies some new energy to extracting an old resource: It engages in oil and natural gas exploration and production. The company has proved reserves of about 283.6 million barrels of oil equivalent; most of its reserves are in the form of crude oil. Nuevo Energy's drilling and exploration activities take place in California (which accounts for the bulk of the company's reserves and production) and Texas and Alabama. It has contracted to sell its California oil production to refiner-marketer Tosco until 2015. The company's international exploration activities all take place offshore of the Republic of Congo and Ghana and inland in Tunisia.

KEY COMPETITORS
Berry Petroleum Company
ChevronTexaco
Royal Dutch/Shell

OCEAN ENERGY, INC.

NYSE: OEI

1001 Fannin St., Ste. 1600
Houston, TX 77002
Phone: 713-265-6000
Fax: 713-265-8008
Web: www.oceanenergy.com

CEO: James T. Hackett
CFO: William L. Transier
HR: Peggy T. d'Hemecourt
Type: Public

2000 Sales: $1,073.6 million
1-Yr. Sales Change: 46.0%
Employees: 1,051
FYE: December 31

At home in the ocean or on land, independent oil and gas company Ocean Energy has onshore and/or offshore operations in eight countries. In the US, Ocean explores and produces in the shelf and deepwater areas of the Gulf of Mexico and in the Permian Basin, Midcontinent, and Rocky Mountain regions. The company also operates in western Africa, Egypt, Indonesia, and Russia; it has proved reserves of more than 460 million barrels of oil equivalent. Riding the wave of higher oil and gas prices, the company has acquired rival Texoil, allowing Ocean to focus more attention on the Gulf Coast region.

KEY COMPETITORS
Anadarko Petroleum
BP
Royal Dutch/Shell

OCEANEERING INTERNATIONAL, INC.

NYSE: OII

11911 FM 529
Houston, TX 77041
Phone: 713-329-4500
Fax: 713-329-4951
Web: www.oceaneering.com

CEO: John R. Huff
CFO: Marvin J. Migura
HR: Janet G Charles
Type: Public

2000 Sales: $307.7 million
1-Yr. Sales Change: (26.2%)
Employees: 3,000
FYE: December 31

Oceaneering International's products are designed to operate in extremely harsh conditions, from the bottom of the sea to the far reaches of space. The company's Offshore Oil and Gas Services and Products unit provides offshore oil companies with underwater drilling support, construction, inspection, maintenance, and repair services. Oceaneering makes subsea systems to test potential offshore oil fields. The company's Advanced Technologies unit makes remotely operated diving vessels, which are often used in search and recovery operations for the US Navy, and makes life-support and robotic systems for use in space. In 2000 Oceaneering located and recovered NASA's Mercury space capsule *Liberty Bell*.

KEY COMPETITORS
Coflexip
Global Industries
Stolt Offshore

OIL STATES INTERNATIONAL, INC.

NYSE: OIS

3 Allen Center
Houston, TX 77002
Phone: 713-652-0582
Fax: 713-652-0499
Web: www.oilstatesintl.com

CEO: Douglas E. Swanson
CFO: Cindy B. Taylor
HR: —
Type: Public

2000 Sales: $304.5 million
1-Yr. Sales Change: 97.3%
Employees: 2,805
FYE: December 31

Oil States International lends a helping hand to oil and gas drillers and producers. The company provides offshore products, including flex-element technology, advanced connectors, and subsea pipeline products, and its well site services range from catering and remote site accommodations to hydraulic well control and rental equipment. Oil States has also added tubular services and offers casing, premium tubing, and line pipe. Drilling its way into e-commerce, the firm has developed a portal for ordering tubular products. Founded in 1949 in Texas, Oil States mainly focuses on deepwater activities in major producing regions, including the Gulf of Mexico and West Africa. Chairman L. E. Simmons owns 63% of the firm.

KEY COMPETITORS
Coflexip
Cooper Cameron
Stolt Offshore

OVERHILL CORPORATION

AMEX: OVH

4800 Broadway, Ste. A
Addison, TX 75001
Phone: 972-386-0101
Fax: 972-386-8008

CEO: James Rudis
CFO: William E. Shatley
HR: William E. Shatley
Type: Public

2000 Sales: $189.1 million
1-Yr. Sales Change: 19.5%
Employees: 1,200
FYE: September 30

A frozen foods and forestry equipment combo doesn't shout synergy, but Overhill (formerly Polyphase) has them both under its corporate roof. Through its Overhill Farms subsidiary, which accounts for more than 75% of its sales, Overhill makes frozen entrees and other food for airline, food service, health care, and retail customers. Jenny Craig, American Airlines, King's Hawaiian, Panda Express, and Delta Airlines are the biggest buyers of its food products, which Overhill cooks up at six plants in California. Subsidiary Texas Timberjack distributes, leases, and finances timber and logging equipment (shears, skidders, loaders), primarily in East Texas. Texas Timberjack president Harold Estes owns 22% of Overhill.

KEY COMPETITORS
ConAgra
Deere
Tyson Foods

PACKAGED ICE, INC.

AMEX: ICY

3535 Travis St., Ste. 170
Dallas, TX 75204
Phone: 214-526-6740
Fax: 214-443-5357

CEO: William P. Brick
CFO: Leonard A. Bedell
HR: Bill Daniel
Type: Public

2000 Sales: $244.0 million
1-Yr. Sales Change: 5.3%
Employees: 1,954
FYE: December 31

Ice is hot stuff, especially when you've got the Ice Factory — technology that lets grocery and convenience stores (where most ice is sold) automatically make and package their own ice. Packaged Ice — the largest US maker of, yes, packaged ice — installs its Ice Factory machines and provides Reddy Ice brand ice in a variety of shapes and sizes (ranging from six pound bags of cubes to 300 pound blocks) to retail, commercial, and industrial users in 30 states (mostly across the southern US) and the District of Columbia. Packaged Ice also leases ice equipment, provides refrigerated warehousing, and produces bottled water. By buying mom-and-pop competitors, Packaged Ice has led the consolidation in its industry.

KEY COMPETITORS
Manitowoc

PALM HARBOR HOMES, INC.

Nasdaq: PHHM

15303 Dallas Pkwy., Ste. 800
Addison, TX 75001
Phone: 972-991-2422
Fax: 972-991-5949
Web: www.palmharbor.com

CEO: Larry H. Keener
CFO: Kelly Tacke
HR: Jennifer Burkhart
Type: Public

2001 Sales: $650.5 million
1-Yr. Sales Change: (16.3%)
Employees: 4,180
FYE: March 31

The old trailer park just ain't what it used to be. A top maker of manufactured homes, Palm Harbor Homes offers a range of floor plans with two to five bedrooms and optional luxury features such as stone fireplaces and whirlpool baths. The company sells its homes under such brands as Palm Harbor, River Bend, and Windsor Homes, through more than 135 company-owned superstores and 300 independent retailers across the US. Palm Harbor operates 15 active plants in the US (primarily in the South and Southwest). It also has financing and insurance subsidiaries. Directors William Thomas and John Wilson control about 35% of the company through Capital Southwest Corporation and Capital Southwest Venture Corporation.

KEY COMPETITORS
Champion Enterprises
Fleetwood Enterprises
Oakwood Homes

 See pages 158–159 for a full profile of this company.

PANDA ENERGY INTERNATIONAL, INC.

4100 Spring Valley Rd., Ste. 1001
Dallas, TX 75244
Phone: 972-980-7159
Fax: 972-980-6815
Web: www.pandaenergy.com

CEO: Robert W. Carter
CFO: Jerry Thurmond
HR: Diane Smith
Type: Private

2000 Sales: $144.0 million
1-Yr. Sales Change: (23.4%)
Employees: 164
FYE: December 30

Pandering to the energy-deprived, Panda Energy International develops, owns, and operates clean, low-cost power plants. The electric generation firm, which was founded in Dallas in 1982, has interests in six operating plants in the US, China, and Nepal (2,560 MW), and has others in development or under construction (13,700 MW). The company has formed a joint venture with TECO Energy to build two generating plants worth $2.3 billion in El Dorado, Arkansas, and Gila Bend, Arizona. It has sold its Oklahoma plant (in development) to Calpine. Subsidiary Panda Power Corporation markets energy from the plants, and Panda Global Services operates and maintains them. The firm is owned by CEO Robert Carter and his family.

KEY COMPETITORS
Calpine
Indeck Energy
Orion Power

PARKER DRILLING COMPANY

NYSE: PKD

1401 Enclave Pkwy., Ste. 600
Houston, TX 77077
Phone: 281-406-2000
Fax: 281-406-2001
Web: www.parkerdrilling.com

CEO: Robert L. Parker Jr.
CFO: James J. Davis
HR: Susan McDonald
Type: Public

2000 Sales: $376.3 million
1-Yr. Sales Change: 15.9%
Employees: 3,542
FYE: December 31

Parker Drilling parks its oil rigs off the beaten path. Its helicopter-transportable rigs allow the drilling contractor to work in remote jungle, mountain, and desert locations in foreign locations, but in recent years it has been targeting offshore markets. Hit hard by the oil crunch of the late 1990s, it sold assets and exited the land drilling business in the US. Since then, however, exploration activity has increased. Parker Drilling, which owns 85 rigs, drills worldwide and has worked in more than 50 countries. Subsidiary Quail Tools provides rental tools for oil and gas drilling and workover activities. Parker Drilling's Partech unit offers rig manufacturing and support services.

KEY COMPETITORS
Noble Drilling
Santa Fe International
Transocean Sedco Forex

PATTERSON-UTI ENERGY, INC.

Nasdaq: PTEN

4510 Lamesa Hwy.
Snyder, TX 79550
Phone: 915-573-1104
Fax: 915-573-0281
Web: www.patenergy.com

CEO: Cloyce A. Talbott
CFO: Jonathan D. "Jody" Nelson
HR: Ronald McClung
Type: Public

2000 Sales: $307.9 million
1-Yr. Sales Change: 103.2%
Employees: 3,062
FYE: December 31

Does bubblin' crude gush up through the ground in your back yard? If not, Patterson-UTI Energy will drill for it. The company, which provides onshore contract drilling for oil and natural gas producers, was formed in 2001 when the former Patterson Energy bought UTI Energy. Patterson-UTI operates 302 rigs, including 286 in the US and 16 in Western Canada. It has the second-largest land-based drilling fleet in North America, behind that of Nabors Industries. Patterson-UTI complements its drilling and completion services with exploration and production operations that have proved reserves of 1.1 million barrels of oil and 3.8 billion cu. ft. of gas in Texas and New Mexico.

KEY COMPETITORS
Grey Wolf
Helmerich & Payne
Nabors Industries

PEGASUS SOLUTIONS, INC.

Nasdaq: PEGS

3811 Turtle Creek Blvd., Ste. 1100
Dallas, TX 75219
Phone: 214-528-5656
Fax: 214-528-5675
Web: www.pegsinc.com

CEO: John F. Davis III
CFO: Susan K. Cole
HR: Gary Siegel
Type: Public

2000 Sales: $161.5 million
1-Yr. Sales Change: 325.0%
Employees: 2,003
FYE: December 31

Pegasus Solutions has no reservations about providing services to the world-wide hotel industry. The company generates about 65% of sales through its hospitality division, which provides reservation representation and marketing services through the Utell and Golden Tulip names. Pegasus Solutions' technology division offers central reservation systems, electronic distribution (connecting some 40,000 hotels to the Internet and the global distribution system), and commission processing, among other services. It also powers the hotel reservations services of more than 1,000 travel Web sites and operates its own site, TravelWeb.com. The company serves more than 40,000 hotels and about 100,000 travel agencies across the globe.

KEY COMPETITORS
Expedia
MICROS Systems
Travel Services

PENNZOIL-QUAKER STATE COMPANY

NYSE: PZL

Pennzoil Place, 700 Milam
Houston, TX 77002
Phone: 713-546-4000
Fax: 713-546-8043
Web: www.pennzoil-quakerstate.com

CEO: James J. Postl
CFO: Thomas P. Kellagher
HR: Mark S. Esselman
Type: Public

2000 Sales: $2,270.6 million
1-Yr. Sales Change: (23.1%)
Employees: 8,428
FYE: December 31

Every three months or 3,000 miles, Pennzoil-Quaker State wants to land your business. Formed by the merger of Pennzoil and Quaker State, the company makes the US's #1 and #2 brands of motor oil: Pennzoil and venerable brand Quaker State. It also owns the US's #1 chain of oil-change centers — Jiffy Lube, which has more than 2,140 outlets (of which about three-quarters are franchised). Pennzoil-Quaker State also owns an arsenal of some 1,300 brand-name auto products, including Gumout, Snap, and Outlaw fuel additives; Fix-A-Flat tire inflator; Medo air fresheners; and Slick 50 engine and fuel treatments.

KEY COMPETITORS
Ashland
BP
ChevronTexaco

See pages 160–161 for a full profile of this company.

PENTACON, INC.

OTC: PTAC

10375 Richmond Ave., Ste. 700
Houston, TX 77024
Phone: 713-860-1000
Fax: 713-860-1001
Web: www.pentacon-inc.com

CEO: Robert L. Ruck
CFO: James C. Jackson
HR: Bruce M. Taten
Type: Public

2000 Sales: $283.7 million
1-Yr. Sales Change: 4.0%
Employees: 740
FYE: December 31

Pentacon isn't hiding any military secrets in its 35 sales and distribution centers across the US, just thousands of fasteners. Through its aerospace and industrial groups, Pentacon distributes fasteners and small parts primarily to original equipment manufacturers. Industrial customers served include diesel engine, locomotive, and power turbine manufacturers. Boeing, GE, and Cummins Engine are some of its largest customers. It distributes more than 100,000 types of fasteners and small parts, such as clamps, springs, and brackets. The company also provides related inventory management and procurement services for its customers. Nearly 90% of its sales are in the US.

KEY COMPETITORS
Federal Screw Works
MNP
PennEngineering

PEROT SYSTEMS CORPORATION

NYSE: PER

12404 Park Central Dr.
Dallas, TX 75251
Phone: 972-340-5000
Fax: 972-340-6100
Web: www.perotsystems.com

CEO: Ross Perot Jr.
CFO: Russell Freeman
HR: Ross Hansen
Type: Public

2000 Sales: $1,105.9 million
1-Yr. Sales Change: (4.0%)
Employees: 7,800
FYE: December 31

If you can't "get under the hood" and fix what's wrong with the US, you might as well fix what's wrong with the world's technology. Perot Systems (founded by twice-thwarted US presidential hopeful and billionaire Ross Perot) provides technology consulting and services to global businesses in systems management and integration, customer management, e-commerce, and strategic consulting. While the company serves customers in a variety of markets, most of its clients are in financial services, health care, and manufacturing industries, including Swiss bank UBS (about 25% of sales), Owens & Minor, and Bank of Ireland. Founder and chairman Perot owns 33% of the company.

KEY COMPETITORS
Computer Sciences
EDS
IBM

 See pages 162–163 for a full profile of this company.

PETRO STOPPING CENTERS, L.P.

6080 Surety Dr.
El Paso, TX 79905
Phone: 915-779-4711
Fax: 915-774-7382
Web: www.petrotruckstops.com

CEO: J. A. "Jack" Cardwell Sr.
CFO: David A. Appleby
HR: Walter Kalinowski
Type: Private

2000 Sales: $983.2 million
1-Yr. Sales Change: 36.6%
Employees: 4,186
FYE: December 31

Petro Stopping Centers is the center of attention for truckers who need a petro stop. The firm operates 57 truck stops (almost half of them franchised) in 32 states. Its truck stops sell Mobil-brand diesel fuel, gas, and travel merchandise such as food, toiletries, truck accessories, and electronics. (Fuel accounts for almost 80% of sales.) The centers also provide Petro:Lube facilities (preventive maintenance services), showers, laundry services, game rooms, and Iron Skillet restaurants (home-style cooking). Chairman and CEO Jack Cardwell, who founded the company in 1975, and his son, SVP Jim, own 52% of the company. Truck maker Volvo has a 29% stake.

KEY COMPETITORS
Flying J
Pilot
Ultramar Diamond Shamrock

PIER 1 IMPORTS, INC.

NYSE: PIR

301 Commerce St., Ste. 600
Fort Worth, TX 76102
Phone: 817-252-8000
Fax: 817-252-8028
Web: www.pier1.com

CEO: Marvin J. Girouard
CFO: Charles H. Turner
HR: E. Mitchell Weatherly
Type: Public

2001 Sales: $1,411.5 million
1-Yr. Sales Change: 14.7%
Employees: 14,600
FYE: February 28

Pier 1 Imports teems with shoppers fishing for furniture and accessories with an exotic flavor. The company sells more than 5,000 items (imported from more than 60 countries) through more than 780 Pier 1 Imports stores in the US and Canada, and nearly 50 outlets abroad, including The Pier chain in the UK. Its stores offer a wide selection of indoor and outdoor furniture, lamps, vases, baskets, ceramics, dinnerware, candles, and other specialty products. Many of the products are handcrafted; the company favors natural materials such as rattan and wood. Through Pier 1 National Bank, the company offers proprietary credit cards, which are used for more than 25% of US sales.

KEY COMPETITORS
Bed Bath & Beyond
Cost Plus
Williams-Sonoma

 See pages 164–165 for a full profile of this company.

PILGRIM'S PRIDE CORPORATION

NYSE: CHX

110 S. Texas St.
Pittsburg, TX 75686
Phone: 903-855-1000
Fax: 903-856-7505
Web: www.pilgrimspride.com

CEO: David Van Hoose
CFO: Richard A. Cogdill
HR: Ray Gameson
Type: Public

2000 Sales: $1,499.4 million
1-Yr. Sales Change: 10.5%
Employees: —
FYE: September 30

Pilgrim's Pride is climbing the barnyard pecking order. The company is the second-largest chicken processor in the US (trailing Tyson Foods) following its purchase of WLR Foods, which also added turkey products to Pilgrim's diet. Pilgrim's operations entail breeding, hatching, raising, processing, distributing, and marketing poultry. Prepared poultry products, which account for 43% of sales, are sold under the Pilgrim's Pride and Wampler Foods brands to restaurants, grocery stores, and frozen entree makers. It also sells fresh whole and cut-up chicken. The company sells its products in North America, Eastern Europe, and Asia. Chairman Lonnie "Bo" Pilgrim and his family own about 61% of the company.

KEY COMPETITORS
Gold Kist
Bachoco
Tyson Foods

 See pages 166–167 for a full profile of this company.

PILLOWTEX CORPORATION

OTC: PTEXQ

4111 Mint Way
Dallas, TX 75237
Phone: 214-333-3225
Fax: 214-330-6016
Web: www.pillowtex.com

CEO: Ralph LaRovere
CFO: Michael R. Harmon
HR: Donald Mallo
Type: Public

2000 Sales: $1,349.6 million
1-Yr. Sales Change: (13.0%)
Employees: 12,500
FYE: December 31

In the stack of home textile manufacturers, Pillowtex is #3, behind #1 Springs Industries and #2 WestPoint Stevens. It is the top US producer of towels, blankets, pillows, and down comforters, and makes other bed, bath, and kitchen textiles and accessories. Pillowtex makes the Fieldcrest, Cannon, and Royal Velvet brands, as well as private and licensed labels. Pillowtex supplies retailers and the institutional markets in North America, including department stores, mass merchants, wholesale clubs, and catalogs. Former CEO Charles Hansen owns about 18% of the company, while Mary Silverthorne, widow of the founder, owns about 20%. Pillowtex filed for Chapter 11 bankruptcy protection in 2000.

KEY COMPETITORS
Dan River
Springs Industries
WestPoint Stevens

See pages 168–169 for a full profile of this company.

PIONEER COMPANIES, INC.

OTC: PIONA

700 Louisiana St., Ste. 4300
Houston, TX 77002
Phone: 713-570-3200
Fax: 713-223-9202
Web: www.piona.com

CEO: Michael J. Ferris
CFO: Philip J. Ablove
HR: Jerry B. Bradley
Type: Public

2000 Sales: $341.5 million
1-Yr. Sales Change: 15.1%
Employees: 895
FYE: December 31

Like all pioneers, Pioneer Companies is facing tough times — but in this case the difficulty is higher energy costs. Pioneer makes chlorine, caustic soda, hydrochloric acid, bleach, and sodium chlorate for use in such industries as agriculture, plastics manufacturing, pulp and paper manufacturing, and water treatment. The company's chemicals are also used in products like detergents, medical disinfectants, and pharmaceuticals. The US accounts for more than 70% of Pioneer's sales. Chairman William Berkley controls more than 50% of the company, which is restructuring about $600 million worth of debt. Pioneer has been selling off units and cutting production at some plants.

KEY COMPETITORS
Dow Chemical
Occidental
PPG

PIONEER NATURAL RESOURCES COMPANY

NYSE: PXD

1400 Williams Sq. West, 5205 N. O'Connor Blvd.
Irving, TX 75039
Phone: 972-444-9001
Fax: 972-969-3576
Web: www.pioneernrc.com

CEO: Scott D. Sheffield
CFO: Timothy L. Dove
HR: Gene Gerber
Type: Public

2000 Sales: $852.7 million
1-Yr. Sales Change: 32.3%
Employees: 853
FYE: December 31

Pioneer Natural Resources is in deep water these days, but it's in the Gulf of Mexico, not in trouble. The large independent oil and gas exploration and production company, which has boosted its Gulf of Mexico properties, holds proved reserves of more than 628 million barrels of oil equivalent. In the US the company focuses its drilling on the Gulf Coast, the midcontinent, and the Permian Basin. Pioneer also explores for and produces oil and gas in Argentina, Canada, Gabon, and South Africa. Texas financier Richard Rainwater (Pioneer's largest single shareholder with a nearly 6% stake) engineered the 1997 merger that created the company from T. Boone Pickens' MESA and other oil and gas companies.

KEY COMPETITORS
Apache
BP
Chesapeake Energy

PITT-DES MOINES, INC.

AMEX: PDM

1450 Lake Robbins Dr., Ste. 400
The Woodlands, TX 77380
Phone: 281-765-4600
Fax: 281-765-4602
Web: www.pdm.com

CEO: William W. McKee
CFO: Richard A. Byers
HR: Tonya G. Cotton
Type: Public

2000 Sales: $317.6 million
1-Yr. Sales Change: (49.5%)
Employees: 1,024
FYE: December 31

Pitt-Des Moines has built a bridge from the 19th century to the 21st. The company, founded in 1892, focuses on its heavy construction unit, which designs and builds steel bridges. Pitt-Des Moines has also built such structures as the Crystal Cathedral and the St. Louis Arch. In 2000 the company announced that it was considering selling some or all of its operations. It has unloaded its steel distribution business, which accounted for two-thirds of sales, as well as units that built water storage and treatment facilities and provided steel fabrication services. Chairman emeritus W. R. Jackson and his family control 37% of the stock of Pitt-Des Moines.

KEY COMPETITORS
Bechtel
Peter Kiewit Sons'
Washington Group

PIZZA HUT, INC.

14841 Dallas Pkwy.
Dallas, TX 75240
Phone: 972-338-7700
Fax: 972-338-7786
Web: www.pizzahut.com

CEO: Michael S. Rawlings
CFO: Tony Bartel
HR: Joe Bosch
Type: Business segment

2000 Sales: $2,469.0 million
1-Yr. Sales Change: (21.1%)
Employees: —
FYE: December 31

If Al Gore invented the Internet, then was The Big New Yorker named after Hillary Rodham Clinton? Pizza Hut is the world's #1 pizza chain; it has more than 12,000 outlets in the US and more than 85 other countries. Besides the popular The Big New Yorker pizza, the company offers its flagship Pan Pizza, Thin n' Crispy, Pizzeria Stuffed Crust, Hand Tossed, and Sicilian. The chain, with its characteristic red roof restaurants, offers dine-in, carry-out, and delivery service. Along with KFC and Taco Bell, Pizza Hut was spun off from PepsiCo in 1997 and is now a division of TRICON Global Restaurants.

KEY COMPETITORS
Domino's Pizza
Little Caesar
Papa John's

PIZZA INN, INC.

Nasdaq (SC): PZZI

3551 Plano Pkwy.
The Colony, TX 75056
Phone: 972-701-9955
Fax: 972-702-9507
Web: www.pizzainn.com

CEO: C. Jeffrey Rogers
CFO: Shawn M. Preator
HR: Susan Milliman
Type: Public

2001 Sales: $63.5 million
1-Yr. Sales Change: (3.9%)
Employees: 211
FYE: June 30

Room and board at Pizza Inn includes a choice of toppings. The company franchises more than 440 pizza restaurants in the US and 12 other countries that feature a variety of pizzas, pastas, and salads. Most of its locations offer full-service menus, while others feature delivery and carryout only, limited-menu express carryout menus (typically at convenience stores and commercial locations), and self-serve buffet bars. Most of its sales come from its Norco division, which supplies franchisees with ingredients, supplies, and equipment. Pizza Inn's US locations are concentrated in southern states such as Arkansas, North Carolina, and Texas. CEO Jeffrey Rogers owns about 36% of the company.

KEY COMPETITORS
LDB Corp
NPC International
Sbarro

PLAINS ALL AMERICAN PIPELINE, L.P.

NYSE: PAA

500 Dallas St.
Houston, TX 77002
Phone: 713-654-1414
Fax: 713-654-1523

CEO: Greg L. Armstrong
CFO: Phillip D. Kramer
HR: Susie Peters
Type: Public

2000 Sales: $6,641.2 million
1-Yr. Sales Change: 41.2%
Employees: 915
FYE: December 31

Expanding north of the border, Plains All American Pipeline's operations now include Canadian units. The limited partnership, in which Plains Resources holds a 39% stake, also owns extensive gathering, terminal, and storage facilities in California, Louisiana, Oklahoma, and Texas. To buy, sell, and transport oil, Plains All American Pipeline owns 2,800 miles of pipelines in 14 states, operates a fleet of more than 250 trucks and owns storage capacity of 9.8 million barrels, mainly in Oklahoma and Texas. Plains All American Pipeline has sold all but a 140-mile stretch of its namesake, the 1,233-mile, 30-inch heated All American Pipeline, which stretches from California to West Texas.

KEY COMPETITORS
Enbridge
EOTT Energy Partners
TransMontaigne

PLAINS COTTON COOPERATIVE ASSOCIATION

3301 E. 50th St.	CEO: Van May	2000 Sales: $633.0 million
Lubbock, TX 79408	CFO: Billy Morton	1-Yr. Sales Change: (31.6%)
Phone: 806-763-8011	HR: Lee Phenix	Employees: 1,000
Fax: 806-762-7333	Type: Cooperative	FYE: June 30
Web: www.pcca.com		

Plainly speaking, the Plains Cotton Cooperative Association (PCCA) is one of the nation's largest cotton handlers. The farmer-owned marketing cooperative has more than 25,000 members in Oklahoma, Kansas, and Texas. PCCA markets about 3 million bales of cotton each year through TELCOT, its computerized trading system that continually updates cotton prices, buyer data, and other information. The co-op has cotton warehouses in Texas and Oklahoma and a denim mill in Texas (Levi Strauss is its largest customer). Through its Mission Valley Fabrics unit, PCCA makes yarn-dyed woven fabric. The co-op was formed in 1953 to enable cotton farmers to obtain the most competitive price for their cotton.

KEY COMPETITORS
Calcot
Dunavant Enterprises
Staplcotn

PLAINS RESOURCES INC.

AMEX: PLX

500 Dallas St., Ste. 700	CEO: James C. Flores	2000 Sales: $6,575.0 million
Houston, TX 77002	CFO: Jere C. Overdyke Jr.	1-Yr. Sales Change: 36.5%
Phone: 713-654-1414	HR: Mary O. Peters	Employees: 1,100
Fax: 713-654-1523	Type: Public	FYE: December 31
Web: www.plainsresources.com		

Plainly resourceful, Plains Resources is an independent energy company that markets, transports, and stores crude oil. The company gets most of its sales from its 39% stake in Plains All American Pipeline LP. The pipeline partnership operates more than 2,800 miles of pipeline in 14 states, primarily in California, Texas, Louisiana, and Oklahoma. It also owns storage capacity of 9.8 million barrels. Plains Resources also acquires, develops, and produces crude oil and natural gas, mainly the underdeveloped, mature fields. It has proved reserves of 238.7 million barrels of oil equivalent concentrated in California, Florida, and Illinois.

KEY COMPETITORS
Enbridge
EOTT Energy Partners
Royal Dutch/Shell

See pages 170–171 for a full profile of this company.

PLAY-BY-PLAY TOYS & NOVELTIES, INC.

OTC: PBYP

4400 Tejasco	CEO: Tomas Duran	2000 Sales: $153.1 million
San Antonio, TX 78218	CFO: James R. Hyslop	1-Yr. Sales Change: (2.2%)
Phone: 210-829-4666	HR: Beverly Echols	Employees: 574
Fax: 210-824-6565	Type: Public	FYE: July 31
Web: www.pbyp.com		

"Play" is the operative word for Play-By-Play Toys & Novelties, one of the major suppliers of stuffed toys to theme parks, family amusement centers, and carnival midways. The debt-ridden company designs and distributes toys and sculpted pillows (Play-Faces) primarily based on its licenses for entertainment characters (Walt Disney, Looney Tunes, Pokémon), sports teams, and universities. Made by third parties in the Far East, Play-By-Play's toys are also sold through retailers, fund-raising groups, and 1,500 company-owned game machines (located mostly in Texas and New Mexico). A growing international business accounts for some 36% of its sales. Founder Arturo Torres owns about a quarter of Play-By-Play.

KEY COMPETITORS
DSI Toys
Grand Toys

POGO PRODUCING COMPANY

5 Greenway Plaza
Houston, TX 77252
Phone: 713-297-5000
Fax: 713-297-5100
Web: www.pogoproducing.com

CEO: Paul G. Van Wagenen
CFO: James P. Ulm II
HR: Kay Tyner
Type: Public

2000 Sales: $498.0 million
1-Yr. Sales Change: 81.0%
Employees: 161
FYE: December 31

Pogo sticks to its core business, although it has bounced to target natural gas rather than oil. Pogo Producing explores for, develops, and produces those resources onshore in Canada, Hungary, and the US (the Permian Basin, South and East Texas, Louisiana, and Wyoming) and offshore in the Gulf of Thailand, the North Sea, and the Gulf of Mexico. All together, it has proved reserves of 1.4 trillion cu. ft. of natural gas equivalent; 61% of its reserves are natural gas. Pogo has increased its reserves by more than 60% by buying NORIC's North Central Oil. The NORIC deal also has changed Pogo's focus to natural gas and bumped up its US reserves to about three-fourths of the total.

KEY COMPETITORS
ChevronTexaco
Exxon Mobil
Royal Dutch/Shell

POWELL INDUSTRIES, INC.

8550 Mosley Dr.
Houston, TX 77075
Phone: 713-944-6900
Fax: 713-947-4435
Web: www.powellind.com

CEO: Thomas W. Powell
CFO: Don R. Madison
HR: Robert J. Murphy
Type: Public

2000 Sales: $223.0 million
1-Yr. Sales Change: 4.9%
Employees: 1,314
FYE: October 31

Powell Industries keeps current by making electrical equipment and computer systems that monitor and control electricity flow in industrial, commercial, and government facilities. Sales and service of switchgear that manages the flow of electricity to motors, transformers, and other equipment account for more than 70% of Powell's total sales. Other products include bus ducts (insulated power conductors housed in a metal enclosure) and process control systems for instrumentation, computer control, communications, and data management. Powell markets to refineries, utilities, paper mills, offshore platforms, and transportation companies. Chairman, president, and CEO Thomas Powell owns about 28% of the company.

KEY COMPETITORS
Baldor Electric
Regal-Beloit

PRENTISS PROPERTIES TRUST

3890 W. Northwest Hwy., Ste. 400
Dallas, TX 75220
Phone: 214-654-0886
Fax: 214-654-5818
Web: www.pplinc.com

CEO: Thomas F. August
CFO: Michael A. Ernst
HR: Gregory S. Imhoff
Type: Public

2000 Sales: $347.6 million
1-Yr. Sales Change: 8.3%
Employees: —
FYE: December 31

Not one to bawl about sprawl, Prentiss Properties Trust is a real estate investment trust (REIT) with interests in about 200 city and suburban office and industrial properties. The properties are spread throughout the United States. The REIT's office holdings include more than 130 buildings containing about 15 million sq. ft. of rentable space; its industrial holdings include more than 60 buildings containing about 5 million sq. ft. of rentable space. The company operates through an acquisition subsidiary and a management subsidiary. Mack-Cali Realty Corporation's planned acquisition of Prentiss was nixed.

KEY COMPETITORS
CarrAmerica
Equity Office Properties Trust
Mack-Cali Realty

PRIDE INTERNATIONAL, INC.

NYSE: PDE

5847 San Felipe, Ste. 3300
Houston, TX 77057
Phone: 713-789-1400
Fax: 713-789-1430
Web: www.prde.com

CEO: Paul A. Bragg
CFO: Earl W. McNiel
HR: Juanita Cerdin
Type: Public

2000 Sales: $909.0 million
1-Yr. Sales Change: 46.8%
Employees: 8,700
FYE: December 31

Proud to be one of the world's largest well-drilling contractors, Pride International offers drilling, maintenance and workover, and engineering services for oil and gas companies. It also designs specialized drilling equipment and provides project management. The company owns a fleet of more than 300 rigs, including ultra-deepwater drillships and semisubmersible, jack-up, tender-assisted, barge, offshore platform, and land-based drilling and workover rigs. Pride International, which operates in more than 20 countries, has been focusing on providing offshore services in the Gulf of Mexico and overseas. The company has agreed to merge with rival Marine Drilling.

KEY COMPETITORS
Nabors Industries
Saipem
Transocean Sedco Forex

PRIME MEDICAL SERVICES, INC.

Nasdaq: PMSI

1301 Capital of Texas Hwy., Ste. C300
Austin, TX 78746
Phone: 512-328-2892
Fax: 512-328-8510
Web: www.primemedical.com

CEO: Brad A. Hummel
CFO: Cheryl L. Williams
HR: Cindy Green
Type: Public

2000 Sales: $130.7 million
1-Yr. Sales Change: 16.7%
Employees: 400
FYE: December 31

Kidney stones rock for Prime Medical Services, a top US provider of lithotripsy services. Lithotripsy is an outpatient procedure that uses shock waves to fragment kidney stones, which are then passed from the body. Prime Medical owns and operates more than 60 lithotripters (most are installed in mobile facilities that travel from hospital to hospital) which serve some 450 hospitals and surgery centers in more than 30 states. Prime Medical also makes mobile lithotripsy, cardiac catheterization lab, and MRI equipment trailers. The company has entered the refractive eye surgery business and now operates 15 laser vision correction facilities.

KEY COMPETITORS
Del Global
HealthTronics
Medstone International

PRIZE ENERGY CORP.

AMEX: PRZ

3500 William D. Tate, Ste. 200
Grapevine, TX 76051
Phone: 817-424-0400
Fax: 817-424-0071
Web: www.prizeenergy.com

CEO: Philip B. Smith
CFO: Lon C. Kile
HR: Shelly Duncan
Type: Public

2000 Sales: $149.5 million
1-Yr. Sales Change: 695.2%
Employees: 139
FYE: December 31

Good oil and gas properties are the prizes that exploration and production company Prize Energy hopes to win. The company operates primarily in the Permian Basin of West Texas and southeastern New Mexico, the onshore Gulf Coast area of Texas and Louisiana, and the midcontinent area of the Texas Panhandle and western Oklahoma. It has proved reserves of nearly 112 million barrels of oil equivalent and 321 billion cu. ft. of natural gas. The new Prize Energy was formed in 2000 when publicly traded Vista Energy Resources acquired privately held Prize Energy in a stock swap that left Prize shareholders in control of the new company, which took the Prize Energy name.

KEY COMPETITORS
Swift Energy
Tom Brown

PRODIGY COMMUNICATIONS CORPORATION

6500 Riverplace Blvd., Bldg. III
Austin, TX 78730
Phone: 512-527-1500
Fax: 512-527-1199
Web: www.prodigy.com

CEO: Paul R. Roth
CFO: Allen Craft
HR: Richard S. Walker
Type: Subsidiary

2000 Sales: $376.4 million
1-Yr. Sales Change: 99.2%
Employees: 455
FYE: December 31

Prodigies sometimes fade away after an auspicious youth. Prodigy Communications Corporation (formerly Prodigy, Inc.), once the leading US online service, is still around and is making a comeback as an international ISP. It has some 3.1 million consumer and small-business subscribers in the US and Mexico, including 700,000 who use high-speed digital subscriber line (DSL) service. Prodigy gained 700,000 subscribers by combining with SBC's consumer and small-business Internet access operations in 2000; as part of the deal, the Baby Bell took a 43% stake in Prodigy. Billionaire Carlos Slim Helu owns about 30% of the company through his interests in Mexico-based Carso Global Telecom and Telmex.

KEY COMPETITORS
America Online
EarthLink
Microsoft

PROMEDCO MANAGEMENT COMPANY
OTC: PMCO

801 Cherry St., Ste. 1450
Fort Worth, TX 76102
Phone: 817-335-5035
Fax: 817-335-8321
Web: www.promedco.com

CEO: Charles W. McQueary
CFO: Robert D. Smith
HR: Lori McBrayer
Type: Public

1999 Sales: $324.5 million
1-Yr. Sales Change: 45.8%
Employees: 4,200
FYE: December 31

ProMedCo has found that it has no dinero. The medical practice management company has filed for Chapter 11 bankruptcy. ProMedCo buys and consolidates physician groups, focusing on practices in areas that have populations between 30,000 and 500,000. The company usually buys the physician groups' non-real-estate assets with cash, common stock, and other securities. Nearly two-thirds of ProMedCo's doctors are primary care physicians, including family practitioners, general internists, pediatricians, and obstetrician/gynecologists. Goldman Sachs has about a 40% stake in the company.

KEY COMPETITORS
IntegraMed America
PhyCor
Sheridan Healthcare

PURE RESOURCES, INC.
NYSE: PRS

500 W. Illinois St.
Midland, TX 79701
Phone: 915-498-8600
Fax: 915-687-0192
Web: www.pureresources.com

CEO: Jack D. Hightower
CFO: William K. White
HR: David Dakil
Type: Public

2000 Sales: $286.8 million
1-Yr. Sales Change: 0.0%
Employees: 228
FYE: December 31

Purely an energy company, Pure Resources was formed when the former Titan Exploration, hardly an oil and gas behemoth, merged its South Central Texas and Gulf Coast assets with major independent oil and gas exploration player Unocal's holdings in the Permian and San Juan basins of West Texas and New Mexico. The company also has interests in the Gulf of Mexico. Pure Resources (65%-owned by Unocal) has proved reserves of more than 1 trillion cu. ft. equivalent. Natural gas accounts for about 60% of its reserves. The oil and gas company boasts daily production of more than 230 million cu. ft. of gas equivalent. Pure Resources has further expanded its asset base with its purchase of oil and gas firm Hallwood Energy.

KEY COMPETITORS
BP
ChevronTexaco
Royal Dutch/Shell

QUANEX CORPORATION

NYSE: NX

1900 West Loop South	CEO: Raymond A. Jean	2000 Sales: $934.2 million
Houston, TX 77027	CFO: Terry M. Murphy	1-Yr. Sales Change: 15.3%
Phone: 713-961-4600	HR: Paul Giddens	Employees: 3,302
Fax: 713-877-5333	Type: Public	FYE: October 31
Web: www.quanex.com		

When it comes to steel, Quanex Corporation runs a seamless operation. The company's MACSTEEL unit produces a variety of seamless steel bars used by OEMs to manufacture camshafts, transmission gears, and bearing cages and rollers. Its Nichols Aluminum unit makes finished and coated aluminum sheet for industrial applications and building products. The engineered products group makes fabricated aluminum and steel products that include aluminum windows, patio doors screens, and similar products using roll-formed aluminum and stamped shapes. Subsidiary Piper Impact makes custom-designed aluminum and steel parts, primarily for Autoliv, for use in automotive airbag systems. Quanex operates 16 production facilities in the US.

KEY COMPETITORS
Alcoa
Commercial Metals
Republic Technologies

QUANTA SERVICES, INC.

NYSE: PWR

1360 Post Oak Blvd., Ste. 2100	CEO: John R. Colson	2000 Sales: $1,793.3 million
Houston, TX 77056	CFO: James H. Haddox	1-Yr. Sales Change: 93.7%
Phone: 713-629-7600	HR: Cindy Nelson	Employees: 13,260
Fax: 713-629-7676	Type: Public	FYE: December 31
Web: www.quantaservices.com		

Without the infrastructure services provided by companies like Quanta Services, electric utilities and telecommunications providers would be all juiced up with no way to go. The company installs, repairs, and maintains electric transmission lines, cable TV, and telephone and data lines in North America. Quanta works on traffic control systems (signal lights, freeway systems) and designs and installs communication towers. The company also installs cable systems for light rail lines, airports, and highways. Major customers include Verizon, Enron, and AOL Time Warner. Other clients include contractors, commercial establishments, and government entities. Utility holding company UtiliCorp owns 35% of Quanta Services.

KEY COMPETITORS
Bracknell
Dycom
MasTec

QUEXCO INCORPORATED

2777 N. Stemmons Fwy.	CEO: Howard M. Meyers	1997 Sales: $2,000.0 million
Dallas, TX 75207	CFO: William Haberberger	1-Yr. Sales Change: 100.0%
Phone: 214-688-4000	HR: Shirley Crary	Employees: 7,000
Fax: 214-630-5864	Type: Private	FYE: December 31

Quexco gets the lead out and puts it back in. A leading secondary lead producer, this private holding company recycles scrapped lead acid batteries into refined lead and lead products. Quexco's RSR Corporation subsidiary is one of the largest lead smelters in the US, with operations in California, Indiana, New York, and Texas. Quexco also owns Eco-Bat Technologies plc, a UK-based battery recycler with operations in Europe and South Africa. The company's RSR Technologies subsidiary (formerly its R&D unit) offers technology and product development services to the metals industry. Chairman and CEO Howard Meyers, who also heads Bayou Steel Corporation, controls Quexco.

KEY COMPETITORS
Exide
Noranda
Renco

RADIOLOGIX, INC.

AMEX: RGX

3600 Chase Tower
Dallas, TX 75201
Phone: 214-303-2776
Fax: 214-303-2778
Web: www.radiologix.com

CEO: Mark L. Wagar
CFO: Sami S. Abbasi
HR: Cindy Brown
Type: Public

2000 Sales: $246.7 million
1-Yr. Sales Change: 23.5%
Employees: 2,000
FYE: December 31

Radiologix is a practice management company for doctors with X-ray vision. The company owns and operates about 120 diagnostic imaging centers located in 18 states and the District of Columbia. About 75% of Radiologix's sales come from its diagnostic imaging business, which includes the production and management of X-rays, magnetic resonance imaging (MRI), and computer tomography (CT). Radiologix also provides its centers with diagnostic imaging equipment, employee recruitment and training, and other management services. The turbulent stock market forced the company to terminate its acquisition by a private investment firm.

KEY COMPETITORS
Alliance Imaging
InSight Health Services
Syncor

RADIOSHACK CORPORATION

NYSE: RSH

100 Throckmorton St., Ste. 1800
Fort Worth, TX 76102
Phone: 817-415-3700
Fax: 817-415-2647
Web: www.tandy.com

CEO: Leonard H. Roberts
CFO: Michael D. Newman
HR: Jeff Bland
Type: Public

2000 Sales: $4,794.7 million
1-Yr. Sales Change: 16.2%
Employees: 43,600
FYE: December 31

RadioShack (formerly Tandy) is sticking with the shack. Through about 5,100 company-owned and more than 2,000 franchised RadioShack stores, the company is one of the leading US electronics retailers. The stores sell audio and video equipment, wireless and conventional telephones, computers, and other items such as parts and gadgets. RadioShack also repairs products and offers Internet and wireless phone services. The chain has been adding "store-within-a-store" units featuring products such as Compaq computers, Sprint phones, RCA electronics, and Microsoft Internet services and software. RadioShack sold its Incredible Universe, McDuff, and Computer City chains, and bought cable installer AmeriLink.

KEY COMPETITORS
Best Buy
Circuit City
CompUSA

 See pages 172–173 for a full profile of this company.

RANDALL'S FOOD MARKETS, INC.

3663 Briarpark
Houston, TX 77042
Phone: 713-268-3500
Fax: 713-268-3812
Web: www.randalls.com

CEO: Frank Lazaran
CFO: Leslie Nelson
HR: Judy Ward
Type: Subsidiary

1999 Sales: $2,585.1 million
1-Yr. Sales Change: 6.9%
Employees: 17,650
FYE: December 31

How do you become one of the largest regional supermarket chains in the US with stores in only a few areas of a single state? Locate them in the big state of Texas, as has Randall's Food Markets. The grocer, which is owned by supermarket giant Safeway, runs more than 125 stores under names Randalls (in Houston and Austin) and Tom Thumb and Simon David (in the Dallas-Fort Worth metro area). Most of the company's stores are in the more well-off areas of those cities and are combination food stores and drugstores; some are more upscale flagship stores. The company also runs 15 gas stations adjacent to stores in Houston and Austin.

KEY COMPETITORS
Albertson's
H-E-B
Kroger

RANGE RESOURCES CORPORATION

NYSE: RRC

777 Main St., Ste. 800
Fort Worth, TX 76102
Phone: 817-870-2601
Fax: 817-870-2316
Web: www.rangeresources.com

CEO: John H. Pinkerton
CFO: Eddie M. LeBlanc III
HR: Carol Culpepper
Type: Public

2000 Sales: $187.0 million
1-Yr. Sales Change: 16.0%
Employees: 139
FYE: December 31

Range Resources is riding the range as an independent acquirer and developer of US oil and gas resources. The company's long-term strategy involves acquiring long-lived established properties and has major development areas in the Appalachian (37% of reserves), Permian (West Texas), midcontinent (western Oklahoma, Texas Panhandle), and Gulf Coast regions. Natural gas accounts for about 72% of Range Resources' proved reserves of about 617 billion cu. ft. of natural gas equivalent. Its Independent Producer Finance subsidiary provides capital to small oil and gas producers.

KEY COMPETITORS
BP
Equitable Resources
Exxon Mobil

RELIANT ENERGY, INCORPORATED

NYSE: REI

1111 Louisiana St.
Houston, TX 77002
Phone: 713-207-3000
Fax: 713-207-3169
Web: www.reliantenergy.com

CEO: R. Steve Letbetter
CFO: Stephen W. Naeve
HR: Preston R. Johnson Jr.
Type: Public

2000 Sales: $29,339.4 million
1-Yr. Sales Change: 91.7%
Employees: 15,633
FYE: December 31

Reliant Energy is growing from a local electric utility to a power provider across the US and in Europe. Its utility distributes electricity and natural gas to nearly 4 million customers in the southern US and Minnesota, and generates 14,000 MW of electricity. Preparing for deregulation, Reliant Energy has transferred its nonregulated operations to subsidiary Reliant Resources, which it plans to spin off. Reliant Resources operates power plants with 12,700 MW generating capacity in the Netherlands and the US, and markets and trades energy in Germany, the Netherlands, the UK, and the US. It also manages Reliant Energy's telecom and e-commerce businesses. Reliant Energy has sold most of its Latin American operations.

KEY COMPETITORS
Entergy
TXU
UtiliCorp

See pages 174–175 for a full profile of this company.

RELIANT RESOURCES, INC.

NYSE: RRI

1111 Louisiana
Houston, TX 77002
Phone: 713-207-3000
Fax: —
Web: www.reliantresources.com

CEO: R. Steve Letbetter
CFO: Stephen W. Naeve
HR: Preston R. Johnson Jr.
Type: Public

2000 Sales: $19,791.9 million
1-Yr. Sales Change: 148.2%
Employees: 4,100
FYE: December 31

Serving up its juice with a transatlantic flavor, Reliant Resources (a subsidiary of Reliant Energy) provides energy and related services in US and European deregulated markets. The firm has more than 12,700 MW of owned or leased generating capacity in the Netherlands and eight states, as well as 2,800 MW under construction. Reliant Resources trades and markets electricity, natural gas, and other commodities to utilities, marketers, and municipalities. It has an option to acquire its parent's regulated Texas plants (14,000 MW capacity) and is selling its 160-MW plant in Argentina. Reliant Resources has taken over its parent's other nonregulated activities, including telecommunications and e-commerce.

KEY COMPETITORS
AES
Mirant
NRG Energy

RENT-A-CENTER, INC.

Nasdaq: RCII

5700 Tennyson Pkwy., 3rd Fl.
Plano, TX 75024
Phone: 972-801-1100
Fax: 972-943-0113
Web: www.rentacenter.com

CEO: Mark E. Speese
CFO: Robert D. Davis
HR: Marc Tuckey
Type: Public

2000 Sales: $1,601.6 million
1-Yr. Sales Change: 13.0%
Employees: 12,554
FYE: December 31

Rent-A-Center wants customers to rent, but its own strategy is to buy. Rent-A-Center (formerly Renters Choice) became the #1 operator of rent-to-own stores in the US through a long string of acquisitions. Nationwide, the company owns and operates more than 2,100 stores and franchises an additional 360 through subsidiary ColorTyme. The stores rent name-brand home electronics (accounting for 40% of sales), furniture and accessories, appliances, and computers; they also offer Internet access. Customers can take ownership of the products after a specified number of payments, but only about 25% of Rent-A-Center's customers actually buy its merchandise. Apollo, a Los Angeles investment group, owns about 29% of the company.

KEY COMPETITORS
Aaron Rents
Best Buy
Rent-Way

 See pages 176–177 for a full profile of this company.

RIVIANA FOODS INC.

Nasdaq: RVFD

2777 Allen Pkwy.
Houston, TX 77019
Phone: 713-529-3251
Fax: 713-529-1661

CEO: Joseph A. Hafner Jr.
CFO: E. Wayne Ray Jr.
HR: Lucille Pagel
Type: Public

2001 Sales: $382.0 million
1-Yr. Sales Change: (12.4%)
Employees: 2,745
FYE: June 30

Riviana Foods is all over the rice business like white on — well, you know. The #1 US seller of rice, Riviana processes, packages, and markets rice under such retail brands as Mahatma, Success, Carolina, River, and WaterMaid. It also supplies food service products, private-label rices for grocery chains, and bulk rice for use in processed foods. Riviana's Central American subsidiaries produce and market canned vegetables, cookies, and fruit drinks. Its Belgian and UK subsidiaries sell rice and packaged foods. It has rice marketing and rice flour partnerships with co-op Riceland Foods. The families of chairman Frank Godchaux III and his brother, VC Charles Godchaux, own nearly 45% of the company.

KEY COMPETITORS
American Rice
Kraft Foods
Mars

See pages 178–179 for a full profile of this company.

ROWAN COMPANIES, INC.

NYSE: RDC

2800 Post Oak Blvd., Ste. 5450
Houston, TX 77056
Phone: 713-621-7800
Fax: 713-960-7660
Web: www.rowancompanies.com

CEO: C. R. Palmer
CFO: E. E. Thiele
HR: Bill S. Person
Type: Public

2000 Sales: $646.0 million
1-Yr. Sales Change: 40.3%
Employees: 4,917
FYE: December 31

Drilling, manufacturing, and flying all have their place in the scheme of things at Rowan Companies. Rowan performs contract drilling of oil and gas wells in Lousiana, Texas, the Gulf of Mexico, and offshore eastern Canada. Its fleet consists of 22 jack-up rigs, one semisubmersible rig, and 14 land drilling rigs. Subsidiary LeTourneau operates a mini-steel mill and manufactures heavy equipment such as front-end loaders and large-capacity trucks for the mining, timber, and transportation industries. LeTourneau's marine group builds offshore jack-up drilling rigs. Rowan's Era Aviation, with more than 110 aircraft, provides contract and charter aircraft services in Alaska, the Gulf Coast area, and the western US.

KEY COMPETITORS
ENSCO
Global Marine
Petroleum Helicopters

RUSH ENTERPRISES, INC.

Nasdaq: RUSH

555 IH 35 S.
New Braunfels, TX 78130
Phone: 830-626-5200
Fax: 830-626-5318
Web: www.rushenterprises.com

CEO: W. Marvin Rush
CFO: Martin A. Naegelin Jr.
HR: Carla Wagner
Type: Public

2000 Sales: $897.4 million
1-Yr. Sales Change: 11.0%
Employees: 1,900
FYE: December 31

Rush Enterprises does everything but spin its wheels to remain the largest Peterbilt truck dealer in the US. The company's 36 truck centers, clustered in the southwestern US, mainly sell Class 8 Peterbilt trucks, but they also offer used trucks by Peterbilt, Mack, and Freightliner. Rush Enterprises also offers aftermarket parts, repair services, financing and insurance, rentals, and leasing. The company sells new and used construction equipment made by Deere through seven Rush Equipment Centers in Michigan and Texas; used equipment by Caterpillar, Komatsu, and others is also available. The company sells farm and ranch supplies through retail stores in Texas. Chairman W. Marvin Rush owns about 39% of the company.

KEY COMPETITORS
Penske
RDO Equipment
Ryder

SABRE INC.

NYSE: TSG

4255 Amon Carter Blvd.
Fort Worth, TX 76155
Phone: 817-963-6400
Fax: 817-931-5582
Web: www.sabre.com

CEO: William Hannigan
CFO: Jeffery M. Jackson
HR: Michael E. Haefner
Type: Public

2000 Sales: $2,617.4 million
1-Yr. Sales Change: 7.5%
Employees: 10,000
FYE: December 31

Sabre helps you hit the road, Jack. Used by travel agencies and corporate travel departments to book airline, car, and hotel reservations, the Sabre system is the world's #1 computerized travel reservation system. Individuals can make travel plans using its 70%-owned Travelocity Web site (the #1 online travel site following its combination with Preview Travel) or its GetThere.com site. Travel reservations bring in about 60% of revenue. In 2001 Sabre sold its information technology (IT) services, which brought in another 30% of its sales, to EDS. Those services included providing airlines with IT outsourcing, software development, and consulting services. American Airlines' parent, AMR, which developed Sabre, spun off its 83% stake in Sabre to AMR shareholders in 2000.

KEY COMPETITORS
Amadeus
Galileo International
priceline.com

 See pages 180–181 for a full profile of this company.

ST. LUKE'S EPISCOPAL HOSPITAL

6720 Bertner Ave., Texas Medical Center
Houston, TX 77030
Phone: 713-791-1000
Fax: 713-794-6182
Web: www.sleh.com

CEO: Michael K. Jhin
CFO: Alan F. Koval
HR: Irene S. Helsinger
Type: Not-for-profit

1996 Sales: $640.2 million
1-Yr. Sales Change: 12.3%
Employees: —
FYE: September 30

St. Luke's Episcopal Hospital has been deep in the hearts of Texans. Affiliate The Texas Heart Institute, under Dr. Denton Cooley, performed the first successful heart transplant in the US and the world's first total artificial heart transplant. Opened in 1954 by the Episcopal Diocese of Texas, St. Luke's has about 1,000 beds. It offers primary and specialty health care services, as well as home health care, outpatient services, and rehabilitation therapy. St. Luke's International Center caters to an international clientele seeking treatment for heart and other serious ailments; through its Episcopal Health Charities, the hospital strives to improve community health.

KEY COMPETITORS
CHRISTUS Health
HCA
MedCath

SAMMONS ENTERPRISES, INC.

5949 Sherry Ln., Ste. 1900
Dallas, TX 75225
Phone: 214-210-5000
Fax: 214-210-5099

CEO: Robert W. Korba
CFO: Joseph A. Ethridge
HR: Carol Cochran
Type: Private

2000 Sales: $2,000.0 million
1-Yr. Sales Change: 27.4%
Employees: 2,300
FYE: December 31

Sammons Enterprises summons its revenues from several sources. The diversified holding company's interests include insurance (Midland National Life Insurance and North American Company for Life and Health Insurance), water bottling (Mountain Valley Spring), industrial equipment distribution (Briggs-Weaver), and industrial trucks (Briggs Equipment). Briggs-Weaver ranks among the leading industrial supply distributors in the US. Sammons Enterprises also owns The Grove Park Inn Resort in Asheville, North Carolina. The late Charles Sammons, an orphan who became a billionaire philanthropist, founded the company in 1962. His estate still owns the company, and his widow, Elaine Sammons, serves as chairman.

KEY COMPETITORS
Nestlé
Prudential
W.W. Grainger

SAMUELS JEWELERS, INC.

OTC: SMJW

2914 Montopolis Dr., Ste. 200
Austin, TX 78741
Phone: 512-369-1400
Fax: 512-369-1500
Web: www.samuels-jewelers.com

CEO: Randy N. McCullough
CFO: Robert J. Herman
HR: Daisy Olivera
Type: Public

2000 Sales: $157.5 million
1-Yr. Sales Change: 94.4%
Employees: 1,535
FYE: May 31

You have to give Samuels Jewelers credit — for not necessarily returning the favor. The retailer (formerly Barry's Jewelers) has tightened up its credit policies and targeted higher-end customers after a couple of trips through bankruptcy. Samuels sells diamond and gemstone jewelry at over 150 stores in 24 states. It operates stores primarily under the Samuels Jewelers and Samuels Diamonds banners and is converting its other stores to those names. Having emerged from Chapter 11 in 1992, the company returned to bankruptcy protection in 1997 before emerging again the following year. Since then Samuels has bought several other chains. DDJ Capital Management owns 49% of the company.

KEY COMPETITORS
Service Merchandise
Signet
Zale

SAN ANTONIO SPURS, LTD.

100 Montana St.
San Antonio, TX 78203
Phone: 210-554-7700
Fax: 210-554-7701
Web: www.nba.com/spurs

CEO: Peter Holt
CFO: Rick A. Pych
HR: Paula Winslow
Type: Private

2000 Sales: $67.4 million
1-Yr. Sales Change: 59.3%
Employees: 100
FYE: June 30

Spurred by David Robinson and Tim Duncan, the San Antonio Spurs basketball team captured its first NBA championship in 1999. The club first hit the court as the Dallas Chaparrals in 1967 as part of the American Basketball Association. The Chaparrals became the San Antonio Spurs in 1973 and entered the NBA in 1976 when the two leagues merged. Success came in the early 1980s behind George "The Iceman" Gervin, who led the Spurs to five division titles. A partnership led by Chairman Peter Holt (with a 32% stake) owns the team. While the Spurs presently call the Alamodome home court, the team is building a new arena: the 18,500-seat, $175 million SBC Center.

KEY COMPETITORS
Dallas Mavericks
Utah Jazz
Minnesota Timberwolves

SAN JUAN BASIN ROYALTY TRUST

NYSE: SJT

500 Throckmorton St.
Fort Worth, TX 76102
Phone: 817-884-4630
Fax: 817-884-4560
Web: www.sjbrt.com

CEO: Lee Ann Anderson
CFO: —
HR: —
Type: Public

2000 Sales: $60.2 million
1-Yr. Sales Change: 89.3%
Employees: —
FYE: December 31

You won't find any crowned heads of state in this royalty trust. San Juan Basin Royalty Trust owns working and royalty interests in oil and gas properties in the San Juan Basin of northwestern New Mexico. Carved from interests owned by Southland Royalty (now part of Burlington Resources Oil & Gas) in 1980, its holding consists of a 75% interest in about 152,000 productive acres in San Juan, Rio Arriba, and Sandoval Counties. The property contains more than 3,300 producing wells with proved reserves of more than 600 barrels of oil and about 300 million cu. ft. of natural gas. Investment firm Alpine Capital owns approximately 30% of San Juan Basin Royalty Trust.

KEY COMPETITORS
Cross Timbers Royalty Trust
Mesa Royalty Trust
Sabine Royalty Trust

SANTA FE INTERNATIONAL CORPORATION

NYSE: SDC

2 Lincoln Centre, Ste. 1100
Dallas, TX 75240
Phone: 972-701-7300
Fax: 972-701-7777
Web: www.sfdrill.com

CEO: C. Stedman Garber Jr.
CFO: Seals M. McCarty
HR: Joe E. Boyd
Type: Public

2000 Sales: $584.0 million
1-Yr. Sales Change: (4.9%)
Employees: 5,500
FYE: December 31

Santa Fe must be this company's patron saint of drilling rigs. Santa Fe International is a contract driller that operates a fleet of 26 marine drillling rigs and 31 land rigs around the world. Key areas of operation include the North Sea, the Middle East, and South America. The company also operates third-party rigs and performs other drilling services; its primary customers are major oil companies. Santa Fe is adding six rigs to its fleet as it plans to launch drilling services in the Gulf of Mexico. SFIC Holdings (Cayman), an entity owned by the government of Kuwait, controls about 39% of the company.

KEY COMPETITORS
Global Marine
Nabors Industries
Transocean Sedco Forex

SBC COMMUNICATIONS INC.

NYSE: SBC

175 E. Houston
San Antonio, TX 78205
Phone: 210-821-4105
Fax: 210-351-2071
Web: www.sbc.com

CEO: Edward E. Whitacre Jr.
CFO: Donald E. Kiernan
HR: Karen E. Jennings
Type: Public

2000 Sales: $51,476.0 million
1-Yr. Sales Change: 4.0%
Employees: 215,088
FYE: December 31

Up the trail from Texas with a herd of telecom operations comes SBC Communications, the #2 local phone outfit in the US after Verizon. SBC has 61 million phone lines in 13 states; its biggest markets are California (Pacific Bell), Texas (Southwestern Bell), and Illinois (Ameritech). The company has combined its US wireless operations with those of BellSouth to form Cingular Wireless, #2 behind Verizon Wireless with more than 20 million subscribers in 38 states. Other services include long-distance (in Connecticut, Kansas, Oklahoma, and Texas) and Internet access (including DSL, through partnership with Covad and Prodigy). SBC also has stakes in telecom operations in more than 20 countries outside the US.

KEY COMPETITORS
AT&T
Verizon
WorldCom

See pages 182–183 for a full profile of this company.

SCHLOTZSKY'S, INC.

Nasdaq: BUNZ

203 Colorado St.
Austin, TX 78701
Phone: 512-236-3600
Fax: 512-236-3601
Web: www.schlotzskys.com

CEO: John C. Wooley
CFO: Richard H. Valade
HR: Alice Klepac
Type: Public

2000 Sales: $59.2 million
1-Yr. Sales Change: 23.6%
Employees: 941
FYE: December 31

Schlotzsky's can't be accused of taking itself too seriously. The company, whose slogan is "funny name, serious sandwich," serves up 15 kinds of deli-style sandwiches, including its popular Schlotzsky's Original, made with ham, two types of salami, three cheeses, and other fixings on a sourdough bun. Schlotzsky's also offers sourdough pizzas, salads, soups, chips, cookies, and other items. It is experimenting with selling its private-label meats, cheeses, and chips in supermarkets, as well as with offering Internet access in select "digital deli" locations. Although Schlotzsky's owns a handful of restaurants, it franchises most of the more than 710 units in 38 states, the District of Columbia, and 10 other countries.

KEY COMPETITORS
Blimpie
Subway
Quizno's

SEACOR SMIT INC.

NYSE: CKH

11200 Richmond Ave., Ste. 400
Houston, TX 77042
Phone: 713-782-5990
Fax: 713-782-5991
Web: www.seacormarine.com

CEO: Charles Fabrikant
CFO: Randall Blank
HR: Rodney Coco
Type: Public

2000 Sales: $339.9 million
1-Yr. Sales Change: 17.4%
Employees: 3,100
FYE: December 31

Smitten by the sea, SEACOR SMIT maintains a fleet of more than 300 marine vessels that support offshore oil and gas operations. Its fleet provides a wide range of services, including cargo and personnel delivery, supply and line handling, towing, and anchoring. Marine services account for the bulk of revenues, but SEACOR also offers standby safety support, logistics services, and oil spill response. More than half of SEACOR's vessels are stationed in the Gulf of Mexico. The company has expanded into drilling through its 27% stake in Chiles Offshore. SEACOR is also investing in telecommunications and data services for the marine industry.

KEY COMPETITORS
GulfMark Offshore
Tidewater
Trico Marine

SEITEL, INC.

NYSE: SEI

50 Briar Hollow Ln., West Bldg., 7th Fl.
Houston, TX 77027
Phone: 713-881-8900
Fax: 713-881-8901
Web: www.seitel-inc.com

CEO: Paul A. Frame
CFO: Debra D. Valice
HR: —
Type: Public

2000 Sales: $163.8 million
1-Yr. Sales Change: 27.3%
Employees: 128
FYE: December 31

There aren't any "Quiet" signs in Seitel's library. With more than 1.1 million linear miles of 2-D and some 16,300 sq. mi. of 3-D data, the firm has the largest seismic databank in North America, which is used to identify underground geologic structures and hydrocarbons. The surveys cover major exploration regions in the US (mainly focused on the Gulf of Mexico area), as well as western Canada and offshore Ireland and the UK. Seitel markets the data to oil and gas firms and partners with them to drive down survey costs. The company contracts with third-party seismic crews to gather data but handles the reprocessing itself. Seitel is spinning off its DDD Energy unit (exploration and production) as Vision Energy.

KEY COMPETITORS
Compagnie Générale de Géophysique
Petroleum Geo-Services

SERVICE CORPORATION INTERNATIONAL

NYSE: SRV

1929 Allen Pkwy.
Houston, TX 77019
Phone: 713-522-5141
Fax: 713-525-5586
Web: www.sci-corp.com

CEO: R. L. "Bob" Waltrip
CFO: Jeffrey E. Curtiss
HR: Helen Dugand
Type: Public

2000 Sales: $2,564.7 million
1-Yr. Sales Change: (22.8%)
Employees: 29,326
FYE: December 31

Service Corporation International (SCI) is to death what H&R Block is to taxes. SCI, the largest funeral services company in the world, owns about 4,400 funeral homes, cemeteries, and crematoria in 18 countries, mostly in the US and Canada (which account for about two-thirds of its sales), and also in Australia, the UK, and France. Its services include embalmment, burial, and cremation. The company also sells prearranged funeral services, caskets, burial vaults, cremation receptacles, flowers, and burial garments. An acquisition binge in recent years has left the company with sizable debt. To bump up finances, SCI has sold its insurance subsidiary and has begun selling funeral locations and cemeteries.

KEY COMPETITORS
Carriage Services, Inc.
Loewen
Stewart Enterprises

 See pages 184–185 for a full profile of this company.

SEVIN ROSEN FUNDS

Two Galleria Tower
Dallas, TX 75240
Phone: 972-702-1100
Fax: 972-702-1103
Web: www.srfunds.com

CEO: Jon Bayless
CFO: John Jaggers
HR: John Jaggers
Type: Private

Sales: —
1-Yr. Sales Change: —
Employees: —
FYE: December 31

With all its investments in high-tech companies, Sevin Rosen Funds may well be the venture capital arm of the Borg. Founded in 1981 by former electrical engineers L.J. Sevin and Benjamin Rosen (the former Compaq Computer chairman), the firm invests in early-stage companies in such fields as telecommunications, software, semiconductors, technology-related health care services, and medical devices. Sevin Rosen was the lead investor in Compaq, Lotus Development, and CIENA. Its investment funds usually provide between $4 million and $15 million in start-up capital.

KEY COMPETITORS
Kleiner Perkins
Safeguard Scientifics
Vulcan Northwest

SHELL OIL COMPANY

One Shell Plaza
Houston, TX 77002
Phone: 713-241-6161
Fax: 713-241-4044
Web: www.shellus.com

CEO: Steven L. Miller
CFO: Nick J. Caruso
HR: David Ohle
Type: Subsidiary

2000 Sales: $29,671.0 million
1-Yr. Sales Change: 53.9%
Employees: 11,140
FYE: December 31

Shell Oil doesn't shilly-shally around. It explores for, produces, and markets oil, natural gas, and chemicals. The company focuses its exploration on the Gulf of Mexico and has proved reserves of 1.5 billion barrels of oil and 4.6 trillion cu. ft. of natural gas. Leading an industry trend toward alliances, Shell has partnered with Texaco and Saudi Aramco in US refining and marketing ventures and with Exxon Mobil in production in California. Shell is also major producer of petrochemical products (Shell Chemical). The company markets natural gas (and electricity) through its Coral Energy unit. Shell's parent, Royal Dutch/Shell Group, is the world's #2 petroleum company (behind Exxon Mobil).

KEY COMPETITORS
BP
ChevronTexaco
Exxon Mobil

 See pages 186–187 for a full profile of this company.

SHELL SERVICES INTERNATIONAL

900 Louisiana St.	CEO: Clive Mather	1999 Est. Sales: $1,200.0 mil.
Houston, TX 77002	CFO: Roy King	1-Yr. Sales Change: 20.0%
Phone: 713-241-1655	HR: Thade van Doesburgh	Employees: —
Fax: 713-241-1376	Type: Business segment	FYE: December 31

The oil business provides Shell Services International (formerly Shell Services International Group) with momentum. Shell Services is a group of accounting, information technology (IT), and procurement companies affiliated with petroleum giant Royal Dutch/Shell Group. Although much of its business comes from other group affiliates, Shell Services draws an increasing portion of sales from outside companies in more than 100 different countries. The group's offerings include management consulting and IT consulting services, including information management, e-business, enterprise resource planning, supply-chain management, data warehouse software, and infrastructure services.

KEY COMPETITORS
Accenture
Computer Sciences
Ernst & Young

SILICON LABORATORIES INC.   Nasdaq: SLAB

4635 Boston Ln.	CEO: Navdeep S. Sooch	2000 Sales: $103.1 million
Austin, TX 78735	CFO: John W. McGovern	1-Yr. Sales Change: 119.8%
Phone: 512-416-8500	HR: Rhonda Berenguel	Employees: 256
Fax: 512-416-9669	Type: Public	FYE: December 31
Web: www.silabs.com		

Silicon Laboratories keeps cooking up new chips for communications devices. The company develops mixed-signal integrated circuits (ICs) for products such as cell phones, set-top boxes, and computer modems. Silicon Laboratories' Direct Access Arrangement products protect wireline devices from telephone line power surges. Its customers include PCTEL (46% of sales), 3Com, and Motorola. The fabless company relies on Taiwan Semiconductor Manufacturing to produce its ICs. Venture capital firm Austin Ventures owns 21% of Silicon Laboratories. Founders Navdeep Sooch (chairman, president, and CEO), David Welland (VP of technology), and Jeffrey Scott (VP of engineering) together own about 41%.

KEY COMPETITORS
Agere Systems
Broadcom
Infineon Technologies

SILVERLEAF RESORTS, INC.   NYSE: SVR

1221 Riverbend Dr., Ste. 120	CEO: Robert E. Mead	1999 Sales: $230.8 million
Dallas, TX 75247	CFO: Harry J. White Jr.	1-Yr. Sales Change: 66.8%
Phone: 214-631-1166	HR: Ben Jenkins	Employees: 3,561
Fax: 214-638-7256	Type: Public	FYE: December 31
Web: www.silverleafresorts.com		

Silverleaf Resorts helps vacationers get away without going far away. The company owns and operates about a dozen time-share resorts in six states. Silverleaf's focus is on "drive-to resorts," which are located near major cities (such as Chicago, Dallas, Houston, and St. Louis) and attract short-stay vacationers. In addition, the company owns "destination resorts" that are more luxurious and expensive. Each resort offers amenities such as fishing, boating, tennis, golf, or horseback riding. Due to financial difficulties, the company began cutting employees to curtail costs. It also defaulted on some of its loans in 2001 and began negotiating with creditors.

KEY COMPETITORS
Cendant
Marriott International
Sunterra

SMITH INTERNATIONAL, INC.

NYSE: SII

411 N. Sam Houston Pkwy., Ste. 600
Houston, TX 77060
Phone: 281-443-3370
Fax: 281-233-5199
Web: www.smith.com

CEO: Douglas L. Rock
CFO: Margaret K. Dorman
HR: Peter D. Nicholson
Type: Public

2000 Sales: $2,761.0 million
1-Yr. Sales Change: 52.9%
Employees: 9,892
FYE: December 31

Smith International helps oil and gas producers pump it up. The company makes premium drill bits, drilling fluids, and related products and offers drilling-related services. Its M-I Fluids unit sells fluids used to cool and lubricate drill bits and prevent pipes from clogging. Its Wilson Supply business provides pipe, valves, fittings and other maintenance devices primarily to oil and mining companies in the US. The Smith Drilling & Completions and Smith Bits units produce diamond polycrystalline drill bits and other drilling equipment. The company owns sites from which it mines some of the barite and bentonite necessary for making drill fluids. More than 50% of Smith International's sales are outside the US.

KEY COMPETITORS
Baker Hughes
Halliburton
Schlumberger

SNELLING AND SNELLING, INC.

12801 N. Central Expwy., Ste. 700
Dallas, TX 75243
Phone: 972-239-7575
Fax: 972-239-6881
Web: www.snelling.com

CEO: Timothy J. Loncharich
CFO: J. Russell Crews
HR: Shelly Walker
Type: Private

2000 Sales: $481.0 million
1-Yr. Sales Change: 48.0%
Employees: 500
FYE: December 31

When your mom yells "Get a job!" twice, its time to check out Snelling and Snelling. The company provides temporary, temp-to-hire, contract, and permanent personnel for a range of positions, including accounting, data input, sales, clerical, marketing, and management. Snelling and Snelling has more than 290 company-owned or franchised branches across the US; it also has a location in Brazil. In addition, the company operates Snelling University, which trains franchisees and their employees. The family-owned company was founded in 1951 by Lou and Gwen Snelling.

KEY COMPETITORS
Adecco
Kelly Services
Manpower

SOFTWARE SPECTRUM, INC.

Nasdaq: SSPE

2140 Merritt Dr.
Garland, TX 75041
Phone: 972-840-6600
Fax: 972-864-7878
Web: www.softwarespectrum.com

CEO: Judy C. Odom
CFO: James W. Brown
HR: Carrie Adams
Type: Public

2001 Sales: $1,213.3 million
1-Yr. Sales Change: 20.7%
Employees: 2,000
FYE: April 30

Software Spectrum's product offerings and services run the gamut. The business software reseller provides applications from Microsoft (about two-thirds of sales), IBM, Attachmate, and others to more than 8,800 clients in North America, Europe, and Asia. It also offers technical services in the core areas of networking infrastructure, outsourcing, and enterprise license management. Software Spectrum generates almost 90% of its sales from volume licensing and maintenance agreements, a practice through which clients receive large-order discounts on products.

KEY COMPETITORS
ASCII Group
CompuCom
CS&T

SOUPER SALAD, INC.

140 Heimer, Ste. 400
San Antonio, TX 78232
Phone: 210-495-9644
Fax: 210-495-9657
Web: www.soupersalad.com

CEO: Rich Kerchenko
CFO: Clint Shackelford
HR: Larry Reeher
Type: Private

2000 Sales: $97.4 million
1-Yr. Sales Change: 21.8%
Employees: 4,500
FYE: December 31

It's a bird, it's a plane, it's Souper Salad! You don't have leap tall buildings in a single bound or change your clothes in a phone booth to dine at this all-you-can-eat restaurant chain's 130 units scattered across 16 states. Souper Salad restaurants offer a 60-item salad bar featuring vegetables, fruit, pasta salads, marinated salads, and dressings made from proprietary recipes. The eateries also offer soup bars, potato bars, sandwiches, and desserts. Ray Barshick founded the company in Houston in 1978 and sold it to merchant bank Saunders, Karp & Megrue in 1994.

KEY COMPETITORS
Buffets
Fresh Choice
Garden Fresh Restaurants

SOUTHERN METHODIST UNIVERSITY

Perkins Administration Building
Dallas, TX 75205
Phone: 214-768-2000
Fax: 214-768-1598
Web: www.smu.edu

CEO: R. Gerald Turner
CFO: Morgan R. Olsen
HR: Bill Detwiler
Type: School

2000 Sales: $218.1 million
1-Yr. Sales Change: (22.1%)
Employees: 1,432
FYE: May 31

What do actress Kathy Bates, TV producer Aaron Spelling, and NFL Hall-of-Famer Doak Walker have in common? They all attended Southern Methodist University (SMU). Founded in 1911, SMU is a nonsectarian private institution that offers undergraduate, graduate, and professional degrees in such fields as engineering, the humanities, science, and theology, as well as top-ranked programs in business, law, and the arts. It has an enrollment of more than 10,000 students, more than 500 faculty members, and an average yearly tuition of more than $18,000. The South Central Jurisdiction of the United Methodist Church owns SMU.

SOUTHERN UNION COMPANY

NYSE: SUG

504 Lavaca St., Ste. 800
Austin, TX 78701
Phone: 512-477-5852
Fax: 512-370-8380
Web: www.southernunionco.com

CEO: George L. Lindemann
CFO: David J. Kvapil
HR: Nancy M. Capezzuti
Type: Public

2001 Sales: $1,932.8 million
1-Yr. Sales Change: 132.4%
Employees: 3,105
FYE: June 30

Bring enough natural gas-related businesses together and you have a Southern Union. The company's utility units, which include Southern Union Gas and Missouri Gas Energy, distribute natural gas to 1.4 million customers in Florida, Massachusetts, Missouri, Pennsylvania, Rhode Island, and Texas, as well as Mexico. In addition, Southern Union operates gas transmission pipelines in Texas and Mexico and sells propane. Its Mercado Gas Services unit markets natural gas to industrial and commercial customers. CEO George Lindemann and his family own about 28% of Southern Union.

KEY COMPETITORS
Atmos Energy
NiSource
TXU

See pages 188–189 for a full profile of this company.

SOUTHWEST AIRLINES CO.

NYSE: LUV

2702 Love Field Dr.	CEO: James F. Parker	2000 Sales: $5,649.6 million
Dallas, TX 75235	CFO: Gary C. Kelly	1-Yr. Sales Change: 19.3%
Phone: 214-792-4000	HR: —	Employees: 29,274
Fax: 214-792-5015	Type: Public	FYE: December 31
Web: www.southwest.com		

Southwest Airlines will fly any plane, as long it's a Boeing 737, and let passengers sit anywhere they like, as long as they get there first. Sticking with what works, Southwest has expanded its low-cost, no-frills, no-reserved-seats approach to air travel throughout the US to serve more than 57 cities in 29 states. To curb maintenance and training costs, the airline uses only Boeing 737s; it operates about 320 planes. Southwest offers ticketless travel to trim back-office costs and operates its own reservation system. The airline boasts a highly participative corporate culture and a strike-free string of 27 profitable years. Southwest is expanding service to the eastern US.

KEY COMPETITORS
AMR
Delta
UAL

See pages 190–191 for a full profile of this company.

SOUTHWEST BANCORPORATION OF TEXAS, INC.

Nasdaq: SWBT

4400 Post Oak Pkwy.	CEO: Paul B. Murphy Jr.	2000 Sales: $315.1 million
Houston, TX 77027	CFO: David C. Farries	1-Yr. Sales Change: 47.8%
Phone: 713-235-8800	HR: —	Employees: 1,313
Fax: 713-439-5949	Type: Public	FYE: December 31
Web: www.swbanktx.com		

Southwest Bancorporation of Texas, Inc., is the holding company for Southwest Bank of Texas, which has more than 30 full-service branches in the Houston area. The bank offers a full range of commercial and private banking services, including financial planning and investment management and is targeting midsize business clients for further growth. Commercial loans make up nearly 40% of Southwest's portfolio and construction loans more than 25%. The bank also offers single-family and commercial mortgages and consumer loans. Each Southwest branch appoints selected customers to a business development board that assists in tailoring services to better meet customer needs.

KEY COMPETITORS
Coastal Bancorp
Sterling Bancshares
Washington Mutual

SOUTHWEST RESEARCH INSTITUTE

6220 Culebra Rd.	CEO: J. Dan Bates	2000 Sales: $315.0 million
San Antonio, TX 78228	CFO: John F. Sprencel	1-Yr. Sales Change: 5.0%
Phone: 210-684-5111	HR: Bill E. Crumlett	Employees: 2,673
Fax: 210-522-3547	Type: Not-for-profit	FYE: September 30
Web: www.swri.edu		

If you're looking for research at an institute in the Southwest, look no further. Founded in 1947 by oilman and rancher Thomas Slick Jr., Southwest Research Institute is an independent, not-for-profit research and development institution that contracts to explore subjects from A (aboveground fuel tanks) to Z (zero gravity fluids). Other research areas include artificial intelligence, bioengineering, electronics, engine design, and mechanics. The institute's more than 2,700 scientists, engineers, and support staff conduct research from laboratories, workshops, and testing facilities (occupying nearly 2 million sq. ft.) in San Antonio. Customers include businesses and government agencies worldwide.

KEY COMPETITORS
Battelle Memorial
SAIC
SRI International

SOUTHWEST TEXAS STATE UNIVERSITY

601 University Dr.
San Marcos, TX 78666
Phone: 512-245-2111
Fax: 512-245-8153
Web: www.swt.edu

CEO: Jerome H. Supple
CFO: William A. Nance
HR: John E. McBride
Type: School

2000 Sales: $231.6 million
1-Yr. Sales Change: 10.2%
Employees: —
FYE: August 31

Although not really in the Southwest, San Marcos, Texas, is the home to Southwest Texas State University (SWT). Originally a teacher's college founded by the state legislature in 1903, SWT now has more than 22,000 students pursuing degrees in more than 100 undergraduate and nearly 70 graduate disciplines. The university has more than 1,000 faculty members and houses eight colleges (as well as a graduate school). SWT is the largest school in the Texas State University system, which includes Angelo State University, Lamar University, Sam Houston State University, and Sul Ross State University. The university's board of regents is considering changing the school's name to Texas State University.

SOUTHWESTERN ENERGY COMPANY
NYSE: SWN

2350 N. Sam Houston Pkwy. East, Ste. 300
Houston, TX 77032
Phone: 281-618-4700
Fax: 281-618-4757
Web: www.swn.com

CEO: Harold M. Korell
CFO: Gregory D. Kerley
HR: Jim Mullins
Type: Public

2000 Sales: $363.9 million
1-Yr. Sales Change: 29.8%
Employees: 536
FYE: December 31

Southwestern Energy is putting a lot of energy into oil and gas exploration and production. The company operates in Arkansas, Louisiana, New Mexico, Oklahoma, Texas, and along the Gulf Coast, where it has proved reserves of 380.5 billion cu. ft. of natural gas equivalent. Southwestern Energy is also engaged in natural gas transportation and marketing. Spurred by an unfavorable court judgment, the company announced plans to sell subsidiary Arkansas Western Gas, which distributes natural gas to more than 136,000 customers in Arkansas, to help pay a $109 million judgment in a lawsuit brought by royalty owners. However, Southwestern Energy has had difficulty in finding a buyer to come up with its asking price.

KEY COMPETITORS
Exxon Mobil
Newfield Exploration
Reliant Energy

SOUTHWESTERN LIFE HOLDINGS INC.
Nasdaq: SWLH

717 N. Harwood St.
Dallas, TX 75201
Phone: 214-954-7111
Fax: 214-954-7906

CEO: Bernard Rapoport
CFO: David A. Commons
HR: David Little
Type: Public

2000 Sales: $251.3 million
1-Yr. Sales Change: (60.5%)
Employees: 187
FYE: December 31

There's still life left in Southwestern Life Holdings (formerly PennCorp Financial Group). The firm, which survived Chapter 11 bankruptcy, is the parent of Southwestern Life Insurance, an underwriter of life insurance, accident and sickness insurance, long-term care insurance, and annuities. The company's products are sold mostly to individuals in the southern US; Texas accounts for more than 25% of premium sales. Southwestern Life Holdings has discontinued its payroll sales and career sales divisions. After the restructuring plan, Inverness/Phoenix Capital (a unit of investment firm Inverness Management) owns about a third of the company; chairman and CEO Bernard Rapoport owns some 20%. Swiss Re has bought the firm.

KEY COMPETITORS
American General
MetLife
Prudential

SPINNAKER EXPLORATION COMPANY

NYSE: SKE

1200 Smith St., Ste. 800	CEO: Roger L. Jarvis	2000 Sales: $121.4 million
Houston, TX 77002	CFO: Robert M. Snell	1-Yr. Sales Change: 253.9%
Phone: 713-759-1770	HR: Judy Schmidt	Employees: 46
Fax: 713-759-1773	Type: Public	FYE: December 31

It's hard to run with the wind on an offshore oil rig, but Spinnaker Exploration is gaining speed in the Gulf of Mexico. The natural gas and oil exploration and production company has proved reserves of 183 billion cu. ft. of natural gas equivalent (90% natural gas) and owns the rights to 3-D seismic information for 39 million deep- and shallow-water acres off the Louisiana and Texas coasts. Spinnaker Exploration has working interests in 37 wells (all but one are natural gas); it plans to continue drilling exploratory wells in its 207 leasehold interests that cover about 740,000 acres. Warburg, Pincus Ventures, a founder, owns about 28% of the company; another founder, Petroleum Geo-Services, has sold its stake.

KEY COMPETITORS
Houston Exploration
Pioneer Natural Resources

STAGE STORES, INC.

OTC: STGSV

10201 Main St.	CEO: James Scarborough	2001 Sales: $952.3 million
Houston, TX 77025	CFO: Michael E. McCreery	1-Yr. Sales Change: (15.1%)
Phone: 713-667-5601	HR: Ron Lucas	Employees: 14,021
Fax: 713-660-3330	Type: Public	FYE: January 31
Web: www.stagestoresinc.com		

Stage Stores is closing the curtains on some of its failing stores. The company operates more than 470 department stores (after closing more than 200), mainly small stores in rural towns throughout about 20 central, southern, and midwestern states. Through its Stage, Bealls, and Palais Royal stores, the company offers moderately priced fashion apparel, cosmetics, gifts, and footwear. Brands such as Liz Claiborne, Calvin Klein, and NIKE make up 85% of sales; Levi Strauss rings up about 6%. Stage Stores also sells private-label merchandise. Shoppers can charge items on the company's private-label credit cards. Due to sluggish sales, the company filed for Chapter 11 bankruptcy and plans to close 121 more stores.

KEY COMPETITORS
J. C. Penney
Target
Wal-Mart

THE STAUBACH COMPANY

15601 Dallas Pkwy., Ste. 400	CEO: Roger Staubach	2001 Sales: $180.0 million
Dallas, TX 75001	CFO: Cathy Sweeney	1-Yr. Sales Change: 9.1%
Phone: 972-361-5000	HR: A. Jeff Lamb	Employees: 1,000
Fax: 972-361-5906	Type: Private	FYE: June 30
Web: www.staubach.com		

Former Dallas Cowboys quarterback Roger Staubach has gone from getting sacked to sacking great real estate deals. The Staubach Company is a real estate firm that provides property location services around the world, focusing on tenant services. Clients include Salomon Smith Barney, Staples, Pfizer, Cisco Systems, Old Navy, and WorldCom. The firm also provides planning and research; financial assistance (through its Wolverine Equities and NLP-Net Lease Properties affiliates); negotiation services; and portfolio, property, and lease management. The company has a global real estate services joint venture, DTZ Staubach Tie Leung, with DTZ Debenham Tie Leung, a real estate firm covering Europe, Africa, and Asia.

KEY COMPETITORS
CB Richard Ellis
Jones Lang LaSalle
Trammell Crow

STERLING BANCSHARES, INC.

Nasdaq: SBIB

15000 Northwest Fwy., Ste. 200
Houston, TX 77040
Phone: 713-466-8300
Fax: 713-466-3117
Web: www.banksterling.com

CEO: George Martinez
CFO: Eugene S. Putnam Jr.
HR: Bambi L. McCullough
Type: Public

2000 Sales: $196.0 million
1-Yr. Sales Change: 28.2%
Employees: 1,094
FYE: December 31

Sterling Bancshares is the holding company for Sterling Bank, which provides commercial and retail banking services through some 30 branches in the Houston, Dallas, and San Antonio areas. The bank's services include checking, savings, money market, and IRA accounts, along with certificates of deposit and automated teller machines. Commercial real estate and business loans make up about two-thirds of its loan portfolio. Residential mortgage, consumer, and construction loans are also offered. Subsidiary Sterling Capital Mortgage (80%-owned) originates and services single-family residential mortgages from 25 offices located primarily west of the Mississippi River.

KEY COMPETITORS
Coastal Bancorp
Southwest Bancorp of Texas
Wells Fargo

STERLING CHEMICALS HOLDINGS, INC.

OTC: STXX

1200 Smith St., Ste. 1900
Houston, TX 77002
Phone: 713-650-3700
Fax: 713-654-9551
Web: www.sterlingchemicals.com

CEO: Frank P. Diassi
CFO: Paul G. Vanderhoven
HR: Robert O. McAlister
Type: Public

2000 Sales: $1,078.4 million
1-Yr. Sales Change: 49.6%
Employees: 1,180
FYE: September 30

Sterling Chemicals Holdings provides the chemistry for making products ranging from Styrofoam cups to hosiery. The company makes petrochemicals, acrylic fibers, and pulp chemicals, which it sells primarily to chemical companies (British Petroleum accounts for 12% of sales). Sterling's principal products include styrene (46% of sales) and pulp chemicals (20%). Its acrylic fiber operations produce textile and technical fibers used in the apparel, industrial, and auto industries. The company also licenses and supervises the construction of large-scale chlorine dioxide generators (used to convert sodium chlorate into chlorine dioxide) for the pulp and paper industries. Sterling operates plants in the US and Canada.

KEY COMPETITORS
Akzo Nobel
ChevronTexaco
Dow Chemical

STEVENS TRANSPORT INC.

9757 Military Pkwy.
Dallas, TX 75227
Phone: 972-216-9000
Fax: 972-289-7002
Web: www.stevenstransport.com

CEO: Steven L. Aaron
CFO: Bob Nelson
HR: Elsa Brewer
Type: Private

2000 Sales: $231.0 million
1-Yr. Sales Change: 12.1%
Employees: 1,425
FYE: December 31

Staying cool is a must for Stevens Transport. An irregular-route, refrigerated truckload carrier (or reefer), Stevens hauls frozen foods throughout 48 contiguous US states. Through alliances it also covers every province in Canada, as well as every state in Mexico. The company maintains 14 service centers and a fleet of about 1,400 trucks and 1,450 refrigerated trailers. Stevens' trailers ride the rails to provide intermodal refrigerated transport around the US. The company also provides customers with third-party logistical support and uses satellite technology to track its fleet. CEO Steven Aaron owns the firm, which he founded in 1980.

KEY COMPETITORS
KLLM Transport Services
Marten Transport
Simon Transportation Services

STEWART & STEVENSON SERVICES, INC.

Nasdaq: SSSS

2707 North Loop West
Houston, TX 77008
Phone: 713-868-7700
Fax: 713-868-7692
Web: www.ssss.com

CEO: Michael L. Grimes
CFO: John H. Doster
HR: Steve Hines
Type: Public

2001 Sales: $1,153.2 million
1-Yr. Sales Change: 26.5%
Employees: 4,100
FYE: January 31

If you need a little drive, consider Stewart & Stevenson Services. The company's Power Products Segment sells and rents engineered power systems (53% of sales), including diesel engines, transmissions, generator sets, and construction equipment. Its suppliers include Detroit Diesel, GM, and John Deere. Stewart & Stevenson's Tactical Vehicles Segment (26% of sales) assembles equipment for the US Army such as troop carriers and dump trucks. Other operations make ground support equipment for the airline industry and exploration and production gear for the petroleum industry. Stewart & Stevenson has operations in the Americas, Europe, and the Middle East. US customers account for 90% of the company's sales.

KEY COMPETITORS
Caterpillar
DaimlerChrysler
Steyr-Daimler-Puch
Aktiengesellschaft

STEWART INFORMATION SERVICES CORPORATION

NYSE: STC

1980 Post Oak Blvd., Ste. 800
Houston, TX 77056
Phone: 713-625-8100
Fax: 713-552-9523
Web: www.stewart.com

CEO: Malcolm S. Morris
CFO: Max Crisp
HR: Nita B. Hanks
Type: Public

2000 Sales: $935.5 million
1-Yr. Sales Change: (12.7%)
Employees: 5,627
FYE: December 31

Stewart Information Services Corporation is a one-stop title insurance shop. Through its Stewart Title, Landata, and National Title subsidiaries, among others, the company writes title insurance policies through some 5,300 agents (mostly independent) in the US and abroad. In addition to title insurance (about 90% of sales), Stewart also provides a variety of real estate information and services to help mortgage lenders close deals. These services include property appraisals, title reports, and flood determinations. Stewart's title insurance and information services customers include government entities, real estate developers, and mortgage lenders.

KEY COMPETITORS
First American Corporation
LandAmerica Financial Group

SUIZA DAIRY GROUP

2515 McKinney Ave., Ste. 1200
Dallas, TX 75201
Phone: 214-303-3400
Fax: 214-303-3838

CEO: Pete Schenkel
CFO: Barry Fromberg
HR: Robert Dunn
Type: Joint venture

2000 Sales: $4,660.3 million
1-Yr. Sales Change: 3.6%
Employees: 17,500
FYE: December 31

Nourished by two of the nation's top fluid milk producers, Suiza Dairy Group has become one of the biggest cows in the dairy. The joint venture between Suiza Foods (which owns 66%) and Dairy Farmers of America (DFA, 34%) was formed in early 2000 when Suiza combined its domestic fluid milk operations with #3 fluid milk producer Southern Foods (50%-owned by DFA). Suiza Dairy Group operates more than 80 dairy processing plants that produce and distribute milk to 46 states. Its brands include Meadow Gold, Borden, Elsie, Foremost, Oak Farms, Country Fresh, Tuscan, Dairymens, Pet, Flav-o-Rich, Broughton, and Suiza Dairy. DFA has announced that it will sell its stake in the venture to Suiza Foods.

KEY COMPETITORS
California Dairies Inc.
Dean Foods
Land O'Lakes

SUIZA FOODS CORPORATION

NYSE: SZA

2515 McKinney Ave., Ste. 1200
Dallas, TX 75201
Phone: 214-303-3400
Fax: 214-303-3499
Web: www.suizafoods.com

CEO: Gregg L. Engles
CFO: Barry A. Fromberg
HR: Robby Dunn
Type: Public

2000 Sales: $5,756.3 million
1-Yr. Sales Change: 28.4%
Employees: 18,000
FYE: December 31

Suiza Foods has become the milk king by taking over other dairies' thrones. The leading producer of fluid milk and dairy products, Suiza has grown rapidly through acquisitions. Its products are made under national brands such as International Delight (creamers) and Second Nature (egg substitute). It also makes private-label and regional brands that are sold to grocery and food service customers, mainly in the US. Suiza Foods also owns a majority interest in Spanish dairy producer Leche Celta and 66% of Suiza Dairy Group, a milk processing joint venture with Dairy Farmers of America. The company is buying rival Dean Foods with plans to merge management of the two companies and possibly take on the Dean Foods name.

KEY COMPETITORS

Dean Foods
Kraft Foods
Parmalat Finanziaria

 See pages 192–193 for a full profile of this company.

SUN COAST RESOURCES INC.

6922 Cavalcade
Houston, TX 77028
Phone: 713-844-9600
Fax: 713-844-9696
Web: www.suncoastresources.com

CEO: Kathy Lehne
CFO: Lisa Smith
HR: Samantha Aycock
Type: Private

2000 Sales: $300.0 million
1-Yr. Sales Change: 34.2%
Employees: 150
FYE: December 31

Breaking the glass ceiling with gushers of Texas tea, woman-owned Sun Coast Resources buys refined oil and sells it to third-party customers such as convenience stores, school districts, and companies in the construction industry. Founded in 1985 by Kathy Lehne with $2,000 in start-up capital, Sun Coast Resources serves customers (including the US Coast Guard) in the South and Southwest US. The company offers transportation services as well as gasoline and diesel fuels, lubricants, and on-site and fleet fueling. Sun Coast carries a full line of Exxon lubricants.

KEY COMPETITORS

George Warren
Martin Resource Management

SWIFT ENERGY COMPANY

NYSE: SFY

16825 Northchase Dr., Ste. 400
Houston, TX 77060
Phone: 281-874-2700
Fax: 281-874-2726
Web: www.swiftenergy.com

CEO: Terry E. Swift
CFO: Alton D. Heckaman Jr.
HR: Peggy Hall
Type: Public

2000 Sales: $189.5 million
1-Yr. Sales Change: 74.0%
Employees: 181
FYE: December 31

No laggard, oil and gas exploration and production company Swift Energy has interests in more than 1,520 producing wells in eight US states, primarily in Texas and Louisiana. The company's core production areas are the AWP Olmos Field in South Texas (37% of Swift Energy's proved reserves) and Master's Creek in West Louisiana. It is also pursuing development and exploration activities in East Texas and New Zealand. Swift Energy attempts to increase reserves and production by adjusting the balance between drilling and acquisition activities in response to market conditions. The company's proved reserves consist of 629.4 billion cu. ft. of natural gas equivalent.

KEY COMPETITORS

Apache
BP
Exxon Mobil

SWS GROUP, INC.

1201 Elm St., Ste. 3500
Dallas, TX 75270
Phone: 214-859-1800
Fax: 214-859-0810
Web: www.southwestsecurities.com

CEO: David Glatstein
CFO: Stacy M. Hodges
HR: Jim Zimcosky
Type: Public

2001 Sales: $470.7 million
1-Yr. Sales Change: (20.1%)
Employees: 1,121
FYE: June 30

Southwest Securities Group is a diversified investment and financial services company. Its major subsidiary, Southwest Securities, provides clearing, brokerage, and asset management services to individual and institutional clients. Brokers and dealers in the US, Canada, and Europe use its clearing services. Southwest Securities' investment banking services target corporate clients in the southwestern US; the company also operates retail brokerages in New Mexico and Texas. Other subsidiaries include Mydiscountbroker.com, an online discount broker, and mutual fund manager Westwood Management. The firm has expanded beyond its home turf, launching underwriting operations in New England.

KEY COMPETITORS
Morgan Keegan
Raymond James Financial
RBC Dain Rauscher

SYNAGRO TECHNOLOGIES, INC.

1800 Bering Dr., Ste. 1000
Houston, TX 77057
Phone: 713-369-1700
Fax: 713-369-1750
Web: www.synagro.com

CEO: Ross M. Patten
CFO: J. Paul Withrow
HR: Mike Allison
Type: Public

2000 Sales: $163.1 million
1-Yr. Sales Change: 188.7%
Employees: 918
FYE: December 31

Ever-growing Synagro Technologies collects, processes, and monitors sludge (known as biosolids) created by the treatment of wastewater. The company performs these services for state and local governments and private companies throughout the US. It markets to landfill operators, agri-businesses, and transportation service companies. The company has a fleet of trucks to pump, collect, and transport sludge wastes to its treatment facilities. Once treated, the sludge can be turned into products such as fertilizer or stored. Other services include biosolid consulting and management. Synagro purchased organic waste treatment company Bio Gro from Waste Management, one of seven acquisitions it made in 2000.

KEY COMPETITORS
CET Environmental
Ecology and Environment
TRC

SYSCO CORPORATION

1390 Enclave Pkwy.
Houston, TX 77077
Phone: 281-584-1390
Fax: 281-584-2721
Web: www.syscosmart.com

CEO: Charles H. Cotros
CFO: John K. Stubblefield Jr.
HR: K. Susan Billiot
Type: Public

2001 Sales: $21,784.5 million
1-Yr. Sales Change: 12.9%
Employees: 43,000
FYE: June 30

SYSCO went from being a small fry to delivering them as the largest food service distributor in North America. The company provides an inventory of some 275,000 products to about 356,000 restaurants, schools, hotels, health care institutions, and other food service customers. Restaurants account for about two-thirds of sales; its SYGMA Network subsidiary focuses on serving chain restaurants such as Wendy's International. SYSCO distributes fresh and frozen meat, poultry, seafood, fruits and vegetables, canned and dry products, paper and disposable products, cleaning supplies, kitchen equipment, and medical supplies. The company has a network of more than 115 facilities throughout the US and in Canada.

KEY COMPETITORS
McLane Foodservice
Performance Food
U.S. Foodservice

📖 See pages 194–195 for a full profile of this company.

TACO CABANA, INC.

8918 Tesoro Dr., Ste. 200
San Antonio, TX 78217
Phone: 210-804-0990
Fax: 210-804-1970
Web: www.tacocabana.com

CEO: Daniel T. Accordino
CFO: James Jenkins
HR: Douglas Gammon
Type: Subsidiary

2000 Sales: $170.7 million
1-Yr. Sales Change: 7.0%
Employees: 5,000
FYE: December 31

Taco Cabana knows salsa is not just a dance. The company offers about 125 Mexican patio cafes (including 10 franchises) primarily in Texas, but also in Georgia, New Mexico, Indiana, and Oklahoma. Taco Cabana serves Tex-Mex and traditional Mexican fare, including fajitas, enchiladas, tacos, margaritas, and breakfast foods. It competes with most sit-down Tex-Mex restaurants, but its prices and service resemble those of fast-food outlets. The company is completing an image makeover that is a departure from the vivid pink walls and flashy neon for which Taco Cabana is known; the restaurants aim for more of a vintage Mexican courtyard look. Privately held Carrols Corp., a large Burger King franchisor, bought the company in 2000.

KEY COMPETITORS
Brinker
Del Taco
Taco Bell

TANDY BRANDS ACCESSORIES, INC.

Nasdaq: TBAC

690 E. Lamar Blvd., Ste. 200
Arlington, TX 76011
Phone: 817-548-0090
Fax: 817-548-1144
Web: www.tandybrands.com

CEO: J. S. Britt Jenkins
CFO: Stanley T. Ninemire
HR: Jan Hancock
Type: Public

2001 Sales: $199.0 million
1-Yr. Sales Change: 4.7%
Employees: 1,224
FYE: June 30

Tandy Brand Accessories would like to belt you — in a gentle way. Primarily a leather goods manufacturer, Tandy Brand garners about 50% of its sales from belts; the rest comes from leather goods such as wallets and handbags, as well as scarves, neckties, and other accessories. Although the company has licenses to make products for national brands (including Bugle Boy, Dockers, Florsheim, Haggar, and Jones New York), most of its products are proprietary brands and private-label items made for companies such as Wal-Mart and J. C. Penney. (Wal-Mart accounts for nearly 40% of sales.) Its proprietary brands include Amity, Rolfs, Prince Gardner, and Princess Gardner. Employees own approximately 16% of Tandy Brands.

KEY COMPETITORS
Fossil
Humphreys
Swank

TANOX, INC.

Nasdaq: TNOX

10301 Stella Link
Houston, TX 77025
Phone: 713-578-4000
Fax: 713-578-5002
Web: www.tanox.com

CEO: Nancy T. Chang
CFO: Michael A. Kelly
HR: Gary M. Glandon
Type: Public

2000 Sales: $12.7 million
1-Yr. Sales Change: 807.1%
Employees: 95
FYE: December 31

Tanox may put an end to your allergy misery. The firm develops monoclonal antibodies, which mimic the human immune system's defenses, to treat autoimmune and inflammatory diseases. Lead drug product Xolair may treat allergic asthma and hay fever by blocking allergic reactions. The Tanox pipeline includes Hu-901, designed to alleviate allergic reactions to peanuts, and 5D12, designed to treat autoimmune diseases such as Crohn's disease. Tanox is collaborating with Novartis and Genentech to develop and market Xolair; other partners include Chiron and Biogen. Novartis owns about 15% of Tanox; co-founders and former spouses Nancy and Tse Wen Chang together own another 15%.

KEY COMPETITORS
Celltech Group
Immunex
Protein Design Labs

TAUBER OIL COMPANY

55 Waugh Dr., Ste. 700
Houston, TX 77210
Phone: 713-869-8700
Fax: 713-869-8069
Web: www.tauberoil.com

CEO: David W. Tauber
CFO: Stephen E. Hamlin
HR: Debbie Moseley
Type: Private

2000 Est. Sales: $1,000.0 mil.
1-Yr. Sales Change: 0.0%
Employees: 45
FYE: September 30

No petrochemical product is taboo for oil refiner and marketer Tauber Oil. The company, which was founded by O. J. Tauber Sr. in 1953, markets refined petroleum products, natural gas, carbon black feedstocks, liquefied petroleum gases, chemicals, and petrochemicals (including benzene, styrene monomer, and methanol). The company is one of the US's leading suppliers of feedstocks for reforming and olefin cracking. Subsidiary Tauber Petrochemical was created in 1997 to beef up the company's international petrochemical business. Tauber maintains a fleet of over 100 rail cars.

KEY COMPETITORS
Exxon Mobil
Lyondell Chemical
Valero Energy

TDINDUSTRIES, LTD.

13850 Diplomat Dr.
Dallas, TX 75234
Phone: 972-888-9500
Fax: 972-888-9482
Web: www.tdindustries.com

CEO: Jack Lowe Jr.
CFO: —
HR: —
Type: Private

2000 Sales: $204.0 million
1-Yr. Sales Change: 22.7%
Employees: 1,500
FYE: December 31

Texans count on air conditioning, and Texas building owners and operators count on TDIndustries. The mechanical contractor installs heating, ventilation, and air-conditioning (HVAC); electrical; and plumbing systems in commercial, industrial, and multifamily residential buildings, primarily through general contractors. TDIndustries also operates, maintains, repairs, and upgrades mechanical systems. The company offers services nationwide, but operates primarily in Texas for companies such as BANK ONE, Hitachi, and J. C. Penney. The father of CEO Jack Lowe Jr. founded TDIndustries in 1946. The employee-owned firm ranked #4 on the 2000 *FORTUNE* list of the best companies to work for.

KEY COMPETITORS
AMPAM
EMCOR
Encompass Services Corp.

TEMPLE-INLAND INC.

NYSE: TIN

1300 S. Mopac Expwy.
Austin, TX 78746
Phone: 512-434-8000
Fax: 512-434-3750
Web: www.templeinland.com

CEO: Kenneth M. Jastrow II
CFO: Randall D. Levy
HR: M. Richard Warner
Type: Public

2000 Sales: $4,286.0 million
1-Yr. Sales Change: 16.4%
Employees: 14,800
FYE: December 31

For Temple-Inland money grows on trees *and* in banks. Through subsidiaries, the company produces paper products (about half of sales) such as corrugated packaging and point-of-purchase displays. Temple-Inland also operates a Financial Services Group (one-third of sales) that includes Guaranty Federal Bank and its roughly 155 branches in Texas and California. Another subsidiary, Temple-Inland Forest Products, produces lumber, particleboard, gypsum wallboard, and other building materials. Temple-Inland Forest Products also manages 2.2 million acres of timberland in Alabama, Georgia, Louisiana, and Texas. The company also has real estate, mortgage, and insurance interests. Temple-Inland operates chiefly in the US.

KEY COMPETITORS
Georgia-Pacific Group
International Paper
Smurfit-Stone Container

 See pages 196–197 for a full profile of this company.

TEPPCO PARTNERS, L.P.

NYSE: TPP

2929 Allen Pkwy.
Houston, TX 77252
Phone: 713-759-3636
Fax: 713-759-3957
Web: www.teppco.com

CEO: William L. Thacker
CFO: Charles H. Leonard
HR: David E. Owen
Type: Public

2000 Sales: $3,087.9 million
1-Yr. Sales Change: 59.6%
Employees: 798
FYE: December 31

TEPPCO Partners has a lot of business in the pipeline. The company's crude oil assets include more than 3,500 miles of pipeline and 1.6 million barrels of storage. It also operates a 4,300-mile pipeline network (including 20 product delivery terminals and 30 storage facilities in 12 states) that moves refined petroleum products from the Texas Gulf Coast to the central and midwestern US and liquefied petroleum gases to central, midwestern, and northeastern states. The company also owns natural gas liquid fractionation facilities in Colorado. Texas Eastern Products Pipeline, the general partner, is an indirect wholly owned subsidiary of Duke Energy Field Services.

KEY COMPETITORS
EOTT Energy Partners
Kinder Morgan, Inc.
Williams Companies

TESORO PETROLEUM CORPORATION

NYSE: TSO

300 Concord Plaza Dr.
San Antonio, TX 78216
Phone: 210-828-8484
Fax: 210-283-2045
Web: www.tesoropetroleum.com

CEO: Bruce A. Smith
CFO: Gregory A. Wright
HR: Thomas E. Reardon
Type: Public

2000 Sales: $5,104.4 million
1-Yr. Sales Change: 70.1%
Employees: 2,100
FYE: December 31

After exiting its exploration and production activities, Tesoro Petroleum has opted for a more refined existence. The independent oil refiner and marketer has three refineries — in Alaska, Hawaii, and Washington — with a combined capacity of 275,000 barrels per day. It makes gasoline, jet fuel, diesel fuel, fuel oil, liquid asphalt, and other fuel products. Tesoro operates some 280 gas stations (100 company-owned) in Alaska, Hawaii, and several Western states. Its marine services unit provides diesel fuel and other products to oil producers in the Gulf of Mexico. The company has agreed to build and operate about 200 Mirastar branded service stations at Wal-Mart stores in 17 states, primarily in the western US.

KEY COMPETITORS
Equilon Enterprises
Phillips Petroleum
Valero Energy

 See pages 198–199 for a full profile of this company.

TETRA TECHNOLOGIES, INC.

NYSE: TTI

25025 I-45 N.
The Woodlands, TX 77380
Phone: 281-367-1983
Fax: 281-364-4306
Web: www.tetratec.com

CEO: Geoffrey M. Hertel
CFO: Joseph M. Abell III
HR: Linden Price
Type: Public

2000 Sales: $224.5 million
1-Yr. Sales Change: 4.3%
Employees: 1,362
FYE: December 31

TETRA Technologies is a smooth operator when it comes to discarded oil wells. The company is made up of three divisions: fluids (53% of sales), well abandonment services (27% of sales), and testing (20% of sales). The fluids division makes clear brine fluids as well as dry calcium chloride that aid in drilling for the oil and gas industry. Its well abandonment segment decommissions offshore drilling platforms and pipelines. In addition to production testing services for oil and gas operations, TETRA's testing division also recycles the oily residuals that are a byproduct of petroleum refining and exploration. The US accounts for 85% of sales.

KEY COMPETITORS
General Chemical
Halliburton
Smith International

THE TEXAS A&M UNIVERSITY SYSTEM

John B. Connally Building, 301 Tarrow, 3rd Fl.
College Station, TX 77843
Phone: 979-845-3211
Fax: 979-845-5406
Web: tamusystem.tamu.edu

CEO: Howard D. Graves
CFO: Tom D. Kale
HR: Patti Couger
Type: School

2000 Sales: $2,619.8 million
1-Yr. Sales Change: 46.2%
Employees: 23,000
FYE: August 31

Everything is bigger in Texas, even its universities. With more than 90,000 students at nine institutions, The Texas A&M University System ranks among the largest in the US. Its flagship school at College Station is well-known not only for its programs in engineering and agriculture, but also for its long-held traditions and school spirit. Other system institutions include Tarleton State University and Prairie View A&M. The system also runs eight state extension agencies and a health sciences center. Texas A&M was founded in 1876 as the Agricultural and Mechanical College of Texas. The A&M system was formed in 1948. It is funded in part by a $7.7 billion state endowment (shared with the University of Texas).

 See pages 200–201 for a full profile of this company.

TEXAS HEALTH RESOURCES

611 Ryan Plaza Dr., Ste. 900
Arlington, TX 76011
Phone: 817-462-7900
Fax: —
Web: www.texashealth.org

CEO: Douglas D. Hawthorne
CFO: Ron Bourland
HR: Bonnie Bell
Type: Not-for-profit

2000 Sales: $1,340.1 million
1-Yr. Sales Change: 3.8%
Employees: 16,000
FYE: December 31

This company is takin' care of Texas, with about 25 health care facilities in the Dallas-Fort Worth and North Texas region. Formed by the merger of Harris Methodist Health System, Presbyterian Healthcare System, and Arlington Memorial Hospital Foundation, the not-for-profit system includes acute-care hospitals, mental health centers, a retirement community and senior care centers, and home health services. Its network includes more than 4,000 physicians and more than 4,200 beds. Texas Health Resources sold its unprofitable St. Paul Medical Center to the University of Texas.

KEY COMPETITORS
Baylor Health
HCA
Triad Hospitals

TEXAS INDUSTRIES, INC.

NYSE: TXI

1341 W. Mockingbird Ln.
Dallas, TX 75247
Phone: 972-647-6700
Fax: 972-647-3878
Web: www.txi.com

CEO: Robert D. Rogers
CFO: Richard M. Fowler
HR: William J. Durbin
Type: Public

2001 Sales: $1,252.2 million
1-Yr. Sales Change: (4.1%)
Employees: 4,400
FYE: May 31

Texas Industries is "steel" rocking. Texas Industries, Inc. (TXI) produces cement, concrete, and steel products for the construction and manufacturing industries. The company's cement and concrete division makes and sells cement, aggregates (sand, gravel, and crushed limestone), ready-mix concrete, and concrete pipe, block, and brick. TXI sells its cement, concrete, and aggregate products primarily to the construction industry in the southwestern US. Subsidiary TXI Chaparral Steel makes beams, merchant-quality rounds, special bar-quality rounds, and channels, all from recycled steel. Its markets include the construction, rail, defense, automotive, mobile home, and energy industries, primarily in North America.

KEY COMPETITORS
Lafarge North America
USX-U.S. Steel
Vulcan Materials

See pages 202–203 for a full profile of this company.

TEXAS INSTRUMENTS INCORPORATED

NYSE: TXN

12500 TI Blvd.	CEO: Thomas J. Engibous	2000 Sales: $11,875.0 million
Dallas, TX 75266	CFO: William A. Aylesworth	1-Yr. Sales Change: 25.4%
Phone: 972-995-3773	HR: Stephen H. Leven	Employees: 42,400
Fax: 972-995-4360	Type: Public	FYE: December 31
Web: www.ti.com		

Say hello to the big Texan. One of the world's largest semiconductor makers, Texas Instruments (TI) is the market leader in analog chips and digital signal processors (DSPs). Over half the wireless phones sold worldwide contain TI's DSPs, which are also found in an array of devices including VCRs, automotive systems, and computer modems; TI is betting that DSPs will become even more pervasive in years to come. Its semiconductors (over 85% of sales) also include logic chips, microprocessors, and microcontrollers. The company also makes calculators and electronic controls and connectors. TI, which derives nearly three-fourths of sales from outside the US, is using acquisitions to strengthen its core chip lines.

KEY COMPETITORS
Analog Devices
Motorola
STMicroelectronics

 See pages 204–205 for a full profile of this company.

TEXAS LOTTERY COMMISSION

611 E. 6th St.	CEO: Linda Cloud	2000 Sales: $3,939.9 million
Austin, TX 78701	CFO: Bart Sanchez	1-Yr. Sales Change: 24.8%
Phone: 512-344-5000	HR: Jim Richardson	Employees: 335
Fax: 512-344-5490	Type: Government-owned	FYE: August 31
Web: www.txlottery.org		

The eyes of Texas are watching the lotto jackpot. The Texas Lottery Commission oversees one of the country's largest state lotteries, which has pumped more than $7 billion into state coffers since it was created in 1991. About 55% of lottery sales are paid out in prize money, while more than 30% goes to the state's Foundation School Fund. The lottery offers four numbers games, including Lotto Texas, Pick 3, Cash 5, and Texas Two Step, and several instant-win games sold through retailers and vending machines around the state. Retailers such as grocery stores, gas stations, and liquor and convenience stores make a small commission on tickets they sell.

KEY COMPETITORS
Multi-State Lottery

 See pages 206–207 for a full profile of this company.

TEXAS PACIFIC GROUP

301 Commerce St., Ste. 3300	CEO: David "Bondo" Bonderman	Sales: —
Fort Worth, TX 76102	CFO: Jim O'Brien	1-Yr. Sales Change: —
Phone: 817-871-4000	HR: Jennifer Dixon	Employees: 75
Fax: 817-871-4010	Type: Partnership	FYE: December 31

Yee-hah! Let's round us up some LBOs. Investment firm Texas Pacific Group has staked its claim on the buyout frontier with a reputation for scooping up and reforming troubled companies other firms wouldn't dare touch. Its holdings include Oxford Health Plans, Magellan Health Services, Ducati Motor, J. Crew Group, semiconductor maker ZiLOG, and airlines. Texas Pacific Group makes money not only from fund management fees but also from the increased values of holdings. With the US buyout frontier becoming increasingly settled and expensive, the company is heading overseas to invest in Europe. CEO David "Bondo" Bonderman is known for turning around Continental Airlines.

KEY COMPETITORS
Clayton, Dubilier
Hicks, Muse
KKR

TEXAS PETROCHEMICALS LP

3 Riverway, Ste. 1500
Houston, TX 77056
Phone: 713-627-7474
Fax: 713-477-8762
Web: www.txpetrochem.com

CEO: Bill Waycaster
CFO: Carl Stutt
HR: Jimmy Rhodes
Type: Private

2001 Sales: $858.7 million
1-Yr. Sales Change: 15.3%
Employees: 316
FYE: June 30

Texas Petrochemicals has kept motoring along thanks to the US Clean Air Act of 1990, which requires an oxygenate in gasoline in heavily populated areas. The company derives 58% of its sales from the production of MBTE, the predominate oxygenate used in US gasoline; however, it plans to reduce dependence on MBTE after several incidents of groundwater contamination. Other products include butadiene, butene-1, high-purity isobutylene, diisobutylene, and isobutylene concentrate, which are used in the manufacture of synthetic rubber, plastic resins, and lubricants. Texas Petrochemicals also operates its own cogeneration power plant and sells the excess capacity. TPC Holdings owns the company, which was formed in 1968.

KEY COMPETITORS
Equistar Chemicals
Lyondell Chemical
Valero Energy

TEXAS RANGERS BASEBALL CLUB

1000 Ballpark Way
Arlington, TX 76011
Phone: 817-273-5222
Fax: 817-273-5174
Web: rangers.mlb.com

CEO: James R. Lites
CFO: John F. McMichael
HR: Brenda Whittenberg
Type: Private

2000 Sales: $126.5 million
1-Yr. Sales Change: 7.7%
Employees: 250
FYE: December 31

These Texas Rangers will need more than a tin star to get to the World Series. Texas Rangers Baseball operates Dallas' pennant-less American League franchise, which won three division titles in the 1990s but posted only one playoff victory. The team is banking its future success on the talents of Alex Rodriguez, who was signed to a $252 million, 10-year deal (the largest contract in sports history) in 2000. The Rangers play host at the historic-looking Ballpark in Arlington (opened 1994). The club first played as the 1961 Washington Senators expansion team and migrated to Texas in 1972. Tom Hicks (who also owns the Dallas Stars) bought the Rangers in 1998 for $250 million from a group led by George W. Bush.

KEY COMPETITORS
Anaheim Angels
Oakland Athletics
Seattle Mariners

TEXAS REGIONAL BANCSHARES, INC.

Nasdaq: TRBS

3900 N. 10th St., 11th Fl.
McAllen, TX 78501
Phone: 956-631-5400
Fax: 956-632-7706
Web: trbsinc.com

CEO: Glen E. Roney
CFO: R. T. Pigott Jr.
HR: Helen Dickerson
Type: Public

2000 Sales: $203.1 million
1-Yr. Sales Change: 26.0%
Employees: 953
FYE: December 31

Don't mess with Texas Regional Bancshares, the bank holding company for Texas State Bank. The bank serves individuals and businesses through more than 25 branches throughout South Texas. It offers such deposit services as checking and savings accounts, CDs, and IRAs. The bank offers commercial real estate and commercial loans, which each account for about 30% of the loan portfolio. Texas State Bank's other loans include residential mortgages and agricultural, construction, and consumer loans. Bank subsidiary TSB Securities is a full-service securities broker-dealer; TSB Properties receives and liquidates foreclosed assets. Texas Regional Delaware, a second-tier holding company, owns the bank.

KEY COMPETITORS
Coastal Bancorp
Cullen/Frost Bankers
International Bancshares

TEXAS SOUTHERN UNIVERSITY

3100 Cleburne Ave.
Houston, TX 77004
Phone: 713-313-7011
Fax: 713-313-1023
Web: www.tsu.edu

CEO: Priscilla Slade
CFO: Quentin Wiggins
HR: Princess Gardner
Type: School

1997 Sales: $60.6 million
1-Yr. Sales Change: (30.5%)
Employees: 1,149
FYE: August 31

Producing such alumni as late US representatives Barbara Jordan and Mickey Leland, Texas Southern University (TSU) is a historically black public institution established in 1947 by the Texas Legislature. The university, located on a 145-acre campus in downtown Houston, offers nearly 80 baccalaureate degrees and more than 30 graduate degrees to 7,000 students from the US and around the world. Its notable programs include education, political science, biology, pharmacy, law, communications, and business administration. TSU is working to improve its fiscal and administrative standing after lawmakers threatened in 1998 to merge it with another university system.

TIG SPECIALTY INSURANCE SOLUTIONS

5205 N. O'Connor Blvd.
Irving, TX 75039
Phone: 972-831-5000
Fax: 972-831-6081
Web: www.tigspecialty.com

CEO: Courtney C. Smith
CFO: R. Scott Donovan
HR: Lon P. McClimon
Type: Subsidiary

2000 Sales: $978.6 million
1-Yr. Sales Change: (8.9%)
Employees: 748
FYE: December 31

More than just a mouthful, TIG Specialty Insurance Solutions is a company that offers a range of property/casualty insurance and reinsurance products. A subsidiary of Fairfax Financial Holdings, the company sells standard and nonstandard auto, medical malpractice, and accident and health coverage; it also provides workers' compensation coverage, traditional commercial property/liability insurance, and risk management services (including insurance for sporting events) to businesses and groups. TIG markets its products and services through independent agents, brokers, and managing general agents. The company is teaming up with eAutoclaims.com to simplify its claims process.

KEY COMPETITORS
GeneralCologne Re
SAFECO
Travelers

TNP ENTERPRISES, INC.

4100 International Plaza
Fort Worth, TX 76109
Phone: 817-731-0099
Fax: 817-737-1343
Web: www.tnpe.com

CEO: William J. Catacosinos
CFO: Theodore A. Babcock
HR: Melissa D. Davis
Type: Private

2000 Sales: $644.0 million
1-Yr. Sales Change: 11.8%
Employees: 836
FYE: December 31

The sleepy little utility from the Southwest has made a big splash in its industry: TNP Enterprises was acquired in 2000 by a private investor group in the first leveraged buyout of a US electric utility. Industry veteran William Catacosinos of Laurel Hill Capital Partners led the buyout and has become TNP's CEO. Other investors include CIBC World Markets. The company's main subsidiary, Texas-New Mexico Power (TNMP), provides electricity to more than 235,000 customers in 85 towns in north-central and West Texas, along the Texas Gulf Coast, and in southern New Mexico. TNP has formed First Choice Power to compete in the Texas electricity market, which is being restructured. It is also selling its 300-MW power plant.

KEY COMPETITORS
El Paso Electric
Reliant Energy
TXU

TRAMMELL CROW COMPANY

NYSE: TCC

2001 Ross Ave., Ste. 3400
Dallas, TX 75201
Phone: 214-863-3000
Fax: 214-863-3138
Web: www.trammellcrow.com

CEO: Robert E. Sulentic
CFO: Derek R. McClain
HR: Robert A. James
Type: Public

2000 Sales: $761.1 million
1-Yr. Sales Change: 21.1%
Employees: 7,300
FYE: December 31

Among the top commercial real estate management companies in the US, Trammell Crow has something to crow about. The firm oversees more than 500 million sq. ft. of commercial property in the US and Canada. It also offers real estate brokerage services, provides major corporations with infrastructure management services, and offers investment advising as well as property development and construction to corporate and institutional clients. Trammell Crow's 170 offices in Canada and the US and its Trammell Crow Savills joint venture serve multinational corporations around the world. Founder Trammell Crow and his family own nearly 20% of the company.

KEY COMPETITORS
CB Richard Ellis
Cushman & Wakefield
Jones Lang LaSalle

 See pages 208–209 for a full profile of this company.

TRANSCONTINENTAL REALTY INVESTORS, INC.

NYSE: TCI

1800 Valley View Ln., Ste. 300
Dallas, TX 75234
Phone: 469-522-4200
Fax: 469-522-4299
Web: www.basiccapitalmgmt.com/transcont.htm

CEO: Ted P. Stokely
CFO: Brent Horak
HR: Michael K. Lane
Type: Public

2000 Sales: $191.7 million
1-Yr. Sales Change: 55.7%
Employees: 0
FYE: December 31

Real estate investment trust (REIT) Transcontinental Realty Investors specializes in commercial and multifamily real estate. Located mainly in Texas and the Southeast, its portfolio includes some 70 apartment complexes, 25 office buildings, 20 warehouses and shopping centers, four hotels, and 15 undeveloped parcels of land. The REIT has merged with Continental Mortgage and Equity Trust, both formerly parts of the now bankrupt Southmark Corp. Southmark's former president, Gene Phillips, owns about 60% of Transcontinental through affiliated firms.

KEY COMPETITORS
Camden Property
Equity Office Properties Trust
Tarragon Realty Investors

TRANSOCEAN SEDCO FOREX INC.

NYSE: RIG

4 Greenway Plaza
Houston, TX 77046
Phone: 713-232-7500
Fax: 713-232-7027
Web: www.deepwater.com

CEO: J. Michael Talbert
CFO: Robert L. Long
HR: David J. Mullen
Type: Public

2000 Sales: $1,229.5 million
1-Yr. Sales Change: 89.7%
Employees: 15,600
FYE: December 31

Transocean Sedco Forex, one of the world's leading offshore drilling contractors, reaches down deep for oil and gas. It specializes in deepwater drilling, and it isn't afraid of harsh environments. The company's fleet, which includes 50 semisubmersibles, 58 jack-up rigs, and 16 drillships, operates in the world's major offshore oil-producing regions. Transocean Sedco Forex also provides well management services. The company was formed in 1999 when Transocean Offshore merged with Sedco Forex, which had been spun off from Schlumberger. It has expanded with the acquisition of rival R&B Falcon

KEY COMPETITORS
Global Marine
Noble Drilling
Saipem

TRANSPORTATION COMPONENTS, INC.

3 Riverway, Ste. 200
Houston, TX 77056
Phone: 713-332-2500
Fax: 713-572-9496
Web: www.transcomusa.net

CEO: T. Michael Young
CFO: David Phelps
HR: —
Type: Public

1999 Sales: $310.5 million
1-Yr. Sales Change: 132.2%
Employees: 1,790
FYE: December 31

Transportation Components helps heavy-duty vehicles keep on trucking. The company, known as TransCom, is a distributor of replacement parts and supplies for commercial trucks, trailers, and other heavy-duty vehicles. Products distributed by TransCom include parts for engines, trailers, and braking systems, as well as axles, wheels, and rims. The company also offers parts installation and repair, fleet services, and remanufactures brake shoes, turbochargers, and fuel injectors. TransCom, which was formed from nine regional parts supply companies, has facilities in the US, Canada, and Mexico. TransCom is operating under bankruptcy protection.

KEY COMPETITORS
Boler
Hawk
Uni-Select

TRANSTEXAS GAS CORPORATION   OTC: TTXG

1300 N. Sam Houston Pkwy. East, Ste. 310
Houston, TX 77032
Phone: 281-987-8600
Fax: 281-986-8866
Web: www.ttxg.com

CEO: John R. Stanley
CFO: Edwin B. Donahue
HR: Jerald Barkley
Type: Public

2001 Sales: $182.9 million
1-Yr. Sales Change: 73.5%
Employees: 186
FYE: January 31

TransTexas Gas waltzes across South Texas and the upper Gulf Coast exploring for oil and gas. An independent exploration and production company, TransTexas Gas has proved reserves of 132 billion cu. ft. of natural gas equivalent. The company emerged from bankruptcy protection in 2000 after having sold noncore assets, including drilling rigs and pipeline assets, to reduce debt. TransTexas founder and CEO John Stanley — no stranger to bankruptcy courts — owned 81% of the company before the bankruptcy filing and wound up with a 20% stake after the reorganization. Entities controlled by investor Carl Icahn own 34%.

KEY COMPETITORS
Abraxas Petroleum
ChevronTexaco
Exxon Mobil

TRAVELOCITY.COM INC.   Nasdaq: TVLY

15100 Trinity Blvd.
Fort Worth, TX 76155
Phone: 817-785-8000
Fax: 817-785-8003
Web: www.travelocity.com

CEO: Terrell B. Jones
CFO: Ramesh K. Punwani
HR: Joe Luna
Type: Public

2000 Sales: $192.7 million
1-Yr. Sales Change: 112.0%
Employees: 1,300
FYE: December 31

If Jimmy Buffett had known about Travelocity.com, he could have had an e-burger in paradise. The company — the result of a 2000 merger of travel reservation firm Sabre's Travelocity Web site and Preview Travel — is the #1 online travel destination. Users of Travelocity.com can make reservations on most of the world's airlines, more than 50,000 hotels, some 50 car rental companies, and more than 5,000 vacation packages. In addition to travel transaction fees, the company collects about 25% of its revenue from online advertising. Travelocity.com is also helping create online travel exchanges for several Asian airlines. Sabre has 15% voting control of the company, although it owns about 70% of its stock.

KEY COMPETITORS
Expedia
Lowestfare.com
Orbitz

TRAVIS BOATS & MOTORS, INC.

Nasdaq: TRVS

5000 Plaza on the Lake, Ste. 250
Austin, TX 78746
Phone: 512-347-8787
Fax: 512-329-0344
Web: www.travisboats.com

CEO: Mark T. Walton
CFO: Michael B. Perrine
HR: Sue McConnell
Type: Public

2000 Sales: $217.7 million
1-Yr. Sales Change: 19.4%
Employees: 701
FYE: September 30

Travis Boats & Motors is making waves in the boat business. The company sells recreational boats, motors, trailers, and other marine accessories through about 40 Travis Boating Center superstores in Alabama, Arkansas, Florida, Georgia, Louisiana, Mississippi, Oklahoma, Tennessee, and Texas. Travis Boats also offers financing, insurance, and repair services and sells personal watercraft, offshore fishing boats, and cabin cruisers in some locations. Its Travis Edition packages (brand-name boats with motors, trailers, and other accessories) account for most of new-boat sales. Travis Boats has grown primarily by acquiring boat dealerships in the South.

KEY COMPETITORS
Holiday RV Superstores
MarineMax
West Marine

TRIAD HOSPITALS, INC.

NYSE: TRI

13455 Noel Rd., 20th Fl.
Dallas, TX 75240
Phone: 972-789-2700
Fax: 972-789-2801
Web: www.triadhospitals.com

CEO: James D. Shelton
CFO: Burke W. Whitman
HR: Rick Thomason
Type: Public

2000 Sales: $1,235.5 million
1-Yr. Sales Change: (7.0%)
Employees: 15,500
FYE: December 31

Triad Hospitals may not have tripled in size, but it has grown noticeably with its purchase of Quorum Health Group; it is now one of the largest hospital operators in the US. Triad Hospitals, which was spun off from HCA - The Healthcare Company in 1999, operates some 50 hospitals and 14 outpatient surgery centers in nearly 20 Sunbelt and western states. Most of its hospitals are in smaller cities, where they face little competition; almost half are in Arizona and Texas. The company, which had already completed some smaller purchases, took a big bite when it said it would buy fellow HCA spinoff Quorum Health.

KEY COMPETITORS
Banner Health System
Catholic Healthcare West
Tenet Healthcare

TRIANGLE PACIFIC CORP.

16803 Dallas Pkwy.
Addison, TX 75001
Phone: 214-887-2000
Fax: 214-887-2221

CEO: Frank A. Riddick III
CFO: —
HR: Jennifer Wisdom
Type: Subsidiary

1999 Sales: $822.6 million
1-Yr. Sales Change: 137.7%
Employees: —
FYE: December 31

People have been walking all over Triangle Pacific for some 55 years, and the company is ready to get stepped on some more. A subsidiary of Armstrong Holdings, Triangle Pacific makes hardwood flooring and cabinets. Its hardwood-flooring division makes solid and engineered hardwood flooring products under such brand names as Hartco, Bruce, and Robbins. The company sells its products through a network of more than 90 independent wholesale distributors. It is also a leading maker of hardwood, kitchen and bathroom cabinets sold under the Bruce and IXL brands.

KEY COMPETITORS
American Woodmark
Masco

TRILOGY

6034 W. Courtyard Dr.
Austin, TX 78730
Phone: 512-425-3100
Fax: 512-794-8900
Web: www.trilogy.com

CEO: Joe Liemandt
CFO: Patrick Kelly
HR: Jim Abolt
Type: Private

2000 Est. Sales: $250.0 mil.
1-Yr. Sales Change: (16.7%)
Employees: 650
FYE: December 31

Trilogy wants to prove that anything can be bought on the Web. Its software suite handles procurement, customer service, and data integration for companies that purchase complex goods online. It can be used to select, customize, and purchase virtually anything, from computers to heavy machinery. The suite provides clients including Toyota, NCR, and Nationwide with integrated product information, compatibility requirements, and customer support. The company, which is cutting its workforce, is refocusing on four core markets — automotive, financial services, computers, and telecommunications. CEO Joe Liemandt is Trilogy's majority shareholder.

KEY COMPETITORS
Calico Commerce
i2 Technologies
Selectica

TRINITY INDUSTRIES, INC.   NYSE: TRN

2525 Stemmons Fwy.
Dallas, TX 75207
Phone: 214-631-4420
Fax: 214-589-8810
Web: www.trin.net

CEO: Timothy R. Wallace
CFO: Jim S. Ivy
HR: Michael J. Lintner
Type: Public

2001 Sales: $1,904.3 million
1-Yr. Sales Change: (30.5%)
Employees: 15,300
FYE: March 31

If Trinity Industries had a theme song, it could easily have been written by Boxcar Willie. The company makes freight cars, box cars, intermodal cars, hopper cars, gondola cars, and tank cars for hauling everything from lumber to corn syrup. Such railcar business accounts for more than half of Trinity's sales. Its industrial group makes metal containers for storing and transporting liquefied petroleum gas and fertilizer, and its highway construction group makes highway guardrails. Trinity also builds barges for transporting commodities such as grain and coal, and it produces ready-mix concrete and aggregates, primarily in Texas and Louisiana.

KEY COMPETITORS
ACF
Bombardier
Duchossois Industries

 See pages 210–211 for a full profile of this company.

TRITON ENERGY LIMITED

6688 N. Central Expwy., Ste. 1400
Dallas, TX 75206
Phone: 214-691-5200
Fax: 214-691-0340
Web: www.tritonenergy.com

CEO: James C. Musselman
CFO: W. Greg Dunlevy
HR: Andy Mormon
Type: Subsidiary

2000 Sales: $328.5 million
1-Yr. Sales Change: 32.5%
Employees: 195
FYE: December 31

Like its patron deity, the sea god, Triton Energy covers the earth. The international oil and gas exploration and production company has operations in Africa, Asia, Europe, Latin America, and the Middle East. Triton Energy's main properties and operations are in Colombia, the Malaysia-Thailand joint development area, and Equatorial Guinea. Proved reserves stack up to 194.7 million barrels of oil and 592.6 billion cu. ft. of gas. The company's current revenues are from its oil and gas production in Colombia, although it has made a major discovery offshore Equatorial Guinea. Investment firm Hicks, Muse, Tate & Furst owns 38% of the company.

KEY COMPETITORS
BP
CMS Oil and Gas Company
Exxon Mobil

TRT HOLDINGS

420 Decker Dr., Ste. 100
Irving, TX 75062
Phone: 972-730-6664
Fax: 972-871-9240
Web: www.omnihotels.com

CEO: —
CFO: —
HR: Joy Rothschild
Type: Private

2000 Sales: $550.0 million
1-Yr. Sales Change: 22.2%
Employees: 10,000
FYE: December 31

No one can accuse TRT Holdings of failing to put its energies into the lodging business. After making a fortune from Texas oil and gas holdings, the members of the Rowling family, whose investments are controlled by TRT Holdings, sold their Teco Pipeline and the production arm of their Tana Oil & Gas subsidiary, then focused on the hotel empire they started building in 1990. The jewel in TRT Holdings' crown is the Omni Hotels chain, a string of more than 40 luxury hotels (about one-third are franchised) in the US, Canada, and Mexico. The company cut its ties to its past in 2000 when it sold essentially all the remaining assets of its Tana Oil & Gas exploration operations to Unocal.

KEY COMPETITORS
Fairmont Hotels
Marriott International
Starwood Hotels & Resorts

TTI, INC.

2441 Northeast Pkwy.
Fort Worth, TX 76106
Phone: 817-740-9000
Fax: 817-740-1622
Web: www.ttiinc.com

CEO: Paul E. Andrews Jr.
CFO: Nick M. Kypreos
HR: Dick Andrews
Type: Private

1999 Sales: $555.0 million
1-Yr. Sales Change: 20.4%
Employees: 1,055
FYE: December 31

TTI is passionate about passives. Each year the company distributes more than 1.7 million electronic components, including passive components such as resistors and capacitors, and interconnects such as cables, sockets, and filter connectors. Suppliers of its 160,000 line items include 3M, Spectrum Control, Koninklijke Philips, and Vishay Intertechnology. TTI also offers services such as component packaging and supply chain management. TTI, which owner and CEO Paul Andrews founded in 1971 as a supplier to the military, serves manufacturers of aerospace and defense systems, computers, telecom equipment, medical devices, and industrial products. The company is expanding its presence in Europe.

KEY COMPETITORS
All American Semiconductor
Arrow Electronics
Smith & Associates

TUESDAY MORNING CORPORATION

Nasdaq: TUES

14621 Inwood Rd.
Addison, TX 75001
Phone: 972-387-3562
Fax: 972-387-1974
Web: www.tuesdaymorning.com

CEO: Kathleen Mason
CFO: Mark E. Jarvis
HR: Cynthia Allison
Type: Public

2000 Sales: $586.9 million
1-Yr. Sales Change: 20.0%
Employees: 6,340
FYE: December 31

Tuesday Morning offers big discounts every day of the week, but not every week of the year. The closeout retailer sells discontinued merchandise from name-brand manufacturers at steep discounts. Its merchandise typically includes linens, china, cookware, and collectibles. Tuesday Morning's roughly 440 stores, located in 41 states, operate only during eight annual sales events, lasting three to eight weeks each. The retailer keeps costs down by selling from low-rent locations and using seasonal help — only about 15% of its employees are full-time. Investment firm Madison Dearborn Partners, which bought Tuesday Morning in 1997, owns about 71% of the company.

KEY COMPETITORS
Bed Bath & Beyond
Linens 'n Things
Target

THE TURNER CORPORATION

Bank of America Plaza, 901 Main St., Ste. 4900
Dallas, TX 75202
Phone: 214-915-9600
Fax: 214-915-9700
Web: www.turnerconstruction.com

CEO: Thomas C. Leppert
CFO: Donald G. Sleeman
HR: Bruce Ruthven
Type: Subsidiary

2000 Sales: $5,800.0 million
1-Yr. Sales Change: 19.8%
Employees: 4,200
FYE: December 31

The Turner Corporation, a subsidiary of German construction group HOCHTIEF, is one of the world's leading general builders. The firm's subsidiaries built Madison Square Garden and the UN Secretariat in New York City, as well as several of the tallest buildings in the world. Turner builds primarily large projects, including airports, office towers, and correctional, entertainment, and manufacturing facilities, and provides project management services. Subsidiaries also do interior construction and renovation, offer environmental engineering services, and own real estate. Subsidiary Turner International provides design-build, general contracting, and management services outside the US.

KEY COMPETITORS
Bechtel
Clark Enterprises
Peter Kiewit Sons'

 See pages 212–213 for a full profile of this company.

TXU CORP.   NYSE: TXU

1601 Bryan St., 33rd Fl.
Dallas, TX 75201
Phone: 214-812-4600
Fax: 214-812-7077
Web: www.txu.com

CEO: Erle Nye
CFO: Michael J. McNally
HR: Richard Wistrand
Type: Public

2000 Sales: $22,009.0 million
1-Yr. Sales Change: 28.6%
Employees: 16,540
FYE: December 31

TXU! TXU! It sells gas and electricity too! Through its subsidiaries, utility holding company TXU (formerly Texas Utilities) supplies energy to more than 11 million customers in Australia, Europe, and Texas. The company holds the largest utility in the Lone Star State and the largest electricity distributor in the UK. TXU Electric serves 2.6 million Texans and has a generating capacity of 21,100 MW; TXU Gas delivers to 1.4 million Texans. TXU Europe has 4.4 million electric and 1.1 million gas customers in the UK, as well as 6,830 MW of generating capacity. TXU Australia Holdings serves 1 million customers in Victoria. Deregulated operations include telecommunications and global energy trading and marketing.

KEY COMPETITORS
AEP
Centrica
Reliant Energy

 See pages 214–215 for a full profile of this company.

UICI   NYSE: UCI

4001 McEwen Dr., Ste. 200
Dallas, TX 75244
Phone: 972-392-6700
Fax: 972-392-6721
Web: www.uici.net

CEO: Gregory T. Mutz
CFO: Matthew R. Cassell
HR: Dennis Wegehoft
Type: Public

2000 Sales: $1,051.4 million
1-Yr. Sales Change: 3.8%
Employees: 2,300
FYE: December 31

UICI sells health insurance to students and the self-employed through subsidiaries MEGA Life and Health Insurance and Chesapeake Life Insurance, and sells niche market life insurance, as well as student loans and technical support for health care providers. The company markets policies through a sales force consisting of some 4,000 independent contractors. UICI is focusing on its self-employed, student insurance, and life businesses, exiting some of its less profitable operations. The company has liquidated United Credit National Bank, its credit card subsidiary. Founder Ronald Jensen and his wife own more than 15% of the company.

KEY COMPETITORS
AFLAC
Aon
Guarantee Trust

ULTRAK, INC.

Nasdaq: ULTK

1301 Waters Ridge Dr.
Lewisville, TX 75057
Phone: 972-353-6500
Fax: 972-353-6513
Web: www.ultrak.com

CEO: George K. Broady
CFO: Chris T. Sharng
HR: Patty Cramer
Type: Public

2000 Sales: $200.0 million
1-Yr. Sales Change: (3.1%)
Employees: 568
FYE: December 31

Ultrak has the inside track on closed-circuit TV. A designer and manufacturer of closed-circuit TV systems for security, professional audio/video, and industrial applications, Ultrak makes cameras, lenses, monitors, switchers, time-lapse and digital recorders, audio equipment, and video transmission systems. Ultrak sells most of its products under its proprietary brand names, which include Diamond Electronics, Exxis, Phoenix, Smart Choice, and Ultrak. The company also sells Mitsubishi, Sony, and Panasonic products under license. Ultrak's sales force markets its products to distributors worldwide. Chairman and CEO George Broady controls about a third of Ultrak's voting power.

KEY COMPETITORS
Checkpoint Systems
Philips Electronics
Sensormatic

ULTRAMAR DIAMOND SHAMROCK CORPORATION

NYSE: UDS

6000 N. Loop 1604 West
San Antonio, TX 78249
Phone: 210-592-2000
Fax: 210-592-2054
Web: www.udscorp.com

CEO: Jean R. Gaulin
CFO: Robert Shapard
HR: Penelope Rhude Viteo
Type: Public

2000 Sales: $17,061.1 million
1-Yr. Sales Change: 22.1%
Employees: 20,000
FYE: December 31

Ultramar Diamond Shamrock Corporation, which rival Valero has agreed to buy, is the ultimate marketing and refining company — almost. The company is the #2 independent oil refining and marketing company in the US, behind Tosco. Its seven refineries (in California, Colorado, Oklahoma, Texas, and Quebec, Canada) have a total capacity of about 850,000 barrels per day. Ultramar Diamond Shamrock has more than 3,900 retail gas station/convenience stores in the US and Canada; most operate under the Beacon, Diamond Shamrock, Total, or Ultramar brand names. The company also operates pipelines and terminals, a home heating oil business, and petrochemical and natural gas liquids ventures.

KEY COMPETITORS
7-Eleven
Exxon Mobil
Phillips Petroleum

UNITED SUPERMARKETS, INC.

7830 Orlando Ave.
Lubbock, TX 79423
Phone: 806-791-0220
Fax: 806-791-7491
Web: www.unitedtexas.com

CEO: Kent Moore
CFO: Keith Mann
HR: Phil Pirkle
Type: Private

2001 Est. Sales: $575.0 mil.
1-Yr. Sales Change: 2.7%
Employees: 5,000
FYE: January 31

United Supermarkets is about as common in the Texas panhandle as tumbleweeds. The grocer has more than 40 supermarkets throughout mostly rural towns in West and North Texas. Its stores feature deli, floral, and bakery shops, as well as traditional supermarket fare and pharmacies. The company's newer store format, called Market Street, is much larger and stocks more specialty foods. United Supermarkets operates its own distribution facility. Henry Snell founded the company in Sayre, Oklahoma, in 1916 as United Cash Store. Snell bucked the norms of the day — when grocers sold their wares on credit — by selling his goods for cash at lower prices. United Supermarkets is still owned and operated by the Snell family.

KEY COMPETITORS
Albertson's
Furrs Supermarkets
Homeland Holding

UNITED SURGICAL PARTNERS INTERNATIONAL, INC.

Nasdaq: USPI

17103 Preston Rd., Ste. 200 North	CEO: Donald E. Steen	2000 Sales: $135.6 million
Dallas, TX 75248	CFO: Mark A. Kopser	1-Yr. Sales Change: 92.6%
Phone: 972-713-3500	HR: Sherry Reinert	Employees: 2,400
Fax: 972-713-3550	Type: Public	FYE: December 31
Web: www.unitedsurgical.com		

Can you say "forceps" in Spanish? United Surgical Partners International brings together surgeons from the US, Spain, and the UK. In the US, the company owns interests in and/or manages some 30 surgery centers and one surgical hospital; it has several additional centers under construction. Its Spanish stakes include six surgical hospitals, two surgery centers, and one diagnostic facility. The firm owns two surgical hospitals in the UK, with a cancer center under development. Former HCA — The Healthcare Company executive Donald Steen founded the company in 1998 with investment firm Welsh, Carson, Anderson & Stowe, which owns about a third.

KEY COMPETITORS
AmSurg
HEALTHSOUTH
Triad Hospitals

UNIVERSAL COMPRESSION HOLDINGS, INC.

NYSE: UCO

4440 Brittmoore Rd.	CEO: Stephen A. Snider	2001 Sales: $232.8 million
Houston, TX 77041	CFO: Richard W. FitzGerald	1-Yr. Sales Change: 70.7%
Phone: 713-335-7000	HR: Rick Klein	Employees: 1,650
Fax: 713-466-0323	Type: Public	FYE: March 31
Web: www.universalcompression.com		

Universal Compression Holdings desired expansion from the start; it was formed in 1997 to acquire the natural gas compression business of Tidewater, a marine oil services company. The company's purchase of Weatherford International's compression operations has made it the world's second-largest natural gas compression services company (after Hanover Compressor), with a 1,800,000-HP capacity. As a result, Weatherford owns 48% of Universal Compression. Universal Compression provides a range of services, including equipment rental, sales, maintenance, operations, and fabrication, to customers throughout the US and in nine foreign countries, including oil producers, transporters, and processors.

KEY COMPETITORS
Enerflex
Hanover Compressor
Schlumberger

UNIVERSITY OF HOUSTON SYSTEM

4800 Calhoun	CEO: Arthur K. Smith	2000 Sales: $514.9 million
Houston, TX 77204	CFO: Randy J. Harris	1-Yr. Sales Change: (11.0%)
Phone: 713-743-1000	HR: Robert Harrington Jr.	Employees: 8,300
Fax: 713-743-8199	Type: School	FYE: August 31
Web: www.uhsa.uh.edu		

Whether you're looking for heat, humidity, or higher education, Houston's the place for you. The University of Houston System can't do much about the first two, but more than 50,000 students are seeking the latter at the Houston-area public universities that the system oversees. Flagship institution the University of Houston was founded in 1927 and offers more than 275 undergraduate and graduate degree programs in fields such as business, education, humanities, and law. Also under the system's umbrella are the University of Houston-Clear Lake, the University of Houston-Downtown, the University of Houston-Victoria, and the University of Houston System at Fort Bend. The system organization was formed in 1977.

UNIVERSITY OF NORTH TEXAS

1501 W. Chestnut	CEO: Alfred F. Hurley	1999 Sales: $256.6 million
Denton, TX 76203	CFO: Phillip C. Diebel	1-Yr. Sales Change: 4.7%
Phone: 940-565-2000	HR: Steve Miller	Employees: 6,447
Fax: 940-565-4382	Type: School	FYE: August 31
Web: www.unt.edu		

Students at the University of North Texas (UNT) really know how to toot their own horns. Its music school (particularly its jazz program) is regarded as one of the best in the nation. Founded in 1890, UNT has more than 20,000 students studying various undergraduate and graduate disciplines through nine schools and colleges at its main Denton campus. UNT opened a new Dallas branch in 2000 and also is affiliated with the UNT Health Science Center at Fort Worth. In athletics, the Mean Green Eagles are leaving the Big West Conference in every sport except football to join the Sun Belt Conference for the 2000-01 season (football will follow in 2001).

THE UNIVERSITY OF TEXAS SYSTEM

601 Colorado St.	CEO: R. D. "Dan" Burck	2000 Sales: $5,943.1 million
Austin, TX 78701	CFO: Kerry L. Kennedy	1-Yr. Sales Change: 43.9%
Phone: 512-499-4200	HR: Gerald Schroeder	Employees: 79,430
Fax: 512-499-4218	Type: School	FYE: August 31
Web: www.utsystem.edu		

These students are hooked on higher education. The University of Texas System runs nine universities throughout the Longhorn State with a total enrollment of some 153,000 students, making it one of the largest university systems in the US. (Its flagship school in Austin, with 50,000 students, is ranked as the university with the largest campus population in the nation.) UT also runs six health centers and four medical schools and receives more than $1 billion a year in research money. Its $10 billion endowment fund (managed by the University of Texas Investment Management Co.) is the third-largest in the country (after Harvard and Yale). Established in 1876, UT Austin opened in 1883. The UT System was formally organized in 1950.

 See pages 216–217 for a full profile of this company.

U.S. CONCRETE, INC.
Nasdaq: RMIX

2925 Briarpark, Ste. 500	CEO: Eugene P. Martineau	2000 Sales: $394.6 million
Houston, TX 77042	CFO: Michael W. Harlan	1-Yr. Sales Change: 135.0%
Phone: 713-499-6200	HR: Michael W. Harlan	Employees: 375
Fax: 713-499-6201	Type: Public	FYE: December 31

U.S. Concrete is a concrete consolidator. The company was formed to buy companies that sell ready-mixed concrete and related materials (bagged cement, rebar, cast cement products) and services. Ready-mixed concrete accounts for most of the company's sales. U.S. Concrete has a fleet of nearly 1,000 mixer trucks and more than 70 operating plants; the plants produce upwards of 5.6 million cubic yards of concrete a year. The company concentrates on major markets and has operations in California, Michigan, New Jersey, Oklahoma, Tennessee, Texas, and Washington, DC, among other places. Director Robert Walker owns about 11% of the company.

KEY COMPETITORS

Cemex
Holnam
Lafarge North America

U S LIQUIDS INC.

AMEX: USL

411 N. Sam Houston Pkwy. East, Ste. 400
Houston, TX 77060
Phone: 281-272-4500
Fax: 281-272-4545
Web: www.usliquids.com

CEO: Michael P. Lawlor
CFO: Earl J. Blackwell
HR: Wendy O'Dell
Type: Public

2000 Sales: $247.9 million
1-Yr. Sales Change: 6.9%
Employees: 1,200
FYE: December 31

U S Liquids stays strong and healthy on a diet of liquid waste. The company collects, treats, and disposes of liquid waste from landfills, restaurants, breweries and soft drink manufacturers, and auto dealers and service centers. Through 43 facilities in 13 states, U S Liquids picks up commercial (68% of sales) and industrial (23%) waste liquids such as bulk liquids, beverages, chemicals, and used antifreeze, then treats the waste and recycles or disposes of leftover solids. The company sells the commercial waste by-products, such as fats, feed proteins, and industrial grade ethanol. U S Liquids also treats and disposes of oil field wastes from six oilfield waste facilities in Louisiana and Texas.

KEY COMPETITORS
EarthCare
Safety-Kleen
Weststar Environmental

US ONCOLOGY, INC.

Nasdaq: USON

16825 Northchase Dr., Ste. 1300
Houston, TX 77060
Phone: 832-601-8766
Fax: 281-775-0201
Web: www.usoncology.com

CEO: R. Dale Ross
CFO: Bruce D. Broussard
HR: Jerry McMorrough
Type: Public

2000 Sales: $1,324.2 million
1-Yr. Sales Change: 21.2%
Employees: 7,716
FYE: December 31

The name says it all. US Oncology is the US's largest outpatient cancer network, treating an estimated 15% of the country's cancer cases. The company (resulting from the 1999 merger of American Oncology Resources and Physician Reliance Network) provides practice management for more than 800 physicians in 26 states. The company manages non-medical aspects of oncology practices — business planning, financial analysis, implementing management information systems, purchasing supplies and equipment, coordinating clinical trials, and managing facilities and non-medical personnel. The company's contract with Texas Oncology accounts for about 25% of revenue.

KEY COMPETITORS
PhyAmerica
Physicians' Specialty
Sheridan Healthcare

USAA

9800 Fredericksburg Rd., USAA Building
San Antonio, TX 78288
Phone: 210-498-2211
Fax: 210-498-9940
Web: www.usaa.com

CEO: Robert G. Davis
CFO: Joe Robles Jr.
HR: Elizabeth Conklyn
Type: Mutual company

2000 Sales: $8,550.0 million
1-Yr. Sales Change: 2.8%
Employees: 22,000
FYE: December 31

USAA has a decidedly military bearing. The mutual insurance company serves more than 4 million customers, primarily military personnel and their families. Its products and services include property/casualty (sold only to military personnel) and life insurance, banking, discount brokerage, and investment management. USAA relies largely on technology and direct marketing to sell its products, reaching clients via the telephone and Internet. The company also has a large mail-order catalog business (computers, furniture, giftware, jewelry, and home and auto safety items), and it offers long-distance telephone services.

KEY COMPETITORS
MetLife
Nationwide
State Farm

See pages 218–219 for a full profile of this company.

USX-MARATHON GROUP

NYSE: MRO

5555 San Felipe Rd.
Houston, TX 77056
Phone: 713-629-6600
Fax: 713-296-2952
Web: www.marathon.com

CEO: Thomas J. Usher
CFO: Robert M. Hernandez
HR: Eileen Campbell
Type: Public

2000 Sales: $33,859.0 million
1-Yr. Sales Change: 39.8%
Employees: 30,892
FYE: December 31

Lean and long-striding, integrated oil company USX-Marathon Group is the major revenue generator of USX Corporation's two business units (USX-U.S. Steel is the other). Marathon explores for, develops, and produces oil and gas in 11 countries. It has net proved reserves of 1.2 billion barrels of oil equivalent (57% are in the US). The company owns 62% of Marathon Ashland Petroleum (MAP), a joint venture with Ashland that conducts downstream activities. In the US, MAP operates pipelines, terminals, seven refineries, and more than 5,900 retail outlets under such brands as SuperAmerica and Speedway. Marathon also invests in independent electric power projects.

KEY COMPETITORS
ChevronTexaco
Phillips Petroleum
Royal Dutch/Shell

 See pages 220–221 for a full profile of this company.

VALERO ENERGY CORPORATION

NYSE: VLO

One Valero Place
San Antonio, TX 78212
Phone: 210-370-2000
Fax: 210-370-2646
Web: www.valero.com

CEO: William E. Greehey
CFO: John D. Gibbons
HR: Keith D. Booke
Type: Public

2000 Sales: $14,671.1 million
1-Yr. Sales Change: 84.3%
Employees: 3,180
FYE: December 31

Valero Energy is on a mission. The company, named after the Alamo (the Mission San Antonio de Valero), is championing clean fuels. It refines low-cost residual oil and heavy crude into cleaner-burning, higher-margin products, including reformulated gasolines and low-sulfur diesels. Valero, the leading independent refiner on the Gulf Coast, operates three refineries in Texas, three in California, and one each in Louisiana and New Jersey; its overall production capacity is 1 million barrels per day. The company markets petroleum products wholesale in 34 states; its retail operations include 350 stores in California. Valero will become the nation's leading independent refiner by buying Ultramar Diamond Shamrock.

KEY COMPETITORS
BP
Exxon Mobil
Phillips Petroleum

 See pages 222–223 for a full profile of this company.

VALHI, INC.

NYSE: VHI

5430 LBJ Freeway, Ste. 1700
Dallas, TX 75240
Phone: 972-233-1700
Fax: 972-448-1445

CEO: Harold C. Simmons
CFO: Bobby D. O'Brien
HR: Kathy Brownlee
Type: Public

2000 Sales: $1,191.9 million
1-Yr. Sales Change: 4.1%
Employees: 7,110
FYE: December 31

Valhi, through its subsidiaries and affiliates, operates in the chemical, component products, waste management, and titanium metals industries. Its NL Industries unit, operating through subsidiary Kronos, is a leading maker of titanium dioxide, a pigment used to whiten, brighten, and add opacity to fiber, paper, paint, and plastic. CompX makes ergonomic computer support systems and office security products. Titanium Metals makes titanium sponge, ingot, slab, and mill products for the aerospace and other markets. Valhi also operates a hazardous waste-treatment facility in West Texas through Waste Control Specialists. Chairman and CEO Harold Simmons controls more than 90% of Valhi through Contran Corporation.

KEY COMPETITORS
DuPont
Kerr-McGee
Millennium Chemicals

VALLEN CORPORATION

13333 Northwest Fwy.
Houston, TX 77040
Phone: 713-462-8700
Fax: 713-462-7634
Web: www.vallen.com

CEO: Richard Harrison
CFO: Ken Bourne
HR: Don Reegi
Type: Subsidiary

1999 Sales: $306.1 million
1-Yr. Sales Change: 3.8%
Employees: 1,100
FYE: December 31

Firemen feel safer dashing into burning buildings accompanied by Vallen, a leading North American manufacturer and distributor of firefighting gear and industrial safety equipment. A subsidiary of Netherlands-based Hagemeyer, Vallen produces gas detection and fire safety instruments, materials-handling equipment, and protective gear and clothing. It also distributes protection products made by such companies as 3M, Wells Lamont, and Walter Kidde. Vallen offers on-site safety inspection and product repair services and provides safety training and consulting. Vallen Technical Services maintains and repairs industrial safety products. Customers include the petroleum and chemical industries.

KEY COMPETITORS
Federal Signal
Mine Safety Appliances
Tyco International

VARI-LITE INTERNATIONAL, INC.

Nasdaq: LITE

201 Regal Row
Dallas, TX 75247
Phone: 214-630-1963
Fax: 214-630-5867
Web: www.vlint.com

CEO: H. R. Brutsché III
CFO: Jerome L. Trojan III
HR: Janis C. Pestinger
Type: Public

2000 Sales: $93.7 million
1-Yr. Sales Change: 2.4%
Employees: 397
FYE: September 30

Vari-Lite International can lighten any mood. It provides computerized lighting systems for concerts; stage, film, and TV productions; and corporate events. The firm's products are used by popular music acts such as the Backstreet Boys, Ricky Martin, and Sting, and it illuminates all the stars of stage and screen at awards shows such as the Grammy Awards and the Academy Awards. Although Vari-Lite had long relied on renting its equipment, it now sells the equipment as well and provides training and maintenance services. About 40% of the company's sales are generated outside North America. Current and former members of rock group Genesis, early backers of the company, own about 10% of Vari-Lite.

KEY COMPETITORS
Clay Paky
High End Systems
Production Resource Group

VARTEC TELECOM, INC.

1600 Viceroy Dr.
Dallas, TX 75235
Phone: 214-424-1000
Fax: 214-424-1555
Web: www.vartec.com

CEO: Sherman Henderson
CFO: Gary Egger
HR: —
Type: Private

2000 Sales: $1,020.0 million
1-Yr. Sales Change: 6.4%
Employees: 2,238
FYE: December 31

Actors and comedians employed promoting 10-10 calling plans can thank VarTec Telecom, a leading provider of "dial-around" long-distance service, which helped pioneer the calling method. VarTec provides residential and business calling plans, as well as Internet access and 800-number service. The company was founded in 1989 by president Joe Mitchell and his wife, EVP Connie Mitchell, along with EVP Ray Atkinson. Holding company Telephone Electronics Corp. owns a majority stake in VarTec, which has agreed to merge with business telecom services reseller Lightyear Communications and has entered into merger talks with Dallas-based long-distance retailer Excel Communications.

KEY COMPETITORS
AT&T
Sprint FON
WorldCom

VERITAS DGC INC.

NYSE: VTS

10300 Town Park Dr.
Houston, TX 77072
Phone: 832-351-8300
Fax: 832-351-8701
Web: www.veritasdgc.com

CEO: David B. Robson
CFO: Anthony Tripodo
HR: Scott Smith
Type: Public

2001 Sales: $477.3 million
1-Yr. Sales Change: 35.2%
Employees: 4,300
FYE: July 31

A veritable leader in seismic data acquisition, Veritas DGC serves the energy industry. The company works on land and at sea to gather seismic data for oil and gas companies, which use the information to manage reserves and to determine suitable locations for drilling exploratory wells. Known as Digicon until its purchase of Canadian firm Veritas Energy Services in 1996, the company uses seven marine research vessels and 17 land and transition zone data acquisition crews. Veritas DGC analyzes the data it uncovers at 19 data processing centers around the world.

KEY COMPETITORS
Compagnie Générale de
  Géophysique
Petroleum Geo-Services
WesternGeco

VHA INC.

220 E. Las Colinas Blvd.
Irving, TX 75039
Phone: 972-830-0000
Fax: 972-830-0012
Web: www.vha.com

CEO: C. Thomas Smith
CFO: Curt Nonomaque
HR: Kim R. Alleman
Type: Cooperative

2000 Sales: $442.0 million
1-Yr. Sales Change: 10.0%
Employees: 1,200
FYE: December 31

Hospital cooperative VHA is keeping the US healthy through a nationwide network of community-owned health care organizations. With more than 2,200 members in 48 states, the co-op represents about one-quarter of US community-owned hospitals. VHA offers networking and education opportunities for health care workers, provides information technology, evaluates clinical effectiveness, and helps build market share. VHA members purchase medical supplies from Novation, a joint venture with University HealthSystem Consortium. VHA's members include Baylor Health Care System in Texas, BJC Health System in Illinois, and the Mayo Foundation in Minnesota.

KEY COMPETITORS
Allegiance
McKesson General Medical
Premier

VIGNETTE CORPORATION

Nasdaq: VIGN

901 S. Mopac Expwy., Bldg. 3
Austin, TX 78746
Phone: 512-741-4300
Fax: 512-741-4500
Web: www.vignette.com

CEO: Gregory A. Peters
CFO: Charles W. Sansbury
HR: Dee Ann Thompson
Type: Public

2000 Sales: $366.7 million
1-Yr. Sales Change: 311.1%
Employees: 2,330
FYE: December 31

Vignette hopes its role in the content management and personalization scene isn't brief. Vignette has repackaged its flagship StoryServer content management product into a suite of e-commerce applications, expanding into online customer personalization and business application integration. Clients such as Motorola, Cisco, and Federal Express use Vignette software to create Web-based applications in the areas of content management, channel integration, and application deployment. The company also offers consulting, implementation, and training services. After fueling its rapid growth primarily through acquisitions, in 2001 Vignette switched gears, and began streamlining operations, reducing its workforce by 25%.

KEY COMPETITORS
Art Technology Group
BroadVision
Interwoven

 See pages 224–225 for a full profile of this company.

VINSON & ELKINS L.L.P.

2300 First City Tower, 1001 Fannin	CEO: Harry M. Reasoner	2000 Sales: $386.5 million
Houston, TX 77002	CFO: John Spire	1-Yr. Sales Change: 18.0%
Phone: 713-758-2222	HR: Patty Calabrese	Employees: 2,000
Fax: 713-758-2346	Type: Partnership	FYE: December 31
Web: www.velaw.com		

Even the law firms are big in Texas. Vinson & Elkins has more than 650 attorneys in five US offices (three in Texas) and four international offices. The firm is a specialist in international energy law and litigation. It has one of the largest health-care practices in the US as well. Besides these fortes, the firm operates in almost all areas of civil law, practicing antitrust, intellectual property, international, securities law, and many other areas for its government, corporate, and individual clients. Texas Judge James Elkins and William Vinson founded the firm in Houston in 1917.

KEY COMPETITORS
Andrews & Kurth
Baker Botts
Fulbright & Jaworski

VOUGHT AIRCRAFT INDUSTRIES, INC.

9314 W. Jefferson Blvd.	CEO: Gordon Williams	2000 Est. Sales: $1,000.0 mil.
Dallas, TX 75211	CFO: William J. McMillan	1-Yr. Sales Change: —
Phone: 972-946-2011	HR: Margo B. Parker	Employees: 5,000
Fax: 972-946-3465	Type: Private	FYE: December 31
Web: www.voughtaircraft.com		

Vought Aircraft Industries is one of the world's largest aerostructures subcontractors. The company provides fuselage subassemblies (doors and fuselage panels), nacelles, thrust reversers, empennage structures, wings, and other components for both military and commercial aircraft manufacturers. It makes parts for almost all of Boeing's commercial fleet, ranging from the 737 to the 777. Other customers include Dassault Aviation, GE, Gulfstream, Lockheed Martin, NASA, and Raytheon. Vought subcontracts for programs that build military cargo planes (C-17), bombers (B-2), and fighters (F-14 and F/A-18). It also provides spare parts, maintenance, repair, and overhaul services. The Carlyle Group owns about 90% of Vought.

KEY COMPETITORS
CPI Aerostructures
Goodrich
LMI Aerospace

VTEL CORPORATION
Nasdaq: FORG

108 Wild Basin Rd.	CEO: Richard N. "Dick" Snyder	2001 Sales: $38.2 million
Austin, TX 78746	CFO: Jay C. Peterson	1-Yr. Sales Change: (71.6%)
Phone: 512-437-2700	HR: —	Employees: 312
Fax: 512-437-2972	Type: Public	FYE: July 31
Web: www.forgent.com		

Forgent Corporation provides sight for sore ears. The company, formerly VTEL, is one of the world's top makers of videoconferencing systems. Its products integrate traditional audio- and videoconferencing with other options, including document and graphics exchanges. Forgent makes desktop conferencing systems, plus systems customized for large and small groups, and sells them to customers such as Kinko's and Citicorp. The company is expanding into Internet-based videoconferencing products and services through Web portal subsidiaries Onscreen24 and ArticuLearn. Forgent markets primarily through its reseller network.

KEY COMPETITORS
Ezenia!
PictureTel
Polycom

WARREN ELECTRIC GROUP, LTD.

2929 McKinney St.	CEO: Cheryl L. Thompson-Draper	2000 Sales: $310.0 million
Houston, TX 77003	CFO: Rita Hausman	1-Yr. Sales Change: 17.9%
Phone: 713-236-0971	HR: Yvonne Oakes	Employees: 613
Fax: 713-236-2261	Type: Private	FYE: December 31
Web: www.warrenelectric.com		

Business gets down to the wire at Warren Electric Group. The wholesaler distributes the wares of more than 250 electrical and communications products companies. Customers for the distributor's thousands of products — which range from batteries and fuses to transformers and fiber optics — include the chemical, paper, energy, process, and telecommunications industries. The group also offers technical support and training for the products it distributes, as well as inventory-management and energy-conservation programs. Founded in 1919, Warren Electric is owned by Mary Claude Thompson and her daughter, chairman and CEO Cheryl Thompson-Draper.

KEY COMPETITORS
Graybar Electric
WESCO International
Wholesale Electric

WASTE MANAGEMENT, INC.   NYSE: WMI

1001 Fannin, Ste. 4000	CEO: A. Maurice "Maury" Myers	2000 Sales: $12,492.0 million
Houston, TX 77002	CFO: William L. Trubeck	1-Yr. Sales Change: (4.8%)
Phone: 713-512-6200	HR: Jimmy D. LaValley	Employees: 57,000
Fax: 713-512-6299	Type: Public	FYE: December 31
Web: www.wm.com		

Waste Management, formerly USA Waste Services, is at the top of the heap in the US solid-waste industry (Allied Waste is #2). The company serves about 27 million municipal, business, and residential customers in the US, Canada, and Mexico. It has a network of landfills and collection operations, as well as waste transfer, disposal, and recycling services. In 1998 USA Waste bought the top-ranked but faltering Waste Management, taking the Waste Management name and many of its problems. To focus on its core North American operations, the company has sold off its international solid- and hazardous-waste management businesses along with its noncore North American assets (hazardous waste and power production operations).

KEY COMPETITORS
Allied Waste
Republic Services
Safety-Kleen

 See pages 226–227 for a full profile of this company.

WEATHERFORD INTERNATIONAL, INC.   NYSE: WFT

515 Post Oak Blvd., Ste. 600	CEO: Bernard J. Duroc-Danner	2000 Sales: $1,814.3 million
Houston, TX 77027	CFO: —	1-Yr. Sales Change: 46.3%
Phone: 713-693-4000	HR: Jon R. Nicholson	Employees: 11,900
Fax: 713-693-4294	Type: Public	FYE: December 31
Web: www.weatherford.com		

When there's oil or natural gas in them there fields, Weatherford International can help get it out. The company supplies equipment and services used in the oil and gas drilling industries. In addition to its drilling and intervention services, the company provides completion products and artificial lift systems (pumping systems). Weatherford operates from about 400 locations in more than 50 countries. As part of its strategy to focus on its core products and services, Weatherford has spun off its Grant Prideco unit, maker of drill system and tubular products, and has sold its natural gas compression operations.

KEY COMPETITORS
Baker Hughes
Halliburton
Schlumberger

WEBLINK WIRELESS, INC.

OTC: WLNKA

3333 Lee Pkwy., Ste. 100
Dallas, TX 75219
Phone: 214-765-4000
Fax: 214-765-4940
Web: www.weblinkwireless.com

CEO: John D. Beletic
CFO: John R. Hauge
HR: James F. Nieves
Type: Public

2000 Sales: $290.0 million
1-Yr. Sales Change: (10.8%)
Employees: 1,899
FYE: December 31

With nearly 2 million subscribers, WebLink Wireless (formerly PageMart Wireless) is one of the largest messaging services providers in the US, behind Arch Wireless and Metrocall. WebLink Wireless' two-way wireless data network covers 90% of the US population, and the company offers service throughout the Americas through affiliations with other carriers. WebLink Wireless hopes continued growth in its wireless data division, which has more than 510,000 customers, will counteract the decline of its one-way paging business, which has 1.4 million customers. In 2001 Metrocall terminated a deal to merge with WebLink Wireless, which then filed for Chapter 11 bankruptcy protection.

KEY COMPETITORS
Arch Wireless
Metrocall
Verizon Wireless

WEINER'S STORES, INC.

OTC: WEIR

6005 Westview Dr.
Houston, TX 77055
Phone: 713-688-1331
Fax: 713-688-6976
Web: www.weiners.com

CEO: Raymond J. Miller
CFO: Michael S. Marcus
HR: Glenis Webb
Type: Public

2001 Sales: $249.1 million
1-Yr. Sales Change: (10.0%)
Employees: 1,557
FYE: January 31

Weiner's Stores has come to the end of its bun. In June 2001 the company announced plans to close all of its stores and begin liquidating its assets. Weiner's runs about 100 outlets, mostly in urban strip malls in Texas, but also in Louisiana, Mississippi, and Alabama. The company primarily sells discounted name-brand apparel and shoes, as well as bed and bath items, fragrances, electronics, and toys. Hispanic and African-American shoppers make up nearly 90% of Weiner's customers. Founded in 1926 by Isidore Weiner, the firm emerged from over two years of bankruptcy protection in 1997, only to file again in 2000. Chase Manhattan owns 47% of the company; the Weiner family still owns 10%.

KEY COMPETITORS
Ross Stores
Stein Mart
Wal-Mart

WEINGARTEN REALTY INVESTORS

NYSE: WRI

2600 Citadel Plaza Dr., Ste. 300
Houston, TX 77008
Phone: 713-866-6000
Fax: 713-866-6049
Web: www.weingarten.com

CEO: Andrew M. "Drew" Alexander
CFO: Stephen C. Richter
HR: Brenda Corn
Type: Public

2000 Sales: $273.8 million
1-Yr. Sales Change: 9.0%
Employees: 222
FYE: December 31

Weingarten Realty Investors is one company that has never said, "Houston, we've got a problem." The real estate investment trust (REIT) owns nearly 300 properties, over a third of them in Houston, about a third elsewhere in Texas, and the rest in 15 other states, mostly in the Southwest. The company's 30 million-sq.-ft. portfolio is focused on neighborhood shopping centers (over 220 of them) anchored by major food, drug, or discount stores such as Albertson's, Eckerd, and Kmart. The firm's other holdings include more than 50 industrial sites, an office building, an apartment complex; it also owns some 40 parcels of unimproved land suitable for an additional 12 million sq. ft. of development.

KEY COMPETITORS
Equity One
New Plan Excel Realty Trust
Regency Centers

W-H ENERGY SERVICES, INC.

Nasdaq: WHES

10370 Richmond Ave., Ste. 990
Houston, TX 77042
Phone: 713-974-9071
Fax: 713-974-7029
Web: www.whes.com

CEO: Kenneth T. White Jr.
CFO: Jeffrey L. Tepera
HR: Monique Peddy
Type: Public

2000 Sales: $230.0 million
1-Yr. Sales Change: 80.3%
Employees: 1,015
FYE: December 31

W-h-a-t is W-H? W-H Energy Services offers diversified oil field services both onshore and off — from wireline logging and perforating to cleaning and maintenance. Products include specialty chemicals, drilling motors and fluids, and measurement-while-drilling systems. Founded in 1989, W-H Energy Services serves major and independent oil and gas firms, petrochemical companies, and other oil field service companies, primarily on the US Gulf Coast and in the Gulf of Mexico and the North Sea. The company, which has grown through acquisitions, is pursuing further international expansion.

KEY COMPETITORS
Baker Hughes
Halliburton
Schlumberger

WHATABURGER, INC.

4600 Parkdale Dr.
Corpus Christi, TX 78411
Phone: 361-878-0650
Fax: 361-878-0673
Web: www.whataburger.com

CEO: Thomas E. Dobson
CFO: John M. McLellan
HR: Peter H. Opel
Type: Private

2000 Est. Sales: $600.0 mil.
1-Yr. Sales Change: 0.0%
Employees: 15,000
FYE: September 30

When you see that familiar orange and white roof, you know you're in for a Whataburger. The more than 560-unit strong hamburger chain stretches across seven southern and southwestern states and Mexico. Open 24 hours a day, Whataburger restaurants also serve breakfast items (taquitos, pancakes), fajitas, chicken, fish, and salads. Loyal Whataburger fans also can don the company's line of apparel sporting the chain's logo and dress their kids in Whatakids duds. The late Harmon Dobson founded Whataburger in Corpus Christi, Texas, in 1950. His family (including Dobson's son, president and CEO Thomas Dobson) owns the company.

KEY COMPETITORS
Burger King
McDonald's
Sonic

WHOLE FOODS MARKET, INC.

Nasdaq: WFMI

601 N. Lamar, Ste. 300
Austin, TX 78703
Phone: 512-477-4455
Fax: 512-477-1301
Web: www.wholefoodsmarket.com

CEO: John P. Mackey
CFO: Glenda Flanagan
HR: Cindy Strunk
Type: Public

2000 Sales: $1,838.6 million
1-Yr. Sales Change: 17.3%
Employees: 18,500
FYE: September 30

With food and other items that are free of pesticides, preservatives, sweeteners, and cruelty, Whole Foods Market knows more about guiltless eating and shopping than most other retailers. The nation's #1 natural foods chain, the firm operates about 117 stores in more than 20 states and Washington, DC. (It pioneered the supermarket concept in health foods retailing.) Although most stores operate under the Whole Foods Market banner, others are Bread & Circus, Fresh Fields, and Wellspring Grocery. Whole Foods is expanding its private labels (Whole Foods, Whole Kids, 365) and has moved into related businesses (nutritional supplements). It also sells items online through a co-branding operation with Gaiam.com.

KEY COMPETITORS
GNC
Trader Joe's Co
Wild Oats Markets

 See pages 228–229 for a full profile of this company.

WILLIAMSON-DICKIE MANUFACTURING COMPANY

509 W. Vickery Blvd.
Fort Worth, TX 76104
Phone: 817-336-7201
Fax: 817-877-5027
Web: www.dickies.com

CEO: Philip C. Williamson
CFO: Britt Ingebritson
HR: Marett Cobb
Type: Private

2000 Sales: $820.0 million
1-Yr. Sales Change: 5.1%
Employees: 6,300
FYE: December 31

Appreciated by the working class and the sophomore class alike, Williamson-Dickie Manufacturing Company is the maker of Dickies khaki pants, bib overalls, jeans, and women's and children's apparel. It also makes Workrite safety uniforms. The company's work clothes were originally tailored with the blue-collar set in mind, but these days the clothes are in favor with hip kids, who like to wear their pants and overalls several sizes too big. Dickies T-shirts are made extra long to prevent the display of "plumber's crack" by squatting workmen. Dickies products are sold worldwide through retailers and directly to businesses. The Williamson family owns the company they co-founded in 1922.

KEY COMPETITORS
Carhartt
Levi Strauss
VF

WINGATE PARTNERS

750 N. St. Paul St., Ste. 1200
Dallas, TX 75201
Phone: 214-720-1313
Fax: 214-871-8799
Web: www.wingatepartners.com

CEO: Frederick B. Hegi Jr.
CFO: Alna Evans
HR: Alna Evans
Type: Private

Sales: —
1-Yr. Sales Change: —
Employees: —
FYE: December 31

Wingate Partners gets by on more than a wing and a prayer, rescuing lackluster manufacturing, distribution, and service businesses. It avoids banking, media, high-tech, insurance, natural resources, and real estate companies, investing instead in firms that are underperforming or that are in industries in transition. The targets often have revenues between $100 million and $500 million and may or may not be profitable at the time of purchase. Wingate's portfolio includes holdings in Loomis, Fargo & Co. (armored car services) and Kevco (manufactured-housing building products distributor).

KEY COMPETITORS
AEA Investors
Clayton, Dubilier
Texas Pacific Group

WYNDHAM INTERNATIONAL, INC.

NYSE: WYN

1950 Stemmons Fwy., Ste. 6001
Dallas, TX 75207
Phone: 214-863-1000
Fax: 214-863-1527
Web: www.wyndhamintl.com

CEO: Fred J. Kleisner
CFO: Richard A. Smith
HR: Mary Watson
Type: Public

2000 Sales: $2,421.6 million
1-Yr. Sales Change: (2.5%)
Employees: 28,000
FYE: December 31

Wyndham International has led many lives. The company formerly operated as Patriot American Hospitality, a paired-share real estate investment trust (REIT) that traded with hotel operator Wyndham International. But a heavy debt burden left the company in dire financial straits, and in 1999 Patriot American Hospitality accepted a $1 billion bailout from investors, shed its REIT status, and merged with Wyndham International. Left standing when all was said and done was Wyndham International, now an owner or operator of some 240 upscale hotels. Investors include Apollo Investment Fund (about 27%) and Thomas H. Lee Equity Fund (19%).

KEY COMPETITORS
Fairmont Hotels
Hilton
Hyatt

See pages 230–231 for a full profile of this company.

XANSER CORPORATION

2435 N. Central Expwy.
Richardson, TX 75080
Phone: 972-699-4000
Fax: 972-644-3524
Web: www.xanser.com

CEO: John R. Barnes
CFO: Howard C. Wadsworth
HR: William H. Kettler Jr.
Type: Public

2000 Sales: $127.6 million
1-Yr. Sales Change: (74.8%)
Employees: 1,131
FYE: December 31

Kaneb Services knows that information technology and technical services is where the growth is. Once an operator of oil pipelines and a wholesale fuel-marketing services business, the company has discontinued these businesses to focus on its technology-oriented operations. Kaneb's technical services segment includes Furmanite Worldwide, which provides on-site leak sealing and other services. Kaneb's fast-growing information technology division provides computer networking and telemedical applications development. The company is changing its name to Xanser Corporation.

KEY COMPETITORS
IBM
NESCO
Team, Inc.

XETEL CORPORATION

2105 Gracy Farms Ln.
Austin, TX 78758
Phone: 512-435-1000
Fax: 512-834-1856
Web: www.xetel.com

CEO: Angelo A. DeCaro Jr.
CFO: David G. Osowski
HR: Ruben D. Gonzales
Type: Public

2001 Sales: $192.9 million
1-Yr. Sales Change: 63.9%
Employees: 632
FYE: March 31

Surface impressions count for XeTel. The contract manufacturer specializes in printed circuit boards using advanced surface-mount technology (SMT) such as fine-chip and chip-scale packages. Such boards pack more circuitry into a small space; components are soldered to the surface, rather than attached with pins. XeTel also offers an array of ancillary services including product development, prototyping, product testing, and systems integration. XeTel's customers — including Visual Networks and Crossroads Systems — are drawn primarily from the computer, networking, and telecommunications industries. The US subsidiary of Japanese electronics company Rohm owns one third of XeTel.

KEY COMPETITORS
Flextronics
Sanmina
Solectron

XTO ENERGY INC.

810 Houston St., Ste. 2000
Fort Worth, TX 76102
Phone: 817-870-2800
Fax: 817-870-1671
Web: www.crosstimbers.com

CEO: Bob R. Simpson
CFO: Louis G. Baldwin
HR: Robert C. Myers
Type: Public

2000 Sales: $600.9 million
1-Yr. Sales Change: 76.1%
Employees: 651
FYE: December 31

XTO Energy (formerly known as Cross Timbers Oil) doesn't have to cross its fingers and hope its fields produce oil and gas. It buys mostly long-lived producing properties, and has begun more exploration of unproved reserves. The large independent's holdings are mainly in Alaska, Arkansas, Texas, Kansas, New Mexico, Oklahoma, and Wyoming. XTO Energy owns interests in about 6,900 wells and operates gas gathering systems in Arkansas, Kansas, Oklahoma, and Texas. Natural gas accounts for 76% of sales. The firm has proved reserves of about 58.4 million barrels of oil, 1.8 trillion cu. ft. of natural gas, and 22 million barrels of natural gas liquids.

KEY COMPETITORS
Apache
BP
Exxon Mobil

THE YORK GROUP, INC.

Nasdaq: YRKG

8554 Katy Fwy., Ste. 200
Houston, TX 77024
Phone: 713-984-5500
Fax: 713-984-5569
Web: www.yorkgrp.com

CEO: Thomas J. Crawford
CFO: Dan E. Malone
HR: Robert T. Monteleone
Type: Public

2000 Sales: $192.5 million
1-Yr. Sales Change: (2.8%)
Employees: 1,667
FYE: December 31

The York Group might like its managers to think outside the box, but it prefers its clients to stay in the box. The nation's #2 casket maker — after Hillenbrand's Batesville Casket — produces metal and wood caskets, memorials and plaques, and cremation containers. (Cremation is the industry's hot trend — a quarter of US deaths are handled this way.) York is staking its vitality on an incentive program designed to boost sales via independent funeral homes. Its caskets are sold almost entirely in the US through company-owned and independent distributors. Wilbert, Inc. owns 14% of York; its offers to buy the rest were rebuffed. Instead, York has agreed to be bought by memorial-products maker Matthews International.

KEY COMPETITORS
Hillenbrand
Matthews International
Rock of Ages

ZALE CORPORATION

NYSE: ZLC

901 W. Walnut Hill Ln.
Irving, TX 75038
Phone: 972-580-4000
Fax: 972-580-5523
Web: www.zalecorp.com

CEO: Robert J. DiNicola
CFO: Sue E. Gove
HR: Gregory Humenesky
Type: Public

2001 Sales: $2,068.2 million
1-Yr. Sales Change: 15.3%
Employees: 20,000
FYE: July 31

Zale is the king of diamonds. The US's largest specialty jewelry retailer, Zale has more than 2,300 stores throughout the US, Canada, and Puerto Rico where it sells diamond, colored stone, and gold jewelry; watches; and gift items. The firm has three large chains aimed at different jewelry markets: Zales Jewelers (moderately priced items), Gordon's Jewelers (more expensive contemporary and regional items), and Bailey Banks & Biddle Fine Jewelers (higher-priced items). Zale also operates more than 65 jewelry outlet stores. It runs about 170 Peoples Jewellers in Canada and sells online. The company also owns about 95% of US kiosk jeweler Piercing Pagoda. Zale offers jewelry insurance as well as a private credit card.

KEY COMPETITORS
Helzberg Diamonds
Signet
Wal-Mart

 See pages 232–233 for a full profile of this company.

Hoover's Texas 500

The Indexes

Norwood Promotional Products,
Inc. 344

Membership Organizations
Boy Scouts of America 255

Miscellaneous Business Services
The Freeman Companies 298
F.Y.I. Incorporated 301

Personal Services
Carriage Services, Inc. 261
Service Corporation
International **184-185**, 365

**Printing, Photocopying
& Graphic Design**
Consolidated Graphics, Inc. 271

**Schools & Educational
Services — Colleges
& Universities**
Angelo State University 245
Baylor University 252
Southern Methodist
University 368
Southwest Texas State
University 370
The Texas A&M University
System **200-201**, 379
Texas Southern University 382
University of Houston
System 390
University of North Texas 391
The University of Texas
System **216-217**, 391

**Security & Protection Products
& Services**
Cornell Companies, Inc. 274
Interlogix, Inc. 320

**Staffing, Outsourcing & Other
Human Resources**
Administaff, Inc. **38-39**, 238
Snelling and Snelling, Inc. 367

**Technical & Scientific Research
Services**
Southwest Research
Institute 369

**Telemarketing, Call Centers
& Other Direct Marketing**
Aegis Communications Group,
Inc. 239

DRUGS
Biotechnology — Research
Tanox, Inc. 376

**Vitamins, Nutritionals & Other
Health-Related Products**
Mannatech, Incorporated 332

ELECTRONICS
& MISCELLANEOUS
TECHNOLOGY
**Contract Electronics
Manufacturing**
Benchmark Electronics,
Inc. 253

XeTel Corporation 401
Electronics Distribution
CellStar Corporation **66-67**, 263
N.F. Smith & Associates, LP 343
TTI, Inc. 387

Miscellaneous Electronics
Ultrak, Inc. 389

Semiconductor — Broad Line
Texas Instruments
Incorporated **204-205**, 380

**Semiconductor Equipment
& Materials**
DuPont Photomasks, Inc. 282

**Semiconductor — Integrated
Circuits**
Cirrus Logic, Inc. 265
Dallas Semiconductor
Corporation 277
Silicon Laboratories Inc. 366

ENERGY
Integrated Oil & Gas
Conoco Inc. **82-83**, 271
Exxon Mobil
Corporation **106-107**, 293
Shell Oil Company **186-187**,
365
USX-Marathon Group **220-221**,
393

Oil & Gas Equipment
Baker Hughes
Incorporated **50-51**, 251
CARBO Ceramics Inc. 260
Cooper Cameron
Corporation 273
Dril-Quip, Inc. 281
Hydril Company 316
Input/Output, Inc. 319
Lufkin Industries, Inc. 331
NATCO Group Inc. 339
Smith International, Inc. 367

**Oil & Gas Exploration
& Production**
3TEC Energy Corporation 236
Anadarko Petroleum
Corporation **46-47**, 245
Apache Corporation **48-49**, 246
Burlington Resources
Inc. **62-63**, 258
Cabot Oil & Gas
Corporation 258
Clayton Williams Energy,
Inc. 266
CMS Oil and Gas Company 267
Comstock Resources, Inc. 270
Denbury Resources Inc. 280
EEX Corporation 284
EOG Resources, Inc. 290
The Houston Exploration
Company 315
Hunt Consolidated Inc. 316
KCS Energy, Inc. 323
Magnum Hunter Resources,
Inc. 332

The Meridian Resource
Corporation 335
Mitchell Energy & Development
Corp. **150-151**, 337
Newfield Exploration
Company 342
Noble Affiliates, Inc. 343
Nuevo Energy Company 345
Ocean Energy, Inc. 345
Pioneer Natural Resources
Company 351
Pogo Producing Company 354
Prize Energy Corp. 355
Pure Resources, Inc. 356
Range Resources
Corporation 359
Southwestern Energy
Company 370
Spinnaker Exploration
Company 371
Swift Energy Company 374
TransTexas Gas Corporation 384
Triton Energy Limited 386
XTO Energy Inc. 401

Oil & Gas Pipelines & Storage
El Paso Corporation **96-97**, 285
El Paso Energy Partners,
L.P. 286
Enbridge Energy Partners,
L.P. 287
Enterprise Products Partners
L.P. 289
EOTT Energy Partners,
L.P. **104-105**, 290
Kaneb Pipe Line Partners,
L.P. 323
Kaneb Services LLC 323
Kinder Morgan Energy Partners,
L.P. 325
Kinder Morgan, Inc. 325
Northern Border Partners,
L.P. 344
Plains All American Pipeline,
L.P. 352
Plains Resources Inc. **170-171**,
353
TEPPCO Partners, L.P. 378

Oil & Gas Refining & Marketing
Adams Resources & Energy,
Inc. **36-37**, 238
Equilon Enterprises LLC 291
Frontier Oil Corporation 300
Genesis Energy, L.P. 303
Holly Corporation 312
Motiva Enterprises
LLC **152-153**, 338
Pennzoil-Quaker State
Company **160-161**, 348
Tesoro Petroleum
Corporation **198-199**, 378
Ultramar Diamond Shamrock
Corporation 389
Valero Energy
Corporation **222-223**, 393

Oil & Gas Services
Atwood Oceanics, Inc. 248
BJ Services Company 253
Cal Dive International, Inc. 259

American National Insurance Company 242

National Western Life Insurance Company 340

Southwestern Life Holdings Inc. 370

Multiline Insurance

USAA **218-219**, 392

Property/Casualty Insurance

Argonaut Group, Inc. 246

GAINSCO, INC. 302

HCC Insurance Holdings, Inc. 310

TIG Specialty Insurance Solutions 382

Surety, Title & Miscellaneous Insurance

Stewart Information Services Corporation 373

LEISURE

Gambling Resorts & Casinos

Hollywood Casino Corporation 312

Gaming Activities

Multimedia Games, Inc. 339

Texas Lottery Commission **206-207**, 380

Lodging

La Quinta Corporation **132-133**, 327

Silverleaf Resorts, Inc. 366

TRT Holdings 387

Wyndham International, Inc. **230-231**, 400

Professional Sports Teams & Organizations

Dallas Cowboys Football Club, Ltd. 276

Dallas Mavericks 276

Dallas Stars L.P. 277

Houston Astros Baseball Club 314

Houston Rockets 315

San Antonio Spurs, Ltd. 362

Texas Rangers Baseball Club 381

Restaurants

Brinker International, Inc. **58-59**, 256

Carlson Restaurants Worldwide Inc. 261

CEC Entertainment, Inc. 262

Dave & Buster's, Inc. **88-89**, 278

El Chico Restaurants, Inc. 285

Furr's Restaurant Group, Inc. 301

La Madeleine French Bakery & Cafe 327

Landry's Restaurants, Inc. 328

LDB Corp. 329

Luby's, Inc. **136-137**, 330

Pizza Hut, Inc. 352

Pizza Inn, Inc. 352

Schlotzsky's, Inc. 364

Souper Salad, Inc. 368

Taco Cabana, Inc. 376

Whataburger, Inc. 399

Sporting Activities

ClubCorp, Inc. **74-75**, 266

Travel Agencies, Tour Operators & Other Travel Services

Hotel Reservations Network, Inc. 314

Pegasus Solutions, Inc. 348

Sabre Inc. **180-181**, 361

Travelocity.com Inc. 384

MANUFACTURING

Agricultural Machinery

Alamo Group Inc. 240

Fluid Control Equipment, Pumps, Seals & Valves

Flowserve Corporation 297

Food Service Equipment

Lancer Corporation 328

Hardware & Fasteners

Industrial Holdings, Inc. 318

Industrial Equipment & Products Distribution

Darr Equipment Company 278

DXP Enterprises, Inc. 282

National-Oilwell, Inc. 340

Rush Enterprises, Inc. 361

Vallen Corporation 394

Warren Electric Group, Ltd. 397

Metal Fabrication

Grant Prideco, Inc. 305

MMI Products, Inc. 338

Miscellaneous & Diversified Industrial Products

AXIA Incorporated 250

Miscellaneous Electrical Products

Cooper Industries, Inc. **86-87**, 273

Powell Industries, Inc. 354

Packaging & Containers

Consolidated Container Company LLC 271

Paper & Paper Products

Temple-Inland Inc. **196-197**, 377

Pollution & Treatment Controls & Filtration Products

Denali Incorporated 280

Rubber & Plastic Products

Gundle/SLT Environmental, Inc. 307

Turbines, Transformers & Other Electrical Generation Equipment

Active Power, Inc. 238

Wire & Cable

Encore Wire Corporation 288

MATERIALS & CONSTRUCTION

Aggregates, Concrete & Cement

Centex Construction Products, Inc. 263

Texas Industries, Inc. **202-203**, 379

U.S. Concrete, Inc. 391

Environmental Services

Synagro Technologies, Inc. 375

Heavy Construction

Austin Industries Inc. 249

The Beck Group 252

H. B. Zachry Company 309

Pitt-Des Moines, Inc. 351

The Turner Corporation **212-213**, 388

Manufactured Buildings

American Homestar Corporation 242

Palm Harbor Homes, Inc. **158-159**, 347

Miscellaneous Building Materials

Associated Materials Incorporated 247

Atrium Companies, Inc. 248

Dal-Tile International Inc. 277

Elcor Corporation 286

Justin Industries, Inc. 322

Kevco, Inc. 324

L.D. Brinkman and Co. 328

NCI Building Systems, Inc. 341

Triangle Pacific Corp. 385

Plumbing & HVAC Equipment

Lennox International Inc. **134-135**, 329

Specialty Contracting & Industrial Maintenance

American Plumbing and Mechanical, Inc. 242

Integrated Electrical Services, Inc. 320

Quanta Services, Inc. 357

TDIndustries, Ltd. 377

Xanser Corporation 401

Waste Management & Recycling

U S Liquids Inc. 392

Waste Management, Inc. **226-227**, 397

MEDIA

Movie, Television & Music Production Services & Products

Vari-Lite International, Inc. 394

Movie Theaters

Cinemark USA, Inc. **70-71**, 264

Publishing

Belo Corp. **52-53**, 252

Radio Broadcasting & Programming

Clear Channel Communications, Inc. **72-73**, 266

Crown Castle International
Corp. 275

**Wireless Communications
Services**

Alamosa Holdings, Inc. 240
WebLink Wireless, Inc. 398

TRANSPORTATION

**Air Delivery, Freight & Parcel
Services**

Dynamex Inc. 283
EGL, Inc. 284
Express One International,
Inc. 293

Airlines

AMR Corporation **44-45**, 244
Continental Airlines,
Inc. **84-85**, 272
Southwest Airlines
Co. **190-191**, 369

**Bus, Taxi & Other Passenger
Services**

Greyhound Lines, Inc. 305

Railroads

Burlington Northern Santa Fe
Corporation **60-61**, 257

Shipping

Kirby Corporation 326

Trucking

Central Freight Lines, Inc. 264
Frozen Food Express Industries,
Inc. 300
Stevens Transport Inc. 372

UTILITIES

Diversified Utilities

TXU Corp. **214-215**, 388

Electric Utilities

Austin Energy 249

Brazos Electric Power
Cooperative, Inc. 256
El Paso Electric Company 285
Lower Colorado River
Authority 330
TNP Enterprises, Inc. 382

Gas Utilities

Atmos Energy Corporation 248
Southern Union
Company **188-189**, 368

**Independent Power Producers
& Marketers**

Dynegy Inc. **94-95**, 283
Enron Corp. **102-103**, 289
Panda Energy International,
Inc. 347
Reliant Energy,
Incorporated **174-175**, 359
Reliant Resources, Inc. 359

Aulbaugh, Carrol 334
Austin Energy 249
Austin, Gene 57
Austin, H. Brent 97
Austin Industries Inc. 249
Austin Ventures, L.P. 224, 249, 336, 366
Australian Radio Network 72, 73
Autoliv (airbags) 357
AutoNation, Inc. 54, 100, 306
Autoshade car care products 161
AV Labs (accelerator venture fund) 224, 249
Availability Reservisor 180
AVCO. *See* Aviation Corporation
Avery Fisher Hall (New York City) 213
Avery, Warren S. 305
The Avia Watch Company 110
Aviall, Inc. 250
Aviation Corporation 44
Avicola Pilgrim's Pride de Mexico, S.A. DE C.V. 167
Avon Products, Inc. 140, 333
AVW Audio Visual (presentation technologies) 298
AWP Olmos Field 374
AXIA Inc. 250
Axius car care products 160
Aycock, Samantha 374
Aylesworth, William A. 205, 380
Azurix Corporation 102, 289

B

BA. *See* British Airways Plc
Babbage's stores 302
Babcock, Amber 238
Babcock, Havilah 128
Babcock, Theodore A. 382
Baby Bells 66, 182, 356
Bacardi spirits 303
Bach, Richard C. 213
Bache & Company 142
Bacherman, Renee 57
Backstreet Boys (musical group) 394
Badawi, Samir 307
Baggett, David C. 242
Bagwell, Jeff 314
Bahorich, Michael 49
Bailey Banks & Biddle Fine Jewelers 232, 233, 402
Bailey, Lee 223
Bajenski, Richard J. 87
Baker Botts L.L.P. 250
Baker, Carl 50
Baker Casing Shoe Company 50
Baker Hughes Inc. **50-51**, 250, 251, 319
Baker, James Addison 250
Baker, James A., III 250
Baker Oil Tools 50, 51
Baker Petrolite 50, 51
Baker, Robert W. 45
Baker, Tom 215
Baker, William 174
Baker's Supermarkets 108
Baldi, John F. 109
Baldwin, Louis G. 401

Balfour (class rings) 268
Balko, J. L. 287
Ballard Medical Products 128
Ballpark in Arlington (Texas) 381
BancTec, Inc. 251
B&B Foods stores 256
B&S electrical products 87
Bangs, Nelson A. 157
Banister, Gaurdie E. 187
Bank of Ireland 162, 349
BANK ONE Corporation 38, 377
Banks, Nicki 295
BAP Management (beef) 299
Bargain Bulletin (San Diego) advertising shopper 117
BariKare beds 326
Barkley, Charles 315
Barkley, Jerald 384
Barker, Myra O. 141
Barnaba, Constance Hall 39
Barnes & Noble, Inc. 302
Barnes, Ben 206
Barnes, Carol 284
Barnes, Jesse 77, 268
Barnes, John (ILEX Oncology) 317
Barnes, John R. (Kaneb Services/Xanser) 323, 401
Barney's clothing stores 126
Barrera, Sylvia 236
Barrett, Colleen C. 190, 191
Barrett Resources (natural gas) 186
Barrington, Michael R. 243
Barrow, Steven G. 137
Barry's Jewelers. *See* Samuels Jewelers, Inc.
Barshick, Ray 368
Barshop, Phil 132
Barshop, Sam 132
Bartel, Tony 352
Barton Creek Resort and Country Club (Texas) 75
Barton, Michael 271
Basic Capital Management, Inc. 243
Basis Petroleum 222
Bass, Anne 330
Bass, James K. 49
Bass, Lee 132
Bass PLC. *See* Six Continents
Bass, Robert 148, 330
Bass, Sid 132
Bates, J. Dan 369
Bates, Kathy 368
Batesville Casket Company 402
Battle, Thomas P. 151
Baugh, John 194
Baum, Herbert M. 160
Baum, Vicki 296
Baumel-Eisner Neuromedical Institute 40
Bay Meadows Operating Company (racetrack) 230
Bayer AG 138
Bayer, James W. 139
Bayless, Jon 365
Bayless, Linda 249
Baylor College of Dentistry 200, 201
Baylor College of Medicine 336

Baylor Health Care System 251, 252, 395
Baylor University 252
Baylor University Medical Center 251
Bayou City Pipelines, Inc. 37
Bayou Steel Corporation 357
BBC. *See* British Broadcasting Corporation
BCE (telecommunications) 292
Beacon gas stations 389
Beacon Manufacturing Company 168, 169
Beaird Industries (rail cars) 210
Beal, Joseph J. 330
Beal Leslie 285
Beale, Michelle 337
Bealls stores 371
Beaman, Rick 193
Bean, Roger 261
The Bear Stearns Companies Inc. 40, 120
Beard, John R. 139
Bearrows, Jeff 290
Beattie, Harold R., Jr. 286
Beauchamp, Lee A. 37
Beauchamp, Robert E. 56, 57, 255
Beaulieu of America (carpets) 328
Beaver Street Fisheries 194
Beazer Homes USA 101
The Beck Group 252
Beck, Henry 252
Beckwitt, Richard 92
Bedell, Leonard A. 346
Beecher, William M. 125, 317
Behrman Capital 237
Behrman, Philip G. 221
Beijing Radio Telecommunications Bureau 66
Beittenmiller, J. Gordon 267
Belco Petroleum 102, 104
Beletic, John D. 398
Bell Atlantic 80
Bell, Bonnie 379
Bell Canada 183
Bell, Paul D. 91
Bell Telephone Company of Missouri 182
Bellcore research consortium 182
BellSouth Corporation 98, 176, 182, 284, 363
Belo, Alfred Horatio 52
Belo Corporation **52-53**, 252
Belridge Oil 186
Ben E. Keith Company 253
Ben Franklin variety stores 148
Benavides, Ross A. 303
Bench, Sherice P. 268
Benchcraft brand 177
Benchmark Electronics, Inc. 253
Bender, Jeffrey M. 49, 246
Benfield Greig (reinsurance) 292
Benjamin Polakoff & Son (food wholesalers) 194
Benoit, Michele M. 294
Benson, Donald T. 336
Berce, Daniel E. 243
Berenguel, Rhonda 366
Berg Electronics 120

Mouser, Jerry H. 199
Moyes, Jerry 264
Moyes, Ron 264
Mr. Gatti's Inc. (pizza) 329
Mr. Payroll Corporation 64, 65, 262
Mrs. Gooch's Natural Foods
  Markets 228
MS Acquisition 332
MSG. *See* Madison Square Garden
MSLO. *See* Martha Stewart Living
  Omnimedia Inc.
MSNBC.com 122
MTech 42
Muchmore, R. Charles, Jr. 115
Mudd casual clothing 301
Mueck, David 264
Muehleman, Frank 91
Mueller, Joe 303
Mullen, David J. 383
Mullins, Charles B. 217
Mullins, Jim 370
Multibanco Mercantil Probursa 162
Multimedia Games, Inc. 339
Mumm champagne 120
Murdy, William F. 267
Murphy, Jeffrey J. 250
Murphy, Kenneth T. 296
Murphy, Paul B., Jr. 369
Murphy, Philip B. 109
Murphy, R. Craig 181
Murphy, Robert J. 354
Murphy, Terry M. 357
Murray, Michael J. 167
Musco Olive Products 243
Muse Air 190
Muse, John O. (Darling
  International) 278
Muse, John R. (Hicks, Muse, Tate &
  Furst) 120, 121
Muse, Lamar 190
Muse, Michael 190
Museum of Contemporary Art (Los
  Angeles) 252
Music Plus 54
Musselman, James C. 386
Musser, Warren V. 80
Mutual Oil 82
Mutz, Gregory T. 388
MVI. *See* Machine Vision
  International
Grupo MVS SA (pay-TV) 121
MW Group (investments) 278
My News (news by e-mail) 52
Mydiscountbroker.com 375
Myers, A. Maurice 226, 227, 397
Myers Electric Products 86
Myers, Robert C. 401
Myers, Rodney S. 49
Myers, Stuart A. 89

N

N&C Boost NV 178, 179
Nabors Industries, Inc. 339, 348
Naegelin, Martin A., Jr. 361
Naeve, Stephen W. 175, 359
NAFTA. *See* North American Free
  Trade Agreement
Nakane, Sam 125
Nakanishi, Greg 51, 251

Nance, William A. 370
Napier, Robert V. 79
NASA. *See* US National Aeronautics
  and Space Administration
Nashville Eagle airline 44
Natalicio, Diana S. 217
NATCO Group Inc. 339
National Basketball
  Association 315, 362
National Broadcasting Company,
  Inc. 53
National Cabinet Lock 270
National Cash Register Corporation.
  See NCR Corporation
National Football League 238, 276,
  368
National Healthcare Logistics 194
National Instruments
  Corporation **154-155**, 340
National League (baseball) 314
National Manufacturing, Inc.
  (aluminum products) 146
National Power & Light
  Company 174
National Processing Inc. 42
National Realty, L.P. 243
National Semiconductor
  Corporation 224
National Tape and Record Center
  stores 66
National Title 373
National Western Life Insurance
  Company 340
National-Oilwell, Inc. 340
Nationwide 386
Nationwide Arena (Columbus,
  OH) 213
Natural by Garelick Farms 193
Natural Gas Clearinghouse 94
Natural Gas Policy Act (1978) 94,
  96
Nature's Finest brand foods 109
Nature's Heartland markets 228
Navajo Refining 312
Naval Sea Systems Command
  Headquarters (Washington,
  DC) 213
Navarro, Imelda 320
Nazer, Hisham 152
NBA. *See* National Basketball
  Association
NBC. *See* National Broadcasting
  Company
NCH Corporation 341
NCI Building Systems, Inc. 341
NCR Corporation 386
NEC Corporation 263
Negra Modelo beer 302
Neiman, A. L. 156
Neiman, Carrie Marcus 156
The Neiman Marcus Group,
  Inc. **156-157**, 341
Nelson, Bob 372
Nelson, Cindy 357
Nelson, Jean 244
Nelson, Jonathan D. "Jody," 348
Nelson, Leslie 358
Neoforma.com 124
NEON Systems 56

Nestaway (dishwasher parts) 250
Nets Inc. 162
Nettle Creek stores 168
Network Telesystems
  (software) 284
NetXtreme inventory system 66
NetZero Internet service 176
Neustadt, Donald H. 237
Neustadt, James C. 149
Nevada Bell 182, 183
Nevares, Hector M., Jr. 193
Nevares, Hector, Sr. 192
Nevarez, Miguel A. 217
New Century Equity Holdings
  Corporation 342
New Dimension (software) 56
New England Energy Group 36, 37
New Jersey Devils (hockey
  team) 314
New Jersey Performing Arts Center
  (Newark, NJ) 213
The New Power Company 102
New York City Department of
  Consumer Affairs 176
New York Mercantile Exchange. *See*
  NYMEX
New York Stock Exchange, Inc. 76,
  164, 172
The New York Times Company 128
New Zealand Radio Network 73
Newco Homes 158
Newfield Exploration Company 50,
  342
Newman, Michael D. 173, 358
Newmark Homes Corporation 342
Newmark, Penny 300
Newport Meat Company 194
Newport News Shipbuilding 100
NewPower Holdings, Inc. 102
Nextel Communications, Inc. 101
N.F. Smith & Associates, LP 343
NFL. *See* National Football League
NGC Oil Trading and
  Transportation 94
NGTS (gas) 332
NI Developer Zone 154
Nichol, Laura 241
Nichols Aluminum 357
Nichols, Michael C. 195
Nicholson, John (Austin
  Ventures) 249
Nicholson, Jon R. (Weatherford
  International) 397
Nicholson, Peter D. 367
Nicklaus, Jack 74
NICOR Energy, L.L.C. 94
Nies, Douglas E. 213
Nieves, James F. 398
Nigbor, Donald E. 253
NIKE, Inc. 371
Nilles, Richard 131
Ninemire, Stanley T. 376
Nissan Motor Company, Ltd. 100,
  245, 279
Nissho Iwai Corporation
  (securities) 208
Nixon, Dennis E. 320
NL Industries, Inc. 272, 343, 393
NLP-Net Lease Properties 371